# Issues in Media

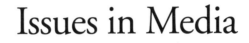

# Issues in Media

# CQ PRESS

A Division of SAGE
Washington, D.C.

SELECTIONS FROM **CQ RESEARCHER**

CQ Press
2300 N Street, NW, Suite 800
Washington, DC 20037

Phone: 202-729-1900; toll-free, 1-866-4CQ-PRESS (1-866-427-7737)

Web: www.cqpress.com

Cover design: Kimberly Glyder
Cover photo: Uyen Le/GETTY Images

⊗ The paper used in this publication exceeds the requirements of the American National Standard for Information Sciences—Permanence of Paper for Printed Library Materials, ANSI Z39.48-1992.

Printed and bound in the United States of America

12  11  10  09  08      1  2  3  4  5

**A CQ Press College Publishing Group Publication**

| | |
|---|---|
| *Executive director* | Brenda Carter |
| *Acquisitions editor* | Aron Keesbury |
| *Development editor* | Dwain Smith |
| *Marketing manager* | Christopher O'Brien |
| *Production editor* | Allyson Rudolph |
| *Compositor* | Olu Davis |
| *Managing editor* | Stephen Pazdan |
| *Electronic production manager* | Paul Pressau |
| *Print and design manager* | Paul Pressau |

**Library of Congress Cataloging-in-Publication Data**

Issues in media : selections from CQ researcher.
    p. cm.
  Includes bibliographical references.
  ISBN 978-0-87289-995-7 (alk. paper)
  1. Mass media--Social aspects. 2. Mass media and culture. 3. Mass media and public opinion. 4. Digital media--Social aspects. I. CQ Press. II. CQ researcher. III. Title.

HM1206.I77 2009
302.23--dc22

                                                                              2008025558

# Contents

# Annotated Contents

The 12 *CQ Researcher* reports reprinted in this book have been reproduced essentially as they appeared when first published. In the few cases in which important developments have since occurred, updates are provided in the overviews highlighting the principal issues examined.

## MEDIA AND CULTURE

### Broadcast Indecency

The supposedly accidental "wardrobe malfunction" that exposed Janet Jackson's right breast during the 2004 Super Bowl halftime show should not have surprised anyone. Radio shock jocks like Howard Stern and Bubba the Love Sponge have been pushing the decency envelope for years, and television has been following suit, raising new complaints about its increasingly risqué—some say indecent—content. Defenders of the media say the First Amendment gives them wide latitude to broadcast sexually provocative material, which simply reflects changing contemporary mores. But critics of today's radio and television content say sexually oriented broadcasting can harm society, especially children. With polls showing that Americans want something done about broadcast content, legislation is now pending in Congress to increase indecency fines dramatically. There is even talk of regulating the cable TV industry.

## Blog Explosion

The blogging phenomenon is sweeping across the United States and around the world. Millions of bloggers are filling the blogosphere with everything from personal journals and family photographs to political advocacy and journalistic commentary. Blogophiles say the blogging revolution is changing politics, business and popular culture for the better by reducing the influence of elites and institutions and allowing for wider public participation and greater interactivity. Some skeptics, however, question whether blogging is anything more than an Internet fad. And some critics say public-policy blogs spew too much unchecked information and overhyped rhetoric into the political process. But with easy-to-use software and growing interest among individuals as well as businesses and government, the blogging phenomenon appears unlikely to peak any time soon.

## Cyber Socializing

Internet socializing has become widely popular, and Web sites that help people meet potential dates, find new friends and keep track of old ones are big business. Hundreds of sites attract millions of users, and more sites come online daily. Born along with the Internet in the early 1970s, online socializing has helped people worldwide link to others with common interests for conversation and support. Nevertheless, social-networking sites like Facebook and MySpace raise more troubling privacy issues than do traditional Internet chat rooms. Visitors to such sites can access not only individuals' posted profiles but also those of their friends. Parents and law-enforcement agencies worry that predators can use the information to contact vulnerable teens. Some states are considering requiring tighter security and confidentiality, and a bill introduced in the House of Representatives would require schools and libraries to block teenagers from the sites.

## Free-Press Disputes

The press has been losing numerous legal battles in recent years, with courts losing sympathy for arguments made by reporters that they cannot testify without revealing confidential sources. In the most celebrated instance, six television reporters and print reporters for national publications eventually gave in to prosecutor demands that they testify in a case involving the leaked identity of a former covert CIA agent. Prosecutors say journalists have the same obligation as anyone else to give evidence in legal proceedings. But journalists say that offering confidentiality to sources wishing to remain anonymous is sometimes necessary to get information about government and corporate wrongdoings, such as the Abu Ghraib prison abuses and the Bush administration's policy of warrantless wiretaps. Meanwhile, media groups are clashing with the Bush administration over restrictions on government information imposed since the 9/11 terrorist attacks.

## Video Games

More than three-quarters of American youths have video-game consoles at home, and on a typical day at least 40 percent play a video game. Some academic scholars claim playing games is good for literacy, problem-solving, learning to test hypotheses and researching information from a variety of sources. Others say gaming may be good for understanding technical information but not for reading literature and understanding the humanities. Enthusiasts claim gaming is preparing young people for the knowledge-based workplace. Critics worry that it is making kids more socially isolated, less experienced in working with others and less creative. Experts remain divided about whether addiction to games is widespread and whether violent games produce violent behavior. Increasingly, researchers are studying why games are so engrossing, and some are urging educators to incorporate games' best learning features into school programs.

# THE ECONOMICS OF MEDIA

## Media Ownership

Media companies are expanding rapidly, integrating broadcast television, cable, radio, newspapers, books, magazines and the Internet under their roofs. Five conglomerates control most prime-time TV programming, and one company—Clear Channel—dominates radio. Yet, in the paradox of today's media landscape, consumers have more choices than ever, although critics say too many choices are low-brow offerings like "reality" TV. Meanwhile, newcomers—such as Web bloggers, viral video and social networking sites—keep sprouting.

Now, as media companies push to grow even bigger, a nationwide debate rages over whether there is enough diversity of content and ownership. In 2007, the Federal Communications Commission voted to relax its media-ownership rules—similar to an attempt it made in 2003 that was rejected in an appeals court—but growing resistance from lawmakers means the changes will have many hurdles to overcome.

### Media Bias

Charges of media bias have never been louder than they are today. Both liberals and conservatives complain about slanted coverage of central events such as the war in Iraq and the 2008 presidential campaign. CBS was universally condemned in 2004 for basing a report about President George W. Bush on fake documents, but every major media outlet has come in for its share of criticism. The Fox News Channel and popular commentator Bill O'Reilly have been called little more than spokespersons for the Republican Party. And the national media as a whole have come under fire recently for the perceived pro-Barack Obama slant of their reporters and political commentators. With distrust so rampant, experts are asking whether the American public as a whole can ever agree about what constitutes the truth. In an era of polarized politics, if citizens cannot even agree about what the facts are because they do not trust major sources of information, it is that much more unlikely that the populace will be able to reach consensus on the major issues of the day.

### Controlling the Internet

Governments and corporations are increasingly concerned about political and economic threats posed by a freewheeling, global Internet. Many experts warn the "Net" may fragment into "walled gardens" that block users' freedom to communicate and innovate. In the United States, telephone and cable companies already have won the right to block competing Internet service providers like Earthlink from using their high-speed broadband lines. Now, advocates for an open Internet worry that broadband providers will use their market power to slow or block access to controversial Web sites or competing businesses like Internet telephone. The activists want Congress to require the companies to treat all Internet content the same. Abroad, more nations are expanding broadband access for economic reasons, even as they crack down on citizens who access controversial material or express dissenting opinions via the Net. In the face of such turmoil, civic groups worldwide are seeking new forms of governance to keep the Internet secure and uncensored.

### Advertising Overload

Consumer advocates say Americans are under siege by advertisers, and that the problem is more serious than just irritating dinnertime phone calls or endless advertisements during movie previews and commercial names in sports stadiums. The advocates blame increasingly intrusive advertising for such societal ills as childhood obesity, rising health-care costs and lost productivity because workplace e-mail boxes are clogged by unsolicited e-mails known as "spam." Public outcry has resulted in a national do-not-call list aimed at curbing telemarketing and may soon trigger a do-not-e-mail list to deter spammers. Other advertising critics are seeking greater restrictions on advertising to children. Advertisers and some advocacy groups warn, however, that many of the proposed restrictions violate First Amendment protections of free speech.

## THE FUTURE OF MEDIA

### Future of Newspapers

The nation's $59 billion newspaper industry is facing an uncertain future even while its biggest companies are enjoying enviable profits averaging around 20 percent. Newspaper circulation has been declining for many years, especially among young adults. Now, newspapers are losing readers and some advertising to the Internet. In fact, only 52 percent of adults read the paper on a typical weekday. Many newspapers are working on redesigns aimed at making their print editions more readable. Most also have created Web sites to deliver news and information, including special features and interactive options not included in the print product. But newspaper executives are struggling to incorporate their online editions into viable business plans. Meanwhile, slipping profit margins are resulting in layoffs at several of the major newspaper companies.

## Future of Television

Television is changing rapidly, and so is the TV audience. Viewers are ignoring broadcast schedules and watching programs via Internet "streams" and iPod downloads. Or they are "time-shifting" and skipping the commercials, using digital video recorders, such as TiVo, or video-on-demand television. Millions are also spending time watching user-generated video on sites such as YouTube. Many TV executives are wondering whether television can sustain its traditional approach to making money—"renting out" millions of viewers at a time to advertisers. For all the ferment, however, Americans are watching more television than ever, using the new devices not to avoid traditional TV but to catch up on shows they otherwise would have missed. There's an atmosphere of experimentation and uncertainty in the industry reminiscent of the dot-com boom, but television and advertising executives insist that the future of TV is bright.

## Future of the Music Industry

The widespread availability of music that can be downloaded for free off the Internet has decimated sales of compact discs in recent years—amounting to hundreds of millions of dollars in losses. The music industry is fighting back, filing high-profile lawsuits against individuals to discourage piracy. And while they have long resisted the new technology, recording labels are finally beginning to offer their music in a multitude of legally downloadable formats. But many observers wonder whether it is too late for the industry to change its ways and successfully compete in the new digital age. As physical distribution of music on plastic discs becomes an anachronism, who will profit from promoting and marketing music that is available everywhere through digital devices—the labels, the artists, legitimate Internet companies or the pirates?

# Preface

Do media conglomerates have too much power? Does the Federal Communications Commission have sufficient authority to punish broadcasters for indecency? Will print papers survive in an online world? These questions—and many more—are at the heart of today's media landscape. How can instructors best engage students with these crucial issues? We feel that students need objective, yet provocative examinations of these issues to understand how they affect citizens today and will for years to come. This collection aims to promote in-depth discussion, facilitate further research and help readers formulate their own positions on crucial issues. Get your students talking both inside and outside the classroom about *Issues in Media*.

This text includes twelve up-to-date reports by *CQ Researcher*, an award-winning publication that chronicles and analyzes the background, current situation and future outlook of a policy discussion or societal topic. This collection is divided into three related areas—media and culture, media economics and the future of media—to cover a range of issues found in most mass communication and media literacy courses.

## CQ RESEARCHER

*CQ Researcher* was founded in 1923 as *Editorial Research Reports* and was sold primarily to newspapers as a research tool. The magazine was renamed and redesigned in 1991 as *CQ Researcher*. Today, students are its primary audience. While still used by hundreds of journalists and newspapers, many of which reprint portions of the reports, *Researcher*'s main subscribers are now high school, college and public libraries. In 2002, *Researcher* won the American Bar Association's coveted Silver Gavel Award for magazine excellence for a series of nine reports on civil liberties and other legal issues.

*Researcher* staff writers—all highly experienced journalists—sometimes compare the experience of writing a *Researcher* report to drafting a college term paper. Indeed, there are many similarities. Each report is as long as many term papers—about 11,000 words—and is written by one person without any significant outside help. One of the key differences is that writers interview leading experts, scholars and government officials for each issue.

Like students, staff writers begin the creative process by choosing a topic. Working with the *Researcher*'s editors, the writer identifies a controversial subject that has important policy and societal implications. After a topic is selected, the writer embarks on one to two weeks of intense research. Newspaper and magazine articles are clipped or downloaded, books are ordered and information is gathered from a wide variety of sources, including interest groups, universities and the government. Once a writer is well informed, he or she develops a detailed outline and begins the interview process. Each report requires a minimum of ten to fifteen interviews with academics, officials and people working in the field. Only after all interviews are completed does the writing begin.

## CHAPTER FORMAT

Each issue of *CQ Researcher*, and therefore each selection in this book, is structured in the same way. Each begins with an overview, which briefly summarizes the areas that will be explored in greater detail in the rest of the chapter. The next section chronicles important and current debates on the topic under discussion and is structured around a number of key questions, such as "Will television remain a viable medium for advertisers?" and "Are tougher limits needed on advertising to children?" These questions are usually the subject of much debate among practitioners and scholars in the field. Hence, the answers

presented are never conclusive but detail the range of opinion on the topic.

Next, the "Background" section provides a history of the issue being examined. This retrospective covers important context, including legislative measures, court decisions and pivotal events. Then the "Current Situation" section examines the most recent events relating to the controversy. Each selection concludes with an "Outlook" section, which addresses long-range projections of where an issue is headed.

Each report contains features that augment the main text: two to three sidebars that examine issues related to the topic at hand, a pro versus con debate between two experts, a chronology of key dates and events and an annotated bibliography detailing major sources used by the writer.

## ACKNOWLEDGMENTS

We wish to thank many people for helping to make this collection a reality. Tom Colin, managing editor of *CQ Researcher*, gave us his enthusiastic support and cooperation as we developed this edition. He and his talented staff of editors and writers have amassed a first-class library of *Researcher* reports, and we are fortunate to have access to that rich cache.

Some readers may be learning about *CQ Researcher* for the first time. We expect that many readers will want regular access to this excellent weekly research tool. For subscription information or a no-obligation free trial of *Researcher*, please contact CQ Press at www.cqpress.com or toll-free at 1-866-4CQ-PRESS (1-866-427-7737).

We hope that you will be pleased by *Issues in Media*. We welcome your feedback and suggestions for future editions. Please direct comments to Aron Keesbury, Acquisitions Editor, College Publishing Group, CQ Press, 2300 N Street, N.W., Suite 800, Washington, D.C. 20037, or akeesbury@cqpress.com.

—*The Editors of CQ Press*

# Contributors

**Thomas J. Colin**, managing editor of *CQ Researcher*, has been a magazine and newspaper journalist for more than 30 years. Before joining Congressional Quarterly in 1991, he was a reporter and editor at the *Miami Herald* and *National Geographic* and editor in chief of *Historic Preservation*. He holds a bachelor's degree in English from the College of William and Mary and in journalism from the University of Missouri.

**Marcia Clemmitt** is a veteran social-policy reporter who joined *CQ Researcher* after serving as editor in chief of *Medicine and Health*, a Washington-based industry newsletter, and staff writer for *The Scientist*. She has also been a high school math and physics teacher. She holds a bachelor's degree in arts and sciences from St. Johns College, Annapolis, and a master's degree in English from Georgetown University.

**Karen Foerstel** is a freelance writer who has worked for *CQ Weekly* and *Daily Monitor*, *The New York Post* and *Roll Call*, a Capitol Hill newspaper. She has published two books on women in Congress, *Climbing the Hill: Gender Conflict in Congress* and *The Biographical Dictionary of Women in Congress*. She currently lives and works in London. She has worked in Africa with ChildsLife International, a nonprofit agency that helps needy children around the world, and Blue Ventures, a marine conservation organization that protects coral reefs in Madagascar.

**Sarah Glazer** specializes in health, education and social-policy issues. Her articles have appeared in *The Washington Post*, *Glamour*,

*The Public Interest* and *Gender and Work*, a book of essays. Glazer covered energy legislation for the Environmental and Energy Study Conference and reported for United Press International. She holds a bachelor's degree in American history from the University of Chicago.

**Alan Greenblatt** is a staff writer for Congressional Quarterly's *Governing* magazine, and previously covered elections and military and agricultural policy for *CQ Weekly*. A recipient of the National Press Club's Sandy Hume Memorial Award for political reporting, he holds a bachelor's degree from San Francisco State University and a master's degree in English literature from the University of Virginia.

**David Hatch** is a freelance writer in Arlington, Virginia, who specializes in media, advertising and consumer issues. A former reporter in the Washington bureau of Crain Communications, he holds a bachelor's degree in English from the University of Massachusetts, Amherst.

**Melissa J. Hipolit** is the former assistant editor of *CQ Researcher*. She graduated magna cum laude from Hobart and William Smith Colleges with a bachelor's degree in history. She has contributed to recent reports, including "American Indians," "Death Penalty Controversies," "Eating Disorders" and "Emerging China."

**Kenneth Jost**, associate editor of *CQ Researcher*, graduated from Harvard College and Georgetown University Law Center, where he is an adjunct professor. He is the author of *The Supreme Court Yearbook* and writer and editor of *The Supreme Court A to Z* (both published by CQ Press). He was a member of the *CQ Researcher* team that won the 2002 American Bar Association Silver Gavel Award.

**Heather Kleba** is a graduate of The George Washington University, where she majored in journalism with a minor in political science. She is currently the research specialist and events coordinator at *Governing* magazine.

**Patrick Marshall** is a freelance writer in Bainbridge Island, Washington, who writes about public policy and technology issues. His recent reports include "Policing the Borders" and "Civil Liberties in Wartime."

**William Triplett** is a veteran writer who is now Washington correspondent for *Variety*. A former *CQ Researcher* staff writer, he previously covered science and the arts for such publications as *Smithsonian*, *Air & Space*, *Washingtonian*, *Nature* and *The Washington Post*. He holds a bachelor's degree in journalism from Ohio University and a master's degree in English literature from Georgetown University.

# Issues in Media

# 1

# Broadcast Indecency

William Triplett

Justin Timberlake prepares to rip Janet Jackson's costume during their controversial halftime show at Super Bowl XXXVIII on Feb. 1, 2004. Critics say the increasingly indecent content on radio and TV harms society and needs to be regulated more strictly. Defenders of the media say the First Amendment provides wide latitude to broadcast sexually provocative material.

From *CQ Researcher,*
April 16, 2004.

Rep. Fred Upton wouldn't have missed this year's exciting Super Bowl game for anything. But the Michigan Republican did miss the fireworks during the halftime show. He was in the kitchen making popcorn when a supposedly accidental "wardrobe malfunction" exposed pop singer Janet Jackson's right breast.

By the time he returned to the TV, the second half had started. For that one day, all he knew was that Super Bowl XXXVIII had been one of those rare, exciting contests between two equally matched teams.

The next day Upton called his 80-year-old father to get his reaction to the game. He expected to hear, "Great!"

"Awful!" his father said. He'd seen singer Justin Timberlake rip Jackson's costume, momentarily exposing her right breast, and it had ruined the entire game for him. Upton felt particularly bad because his father had watched it on the high-definition television set Upton had encouraged him to buy — which gave him a superb view of something he'd rather not have seen at all.

A few weeks later, Rep. Christopher Cox, R-Calif., and his 5-year-old son were horsing around in the living room. Out of breath, Cox called for a break, saying, "Halftime!" That prompted his son to jump on the coffee table, yank off his shirt and shout, "Halftime show!" He had not seen the Timberlake-Jackson incident but had heard other kids and adults talking about it.

As Upton and Cox discovered, it was impossible to escape the infamous breast-baring — even if one hadn't seen it — and even more difficult not to have a reaction to it.

Ironically, the House Subcommittee on Telecommunications

## Majority of TV Shows Have Sexual Content

Sexual content is in the vast majority of top teen TV shows and nearly two-thirds of all the programs on broadcast TV. During prime time, nearly three-quarters of the shows have sexual content.

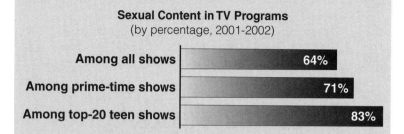

**Sexual Content in TV Programs**
(by percentage, 2001-2002)

| | |
|---|---|
| Among all shows | 64% |
| Among prime-time shows | 71% |
| Among top-20 teen shows | 83% |

*Note:* The survey included all types of shows (except sports, news and children's) and all segments of the TV industry, including broadcast network, syndicated programming, basic and premium cable and public TV. Ten channels were included: ABC, NBC, CBS, Fox, Lifetime, TNT, HBO, PBS, USA and the WB affiliate in Los Angeles, KTLA.

*Source:* "Sex on TV: Content and Context," Kaiser Family Foundation, February 2003.

and the Internet, which Upton heads and Cox sits on, had been holding hearings into charges that radio and network television have become regular purveyors of indecent material, in violation of rules set by the Federal Communications Commission (FCC). But neither congressman — nor millions of other Americans — was prepared for such a brazen display of female anatomy in the middle of what had become an annual family-viewing tradition.

Nor, presumably, had viewers been prepared for the NBC comedy special that aired in May 2003 at 8 p.m. — during what the networks once dubbed the "family hour." The show included a sexually suggestive skit featuring comedian Dana Carvey as the Church Lady, a character he'd originated on "Saturday Night Live," interviewing former child star Macaulay Culkin about his "sleep-overs" with pop singer Michael Jackson, who is facing child sex-abuse charges. Crude commentary by TV gangster Michael Imperioli, of "The Sopranos," added to the vulgarity.

In the weeks following the Super Bowl, the FCC ultimately received more than 530,000 complaints about the Jackson incident. The loudest came mostly from those who had been complaining for years that the public airwaves had become increasingly saturated with inde-

cency; to them, the Jackson episode was unavoidable proof of what they'd been saying.

Others argued, however, that while the halftime show was neither tasteful nor smart, it was just another example of television doing what it always does: trying to grab the viewers' attention. Ultimately, no one had gotten hurt, they said, and after all, it was just a TV show in a country where free speech and freedom of expression are constitutionally protected.

Defenders of the media say the First Amendment gives them wide latitude to broadcast sexually provocative material, which simply reflects changing contemporary mores. But critics of today's radio and television content say sexually oriented broadcasting can harm society, especially children.

They blame the increasing amounts of broadcast indecency on the intense competition between the networks and the cable industry. Networks have been losing market share to cable for the past two decades, mostly, because cable — which is unregulated — offers racier, more violent content. As a result, say some critics, the FCC should be authorized to regulate cable as well as TV broadcasting.

Others say indecency on the airwaves has increased since Congress deregulated the industry in 1996, which has contributed to media concentration into a tiny group of conglomerates. "Deregulation has simply greased the pockets of [broadcast executives], while spawning a fundamental lack of accountability," said James P. Steyer, author of *The Other Parent: The Inside Story of the Media's Effect on Our Children.* [1]

The simmering debate — which perennially erupts during presidential elections — includes questions about whether anyone is really harmed by broadcast indecency. Does a naked body presented as titillating entertainment affect or influence public perceptions — especially children's perceptions — of sex and sexuality? Are the media helping to shape the culture, or just reflecting it?

The current national upset over indecency is just another flareup in a very old debate, says Robert J. Thompson, professor of popular culture and director of the Center for the Study of Popular Television at Syracuse University. "Before television, it was radio, and before radio it was comic books, and before that vaudeville," he says. "Plato talked about whether art should show how the world is or how it should be. We're having the same conversation now."

However, recent studies show there is more sexual content on network prime-time television now than ever before. And some say the problem is even more acute on radio, where some disk jockeys have offered prizes to listeners willing to describe their experiences having sex in public places, invited porn stars into the studio to discuss their work in detail and even castrated a pig during a broadcast.

Left unchecked, some critics say, the networks and cable companies will only compete to outdo each other with increasingly shocking content. A prime-time episode of NBC's "Friends" shows roommates unable to tear themselves away from the television after learning they were mistakenly receiving a pornography channel for free. A rock star says the F-word on live television, followed a few weeks later by a movie star saying the S-word on a similar program. Then a pop singer's breast "accidentally" appears before a U.S. television audience of 143 million people.

The networks are competing in a "race to the bottom," said FCC Commissioner Michael J. Copps. [2]

Some observers and critics say broadcast indecency has seemingly accelerated since the 1980s due to the combined impact of the advent of cable television, videocassette recorders and industry deregulation. And the phenomenon seems even more rapid, according to Thompson, because during the 1950s and '60s, television insisted on presenting an idealized view of the world, while American culture and values were, in fact, changing dramatically.

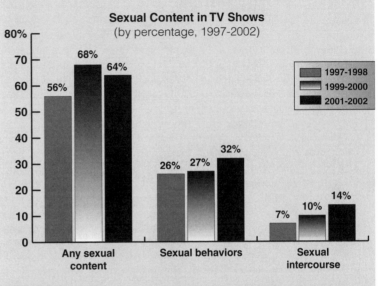

## Sexual Behavior on TV Increased

Although the percentage of shows with sexual content declined slightly in recent years, the percentage exhibiting specific sexual behaviors increased. The percentage of programs that referred to or depicted sexual intercourse in 2001-2002, for instance, was double that of 1997-1998.

**Sexual Content in TV Shows**
(by percentage, 1997-2002)

*Note:* The survey included all types of shows (except sports, news and children's) and all segments of the TV industry, including broadcast network, syndicated programming, basic and premium cable and public TV. Ten channels were included: ABC, NBC, CBS, Fox, Lifetime, TNT, HBO, PBS, USA and the WB affiliate in Los Angeles, KTLA.

*Source:* "Sex on TV: Content and Context," Kaiser Family Foundation, February 2003.

"Now, you're seeing this catch-up, and it seems to be happening really fast, because nothing happened for 50 years," Thompson recently said. "Cultural standards changed and broadcasting didn't. Now it seems like it's unbelievably out of control." [3]

But some warn that the catching-up can be far from benign. Texas Republican Joe Barton, chairman of the House Energy and Commerce Committee, says an increasing amount of indecency could harm the national culture. "The media can be one of three things: Neutral on values, reinforcing values or dismissive/destructive of values," Barton says. "Some of the music and language you hear on radio and TV have been dismissive, if not destructive of values. Over time, that could be very corrosive."

# Supreme Court Internet-Indecency Decision Due

Congress has tried twice to limit children's access to sexually explicit material on the Internet, but the effort has been tied up in constitutional knots.

The Supreme Court ruled the first attempt unconstitutional on free-speech grounds. Now, however, a majority of the justices appear receptive to the lawmakers' second try, after hearing a legal challenge to the law in March.

The government is asking the high court to reinstate the 1998 Child Online Protection Act (COPA), which makes it a crime for commercial organizations to make sexual material deemed "harmful to minors" available to children under 17.

"Internet porn is widely accessible, as equally accessible to children as a TV remote," Solicitor General Theodore Olson told the justices during March 2 arguments.

But a lawyer for the American Civil Liberties Union (ACLU) insisted the law violates the First Amendment because it "suppresses" materials that adults have a right to view. "COPA criminalizes speech that adults under any definition have the right to access," Ann Beeson told the justices. The government has "less restrictive alternatives" to controlling minors' access to indecent materials, she said, such as encouraging parents to install software filters that block sexually explicit sites.

The case — *Ashcroft v. American Civil Liberties Union* — marked the third time the Supreme Court has heard arguments on efforts to limit minors' access to Internet pornography. In pre-Internet cases, the Supreme Court ruled the government can prohibit children from having access to sexually explicit materials, but only if the law does not unduly interfere with adults' rights to read or view anything short of the stringent definition of legal obscenity.

In its first ruling on Internet porn, the court in 1997 struck down the 1996 Communications Decency Act. In a mostly unanimous decision, the court in *Reno v. American Civil Liberties Union* agreed with the ACLU's arguments that the law unconstitutionally interfered with adults' access to protected materials.

Congress tried to meet the court's objections when it approved the COPA in 1998. The new law applies only to commercial publishers on the World Wide Web, not to e-mail, chat rooms or news groups. In contrast to the earlier prohibition against "patently offensive" materials, the new law covers material found to be "harmful to minors" — defined as sexually explicit, patently offensive and lacking serious value for minors. The new law — like the earlier one — protects a Web publisher if it requires users to establish

---

By itself, Jackson's bared breast might have provoked only momentary outrage. But coming in the wake of growing charges of indecency against radio shock jocks and broadcast television shows — and prompting Rep. Upton to hold hearings — it electrified the indecency debate with contemporary urgency.

In many ways the debate is a Rorschach test revealing our national values. To some, it is nothing less than part of a fight for the very soul of the culture.

"Historically, culture was something for more than just enjoyment," says Robert Peters, president of Morality in Media. "It was what knit a civilization together, to encourage the values that the particular civilization believed were important. When your popular culture begins to undermine everything you think is good in your society, you're headed for trouble. There's a lot of good in America, and, relatively speaking, not much good makes the news or the entertainment media.

To me, it's literally a life and death issue for our society."

As the debate over broadcast indecency rages, here are some of the questions being raised over the meaning and implications of recent events:

### Does indecency over the airwaves undermine American society?

"It's easy to dismiss how influential television can be or how much power it has to undermine values," says Melissa Caldwell, director of research and publications at the Parents Television Council, a conservative group that supports family-oriented TV programming. "But when you look at the . . . thousands of studies pointing to a causal relationship between media violence and real-life aggression, you see that children who watch lots of violent TV as kids can grow up to be violent adults. There is a huge body of evidence out there for that."

Likewise, a "growing body of evidence shows that

their age by a credit card, adult identification number or other device.

Despite the modifications, the ACLU immediately challenged the new law on behalf of an array of Web publishers. Plaintiffs included Internet privacy advocates, gay and lesbian services and the online magazine *Salon* — which publishes a widely read sex-advice columnist, Susie Bright.

The lawsuit had first reached the Supreme Court in 2002 after the statute was ruled unconstitutional, first in a broad ruling by a federal district court in Philadelphia and then on a narrower ground by the federal appeals court in Philadelphia. The high court said the appeals court was wrong to strike the statute on the ground that it allowed local community standards to be used in defining the scope of the law. [1] The decision sent the case back to the appeals court to rule on other issues. The appeals court again ruled the law unconstitutional, and the Bush administration brought the case back to the high court.

Meanwhile, a third law aimed at protecting children from Internet porn — the Children's Internet Protection Act — was upheld by the court in June 2003. It required schools and libraries to install software filters on computers to restrict children's access to sexually explicit materials. [2]

In the March 2 arguments in the COPA suit, Olson stressed Congress' efforts to target commercial pornography. Beeson countered by claiming the law threatened sites that provided safe-sex education. For instance, Bright's *Salon* columns would be covered, Beeson said, because they discuss "sexual pleasure."

Justice Stephen G. Breyer appeared unconvinced. "I don't think that's prurient," he said. "A discussion about sex is a totally different thing from a discussion that is itself supposed to be part of a sexual response." In previous cases, Breyer has sometimes joined with members of the court's conservative majority to uphold government regulation of speech and expression.

Among the nine justices, only two — Anthony M. Kennedy and Ruth Bader Ginsburg — appeared strongly skeptical of the law. Kennedy questioned the breadth of the law, while Ginsburg voiced concerns that adults would be deterred from looking at sexually explicit materials if they had to identify themselves by using a credit card. Justice David H. Souter, who had voted to invalidate other Internet porn laws, was silent during the hourlong argument.

A decision is due by the end of June.

— **Kenneth Jost**

---

[1] The 8-1 decision is *Ashcroft v. American Civil Liberties Union*, 535 U.S. ___ (May 13, 2002). Justice John Paul Stevens dissented.

[2] The 6-3 decision is *United States v. American Library Association*, 539 U.S. ___ (June 23, 2003). Justices Stevens, David H. Souter, and Ruth Bader Ginsburg dissented. For background, see Kenneth Jost, "Libraries and the Internet," *CQ Researcher*, June 1, 2001, pp. 465-488.

---

kids' sexual behavior is influenced by what they see on television," she says. Although the evidence linking youngsters' behavior to sexual content on TV is still relatively small, it is notable, she says.

For instance, the Medical Institute for Sexual Health, in Austin, Texas, which promotes abstinence as the only foolproof method of birth control and avoidance of sexually transmitted diseases, recently reviewed more than 2,500 biomedical and social science studies conducted over the last 20 years. Only 19 — less than 1 percent — examined the effects of mass media on adolescent sexual behavior or attitudes.

Those 19 studies found that teenagers are exposed to "extensive sexual imagery and content" in mass media. Researchers found that television, for example, showed 6.7 scenes featuring topics related to sexuality every hour, and the average teenager watches three to four hours of television a day. Adolescents exposed to such content were more likely to have more permissive views of premarital sex and more likely to think that "having sex is beneficial," according to the study. [4]

"Children exposed to lots of sexual content believe that everyone's having sex," Susan Tortolero, a study author and an epidemiology professor at the University of Texas School of Public Health. "That is bad, especially for young ages," particularly since most sex on television is casual or between unwed couples, and married sex is usually portrayed negatively, she says.

"Psychologists [say] it can confuse children when they're exposed to a lot of sexual material. It can cause harm in that it's too much information," which kids aren't capable of understanding at young ages. "We see lots of kids having oral sex and at early ages. They say they see it on television and hear it in music, mostly rap music."

Similarly, a recent report from the Kaiser Family

## Teen Shows Often Mention 'Safer Sex'

Among the most-popular teen shows with intercourse-related content, nearly half mentioned safer-sex practices, such as using condoms or practicing abstinence.

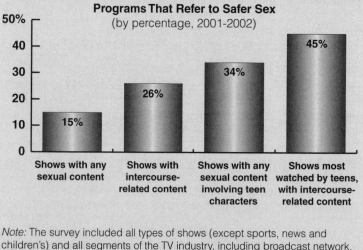

**Programs That Refer to Safer Sex**
(by percentage, 2001-2002)

- Shows with any sexual content: 15%
- Shows with intercourse-related content: 26%
- Shows with any sexual content involving teen characters: 34%
- Shows most watched by teens, with intercourse-related content: 45%

*Note:* The survey included all types of shows (except sports, news and children's) and all segments of the TV industry, including broadcast network, syndicated programming, basic and premium cable and public TV. Ten channels were included: ABC, NBC, CBS, Fox, Lifetime, TNT, HBO, PBS, USA and the WB affiliate in Los Angeles, KTLA.

*Source:* "Sex on TV: Content and Context," Kaiser Family Foundation, February 2003.

Foundation — which has been tracking sexual content on television for several years — found that in the top 20 shows watched by teens, eight in 10 episodes included some sexual content and one in five involved sexual intercourse.* And the amount of sexual content was increasing on nearly every channel, the report noted. Approximately 64 percent of all shows now have some kind of sexual content, up from roughly 50 percent just four years ago. And 14 percent of shows specifically include sexual intercourse, either depicted or strongly implied, an increase from 7 percent four years ago. [5] (*See graph, p. 3.*)

However, the report also notes that references on these shows to safe, or at least safer, sex practices are also increasing, thus presenting at least in part an arguably more responsible view toward sex. (*See graph, p. 6.*)

---

* In the past few years, top-rated teen shows have included "Dawson's Creek," "That '70s Show," "One on One," "Just Deal" and "Beverly Hills 90210," all of which contain scenes involving sex or talk of sex.

Are kids being corrupted by sexual imagery on television? No, according to a 17-year-old high school girl in North Carolina. "People don't give people our age enough credit," she recently said. "We understand what's going on. We're a lot wiser. [Networks] just have to keep getting more shocking to keep people tuning in."

But asked about Madonna's televised open-mouth kiss with Britney Spears during last year's MTV music video awards show, the girl acknowledged: "It's more common to see girls making out now as a tactic to get guys. Nobody's going to say it's because Britney and Madonna did it, but it is." [6]

And the effect isn't just on children, says Patrick Trueman, senior legal adviser to the conservative Family Research Council. He says formerly inhibited or prohibited behaviors are becoming commonplace as a result of programming standards that he says have hit bottom. "What used to be sort of extreme activity has become normal for a good segment of society," he says.

"The shock-jock routine has taken the shock out of taboo in America," continues Trueman, former chief prosecutor in the Department of Justice's child exploitation and obscenity division. "I was recently with the Philadelphia vice squad on a drive around to 'massage' parlors, and the clientele were normal, regular businessmen — ordinary Joes doing what seems a casual, regular thing." Although Trueman doesn't blame shock jocks for all such adult behavior, indecent programming is partly responsible, he says.

No one argues that the airwaves are pure, or even harmless. The debate surrounds how much harm occurs from broadcast indecency and whether it's appreciably worse now than ever before. "I'm sure indecency undermines some people's values," says Frank Couvares, professor of history and American studies at Amherst College in Massachusetts. "And I'm sure it has no effect on other people."

Others note that as cultural standards in broadcast, print and the newer electronic media have become more permissive, large parts of American life have substantially improved. Women and blacks, for example, have achieved a status long previously denied to them. U.S. church attendance remains steady as ever and is significantly higher than in most European societies. Overall, violent crime has been declining since the early 1990s, and more public interest and advocacy groups are fighting poverty, homelessness, hunger and illiteracy today than ever before. [7]

Perhaps most significant: At a time when sexual content increasingly pervades television and radio, pregnancy rates among U.S. teenagers have dropped to the lowest level ever recorded, and fewer teenagers are having sex. [8]

"There's not much [evidence of] children being corrupted by media . . . [or] being led here in radically dysfunctional directions," Couvares says, adding that many children are, however, "being corrupted by abusive parents and terrible events in their lives."

While to some extent television and radio simply reflect the culture, some evidence suggests the media also influences culture. But the influence is minimal, at best, Syracuse's Thompson says. "It always amazes me to hear claims that television sets the agenda," he says, noting that school segregation was ruled unconstitutional in 1954, but not until 1971 did civil rights get regular mention on television, in "All in the Family." "Other institutions push envelopes, television licks the envelope only when it's safe to do so.

"Ultimately," he continues, "if we're looking at the 500 major things threatening American life today — including the welfare of our children — the content of television isn't even in the top 100." If children are suffering any ill effects from exposure to sexual content on either television or radio, he says, then parents are failing to restrict access as they should. (*See "At Issue," p. 17.*)

But parents say that's almost impossible today, given the pervasiveness of sexual content throughout American media and culture.

### Does the FCC have sufficient authority to punish broadcasters for indecency?

"Yes, we do have the authority," says FCC Commissioner Copps. "I've been talking about this issue [since] I arrived here two and half years ago." But until recently, he says, the commission had been unwilling to tackle the problem, largely due to institutional fears of

"Dawson's Creek" created waves from its first show, which featured a love affair between a female high school teacher and one of her male students. Most teen-oriented shows today have high amounts of sexual content.

running afoul of the First Amendment and the commission's free-market stance that the public was free to turn off the TV or radio if they did not like the content.

"The Super Bowl became a galvanizing incident," Copps says, precisely because "it gave the lie to these arguments. Here's all of America gathered round to watch the Super Bowl, and they're supposed to turn it off?"

The FCC's historical stance of letting market forces influence content has angered some parents. "A major responsibility of the FCC is to ensure that those who use the public airwaves adhere to standards of decency," L. Brent Bozell III, president of the Parents Television Council, recently told a House subcommittee. "Yet, looking at the FCC's track record on indecency enforcement, it becomes painfully apparent that the FCC could care less about community standards of decency or about protecting the innocence of young children."

In the past two years, Bozell continued, the FCC has received "literally hundreds of thousands of complaints of broadcast indecency from fed-up, angry, frustrated parents." Yet it "hasn't seen fit to agree with a single complaint." In fact, in its entire history the FCC has issued only three fines to television stations for broadcast indecency.

The FCC, he concluded, is "a toothless lion, and its non-actions are not only irresponsible, they're inexcusable. Either the FCC has no idea what it's doing, or it just doesn't care what the public thinks." [9]

Excluding this year's Super Bowl, the FCC has received more than 308,000 complaints of indecent broadcasts over the last 10 years, but issued only 52 notices of liability for violations. [10]

FCC Chairman Michael K. Powell has maintained that regulating content "gets tricky" because it is difficult to define a violation for which a licensee can be fined. [11]

Nevertheless, Copps says, "I don't think commissioners need to sit and debate whether we have the authority. We've been given a law that says when kids are watching television, you shouldn't have obscene, indecent or profane material."

The law stems from a 1978 Supreme Court decision following the 1973 airing by Pacifica Radio of comic George Carlin's now-famous "Seven Words You Can't Say on Television" monologue. After the high court affirmed in *FCC v. Pacifica Foundation* that the FCC has a right to police indecent broadcasts, the commission defined indecency as "language that describes, in terms patently offensive as measured by contemporary community standards . . . sexual or excretory activities or organs," when "there is a reasonable risk that children may be in the audience." [12]

However, Robert Corn-Revere, a former FCC attorney now specializing in communications law, says the *Pacifica* decision — which split the court 5-4 — was a limited affirmation of FCC authority. Moreover, he says, subsequent changes in technology, society and especially the law have weakened the constitutional basis for the FCC's definition of indecency.

For instance, last fall FCC Enforcement Bureau Chief David Solomon decided not to fine rock singer Bono, who exclaimed, "This is really, really f—ing brilliant!" after receiving an award during NBC's 2003 live broadcast of the Golden Globe Awards. Solomon said he was prevented from fining NBC in part because FCC regula-

tions only prohibit such words from being used as verbs or nouns, not as adjectives or adverbs.

Moreover, the Supreme Court's *Pacifica* decision had also said that for a broadcast to be indecent or obscene, the violations must be repeated and willful, so FCC rules also require the context of an alleged violation to be considered.

Solomon didn't have the authority to fine NBC, says Corn-Revere, "because with the Bono case, you were talking about a live, unscripted program and a single, fleeting reference."

The Parents Television Council successfully pressed the FCC to reconsider the Bono decision, and in March the commission declared that the incident did indeed violate decency standards. In the future, the FCC said, use of the F-word in any form would be fined. But the panel again refused to issue a fine, saying no stations had been warned first that broadcasting such profanity would violate FCC decency rules. [13]

However, some observers say the reconsidered decision is consistent with the FCC's longstanding pattern of avoiding fines in indecency cases to prevent being challenged in court on First Amendment grounds. Instead of going to court, the FCC typically collects fines by holding up other business — such as a merger or a license renewal — that the station wants to effect. As such, the agency avoids a legal challenge to whether its indecency standard is constitutional. All the cases filed by the FCC over the last 10 years have been settled out of court.

Thus, for at least the last 20 or 25 years, getting involved in "content stuff" was the "last thing the commission wanted to do," says Christopher Sterling, a former special assistant for media affairs at the FCC and now a professor of media and public affairs at George Washington University. "The FCC has washed its hands [of the matter] and said there's no role it can play here. So [people] write to Congress, which is why we're having hearings."

"The FCC is caught between statutory and constitutional demands in an area that from time to time is highly politicized," says Corn-Revere, who often had to determine whether allegations of indecency merited action when he worked at the commission. "The people who are howling for blood simply don't have a clue about what the [commission's] legal dilemma is."

Chairman Powell acknowledged the statutory-constitutional tension in a statement accompanying the reconsidered Bono decision. "This sends a signal to the industry that the gratuitous use of such vulgar language on broadcast television will not be tolerated," Powell said. "Going forward, as instructed by the Supreme Court, we must use our enforcement tools cautiously. As I have said since becoming a commissioner, government action in this area can have a potential chilling effect on free speech." [14]

However, Rep. Barton doesn't think the FCC needs any additional or revised authority to do its job. "In the past," he says, "they've been lax in enforcement."

### Should the FCC regulate cable television?

Radio and network television broadcasts travel over the public airwaves and thus can be tuned in for free by anyone with a TV or radio. The courts have said that because these broadcasts are "pervasive" and an "uninvited guest" in homes, the FCC has authority to regulate them.

But because cable and satellite programs are privately transmitted for a fee and those who watch them must first "invite" them into their homes, cable and satellite programs are not subject to FCC authority.

But that may change.

More than 85 percent of viewers — including those who could receive broadcast directly over the airwaves — now receive their broadcast television through cable or satellite transmissions. [15] And viewers increasingly discern little difference between broadcast and cable, except when changing channels from, say, a Disney show to something like "The Sopranos," the popular HBO Mafia series that includes graphic language, sex and violence.

"That changes the argument a little," says Copps, "especially when the Supreme Court has already said there's a compelling governmental interest in protecting children from indecency on cable." [16]

Nielsen Media Research reported last year that for the first time more viewers watch TV through cable than via broadcast, though the top-rated broadcast shows still draw larger audiences than most top-rated cable programs. But with more families receiving television through cable and satellite transmission — and the prospect that even more people will do so in the future — some argue that the FCC should have domain over cable and satellite as well.

"I'm sympathetic to the many people who ask why our indecency regulations apply only to broadcast," FCC Commissioner Kevin Martin recently testified. "Increasingly, I hear a call for the same rules to apply to

everyone, for a level playing field. And if cable and satellite operators continue to refuse to offer parents more tools for blocking unwanted content, then basic indecency and profanity restrictions may be a viable alternative that also should be considered." [17]

Bozell, of the Parents Television Council, agrees. "More and more, the audience is gravitating to cable, so you have to address the sewage that's seeping through there," he said recently. [18]

Even Rep. Barton, who describes himself as a "free-market, pro-competition guy," believes FCC regulation of cable and satellite should be considered. "As satellite and cable become more ubiquitous," he says, "the distinction between over-the-air and cable lowers."

The cable industry says regulation is unnecessary. Cable has become popular precisely because it provides networks offering appropriate programs targeting children and families, says Brian Dietz, a spokesman for the National Cable and Telecommunications Association.

"Cable also has specific technology that allows customers to block out certain channels," Dietz adds. "Analog boxes offer simple technology to block whole channels, while digital boxes offer advanced technology that will allow the channel to come in, but not certain shows if you don't want them."

Parents' groups have complained that children often are more technologically sophisticated than adults and can circumvent such control devices. But Dietz points out that with cable, children cannot access the control system without knowing the parents' password, or PIN number. "If a kid doesn't have the PIN code, he's not going to get in."

The FCC's Martin and others have pressed the cable and satellite industries to at least consider offering family-friendly tiers or à la carte bundles of channels, instead of forcing consumers to subscribe to packages that include every available channel. That way, parents who prefer their kids not to see, for example, "The Sopranos" or anything on MTV, could order packages without those channels.

"Tier or à la carte delivery would undermine the economics of the industry and have a detrimental impact on the diversity and variety of programming," Dietz claims. Cable advertising rates are based on the total number of homes served — about 70 million. "If a network was sold à la carte or by a tier, that base of 70 million might go down to 5 million." With fewer viewers in a tier, the

## CHRONOLOGY

1950s *Television experiences its "Golden Age"; networks voluntarily impose decency rules.*

**1950-51** Complaints of starlets' plunging necklines prompt the first congressional hearings into TV content. Broadcasters establish a voluntary ethics code.

**1952** Network censors forbid the word "pregnant" from being uttered in any "I Love Lucy" episode.

**1957** Actress Jayne Mansfield's breasts "accidentally" pop out of her low-cut gown during live TV Oscar show.

1970s *Television is allowed to show more realism.*

**1971** "All in the Family" debuts, addressing taboo subjects like racism, bigotry, homosexuality and rape.

**Feb. 4, 1975** National Association of Broadcasters TV code board adopts "Family Viewing Hour" prohibiting programming "inappropriate for general family viewing" during the 7-9 p.m. time period.

**Nov. 4, 1976** A federal judge rules the family-viewing hour unconstitutional; the networks voluntarily re-establish it.

**1978** Supreme Court's *FCC v. Pacifica Foundation* decision grants the FCC limited authority to regulate broadcast indecency.

1980s-1990s *Advent of unregulated adult fare on cable and video forces commercial broadcasters to compete.*

**1981** "Hill Street Blues" introduces edgy dialogue and implied or discussed sex to prime-time drama.

**1983** Broadcasters abandon voluntary code of ethics after Justice Department alleges it violates antitrust laws.

**1987** A character on NBC's "St. Elsewhere" moons his boss.

**1988** "Married . . . with Children" debuts, becomes an instant hit.

**1992** When unwed TV character "Murphy Brown" decides to have a baby, Vice President Dan Quayle denounces TV's disrespect for "family values."

**1993** Premiere episode of "NYPD Blue" shows a woman's dimly lit breast and backside during a lovemaking scene.

**1995** FCC fines Infinity Broadcasting a record $1.7 million for indecency by radio shock jock Howard Stern.

**1996** Telecommunications Act requires networks to develop content ratings and for all televisions to eventually contain "V-chips" allowing parents to block objectionable programs.

**Jan. 1, 1997** Television industry begins ratings system with age-based advisories; made more descriptive later that year.

**1999** Critically acclaimed show "The Sopranos" debuts on cable's HBO, featuring profanity, graphic violence and sex.

2000s *Broadcasters continue to push the decency envelope, prompting a regulatory and congressional backlash.*

**2000** Contestant Richard Hatch appears naked several times on CBS' reality TV show "Survivor."

**2001** Characters on the animated cable satire "South Park" say the S-word 162 times in one episode.

**2002** The FCC fines Infinity Broadcasting $357,500 after radio shock jocks Opie and Anthony broadcast a live description of a couple having sex during a church service.

**2003** Rock singer Bono says the F-word during a live broadcast; FCC refuses to fine the network.

**January 2004** Viewer complaints prompt Congress to hold hearings on broadcast indecency and FCC inaction.

**February 2004** Janet Jackson's right breast is exposed during the Super Bowl halftime show.

**March 2004** Senate and House pass bills increasing fines against indecency from $27,500 per infraction to as much as $500,000.

ad rates would have to drop, lowering the company's overall profitability.

"To stay in business," Dietz says, "subscription prices would have to be significantly higher." Consumers currently paying $40 a month for 70-80 channels could end up paying $40 a month for only 10 channels, he says.

Caldwell, of the Parents Television Council, isn't persuaded by such economic arguments. "I don't know what all the economic ramifications are," she says, "but if you're taking a free-market position, let the viewers pay for what they want."

Dietz counters: "Cable is sold as a bundled product similar to a newspaper or a magazine. You can't buy just the business section of *The Washington Post* or *The New York Times.*"

Ultimately, the courts probably will declare it unconstitutional for the FCC to gain authority over the cable and satellite industries, according to attorney Corn-Revere.

"In every other medium and in every other situation, the courts — including the Supreme Court — have struck down attempts to extend an indecency or indecency-type regime outside of the network-broadcasting context," he says. "Broadcasting is the sole and very narrow exception."

Others don't view the situation in such absolute terms. "The First Amendment is to benefit everyone, but that's not to say we can't have laws against indecency," says the Family Research Council's Trueman. "Because it's a freedom that turns into a slavery if we are no longer allowed to protect our children and instead enslave them in this culture we're developing."

## BACKGROUND

### Early TV Taboos

The federal government began regulating America's media industry in the early 1900s, driven by a concern that had nothing to do with content. Fearing that the infant broadcast companies might acquire too much market power, possibly violating antitrust laws, Congress passed the 1927 Federal Radio Act, establishing the Federal Radio Commission — a precursor of the FCC.

Seven years later, Congress passed the watershed 1934 Communications Act, which established the FCC as an independent agency and set guidelines for regulating the amount of public airwaves any one company could use.

An infamous science-fiction radio program in 1938 — Orson Welles' eerily realistic adaptation of H.G. Wells' novel, *War of the Worlds* — triggered the government's first interest in controlling broadcast content. On Halloween night, Welles introduced the show as a fictional drama, but most listeners tuned in later and didn't hear the disclaimer. The broadcast, crafted as a breaking news story, convinced thousands of people that Martians had landed and were taking over the Earth. Panic ensued.

In response, the head of the FCC warned radio to police itself and its programming better if it wanted to avoid government intervention. [19]

A dozen years later, however, television presented a bigger problem. "Television in the beginning was almost all live," says Louis Chunovic, author of the 2000 TV history, *One Foot on the Floor: The Curious Evolution of Sex on Television from "I Love Lucy" to "South Park."* "The first people who put shows on reasoned that they were being invited into viewers homes," so they dressed up for the occasion, with men often in tuxedos and women in evening gowns.

"The very first thing that got Congress up in arms was the plunging neckline debate," Chunovic says of the ambitious starlets who wore gowns with revealing necklines, out of which they might "accidentally" tumble. "This was a great way to get publicity in those days, and it happened time after time after time on these live programs."

One buxom starlet — Virginia Ruth Egnor, known to millions as Dagmar — provoked government intervention. "Her job was just to wear spectacular strapless evening gowns and view the proceedings, from a stool set up near the band," Chunovic says. Soon she was receiving 500 fan letters a week.

But other viewers, offended by Dagmar's ample décolletage, complained to Congress, prompting the first congressional hearings into television morality. Knowing that broadcast licenses had to be periodically renewed and that Congress was already hotly pursuing suspected communists in Hollywood, the industry wilted under the political glare. Executives ordered backstage seamstresses to sew gauze onto the tops of low-cut gowns. CBS declared it would henceforth ban any mention, in any context, of the word "sex" over the airwaves.

Most significantly, the industry adopted a voluntary code of conduct dictating what could and could not be broadcast. The National Association of Broadcasters, the industry trade group, specifically banned "profanity,

# Policing the F-word . . . and Its Cousins

Viewers were outraged a year ago, when rock star Bono — in response to receiving a Golden Globe award — said on a live NBC television broadcast, "This is really, really f—ing brilliant."

But they were even more outraged when the Federal Communication Commission's (FCC) Enforcement Bureau announced it would not fine either Bono or NBC for the incident.

The FCC's indecency rules prohibit offensive words describing sexual or excretory acts or organs, but only when used as verbs or nouns. Because Bono had used the word as an adjective, it did not officially violate the FCC rule.

Incensed at what they considered a technicality, many people complained to Congress. In January, Rep. Doug Ose, R-Calif., introduced a bill to amend FCC rules so that any mention in any context of the F-word — as well as several other words and phrases considered obscene or indecent — would violate FCC rules and therefore be subject to fines.

The measure has triggered debate on several topics, including whether such a zero-tolerance policy is artistically harmful. For example, in 2001 ABC aired Steven Spielberg's Academy Award-winning movie *Saving Private Ryan*, with its multiple use of the F-word (and gory scenes of battlefield carnage) fully intact. Network censors decided that the context in which the word was used — among sol-

diers fighting and dying in the bloody D-Day landing of World War II — made the language relevant and necessary.

If Ose's bill passes — it has more than 40 cosponsors and has been referred to the House Subcommittee on the Constitution — uncensored versions of *Saving Private Ryan* or other movies with similar content could not air on network television without incurring fines.

After receiving thousands of outraged letters about the FCC's Bono decision, FCC commissioners recently reconsidered the case and issued a unanimous decision that the rocker's use of the word "is within the scope of our indecency definition because it does depict or describe sexual activities." However, because existing precedents had allowed such utterances, the commission did not fine NBC or Bono. [1]

"Bono may have used the F-word as an adjective, but today's FCC ruling turned it into a verb directed at American families," responded an angry L. Brent Bozell III, president of the Parents Television Council, which advocates family-friendly TV content. [2]

However, the FCC warned that future utterances of the F-word would trigger fines. Ose's bill would simply clarify and strengthen the FCC's statutory authority to do so.

But some in the broadcast industry question the FCC's constitutional authority to police indecency more stringently. For one thing, a 1978 Supreme Court decision on

obscenity and smut," including "camera angles that emphasize anatomical details indecently." Moreover, "illicit sexual relations" should not be treated as "commendable." [20]

During the 1950s and the beginning of the '60s, life was depicted on television as remarkably — absurdly, to some — free of almost anything that even hinted at sex or sexuality. For instance, the married characters Lucy and Ricky Ricardo of the "I Love Lucy" show slept in separate twin beds, as did Rob and Laura Petrie of "The Dick Van Dyke Show." When Lucille Ball (Lucy) became pregnant by real-life husband Desi Arnaz (Ricky), and producers incorporated the development into the show's story line, the word "pregnant" could not be used.

On the eve of the social and sexual revolutions of the 1960s, American television remained a safe haven ruled

by network censors acutely sensitive to anything that might be the least bit offensive. For example, the still relatively new "Tonight Show" featured host Jack Paar, who could be sharp, edgy and impatient. When a network censor forbade him from telling a joke using the word "W.C." — the abbreviation for water closet, or bathroom toilet — Paar walked off the set.

Television continued to reflect a world in which nothing really sexual or even remotely bad happened, even as the cultural upheavals of the decade burst forth: the rise of the counterculture, the war in Vietnam, the surge of feminism and the appearance of explicit sex in the cinema. In 1968 — the year of North Vietnam's Tet Offensive, the Chicago Democratic convention, the assassinations of the Rev. Martin Luther King Jr. and Sen. Robert F. Kennedy — one of the top-ranked television shows was "Gomer Pyle,

broadcast indecency, *FCC v. Pacifica Foundation*, says that for an utterance to be indecent, it must be "repeated" and "willful" — a standard the single Bono comment, in a moment of excitement, apparently does not meet.

Moreover, says *Radio Business Report*, an online trade newsletter, the agency's indecency standard is so vague it is hard to enforce.

The standard describes indecency as "language that describes, in terms patently offensive as measured by contemporary community standards . . . sexual or excretory activities or organs, at times of the day when there is a reasonable risk that children may be in the audience." Indeed, the standard is so vague that within the last 10 years the agency has settled all its indecency cases, avoiding taking them to court and risking defeat.

In addition, says the newsletter, the commission's indecency enforcement has been "erratic and inconsistent" and the defense could easily prove that no one at the FCC has a

AFP Photo/Jeff Haynes

The rock singer Bono used the F-word on live TV last year, but the FCC declined to fine him or NBC. Here he performs during halftime at the 2002 Super Bowl.

really clear idea of what the FCC's indecency standard really is. [3]

For that reason, says Robert Corn-Revere, a former FCC attorney now specializing in communications law, Ose's bill — if enacted — "would be reversed in 10 minutes" if it were challenged in court. "People will argue the [overall] indecency standard is vague, which it is, so why don't you fix it by making it specific?"

FCC Chairman Michael K. Powell nevertheless believes the agency is moving in the right direction. "We will continue to respect the delicate balance of protecting the interests of the First Amendment with the need to protect our children," he said recently. [4]

---

[1] See *Radio Business Report*, www.rbrepaper.com/epaper/pages/march04/04-55_news6.html.

[2] See Jonathan D. Salant, "FCC cites Howard Stern and Bono for Indecency," The Associated Press, March 18, 2004.

[3] *Radio Business Report*, *op. cit.*

[4] Statement, March 18, 2004.

USMC." "It was set in the contemporary Marine Corps," notes Thompson of Syracuse University, "but never even once mentioned Vietnam." Meanwhile, NBC ran a comedy series called "I Dream of Jeannie," about an astronaut and the confounding hijinks that always resulted when his 2,000-year-old, live-in genie tried to help him. Costumers dressed Barbara Eden, who played the genie, in stereotypical Middle Eastern female garb, complete with bare midriff, but NBC censors insisted that her navel always be hidden.

The first prime-time show to address contemporary issues was "All in the Family," producer Norman Lear's groundbreaking comedy series that debuted on CBS in 1971. One episode dealt with impotence, another with rape and still another with marital problems. Subjects previously taboo — particularly racism — became staples as the show proved a hit with viewers and advertisers.

Chunovic attributes the show's enormous success to the fact that the first generation of Baby Boomers was at the age — the mid-20s — to start demanding a more realistic and representative portrait of the world from network television. Also, as critics pointed out, the show treated its volatile subjects with an unprecedented balance of biting satire and serious respect.

Then in 1973, WBAI, the Pacifica network radio station in New York City, played Carlin's "Seven Words" routine. But in just a few years, technology and market forces enormously complicated the applicability of the Supreme Court's ensuing *Pacifica* ruling.

### The Cable Challenge

During the network era, the business model had been one of homogenization, Thompson says. "The networks

Getty Images

The popular HBO Mafia series "The Sopranos" includes graphic language, sex and violence. Some critics say the Federal Communications Commission should regulate cable television because most broadcast TV comes into homes on cable, and viewers increasingly discern little difference between broadcast and cable. From left: Steven Van Zandt as Silvio Dante, James Gandolfini as Tony Soprano and Tony Sirico as Paulie Walnuts.

were airing pretty much the same shows, trying to appeal to the biggest audience possible," he explains. "That made the most marketplace sense at the time. Then cable came along and flipped that business model on its ear."

The cable industry's underlying market theory was "different strokes for different folks." Not everyone liked the same thing, so industry executives figured a bundled subscription package of multiple channels offering diverse programming — effectively fragmenting the audience — would become reasonably profitable. And because cable shows were not broadcast over public airwaves, programmers did not have to abide by the FCC's indecency rules. Cable shows almost immediately pushed the envelope of taste and propriety.

The videocassette recorder (VCR) appeared almost simultaneously with the rise of cable. VCRs allowed viewers not only to tape edgy cable programs but also to watch adult videos in the privacy of their own homes. And Americans quickly displayed a substantial appetite for pornography: By 1984, adult videos accounted for 13 percent of all video rentals nationwide. [21]

Cable and VCRs delivered a powerful one-two punch to the networks. Even with popular shows like "Three's Company" — in which two single young women roomed with a single male who pretended to be homosexual — the networks began to look hopelessly prim

and out-of-date compared with the more realistic and gritty programs on cable, not to mention the tantalizing allure of adult videos. Networks felt pressure to compete, and by then they had little reason not to: In 1983, they had abandoned their voluntary code of ethics after the Justice Department ruled that parts of the code violated antitrust laws.

Meanwhile, as the Reagan administration proselytized for deregulation in almost all areas, the White House appointed Mark S. Fowler as FCC chairman. Fowler's FCC essentially left the networks to self-regulate content, per the guidelines established in the *Pacifica* decision. The three major broadcast networks continued to maintain their standards-and-practices departments — the censors' bailiwick.

But then the Fox network appeared in the late 1980s. "When Fox came on the air as the fourth network," Chunovic says, "part of its commercial campaign was to tout, 'Hey, we're the network that doesn't have standards and practices!'"

Fox positioned itself as the only broadcaster offering the kind of edgy, hip material typically reserved for cable. "Married . . . with Children," for example, dished up lowbrow jokes about such topics as menstruation, sexual devices and penis size — raunchy humor never before seen in prime-time television. "'Married' was immensely influential, both for Fox . . . and for other broadcast networks," Chunovic writes in his history of sex on television. "Not only because it extended the reach of what was permissible for over-the-air TV, but because its no-taste humor was genuinely funny." [22] Fox now has a standards-and-practices department.

Syracuse University's Thompson says until then the barriers establishing what was acceptable on network television had been broken by "classy stuff" — quality shows like "Hill Street Blues" and "St. Elsewhere."

"However, once that's done, one can't make laws that take into account quality, because that's completely subjective," he says.

## Shock Jocks

With few FCC regulators looking over their shoulders, the networks began ratcheting up sexual content in all sorts of prime-time shows. For instance, the hugely popular '90s series "Seinfeld" devoted an entire episode to a bet over which of the characters could go the longest without masturbating.

Although shock jocks like sex-obsessed Howard Stern in New York were beginning to make names for themselves on radio, television drew most of the criticism at the time. During the 1992 presidential campaign, for example, Vice President Dan Quayle attacked the series "Murphy Brown" as morally irresponsible because the lead character bore a child out of wedlock. (Defenders of the show accused Quayle of playing politics: The previous year the same thing had happened on another show, "The Days and Nights of Molly Dodd," but passed without comment from Washington.)

Sexy talk and double-entendres proliferated on prime time throughout the '90s, and shows that featured such content were among the most critically acclaimed and widely popular, such as "NYPD Blue," "Seinfeld," "Northern Exposure," "Mad About You" and "Law and Order." In the late 1990s, cable's HBO introduced "The Sopranos," a hit almost from the very first episode, featuring not only nudity and sex but also a torrent of four-letter words and violence as a way of life.

However, as both sexual and violent content increased, parents and concerned groups again pressured Washington to do something. President Bill Clinton responded in 1996 with an omnibus telecommunications bill, which, among many other things, mandated that television manufacturers equip new sets with a computerized "V-chip," which could be used in conjunction with a new industry ratings system. Parents could program the chip to block reception of specific shows based on their ratings. [23]

Politicians and cultural critics continued to denounce broadcast indecency. For instance, in 1997 Sen. Joseph I. Lieberman, D-Conn., said in a speech at the University of Notre Dame, "The media [are] speeding the moral breakdown of our society."

Former Secretary of Education William J. Bennett, a Republican, joined forces with Lieberman, calling their movement the "Revolt of the Revolted," which they said represented the "disgust millions of Americans feel toward the growing culture of violence, perversity and promiscuity" in the media. [24]

While groups like the Parents Television Council steadily complained about indecent and violent content on television, radio shock jocks seemed to be pushing the broadcast envelope the farthest, prompting a new round of concern about indecency on the airwaves. Throughout the early '90s, Stern, who seemed to interview a different

The gritty ABC-TV police drama "NYPD Blue" debuted in 1993 with violent, sexually oriented content. In recent years, the actors have begun using mild profanity. Dennis Franz, right, still stars as Det. Andy Sipowicz; Jimmy Smits played his partner for several years.

porn actress almost every time he was on the air, asking detailed questions about their work, racked up indecency fines totaling a record $1.7 million, which station owner Infinity Broadcasting eventually paid.

In 2001, Bubba the Love Sponge, a Florida shock jock whose real name used to be Todd Clem, graphically discussed sex acts during several different broadcasts, resulting in $755,000 in fines against station owner Clear Channel Communications, Inc., a major player in the radio market.

In 2002, the shock duo Opie and Anthony, at WNEW-FM in New York, outraged listeners when they held a contest calling for couples to have sex in risky places. After broadcasting a live encounter between a couple in a Manhattan church during services, Infinity Broadcasting — which owned the station — fired the DJs, and the FCC levied a $375,500 fine against Infinity.

Ironically, the Center for Media and Public Affairs, which studies the news and entertainment media, announced findings around the same time showing that sexual content on television had decreased by almost a third in recent years. But television returned almost instantly to the front of the indecency debate in January 2003, when rock singer Bono uttered the F-word on live television.

The FCC's subsequent decision not to fine NBC for the incident provoked even more outrage, the brunt of which hit Congress. Rep. Upton, who personally signs every letter his office sends in response to constituents' queries or complaints, says, "Last year, I signed about 50,000 letters." Broadcast indecency "was the No. 1 mail item — above Iraq, above abortion — and it only really started coming in the last weeks of 2003, after the FCC's decision on Bono."

Upton began holding hearings on the issue last January, before the Super Bowl incident.

## CURRENT SITUATION

### Raising Fines

In late February, just after the Super Bowl, Clear Channel Radio President John Hogan sat contritely before the House Subcommittee on Telecommunications and the Internet. The subcommittee wanted to know whether increasing the fine for broadcasting indecency from $27,500 per incident to $500,000 would indeed curb indecency on the airwaves.

Hogan answered by announcing that Clear Channel had fired Bubba the Love Sponge. "More than anything else," he said, "I am embarrassed by Bubba's broadcasts." The DJ's shows in general, he added, "are tasteless, they are vulgar and they should not, do not and will not represent what Clear Channel is about." He also said Stern's show would be dropped by the six Clear Channel stations that carried it. Finally, he said that he had begun a "zero tolerance" policy regarding indecency on any Clear Channel airwaves. [25]

Hogan argued that because he had taken these measures without the threat of higher fines, the amount of the fines did not need to be raised. Television executives from ABC, NBC and Fox — all of whom said their networks oppose indecency — supported Hogan's point. They also spoke in conciliatory tones and made clear their desire to cooperate.

But author Steyer questions the media's professed sincerity. "For Clear Channel to say after eight years of

Howard Stern, 'Oh, no, he's saying that on the air?' — it's a joke! These guys have laughed all the way to the bank, being completely irresponsible to kids and families as they've pursued the almighty buck," says Steyer, who is executive director of Common Sense Media, which calls itself "the leading nonpartisan organization dedicated to improving media and entertainment choices for kids and families."

Still, broadcast executives have responded positively to some suggestions from Congress, such as airing public-service announcements informing parents how to block programs with certain ratings using the V-chip technology. More than half of parents who own televisions with V-chips don't know how to use them, industry executives say. TV executives also have agreed to flash ratings of shows following every commercial break, so parents tuning in after the start of a program — the only time the ratings now are shown — can be better informed about content.

"The industry will do whatever it has to do, and that includes acceding to censorship of some sort, which they've done repeatedly when they feel a danger of getting caught in the crossfire of public outrage," says Couvares of Amherst College. Moreover, as author Chunovic and others say, the industry believes a willing attitude will result in less governmental intrusion into the marketplace.

Nevertheless, Congress is working on a bill to raise indecency fines to $500,000. The House passed its version on March 11 establishing a $500,000 ceiling, applicable even for first offenses. The Senate version — passed by committee on March 9 but still awaiting a floor vote — would establish a climbing scale, with $500,000 applicable for third and subsequent offenses. Both versions for the first time would allow the FCC to fine individual artists as well as licensees for indecency violations.

Edward O. Fritts, president and CEO of the National Association of Broadcasters, said voluntary industry initiatives are "far preferable to government regulation" when dealing with programming issues. While the group does not support the legislation as written, he said, "We hear the call of legislators and are committed to taking voluntary action to address this issue." [26]

### Media Consolidation

The Senate's version of the bill also includes a temporary moratorium on media mergers or expansions, so Congress can study whether media consolidation is

# Are parents who seek stricter broadcast-indecency rules asking the government to do their job as parents?

## YES

**Robert Thompson**
*Professor of Popular Culture*
*Director, Center for the Study of Popular*
*Television, Syracuse University*

Written for *CQ Researcher*, March 2004

Once upon a time a parent, in reasonably good conscience, could sit a kid in front of just about anything on TV. Not today. The industry has changed, the culture has changed and much of what's on television today is patently inappropriate for the very young.

So what's a parent to do?

Rudimentary childproofing technologies such as the V-chip and the ratings system are available, but most parents never bother to learn how to deploy them. Instead, many depend upon the federal government to tell kids what they can't watch by never letting it go on the air in the first place.

Children are at the center of nearly every discussion about broadcast indecency today. Most adults, after all, aren't going to be damaged by a vulgar word or a peek at an exposed breast. The outrage over the Super Bowl halftime show was nearly always expressed in terms of the fact that there were little kids in the audience.

Citizens have every right to demand more programming in the public interest. But in calling for the enhancement and enforcement of indecency rules, people aren't asking for the introduction of better programming but merely for the elimination of naughty words and sexual content. And millions of parents, many of whom object to the federal government's regulation of prayer in the classroom and resent it when public schools teach sex education, want the FCC to police the airwaves more aggressively than ever before.

The power to enforce the prior restraint of content in any medium, even a regulated one like broadcasting, is not one to be granted lightly, and especially not as a form of child care. If we legislate against anything inappropriate for a child, we may also eliminate good programming for adults. Little children shouldn't listen to Howard Stern; neither should they watch a performance of *King Lear*. And, as much as we want to protect them, they shouldn't determine the content of everything seen on TV before 10 p.m.

Like liquor and toxic cleaning products, some TV content is a potential household hazard to children, to be responsibly managed by parents but not necessarily removed by federal fiat.

## NO

**Robert Peters**
*President, Morality in Media*

Written for *CQ Researcher*, March 2004

In *FCC v. Pacifica Foundation*, the Supreme Court listed two characteristics of the broadcast media that justify regulation of indecent language. First, broadcasting is "a uniquely pervasive presence in the lives of all Americans" and confronts the citizen in the privacy of the home so that prior warnings alone cannot protect consumers from unexpected program content.

I would add that if adults can use a helping hand in shielding themselves from indecent programming, they can also use some help protecting their children.

Secondly, the court said, "broadcasting is uniquely accessible to children, even those too young to read." The government has an interest in protecting the "well-being of its youth," the court continued, and in "supporting parents' claim to authority in their own household."

Common sense ought to inform us that *Pacifica* was right about the government interests. Many children do not enjoy the blessings of a responsible parent. Consider parents who place no restrictions on what their kids, regardless of age and maturity, watch on TV or how long they watch. Some of these children may need the government's help, regardless of what a parent thinks.

As for the government supporting parents, most parents would welcome government's help in keeping their children away from indecent entertainment on radio and TV. The reasons should be obvious. Parents can't monitor their children every hour of every day from birth to full legal age. And despite their efforts, many parents fail to inculcate their children with a perfect moral sense and the strength to act on it. Moreover, parents can't always control the actions of someone else's kids.

As I see it, parents bear the primary responsibility for raising children, and undoubtedly there are parents who don't fulfill that responsibility and then blame others for their children's problems. But that does not mean that the whole job of raising children should fall on parents!

Human beings are gregarious in nature. We form governments to help order the communities in which we live and to protect us from irresponsible and unscrupulous persons who would harm the community or individuals in it — including children, who often need special protections.

Most parents aren't asking the FCC to do their job; they are asking the FCC to do its job.

AFP/Getty Images/Luke Frazza

Federal Communications Commission Chairman Michael K. Powell testifies on Feb. 11, 2004, on Capitol Hill on broadcast indecency following the Janet Jackson incident. "We must use our enforcement tools cautiously," Powell said. "Government action in this area can have a potential chilling effect on free speech."

contributing to broadcast indecency. Eighty percent of the 91 major cable TV networks, serving more than 16 million homes, are owned or co-owned by only six media conglomerates. [27]

Both conservative and liberal organizations have claimed that having fewer companies controlling what's on the air leads to less concern for community tastes and standards. In turn, they argue, that allows networks to pursue the large, lucrative market of 18- to 34-year-old (mostly male) viewers with increasingly racy and raunchy content.

Both constituencies were concerned last fall when Congress debated whether to include a provision in the fiscal 2004 omnibus appropriations bill relaxing media-ownership rules. The White House and FCC Chairman Powell had favored allowing individual broadcast companies to own as much as 45 percent of the national television market, up from 35 percent. Congress eventually settled on a compromise of 39 percent, which still angered the two constituencies.

"Congress is basically an un-indicted co-conspirator here," says Jeff Chester, executive director of the Center for Digital Democracy, a media-policy group opposed to relaxing media ownership rules. "Congress has basically given to the broadcasters and cable every special-interest request they have made over the last decade."

FCC Commissioner Copps opposes the continued consolidation of the nation's media. For instance, when the agency last summer approved the merger between Spanish-language broadcaster Univision and the Hispanic Broadcasting Corporation, Copps said the deal would "take consolidation to new and threatening heights for those who receive their news and entertainment in Spanish. It involves not just TV, radio and cable, but Internet portals, recording labels and other promotional enterprises."

Univision was already the fifth-largest network and owns local stations reaching more than 40 percent of the country, Copps noted. [28]

When the agency approved News Corporation's acquisition last December of a multichannel distribution system plus a television station in the same market, Copps called the deal "an unprecedented level of consolidation," and asked rhetorically, "When is 'Big Media' big enough?" [29]

Rep. Barton, however, argues that greater media consolidation may lead to less indecency or vulgarity, rather than more. "If you've got a hundred people trying to get a piece of the market, the probability is that at least one of those hundred will do whatever it takes to get share. But when you have only four or five, there's a higher degree of probability that they're more willing to listen to community standards and are more responsive."

In fact, the Parents Television Council does see progress being made. Caldwell notes that merely the threat of FCC action "has been enough for broadcasters to start doing some things they should've been doing all along," such as firing Bubba the Love Sponge and the networks' recent decision to put live broadcasts — including sporting events — on 10-second delay transmission, which allows them to delete objectionable words. "I hope they continue to be more proactive in restricting content, rather than responding to an FCC fine," he says.

However, Peters of Morality in Media thinks the networks still aren't getting the message. "A lot more people in America would watch any one of the networks," he says, "if they'd stop crapping in our face."

## OUTLOOK

### Political Posturing

"The attention directed toward indecency really tends to be cyclical," FCC Chairman Powell said recently. "The envelope will be pushed until someone barks. Then, we recalibrate again and move forward." [30]

Whether the current debate recedes as part of a cycle depends on some factors that didn't figure into previous clashes over indecent programming. One is the dramatically increased fines. Predictions of their effectiveness vary widely.

"If you're the general manager of a television station [facing] a potential $500,000 fine, and any violation will be considered when you apply for re-licensing, that's going to get your attention," says Rep. Heather Wilson, R-N.M. At the network level, though, it might not draw much attention at all. At the Feb. 26 hearing of the House Subcommittee on Telecommunications and the Internet, Rep. John Dingell, D-Mich., asked three network executives if the higher fines would be a credible deterrent. Two replied they didn't think so.

"Some fines may be levied, and some may actually stick," says Sterling of George Washington University. "But I'll be surprised if there's any fundamental change in the industry. You may see it for a season or two, but after that, it'll be business as usual.

"Let's not lose track of the fundamental issue here: money. Lots of it," he continues. "There's huge money to be made, and with the broadcast industry panicking over survival in a multichannel world, one way to do that is to shoot for the lowest common denominator. Clearly that's what's happened, and it's not going to stop. Maybe slow down a little, but not stop."

Others are even less optimistic, saying that the only reason Washington is paying any serious attention to the indecency issue right now is because 2004 is an election year.

"If I were a betting man, I'd bet that after a certain Tuesday in November this will all go away," author Chunovic says.

"It's a front-and-center controversy now," says Chester of the Center for Digital Democracy. "But after the election, this will fade into obscurity."

While hardly optimistic, Peters of Morality in Media is hopeful. "Is all this just a moment of political posturing? Well, the industry isn't going to change on its own," he says. "It's the old carrot-and-stick approach, and if the stick isn't there, they are not going to do what is right. But the potential for change is there." It all depends on whether the FCC maintains its current resolve to crack down on indecent programming, he says. "If they mean business and start taking their responsibility to uphold indecency standards, there's going to be a change."

In theory, the FCC is an independent agency, although the White House designates the commissioners, who must be confirmed by the Senate, and Congress authorizes funding and maintains oversight. Since many argue that the FCC is only as effective and engaged as Congress is, the ultimate question may be whether Congress means business.

"The industry is so powerful and the political leadership so spineless on this that the near-term changes will be small," predicts Steyer of Common Sense Media.

Rep. Wilson acknowledges that Congress hasn't been as diligent on indecency as it could have been, but she and several colleagues vow to follow the issue after the November elections.

Rep. Upton, whose father was appalled by the Super Bowl halftime show, intends to watch the issue, too. "Once our bill is law and it's in effect for a while, we'll come back and see how they're doing, probably around the end of the year," he says. "Are broadcasters and shock jocks meeting limits, or are they still getting fines?"

If they are still exceeding limits, he says, the industry can prepare for more government intervention.

## NOTES

1. Quoted in Patrick Goldstein, "The Decency Debate: The Zipping Point," *Los Angeles Times*, March 28, 2004.

2. *Ibid.*

3. See Lynn Smith, "Can You Say That on TV?" *Los Angeles Times*, Jan. 19, 2004, p. E1.

4. See http://cme.kff.org/Key=1959.CJr.J.D.MW2Tr9.

5. See Kaiser Family Foundation, *Sex on TV 3: Content and Context*, February 2004.

6. See Scott Dodd, "America Divided on Decency; Culture War Especially Hot in States Bush Won, Including the Carolinas," *The Charlotte Observer*, Feb. 23, 2004, p. 1A.

7. See Eric Adler and Steve Paul, "The Debate Over Decency: Media and Morality Face Off," *The Kansas City Star*, Feb. 12, 2004. See also U.S. Department of Justice, "Uniform Crime Reports, January-June 2003," Dec. 15, 2003, p. 1.

8. National Campaign to Prevent Teen Pregnancy, "Recent Trends in Teen Pregnancy, Sexual Activity and Contraceptive Use," Fact Sheet, February 2004. See also Nina Bernstein, "Behind Fall in Pregnancy, A New Teenage Culture of Restraint," *The New York Times*, March 7, 2004, p. A1, and Kathy Koch, "Encouraging Teen Abstinence," *CQ Researcher*, July 10, 1998, pp. 577-600.

9. Testimony before U.S. House Subcommittee on Telecommunications and the Internet, Jan. 28, 2004.

10. Michael K. Powell, FCC chairman, letter to Rep. John Dingell, March 2, 2004.

11. See "Powell's Agenda for '04; FCC chief discusses initiatives on content, localism, indecency," *Broadcasting and Cable*, Jan. 26, 2004, p. 30.

12. See Charles S. Clark, "The Obscenity Debate," *CQ Researcher*, Dec. 20, 1991, pp. 969-992.

13. See Frank Ahrens, "FCC Says Bono Profanity Violated Standards, but Won't Fine NBC," *The Washington Post*, March 19, 2004, p. E1.

14. See http://hraunfoss.fcc.gov/edocs_public/attach match/FCC-04-43A2.doc.

15. See Frank Ahrens, "Over the Line? Only if Over the Air," *The Washington Post*, Feb. 3, 2004, p. E1.

16. In 1996, Playboy Entertainment Group sued the government over the FCC's attempt to force adult cable channels to scramble their signals. Playboy won, but the government appealed, ultimately to the Supreme Court, which upheld the initial decision that the attempt violated First Amendment rights. However, the court asserted that the government did have "compelling interest" in protecting children from indecency on cable. See http://hraunfoss.fcc.gov/edocs_public/attachmatch/FCC-01-340A1.pdf.

17. Testimony before U.S. House Subcommittee on Telecommunications and the Internet, Feb. 11, 2004.

18. See Ahrens, *op. cit.*, Feb. 3, 2004.

19. See Steve Carney, "Around the Dial; FCC Official's Plea Goes Unheeded," *Los Angeles Times*, March 22, 2004, p. 28.

20. See Louis Chunovic, *One Foot on the Floor: The Curious Evolution of Sex on Television from "I Love Lucy" to "South Park"* (2000), pp. 19, 27.

21. See Clark, *op. cit.*, p. 973.

22. See Chunovic, *op. cit.*, p. 114.

23. See Kenneth Jost, "Children's Television," *CQ Researcher*, Aug. 15, 1997, p. 736.

24. Quoted in Koch, *op. cit.*, p. 588.

25. Testimony before House Subcommittee on Telecommunications and the Internet, Feb. 26, 2004.

26. Statement, March 3, 2004.

27. Goldstein, *op. cit.* For background, see David Hatch, "Media Ownership," *CQ Researcher*, Oct. 10, 2003, pp. 845-868.

28. Statement, Sept. 22, 2003.

29. Statement, Dec. 19, 2003.

30. See "Powell's '04 Agenda," *op. cit.*

## BIBLIOGRAPHY

### Books

**Chunovic, Louis, *One Foot on the Floor: The Curious Evolution of Sex on Television from "I Love Lucy" to "South Park,"* TV Books, 2000.**
A former television journalist argues that, despite changing audience tastes and standards, network executives and censors face the same challenges they did when commercial television first appeared, such as: How best to hook large numbers of viewers without offending too many of them?

**McChesney, Robert, *Rich Media, Poor Democracy: Communication Politics in Dubious Times*, University of Illinois Press, 1999.**
A left-leaning media scholar says television's mercantile demands, including racy material to draw viewers, should be balanced by governmental subsidies for nonprofit television, antitrust suits against media conglomerates and vigorous regulation of commercial broadcasters.

Minow, Newton, and Craig LaMay, *Abandoned in the Wasteland: Children, Television, and the First Amendment*, Hill & Wang, 1995.
As chairman of the Federal Communications Commission (FCC) in 1961, Minow shook the industry with his description of television as "a vast wasteland." Writing with a communications scholar, he charges broadcasters with exploiting children for profit while hiding behind First Amendment guarantees.

Steyer, James P., *The Other Parent: The Inside Story of the Media's Effect on Our Children*, Atria Books, 2002.
A Stanford University professor argues that today's media constantly bombard children with images of commercialism, sex and violence, forcing them to confront an adult world long before they are ready.

### Articles

Brown, Patricia Leigh, "Sex Appeals; Hey There, Couch Potatoes: Hot Enough for You?" *The New York Times*, July 27, 2003, Section 4, p. 1.
A cultural reporter asks whether "the current deluge of sex-charged programming indicates a healthy affirmation of American sexuality or the transformation of prime time into a Hooters franchise."

Rutenberg, Jim, "Few Viewers Object as Unbleeped Bleep Words Spread on Network TV," *The New York Times*, Jan. 25, 2003, Section B, p. 7.
Even following rock singer Bono's saying the F-word on live television and other similar incidents, the FCC reported receiving few complaints.

Smith, Lynn, "Can You Say That on TV? Just When It Seems As If Nothing Is Too Profane, Recent Incidents Have Gotten the Feds Involved," *Los Angeles Times*, Jan. 19, 2004, Section E, p. 1.
The author reviews the current controversy over FCC indecency standards and television's historical attempts to test their limits.

Teitelman, Bram, "Radio Reacts to Indecency Flak," *Billboard.com*, March 13, 2004.
Major radio corporations have issued guidelines to their stations regarding new limits on indecent content, signaling the industry's willingness to cooperate with Congress and the FCC.

Witte, Griff, "Broadcasters Promise to Curtail Indecency," *The Washington Post*, Feb. 27, 2004, p. E01.
The threat of new legislation to strengthen anti-indecency rules prompts broadcasting executives to tell Congress they will be more vigilant about content

### Reports and Studies

"Dereliction of Duty: How the Federal Communications Commission has Failed the Public," Parents Television Council, 2004. See www.parentstv.org/ptc/publications/reports/fccwhitepaper/main.asp.
The group says the FCC has a poor record of holding corporate broadcasters accountable for indecent programming.

"Impact of the Media on Adolescent Sexual Attitudes and Behaviors," Medical Institute for Sexual Health, 2004. See www.medinstitute.org/media/index.htm.
The institute found a significant lack of knowledge about how media sex imagery affects children and youth.

"Middletown Media Studies," Ball State University Center for Media Design, 2004. See www.commonsensemedia.org/information/index.php?article=latestresearch.
A team of researchers discovered that 101 Americans' exposure to media in almost all forms was nearly twice as much as the participants had estimated.

"Sex on Television 3: Content and Context," The Kaiser Family Foundation, 2003. See www.kff.org/entmedia/3325-index.cfm.
The third biennial study sponsored by the prestigious foundation finds that while the amount of sex on television remains high, there are also increased references to safe sex and abstinence.

# For More Information

**Center for Digital Democracy**, 1718 Connecticut Ave., N.W., Suite 200, Washington, DC 20009; (202) 986-2220; www.democraticmedia.org. A media-policy organization committed to encouraging non-commercial, public-interest programming and free access to the Internet.

**Center for the Study of Popular Television**, S. I. Newhouse School of Public Communications, Syracuse University, Syracuse, NY 13244; (315) 443-4077; http://newhouse.syr.edu/research. Examines the impact of entertainment television on popular culture.

**Common Sense Media**, 500 Treat Ave., Suite 100, San Francisco, CA 94110; (415) 643-6300; www.commonsense media.org. A nonpartisan, nonprofit organization advocating media programming that serves children's interests.

**Family Research Council**, 801 G St., N.W., Washington, DC 20001; (202) 393-2100; www.frc.org. A public-policy group promoting traditional societal and cultural values.

**The Henry J. Kaiser Family Foundation**, 2400 Sand Hill Rd., Menlo Park, CA 94025; (650) 854-9400; www.kff.org. A nonpartisan, nonprofit foundation that studies major health-care issues confronting America.

**Morality in Media**, 475 Riverside Dr., Suite 239, New York, NY 10115; (212) 870-3222; www.moralityin media.org. A national, nonprofit organization "established in 1962 to combat obscenity and uphold decency standards in the media."

**National Association of Broadcasters**, 1771 N St., N.W., Washington, DC 20036; (202) 429-5300; www.nab.org. The main trade association representing television and radio broadcasters, though the Big Four TV networks are no longer members.

**National Cable and Telecommunications Association**, 1724 Massachusetts Ave., N.W., Washington, DC 20036; (202) 775-3550; www.ncta.com. The major trade association for cable companies.

**Parents Television Council**, 707 Wilshire Blvd., Suite 2075, Los Angeles, CA 90017; (213) 629-9255; www.parentstv.org. A conservative organization focusing on improving the quality of television programming.

# 2

Getty Images/Andrew H. Walker

Former conservative socialite Arianna Huffington created HuffingtonPost.com, a year-old liberal political blog that has risen to the top rank of blogs, with an estimated 1.3 million visitors in April 2006. Huffington says blogging has "leveled the playing field" between the traditional media and the new, independent media who have only a laptop and an Internet connection.

From *CQ Researcher*,
June 9, 2006.

# Blog Explosion

Kenneth Jost and Melissa J. Hipolit

*T*ime magazine's special issue promised to reveal "the lives and ideas of the world's most influential people," and many of the faces on the May 8 cover were instantly recognizable: President Bush, Al Gore and Hillary Rodham Clinton from the world of politics. Computer billionaire Bill Gates. Entertainment queen Oprah Winfrey. Rock star turned global activist Bono.

Down toward the bottom, however, *Time* anointed two media stars less familiar to most Americans but well known to the increasing number of news junkies who turn to cyberspace for information and opinion about the day's events.

Matt Drudge appeared in his trademark fedora, looking much the same as the taboo-defying conservative did in 1998 when his online Drudge Report broke the story of President Bill Clinton's liaison with White House intern Monica Lewinski.

Off to Drudge's left, Arianna Huffington presented an image of pensive glamour evoking her dual life as celebrity socialite and proprietress of HuffingtonPost.com, a new but widely read liberal compendium of political news and opinion.

*Time's* selection of Drudge and Huffington from among many better-known media heavyweights represented the kind of event the weekly news magazine might have noted on its "Milestones" page:

"**ARRIVED**. *The Age of the Blog, the interactive, globally connected medium of communication with revolutionary potential to make politics more democratic, business more productive and knowledge and culture more diffuse.*" [1]

The word "blog" — short for "Web log" — may nevertheless still seem like somewhat obscure jargon to many Americans. A countercultural computer geek coined the word less than 10 years ago to

23

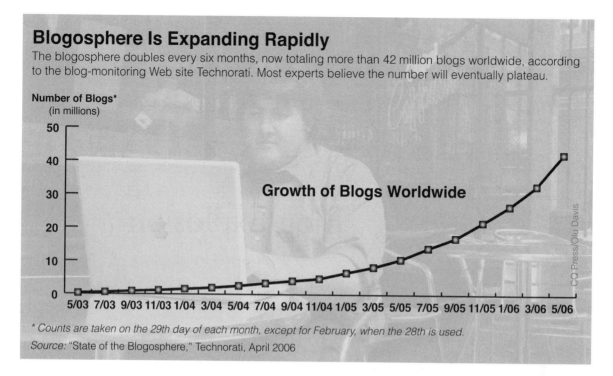

## Blogosphere Is Expanding Rapidly

The blogosphere doubles every six months, now totaling more than 42 million blogs worldwide, according to the blog-monitoring Web site Technorati. Most experts believe the number will eventually plateau.

**Number of Blogs***
(in millions)

**Growth of Blogs Worldwide**

*Counts are taken on the 29th day of each month, except for February, when the 28th is used.*

*Source:* "State of the Blogosphere," Technorati, April 2006

CQ Press/Olu Davis

describe the process of logging on a personal site items he found interesting while surfing the World Wide Web. Nearly three-fourths of the country's Internet users had never read a blog as of November 2004, according to a survey by the Pew Internet and American Life Project. [2]

Today, however, the so-called blogosphere has exploded, with more than 42 million sites and counting, according to the blog-finding service Technorati. Admittedly, many of them are little more than personal diaries, such as the growing number of intimacy-revealing blogs published by high-school and college students. (*See sidebar, p. 36.*) But businesses, politicians and even government agencies are now starting blogs to provide information to — and invite feedback from — customers and constituents. (*See sidebar, p. 34.*)

In addition, a growing number of political blogs provide breaking news not found in mainstream media along with corrections or complaints about news coverage and sharp, often vituperative commentary about national and world events. "Blogs have become the new information ecosystem, part of the conversation about policy," says Rebecca MacKinnon, a research fellow at the Berkman Center for Internet and Society at Harvard Law School in Cambridge, Mass. (*See chart, p. 28.*)

Blogging has also become a global phenomenon and a valuable tool for human-rights and pro-democracy activists in challenging repressive regimes. Bloggers and other Web activists face risks, however. The Egyptian government jailed at least six bloggers among other dissidents in May 2006. China has jailed several Web activists and — with the assistance of U.S.-based Internet service providers — blocked some anti-government sites. And Iran jailed some 20 online journalists and bloggers in January 2005. Some were released after international criticism, but human-rights groups say the government continues to persecute bloggers critical of the regime. [3]

Blogs offer two comparative advantages over other media. Bloggers face few barriers to entry: Anyone with a computer and the nominal costs of easy-to-use software and a Web hosting service can start a blog. The ease of start-up is beguiling, however. The vast majority of blogs go idle after a short period of time. For readers, blogs offer the opportunity to provide instantaneous feedback and to engage in freewheeling dialogue with other blog readers unlimited by space or time.

"Blogs give people the ability to talk to each other, and they're finding that they have more trust in people like themselves, at least in some key areas, than they have in traditional sources of information," says David Kline, a business journalist, consultant and co-author of the book *blog! how the newest media revolution is changing politics, business and culture.*

Drudge himself reportedly dislikes the word "blog," and the Drudge Report invites e-mail and tips but, unlike true blogs, no interactive feedback. Huffington sees her recognition from Time, however, as "a tribute to the influence of the blogosphere," which she says "has leveled the playing field between the media haves and the media have-only-a-laptop-and-an-Internet-connection crowd."

In fact, both Drudge and Huffington have clearly arrived in terms of their visibility in political and media circles. Drudge's site drew around 2.7 million "unique" visitors in April 2006, according to the media-tracking service Nielsen/Net. * "Anybody who's dealing with the political world or the political media world, they're checking Drudge's site every day," says Robert Cox, managing editor of TheNationalDebate.com and president of the newly founded Media Bloggers Association.

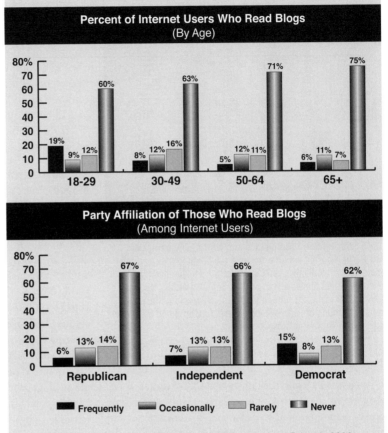

**Most Blog Readers Are Young and Democrats**

Internet users between ages 18-29 read blogs more than other age groups, and 28 percent of them read blogs frequently or occasionally. Democrats read blogs more often than Republicans or Independents.

**Percent of Internet Users Who Read Blogs**
(By Age)

*Source:* The Gallup Poll, "Blog Readership Bogged Down," Feb. 10, 2006.

Huffington's site, which debuted on May 9, 2005, rose within a year to the top rank of blogs. Nielsen/Net estimated 1.3 million visitors in April 2006. "It creates a place for liberals to gather and takes some of the oxygen from conservative sites like the Drudge Report," says the liberal political satirist Al Franken. [4] In the *Time* issue, he claims tongue-in-cheek credit for converting the onetime Newt Gingrich acolyte to her self-described views today as "a compassionate and progressive populist."

The mainstream print and broadcast media continue to draw far more readers and viewers than blogs, however — even in head-to-head competition online. NewYorkTimes.com, for example, was reporting 29 million unique visitors per month in March 2006. [5] "We haven't gotten to the point that blogs swamp in readership the aggregate of all newspapers and magazines," says Eugene Volokh, a UCLA law professor and author of a widely read legal-affairs blog, The Volokh Conspiracy.

In contrast to traditional media, bloggers have no established career path, no prescribed course of dues-paying jobs before reaching prime time or the front page.

---

* A "unique visitor" is anyone who goes to a site at least once during the time period.

AFP/Getty Images/Stephen Jaffe

At Sen. Strom Thurmond's 100th birthday bash on Dec. 5, 2002, Sen. Trent Lott, R-Miss., center, fondly recalled Thurmond's 1948 campaign on a segregationist platform. The gaffe went largely unreported until it erupted in the blogosphere, and the mainstream media then took up the story. An abashed Lott eventually had to give up his post as Senate majority leader — an incident many attribute to bloggers' newfound political muscle. Among others, President Bush, left, attended the party, along with Thurmond's daughter Julie, right.

Drudge used a job in the gift shop at CBS Studios in Los Angeles in the early 1990s to gather Hollywood-type gossip for a report that started as an e-mail newsletter and then broadened into political gossip as it moved onto the World Wide Web in 1996. Before starting her blog, Huffington was a columnist and critic in London in the 1970s and an author and socialite after moving to the United States in the 1980s.

Easy access makes the blogosphere "extremely competitive," according to media historian Paul Starr, a professor of sociology and public affairs at Princeton University in New Jersey. But it is unclear "how deeply entrenched the early leaders will be, how long they will be able to maintain the edge that they now enjoy," says Starr, author of the Pulitzer Prize-winning *The Creation of the Media.*

The biggest blogs, however, not only appear to have staying power but also — thanks to advertising — are

making their creators rich. Drudge's site has been estimated to be worth as much as $120 million; Huffington has made lucrative deals with Internet giants AOL and Yahoo. *Time* itself hosts one of the older blogs: Andrew Sullivan's Daily Dish, while Mickey Kaus's Kausfiles is featured on the online magazine *Slate.com.*

Still, media watchers emphasize that blogs depend on mainstream media for much of their raw material. "They don't go out and do investigative reporting," says Kline. "But as a complement to traditional media, blogs have been very helpful, adding a real slice of life to reporting, uncovering a lot of mistakes in the mainstream media and allowing more diverse voices to be heard."

As the number of blogs and blog readers continues to grow, here are some of the questions being debated:

## Should policymakers be influenced by political blogs?

One month away from becoming Senate majority leader, Sen. Trent Lott, R-Miss., put his foot in his mouth at Sen. Strom Thurmond's 100th birthday bash on Dec. 5, 2002, by fondly recalling the presidential campaign the South Carolinian waged in 1948 on a segregationist platform. Noting that his home state of Mississippi had voted for Thurmond, Lott remarked, "If the rest of the country had followed our lead, we wouldn't have had all these problems over all these years."

Initially, Lott's gaffe went unreported except for a brief mention on ABCNews.com. But the story erupted in the blogosphere, pushed initially by the liberal Joshua Micah Marshall (talkingpointsmemo.com) and the conservative Glenn Reynolds (Instapundit.com). Eventually, the mainstream media took up the missed story, and an abashed Lott had to give up the GOP leadership.

Even as bloggers were demonstrating their impact, however, a noted journalism professor was dismissing their abilities and their role. "Bloggers are navel gazers," Elizabeth Osder, a visiting professor at the University of Southern California's Annenberg School of Journalism, told *Wired News* in 2002. "This is opinion without expertise, without resources, without reporting." [6]

Osder reflected a common view of blogging among journalists and media-watchers in the early years of the phenomenon. But now, blogging is getting respect. "It's moving out of the toddler stage and into the early elementary school age," says Lee Rainie, director of the Pew Internet and American Life Project. Bloggers influence

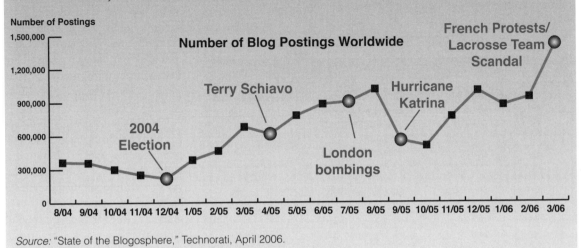

## Daily Blog Postings Approach 1.5 Million

By the end of March, blog postings had surpassed 1.4 million per day — or nearly 60,000 per hour. Postings depend on the news. For instance, postings spiked after the 2004 presidential election, Hurricane Katrina, the death of Terry Schiavo, the subway bombings in London and the youth protests in France and the Duke University lacrosse team scandal.

**Number of Blog Postings Worldwide**

Number of Postings

French Protests/ Lacrosse Team Scandal

Terry Schiavo

2004 Election

Hurricane Katrina

London bombings

*Source:* "State of the Blogosphere," Technorati, April 2006.

mainstream news coverage by checking facts, adding material and prolonging stories, he says. "In some respects bloggers can keep a story alive a lot longer than it would've been alive in the pre-Internet era."

With literally millions of bloggers, generalizations are necessarily treacherous. But among the highest-profile political bloggers, several of them started — like Huffington and Drudge — without the kind of background or experience ordinarily associated with admission into the top echelons of the commentariat. Marshall, for example, had been in journalism for only two years when he started Talking Points Memo in 2000 at the age of 31. Reynolds was a 41-year-old professor at the University of Tennessee Law School when he started Instapundit in 2001.

But legal-affairs blogger Volokh bristles at the insinuation that bloggers have not paid their dues. "Some bloggers have many more qualifications than the average journalist writing on a particular field," he says. Others may have no special expertise but "end up producing good stuff because they're smart people."

Author Kline acknowledges the uneven quality of some blog content. "A great deal of it is uninformed — maybe 95 percent," he says. "But much of what I read in the newspapers is garbage. And most academic writing is terrible."

As with the Lott story, however, Huffington says bloggers have played an important role by running ahead on controversies that mainstream media were either missing or downplaying, such as the re-examination of the "60 Minutes II" story on President Bush's Air National Guard service and the reassessment of the pre-war coverage of Iraq's supposed weapons of mass destruction. "These stories would not have gotten the traction they did without the blogosphere," she says.

But Tom Rosensteil, director of the Washington-based Project on Excellence in Journalism, says bloggers depend on mainstream media to have an impact on events. "If you track the cases where blogs have been influential, it's because they've influenced other political leaders or the media," the former *Los Angeles Times* media critic says.

Whether direct or indirect, bloggers' influence appears to have become a recognized fact of political life. "They have a considerable readership," says Princeton's Starr, who is co-editor of the liberal monthly *The American Prospect*. "I don't see how anybody can ignore them."

Geneva Overholser, a longtime journalist and now a professor at the University of Missouri School of

## Liberal Political Blogs Are Most Popular

Although conservative blogs dominated immediately after the 9/11 terrorist attacks, most of the top 12 political blogs today are liberal. A blog's popularity is measured by how many other sites link to it, considered a vote of confidence for that blog. The rankings refer to how the Web site ranks among the 100 most popular blogs of all types.

### Top 12 Political Blogs

| Overall Rank Among All Blogs | Blog/Blogger | Site | No. of Web Sites Linking to This Blog |
|---|---|---|---|
| 6 | **Daily Kos** Liberal political analysis written by conservative-turned-liberal author Markos Moulitsas Zuniga. | www.dailykos.com | 11,798 |
| 10 | **Huffington Post** Liberal commentary by conservative-turned-liberal Arianna Huffington. | www.huffingtonpost.com | 8,960 |
| 16 | **Michelle Malkin** Written by conservative journalist and author Michelle Malkin; focuses on immigration issues. | www.michellemalkin.com | 7,165 |
| 17 | **Instapundit** Libertarian/conservative; written by University of Tennessee law Professor Glenn Reynolds. | www.instapundit.com | 6,460 |
| 19 | **Crooks & Liars** Liberal virtual magazine by former Duran Duran musician John Amato; features audio and video clips. | www.crooksandliars.com | 6,406 |
| 5 | **Think Progress** Liberal; edited by Judd Legum, research director at the Center for American Progress and former Clinton-era assistant to White House Chief of Staff John Podesta. | www.thinkprogress.org | 5,586 |
| 35 | **Wonkette** Gossipy, satirical blog on Washington, D.C., politics created by journalist Ana Marie Cox. | www.wonkette.com | 4,177 |
| 39 | **Talking Points Memo** Liberal political commentary, reporting from Joshua Micah Marshall, a columnist for the Capitol Hill newspaper, *The Hill*. | www.talkingpointsmemo.com | 3,879 |
| 55 | **AMERICAblog** Liberal blog with focus on the Bush administration, the radical right and gay civil rights; edited by writer and political consultant John Aravosis. | www.americablog.blogspot.com | 3,402 |
| 56 | **Little Green Footballs** Neoconservative war blog by software engineer and guitarist Charles Johnson. | www.littlegreenfootballs.com | 3,401 |
| 59 | **Power Line** Conservative blog dealing with policy issues such as income inequality and campaign finance reform written by lawyers John H. Hinderaker and Scott W. Johnson. | www.powerlineblog.com | 3,346 |
| 71 | **Eschaton** News and politics from liberal points of view; edited by Duncan Black, a senior fellow at Media Matters for America. | www.atrios.blogspot.com | 3,147 |

*Source:* Technorati.com, as of June 1, 2006.

Journalism in Columbia, agrees, but says readers need better information to evaluate individual blogs. She also worries about a seeming lack of diversity in the blogosphere. "We're not seeing the diversity of voices across the old lines of sex, race, socioeconomic level," she says. "Could we really say it's just as easy to find a poor Latina writing a blog that will be heard as it is to find some 35-year-old white guy writing for us?"

Meanwhile, Osder sounds different on the subject today from four years ago. Blogging is "absolutely a wonderful new way to hear the voices of people you might not have heard before," she says. "I think of it more as a way for people in public office to have a new and legitimate ear on their community."

### Should blogs tone down their political rhetoric?

Barely an hour after the American Bar Association (ABA) announced it had rated as "unqualified" President Bush's judicial nominee Michael Wallace, one of the bloggers on the pro-Bush site ConfirmThem.org vented his reaction.

"This is complete and utter b.s.," wrote Stephen Dillard ("feddie") in his May 10 posting. "Mike Wallace is clearly qualified to serve as a federal appellate judge, and the hacks that issued this rating ought to be ashamed of themselves. Lord, how I loathe the ABA."

A few days later, the liberal blogger Jerry Tenuto ("Lone Star Iconoclast") weighed in from the opposite perspective on another Bush nominee, Brett Kavanaugh.

"Brett Kavanaugh is just another shiftless Republican sycophant, ready to do the bidding of the King . . . er, Herr Oberst Karl Rove, that is," Tenuto wrote in the posting on OpEdNews.com. "They've really got this Fuhrer prinzip concept working overtime."

Although such caustic blogosphere rhetoric cheers partisans, some fear it risks aggravating political divisions and coarsening political dialogue. Media historian Starr, however, says blogs cannot be blamed for the political divisions in the country.

"You have, in general, a more polarized and more partisan politics, and at the same time you have the development of the blogs," says Starr. "The two feed off each other."

Bloggers themselves defend the sharp language as part of an American tradition and an essential element of their appeal. "There is a long, proud tradition of incendiary, controversial political rhetoric in America that goes back to the days before the Declaration of Independence," says Cox, of the Media Bloggers Association.

At the same time, blog expert Kline is one of many media watchers who expect the tone to change over time. "I don't think the degree of snarkiness is going to last," Kline says. "This phenomenon is going to evolve. The political conversations now, people just talk at each other. Over time, they'll become more reasoned."

Starr notes that blog technology invites intemperate postings. "There is less of a filter with the blogs because somebody's keystrokes go up immediately," says Starr. "Even if that writer has second thoughts, it's too late."

But Rosenstiel of the Project on Excellence in Journalism says some bloggers do claim to filter out inflammatory rhetoric. "They try to be more provocative, but the most obstructionist and divisive stuff is kept out," he says.

For some bloggers, sharp rhetoric is part of their appeal. "I'm preaching to the choir for a reason," says Markos Moulitsas Zuniga, whose liberal blog DailyKos reportedly draws 500,000 visitors monthly. "It's because we're trying to organize, we're trying to fundraise, we're trying to win elections." [7]

Huffington, however, says she aims at a wider audience. "I don't think we just preach to the choir," she says. Huffington says her blog is bookmarked by many people in the media and in government. "Obviously, these are not all people of the same political persuasion," she says.

UCLA's Volokh cautions against overgeneralizing about blogs. "Some are highly partisan, some are less partisan and some are not partisan at all," he says. In fact,

Bloggers post on their Web logs in a special section reserved for them during the Democratic National Convention in July 26, 2004, in Boston, Mass. Bloggers marked an important milestone when both the Republican and Democratic parties credentialed some bloggers to cover their 2004 national conventions.

legal affairs blogs include several widely read primarily informational sites, such as SCOTUSBlog about the Supreme Court and How Appealing, which covers appellate litigation.

For his part, Cox of TheNationalDebate.com says the marketplace will operate over time as a check on the kind of rhetoric seen in the blogosphere now. "Bloggers, like anyone else advocating a political point of view, must compete in the marketplace of ideas," he says. "This marketplace is self-correcting. Those that employ language in a way that offends the sensibilities of their readers will find themselves with a dwindling audience and decreased influence."

Journalism Professor Overholser agrees. "There are all kinds of blogs," says Overholser. "Some will seek to be balanced, though most are indeed opinionated. Among the opinionated, some will be shrill, others more thoughtful and fair-minded. We consumers will choose among them, and the ones we choose will flourish."

## Should bloggers have the same rights and privileges as reporters?

Sen. Richard J. Lugar, R-Ind., cheered journalism groups in May when he and a group of four bipartisan cosponsors introduced a bill to establish a federal shield law giving reporters a qualified privilege to protect confidential sources of information. "This is important legislation that all Americans should support," David Carlson, president of the Society of Professional Journalists, said in a May 18 press release. [8]

Bloggers had less reason to cheer, however. Lugar's bill would limit the protection to established print, broadcast and cable media — and exclude bloggers. "This bill is more like an 'affirmative action' program for corporate media," says Cox. "It grants special privileges to entities or persons based solely on their relationship to a corporate media organization."

Lugar says the issue is still open for discussion. "As to who is a reporter, this will be a subject of debate as this bill goes farther along," Lugar said in an online reply to a question after introducing the bill. [9] And journalists and media watchers are themselves uncertain about how far into the blogosphere to extend special privileges established for journalists.

"There's so much variety," says Steve Outing, a columnist for *Editor and Publisher Online* who covers interactive media. "Anything from a high-school student who has a personal blog all the way up to a *New York Times* reporter who might be blogging for *The New York Times* or maybe they have a personal blog."

As free-speech expert Volokh notes, the First Amendment itself guarantees certain rights to anyone — whether or not in the news media. The government cannot censor blogs, for example. But journalist shield laws passed by some states are the only protection for guarding confidential sources after the Supreme Court in 1974 refused to recognize a journalists' privilege under the First Amendment.

In addition, governmental and private organizations routinely must decide who qualifies as a member of the media in order to grant them special seating or access to news events. Bloggers marked an important milestone in 2004 when both the Republican and Democratic parties credentialed online journalists — including some bloggers — to cover their national conventions. [10]

For his part, Cox says the rule for bloggers is simple: "When bloggers are acting in a journalistic capacity, they should have the full protections afforded to anybody else who's operating as a journalist. If a blogger is reporting on a story — interviewing people, gathering information, reporting facts and putting together a story — they are a journalist. How they publish is irrelevant. The fact that bloggers are self-published doesn't speak to the issue of what they're doing to produce their content."

Carlson, director of the Interactive Media Lab at the University of Florida in Gainesville, agrees on protections for journalist bloggers but says it is necessary to draw a line between bloggers who are journalists and those who are not. One way to draw the line, Carlson says, is between bloggers who are doing "original reporting" and those who are only "stating opinion" or "regurgitating what others have written."

"You can't necessarily say someone who only does opinion is not a journalist, but often they are not," Carlson continues. "And you can't necessarily say anyone who's doing original reporting is a journalist. But most often they are."

However, Duncan Black, a senior fellow at Media Matters for America and a blogger, says original reporting should not be a prerequisite for a blogger to be treated like other journalists. "What bloggers do fits well within the news media if we broaden [the definition of media] to include the kind of talk shows we find on cable news, public-affairs programs that include news analysis, AM talk radio," he says. "The news media is much broader than people like to think sometimes."

Corporate affiliation should be irrelevant, Black adds. "A press ID from *The New York Times* shouldn't give you special privileges," he says. Rosensteil agrees. "From a journalistic point of view, the technology exists now that you don't need an organization to practice journalism," he says.

Moreover, Cox notes, the mainstream media now are moving rapidly into the blogosphere themselves. "It's not an us [bloggers] versus them [mainstream media] issue," says Cox. "It very much used to be, but now it's gone. When *The New York Times*, *Washington Post*, *National Journal*, CBS News all have bloggers, there's no longer a dichotomy."

## BACKGROUND

### Before Blogs

Modern-day bloggers trace their antecedents back to Ice Age cave painters and to the political pamphleteers of the early centuries of the print revolution. In U.S. history, their ancestry can be seen in the openly partisan press of the 19th and early 20th centuries, the muckraking journalists of the progressive era and the rambunctious hosts of mid- and late 20th-century talk radio. Now with an inexpensive platform that was available to none of those ancestors, bloggers have a unique ability to disseminate their messages — chatty or substantive, informational or opinionated — in real time, 24/7, to an audience as large and far-flung as a global computer network will allow. [11]

The connection between bloggers and cave painters came to blog expert Dan Burstein on a visit to southwestern France. [12] Burstein writes of learning for the first time that the pictorial decorations went on in some instances for generations or longer. With no written language, the painters and storytellers of prehistory used visual images to describe and comment on their ideas and beliefs on the topics of their day — hunting, initiation rites, sickness, mortality, the afterlife. The automotive blog Inside Line sees the same connection. "People blog because cave paintings are obsolete," a Jan. 10, 2006, post reads.

Cave painting was indeed a limiting medium. Reaching a wider audience awaited the development of written languages and a writing "platform." The Egyptians came up with papyrus around 3000 B.C. Europeans used sheepskin parchment. The Chinese initially used bamboo and silk, but around 200 B.C. developed a technique of using wood pulp to make what came to be called "paper" when it reached Europe more than 1,000 years later. Despite modern-day derision of "dead tree" media, paper was truly a breathtaking breakthrough: it used an abundant natural resource to produce a communications medium both portable and durable.

Publishing was a labor-intensive process dependent on monks and Talmudic scholars, however, until the development of movable type and the printing press. The Chinese pioneered movable type beginning in the 11th century. Clay type was used first, then wood and finally metal.

In the mid-15th century German goldsmith Johann Gutenberg combined metal type with a mechanical printing press. The invention spread quickly, and books — once a luxury — became by contemporary standards cheap and plentiful, as did pamphlets, like the anticlerical writings of the English Puritan John Milton in the mid-17th century or the political satire of the Anglo-Irish author Jonathan Swift in the early 18th. In America, Thomas Paine's pro-independence pamphlet "Common Sense" (1776) sold half a million copies and is widely credited with helping swing popular sentiment toward revolution. [13]

The Industrial Revolution made printing even cheaper in the 19th century, as the United States was developing what was then the world's most efficient and reliable postal system. News was cheap: It was the era of the "penny newspaper." And with the invention of the telegraph, news could travel even faster.

Throughout this period, U.S. newspapers were highly partisan. "There's nothing that we see on any blog that compares to the scurrilous kind of attacks newspapers would print about politicians in those days," says author Kline. At the turn of the century, journalist-authors like Ida Tarbell, Lincoln Steffens and Upton Sinclair created the model of investigative reporting. President Theodore Roosevelt labeled them "muckrakers," even as he congratulated them for attacking the "grave evils" of the day.

The advent of radio and television made news even cheaper and quicker. Advertising-supported over-the-air broadcasting gradually became a big business — "the biggest of Big Media," as journalist-turned-blogger Dan Gillmor puts it. [14] Broadcasting became too profitable to risk being too controversial. Simultaneously, newspapers generally were moving away from outright partisanship toward an ethos of objectivity and professionalism. In the process, today's bloggers suggest, print and broadcast media alike became more centralized and homogenized — and less interesting.

The era gave rise, however, to a few mavericks who can be viewed as forerunners of today's bloggers, with the best example being I. F. Stone (1907-1989), says media historian Starr. After two decades as a journalist and author, Stone in 1953 started his own publication, *I. F. Stone's Weekly*, and filled it for 18 years with hard-hitting articles often based on close examination of government documents left unread by mainstream reporters.

Talk-radio hosts can also be seen as antecedents for bloggers. Call-in shows date from 1945, but the format exploded in the late 1980s when the Federal Communications Commission's repeal of the Fairness Doctrine eliminated stations' need to ensure balanced viewpoints. Over the next decade the rise of conservative hosts like Rush Limbaugh — and the eventual emergence of a few, less successful liberal counterparts — stemmed from a shared distrust between host and listeners of "the media" and the listeners' ability to voice their opinions on the air.

Meanwhile, a new communications technology was emerging. Rudimentary elements of computer network-

1970s-1980s *Early days of computer networking; electronic bulletin boards emerge, Internet is born.*

1990s *World Wide Web launched; first weblogs follow.*

**1991** First World Wide Web site brought online by British computer scientist Sir Tim Berners-Lee.

**1993** Mosaic Web browser simplifies creating Web pages.

**1994** Swarthmore College student Justin Hall starts Web-based diary "Justin's Links from the Underground," seen as forerunner of personal blogging.

**1996** Matt Drudge migrates gossipy Hollywood-based Drudge Report from e-mail distribution to Web.

**1997** Jorn Barger begins publishing "RobotWisdom," coins the word "weblog" to describe process of logging the Web as he surfed.

**1998** Drudge Report breaks story of President Clinton's liaison with White House intern Monica Lewinsky.

**1999** Pyra Labs creates "Blogger," easy-to-use software for creating blogs. . . . Fewer than 100 blogs known to be in existence.

2000-Present *Blogs number in the millions, but are unread by most Americans.*

**2001** Terrorist attacks of 9/11 bring outpouring of conservative, pro-war sentiments on "war blogs."

**2002** *New York Times* word maven William Safire devotes July 28 column to origins, usage of "blog" . . . Bloggers Glenn Reynolds (Instapundit) and Joshua Micah Marshall (TalkingPointsMemo) publicize Senate GOP Leader Trent Lott's praise for Strom Thurmond's segregationist presidential campaign in 1948; controversy picked up by mainstream media, forces Lott to relinquish post.

**2003** Teen blog site MySpace.com is founded; acquired by Rupert Murdoch's NewsCorp in 2005 for $580 million. . . . Howard Dean uses Internet, blogs to raise funds, mobilize support for 2004 presidential campaign; folds campaign in February 2004 after faring badly in Iowa, New Hampshire.

**May 2004** Senate staffer Jessica Cutler fired for writing sexy "Washingtonienne" blog from office computer but gets six-figure book deal from episode.

**July 2004** Bloggers credentialed for political party conventions.

**September-Novemer 2004** Conservative blogs sharply attack CBS report questioning President Bush's service in Texas Air National Guard; controversy hastens Dan Rather's retirement as news anchor, forces network to acknowledge flaws in report. . . . Bush and Democratic challenger John Kerry both use blogs in presidential campaigns. . . . Media Bloggers Association formed.

**January 2005** Iran jails 20 online journalists and bloggers.

**February 2005** Gallup Poll shows a third of Internet users read blogs at least occasionally, but nearly two-thirds never do.

**May 2005** *Business Week* cover story tells businesses to use blogs for market research, consumer feedback. . . . Ariana Huffington debuts liberal blog HuffingtonPost.com.

**March 2006** Federal Election Commission says political blogs not subject to federal campaign finance laws.

**April 2006** *Los Angeles Times* columnist's blog on California politics is suspended after he was found to have posted comments on site and elsewhere under an assumed name.

**May 2006** Matt Drudge, Ariana Huffington named by *Time* magazine as among world's 100 most influential people. . . . California state appeals court says bloggers entitled to same protection for confidential sources as other journalists. . . . Bloggers tracked by Technorati surpass 42 million. . . . Egypt jails at least six bloggers among other dissidents.

ing dated from the 1960s. The electronic bulletin boards of the 1980s allowed computer users to dial up individual sites for information. Then in the early 1990s came the World Wide Web: a global information space accessible to any Internet-connected computer with the use of click-and-point technology. A new chapter in media history was about to begin.

## Birth of Blogs

The first bloggers began blogging in the mid-'90s before the word "blog" had been coined or the technology for widespread use had been developed. The pioneers were computer experts who were and remain little known outside the information-technology community. The advent of easy-to-use software at the end of the decade allowed non-geeks to begin blogging. Then, in the first years of the new century, the Sept. 11, 2001, terrorist attacks showed that the new technology could facilitate national conversation about cataclysmic events while the toppling of Senate Republican leader Lott demonstrated that bloggers could have real impact on politics and government. [15]

The British computer scientist Sir Tim Berners-Lee brought the first World Wide Web site online on Aug. 6, 1991. He had developed the concept of hypertext in the 1980s as a means of facilitating the sharing and updating of computer-stored information among researchers. In 1989 he saw the potential to join his hypertext markup language (HTML) software with the Internet to allow information-sharing globally. And, as blogger Gillmor notes, Berners-Lee also envisioned two-way communication: the ability to read from and to write to documents found on the Web. [16]

Programmers at the National Center for Supercomputing Applications in Champaign, Ill., made the next breakthrough: the development of Mosaic, the first Web browser to provide a multimedia, graphical user interface to the Internet. The leader of the team, Marc L. Andreessen, went on to found the company that later became Netscape. With Mosaic, Web pages were relatively easy to create, and some early forms of what Gillmor calls "personal journalism" emerged. He counts Justin's Links from the Underground by Swarthmore College student Justin Hall as "perhaps the first serious weblog."

"It was journalism," Hall explained later, "but it was mostly about me." [17]

Credit for naming the practice goes to Jorn Barger, a computer geek from the age of 11 and an active par-

ticipant in the early 1990s in Usenet, the pre-Web computer communications network. On Dec. 17, 1997, Barger began posting short comments and links on his Robot Wisdom Web site. He coined the term "weblog," which he defined in a September 1999 posting as "a webpage where a weblogger . . . 'logs' all the other webpages she finds interesting." By then, Barger was reporting getting 1,500-2,000 hits a day, the term was being shortened to "blog," and the new phenomenon was being heralded — in the words of tech journalist Jon Katz — as "the freshest example of how people use the Net to make their own, radically different new media." [18]

Pyra Labs, a start-up company in San Francisco founded in 1999 by Evan Williams and Meg Hourihan, provided the last of the initial building blocks: an easy-to-use software dubbed "Blogger." The service was made available, for free, in August 1999 — at a time when blogs may have numbered fewer than 100. As software developer Matthew McKinnon wrote two years later, Blogger allowed anyone with a Web site to set up a blog "in about two minutes" and to update the site any time from anywhere. [19] As word of the free service spread, the number of blogs grew. The software was rewritten in 2002 so that it could be licensed, and the advertising-supported blogspot began to emerge as the dominant software. By then, the number of blogs was estimated at 40,000. [20]

At that point, blogging was also generating its first intramural spat: complaints from early bloggers about the rise of so-called "war bloggers" in the aftermath of the Sept. 11 terrorist attacks. As the U.S.-led invasion of Afghanistan got under way, several hawkish blogs emerged — notably, Glenn Reynolds' Instapundit — to vent indignation and to chronicle and support the military actions. In contrast to the techies' "inward-looking" sites, Reynolds said his and other sites were "outward-looking" — focused on a larger audience. [21] Old-line bloggers flinched at the newcomers' political slant and at the spike in attention, but the visibility was paying off in eyeballs. Reynolds was counting nearly 20,000 visitors a day by mid-2002.

By the end of the year, the broader-focused blogs were being depicted as a new power center, based on their role in forcing Lott to step down as Senate Republican leader. Mainstream media missed the story of Lott's Dec. 5 remarks at first, but the story gained legs thanks to vent-

# Businesses Ignore Blogosphere at Their Peril

The Kryptonite lock company's slogan — "Tough Locks for a Tough World" — refers to the protection its locks offer against "real world" thieves. But the Canton, Mass., manufacturer of high-end bicycle locks learned that cyberspace is a tough world, too, especially for businesses that ignore the blogosphere.

Kryptonite still feels the impact of the September 2004 blogosphere eruption that occurred when someone using the name "unaesthetic" posted on a discussion site the fact that the company's ubiquitous U-shaped lock could be picked with the plastic casing of a ballpoint pen. Within two days, a number of blogs, including the consumer electronics site engadget, had posted a video demonstrating how to perform the trick. Hundreds of thousands of people read about the lock's flaw, and cyclists in chatrooms and blogs expressed their alarm.

Two days later the company promised a tougher line of locks, but bloggers stayed on the case. The blog-monitoring Web site Technorati estimated that 1.8 million Internet users read about the lock's flaws. Finally, 10 days after word initially broke, the company said it would exchange any lock for free. [1] The incident cost the company's parent company Ingersoll-Rand an estimated $10 million. [2]

Donna Tocci, the company's media chief, now checks 30-40 blogs a day for discussions about its products. [3]

"This wouldn't happen today," says Steve Rubel, a senior vice president and author of the blog "Micro Persuasion" at the Edelman public relations firm. "Kryptonite didn't respond fast enough, and it spun out of control."

Love it or hate it, businesses are coming to grips with the blogosphere and learning that when managed well it can help the bottom line — or at least public relations. For instance, when a Manhattan blogger complained that he could not find Degree Sport deodorant in his neighborhood, manufacturer Unilever not only e-mailed him to tell him where he could find it but also sent him a free case of the antiperspirant, Rubel says.

In another example of how blogs can improve customer relations, Microsoft employee Robert Scoble's blog (http://scobleizer.wordpress.com/) was credited with helping reduce external criticism of the company's launch of MSN Space in 2004. Scoble then co-authored *Naked Conversations*, describing how blogs are changing communications between business and customers. Microsoft Chairman Bill Gates wrote admiringly on the book jacket that Scoble was "building a connection" to customers, adding, "Maybe they'll tell us how we can better improve our products."

Everyone who follows business blogs has a favorite story about how they have helped or hurt any given firm, says David Kline, co-author of *blog! how the newest media revolution is changing politics, business, and culture.*

Nevertheless, only a fraction of America's biggest companies have embraced the blog's power so far. As of April 18 of this year, 29 — or only 5.8 percent — of *Fortune* 500 companies were blogging, according to a "wiki" launched by Chris Anderson of *Wired* magazine and Ross Mayfield of Socialtext, a maker of enterprise social software for collaboration. *[4]

But companies ignore the blogosphere at their peril, as

---

* A wiki — the Hawaiian word for quick — is a Web page that readers can edit.

ing from hundreds of bloggers ranging across the political spectrum. "The Internet's First Scalp," the *New York Post* declared in a headline. [22]

Reynolds and liberal counterpart Joshua Micah Marshall demurred. "I think you can exaggerate the role of the blogs in this," Reynolds said, while Marshall took exception to what he called "blog triumphalism." [23]

Whether exaggerated or not, the episode sent a clear warning to journalists and politicians alike: Ignore the bloggers at your peril.

## Power of Blogs

With blogging still in its first decade, the number of blogs has skyrocketed along with readership. Bloggers continued to demonstrate their power by helping force the resignations of two media heavyweights in 2005: CBS News anchor Dan Rather and CNN President Eason Jordan. Political candidates also began to use blogs as fund-raising and mobilizing tools — most notably, former Vermont Gov. Howard Dean in his unsuccessful bid for the Democratic presidential nomination in 2004. But the intermingling of journalistic

Dell computer manufacturer found out. Writer, publisher and interactive journalism expert Jeff Jarvis complained on his blog (Buzzmachine) that his Dell laptop kept crashing and recounted his fruitless efforts to get Dell customer support to help. His subsequent blog post announcing that he planned to buy an Apple laptop became one of the most trafficked posts for weeks.

"If something is happening on the Internet and you're not aware of it, whether you're a company or a major brand or a government agency, there's a price to pay," says Sue MacDonald, marketing manager at Nielsen Buzzmetrics, which helps companies navigate "consumer-generated media," including blogs. Many firms now check what people are saying about them online, but they do so only on an ad hoc basis.

Yet Kline says when people shop online, it is the customer comments rather than advertising or newspapers that have the most important impact on purchasing decisions. He cites *Edelman Annual Trust Barometer*, a survey of 2,000 opinion leaders in 11 countries conducted by the world's biggest public relations firm. Its most recent survey found that participants believe what "a person like me" says about a company or its products more than what anyone else says. Among U.S. participants this tendency leapt from just 20 percent in 2003 to 68 percent in 2005. [5]

Word spread through cyberspace like wildfire in 2004 after a blogger mentioned that the famous U-shaped Kryptonite-brand lock could be easily opened with the plastic casing of a ballpoint pen.

Jason Goldman, product manager for Google's blogging service called Blogger, says that at conferences and other gatherings in the last 18 months, there has been a "groundswell" of people getting specifically involved in helping businesses start their own blogs. "The fact that it has already penetrated close to 6 percent among the last bastion of traditional businesses is rather surprising," he says. The percentage of smaller companies blogging, particularly Internet start-ups, was far higher, he adds.

Kline says blogging will dramatically change the way companies advertise. "Now people can go on their blogs and say, I had a lousy experience with a Dell computer, and it has an evident, noticeable impact. In the future, the database miners will be less important than those who can derive relevant meaning from even a small sample of consumers in their own words," he says. "Customers are going to become co-creators in terms of marketing strategy."

— *Elaine Monaghan*

[1] See David Kirkpatrick, *et al.*, "Why There's No Escaping the Blog," *Fortune*, Jan. 10, 2005.

[2] Ben Delaney, "Kryptonite on level ground six months after U-lock publicity crisis," *Bicycle Retailer*, April 1, 2005.

[3] See "The Blog in the Corporate Machine — Corporate Reputations," *The Economist*, Feb. 11, 2006.

[4] www.socialtext.net/bizblogs/index.cgi.

[5] www.edelman.com/news/ShowOne.asp?ID=102.

---

and political roles by some bloggers raised a variety of legal and ethical issues.

The blogosphere's growth has been nothing short of phenomenal. From fewer than 1 million blogs at the start of 2003, the number doubled every six months through early 2006. News coverage of blogs also increased. *The New York Times* used the word in 28 articles in 2002 and 553 articles in 2005. Blog readership also grew rapidly, as the number of adults who have read blogs increased more than fourfold — from 13.2 million in May 2003 to 57 million by January 2006, according to the Pew

Internet center. Significantly, more than one out of 10 Internet users have also posted material or comments on other people's blogs. [24]

In 2004 Dean's Internet-driven presidential campaign created a surge of interest in blogs and other online tools among politicians, voters and political journalists. Dean went from a blip on the political radar screen in early 2003 to the presumed Democratic front-runner by the end of the year primarily on the strength of using the Internet to raise more than $40 million from 300,000 donors. At one point his campaign weblog drew 100,000

# Teens and 'Gen-Y' Love to Blog

Alongside her photograph and personal information on her MySpace weblog, 19-year-old Jenna from Cross Plains, Tenn., praises her "wonderful" boyfriend Jeremy, adding, "even though he can be a dork sometimes."

A 22-year-old from Salt Lake City wrote on his blog that when he revealed that he was homosexual, his father had kicked him in the groin. "The only people I can really count on in this difficult time is you all," he wrote.

Teens and Internet users who belong to Generation Y — the 18-to-28 age group — are in the vanguard of the blogging revolution, revealing their true loves, rating their teachers, coming out, finding dates, sharing passions and even mourning deaths in public.

"The younger generations have no problem expressing their whole life on their blog," says Mark Jen, a product manager at Plaxo, a company that maintains contact information for more than 10 million Internet users. In fact, 38 percent of Internet users ages 12 to 17 read blogs, while 19 percent say they have created one. Forty-one percent of Generation Y Internet users read blogs and one in five have created one of their own, according to a survey released in December 2005 by the Pew Internet and American Life Project. Blog creation trails off significantly in older age groups, dropping to 9 percent for the 29-40 and 51-59 age groups, 3 percent for the 41-50- and 60-69-year-olds and 4 percent for those 70-plus. [1]

But for young people, blogging has opened the door to a new sense of community, says Jen, 23. For instance, Sara, a 23-year-old from San Francisco, reported finding 42 new "friends" in her first day of MySpace membership.

The enormously popular teen blogging site attracted 48 million visitors in April and was the eighth most trafficked site. Founded in 2003, the site was bought for $580 million in July 2005 by Rupert Murdoch's News Corp.

Teens also use blogs — and flex their blog muscle — in innovative ways. Eight million students around the world use RateMyProfessors.com, which allows college and university students to give frank, anonymous assessments of their teachers. More than 3 million school kids in the United States, Canada, the United Kingdom and Ireland have posted 9.2 million ratings on a sister site, RateMyTeachers.com.

The most rated college is Grand Valley State University in Allendale, Mich., where teachers get marks of good, average or poor — and a red chili pepper if they are "hot." Here, a teacher can learn a student was so bored he counted 137 tiles on the ceiling during a lecture.

Similarly, Facebook.com, a two-year-old online social directory, claims 7.5 million members from more than 2,200 colleges, 22,000 high schools and 2,000 companies and is the seventh-most trafficked site. Two-thirds of the membership visits the site daily, spending an average of 20 minutes viewing photos and profiles of peers or updating their own information.

Bearing in mind recent examples of online predators taking advantage of teens on the Internet, Rep. Michael Fitzpatrick (R-Pa.) has introduced a bill that would restrict minors from accessing commercial social networking Web sites and chat rooms at schools and public libraries. [2] Mobilizing America's Youth, a group that works to increase political participation by the young, opposes the bill,

visitors a day. The excitement about Web-based politics deflated when Dean's Web support failed to materialize at the polls: he ended his campaign on Feb. 18 after losing badly in the Iowa caucuses in January and the New Hampshire primary in early February 2004. [25]

Both President Bush and the eventual Democratic nominee John Kerry did pick up Dean's idea of using blogs as a tool to communicate with supporters and volunteers — but in different formats. An Associated Press Internet reporter described Bush's campaign blog as "flashier," Kerry's more substantive, and noted that

Kerry's blog allowed visitors to post comments, while Bush's did not. [26] Bush "didn't get in trouble" for not having an interactive blog, Professor Davis remarks today. "His supporters didn't punish him for it, and he won."

Bloggers did play an important part, however, in helping the president's campaign combat questions that resurfaced late in the campaign about Bush's service in the Texas Air National Guard in the 1960s. The CBS program "60 Minutes II" aired a story on Sept. 8, 2004, claiming that newly discovered documents provided by an anonymous source showed that then-Lt. Bush had

although it agrees with the intent: to protect Internet users. Spokesman Damien Power said Facebook.com allows users to block other users and to report unsolicited messages to site administrators. [3]

However, the ease with which teenagers and young adults "let it all hang out" on their blogs — particularly descriptions of illegal activities like drug or alcohol use — could come back to haunt them. Police regularly trawl MySpace for evidence of crimes both big and small.

Rayann VonSchoech, a community-services officer with the Sacramento Police Department's gang-suppression unit, has bookmarked about 30 MySpace blogs to check for faces matching gang street names or other signs of a looming crime. [4] "I already have a bank full of gangsters," she said. Her colleague Detective Sam Blackmon estimated that the Internet helps provide clues to about 10 percent of the city's gang arrests. [5]

And in Riverton, Kan., five students were arrested in April on suspicion of plotting a school shooting attack after posting a threatening message on MySpace.com. [6]

Georgia State University student Pamela Elder accesses her Facebook.com blog, where she has reconnected with old friends. The two-year-old online social directory claims 7.5 million members from more than 2,200 colleges, 22,000 high schools and 2,000 companies.

Marketers have begun to view the popularity of such sites among the youthful market sector as a vast untapped advertising opportunity. But the younger generation is suspicious of advertisers, so companies are cautious.

"We don't tell clients to market *to* teens," says Steve Rubel, a prominent blogger and senior vice president at the global public relations firm Edelman. "We say you should market *with* teens."

He adds, "You need to figure out what their motivations are and help them succeed, and at the same time . . . integrate your brand into that experience."

— *Elaine Monaghan*

[1] The Pew survey can be found at www.pewinternet.org/PPF/r/144/report_display.asp.

[2] See Timothy Taylor and Stephanie Woodrow, "Youths to Congress: Don't Block MySpace," *Roll Call*, May 22, 2006.

[3] *Ibid.*

[4] Carrie Peyton Dahlberg, "Many eyes on teens' space; Law enforcement combs popular Web site where youths let it all hang out," *The Sacramento Bee*, May 30, 2006.

[5] *Ibid.*

[6] Marcus Kabel, "Five Students Arrested in Foiled Southeast Kansas School Shooting," *Belleville News-Democrat*, April 20, 2006.

received favorable treatment in the Guard and failed to fulfill some service requirements. Rather, a correspondent on the program and then in his 24th year as "CBS Evening News" anchor, reported the story.

An array of conservative bloggers — led by FreeRepublic.com — immediately questioned the authenticity of the documents and accused Rather and CBS of political bias. "You can almost say that conservative bloggers acted as a fire brigade" on the story, says David Perlmutter, a professor of journalism at the University of Kansas who is writing a book on political blogs. Under

heavy attack, Rather announced in November that he would step down as anchor in March 2005. Then, after an independent investigation, CBS News conceded in January 2005 that it could not authenticate the documents, fired the story's producer and demoted three other executives connected with the program.

In another episode, CNN President Jordan was forced to resign in February 2005 after comments he made two weeks earlier blaming the U.S. military for the deaths of 12 journalists in Iraq. As with the so-called Rathergate story, conservative blogs publicized the comments as evidence of liberal bias by CNN and eventually dragged mainstream media into covering the story. Jordan's resignation under pressure cheered conservatives but left one leading blogger ambivalent. "I wish our goal were not taking off heads but digging up truth," Jeff Jarvis of buzzmachine.com told *The New York Times.* [27]

Different ethical issues were raised by the role of two political bloggers in South Dakota's hotly contested 2004 Senate race. Senate Democratic Leader Tom Daschle was running neck and neck with Rep. Jim Thune, a Republican strongly supported by national GOP leaders. It turned out that two bloggers, Jon Lauck and Jason Van Beek, who sharply attacked Daschle on their sites, were paid $27,000 and $8,000, respectively, by the Thune campaign, though the campaign did not disclose the payments until after the election. Thune won by about 4,700 votes, and Van Beek now has a full-time job in Thune's Senate office. The campaign insisted at the time that the bloggers were paid for research, not for blogging. [28]

## CURRENT SITUATION

### Gaining Respect

Bloggers and other Internet sites are savoring two important legal victories that recognize confidential-source protections for online journalists and exempt all unpaid Internet political activity from federal campaign-finance regulation.

In a closely watched trade-secrets case, a state appeals court in California ruled on May 26 that online journalists are entitled to the same protection as other news organizations against being forced to divulge confidential sources. The ruling blocks Apple Computer from learning the identities of individuals who leaked inside information to two bloggers in 2004 about a then unreleased digital-music device the company was developing. [29]

Meanwhile, the Federal Election Commission (FEC) decided on March 27 to extend to bloggers and other online publications the same exemption enjoyed by traditional news media: Bloggers will not be required to disclose their costs of covering federal election campaigns. Under the commission's decision, even overtly partisan blogs organized to support a particular candidate or party need not disclose their expenditures unless actually controlled by the candidate or party. [30]

Blogging advocates praised both decisions. "Bloggers should be treated the same as the media under campaign finance law," says Adam Bonin, a Philadelphia lawyer who represented three liberal bloggers before the FEC.

Media Bloggers Association President Cox calls the California decision "another step up in the ladder of building the case law around blogging."

The Apple case stemmed from the pre-release publication of details of the company's new "Asteroid" device in November 2004 on two Web sites devoted to Apple products: Power Page, published by Pennsylvania blogger Jason O'Grady, and Apple Insider, published by the pseudonymous "Kasper Jade." Apple filed suit in state court claiming the two sites had appropriated valuable trade secrets and then tried to use pretrial discovery to find out who leaked the information.

O'Grady and "Jade" both invoked California's journalist shield law in refusing, but the trial judge said the privilege did not apply because the theft of trade secrets amounted to a crime. On appeal, Apple pressed its argument that the bloggers could not claim protection of the law at all, but the San Jose-based appeals court disagreed. "The shield law is intended to protect the gathering and dissemination of news, and that is what petitioners did here," Justice Conrad Rushing wrote in the 69-page opinion.

"Bloggers who practice journalism are journalists . . . and therefore are entitled to the same protection afforded to any other journalist. Period," says Cox.

The FEC's decision largely reaffirmed the agency's initial stance to leave Internet political activity essentially unregulated. A federal judge in Washington in 2004 ordered the agency to reconsider the issue in a suit brought by the House sponsors of the Bipartisan Campaign Reform Act (BCRA), the 2002 measure commonly known by the names of its Senate sponsors: Sens. John McCain, R-Ariz., and Russ Feingold, D-Wis.

In its new regulation, the FEC decided federal candidates must disclose expenditures for paid political advertising on the Internet but left all other Internet political communications unregulated. The rules "totally exempt individuals who engage in political activity on the Internet from the restrictions of the campaign-finance laws," FEC Chairman Michael Toner said before the March 27 vote.

For bloggers, the FEC action adds Web sites and any other Internet or electronic publications to the definition

# Is blogging increasing public participation in politics?

## YES  Robert Cox
*President, Media Bloggers Association*

Written for *CQ Researcher*, June 2006

Since blogs first "arrived" on the political scene during the 2004 election, blogging has increased popular participation in politics. Blog readership and blog creation have been growing at a phenomenal rate, with political blogging the most active part of the blogosphere.

The question is not whether blogging has increased political participation but rather will that continue as political professionals strive to co-opt blogging for their own ends. Professor Richard Davis (at right) has rightly warned that those in the past who have heralded a new technology as transforming American democracy have been disappointed. Television was to allow more Americans to engage in the great issues of the day, but in the years since the watershed Kennedy-Nixon debates the long-term trend has been a decline in voter turnout.

It is certainly reasonable to fear that political power brokers will seek to control spin on the blogs, just as they do in the rest of the media. Meanwhile, with Rupert Murdoch's purchase of MySpace and the acquisition of About.com by *The New York Times*, large media institutions are already staking out their online claims.

Blogs are fundamentally different from previous mass-communications technologies like newspapers, radio and television. Because they reside on the Internet and are inexpensive to own and operate, anyone with online access can utilize an infinitely scalable, near-free distribution system to reach a global audience. They not only are interactive but also permit information to flow in multiple directions and to be distributed on multiple levels. More important, as Davis notes, blog reading is "purposive," requiring "affirmative steps" that make it ideal for attracting and organizing citizens willing to actively engage in a political campaign. The "netroots" efforts on behalf of Howard Dean's campaign in 2004 demonstrated the power of blogs as a fundraising tool.

The question is not whether blogs increase political participation — they do — but how that participation will manifest itself in the political process. Politicians now realize that blogs have the potential to be a disruptive force in the political power structure. Professor Davis is right to worry that politicians are taking steps to avoid being disintermediated out of the political process, but squelching bloggers is about as effective as squeezing mercury. Traditional gatekeepers in the political process are fighting a rearguard action as blogging redefines the political landscape, levels the information playing field and gives millions of Americans a voice they never had in our national political dialogue.

## NO  Richard Davis
*Professor of Political Science, Brigham Young University*

Written for *CQ Researcher*, June 2006

Blogs provide another vehicle for political expression. In that sense, they increase political participation. But if political participation is defined more broadly, blogs potentially fall short.

For example, if we mean increased involvement by bloggers in political activities such as voting, donating, communicating with public officials, community service, and so forth, then there is no evidence blogs have performed that function.

And if we mean involving more people who have not previously been involved in politics, then that seems unlikely as well. That's because the political-blog audience consists of the already highly political. According to a recent survey by Harris Interactive, 52 percent of daily, political-blog readers also listen to talk radio at least several times a week and 86 percent watch network or cable news broadcasts. Among the general public, only 37 percent listen to talk radio, and 71 percent watch network news.

But some might say that will change as blog use grows. That argument is based on a premise that fails to consider human behavior. The mere existence of a technology does not change people's interests, attitudes and political behavior. For example, when people go online, they do much the same thing they used to do through other means: write to family and friends, trade stocks, follow sports scores or pay attention to politics. They are not more likely to engage in activities in which they have little interest.

Political blogs are even less likely than the Internet generally to reach citizens who are not politically interested or active. They are a niche of the blogosphere and of the Internet that the less politically interested must search out and find. Why would they do so? Perhaps if they were angry about some governmental decision, they would. But the stimulus would be their anger, not blogs.

The digital divide between rich and poor feared in the 1990s actually became a divide between the politically interested and active — who found e-mail, Web sites, and online discussion a new mechanism for gathering political information and expressing themselves — and the politically less interested, who used the Internet for other things.

Political blogs are part of that digital divide as well. The politically interested will gravitate to them while the majority who see politics primarily as a civic duty, if even that, will go elsewhere.

of news media in a longstanding exemption from having to report the costs of news coverage, editorials or commentaries. "Bloggers and others who communicate on the Internet are entitled to the press exemption in the same way as traditional media entities," the commission wrote in explaining the rule.

The commission had taken the same stance in an advisory ruling in November 2005, telling the pro-Democratic blog Fire Up that it did not need to disclose its spending as campaign contributions. A coalition of public-interest groups favoring campaign finance regulation had opposed the exemption. "This looked much more like a partisan political organization," explains Paul Ryan, FEC program director for the Campaign Legal Center.

Prominent bloggers on the left and right both praised the FEC's rule. "This is a tremendous win for speech," said Mike Krempasky of the conservative blog RedState.org. Liberal blogger Duncan Black, writing under the pseudonym Artios, said: "This could have been an utter disaster, but it appears to have all worked out in the end." [31]

For their part, the campaign-finance groups say they are satisfied with the FEC's overall position, but Ryan still voices concern about the broad media exemption. "Whenever the FEC opens an exemption, the window for abuse opens," he says.

### Blogging at Work

A police union in suburban Washington, D.C., is watching its online message board more carefully these days after some officers were discovered to have posted racist, sexist and anti-immigrant comments on the site.

A *Los Angeles Times* columnist is no longer writing a political blog for the newspaper because he posted comments on the newspaper's Web site and elsewhere on the Web under pseudonyms.

A marine zoologist is out of a job after the Academy of Natural Sciences in Philadelphia fired her for posting comments about her job on her site and on MySpace.com.

Along with all the marvels of blogging come at least a fair share of new problems. Blogging culture invites the posting of information that in the pre-Internet world might have been kept private and messages that might have been left unwritten — or at least undelivered.

Employers and employees are among those working out rules for blogging — mostly by trial and error. The vast majority of companies appear to have no written

policies on the subject. But a blogger activist who says he lost out on a job because of one of his postings counts more than 60 other bloggers who have been fired or disciplined for blog-related reasons.

The most famous workplace victim is Jessica Cutler, a twenty-something former staffer for Sen. Mike DeWine, R-Ohio, who was fired in May 2004 for writing up her active sex life under the cyberhandle "Washingtonienne." Cutler thought the anonymous blog would amuse her girlfriends, only to discover that others were not amused after the blog was publicized through another blog: Wonkette, a widely read Washington gossip and politics site.

Cutler landed on her feet, however. She received a six-figure advance to write a thinly fictionalized account of her experiences under the title *The Washingtonienne: A Novel.* [32]

Curt Hopkins, a journalist-blogger (MorphemeTales) and founder of the now-defunct Committee to Protect Bloggers, began counting blog-related job actions in December 2004 shortly after a public-radio network cited one of his postings in rejecting him for a staff position. By May 2006, Hopkins' list included 61 individuals who had been fired, four who had been disciplined and two, including himself, who were "not hired." Hopkins shut down the blog-protection committee in May for lack of funding.

While no one was fired in the police blog episode, the Montgomery County (Md.) Fraternal Order of Police suffered a black eye in March 2006 when *The Washington Post* disclosed that some officers had anonymously posted offensive comments on the union's password-protected message board. One referred to immigrants as "beaners," and another called a black policewoman a "ghetto" officer. The department responded by restricting access to the site from county computers, while the union promised to monitor the site and remove offensive messages. [33]

*The Los Angeles Times* suspended columnist Michael Hiltzik's Golden State blog in April after he acknowledged posting comments on his own blog and other sites under two assumed names. (The pseudonymous postings were disclosed by another blogger.) *The Times* said it was suspending the blog because Hiltzik had violated ethics guidelines requiring editors and reporters to identify themselves when dealing with the public. Hiltzik continues to write a political column with the same name, however, for the newspaper's print editions. [34]

Meanwhile, the blogosphere is treating marine zoologist Jessa Jeffries as a martyr of sorts after the Academy of Natural Sciences in Philadelphia fired her because her blog (Jessaisms) contained identifiable references to the museum along with racy details about sex and drinking. "Blogger Fired for Actually Having a Life," the widely read Thought Mechanics blog declared in a May 18 posting. Jeffries was unapologetic in her blog post about the firing, but she later told *The New York Times*: "I probably shouldn't have been blogging about work." [35]

Workplace policies on blogging, however, are murky at best. In a survey by the Society for Human Resources Management, only 8 percent of the HR professionals responding said their companies had written policies on the subject. But Jonathan Segal, a Philadelphia employment-law attorney, says it may be too early to try to write detailed policies on employee blogging. "It's so gray, every time you try to write a rule you can come up with a hundred ways that the rules won't work," he says.

For its part, the Electronic Frontier Foundation, a San Francisco-based advocacy group, cautions that more and more bloggers are getting in trouble over the issue and that legal protections for work-related blogging are limited.

"None of this should stop you from blogging," the group says. "Freedom of speech is the foundation of a functioning democracy, and Internet bullies shouldn't use the law to stifle legitimate free expression." [36]

## OUTLOOK

### 'Starting Discussions'

Blogging enthusiasts see the phenomenon as far more than an entertaining hobby or short-lived fad. They see blogs as the dawning of a new media age that will replace top-down journalism and government- and corporate-controlled information with ever more interactive communication and ever more democratic political and economic life.

"Traditional media send messages," the French software executive Loïc le Meur proclaims on his blog. "Blogs start discussions."

Clearly, blogging has yet to reach its potential — in politics, business or culture. Blogs are continuing to increase in number and applications: podcasting and videoblogs are now emerging. "There's lots more innovation and development to be done," says the Pew center's Rainie. "It's very much an unfolding, evolving form."

But a Gallup Poll in February suggests that popular interest in blogging may be leveling off — and at a somewhat low level. Under the headline "Blog Readership Bogged Down," Gallup reports that only 9 percent of Internet users say they frequently read blogs and another 11 percent occasionally. The figures are essentially unchanged from a year earlier. [37]

The number of blogs may itself be misleading, since most are inactive after a couple of weeks. "Most blogs are like diets," says Rosensteil at the Project for Excellence in Journalism. "They're started and then abandoned."

Blogging's influence may also be blunted by its very successes, as the institutions that bloggers are self-consciously challenging adapt the tool for their own uses. Businesses, political candidates and government agencies are learning how to use blogs to promote their products, campaigns or services. It remains to be seen whether they will be transformed by the bottom-up communication that results or whether they will simply learn how to use blogs to manipulate consumer taste and voter behavior.

News organizations are also rapidly adding blogs to their Web sites. "The blogosphere and the mainstream media world are getting blended now and will probably blend more in the future," says Rainie. "The notion that they are separate realms and competing realms will fade."

Blogging has certainly increased the number of voices in the news media and the amount of information and opinion available for news junkies. Independent blogs are making "big media" somewhat more accountable through the fact-checking and agenda-setting functions Rainie cites. At the same time, Rosensteil says readers take the independent blogs with a grain of salt.

"People who read blogs don't necessarily think of them as accurate," he says. "They view them as interesting opinion, but they don't think of them as The Associated Press. They have a feel for what they're getting."

In addition, some in the "old media" fret that minute-by-minute postings in short bursts have little, if any, lasting value, informational or literary. "Blogging is the closest literary culture has come to instant obsolescence," Washington writer Trevor Butterworth concludes in a lengthy critique in the London-based *Financial Times*. "No Modern Library edition of the great polemicists of the blogosphere to yellow on the shelf; nothing but a virtual tomb for a billion posts. . . ." [38]

Bloggers are also worried about a potential threat to their most valuable resource: unhampered access to the Internet. Some major telephone and cable companies want to charge extra for delivering some high-bandwidth services through their wires faster than others. They say they need the revenue to pay for network infrastructure improvements. But bloggers are part of a coalition that wants Congress to block the idea by requiring non-discriminatory access to the Internet — so-called net neutrality. They argue that the proposed charges would make it harder for "everyday people" to have their voices heard on the Web. [39]

Despite all those reservations and caveats, blogging advocates remain convinced that blogs are an important and lasting tool for self-expression and self-empowerment. "The fact that anybody, anywhere, can create their own media, publish their own opinions and information on the Web — that is not going away," says MacKinnon at Harvard's Berkman Center. "In fact, that is going to become more pervasive."

"Blogging will last," says UCLA's Volokh, "because it taps into one of the most fundamental desires of many humans, which is to express their views — and to get the pleasures both selfish and selfless of knowing that others are listening and — one hopes — being enlightened and helped by the spreading of those views."

Author Kline agrees. "The idea of ordinary people talking to each other about what's important in the world, the ability to reach vast audiences and to maneuver around the official sources of power — that's going to survive," he says. "There's no way this is going to fade, and people are just going to go back and be passive recipients of politics, business, information, products and services. That genie is definitely out of the bottle."

## NOTES

1. See "The People Who Shape Our World," *Time*, May 8, 2006, (www.time.com). For individual entries, see Ana Marie Cox, "Matt Drudge: Redefining What's News," p. 171; Al Franken, "Arianna Huffington: The Woman Who Made a Sharp Left," p. 172. Some background on Drudge and Huffington drawn from Wikipedia (visited May 2006).

2. Pew Internet and American Life Project, "The state of blogging," January 2005; www.pewinternet.org/PPF/r/144/report_display.asp.

3. See Daniel Williams, "New Vehicle for Dissent Is a Fast Track to Prison; Bloggers Held Under Egypt's Emergency Laws," *The Washington Post*, May 31, 2006, p. A10; Tom Zeller Jr., "Internet Firms Facing Questions About Censoring Online Searches in China," *The New York Times*, Feb. 15, 2006, p. C3; Megan K. Stack, "Iran Attempts to Pull the Plug on Web Dissidents," *Los Angeles Times*, Jan. 24, 2005, p. A3.

4. Quoted in Eric Deggans, "Huffington Beats Odds as Blogger," *St. Petersburg* (Fla.) *Times*, May 10, 2006, p. 1A.

5. *Ibid.*

6. Noah Schachtman, "Blogs Make the Headlines," *Wired News*, Dec. 23, 2002.

7. Quoted in David Kline and Dan Burstein, *blog! how the newest media revolution is changing politics, business, and culture* (2005), p. 17.

8. For background, see Kenneth Jost, "Free-Press Disputes," *CQ Researcher*, April 8, 2002, pp. 293-316.

9. www.nationalreview.com.

10. See Anick Jesdanun, "Democrats Credential Bloggers; Republicans Say They Will, Too," The Associated Press, July 9, 2004.

11. For background, see Kline and Burstein, *op. cit.*; Dan Gillmor, *We the Media: Grassroots Journalism by the People, for the People* (2004).

12. Dan Burstein, "From Cave Painting to Wonkette: A Short History of Blogging," in Kline & Burstein, *op. cit.*, pp. xii-xiii.

13. See Emily Eakin, "The Ancient Art of Haranguing Has Moved To the Internet, Belligerent as Ever," *The New York Times*, Aug. 10, 2002, p. B9.

14. Gillmor, *op. cit.*, p. 4.

15. Some background drawn from Wikipedia entries on individuals and computer technologies. For an overview, see Steven Levy, *et al.*, "Living in the Blogosphere," *Newsweek*, Aug. 26, 2002, p. 42.

16. Gillmor, *op. cit.*, pp. 11-12. For a first-person account, see Tim Berners-Lee and Mark Fischetti, *Weaving the Web: Origins and Future of the World Wide Web* (1999). Berners-Lee, who was knighted in 2004, is now director of the World Wide Web Consortium.

17. Gillmor, *op. cit.*, p. 12.

18. Jon Katz, "Here Come the Weblogs," Slashdot.com, May 24, 1999, reprinted in Editors of Perseus Publications, *We've Got Blog: How Weblogs Are Changing Our Culture* (2002). As reprinted, the article carries the date May 24, 2001, an apparent mistake.

19. Matthew McKinnon, "King of the Blogs," *Shift*, summer 2001, linked from "Pyra Labs," *Wikipedia* (visited May 2006).

20. Steven Levy, "Will the Blogs Kill Old Media?" *Newsweek*, May 20, 2002, p. 52.

21. Quoted in David F. Gallagher, "A Rift Among Bloggers," *The New York Times*, June 10, 2002, p. C4.

22. John Podhoretz, "The Internet's First Scalp," *The New York Post*, Dec. 13, 2002, p. 41.

23. Quoted in Mark Jurkowitz, "The Descent of Trent Lott Brings the Rise of Bloggers," *The Boston Globe*, Dec. 26, 2002, p. D1.

24. Total readership from Pew Internet and American Life Project, forthcoming report, July 2006; blog posting data from previous report, January 2005.

25. Some background from Liz Halloran, "The Blogger's Life: Online Deaniacs Vow to Stay Involved," *Hartford Courant*, Feb. 20, 2004, p. D1; Michael Cudahay and Jock Gill, "The Political Is Personal — Not Web-Based," *Pittsburgh Post-Gazette*, Feb. 1, 2004, p. E1.

26. Anick Jesdanun, "Product Review: Bush, Kerry sites lackluster after bar raised in Democratic primaries," The Associated Press, July 15, 2004.

27. Quoted in Katharine Q. Seelye, "Bloggers as News Media Trophy Hunter," *The New York Times*, Feb. 14, 2005, p. C1.

28. See Eric Black, "In New Era of Reporting, Blogs Take a Seat at the Media Table," *The* (Minneapolis) *Star Tribune*, March 9, 2005.

29. The case is *O'Grady v. Superior Court, Calif. Court of Appeal, Sixth District* (May 26, 2006). For coverage, see Howard Mintz, "Apple Loses Case Against Bloggers," *San Jose Mercury News*, May 27, 2006, p. A1.

30. See Federal Election Commission, "Internet Communications," Notice 2006-8, published in *Federal Register*, Vol. 71, No. 70 (April 12, 2006), p. 18589. For coverage, see Adam Nagourney, "Agency Exempts Most of Internet From Campaign Spending Laws," *The New York Times*, March 28, 2006, p. A15; Eric Pfeiffer, "FEC to Leave Alone Web Political Speech," *The Washington Times*, March 28, 2006, p. A6.

31. Both quoted in Thomas B. Edsall, "FEC Rules Exempt Blogs From Internet Political Limits," *The Washington Post*, March 28, 2006, p. A3.

32. See April Witt, "Blog Interrupted," *Washington Post Magazine*, Aug. 15, 2004, p. W12; Jonathan Yardley, "Capitol Hill Siren's Tell-All Fiction," May 24, 2005, p. C1.

33. See Ernesto Londono, "Union's Online Controls Greeted Warily," *The Washington Post*, April 1, 2006, and earlier stories by same writer March 28 and March 31.

34. See Katie Hafner, "At Los Angeles Times, a Columnist Who Used a False Web Name Loses His Blog," *The New York Times*, April 24, 2006, p. C1.

35. Anna Bahney, "Interns? No Bloggers Need Apply," *The New York Times*, May 25, 2006, p. G1.

36. See Electronic Frontier Foundation, "Legal Guide for Bloggers," April 20, 2006.

37. "Blog Readership Bogged Down: Audience Skews Slightly Young," Gallup News Service, Feb. 10, 2006. The results were based on a telephone survey of 1,013 randomly selected adults Dec. 5-8, 2005; the margin of error is plus or minus 3 percentage points. See also "Bloggy, We Hardly Knew Ye," *Chicago Tribune* (editorial), Feb. 22, 2006, p. C16; for a reply, see Eric Zorn, "Post This: Blogs' Demise Highly Exaggerated," *Chicago Tribune*, Feb. 23, 2006, p. C5.

38. Trevor Butterworth, "Time for the Last Post," *Financial Times*, Feb. 18, 2006, *Weekend Magazine*, p. 18.

39. For opposing views, see Hands Off the Internet, www.handsoff.com, and www.SavetheInternet.com. For background, see Marcia Clemmittt, "Controlling the Internet," *CQ Researcher*, May 12, 2006, pp. 409-432.

# BIBLIOGRAPHY

## Books

**Armstrong, Jerome, and Markos Moulitsas Zuniga,** *Crashing the Gates: Netroots, Grassroots, and the Rise of People-Powered Politics,* **Chelsea Green, 2006.**
Liberal bloggers Armstrong (MyDD) and Moulitsas (DailyKos) present strategies for revitalizing progressive politics and "revolutionizing" the Democratic Party.

**Davis, Richard,** *Politics Online: Blogs, Chatrooms and Discussion Groups in American Democracy,* **Routledge, 2005.**
A professor of political science at Brigham Young University calls online political discussion "a new force in American politics," examines the kind of people who participate and evaluates its potential as a tool for democratic governance.

**Editors of Perseus Publishing,** *We've Got Blog: How Weblogs Are Changing Our Culture,* **Perseus Publishing, 2002.**
This collection of 34 first-person accounts and essays from bloggers includes an eight-page glossary and two-page list of "helpful" sites in building your own blog and understanding weblog culture.

**Gillmor, Dan,** *We the Media: Grassroots Journalism by the People, for the People,* **O'Reilly Books, 2004.**
A former business columnist for the *San Jose* (Calif.) *Mercury News* and now president of the Center for Citizen Media writes with conviction about "journalism's transformation from a 20th-century mass-media structure to something profoundly more grassroots and democratic."

**Kline, David, and Dan Burstein,** *blog! how the newest media revolution is changing politics, business, and culture,* **CDS Books, 2005.**
The authors provide overviews and more than 30 interviews with or commentaries by major bloggers covering the impact of blogs on politics and policy, business and economics, and media and culture. Appendices list most popular blogs as of May 2005 and the authors' recommended blogs by subject matter. Kline, a journalist, and Burstein, a journalist and venture capitalist, are also co-authors of *Road Warriors: Dreams and Nightmares Along the Information Highway* (Dutton, 1995).

**Reynolds, Glenn,** *An Army of Davids: How Markets and Technology Empower Ordinary People to Beat Big Media, Big Government, and Other Goliaths,* **Nelson Current, 2006.**
Conservative blogger Reynolds (Instapundit) argues that technology is evening out the balance of power between the individual and the organization.

**Scoble, Robert, and Shel Israel,** *Naked Conversations: How Blogs Are Changing the Way Businesses Talk With Customers,* **John Wiley, 2006.**
Business blogger Scoble and former public relations executive Israel use 50 case histories to argue that blogging is an efficient and credible method of business communication. Includes overview of blogging culture internationally and suggestions for how to blog successfully in a crisis.

## Articles

**Bai, Matt, "Can Bloggers Get Real?"** *The New York Times Magazine,* **May 28, 2006, p. 13.**
The writer questions whether blogs and other online political tools will fundamentally change the nature of U.S. politics.

**Baker, Stephen, and Heather Green, "Blogs Will Change Your Business,"** *Business Week,* **May 2, 2005, p. 56.**
The cover story — written in the form of blog postings over a five-day period — advises businesses to consider blogs as an invaluable tool for market research and consumer feedback.

**Butterworth, Trevor, "Time for the Last Post,"** *Financial Times*, **Feb. 18, 2006,** *Weekend Magazine*, **p. 16.**
The writer debunks blogging's "evangelists," insisting most blogs are "overblown, boring and don't make a penny."

**Perlmutter, David D., "Political Blogs: the New Iowa?"** *The Chronicle of Higher Education*, **May 26, 2006, p. 38.**
The article raises questions about the role of blogs in the next presidential election. Perlmutter, who recently joined the faculty of the University of Kansas School of Journalism and Mass Communications, also publishes a political-analysis blog: www.policybyblog.squarespace.com.

**Rosen, Jeffrey, "Your Blog or Mine?"** *The New York Times Magazine*, **Dec. 19, 2004, p. 19.**
Blogs are transforming "the boundaries between public and private," according to Rosen, a journalist and law professor at George Washington University.

### Reports and Studies

**Pew Internet and American Life Project, "The state of blogging," January 2005 (www.pewinternet.org/PPF /r/144/report_display.asp).**
The four-page data memo shows blog readership increasing despite most Americans' unfamiliarity with the practice. An updated report is to be published in July 2006.

# For More Information

**Berkman Center for Internet and Society**, Harvard Law School, Baker House, 1587 Massachusetts Ave., Cambridge, MA 02138; (617) 495-7547; http://cyber.law. harvard.edu. A research program investigating legal, technical and social developments in cyberspace.

**Electronic Frontier Foundation**, 454 Shotwell St., San Francisco, CA 94110-1914; (415) 436-9333; www.eff.org. A nonprofit working to protect digital rights; represented two of the Web sites involved in the Apple case.

**Media Bloggers Association**, (928) 223-5711; http://mediabloggers.org. A nonpartisan organization dedicated to promoting blogging as a distinct form of media and helping to extend the power of the press, with all the rights and responsibilities that entails, to every citizen.

**Pew Internet and American Life Project**, 1615 L St., N.W., Suite 700, Washington, DC 20036; (202) 419-4500; www.pewinternet.org. Explores the impact of the Internet on families, communities, work and home, daily life, education, health care and civic and political life.

**Project for Excellence in Journalism**, 1850 K St., N.W., Suite 850, Washington, DC 20006; (202) 293-7394; www.journalism.org. A Columbia University Graduate School of Journalism initiative aimed at raising journalism standards.

**Reporters Committee for Freedom of the Press**, 1101 Wilson Blvd., Suite 1100, Arlington, VA 22209; (703) 807-2100; www.rcfp.org. A nonprofit providing free legal assistance to help journalists defend their First Amendment rights.

**Society of Professional Journalists**, 3909 N. Meridian St., Indianapolis, IN 46208; (317) 927-8000; www.spj.org. Dedicated to the perpetuation of a free press as the cornerstone of democracy.

# 3

# Cyber Socializing

Marcia Clemmitt

Katherine Lester, 17, and her father leave the courthouse in Caro, Mich., on June 29, 2006, after prosecutors decided not to treat her as a runaway for flying to the Middle East to meet a man she had met on the Internet. As cyber socializing grows, so do fears that the Internet exposes the vulnerable — especially the young — to sexual predators.

From *CQ Researcher,*
July 28, 2006.

L ast year, Eddie Kenney and Matt Coenen were kicked off the Loyola University swim team after officials at the Chicago school found they belonged to a group that posted disparaging remarks about their coaches on the Internet social-networking site Facebook. [1]

Like many people who post profiles and photos and exchange messages on cyber-networking sites like Facebook, MySpace, Xanga and Bebo, the students were shocked to find that university officials, not just their friends, were checking out the site. But Facebook, whose 8 million members are high-school or college students, alumni or faculty and staff members, is considered slightly less risky than sites with open membership rolls.

Nevertheless, said Kenney, who has since transferred to Purdue, "Facebook is dangerous right now. I've learned my lesson. You're supposed to have fun with this Facebook thing, but you need to be careful." [2]

But others see greater dangers than a lack of privacy lurking on social-networking Web sites. Last month, a 14-year-old Texas girl and her mother filed a $30 million lawsuit against MySpace, claiming the girl had been sexually assaulted by a 19-year-old man she met on the site. The man allegedly contacted the girl through her MySpace site in April, posing as a high-school senior. After a series of e-mails and phone calls, they arranged a date, when the alleged assault occurred. [3]

MySpace shares blame for the incident, the lawsuit argues, because users aren't required to verify their age, and security measures intended to prevent contacts with children under age 16 are "utterly ineffective." [4]

**47**

## Teens Feel Safe on MySpace

More than 80 percent of teens believe the cyber-networking site MySpace is safe. Teens spend an average of two hours a day, five days a week on the site. However, 83 percent of parents of MySpace users worry about online sexual predators.

| What Teens Say About MySpace | What Parents of MySpace Users Say |
|---|---|
| • Typically visit 2 hours a day, 5 days a week | • 38% have not seen their teen's MySpace page |
| • 7-9% have been approached for a sexual liaison | • 43% don't know how often their teens are on MySpace |
| • 20% feel MySpace negatively affects school, job, family and friends | • 50% allow their teen to have a computer in the bedroom |
| • 83% believe MySpace is safe | • 62% have never talked to their teen about MySpace |
| • 70% would be comfortable showing their parents their MySpace page | • 83% worry about sexual predators on MySpace |
| • 35% are concerned about sexual predators on MySpace | • 75% worry MySpace fosters social isolation |
| • 15% are concerned that MySpace fosters social isolation | • 81% worry about their teen meeting online friends in person |
| • 36% are concerned about meeting online friends in person | • 63% believe there are "quite a few" sexual predators on MySpace |
| • 46% believe there are "some, but not too many," sexual predators on MySpace | |

*Source:* Larry D. Rosen, "Adolescents in MySpace: Identity Formation, Friendship and Sexual Predators," California State University, Dominguez Hills, June 2006

Though computer networking was developed in the late 1960s to allow scientists to access remote computers for research, its users — initially just academic researchers — quickly saw its possibilities as a socializing tool. As early as 1973, for example, 75 percent of electronic traffic was e-mail, much of it purely social in nature.

Over the past 15 years, a slew of new Internet applications — from chat rooms to instant messaging and, most recently, social-networking Web sites — have made online socializing easier than ever. By the end of 2004, for example, about 70 million adults logged onto the Internet every day in the United States alone — up from 52 million four years earlier — and 63 percent of American adults were Internet users. Teens were logging on at even higher rates — 87 percent of those ages 12 to 17. [5]

Today, a great deal of online activity remains social in nature. For example, in a survey by the nonprofit Pew Internet and American Life Project, 34 percent of the people who said the Internet played an important role in a major decision they'd made said they had received advice and support from other people online. [6] And 84 percent of Internet users belong to a group or organization with an online presence; more than half joined only after they got Internet access. Members of online groups also say the Internet brings them into more contact with people outside their social class or their racial or age group. [7]

But as Internet socializing grows, so do fears that the practice exposes the vulnerable — especially young people — to sexual predators. [8] Some also worry that networking sites create added peer pressure for teens to engage in risky behavior, such as posting risqué pictures of themselves.

In the cyber social world, there has always been the possibility that the friendly stranger chatting about mountain biking or a favorite rock band is not who he says he is. Older socializing technologies, such as Internet discussion boards and chat rooms, allow users to converse about favorite topics, from quilting to astrophysics. Participants generally use screen names — pseudonyms — and conversation centers on the forum topic, often with a minimum of personal information exchanged.

But social-networking sites have greatly increased Internet users' ability to discover other users' full personal information. For instance, newer social-networking sites utilize a personal profile — usually with photos and detailed descriptions of the person's likes and dislikes — as well as the names of friends with whom the person e-mails or instant messages. The page owner also can post comments and message on friends' pages.

Thus, while most Internet social networkers use pseudonyms, the wealth of information on their pages —

plus information gleaned by reading their friends' pages — allows strangers to learn far more about a user than they could about someone posting a comment in a traditional cyber chat room. [9]

Moreover, today most cyber social-network users are between 12 and 25 years old. The largest networking site, MySpace, had more than 51 million unique U.S. visitors in May and boasts about 86 million members. [10] Traffic on the site jumped 367 percent between April 2005 and April 2006 while overall traffic on the top 10 social-networking sites grew by 47 percent. [11] Similarly, adult-oriented online dating sites are also attracting tens of millions of users. (*See sidebar, p. 58.*)

By now, most people — including teens — know it's risky to post personal information such as last name and phone number on the Internet, says Michelle Collins, director of the exploited child unit at the National Center for Missing and Exploited Children (NCMEC). But on today's social-networking sites, "You're only as safe as your friends are," says Collins. For example, a teenage girl may think she's playing it safe by not naming her school on MySpace, "but if she has four friends who all reveal the name of their school, then anyone who reads their pages can surmise" that she also goes there and could potentially track her down.

Last spring, concern about child predators spurred the Suburban Caucus — a new group in the House of Representatives — to introduce the Deleting Online Predators Act (DOPA). Building on the 2000 Children's Internet Protection Act (CIPA), DOPA would require schools and libraries to block young people's access to Internet sites through which strangers can contact them. [12]

The bill's purpose is to shield children from being approached by strangers when using the Internet away from home, an aim that's important to suburban families, according to sponsor Rep. Michael Fitzpatrick, R-Pa. "One-in-five children has been approached sexually on the Internet," he told a House subcommittee on June 10. "Child predation on the Internet is a growing problem." [13]

But many wonder if DOPA addresses the right problem. For one thing, the "one-in-five" figure is "more complicated than is being implied," given today's cultural norms, says Tim Lordan, executive director of the nonprofit Internet Education Foundation. As one teenage girl admitted, " 'Dad, if I wasn't getting sexually solicited by my peers, I would be doing something wrong,' " says Lordan.

## Young Adults Are Most Likely to Date Online

About one-in-10 Internet users — or 16 million people — visited an online dating site in 2005. Those ages 18-29 were most likely to have used an online dating site.

**Online Daters**
(% of Internet users who have visited a dating site)

| | |
|---|---|
| **All Internet Users** | **11%** |
| **Sex** | |
| Men | 12% |
| Women | 9 |
| **Race/Ethnicity** | |
| White | 10% |
| Black | 13 |
| Hispanic | 14 |
| **Location** | |
| Urban | 13% |
| Suburban | 10 |
| Rural | 9 |
| **Age** | |
| 18-29 | 18% |
| 30-49 | 11 |
| 50-64 | 6 |
| 65+ | 3 |
| **Education Level** | |
| Less Than High School | 14% |
| High School Grad | 10 |
| Some College | 11 |
| College+ | 10 |

*Source:* Pew Internet and American Life Project, March 5, 2006

"The media coverage of predators on MySpace implies that 1) all youth are at risk of being stalked and molested because of MySpace; and 2) prohibiting youth from participating in MySpace will stop predators from attacking kids," said Danah Boyd, a University of

# Survival Tips for Online Socializing

In the long run, the Internet is good for teens, bolstering their social development, creativity and even writing skills. Dangers do exist, however, mainly caused by teenagers not understanding how easily strangers can access posted information.

There's clear evidence that writing and creating art, music and videos on the social Internet is building literacy and creative skills in today's teens, says Northwestern University Professor of Communications Studies Justine Cassell.

In the early 1990s, educators were concerned about seriously declining interest in writing by American students. But today, "we have striking evidence that kids are willing to write, when they weren't before," a change that many analysts attribute to the popularity of e-mail, instant messaging and blogging, says Cassell. Today's teens even show sophisticated understanding of literary niceties such as tailoring one's writing style to suit the audience. "They don't use emoticons [symbols] with parents," for example, because they "understand that's a dialect," she says.

Benefits aside, however, dangers and misunderstandings also exist, exacerbated by the fact that kids have raced ahead of many adults in their use of Internet socializing tools, says John Carosella, vice president for content at the Internet security company Blue Coat. "We are the first generation of Internet parents, and we need to learn how our job has changed," Carosella says.

Here are experts' tips for handling the online social world:

- Parents must learn how to use the technology, says Cassell. "At the very least, IM (instant message) your kids." Parents who IM "report much less fear about the technology and more happiness because their kids keep in touch," she says.
- Parents should play with Internet search engines "to learn how easily they turn up information and then share that knowledge as they talk with their children about Internet privacy," she says.
- Privacy rules between parents and kids can't remain the same in an Internet world, says Kaveri Subrahmanyam, an associate professor of psychology at California State University, Los Angeles. "If it's a kid's diary, you don't look at it." But diaries are different from MySpace pages, "because nobody else is looking at them," Subrahmanyam says.

  When it comes to publicly posted information that strangers can access, "You do need to know what they do," she says. "You can say to your child, 'I don't need to know the content of the IM, but I do need to know whom you're sending it to.'"
- Age matters when it comes to teens understanding Internet privacy issues, according to Zheng Yan, an education professor at the State University of New York at Albany. Only children ages 12 to 13 or older can grasp the Internet's "social complexity," such as the large number of strangers who can access information posted on Web sites. [1]
- Web sites vary widely in how much public and private access they allow to posted material, and it's important to think about this when posting, says Alex Welch, founder and CEO of the photo-sharing Web site Photobucket. On Photobucket, the photo albums of people under age 18 are automatically kept private.

  However, even if they weren't, posting photos on Photobucket would be less risky than posting the same pictures on a social-networking site like MySpace, says Welch. That's because on MySpace photos are linked to additional personal information that may pique strangers' interest and provide clues to help them contact posters.
- It's also important to consider the future, including how employers or college admissions officers might view your online postings, says Henry Jenkins, director of the comparative media studies program at the Massachusetts Institute of Technology. Much of what appears on the Internet today ends up archived somewhere and can be retrieved tomorrow, he says. "Kids don't recognize the permanence of what they put up there."
- Adults will probably learn a lot about the Internet from their children, and they should be open to that, says Jenkins. Parents "need to recognize that some unfamiliar experiences look scarier from the outside than they are. Take time to understand what you're seeing."

  Talking about teens' MySpace pages can open the door to family discussions of important, sometimes touchy issues, like contemporary fashion, media images and ideals, Jenkins says. "Ask your kid how they choose to represent themselves" on their MySpace pages "and why."
- Teens — and adults — who socialize on the Web should remember that, "when it comes to the rules for getting to know people," the Internet "parallels our world perfectly," says Patricia Handschiegel, founder and CEO of StyleDiary.net, a social-networking site focused on fashion.

  Often, young people have "a false sense that you can't be tracked" by people they correspond with online, Handschiegel says. "If you want to correspond, fine, but take your time getting to know people. Watch for cues" to ulterior motives, "such as somebody pushing too fast to know you."

---

[1] Bruce Bower, "Growing Up Online," *Science News*, June 17, 2006, p. 376, www.sciencenews.org/articles/20060617/bob9.asp.

California, Berkeley, doctoral student who studies how teens use online technology. "Both are misleading; neither is true. . . . Statistically speaking, kids are more at risk at a church picnic or a Boy Scout outing than . . . when they go to MySpace." [14]

In fact, the NCMEC report from which the one-in-five figure originates shows that 76 percent of online sexual solicitations "came from fellow children," and 96 percent of the adult solicitations came from adults 18 to 25, said Boyd. "Wanted and unwanted solicitations are both included. In other words, if an 18-year-old asks out a 17-year-old and both consent, this would still be seen as a sexual solicitation." [15]

Cyberspace presents no more danger than the real world, says Michigan State University Professor of Psychology Linda Jackson. "But there are dangers," she says, "such as the ease with which you can give away your information."

Unwary users giving out private information — perhaps permanently, since so much Internet content is archived — is the chief new danger posed by social networking, say many analysts.

Most teenagers who post MySpace pages "seem to have the sense that nobody is watching" except their closest friends, says Tamyra Pierce, an assistant professor of mass communication at California State University, Fresno, who is studying social-networking use among high-school students. For example, "a boy who posted about banging a mailbox last night" apparently was unaware that the posting exposed him to vandalism charges, she says.

"Teenage girls would be petrified if you read their diary, yet they are now posting online stuff that is much more personal," said Jeffrey Cole, director of the University of Southern California's Center for the Digital Future. "Clearly kids need guidance." [16]

Given the popularity of online socializing, it would be impossible to ban it, says Kaveri Subrahmanyam, an associate professor of psychology at California State University, Los Angeles. "The Internet is here to stay. If you ban it, they'll find a way to get around the ban. It will become a cat-and-mouse game," she says. "We need to teach kids how to keep safe."

Unfortunately, the new dangers posed by sites like MySpace "have not been integrated into the society's knowledge base," said Kevin Farnham, author of a book of safety tips for social-networking. "Common-

Shortly after graduating from Hobart and William Smith Colleges in 2004, Jessica Ostrowski joined the popular college social-networking site Facebook. She lives in Boston but stays connected to friends nationwide through the site, which has 8 million members.

sense teaching is [not] automatically passed from parents to child." [17]

But predators are not the only ones reading social-networking sites. Some employers routinely scan pages posted by job candidates, with potentially disastrous results, says Matthew Smith, a professor of communications at Ohio's Wittenberg University. "You may put up a birthday-party picture of yourself in your underwear, thinking you are showing how carefree you are," says Smith. "But a future employer may see it and decide you're irresponsible."

And the federal government may be next. The National Security Agency (NSA) is funding "research into the mass harvesting of the information that people post about themselves on social networks," according to Britain's *New Scientist* magazine. [18]

"You should always assume anything you write online is stapled to your résumé," said Jon Callas, chief security officer at PGP, a maker of encryption software. [19]

As lawmakers, parents and Internet companies confront new Internet security issues, here are some of the questions being discussed:

## MySpace Users Are Most Loyal

Two-thirds of the visitors to MySpace return each month — more than any other social-networking site. MSN Groups caters to those with special interests, such as computers, cars, music, movies or sports.

### Top Five Socializing Sites
(based on retention rate)

| Site | Retention Rate (%)* |
|------|---------------------|
| MySpace | 67.0 |
| MSN Groups | 57.6 |
| Facebook | 51.7 |
| Xanga.com | 48.9 |
| MSN Spaces | 47.3 |

* Based on the number of March 2006 visitors who returned to the site in April

Source: Nielsen/NetRatings

### Is cyberspace more dangerous than real space?

Some legislators and worried parents warn that the online world increases opportunities for sexual predators to reach victims. Likewise, some women won't use online dating services because they fear they might meet unsavory characters. But defenders of online socializing argue that real-life encounters pose just as much risk of unwanted sexual advances or of being bullied or defrauded.

"There's a child-abuse epidemic that we don't even know about on the Internet, which is how it stays so invisible, when a 45-year-old man engages in sexually explicit dialogue with a 12-year-old girl," says John Carosella, vice president for content control at Blue Coat Systems, a maker of security software and other tools for online communication.

"When it happens in real life you know it's happening," but on the Internet, even the girl herself may not know it's happening initially, he says. "This is why it can

go on with such facility, and it's so easy to escalate because nobody can overhear it."

Internet communication is riskier than real-life meetings, according to Carosella, because many of the cues humans use to size up other people — such as gestures and tone of voice — are missing. "Most of our evolutionary clues [to risk] are stripped out" of online encounters, he says.

In addition, online acquaintances can do harm — especially to young people — even without offline meetings, he says. The Internet "is the most powerful tool yet invented" capable of bringing "every aspect of human behavior from the most sublime to the most debauched and depraved" right into our own homes, he says. And it's burgeoned so fast that "we've had no time to figure out how to deal with it."

Carosella also suggests that — while there is not enough research yet to prove it — easy access to online porn may prime some people to become aggressive or engage in sexual predation. "Lots of data suggest that pornography is a very significant factor in the emergence of criminal, aggressive behavior," he says. "You're whipping around the most powerful urge that people have. And the Internet has made pornography more accessible, more private, more extreme."

Moreover, peer pressure among teens may encourage risky sexual expression on cyber-networking sites, says Pierce of California State University. "The more stuff they have that is graphic and shocking, like links to porn and photos in risqué poses, the more friends they have on their lists," she says of recent studies of MySpace and Xanga and their use by more than 300 local high-school students. "Most who have upward of 500 friends have links to porn sites and graphic stuff."

Looking at social-networking sites can sometimes expose teenagers to porn, even when they don't seek it out, says Pierce. For example, in a group of 50 to 60 sites she recently examined, 10 contained automatic links that unexpectedly shift the viewer to a pornography site.

It "concerns me that our youth may be exposed to pornography" at the inadvertent click of a mouse, she says. "I don't know if individuals in the porn industry are creating 'fake' MySpace sites and then autolinking them or if the young persons themselves are getting involved. I just know that what appeared to be an innocent, young person's site automatically turned into porn" when the site user's photo was clicked.

Collins of the National Center for Missing and Exploited Children says the Internet provides a "target-rich environment" for pedophiles. "Twenty years ago, people had to go to a park or a soccer game" to meet children and teens, she says. And the Internet allows predators to learn more about a potential victim, which may help him build a relationship.

There's little disagreement that dangers can lurk on the Internet. However, many analysts note that, even as Internet socializing has burgeoned, sex crimes have been decreasing, and data do not indicate an increase in sexual predation due to teens going online. "There is no evidence that the online world is more dangerous," says Justine Cassell, a professor of communications studies at Northwestern University.

In fact, predatory crimes against girls have declined during the past decade, even as the Internet was bringing more young people online, she says. All national data sets show that from 1994 to 2004, single-offender crimes, including assaults, by men against 12-to-19-year-old girls decreased, demonstrating that the online world has not put young people in more danger, says Cassell.

The number of sexual-abuse cases substantiated by child-protection agencies "dropped a remarkable 40 percent between 1992 and 2000," and evidence shows it was a "true decline," not a change in reporting methodology, wrote sociology Professor David Finkelhor and Assistant Professor of Psychology Lisa M. Jones, of the University of New Hampshire's Crimes Against Children Research Center. [20]

Meanwhile, says Collins, tips about online enticement of young people reported to the NCECM have risen from 50 reports a week in 1998 to about 230 a week. But does that mean there are more online incidents today? Probably not, says Collins. "More people know where to report it today," thanks to the center's education campaigns and social-networking companies' putting links to NCECM's tipline on their sites. In addition, "more people, more kids, are wired today than ever before," Collins notes.

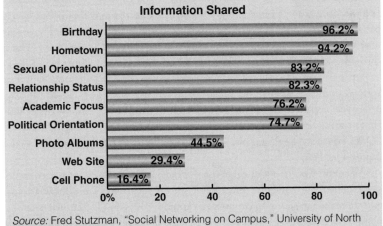

## Freshmen Share Many Personal Details

Most University of North Carolina freshmen reveal their birthday and hometown on social-networking sites. But only 16 percent give out more detailed personal information, like cell phone numbers.

**Information Shared**

| | |
|---|---|
| Birthday | 96.2% |
| Hometown | 94.2% |
| Sexual Orientation | 83.2% |
| Relationship Status | 82.3% |
| Academic Focus | 76.2% |
| Political Orientation | 74.7% |
| Photo Albums | 44.5% |
| Web Site | 29.4% |
| Cell Phone | 16.4% |

*Source:* Fred Stutzman, "Social Networking on Campus," University of North Carolina, Chapel Hill, 2006

Even teenagers' fascination with online porn may be something of a passing fancy, not a long-term, negative behavior change, says Michigan State's Jackson, who recently completed research that tracked teens' Internet usage. "We went everywhere they went for 16 months," she says. "Porn sites were popular for the first three months, then it really died down."

As for the dangers of online dating, Eric Straus, CEO of Cupid.com, a popular dating site, rates the dangers of online and offline dating as about equal. Meeting potential romantic partners online is "a numbers game," and the Web lets you search for geographic proximity or mutual interests across a wide variety of potential dates. But "you shouldn't be fooled into feeling safe" from deception in either environment, he says. "If you talk to 100 people online, some are going to be unsavory. If you meet them in a bar, and they say they're not married, you shouldn't believe that either, and if you give them your phone number, that's dangerous."

New technology always spurs panic, says Paul DiMaggio, a sociology professor at Princeton. "MySpace is generating the same fear reaction that films and vaudeville got," says DiMaggio. "And all new technology and media generate more hysteria than threat."

"A lot of the behavior on sites like MySpace has been going on in teen hangouts for generations," wrote Anne Collier, editor of *NetFamilyNews.* [21] Dangerous behavior existed, "but parents weren't privy to it."

"One child being molested by an online predator is too many and has to be addressed," says Lordan, of the Internet Education Foundation. "Nevertheless, statistically, most molestations are family and acquaintance molestations, and the chance of your child being dragged through the computer screen by a predator is low."

Furthermore, "a lot of the stories that you hear" about teens running off with adults they met on MySpace, for example, "appear to be kids who would get in trouble in some other way if it weren't for the Internet," he says. "Once you start digging down, these don't appear to be typical families."

All youngsters are not at equal risk of being victimized, says Collins. "Some kids are using the Internet to fill a void, and these kids are going to be more susceptible," she says.

## Should schools and public libraries block access to social-networking sites?

Rep. Fitzpatrick and other members of the Suburban Caucus have introduced legislation that would require public schools and libraries to bar access to social-networking sites and chat rooms as well as to pornography sites.

For adults, online social-networking sites "are fairly benign," but "for children they open the door to many dangers," including online bullying and exposure to child predators that have turned the Internet into a virtual hunting ground for children," Fitzpatrick said on the House floor May 9. [22]

"There are thousands of online predators who are trying to contact our kids using powerful engines like MySpace.com," said Rep. Mark Kirk, R-Ill. [23]

Blocking Internet social tools, at least temporarily, is a valid response, says Carosella of Blue Coat Systems. While educational responses are vital in the long run, "we haven't invented [that education] yet."

Furthermore, "while we are developing our educational response, predators are building and improving their game plans. It's an arms race," says Carosella. Blocking access in schools and libraries "is absolutely an answer," because supervision currently "is completely inadequate."

But critics of such proposals say blocking access is nearly impossible without inadvertently blocking valuable portions of the Internet. "It's brain-dead to say you

should stop people from using some technology," says John Palfrey, clinical professor of law and executive director of Harvard Law School's Berkman Center for Internet and Society, pointing out that the technology isn't going away.

Boyd, of the University of California, pointed out that because technology plays a major role in the business world, it is unwise to deprive students of it in schools and libraries. "The law is so broadly defined that it would limit access to any commercial site that allows users to create a profile and communicate with strangers." While it ostensibly targets MySpace, as written it would block many other sites, she said, including blogging tools, mailing lists, video and pod-cast sites, photo-sharing sites and educational sites like NeoPets, where kids create virtual pets and participate in educational games. [24]

Moreover, she continued, many technology companies now are using social software, such as features that help users find information, get recommendations and share ideas. "This would all be restricted," she wrote. [25]

Lynn Bradley, director of the American Library Association's government relations office, agrees. Fitzpatrick's proposal "is like using a water hose to brush your teeth." The legislation could also affect distance-learning programs, which use many technologies that the legislators want blocked. "Rural schools have increasingly started to rely on distance learning to supplement their curricula," said Bradley. "It would appear to us on reading this bill that [such programs] would be swept up in the blockage." [26]

Henry Jenkins, director of comparative media studies at the Massachusetts Institute of Technology (MIT), says it would be unwise to keep teachers and librarians away from social-networking technology because "they are the best people to teach people how to use it constructively and safely." And, while Fitzpatrick's bill contains loopholes for educational uses, history suggests that fear and uncertainty would likely stop many schools from using those loopholes, he adds.

Blocking access at public schools and libraries would also worsen the already troubling "digital divide," says Jenkins. [27] Children in wealthier families could still access school-blocked Internet sites from home, but students without Internet at home "will be shut out," he says.

Policymakers who propose blocking as a "silver bullet" don't know how important online socializing is to teenagers, says the Internet Education Foundation's

Lordan. "Kids feel quite attached to their own space," whether on MySpace or another site, and are "incredibly worried" about it being taken away, he says. If sites are blocked, "they'll go underground."

The bill should be called the "Send Social Networking Sites Off Shore Act," says Lordan, because there are social-networking sites all over the world and "stories of kids creating these sites themselves." If that happens, "we can't even help them."

Moreover, there are serious technical barriers, such as age verification, he says. Many blocking proposals would depend on age verification of site users, either to block out older users who might prey on kids or to keep younger kids from using the sites. But "age verification is a problem even in the real world," where kids use fake ID cards to buy alcohol and cigarettes, says Loran, and the problem is "worse in the online world."

## Does Internet social networking foster good relationships?

For nearly as long as the Internet has existed, people have used it to stay in touch with old friends and meet new ones. [28] For just as long, skeptics have argued that online relationships are less rich, real and reliable than real-world interactions and that Internet socializing actually isolates people. Over the years, studies have found evidence bolstering both sides of the question.

No online community can support human bonding the way real-world communities do, said Clifford Stoll in his 1996 best-seller *Silicon Snake Oil: Second Thoughts on the Information Superhighway*. "What's missing from this ersatz neighborhood? A feeling of permanence, a sense of location, a warmth from the local history. Gone is the very essence of a neighborhood: friendly relations and a sense of being in it together." [29]

Some studies have found that Internet usage pulls people away from their real-world friends and family and isolates the user. Research by Stanford University's Institute for the Quantitative Study of Society (SIQSS), for example, finds that Internet use directly relates to social isolation. Based on survey findings, the Stanford researchers say that for every hour a person spends online, their face-to-face time with family and friends decreases by 23.5 minutes. [30]

Furthermore, "face-to-face interaction with close [friends and family] qualitatively differs from interactions in the virtual world online and is more important

to one's psychological wellness," according to Lu Zheng, a Stanford doctoral student in sociology. [31]

Another SIQSS analysis found that "the more time people spend using the Internet the more they lose contact with their social environment." Internet users, for example, spend much less time talking on the phone to friends and family, according to the study. [32]

"E-mail is a way to stay in touch, but you can't share a coffee or a beer with somebody on e-mail or give them a hug," said SIQSS Director Norman Nie. "The Internet could be the ultimate isolating technology that further reduces our participation in communities." [33]

But other analysts insist that Internet socializing strengthens online and offline relationships. What looks to some like a "fading away" of social life as Internet usage increases is actually just a shift to new communication modes that strengthen many people's social ties, says a recent report from the Pew Internet and American Life Project and the University of Toronto. [34]

"The traditional human orientation to neighborhood- and village-based groups is moving toward communities . . . oriented around geographically dispersed social networks," the Pew report said. "The Internet and e-mail play an important role in maintaining these . . . networks" and "fit seamlessly" into people's social lives. As a result, the study concluded, Americans today "are probably more in contact with members of their communities and social networks than before."

For example, the analysts found that those who e-mail 80-100 percent of their closest friends and family weekly also speak regularly by phone with 25 percent more of their closest associates than those who e-mail less. For so-called second-tier (or "significant") social ties, the effects were even more pronounced: Those who weekly e-mail 80-100 percent of their second-tier contacts also regularly telephone twice as many of those contacts as do people who do not e-mail their friends. [35] Furthermore, 31 percent of those surveyed said their Internet use had increased their number of second-tier contacts — while only 2 percent said it had decreased them. [36]

A Canadian study of a housing development found similar results. University of Toronto researchers found that residents with high-speed connections had more informal, friendly contact with neighbors than residents who were not on the Internet. [37] Residents with broadband service knew the names of 25 neighbors, on average, compared to non-wired residents, who knew eight.

# CHRONOLOGY

1960s-1980s *As the Internet develops, its academic and technical users begin socializing online.*

**1967** The term "six degrees of separation" enters the lexicon after Yale University psychologist Stanley Milgram claims to experimentally validate the theory that any two people on Earth are connected by an average of six intermediate contacts.

**1972** E-mail is invented and quickly becomes the most widely used tool on the first wide-scale computer network, ARPANET.

**1975** First ARPANET mailing lists link people with shared interests.

**1979** First Usenet newsgroups are established.

**1982** Carnegie Mellon University computer-science Professor Scott Fahlman invents the first emoticon, the smiley :-)

**1988** Internet Relay Chat is invented, allowing computer users to exchange real-time messages with a group.

1990s *People flock to the Internet, mostly drawn by socializing tools like e-mail and chat rooms. Worries grow about sexual predators contacting teens through online socializing, but sex crimes against teenagers decrease overall.*

**1990** John Guare's play "Six Degrees of Separation" captures the public imagination with its portrayal of the power of social networks.

**1994** Netscape's Mosaic Web browser is offered free on the company's Web site, helping draw millions of non-technical users online.

**1996** AOL introduces the Buddy List, which alerts users when friends are online and ready to IM (instant message) each other.

**1997** Sixdegrees.com becomes one of the first Internet social sites to link users to friends of friends, through three "degrees of separation." . . . AOL introduces AIM, allowing users for the first time to IM non-AOL users.

**1998** eHarmony.com, the first online dating site to require users to complete a personality-matching test, is founded by evangelical Christian Neil Clark Warren.

2000s *Social-networking sites become teenagers' socializing tool of choice, while rock bands and other performers begin using the sites to build and strengthen their fan bases. Lawmakers become concerned that cyber social networking makes it easier for sexual predators to find teens.*

**2000** President Bill Clinton signs the Children's Internet Protection Act (CIPA), requiring federally subsidized public and school libraries to use filtering software to block children's access to pornography.

**2001** Columbia University Professor Duncan Watts uses forwarded e-mails to confirm Milgram's six-degrees-of-separation finding.

**2003** MySpace is founded. . . . The U.S. Supreme Court upholds CIPA's requirement for public libraries to block Internet sites. . . . Vermont Gov. Howard Dean becomes a leading contender for the 2004 Democratic presidential nomination by using the social-networking site Meetup to spur grass-roots organization.

**2005** News Corp., a global company headed by Australian media mogul Rupert Murdoch, buys MySpace for $580 million. . . . Several state legislatures consider bills requiring online dating sites to conduct background checks of users.

**2006** NBC's television newsmagazine "Dateline" films sting operations around the country in which adults pose as teens in Internet chat rooms and arrange to meet sexual predators. . . . The Deleting Online Predators Act is introduced in Congress to require federally subsidized schools and libraries to block children's access to social-networking sites, chat rooms and other socializing technology. . . . Social software continues to spread with Internet companies including AOL, Netscape, Google and Yahoo jumping on board. . . . Americans spend $521 million on online dating, making it one of the biggest income generators on the World Wide Web.

Wired residents made 50 percent more visits to neighbors' homes than non-wired people, and their visits were more widely scattered around the housing development, according to the paper. [38]

And in a new and interesting wrinkle, the Internet may be helping to keep the lines of communication open between people on both sides of the recent Middle East violence. Since the cross-border shelling between Israel and Lebanon erupted earlier this month, Internet message boards, discussion forums and blogs have exploded with posts from Israeli and Lebanese nationals commenting on the fighting. "The fact that the citizens of two warring countries are maintaining a dialogue while a war is going on cannot be ignored," said Lisa Goldman, a Canadian-born freelance journalist who blogs from Tel Aviv and who points out that Internet discussions and socializing between Israelis and Lebanese predated the current conflict. [39]

Another significant new phenomenon among adolescents equipped with cell phones, instant messaging and social-networking pages is "tele-cocooning," says MIT's Jenkins. Coined by Mimi Ito, a research scientist at the University of Southern California's Annenberg Center for Communication, tele-cocooning refers to "carrying your friends around with you, using technology to be literally in contact with them all the time."

Online socializing also helps kids who would otherwise have a hard time finding friendships, says Jenkins. "Kids who may be outcasts, or pariahs, or have interests that nobody in their school shares now can go online and meet kids all around the country who like the same comic books, music and sports," Jenkins says. "I watched my son go through that."

In addition, while online socializing creates opportunities for deception or misunderstanding, meeting people online first can sometimes help avoid superficial judgments. The Internet allows disadvantaged or physically different people to socialize without suffering the instantaneous negative judgment that may happen in person.

"If people consider you unattractive, for example — you have moles, a big nose — . . . you can get negative reactions in public," says Wittenberg's Smith. "Online, I can talk about my love of pets or my work with my church. I can put down what is lovable about me and bypass whatever I think is keeping me from getting fulfilled relationships" offline.

Internet dating also saves time, says Mark Brooks, editor of *Online Personals Watch.* "The great thing about Internet dating is being able to find the right people," something that is harder in the real world, where there's no search function," he says. By meeting someone online first, "I don't need to go out with somebody who smokes or who has kids. You can ask the difficult questions up front."

Social-networking sites also draw criticism for their emphasis on having a lengthy list of friends, as sites like MySpace tend to do. Encouraging the how-many-friends-do-my-friends-have game sets up bad behaviors, according to technology entrepreneur Christopher Allen. "It is not the number of connections but the quality" that counts, a fact obscured by concentration on long friend lists, he said. [40]

Social networking is based on a faulty view of friendship — the "premise that . . . if A is a friend of B, and B is a friend of C, then A can be a friend of C, too," said the University of California's Boyd. "Just because you're friends with somebody doesn't mean their friends are similar" to the friends you would choose. [41]

A social-networking site can also be used as "an electronic bathroom wall," potentially increasing the reach of school bullying, says NCMEC's Collins. "There's capacity for large-scale humiliation," Collins says, citing an incident in which a girl created a page laden with pornography and put an ex-friend's name on it.

But Boyd isn't so sure. "Bullying, sexual teasing and other peer-to-peer harassment are rampant among teenagers" because they are "tools through which youth learn to make meaning of popularity, social status and cultural norms," she said. It is unclear whether online embarrassment is any more damaging than offline humiliation, she added, conceding the Internet "may help spread rumors faster." [42]

## BACKGROUND

### Wired Love

Virtually all communications technology, no matter why it was developed, has quickly become a socializing tool, with teenagers usually leading the way. And — from the telegraph to MySpace — parents have always worried what kind of trouble teens may get into with the new technology.

# Do You Take This Online Stranger . . . ?

Soon after moving to Washington, D.C., from upstate New York to attend community college, Cait Lynch signed up with the popular Internet dating site Match.com. "I'd just moved to the area and I didn't really know anyone. I was interested in meeting new people," she says. Moreover, her mother had met her husband of eight years online. "I figured if it went well for her, I should give it a shot."

After a few months, Lynch came across a promising profile. Paul Schnetlage was getting his master's degree at Johns Hopkins University, and they shared an interest in cafes, movies, reading and art. Moreover, they were the same age — 22 — and both were in school full time while working.

After e-mailing for a month, they met for coffee, and Paul admitted he had "met several really strange girls" before meeting her. For her part, Lynch says she "didn't take anything seriously at all" on the site. Nonetheless, their relationship slowly blossomed, and last March, nearly two years after meeting, they married. Without Match.com, "I don't think I ever would have met someone like Paul," says Lynch, who works for a real estate developer. Her husband is a software designer.

Launched in 1995 as the first online dating service, Match.com now has some 15 million paid members. It claims that more than 300 marriages or engagements occur between members or former members each month and that 400,000 people find the person they are seeking each year. The "vast majority aren't marriages," says spokesperson Kristin Kelly, "but a lot of people are telling us they found a great relationship."

Today, Internet sites devoted to matchmaking constitute one of the top online income generators, with the U.S. market valued at $521 million. [1] Nearly one-third of American adults know someone who has used a dating Web site, according to the Pew Internet and American Life Project. [2]

But after steady increases in membership, the 25 most-visited online dating sites showed a 4 percent decline in American visitors in the past year compared to a 4 percent increase in the total U.S. Internet audience. [3]

"There is a natural limit to the number of people who want to participate in this industry, and they are getting to that number," explained Jupiter Research analyst Nate Elliot." [4]

And Mary Madden, a Pew senior research specialist, points out the Internet is still very low on the list of ways people meet their significant others. "We asked all Internet users who are married or in a committed relationship if they met their partner online or offline, and only 3 percent said they met them online," she says.

There are clearly cases where online dating does foster meaningful relationships, says Barbara Dafoe Whitehead, co-director of Rutgers University's National Marriage Project. "But to what degree it's a very reliable source of finding a partner is the open question," she says.

Stan Woll, a psychology professor at California State University, Fullerton, says Internet dating sites are good at introducing people to large numbers of potential mates they might not otherwise meet. However, he finds that the number of possibilities tends to make members overlook people they would ordinarily enjoy. "There is an array of other people, and you keep wanting to go on and find somebody better or closer," argues Woll.

Andrea Baker, a sociology professor at Ohio University and author of the 2005 book *Double Click: Romance and Commitment of Online Couples*, argues that online dating sites are better than chance meetings at helping members find partners with common interests.

---

Northwestern's Cassell recounts a newspaper story entitled "Wired Love," which describes how a father followed his 16-year-old daughter to a tryst she'd arranged with a man she had met online and was arrested after threatening to kill the man and the girl. The father had bought his daughter the new technology — a telegraph — according to the 1886 story in the magazine *Electrical World*.

"At first people thought the telegraph would be good for girls," who might land jobs as telegraph operators, says Cassell. "But in the 1880s, an attempt was made to legislate who could be a telegraph operator because people worried that girls would contact men through the device," she says.

In the early 1900s, similar worries and proposals for legislation arose about the telephone, she says. The anti-telephone "rhetoric was identical to anti-MySpace rhetoric today," stressing "fears that girls were at risk," she says.

But online dating has its drawbacks. Whitehead says she often hears criticism about untruthful member profiles. Lynch says members she met online often embellished their résumés to enhance their appeal, such as the man who said he liked chess but didn't know the rules when they sat down to play. And the Pew project found that 66 percent of Internet users think cyber dating is dangerous because its puts personal information online. [5]

Online-dating experts have found that people are turning to the Internet to find love for a number of different social and cultural reasons. For instance, busy work schedules make it harder for people to find compatible partners in the offline world, Baker says.

The Internet also allows busy singles to meet people who live across town whom they would not normally bump into, contends Kelly. It can "cut across boundaries that used to limit people's opportunities to meet people, like geography," adds Whitehead.

Compared to a generation ago, people are much more likely to live in a city where they did not grow up, Kelly points out. Because people's lives are no longer dictated by geography, traditional "friendship networks are down," says Bernardo Carducci, a professor of psychology at Indiana University Southeast. He argues that people are lonely and don't have a local friendship network that can produce dates.

And Whitehead and Kelly agree that singles are also turning to the Internet to find a mate because they are not finding them in the old places, such as college or high school.

While online-dating sites do provide more conveniences, Madden says the majority of people she surveyed did not find online dating more efficient than offline dating. Users "still have the complex challenges of negotiating relationships [including] norms and social skills that are different from face-to-face communication."

Some, like Carducci, describe online dating as just one more tool in the dating arsenal. Others, including Whitehead, think it is a big tool that is going to have a lasting force in society.

Kelly predicts that "some of the stigma about online dating is a generation gap" that will disappear over time.

— *Melissa J. Hipolit*

## Yahoo Drew Most Visitors

Each month Internet dating sites entice millions of hopeful visitors searching for the perfect mate.

### Top 10 Dating Sites

| Site | Unique Visitors (in thousands) |
|------|-------------------------------|
| Yahoo! Personals | 6,052 |
| Match.com Sites | 3,893 |
| MarketRange Inc. | 2,676 |
| Spark Networks | 2,638 |
| Mate1.com | 2,354 |
| True.com | 2,093 |
| eHarmony.com | 1,796 |
| Love@AOL | 1,516 |
| Zencon Technologies Dating Sites | 1,091 |
| Lovehappens.com | 976 |

*Source:* comScore Media Metrix, a division of comScore Networks, Inc., January 2006

---

[1] Ginanne Brownell, "The Five-Year Itch," *Newsweek*, Feb. 27, 2006.

[2] Pew Internet and American Life Project, "Online Dating," March 5, 2006.

[3] comScore Media Metrix, January 2006.

[4] Brownell, *op. cit.*

[5] Pew Internet and American Life Project, *op. cit.*

Yet socializing has always been a top human need, as the history of communications technology has shown, says Wittenberg's Smith. When new technologies change how people communicate, people always use them for social interactions — rather than just for business or educational use, he says.

The telephone, for example, was first marketed as a tool to speed up workplace transactions, says Smith. When the fledgling phone industry found that people were getting on and talking for a long time, they "were horrified," he says. For example, for efficiency's sake a single party line was usually assigned to several families to share. "But people wanted to get on and yak," clogging up the lines for their neighbors, he says.

Internet socializing, which began almost as soon as computer networks were established in the late 1960s, also took network developers by surprise. By 1973, e-mail — much of it purely social in nature — made up

# What's Next for the Social Net?

The mega social-networking site MySpace boasts more than 30 million visitors a day. But with the bulk of its users teenagers, Internet industry observers say the MySpace phenomenon may have peaked and that teens are ready to move on to the next big thing.

But social-networking technology — from people searches to video sharing — is here to stay. And Internet entrepreneurs are scrambling to develop new ways to give social-networking sites more staying power and attract a broader — and older — audience.

"Could it be that MySpace peaked this past April?" mused Scott Karp, a technology and publishing analyst. "When a fad becomes overhyped, teens will eventually retreat," and MySpace daily traffic began falling off somewhat in late spring, Karp said. [1]

Some observers seconded Karp's observation. "MySpace is hot now, but teen audiences are the most fickle market ever invented," wrote Mathew Ingram, an online business writer for the Toronto *Globe and Mail.* "MySpace has gone (or is becoming) mainstream, and mainstream is the kiss of death." [2]

Media mogul Rupert Murdoch, whose News Corp. bought MySpace last year for $580 million, has been reticent about how he plans to make money on the free site. But the man who once described newspapers' paid classified advertising as "rivers of gold," confounded the industry recently when he announced that he will offer free classified advertising on MySpace. [3]

Social-networking sites are really about communicating with people you know or specifically want to know, not publication to strangers, according to Dalton Caldwell, founder and CEO of the social-networking site imeem.com. "You don't want to see strangers' home movies," Caldwell says.

Some people in the social-networking business think of the sites as "destinations," cool places to hang out and spend time, says Caldwell. But that's a recipe for a site whose popularity wanes fairly quickly, Caldwell believes. "The site'll be like a night club. It'll be cool for a while, but then it'll fade."

But a site envisioned as a collection of popular, useful, top-of-the-line communication tools won't likely suffer that fate, because "you're plugging into something that people always do." IM — instant messaging — for example, "is not a fad. It hasn't changed since its inception" because it's "a cool tool that people continue to want to use," Caldwell says.

A big draw of social networking will always be connection, especially for the older-than-teenage crowd that entrepreneurs hope to lure in bigger numbers, says Mark Brooks, editor of *Online Personals Watch.* Facebook — a site that caters to college students — has an advantage for the long run in that regard, says Brooks. Providing a connecting point for school pals that will help them avoid losing touch with old friends, Facebook "hits people at their point of pain," Brooks says.

The fact that the site provides a venue to keep in touch with old school mates will eventually "drive Facebook beyond MySpace," Brooks predicts.

To draw older, hopefully more permanent users than MySpace's teens, some entrepreneurs are developing sites where people can join groups discussing topics of interest rather than hanging out and posting personal profiles. Such sites are similar to traditional Internet social venues like Yahoo Groups, whose thousands of discussion groups are focused on individual topics like hobbies or alternative sexual lifestyles.

---

75 percent of traffic on ARPANET, the computer network designed by the Department of Defense to allow researchers to exchange data and access remote computing capability. [43]

By 1975, ARPANET users had developed the first Internet communities, mailing lists through which people could send messages on topics of interest to a whole list of others who shared their passions. Some lists were work-related, but lists linking science-fiction fans and wine-tasting enthusiasts were among the most popular.

In 1978, computer scientists developed Usenet, a network intended to allow Internet users to exchange technical information about the Unix computer operating system. Again, to the surprise of its developers, Usenet almost immediately became a tool for long-distance socializing. Usenet's "originators underestimated the hunger of people for meaningful communication," wrote Internet historians Michael and Ronda Hauben, pointing out that the possibility of "grass-roots connection of people" around the globe is what attracted users. [44]

Although other online groups joined Usenet, until the early 1990s most users were technical people and academics. In the early 1990s, however, America Online and Netscape began making it easy for non-technical

Unlike traditional discussion groups, however, the new "social media" groups capitalize on social networking's ability to connect an individual not only to friends but also to friends of friends, says Tom Gerace, founder and CEO of Gather.com, a social-networking site aimed at adults.

Gather's approach is to encourage its users — envisioned as the sort of folks who are regular listeners to National Public Radio, for example — to post thoughts on subjects ranging from politics to recipes. Those postings constitute a new "social media," movie reviews and political rants composed not by professional journalists but by any interested Internet user. Sites like Gather then use social networking's "friends of friends" structure to help people link up to the posting they'll be most interested in, because they interest others in their circle of contacts, says Gerace.

Gather users will also provide "social filtering" of the media they create, providing links and reviews that will bring the best socially created content to the top of the heap, Gerace says. The site currently pays members a modest fee if content they create gets high marks from fellow users. And "eventually some writers will earn a living" by creating top-ranked Gather content, Gerace says.

Content is also king at Buzznet, a social-networking site on which users share writings, photo, music and video celebrating popular culture, especially music. "A classic social network is all about your profile, but on Buzznet our emphasis is 100 percent focused on what you're producing," says co-founder Anthony Batt.

Buzznet "is the upside-down version of MySpace," says Batt. It's a catalog of people. We're about . . . what people are interested in. You connect with an interest, then you meet the people." Buzznet founders plan to build on its success to found other communities linked by different interests, potentially attracting different age groups, says Batt.

But Buzznet is not the replacement for MySpace that its founders expected it to be, says Batt. "People tend to have three stops. They hang out on MySpace, write a bit at LiveJournal" — a blogging and social-networking site — "and then spend time with us."

Online dating services will ultimately succumb to the social-networking boom, predicts Markus Frind, creator and owner of the Canada-based dating site Plentyoffish.com. Unlike most other dating sites, Plentyoffish is free to users. Frind's operation is "half social networking," because, unlike most other dating sites, Plentyoffish doesn't attempt proactive matchmaking. Instead, like MySpace, Plentyoffish simply allows members to post profiles, converse and arrange outside meetings — one-on-one dates or multi-member parties — on their own.

Contrary to what MySpace and Facebook members claim, the social-networking sites "are all about sex," says Frind. "People go there to hook up," and they're succeeding at it, he says. Eventually, that success will pull most people away from online dating services — which charge — to social-networking sites, which are free. "The hot girls are only on the social-networking sites now, not on dating sites. It's socially unacceptable for hot girls to say they're looking for dates," Frind says. "Eventually, all the guys will follow them there."

---

[1] Scott Karp, "Has the MySpace Downturn Begun?" *Publishing 2.0*, May 25, 2006, http://publishing2.com.

[2] Quoted in *ibid.*

[3] Murdoch was interviewed on "The Charlie Rose Show," on July 20, 2006. Also see "Murdoch predicts demise of classified ads," *Financial Times*, Nov. 24, 2005.

users to move online. AOL, in particular, popularized chat rooms, where people can exchange messages in real time. The live nature of chat room discussions raised new fears among parents because users were generally anonymous. Some chat rooms were eventually found to be heavily trafficked by pedophiles. By 1997, AOL had 14,000 chat rooms, which accounted for about a third of the time AOL members spent online. [45]

Later, AOL introduced instant messaging (IM) — real-time e-mail discussions with one person — and buddy lists, which alert users when friends are online and available to receive IMs.

"Community is the Velcro that keeps people there," said AOL President Theodore Leonsis. [46]

## Six Degrees

In the 1960s, Yale University psychologist Stanley Milgram tested and apparently verified the theory that any two people on Earth are connected to each other by an average of six intermediate contacts. [47]

Scientific doubt remains about the validity of Milgram's so-called "six-degrees-of-separation" theory, but the idea has intrigued the popular imagination. In the late 1990s, Internet developers recognized that the

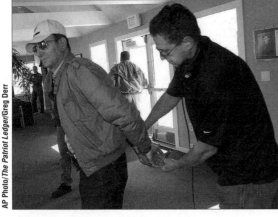

Flight instructor Harold Spector, 67, is arrested last April in Marshfield, Mass., where he'd flown in his private plane to meet what he thought was a 15-year-old girl he'd been "talking" to in an Internet chat room. Spector was charged with attempted statutory rape and attempting to entice a minor under age 16 for sex after the "girl" turned out to be two police officers.

Internet provides tools to seek and contact others in the farther circles of connection. For example, those who post personal Web pages invite friends to link their personal pages to theirs, then their friends link to their friends, creating a chain of social linkages.

In 1997, the pioneering Web site Sixdegrees.com allowed users to send and post messages viewable by their first, second and third-degree contacts. [48] Founder Andrew Weinreich, a lawyer-turned-entrepreneur, explained social networking's usefulness in business and social terms.

"Say you're coming out of college and you want to be a lawyer in Dallas. You ask, 'Who knows an environmental lawyer in Dallas?' You want advice. We give you a shot at that." Less serious queries also pay off, said Weinreich. "You can get a movie review from Siskel and Ebert, but wouldn't you rather hear it from friends you trust?" [49]

The first really big-name social-networking site, Friendster, was launched in 2002, and the blockbuster site, MySpace, quickly followed, in 2003. While other sites also attract visitors in the millions, MySpace struck gold with a concept that, for the first time, brought teen Internet users together at a single spot.

"Curiosity about other people" drove social networking's initial fast growth, says Brooks, of *Online Personals*

*Watch.* "But to make a site grow you need to hit something more powerful than curiosity," something that attracts key people or "connectors" — the "socialites . . . or loudmouths . . . those who run into hundreds of other people all the time," Brooks says.

MySpace seized upon music as a tool to reach the young "connectors." The site contacted music promoters and got band members to engage with the popular people on the site, said Berkeley's Boyd. The bands then created their own pages on MySpace, giving musicians an opportunity to link to multiple kids' pages. "Eventually, other young people followed the young people that followed the music," she says. [50]

And follow they have. With more than 80 million members, MySpace was growing by about 250,000 members a day in early 2006. [51] Exact rankings among the world's top Web sites shift daily, but MySpace averages the sixth-highest number of daily visitors, alongside English-language sites Yahoo, Microsoft Network, Google and eBay, and several Chinese-language sites. That translates to more than 30 million users visiting MySpace daily. [52]

Following right behind have been advertisers, with everybody who wants to contact young people putting up a MySpace page. Even the Marine Corps began collecting "friends" in early 2006. Some 12,000 people now link their pages to the Corps' page, and at last count 430 people had contacted recruiters through the site. [53]

## Techno Kids

What has really brought MySpace to public attention, however, is not its sheer numbers, but its demographics.

Teens and young adults make up the overwhelming majority of users, triggering fear among parents, law-enforcement agencies and some legislators that the site may offer sexual predators easier access to young victims or encourage adolescents to engage in unhealthy behavior, such as posting sexually suggestive photos of themselves.

"The dangers our children are exposed to by these sites are clear and compelling," said Rep. Fitzpatrick. [54]

These worries aren't new and didn't start with social networking, says MIT's Jenkins. "Children and young people have always been early adopters of technology," he says, noting that the Boy Scouts were early users of radio, and in the 19th century children used toy printing presses to create magazines and newspapers.

# Should Congress require schools and public libraries to block social-networking Web sites?

## YES

**Rep. Michael Fitzpatrick, R-Pa.**
*Sponsor, Deleting Online Predators Act*

From remarks on House floor, May 9, 2006

My most important job is my role as a father of six children. In a world that moves and changes at a dizzying pace, being a father gets harder all the time. Technology is one of the key concerns I have as a parent, specifically the Internet and the sites my kids visit, register with and use on a daily basis.

One of the most interesting and worrying developments of late has been the growth in what are called "social-networking sites." Sites like MySpace, Friendster and Facebook have literally exploded in popularity in just a few short years.

For adults, these sites are fairly benign. For children, they open the door to many dangers, including online bullying and exposure to child predators that have turned the Internet into a virtual hunting ground for children. The dangers our children are exposed to by these sites are clear and compelling. MySpace, which is self-regulated, has removed an estimated 200,000 objectionable profiles since it started in 2003.

This is why I introduced the Deleting Online Predators Act as part of the Suburban Caucus agenda. Parents have the ability to screen their children's Internet access at home, but this protection ends when their child leaves for school or the library. The Deleting Online Predators Act requires schools and libraries to implement technology to protect children from accessing commercial networking sites like MySpace.com, and chat rooms, which allow children to be preyed upon by individuals seeking to do harm to our children.

Additionally, the legislation would require the Federal Trade Commission [FTC] to design and publish a unique Web site to serve as a clearinghouse and resource for parents, teachers and children for information on the dangers of surfing the Internet. The Web site would include detailed information about commercial networking sites like MySpace. The FTC would also be responsible for issuing consumer alerts to parents, teachers, school officials and others regarding the potential dangers of Internet child predators and others and their ability to contact children through MySpace.com and other social-networking sites.

In addition, the bill would require the Federal Communication Commission to establish an advisory board to review and report commercial social-networking sites like MySpace.com and chat rooms that have been shown to allow sexual predators easy access to personal information of, and contact with, our nation's children.

## NO

**Henry Jenkins**
*Director, Comparative Media Studies program, Massachusetts Institute of Technology*

From interview posted online by the MIT News Office, accessed July 2006

As a society, we are at a moment of transition when the most important social relationships may no longer be restricted to those we conduct face-to-face with people in our own immediate surroundings. We are learning how to interact across multiple communities and negotiate with diverse norms. These networking skills are increasingly important to all aspects of our lives.

Just as youth in a hunting society play with bows and arrows, youth in an information society play with information and social networks. Rather than shutting kids off from social-network tools, we should be teaching them how to exploit their potential and mitigate their risks.

Much of the current policy debate around MySpace assumes that the activities there are at best frivolous and at worst dangerous to the teens who participate. Yet a growing number of teachers around the country are discovering that these technologies have real pedagogical value.

Teachers are beginning to use blogs for knowledge-sharing in schools; they use mailing lists to communicate expectations about homework with students and parents. They are discovering that students take their assignments more seriously and write better if they are producing work that will reach a larger public rather than simply sit on the teacher's desk. Teachers are linking together classrooms around the country and around the world, getting kids from different cultural backgrounds to share aspects of their everyday experience.

Many of these activities would be threatened by the proposed federal legislation, which would restrict access to these sites via public schools or library terminals. In theory, the bill would allow schools to disable these filters for use in educationally specified contexts, yet, in practice, teachers who wanted to exploit the educational benefits of these tools would face increased scrutiny and pressure to discontinue these practices. Teens who lack access to the Internet at home would be cut off from their extended sphere of social contacts.

Wouldn't we be better off having teens engage with MySpace in the context of supervision from knowledgeable and informed adults? Historically, we taught children what to do when a stranger telephoned them when their parents are away; surely, we should be helping to teach them how to manage the presentation of their selves in digital spaces.

## Many Americans Know Online Daters

Nearly one-third of American adults know at least one person who has used an online dating Web site.

| Percent (of U.S. adults) | No. of People | Who Know Someone Who Has . . . |
|---|---|---|
| 31% | 63 million | used a dating Web site |
| 26 | 53 million | dated a person they met on a dating site |
| 15 | 30 million | been in a long-term relationship or married someone they met online |

*Source:* Pew Internet and American Life Project, "Online Dating," March 5, 2006

But the speed with which new technologies appear on the scene today, combined with teens' propensity to quickly embrace new technologies, makes it especially difficult for parents, lawmakers and technology companies to figure out how to respond, says Blue Coat's Carosella. "The social behaviors that involve the Internet are not going to go away." In fact, "the kids . . . are inventing these behaviors."

"Kids are always one or two steps ahead" of older generations, says California State University's Subrahmanyam. "Chat, IM, social networking have all developed as teen-heavy technology," she says. "That makes sense, because figuring out sex and their own place in the social order . . . makes talking with peers very important."

But while teens have long discussed sex and relationships via instant messaging, adolescent interchanges on sites like MySpace "can now be seen by others," she adds.

### Background Checks

While most of the uproar over potential dangers in online socializing concerns teenagers and children, some fear that online dating sites may also make it easier for sexual predators to reach adult victims.

In the past year and a half, legislators in several states, including California, Florida, Illinois, Michigan, Ohio, Texas and Virginia, proposed requiring online dating sites to conduct criminal background checks of all prospective members or prominently inform users that they do not conduct such checks. [55]

The bills were suggested by Herb Vest, founder and CEO of the True.com dating service, which checks the criminal and marital backgrounds of its members. "The primary motivation is to protect people from criminal predation online," said Vest. "I can't imagine anyone with a hatful of brains being against that." [56]

Many online daters think dating sites already take such precautions, said Republican Florida state Rep. Kevin Ambler, who sponsored a similar bill in Florida last year after hearing that 20 percent of survey respondents thought background checks were already required on dating sites. "Many online daters have a false sense of security," he said. [57]

But some Internet companies and dating sites say the bills aren't needed or would create a false sense of security. "It would be just as easy to argue that True.com should be required to post labels on each page, saying, 'Warning. True.com's background searches will not identify criminals using fake names,'" said Kristin Kelly, a spokeswoman for the Match.com dating site. [58]

True.com has contracted with Rapsheets.com, a private firm trying to build a national database of criminal convictions, according to the Internet Alliance, an advocacy group whose members include the dating sites Match.com and eHarmony.com, as well as other Internet companies such as eBay, AOL and Yahoo. But mechanisms for tracking criminal convictions are state-based, the group points out, and some states decline to participate in national databases. So it is impossible for Rapsheets to have complete information, they said. [59]

Internet Alliance also argues that new laws aren't needed because unregulated dating services — such as newspaper ads and singles hotlines — have run "smoothly for years without legislative interference," while "providing even less information [than] a typical online profile."

So far, the bills have gone nowhere. The Michigan House passed a bill, but it later died in the state Senate. In Florida, bills were approved in committee last year but did not advance. A California bill that would have fined online dating services $250 for each day they don't conduct background checks was introduced but later pulled from consideration.

## CURRENT SITUATION

### Big Brother

Nowadays, teenagers aren't the only ones hanging out on MySpace.com. Law-enforcement officials now are increasingly staking out the site, looking to head off crimes. Some high-profile arrests in MySpace-related cases have raised concerns about social networking similar to worries that arose in the 1990s about chat rooms.

For example, a 39-year-old Pennsylvania man faces federal charges that he molested a 14-year-old Connecticut girl he met through her MySpace page. The girl had listed her age as 18. In another Connecticut case, a 22-year-old man traveled from New Jersey to visit an 11-year-old girl, whom he molested in her home while her parents slept. [60]

Besides monitoring for sexual predation, law-enforcement officials worry that teenagers may use MySpace to plot violence or vandalism. For example, a 15-year-old New Jersey girl was charged with harassment when school officials found an apparent "hit list" on her MySpace page. In Denver, a 16-year-old boy was arrested after allegedly posting photos of himself holding handguns on MySpace. [61] And in Riverton, Kan., five high-school boys were arrested in April after school officials found a message on one boy's MySpace page apparently threatening a Columbine-style shooting. Law-enforcement officers later found weapons and documents related to a plot in a student's bedroom and in school lockers. [62]

Meanwhile, the NBC program "Dateline" recently highlighted potential online dangers to children from adults. In a series of programs, "Dateline" photographed men who had arranged to meet what they thought were young teenagers but were actually adult members of an activist group. While the encounters took place in chat rooms, not on social-networking sites, the shows raised further alarms.

In response, Rep. Fitzpatrick introduced his Deleting Online Predators Act. It would expand the anti-pornography Children's Internet Protection Act (CIPA) by requiring schools and libraries to prohibit access to any commercial social-networking site or chat room through which minors could access sexual material or be subject to sexual advances.

"This is a new and evolving problem" that requires amendments to CIPA, since social networking didn't exist when that law was written, said Michael Conalle, Fitzpatrick's chief of staff. [63]

But the American Library Association said the bill is so broadly written that it would block not only education that would teach kids to go online safely but also "a wide array of other important applications and technologies." [64]

Lordan of the Internet Education Foundation said evidence suggests that more teens are abused in their own homes and neighborhoods than online. "We could end up diverting resources" to attack online predation "when the main need is really elsewhere," he says.

Although the House Energy and Commerce Committee has held subcommittee hearings on Fitzpatrick's bill, and it has been discussed on the House floor, discussions so far have focused heavily on child pornography on the Internet. No action on the legislation has yet been scheduled, and no bills have been introduced in the Senate.

### Safety First

State attorneys general, parents, entrepreneurs and social-networking companies recently have launched safety initiatives for online socializing.

Connecticut Attorney General Richard Blumenthal, for example, has asked social-networking companies to implement tougher measures to block teenagers' access to pornography and rid the sites of sexual predators. Voluntary efforts, once the state and businesses agree on what steps should be taken, would "avoid the costs and time required for any sort of legal action," he said. [65]

In April, MySpace hired Hemanshu Migam — Microsoft's former director of consumer security and child safety and a former federal prosecutor of online child-exploitation cases — to manage its safety, privacy and customer-education programs. The company also partnered with the National Center for Missing and Exploited Children and the Advertising Council to post public-service announcements about online safety on TV, MySpace and other Internet sites. [66]

While acknowledging the company's first steps, Blumenthal said he had urged MySpace to adopt other, "more significant, specific measures," such as tougher age-verification efforts and free software for parents to block MySpace from home computers. [67]

Alarms about social networking also are drawing interest from parents' groups and some entrepreneurs. In Utah, for example, the state parent-teacher association is creating materials to teach parents how to make their children safe online. It will also recommend filtering and blocking software to parents in collaboration with Blue Coat, the Internet security company. [68]

Other Internet-technology developers also are offering help. Sales have tripled in the last three years for programs like eBlaster, Content Protect, IM Einstein and Safe Eyes, which allow parents to monitor their kids' e-mails, instant messages and online chats in real time from a separate computer — such as while the parent is at work. [69] Software developer Alex Strand, for instance, has established MySpacewatch.com, where users can sign up to monitor changes — such as new photos, additional listed friends — on a MySpace Web page for free.

"I started it as . . . a way for parents to check out what their kids are doing," said Strand. [70]

## OUTLOOK

### Here to Stay

In the future, online communications and social networking will become even more deeply rooted in our lives, say most analysts.

That makes it imperative to learn as much as possible about how online activities affect people, says Carosella, of Blue Coat Systems. "There's a critical role for mental health and social scientists," he says. "We should be doing studies on why there are so many sexual predators out there. Where did they all come from? Is there a vicious cycle between easy access to pornography online and the emergence of online predators?"

Future generations will make even more use of social networking, predicts Diane Danielson, who created www.DWCFaces.com, a social-networking site for businesswomen. "We will see Generation Y bringing their social networks into the workspace," she says, referring to the 20-25-year-old age group. "They will also remain connected to more people from their high schools and colleges" thanks to the persistent presence on social-networking sites of links to Web sites like Classmates.com. "In a transient society, a social network Web page might be your most consistent address."

Social networking may also transform some political campaigns into more grass-roots affairs, says Zephyr Teachout, a professor of constitutional law at Vermont Law School, who directed Internet organizing for Howard Dean's 2004 presidential campaign. Dean encouraged people around the country to communicate on their own via social-network software, allowing local and individual momentum to drive many activities. "We discovered that the human need to be political is important" and, if tapped, increases participation, she says. "But to do it you need a candidate willing to devolve power."

When media mogul Rupert Murdoch's News Corp. bought MySpace last year for $580 million, some speculated that the conservative Murdoch might use the site to influence the politics of the site's young users, perhaps by pushing Republican-slanted commentary on the site during the 2008 presidential election cycle. Many analysts doubt whether such an effort could succeed, though, since social-networking users have notoriously fled sites when owners have tried to exercise regulatory clout.

But Murdoch says he spent $1.5 billion in the past year to buy MySpace and other online companies to empower people to create their own content. "Technology is shifting power away from the editors, the publishers, the establishment, the media elite. Now it's the people who are taking control," he said. [71]

As Internet technology draws more people to publish their personal information in cyberspace, a new set of ethics is needed for presenting oneself, says Bill Holsinger-Robinson, chief operating officer of Spout.com, a social-networking site focused on film. "I see it as harking back to earlier, simpler times — a town square where people can gather."

When town squares were common, he says, "there was a certain sense of responsibility on how we presented ourselves. We've lost that. Now we have to reinvent it for a new generation."

## NOTES

1. Erik Brady and Daniel Libit, "Alarms Sound Over Athlete's Facebook Time," *USA Today*, March 8, 2006.

2. Quoted in *ibid*.

3. Clair Osborn, "Teen, Mom Sue MySpace.com for $30 Million," *Austin American-Statesman*, June 20, 2006.

4. Quoted in *ibid*.

5. "Internet: The Mainstreaming of Online Life," Pew Internet and American Life Project, www.pewinternet.org.

6. John Horrigan and Lee Rainie, "The Internet's Growing Role in Life's Major Moments," Pew Internet and American Life Project, April 19, 2006.

7. "Internet: The Mainstreaming of Online Life," *op. cit.*

8. For background, see Brian Hansen, "Cyber-predators," *CQ Researcher*, March 1, 2002, p. 169-192.

9. For background, see David Masci, "Internet Privacy," *CQ Researcher*, Nov. 6, 2998, pp. 953-976.

10. "Social Networking Sites Continue to Attract Record Numbers as MySpace.com Surpasses 50 Million U.S. Visitors in May," PRNewswire, comScore Networks, Inc., June 15, 2006.

11. Marshall Kirkpatrick, "Top 10 Social Networking Sites See 47 Percent Growth," the socialsoftwareweblog, May 17, 2006, http://socialsofware.weblogsinc.com.

12. For background, see Kenneth Jost, "Libraries and the Internet," *CQ Researcher*, June 1, 2001, pp. 465-488.

13. Michael Fitzpatrick, testimony before House Energy and Commerce Subcommittee on Oversight and Investigations, June 10, 2006.

14. Henry Jenkins and Danah Boyd, "Discussion: MySpace and Deleting Online Predators Act," interview published online by Massachusetts Institute of Technology News Office, May 24, 2006, www.danah.org/papers/MySpaceDOPA.html.

15. *Ibid.*

16. Quoted in Anne Chappel Belden, "Kids' Tech Toys: High-Tech Communication Tools," Parenthood.com, http://parenthood.com.

17. Kevin Farnham, reply to "Friendster Lost Steam. Is MySpace Just a Fad?" Corante blog, March 21, 2006, http://man.corante.com.

18. Paul Marks, "Pentagon Sets Its Sights on Social Networking in Washington," *NewScientist.com*, June 9, 2006, www.newscientist.com.

19. Quoted in *ibid.*

20. David Finkelhor and Lisa M. Jones, "Explanations for the Decline in Sexual Abuse Cases," *Juvenile Justice Bulletin*, U.S. Department of Justice, Office of Juvenile Justice and Delinquency Prevention, January 2004, www.ojp.usdoj/gov/ojjdp.

21. Quoted in Larry Magid, "Plug In, or Pull the Plug," Staysafe.org for Parents, www.stay safeonline.com.

22. *Congressional Record*, House, May 9, 2006, p. H2311.

23. *Ibid.*, p. H2315.

24. Jenkins and Boyd, *op. cit.*

25. *Ibid.*

26. Quoted in Robert Brumfield, "Bill Calls for MySpace Age Limit," *eSchoolNews online*, May 16, 2006, www.eschoolnews.com.

27. For background, see Kathy Koch, "The Digital Divide," *CQ Researcher*, Jan. 28, 2000, pp. 41-64.

28. For background, see Marcia Clemmitt, "Controlling the Internet," *CQ Researcher*, May 12, 2006, pp. 409-432.

29. Clifford Stoll, *Silicon Snake Oil: Second Thoughts on the Information Highway* (1996), p. 43.

30. Killeen Hanson, "Study Links Internet, Social Contact," *The Stanford Daily Online Edition*, Feb. 28, 2005.

31. Quoted in *ibid.*

32. Norman H. Nie and Lutz Erbring, "Internet and Society: A Preliminary Report," Stanford Institute for the Quantitative Study of Society, Feb. 17, 2000.

33. Quoted in *ibid.*

34. Jeffrey Boase, John B. Horrigan, Barry Wellman and Lee Rainie, "The Strength of Internet Ties," Pew Internet and American Life Project, Jan. 25, 2006.

35. *Ibid.*

36. *Ibid.*

37. Barry Wellman, Jeffrey Boase and Wenhong Chen, "The Networked Nature of Community: Online and Offline," *IT & Society*, summer 2002, pp. 151-165, www.itandsociety.org.

38. *Ibid.*

39. Sheera Claire Frenkel, "Israelis and Lebanese Are Still Talking — on the Net," *The Jerusalem Post*, July 21, 2006.

40. Christopher Allen, "My Advice to Social Networking Services," Life With Alacrity blog, Feb. 3, 2004, www.lifewithalacrity.com.

41. Quoted in Michael Erard, "Decoding the New Cues in Online Society," *The New York Times*, Nov. 27, 2003.

42. Quoted in Jenkins and Boyd, *op. cit.*

43. For background, see *The Internet's Coming of Age* (2000).

44. Michael Hauben and Ronda Hauben, "The Social Forces Behind the Development of Usenet," First Monday, www.firstmonday.org.

45. "Internet Communities," *Business Week Archives*, May 5, 1997, www.businessweek.com.

46. Quoted in *ibid.*

47. For background, see Judith Donath and Danah Boyd, "Public Displays of Connection," *BT Technology Journal*, October 2004, p. 71.

48. Doug Bedell, "Meeting Your New Best Friends," *The Dallas Morning News*, Oct. 27, 1998.

49. Quoted in *ibid.*

50. Danah Boyd, "Friendster Lost Steam. Is MySpace Just a Fad?" March 21, 2006, www.danah.org.

51. Dawn Kawamoto and Greg Sandoval, "MySpace Growth Continues Amid Criticism," ZDNet News, March 31, 2006, http://news.zdnet.com.

52. MySpace traffic details from www.alexa.com.

53. Audrey McAvoy, "Marines Trolling MySpace.com for Recruits," *Chicago Sun-Times*, July 25, 2006.

54. *Congressional Record, op. cit.*, p. H2310.

55. For background, see Javad Heydary, "Regulation of Online Dating Services Sparks Controversy," *E-Commerce Times*, March 3, 2005, www.ecommercetimes.com.

56. Quoted in "Online Dating Background Checks?" CNNMoney.com, April 25, 2006, http://cnnmoney.com.

57. Quoted in *ibid.*

58. Quoted in Declan McCullagh, "True Love With a Criminal Background Check," C/Net News.com, Feb. 28, 2005, http://news.com.com.

59. "Online Dating," white paper from Internet Alliance, www.internetalliance.org.

60. "Twenty Youths Suspended in MySpace Case," The Associated Press, March 3, 2006.

61. "MySpace in the News," *Bergen* [New Jersey] *Daily Record*, May 14, 2006, www.dailyrecord.com.

62. "Charges Mulled in Alleged School Shooting Plot," The Associated Press, April 23, 2006. For background, see Kathy Koch, "School Violence," *CQ Researcher*, Oct. 9, 1998, pp. 881-904.

63. Quoted in Declan McCullagh, "Congress Targets Social Network Sites," C/Net News.com, May 11, 2006, http://news.com.com.

64. Michael Gorman, "ALA Opposes 'Deleting Online Predators Act,' " May 15, 2006, statement, American Library Association.

65. Quoted in "Making MySpace Safe for Kids," Newsmaker Q&A, *Business Week online*, March 6, 2006, www.businessweek.com.

66. Maria Newman, "MySpace.com Hires Official to Oversee Users' Safety," *The New York Times*, April 12, 2006.

67. Quoted in *ibid.*

68. "Utah PTA and Blue Coat Systems Join Forces to Drive Greater Internet Safety, Community Action," Blue Coat Systems press release, June 20, 2006, www.bluecoat.com.

69. See Ned Potter, "Watching Your Kids Online," ABCNews.com, July 24, 2006.

70. Quoted in Stefanie Olsen, "Keeping an Eye on MySpace," C/Net News.com, June 29, 2006, http://news.com.com.

71. Spencer Reiss, "His Space," *Wired*, July 14, 2006, www.wired.com.

## BIBLIOGRAPHY

### Books

**Farnham, Kevin M., and Dale G. Farnham, *MySpace Safety: 51 Tips for Teens and Parents*, How To Primers, 2006.**
Parents of a veteran teenage MySpace user explain what their experiences have taught them about how social networking works and what safety rules families should follow.

**Rheingold, Howard, *The Virtual Community: Homesteading on the Electronic Frontier*, The MIT Press, 2000.**
A technology analyst and longtime participant in Internet communities recounts the history of the social Internet and his two decades of personal experience with it.

## Articles

**Armental, Maria, "Site Started by New Jersey Teens Is Growing Fast,"** *Asbury Park Press,* **May 16, 2006, www.app.com.**
MyYearbook.com, a social-networking site created by two New Jersey high-school students in 2005, has membership rolls that are growing by about 40 percent a month. The brother and sister team who created it became millionaires before high-school graduation earlier this year when an investor paid $1.5 million for a 10-percent stake in the operation.

**Bower, Bruce, "Growing Up Online,"** *Science News Online,* **June 17, 2006, www.sciencenews.org.**
Research psychologists dissect the appeal of Internet social-networking software to teenagers and describe the findings in several recent studies of how teenagers behave online.

**Brumfield, Robert, "Bill Calls for MySpace Age Limit,"** *eSchoolNews online,* **May 16, 2006.**
Educators discuss the possible effects on schools and students of a congressional proposal to require schools and public libraries to block social software.

**Hof, Robert D., "Internet Communities,"** *Business Week,* **May 5, 1997,** *Business Week Archives,* **www.businessweek.com.**
As women, teenagers and non-technical users flock online, Internet use turns away from pre-created content toward socializing and Internet communities sharing common interests.

**Koppelman, Alex, "MySpace or OurSpace?"** *Salon.com,* **June 8, 2006, www.salon.com.**
A growing number of school administrators and law-enforcement officials regularly monitor MySpace and other social-networking sites in search of evidence of rule-breaking and criminal activity. The practice is raising awareness among teens that spaces they believed were private are not and also is raising questions about how far schools can go in policing students' out-of-school activities.

**Leonard, Andrew, "You Are Who You Know,"** *Salon.com,* **June 15, 2004.**
Social-networking entrepreneurs and Internet analysts explain why Internet technology led to development of social software and why they believe social networks matter, online and off.

**Marks, Paul, "Pentagon Sets Its Sights on Social Networking Websites,"** *New Scientist,* **June 9, 2006, NewScientist.com.**
The National Security Agency is researching the possibility of mining social-networking sites for data to assemble extensive personal profiles of individuals and their social circles to help sniff out terrorist plots.

**Reiss, Spencer, "His Space,"** *Wired,* **July 14, 2006, www.wired.com.**
Since media mogul Rupert Murdoch paid $580 million to buy MySpace in 2005, technology and business analysts have argued about whether Murdoch can make the investment pay by selling advertising and/or using the site as a distribution channel for music and video content.

## Studies and Reports

**Boase, Jeffrey, John B. Horrigan, Barry Wellman and Lee Rainie,** *The Strength of Internet Ties,* **Pew Internet and American Life Project, January 2006.**
Statistics show that the Internet and e-mail aid users in maintaining social networks and providing pathways to support and advice in difficult times, according to University of Toronto and Pew researchers.

**Finkelhor, David, Kimberly J. Mitchell and Janis Wolak,** *Online Victimization: A Report on the Nation's Youth,* **Crimes Against Children Research Center, University of New Hampshire, June 2000.**
In cooperation with the National Center for Missing and Exploited Children and the U.S. Department of Justice Office of Juvenile Justice and Delinquency Prevention, University of New Hampshire researchers detail national statistics on online crimes against children and teens, online sexual solicitation of young Internet users and responses to Internet sexual solicitations by young people, their families and law enforcement.

**Lenhart, Amanda, and Mary Madden,** *Teen Content Creators and Consumers,* **Pew Internet and American Life Project, November 2005.**
Creating and sharing content through blogs, videos and other sites is an integral part of online social life for today's teens.

# For More Information

**Apophenia: Making Connections Where None Previously Existed**, www.zephoria.org/thoughts/. News, data and commentary on the social Internet by social-media researcher Danah Boyd.

**Berkman Center for Internet and Society**, Harvard Law School, Baker House, 1587 Massachusetts Ave., Cambridge, MA 02138; (617) 495-7547; http://cyber.law.harvard.edu. A research program investigating legal, technical and social developments in cyberspace.

**Center for the Digital Future**, University of Southern California Annenberg School, 300 South Grand Ave., Suite 3950, Los Angeles, CA 90071; (213) 437-4433; www.digitalcenter.org. A research program investigating the Internet's effects on individuals and society.

**Crimes Against Children Research Center**, University of New Hampshire, 20 College Rd., #126 Horton Social Science Center, Durham, NH 03824; (603) 862-1888; www.unh.edu/ccrc/. Studies criminal victimization of young people and how to prevent it, including online.

**Internet Education Foundation**, 1634 I St., N.W., Suite 1107, Washington, DC 20006; (202) 638-4370; www.neted.org. Educates the public and lawmakers about the Internet as a tool of democracy and communications; the industry-supported GetNetWise project (www.getnetwise.org) disseminates information on safety and security.

**Many2Many**, http://many.corante.com/. Academics and technical experts provide information and commentary on social networking in this blog.

**National Center for Missing and Exploited Children**, 699 Prince St., Alexandria, VA 22314-3175; (703) 274-3900; www.missingkids.com. Provides education and services on child exploitation to families and professionals; maintains a CyberTipline and other resources for reporting and combating exploitation via the Internet.

**Online Personals Watch**, http://onlinepersonalswatch.typepad.com. A blogger and industry veteran provides news and commentary on social networking and online dating.

**Pew Internet and American Life Project**, 1615 L St., N.W., Suite 700, Washington, DC 20036; (202) 419-4500; www.pewinternet.org. Provides data and analysis on Internet usage and its effects on American society.

**Progress and Freedom Foundation**, 1444 I St., N.W., Suite 500, Washington, DC 20005; (202) 289-8928; www.pff.org. A free-market-oriented think tank that examines public policy related to the Internet.

4

# Free-Press Disputes

Kenneth Jost and Alan Greenblatt

*New York Times* reporter Judith Miller talks to the press after being found in contempt in Washington, D.C., on Oct. 7, 2004, for refusing to reveal confidential sources during an investigation into the unmasking of covert CIA officer Valerie Plame. Miller, here with Executive Editor Bill Keller, spent eighty-five days in jail in 2005 before a source released her from their confidentiality agreement, allowing her to testify.

From *CQ Researcher,*
April 8, 2005. (Updated Jun 1, 2008)

oni Locy is an assistant professor of journalism at West Virginia University. When it comes to freedom of the press, she has a lot to tell her students, based on her own experience. A federal judge in 2008 ordered her to reveal her sources for stories she had written as a *USA Today* reporter seven years earlier, or pay fines of up to $5,000 per day. He also ordered that she pay the fines herself and receive no reimbursement from the newspaper, or anyone else. Locy had written a pair of stories about Steven Hatfill, a former Army scientist identified by the Justice Department as a "person of interest" in the investigation into the deaths of five people killed by anthrax that had been sent through the mail. Hatfill was never charged in the case, despite what was called the largest investigation in the FBI's history.

Hatfill sued the Justice Department for revealing information that damaged his reputation — one of several civil cases former government employees have filed citing the Privacy Act, which is meant to keep official documents about such workers secret. In order to find out who leaked information from his personnel files, Hatfill subpoenaed Locy, who refused to disclose any names.

An appellate court stayed the large fines imposed on Locy, but it was not clear that she would enjoy any further legal protection. In recent years, courts have grown increasingly skeptical about reporters' claims that they cannot reveal information provided to them by confidential sources. "The culture of the press as an independent body is now under attack and if this continues will come to be seen as an investigative arm of the government," Eve Burton, general counsel of the Hearst Corporation, told *The New York Times*. In 2005 and 2006, Burton said that her company had

# Most States Protect Reporters' Sources

Thirty-one states and the District of Columbia have enacted so-called shield laws that permit reporters to protect confidential sources. In many states without such laws, reporters have been granted some privilege to protect their sources through state constitutions, common law or court rules.

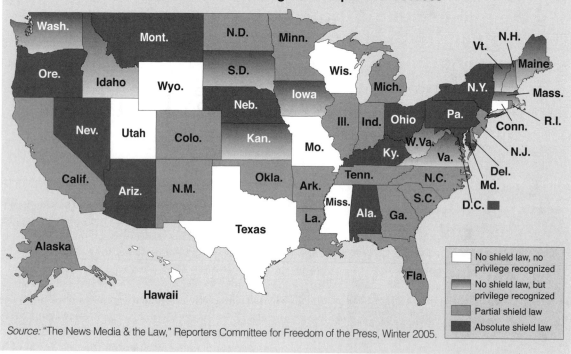

### Shield Laws and Privileges for Reporters' Sources

Legend:
- No shield law, no privilege recognized
- No shield law, but privilege recognized
- Partial shield law
- Absolute shield law

*Source:* "The News Media & the Law," Reporters Committee for Freedom of the Press, Winter 2005.

received eighty newsgathering subpoenas for its broadcast stations, newspapers, and magazines. [1]

Shield laws are on the books in thirty-one states, protecting reporters (to varying degrees) from being compelled from revealing their sources. Virtually every other state, save Wyoming, has case law that has grown out of court proceedings offering similar protection. But there is no media shield law on the federal books, and the federal courts have been where most of the recent cases concerning press freedom have been heard. The House in October 2007 passed media shield legislation, shortly after a Senate committee had passed its own version. But the Justice Department opposed the bills and President Bush threatened a veto. Prospects for a media shield law will brighten following the 2008 election, however, as both Republican senator John McCain of Arizona and Democratic senator Barack Obama of Illinois have each endorsed the idea.

Critics of the shield law concept maintain that it poses potential dangers to national security and criminal investigations. "On a practical level, the bill would cause delays — measured in years — in national security investigations, because prosecutors would be litigating (and appealing) instead of investigating serious crimes," writes Patrick Fitzgerald, the U.S. attorney in Chicago — and special counsel in the most significant case touching on press freedom in recent years. [2] Fitzgerald was appointed special counsel to investigate who leaked the identity of Valerie Plame, a CIA agent whose husband, Joseph Wilson, had criticized the Bush administration's policies in Iraq. Columnist Robert Novak had revealed Plame's identity in 2003, citing two administration sources. In seeking to determine the source of the leak, Fitzgerald subpoenaed several prominent Washington reporters.

Novak and reporters for the *Washington Post* and NBC cut deals with Fitzgerald to provide limited testimony. But two other reporters, Judith Miller of the *New York Times* and Matt Cooper of *Time*, refused to cooperate. Ultimately, *Time* decided to hand over Cooper's notes after the Supreme Court upheld lower court decisions that Cooper was in contempt for refusing to testify. And Miller, after spending eighty-five days in jail in 2005, testified as well after her primary source, vice presidential chief of staff I. Lewis "Scooter" Libby, released her from their confidentiality agreement. At Libby's subsequent trial, ten of the nineteen witnesses were journalists, which the *New York Times* called "a spectacle that would have been unthinkable only a few years ago." [3] (Libby was found guilty of perjury and obstruction of justice in 2007. Bush commuted his sentence, sparing Libby any time in prison.)

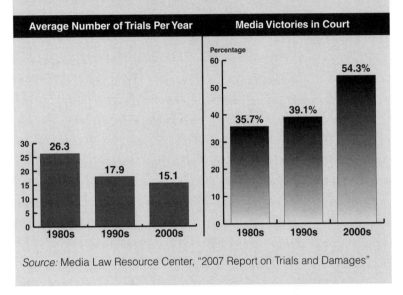

## Media Facing Fewer Libel Trials

The number of libel, privacy and related claims against the media has decreased significantly over the last 27 years (graph at left) while the win rate for media defendants has risen (graph at right). Three-quarters of the claims against the media involved defamation. A total of 572 cases involved media defendants during the 27-year period.

**Average Number of Trials Per Year**

- 1980s: 26.3
- 1990s: 17.9
- 2000s: 15.1

**Media Victories in Court**

Percentage
- 1980s: 35.7%
- 1990s: 39.1%
- 2000s: 54.3%

*Source:* Media Law Resource Center, "2007 Report on Trials and Damages"

"Every tenet and every pact that existed between the government and the press has been broken," said Theodore J. Boutros, a media lawyer who represented *Time* in the case. Burton, the Hearst counsel, noted that the heavy amount of traffic in subpoenas her company receives all came "after the Judith Miller case. In the two years before that, we had maybe four or five subpoenas. We didn't even keep track."

Fitzgerald proved that a prosecutor could force testimony even from prominent journalists working for major news organizations willing to spend millions of dollars on their legal cases. Several other high-profile cases have similarly pointed to an erosion of the media's traditional arguments that reporters must be able to guarantee anonymity to sources who provide sensitive information.

Reporters and media companies have been losing battles to the Bush administration over subpoenas into reporters' phone records and have had to pay hundreds of thousands of dollars to a former government scientist for publishing information from his personnel files. Judges in cases ranging from baseball's steroids scandal to street demonstrations have shown no compunction about leveling big fines or sending journalists to jail.

Journalism groups say the flurry of subpoenas — amid ongoing post-September 11 access disputes between the news media and the Bush administration — threatens reporters' ability to gain cooperation from sources wishing to remain anonymous. "This is a wholesale assault on the media's ability to gather information," says Lucy Dalglish, executive director of The Reporters Committee for Freedom of the Press. Without such protections, former tobacco industry scientist and whistleblower Jeffrey Wigand might never have revealed anonymously, and famously, to CBS' *Sixty Minutes* that the tobacco industry not only knew that cigarettes were addictive and harmful but also had deliberately increased their addictiveness. Nor would the Enron accounting fraud or the Abu Ghraib prison-abuse scandals have been exposed, argues Sandra Baron, executive director of the Media Law Resource Center, in New York.

Journalists have long used the promise of confidentiality to pry information from people who, for various

During the rape trial of basketball star Kobe Bryant, a Colorado judge barred news media from publishing testimony from a closed-door pretrial hearing. Journalists are concerned that judges have begun prohibiting publication of information already in the hands of news organizations. The charges against Bryant were dropped on Sept. 1, 2004, after the alleged victim refused to testify.

reasons, do not want their names in print. In 1972, however, the U.S. Supreme Court rejected journalists' arguments that the First Amendment gives them a privilege to protect confidential sources comparable to such well-established privileges as attorney-client, doctor-patient, and priest-penitent. In a significant concurring opinion in the 5-4 *Branzburg v. Hayes* decision, however, Justice Lewis F. Powell Jr. suggested reporters could claim such a privilege on a case-by-case basis. [4]

Many journalism groups support legislation creating explicit press protections, but some journalists worry that a media shield law could be counterproductive if it defines

the reporter's privilege more narrowly than existing court decisions. However, some legal observers — generally with conservative or pro-law enforcement views — argue that reporters should have no special privileges in criminal cases.

The confidential-source disputes have flared at a time when the judicial climate toward press freedom is mixed, according to journalism groups and First Amendment experts. Supreme Court decisions on libel and privacy beginning in the 1960s have given the media significant protections against liability in private lawsuits. But many state courts and the Bush administration — particularly after the September 11, 2001, terrorist attacks — have restricted the press' access to government information and some legal proceedings. "Overall, it is not a particularly positive time," says Rodney Smolla, dean of the Washington and Lee University Law School in Virginia and author of several books on First Amendment issues. "There's very little doctrinal expansion of rights for the press; and, in a number of instances, there's retreat."

Charles Davis, executive director of the freedom of information program at the University of Missouri's School of Journalism, in Columbia, says that after "tremendous expansions" of press rights in the 1970s and 1980s, there has been "some retrenchment" since the 1990s. "On the issue of confidentiality, we're seeing a revisiting of what we had thought of as an unassailable right," says Davis, who also sits on the freedom of information committee of the Society of Professional Journalists (SPJ). Despite the increasingly dire environment, advocates of press freedom are hopeful that the election of either McCain or Obama will signal a period of greater openness in general — and bright prospects for passage of a media shield law in particular.

If the final result of the Valerie Plame case is not greater threats to press independence, as currently seems to be the case, but a prod for Congress to pass such a law, media lawyer Nathan Siegel predicts, it will simply be the latest example of a scenario that has played itself out in nearly every generation of American history. "Every time this crisis has erupted," Siegal writes, "the jailing of journalists has been the catalyst for changes in the law that protected a subsequent generation of journalists." [5] That kind of long-term perspective, however, offers little comfort to journalists such as Toni Locy who are facing jail time or hefty fines if they fail to cooperate with prosecutors. "I don't have that kind of money," Locy said when the judge in her case fined her thousands of dollars per day. [6]

As disputes over confidential sources continue in federal courts, one of the questions being debated is whether the government is increasingly blocking press access to information. For example, Gov. Robert Ehrlich, R-Md., had a prickly relationship with the news media during his single term in office. But the capital press corps was still surprised in November 2004 when Ehrlich ordered all state agencies not to speak with two *Baltimore Sun* reporters who had written critical articles about his administration. The *Sun* promptly challenged the order in federal court as a violation of the First Amendment. In February 2005, however, Judge William Quarles rejected the suit. "A government may lawfully make content-based distinctions in the way it provides press access to information not available to the public generally," Quarles ruled. [7]

Quarles' decision — which was upheld by the Fourth Circuit Court of Appeals in 2006 — cites Supreme Court rulings saying reporters have no greater right of access to government information than the general public. But a leading media-law expert strongly criticizes both Ehrlich's order and the judge's ruling. "The decision is just dead wrong," says Baron, of the Media Law Resource Center. "How can any nation hold itself up as a model of democracy and yet allow a chief executive to cut off access to those who disagree with him?"

Most clashes between the news media and public officials do not wind up in court, and those that do produce mixed results. The University of Chicago's Geoffrey R. Stone, author of a recent book on free speech in wartime, says the press "has fared reasonably well in the courts" through history. Still, for every celebrated press victory — such as the Supreme Court's 1971 decision permitting the *New York Times* and the *Washington Post* to publish the secret Defense Department study of the Vietnam War known as the Pentagon Papers — there are numerous small-scale judicial rulings barring news media access to information.

The number of such clashes has increased as a result of Bush administration policies adopted after the September 11, 2001, attacks, according to journalism groups and First Amendment experts. "Sources are going to dry up, and the public is not going to be getting the level . . . or the quality of information that they have been getting in those isolated circumstances where [confidentiality] is appropriate," Stone says. The government "has been obsessively and unduly secretive" since September 11.

In the most clearly drawn fight, the administration imposed what the Reporters Committee called "unprecedented secrecy" on the immigration proceedings against hundreds of people — mostly men of Arab and/or Muslim backgrounds — rounded up immediately after September 11, 2001. The administration refused to release the names of the detainees and later closed the immigration hearings to the press and public. News organizations and others unsuccessfully challenged both policies. [8] The administration justified the restrictions by saying that the information could have helped terrorists track the course of the government's investigations. But press groups and other critics said the policies were aimed at preventing scrutiny of the government's actions. "No doubt, the motives were a mix of the two," Stone says.

At the same time, Attorney General John Ashcroft rankled press groups by directing government lawyers whenever possible to defend agency refusals to release records under the federal Freedom of Information Act (FOIA). The Reporters Committee and several other press groups complained about the directive. "This is an administration that has an intrinsic belief that secrecy is a good thing," Dalglish says. "This is policy that is coming down from on high."

Viet Dinh, a professor at Georgetown University Law Center in Washington who helped fashion the post-September 11 policies as assistant attorney general, defends the closure of the immigration hearings. "The judge made the determination that if information had gotten out to the general public, it would have helped the enemy follow the progress of the investigation," Dinh says. "I think he made the right decision based on the facts at the time."

Richard Samp, chief counsel of the conservative Washington Legal Foundation, guardedly agrees but adds that immigration proceedings should usually be open. More broadly, he disputes the criticism of the administration's information policies. "I would deny that this administration has a terrible record of operating in the dark and that the press is being censored," Samp says. He says that there have been "far fewer instances of censorship" in the Iraq war than in the Persian Gulf War under the President George H.W. Bush and that the press has been given "relatively free access" to the military tribunal proceedings at Guantanamo Bay for foreign detainees captured in the Afghanistan war. [9]

White House spokesmen periodically defend the administration against charges of limiting access to information. At the same time, President Bush has said he rarely reads newspaper stories, preferring to rely on the "objective sources" on the White House staff. Andrew Card, then Bush's chief of staff, was quoted in 2005 as saying of the press, "I don't believe you have a check-and-balance function." [10] For his part, the University of Missouri's Davis charges that the Bush administration is "overtly hostile" to the press and that the attitude is filtering down to state and local governments — as in the Ehrlich case. "We're seeing government at the state, local and federal level less willing to pay homage to the press and more willing to take the press on directly," Davis says. "There seems to be this tacit recognition, 'What do we need the press for? We can just go around them. We can control the message a lot better that way.'"

But conservative commentator Bruce Fein, a columnist for the *Washington Times,* thinks the press exaggerates its difficulties. "There is such enormous respect for the press and its power and utility in democracy," says Fein, a Justice Department official under President Ronald Reagan. "There doesn't seem to be in First Amendment doctrine any weakening of protections of the press."

### Should judges jail reporters for refusing to disclose confidential sources?

When he sentenced TV reporter Jim Taricani for contempt of court, Judge Torres justified his decision with a nearly hour-long peroration from the bench. "A reporter should be chilled from violating the law in order to get a story," the judge said, or "from making ill-advised promises of confidentiality in order to encourage a source" to talk. [11] Some evidence indicates popular approval of that sentiment. In the days after Taricani's sentence, *Providence Journal* columnist Mark Patinkin reported that out of "a few dozen" e-mails he received after criticizing Torres's decision, nearly 70 percent agreed with the judge. "I am outraged at the way you and the rest of the news media are circling the wagons to defend your profession as if it is holy ground," wrote one reader. [12]

Journalism groups defend the need to protect confidential sources as an important component of investigative reporting. "Clamping down on confidential sources ignores the role of confidentiality in whistle-blowing and investigative reporting, two very important checks on governmental power," says SPJ's Davis. "What [govern-

ment officials are] saying is, 'Don't speak to the press,'" Davis adds. "The end result is total reliance on government press releases."

Current and former prosecutors, however, generally defend questioning reporters who have information about criminal activity if it cannot be obtained in other ways. "The law is very clear that reporters do not have an absolute or even a qualified privilege to resist grand jury subpoenas in criminal investigations," Joseph di Genova, a Washington lawyer and former independent counsel, told a television interviewer after *Time* reporter Cooper was first held in contempt. "A prosecutor who is doing his or her duty must subpoena reporters if that is the only other source of the information available to them." [13]

The Supreme Court's decision rejecting a First Amendment privilege came in three consolidated cases involving reporters with the *Louisville Courier Journal*, the *New York Times* and a New Bedford, Massachusetts, television station. The *Courier Journal* reporter had observed and written about the manufacture of illegal drugs; the other two reporters had attended and written about activities of the Black Panther Party. All three reporters said they could not have obtained their stories without promising confidentiality. Journalism groups today cite similar examples in arguing that compelled disclosure of confidential sources will eventually hurt what they call the public's right to know. "Sources are going to dry up, and the public is not going to be getting the level of information they've been getting or the quality of information that they have been getting in those isolated circumstances where confidentiality is appropriate," Dalglish of the Reporters Committee says.

Whatever the merits of that general argument, even some journalists question the claim of confidentiality in the Plame investigation. Stephen Chapman, an editorial board member and columnist for the *Chicago Tribune*, called the clash over the Cooper and Miller subpoenas "absolutely the worst case for the press." "We have the same obligation as any citizen has to cooperate with law enforcement," Chapman says. "In cases like this, the promise that reporters give to sources to protect their confidentiality should be to do it within the limits of the law."

For his part, Fein sharply criticizes Cooper and Miller. "It seems to me exceptionally obtuse for the two reporters to suggest that they are falling on their swords to protect the public's right to know," Fein says. "You have the reporters helping to conceal from the public what it has a right to know, namely, whether someone in the government committed a crime." In other cases, journalism groups say a prosecutor's burden in subpoenaing a reporter should be very high. Dalglish, for example, says a reporter should be able to claim confidentiality unless the information sought would prevent serious bodily harm or a life from being threatened. "I haven't been presented with a set of circumstances that would override that privilege," she says.

Fein says the government should take care before deciding to subpoena reporters, but he says news organizations also should show more flexibility in such cases. "The press does a disservice to itself in being so rigid in its insistence that there are no circumstances [in which] it can reveal a confidential source," he says. "When the press makes a claim for an absolute privilege, it loses what needs to be a very cherished reverence for its job of checking the government and informing the public."

### Should courts issue "gag" orders to limit publicity in high-profile cases?

When a Jacksonville, Florida, television reporter quoted from a secret grand jury transcript in a high-profile murder case in July 2004, the judge threatened his stations with criminal prosecution or contempt of court. The judge's order remained on the books, even though the transcript became public record and the reporter had obtained his copy from the state prosecutor in the case. [14]

The judge's order — which the U.S. Supreme Court refused to overturn in 2005 — is an extreme example of the increasing number of free press versus fair trial disputes in high-profile cases. In many instances, judges limit out-of-court comments by attorneys or — as in the ongoing Michael Jackson sexual-molestation trial — even witnesses. Courts also are increasingly using "anonymous" juries to shield jurors from post-trial questioning by news media.

But journalists are especially concerned that a small number of judges have begun prohibiting publication of information already in the hands of news organizations or — as in the Jacksonville case — to threaten legal sanctions for doing so. For example, the Colorado judge in the rape case of basketball star Kobe Bryant [15] barred news media from publishing testimony from a closed-door pre-trial hearing after a court clerk accidentally e-mailed the transcript to several news organizations. The Colorado Supreme Court upheld the order, but the trial judge eventually released an edited transcript. [16] "We are seeing

a lot more gag orders in all levels of courts," Dalglish says. "We see judges periodically kicking reporters out of [pre-trial proceedings]. We are seeing prior restraints." "The press has to be vigilant about the possibility of prior restraints," says Jay Wright, a professor at Syracuse University's Newhouse School of Communications and coauthor of a leading media law casebook. "It never fails to amaze me how we can hear every year about prior restraints in some form or another."

A prominent criminal defense lawyer notes, however, that judges have very little leeway in prohibiting the press from publishing information. "Gag orders against the press traditionally have to be very, very narrow," says Nancy Hollander, an Albuquerque, New Mexico, lawyer and one-time president of the National Association of Criminal Defense Lawyers. "Courts can gag the lawyers far more easily than the courts can gag the press once the press finds out information."

The Supreme Court in 1976 unanimously struck down an effort by a Nebraska judge to bar the press from publishing accounts of open-court proceedings in a high-profile murder trial. In the main opinion, however, Chief Justice Warren E. Burger left open the possibility of upholding a prior restraint under some, unspecified circumstances. Fourteen years later, however, the court declined to review a federal appeals court decision barring CNN from broadcasting excerpts of a tape recording between former Panamanian President Manuel Noriega and lawyers representing him in a drug-conspiracy case in Florida. [17]

Prosecutors and defense lawyers sometimes have a common interest in limiting publicity about criminal trials. Defense lawyers fear the potential influence of media coverage on jurors while prosecutors worry it could jeopardize any conviction on appeal. "A gag order certainly might be justified to the extent that the judge believes that if the testimony leaks out it would meaningfully interfere with the right of the defendant to get a fair trial," says Alfredo Garcia, dean of the St. Thomas School of Law in Miami, who has been both a prosecutor and criminal defense lawyer.

In the Jacksonville case, attorney George Gabel, representing two local TV stations, says Judge Robert Mathis ignored state law when he tried to prevent publication of the grand jury transcript in the murder trial of Justin Barber. The transcript of Barber's grand jury testimony — denying that he had killed his wife — became public record under Florida law when prosecutors turned it over to the defense, according to Gabel. In addition, the prosecutor in the case gave a copy of the transcript to the stations' reporter, Daryl Tardy. Yet Mathis on July 30, 2004, prohibited the stations from airing information from the transcript on the basis of another Florida law mandating secrecy of grand jury proceedings. Ten days later, Mathis specified that the station would be subject to prosecution or criminal contempt for revealing contents of the transcript. "There are no reasons for secrecy," Gabel says. In any event, the lawyer continues, "Where the news media receive information lawfully — even if it's stolen — the press can't be restrained from publishing it."

"It's healthy for the press to be very vigilant about these things," says the University of Chicago's Stone, "because if it isn't made a big issue, then the temptation to [subpoena reporters] comes more often."

## BACKGROUND

### Freedom of the Press

The United States began its history with an already established tradition of a robust, even rambunctious press and a strong but inchoate commitment to press freedom enshrined in the Bill of Rights and in state constitutional provisions. [18]

Despite the First Amendment's guarantee of freedom of the press, courts have sometimes served as the government's instrument for restraining the press. Over time, however, courts have strengthened press protections and, to a lesser extent, interpreted the First Amendment as safeguarding press access to some government information and proceedings.

The press played an important role in the American Colonies' fight against British authorities and eventually for independence from Britain. Early in the struggle, a legal battle between New York's royal governor, William Cosby, and an opposition newspaper helped give birth to a distinctively American view of freedom of the press. In 1735 Cosby obtained an indictment for seditious libel against John Peter Zenger, who printed (but did not write or edit) *The Weekly Journal*, in New York. In defending Zenger, attorney Andrew Hamilton successfully argued for an acquittal by using truth as a defense — a position that was contrary to English law at the time. Although jury verdicts do not establish binding

precedent, similar prosecutions nonetheless "petered out" after the case, according to the prominent constitutional historian Leonard Levy. [19]

As drafted in 1787 and ratified a year later, the Constitution included no protection for freedom of the press or other individual rights — an omission criticized by opponents and remedied by the adoption of the Bill of Rights. As originally drafted by James Madison, the First Amendment would have prohibited either Congress or the states from enacting any law to abridge "the freedom of speech, or of the press." The states were dropped from the final language. Levy argues that the drafting history and the debate in Congress give few clues about whether the Framers intended simply to prohibit prior government censorship or also to bar subsequent punishment for "seditious" publications.

A decade later, the Federalist-controlled Congress found the First Amendment no barrier to passing the notorious Sedition Act of 1798, which made it a crime to publish "any false, scandalous, and malicious" writing about the president, Congress, or the U.S. government. [20] The law was ostensibly designed to strengthen the government in the looming conflict with France but was aimed at and used against the Federalists' Republican opponents. Ten people were convicted under the act, including at least three journalists. Supreme Court justices, sitting as trial judges, refused to find the law unconstitutional, but the issue never reached the full court; the act expired in March 1801.

The Civil War provided the next occasion for the federal government to move against journalists. Early in the war, the government barred three pro-secessionist newspapers in Maryland from being distributed via the U.S. mail and later had their editors arrested. By one estimate, some 300 Democratic newspapers were suspended for at least a brief period — including papers in such major cities as Chicago, Philadelphia, and St. Louis — typically for expressing anti-war or anti-administration views. In his account, however, Professor Stone depicts most of the actions as initiatives by Union generals in the field, not by President Lincoln himself, whom he credits with "an admirable respect for free expression — even when he was the target of attack." [21]

A half-century later, World War I produced more thoroughgoing repression of dissent, though the government's actions were aimed primarily at radical activists and pamphleteers and not the mainstream press. At

President Woodrow Wilson's urging, Congress passed two laws allowing the government to punish anti-war expression. The Espionage Act of 1917 made it a crime to promote insubordination in the military or to obstruct recruitment. The act also authorized the postmaster general to bar such publications from the mails, but significantly Congress rejected a provision to authorize government censorship. A year later, Congress passed the Sedition Act of 1918; broader than the 1798 law, it criminalized criticism of the U.S. government, the Constitution, or the military.

Although the new Sedition Act was little used before the war ended, the Espionage Act was widely invoked to bar radical materials from the mails and prosecute anti-war activists. With the war's end, the Supreme Court began to receive appeals stemming from some of those convictions as well as appeals of convictions under state laws against political dissidents. Until then, the court had had scant opportunity to define the scope of the First Amendment. But it began to lay the foundations of modern free-speech and free-press law in the 1920s and 1930s. Two cases in particular helped create the basis for a more extensive protection for freedom of the press. In *Gitlow v. New York* (1925), the court ruled that the First Amendment applies to both the states and the federal government. The decision nonetheless upheld the conviction of a radical journalist under New York's Criminal Anarchy Act. Six years later, in *Near v. Minnesota* (1931), the court struck down a state law allowing officials to prohibit publication of "malicious, scandalous or defamatory" newspapers or magazines. Writing for the 5-4 majority, Chief Justice Charles Evans Hughes said prior restraint against the press could be justified only under limited circumstances, such as wartime military information, obscenity or incitement to violence or the overthrow of the government. [22]

## Press Privileges

The Supreme Court substantially enlarged press protections with landmark decisions on libel, privacy, and courtroom access between the 1960s and 1980s. At the same time, however, it rebuffed press efforts to gain privileges against compelled disclosure of sources or newsroom searches. Meanwhile, Congress and many states passed freedom of information and open-meetings laws that guaranteed the public and the press access to more government records and proceedings. The web of statutory and constitutional provisions gave the press valuable tools for gathering news and fairly strong protections against the most common forms of private lawsuits.

In the first and most important of the rulings, the high court gave the news media an all-but-impenetrable shield against the financial threat of libel suits by public officials. The court's landmark ruling in *New York Times Co. v. Sullivan* (1964) held that a public official could recover in a libel suit only by proving "actual malice" — that is, that the news organization published a defamatory statement knowing that it was false or with reckless disregard of its truth or falsity. [23] The ruling dismissed a $500,000 award won by an Alabama police commissioner for the *Times'* publication of an advertisement by a civil-rights group that included several inconsequential inaccuracies about police behavior against demonstrators. The court later extended the *Times v. Sullivan* rule to libel suits by public figures who were not officials and created less stringent protections against suits filed by private individuals. [24]

News organizations sought an analogous legal privilege to limit civil liability for invasions of privacy for publishing truthful information, however personally embarrassing. The Supreme Court refused to go that far, but in two significant decisions it barred liability for publishing information lawfully obtained from government sources. In one case, the court in 1975 threw out a privacy suit by the family of a rape-murder victim after a local television station obtained the victim's name from court records. In 1989, the court similarly blocked a rape victim's suit after a newspaper reporter published her name after it was mistakenly released by the local sheriff's office. The high court steered clear of privacy-invasion suits involving non-official information, but plaintiffs through the 1980s generally had only limited success in lower courts. [25]

The Supreme Court gave the news media a less qualified victory in 1980 with a decision recognizing a right of access for the press and public to criminal trials — except in extraordinary circumstances. The ruling in *Richmond Newspapers, Inc. v. Virginia* came after a handful of courts in various states had closed pretrial hearings or in a few cases actual trials in an attempt to protect defendants from prejudicial publicity. Two subsequent decisions, extending the right of access to jury selection and preliminary hearings, effectively established a rule that criminal proceedings can be closed only if narrowly

## CHRONOLOGY

**Before 1900** *Congress, but not states, is barred under First Amendment from abridging freedom of the press; there are only few court rulings to interpret provision.*

**Early 1900s** *Supreme Court restricts free press and speech rights during World War I; later, the Court extends First Amendment rights to states, limits "prior restraints."*

**1925** Supreme Court says First Amendment bars states from violating freedom of speech.

**1931** Supreme Court says states cannot censor press except under limited circumstances (*Near v. Minnesota*).

**1960s–1980s** *Supreme Court gives press major victory by limiting libel suits by public officials, public figures. . . . The Court later rebuffs effort to establish reporter's privilege to protect confidential sources, but many states pass reporter shield laws in response.*

**1964** In *New York Times v. Sullivan*, the Supreme Court establishes constitutional protections against libel suits by public officials; three years later, rule expanded to suits by public figures.

**1966** Congress passes Freedom of Information Act (FOIA) guaranteeing access to federal agency records, subject to various exceptions; over time, many states and municipalities enact similar laws.

**1971** Government's effort to block publication of Pentagon Papers rejected by the Supreme Court.

**1972** The Supreme Court, in a 5-4 ruling, rejects efforts by three reporters to avoid contempt for defying grand jury subpoenas to disclose confidential sources; Justice Powell's concurring opinion is seen by some as backing reporter's privilege in some cases (*Branzburg v. Hayes*).

**1974** The Supreme Court gives press partial victory with a ruling to raise hurdles for libel suits by private figures.

**1978** Supreme Court refuses to recognize First Amendment privilege against newsroom searches.

**1980** First Amendment gives public and press right to attend criminal trials except under limited circumstances, Supreme Court rules (*Richmond Newspapers v. Virginia*).

**1989** The Supreme Court gives media protection against privacy suits by barring liability for publishing information lawfully obtained from government.

**2000s** *Free-press disputes proliferate after access restrictions are imposed following the September 11, 2001, attacks; court disputes over confidential sources increase.*

**2001** Vice President Cheney limits access to meetings, records of energy task force. . . . Attorney General John Ashcroft tells federal agencies to take stricter approach toward FOIA requests.

**2003** The Supreme Court won't hear a challenge to immigration hearings closure in 2001. . . . Justice Department opens probe of leak of name of CIA operative Valerie Plame after publication in July.

**2004** Several reporters subpoenaed in the Plame case; Matthew Cooper of *Time* and Judith Miller of *The New York Times* decline to answer questions about confidential sources and are held in contempt of court in October; fines and jail sentences stayed pending appeal. . . . Five reporters held in contempt in August for defying a subpoena in a privacy suit by nuclear scientist Wen Ho Lee. . . . A Rhode Island federal judge in November holds TV reporter James Taricani in contempt for refusing to identify confidential source; Taricani sentenced to six months' home confinement in December.

**2005** Federal appeals court upholds contempt citations against Cooper, Miller; lawyers seek rehearing, vow Supreme Court appeal if necessary. . . . Miller spends eighty-five days in jail on contempt charges before agreeing to testify after vice presidential chief of staff I. Lewis "Scooter" Libby releases her from their confidentiality agreement.

**2006** The U.S. government and five news organization agree to pay Lee $1.65 million to settle his privacy lawsuit. . . . A federal judge sentences two *San Francisco Chronicle* reporters up to eighteen months in jail for refusing to name sources of leaked documents from a grand jury; the sentence is subsequently dropped when their source is revealed through other means.

**2007** Libby is found guilty of perjury and obstruction of justice in the Plame investigation; his jail sentence is subsequently commuted by President Bush. . . . San Francisco blogger Josh Wolf is freed after spending nearly eight months in jail — the longest contempt-of-court sentence ever served by someone in the U.S. media — for refusing to turn over a video he had shot of a protest at a G-8 summit meeting.

**2008** Toni Locy, a former reporter for *USA Today*, is ordered by a federal judge to pay fines of up to $5,000 per day for refusing to name her sources for stories about Steven Hatfill.

tailored to serve an overriding interest that cannot be protected by some alternative step. [26]

The libel, privacy, and courtroom access rulings all involved issues that journalists confronted on a regular basis. The news media's most dramatic victory in the period, however, came in an all-but-unique setting: the government's effort in 1971 to block *The New York Times* and later *The Washington Post* from publishing the Pentagon Papers. President Richard M. Nixon instructed the Justice Department to block stories on the report, leaked to the newspapers by Pentagon-consultant-turned-antiwar-activist Daniel Ellsberg. Lower courts temporarily restrained the publications, but the Supreme Court — citing *Near v. Minnesota* — voted 6-3 that the government had failed to carry the "heavy burden" needed to justify an injunction. [27]

Against these news-media victories, the *Branzburg* decision stood as the most important setback for journalists. For the majority, Justice Byron R. White rejected warnings from news organizations that refusing to recognize a reporter's privilege would be "a serious obstacle to either the development or retention of confidential news sources by the press." Four years later, the court similarly ruled that news organizations have no right to prevent police from searching newsrooms for evidence — in the specific case, photographs by a college newspaper of a student demonstration. And in the same year the federal appeals court in Washington, D.C., allowed the government to subpoena reporters' telephone records despite the possible intrusion on confidentiality. [28]

Congress and state legislatures softened the effects of the adverse rulings with some legislative relief. State shield laws gave journalists qualified privileges to resist disclosure of confidential sources. Congress did not pass a comparable federal law, but the Justice Department adopted guidelines that ostensibly limited subpoenas to reporters for confidential sources. And Congress in 1980 passed a law prohibiting newsroom searches by federal authorities unless journalists were themselves suspected of crimes. In addition, both Congress and the states had been passing laws since the mid-1960s to provide access to government records and proceedings. The freedom of information acts and so-called government-in-the-sunshine laws typically included various exceptions, which courts — including the Supreme Court — construed narrowly in some cases and more broadly in others. Still, by the end of the 1970s governments at all levels generally operated under statutory provisions that gave journalists and the public at large a presumptive right of access to government information and meetings.

## Press Complaints

Almost as soon as he was inaugurated, President George W. Bush came under fire from media groups complaining that his administration was limiting press access to government information. The criticism intensified after sweeping restrictions on press access were instituted following the September 11, 2001, terrorist attacks, but the policies survived legal challenges. Frustrated by their lack of success, journalist groups and others said the administration's policies were contributing to an anti-press climate at all levels of government. The complaints grew in 2004 with the flurry of cases involving efforts to subpoena reporters who insisted on protecting their confidential sources.

From the start of his presidency in January 2001, Bush minimized the number of full-dress White House news conferences, holding only three by one count in his first seven months in office. [29] With little public notice, he also used his power under the Presidential Records Act to delay release of President Reagan's personal papers. In a higher-profile dispute, Vice President Dick Cheney blocked access to a high-level task force on energy policy created in spring 2001. The group met in secret and refused to release even the names of industry executives who participated. Also in 2001, the Justice Department rankled press advocates in August by subpoenaing the telephone records of a reporter covering a corruption investigation of Democratic New Jersey senator Robert Torricelli. [30]

Shortly after the September 11, 2001, attacks, the administration began imposing broad press restrictions. In an unannounced order on September 21, Chief Immigration Judge Michael Creppy of the Justice Department barred access to immigration hearings for the hundreds of individuals rounded up for alleged immigration violations following the attacks. The order barred releasing even the names of those detained, mostly men of Arab or Muslim backgrounds. [31]

The Justice Department justified the order by saying that terrorists could use the names or information to track the course of the investigation of the attacks. News organizations challenged the closures in courts in Michigan and New Jersey, largely on First Amendment grounds. Separately, a public-interest group sued in fed-

# Are Bloggers Journalists?

The line that used to be drawn between bloggers and professional journalists has become hopelessly blurred in recent years. People who write strictly for blogs have broken numerous studies that were later picked up by reporters in the so-called mainstream media of print and broadcast journalism. Most of the mainstream outlets, in turn, have either hired bloggers or commissioned reporters on staff to write their own blogs on company Web sites. But despite the deluge of mainstream media attention, controversy over bloggers' use of confidential sources has raised a fundamental question: Are bloggers true journalists or just overcaffeinated computer jockeys with attitude?

For instance, in a California case, Apple Computer argued that three blogger sites — Thinksecret.com, Appleinside.com, and Powerpage.org — should disclose their sources of leaked company secrets. The sites say California's shield law and the Constitution's First Amendment give them the privilege to protect the identities of their confidential sources. The bloggers won the case in 2006.

Since blogs are such a new and relatively unstudied media phenomenon, not everyone agrees on whether bloggers merit the same protections enjoyed by mainstream journalists. The issue is confused by the wide variety of blogs. While bloggers can take credit for discovering the information that took down the careers of both CBS's Dan Rather and CNN's chief news executive Eason Jordan, most of their colleagues seem to be posting mundane items about their own lives, material with little or no news value.

"The question should not be whether [all] bloggers are journalists, but which bloggers are journalists?" says Kurt Opsahl, a staff attorney with the Electronic Frontier Foundation, which represented two of the Web sites involved in the Apple case. "The medium of expression should not be the determinate of whether or not you're a journalist. What makes journalism "journalism" is not the format but the content, and my clients have been publishing daily news, feature stories, and the latest happening about Apple products for years," Opsahl says. "Apple would never go after a mainstream media organization in the same way," he adds.

The decision by the California Court of Appeals reflected many of the concerns raised by the Electronic Frontier Foundation. The court's opinion stated, "We can think of no workable test or principle that would distinguish 'legitimate' from 'illegitimate' news. Any attempt by courts to draw such a distinction would imperil a fundamental purpose of the First Amendment, which is to identify the best, most important, and most valuable ideas not by any sociological or economic formula, rule of law, or process of government, but through the rough and tumble competition of the memetic marketplace."

Garrett Graff of FishbowlDC.com in 2005 became the first blogger to receive White House press credentials and considers his work journalism. He agrees that the material published on the Web sites involved in the Apple case is journalism worthy of protection because the sites are "designed to report, break, and disseminate news." But he says the work of those bloggers is more the exception than the rule. "There are a small number — maybe several thousand of the about eight

eral court in Washington seeking the names of the detainees under the Freedom of Information Act. News groups won in the Michigan case but lost both the New Jersey case and the FOIA case in Washington. The Supreme Court in 2003 declined to take up the issues. [32]

Meanwhile, Attorney General Ashcroft in October 2001 directed government agencies to take a more skeptical view of FOI requests. The memo told agencies to "carefully consider" reasons for withholding government records and promised to defend any decisions unless they were "without sound legal basis." The memo reversed a Clinton administration policy that called for releasing government records unless disclosure would be "harmful." [33]

## CURRENT SITUATION

### A String of Losses

The most significant case of the decade involving press freedoms was clearly the Valerie Plame matter. Ultimately, special counsel Patrick Fitzgerald did not file charges against anyone that Plame's identity as a CIA agent had been illegally leaked. And it turned out that Richard Armitage, who served as deputy secretary of State during Bush's first term, was the source for columnist Robert Novak's initial piece mentioning Plame. But Fitzgerald successfully prosecuted Scooter Libby, Vice President

million bloggers — who would consider themselves journalists, but the vast majority of bloggers would not consider their blogs journalism," Graff says.

"What I do on Wonkette is not journalism," said Ana Marie Cox of her "gossipy, raunchy, and potty-mouthed" blog back in 2005. . . . [1] She has since become a staff writer for *Time*, contributing to its political Swampland blog. "If bloggers are presenting their work as reporting, then we judge it by the standards of reporting. And if they present it as commentary and analysis and snarkiness, then there are fewer standards to go by."

Lucy Dalglish, executive director of The Reporters Committee for Freedom of the Press, in Arlington, Va., agrees. Her organization does not think anybody with a computer can call himself or herself a journalist. "That's not journalism," she says, of those posting musings or family information on the Web.

A federal media shield bill pending in Congress would not distinguish between bloggers and traditional reporters, defining journalists as anyone who "regularly" reports and disseminates news and does so as a substantial portion of his or her

Former Wonkette writer Ana Marie Cox.

income. *Los Angeles Times* media columnist David Shaw believes extending any federal shield law to bloggers would harm journalism as a whole. "If the courts allow every Tom, Dick, and Matt who wants to call himself a journalist to invoke the privilege to protect confidential sources, the public will become even less trusting than it already is of all journalists," Shaw wrote. "That would damage society as much as it would the media." [2]

But Tim Rutten, another *Los Angeles Times* media writer, offers precisely the opposite argument. "If the First Amendment and its attendant protections don't cover bloggers, then they've lost their intrinsic meaning," he writes. Bloggers, Rutten argues, "would have been entirely familiar types to the Framers: practitioners of pure political speech, which is what the First Amendment was written to protect." [3]

— *Kate Templin*

[1] Julie Bosman, "First With the Scoop, if Not the Truth," *New York Times*, April 16, 2004, Sect. 9, p. 10.

[2] David Shaw, "Do Bloggers Deserve Basic Journalistic Protections?" *Los Angeles Times*, March 27, 2005, p. E14.

[3] Tim Rutten, "How to Decide Who Gets a Shield," *Los Angeles Times*, Aug. 18, 2007, p. E1.

---

Cheney's chief of staff, for perjury, obstruction of justice, and lying to federal investigators. As part of his investigation, which lasted more than three years, Fitzgerald compelled testimony from journalists at some of the nation's most prestigious news outlets, weakening other journalists' ability to promise confidentiality to their sources.

Fitzgerald in early 2004 began demanding testimony from five nationally prominent reporters in his investigation of the leak of Plame's name to columnist Novak. Three of the reporters — Tim Russert of NBC and Glenn Kessler and Walter Pincus of *The Post* — provided limited testimony that satisfied Fitzgerald, but he went forward with subpoenas for Matt Cooper of *Time* and Judith

Miller of the *New York Times*. Chief U.S. District Judge Thomas Hogan held Miller and Cooper in contempt of court on in October of that year; fined them $1,000 per day; and ordered them jailed until they testified. The fines and sentences were stayed pending appeal. Cooper and Miller strongly defended the importance of confidentiality and each vowed they would go to jail rather than disclose their sources to the grand jury investigating the leak of CIA operative Plame's identity. "People with information about waste, fraud, abuses, dissenting assessments and yes, even gripes, must feel that we will protect them if they trust us with sensitive information," Miller told *Time* in 2005. "That's why I cannot disclose their identities." [34]

Texas writer Vanessa Leggett spent 168 days in jail — a record surpassed only by blogger Josh Wolf, whose sentence of nearly eight months ended in 2007 — after refusing a grand jury subpoena to give federal authorities her notes of interviews with confidential sources during the investigation of the 1997 murder of Dallas socialite Doris Angleton. Leggett was released from jail on Jan. 4, 2002.

Those concerns failed to sway Judge Hogan, who held the reporters in contempt in October 2004, or the three-judge appeals court panel that heard the case two months later. In separate opinions issued in February 2005, the three judges all upheld the contempt citations. Significantly, two of the judges — David Sentelle and Karen Henderson — specifically held that the First Amendment creates no privilege for reporters in regard to grand jury investigations. That holding challenges the prevailing view among media attorneys that the Supreme Court's 1972 *Branzburg* decision recognizes a limited privilege even though the ruling upheld the reporters' subpoenas being challenged in that case. Under the panel's earlier decision, attorneys for Cooper and Miller wrote in a petition for a rehearing filed with the full nine-judge court, journalists "are now faced with a disturbing new landscape." Instead of having a "qualified privilege,"

the lawyers continue, reporters "now proceed with news-gathering at peril of having no protection at all."

The argument of the reporters' attorneys turns on the meaning of Justice Powell's stance in *Branzburg*. He joined the majority in the 5-4 decision but wrote in a concurring opinion that any privilege claim "should be judged on its facts by the striking of a proper balance between freedom of the press and the obligation of all citizens to give relevant testimony with respect to criminal conduct." In a note discovered recently among Powell's papers, the justice wrote, "We should not establish a constitutional privilege" that would cause problems that were "difficult to foresee." But he added that "there is a privilege analogous to" those protecting communication with lawyers, doctors, priests ,and spouses. [35] Since the *Branzburg* decision, many courts have interpreted Powell's opinion as effectively modifying the majority opinion's rejection of a reporter's privilege. However, both Sentelle and Henderson decisively reject that interpretation. "Whatever Justice Powell specifically intended," Sentelle writes for the two judges, "he joined the majority."

Sentelle also rejects any privilege for reporters under federal common law. Henderson avoided that direct issue but said special prosecutor Fitzgerald had established sufficient grounds to override any privilege that might exist. The third judge — David Tatel — recognized a common-law privilege but said the special prosecutor had adequate basis for enforcing the subpoena. In urging the appeals court to let the panel's decision stand, Fitzgerald emphasized that all three judges agreed that he had presented evidence to overcome any privilege. In addition, he argued that the reporters' lawyers were misreading Powell's opinion in *Branzburg*. "The simple fact is that Justice Powell joined the majority opinion," Fitzgerald wrote.

Smolla at the University of Richmond Law School calls the panel's decision "extraordinary" in rejecting any reporter's privilege. The decision "attacks at its heart what had been the orthodoxy, that the Powell opinion did in fact narrow the plurality opinion," he says. But the Supreme Court rejected *Time*'s final appeal. Norman Pearlstine, *Time* Inc.'s editor-in-chief, then decided to comply with a court order and turn over Cooper's notes, showing that he had discussed Plame and her husband Joe Wilson with White House aide Karl Rove. Pearlstine defended the decision, drawing a distinction between "confidential" and "anonymous" sources that didn't sit well with *Time*'s own reporters. [36]

Miller, by contrast, refused to cooperate with Fitzgerald, spending eighty-five days in jail in 2005. Libby released her from their confidentiality agreement and she then agreed to testify on condition that Fitzgerald ask her only about him and no other source. Having been briefly hailed as a champion of press freedom, she was widely castigated for seeming to care more about protecting a source who had sought to enlist her in a smear campaign than about informing the public. Her role was scrutinized at length in her own paper and she subsequently left the *Times.*

## Media's Losing Streak

The Plame case has been widely viewed as strengthening the hands of prosecutors who would seek to compel reporters to testify. They have won a string of other victories in recent years. In 2006, two reporters for the *San Francisco Chronicle* were sentenced to up to eighteen months in jail for refusing to reveal who had leaked them secret grand jury testimony on steroid use by Barry Bonds and other star athletes. They were subsequently spared from testifying when the defense attorney who had leaked the documents to them pleaded guilty to disobeying a court order not to disclose grand jury information, along with other charges.

In another Bay Area case, Josh Wolf, a 24-year-old blogger, was released in April 2007 after spending nearly eight months in prison for refusing to turn over video he had shot at a 2005 protest outside a G-8 summit meeting in San Francisco. It was the longest contempt of court sentence ever served by someone in the U.S. media. Prosecutors sought the video to help identify protesters at the violent protest. Wolf had sold portions of the video to local television stations but held out against allowing prosecutors to view it in full. He felt that helping to identify protesters would turn him into a de facto investigator for the government. He ultimately struck a deal that allowed him to avoid testifying. In response to written questions, he said he could not identify any protesters and had not witnessed an assault on a police officer. Wolf consistently rejected claims by prosecutors that he was not a working journalist but instead "simply a person with a video camera." "It was journalism to the extent that I went out to capture the truth and present it to the public," he said. [37] "The whole issue of whether or not I am a journalist is irrelevant. The First Amendment was written to protect pamphleteers." [38]

Another case involving video led to a lengthy house arrest. Back in February 2001, Jim Taricani, a reporter for WJAR, Channel 10 in Providence, Rhode Island, aired a leaked FBI videotape of a bribe to a local official — part of an anti-corruption probe that ended with the conviction of Providence's former mayor, Vincent A. "Buddy" Cianci. Taricani was subpoenaed and told to reveal the source. When he refused, Chief U.S. District Judge Ernest Torres convicted him of criminal contempt of court in 2004 and sentenced him to six months of home confinement. The judge spared Taricani a prison sentence for medical reasons — he had a heart transplant several years earlier. Taricani ended up serving four months of the sentence. Taricani's case was also unusual because his confidential source acknowledged his role three days before Judge Torres handed down the contempt sentence. Attorney Joseph A. Bevilacqua Jr. admitted giving FBI videotapes to Taricani despite a court order barring their release. Channel 10 aired the tapes in February 2001.

The Bush administration, which has earned a reputation for being unusually secretive, remained combative with the media into its final months. President Bush has vastly expanded the number of documents that are labeled as secret or classified — more than twenty million documents in 2006 alone, up from less than six million under President Clinton in 1996. After the *New York Times* broke the story in 2005 that the National Security Agency had engaged in widespread, warrantless wiretapping of U.S. citizens, the Justice Department began a criminal investigation of possible leaks to the paper.

Former government officials have been called before a grand jury and questioned about phone records that showed they had spoken to one of the *Times* reporters. The reporter, James Risen, has been fighting a grand jury subpoena seeking his testimony about sources for a book he wrote about the CIA. [39] In 2006, the administration sought to force the American Civil Liberties Union to turn over copies of a classified document it had received unsolicited from a source. Typically, grand jury subpoenas are used to gather information, but since the subpoena in this case sought "any and all copies" of the document, it was clear that the government wanted to prevent further dissemination of it. Legal experts said it was the first time a criminal grand jury subpoena was used in an attempt to seize leaked material. [40]

# Student Journalists Fight Campus Censorship

As editors of their college newspaper, Margaret Hosty and Jeni Porche made a lot of waves with critical investigative articles about the faculty and administration at Governors State University, outside Chicago. When Dean of Students Patricia Carter decided in October 2000 that all future issues would require administration approval before publication, the students suspended publication. The dispute left the 9,000-student university without a campus paper for more than four years. And it triggered a major legal battle over college press freedom that ended with the Seventh Circuit Court of Appeals finding in 2005 that the students' rights were not violated. [1]

The case of *Hosty v. Carter* illustrates the sometimes contentious and often unsettled legal environment for high school and college journalists today. Student reporters and editors have to deal with legal issues comparable to those facing mainstream journalists, such as getting access to campus crime reports. But they also have to deal with oversight — or more — from high school principals or college administrators who may wield power over newspaper or broadcast budgets as well as the individual educational careers of student journalists.

A Supreme Court ruling in 1988 held that high school administrators have discretion to censor student newspapers. By a 5-3 vote, the court said in *Hazelwood School District v. Kuhlmeier* that administrators can block publication of material inconsistent with a school's "basic educational mission." Justice Byron R. White cited as examples materials that are "ungrammatical, poorly written, inadequately researched, biased or prejudiced, vulgar or profane, or unsuitable for immature audiences." [2]

In response, eight states have adopted so-called anti-*Hazelwood* laws aimed at protecting high school journalists' freedom of expression. [3] In other states, however, high school journalists have "an uphill battle" in resisting growing interference from school administrators, according to Mark Hiestand, an attorney with the Student Press Law Center. "School officials seem to be more interested in good PR, and oftentimes that will conflict with good journalism," Hiestand says. "It's very unfortunate, but I think the First Amendment is kind of an afterthought for many school officials these days." College newspapers operate with greater freedom, Hiestand says. But when students Horsty and Porche and reporter Steven Barba sued Carter, the Illinois attorney general's office answered by seeking to extend the *Hazelwood* principle to colleges and universities. College journalists' First Amendment rights are not "greater than the limited rights accorded to the [high school] students in *Hazelwood*," the state argued in a legal brief. A three-judge panel of the Seventh U.S. Circuit Court of Appeals soundly rejected that argument in April 2003. Treating college students "like fifteen-year-old high school students and restricting their First Amendment rights by an unwise extension of *Hazelwood* would be an extreme step," the court wrote.

In the meantime, a lower federal court in Michigan issued a ruling that student-press advocates welcomed as limiting high school administrators' powers under *Hazelwood*. The ruling stemmed from a decision by Utica Community Schools officials in 2002 to censor an article by Utica High School student journalist Katy Dean about a lawsuit alleging that diesel fumes from the Michigan school's garage exacerbated a nearby resident's lung cancer. In a strongly worded opinion, U.S. District Judge Arthur Tarnow said student journalists "must be allowed to publish viewpoints contrary to those of state authorities without intervention or censorship by the authorities themselves." [4]

The issue of editorial-viewpoint control has divided other federal appeals courts, according to the Student Press Law Center. Of the six appeals courts to consider the issue, three have ruled that high school administrators can censor articles or editorials solely because they disagree with the views expressed, while three others say such actions go beyond the authority recognized in *Hazelwood*. Apart from court battles, Hiestand says student-press advocates also worry about signs of limited support for First Amendment freedoms among high school students today. In a 2004 nationwide study, nearly one-third of the 112,000 high school students surveyed — 32 percent — said the press has too much freedom. [5] On the other hand, a majority — 58 percent — said high school students should be allowed to report controversial issues in their student newspapers without approval of school authorities. Among principals surveyed, only 25 percent agreed.

---

[1] For coverage and legal materials from both sides, see "*Hosty v. Carter:* The Latest Battle for College Press Freedom," Reporters Committee for Freedom of the Press, www.rcfp.org. See also Richard Wronski, "Court Rips College for Censoring Paper," *Chicago Tribune*, April 11, 2003, Metro, p. 6.

[2] The citation is 484 U.S. 260 (1988). For earlier coverage, see Charles S. Clark, "School Censorship," *CQ Researcher*, Feb. 19, 1993, pp. 145-168.

[3] The states are Arkansas, California, Colorado, Iowa, Kansas, and Massachusetts (statutes); and Pennsylvania and Washington (regulations).

[4] The case is *Dean v. Utica Community Schools*, No. 03-CV-71367DT (Nov. 17, 2004).

[5] The survey was conducted in spring 2004 by researchers at the University of Connecticut and sponsored by the John S. and James L. Knight Foundation. See "Future of the First Amendment: What America's High School Students Think about their Freedoms," Jan. 31, 2005 (http://firstamendment.jideas.org).

# Should Congress pass a federal shield law for journalists?

## YES
**Sandra Baron**
*Executive Director, Media Law Resource Center*

Written for *CQ Researcher*, April 2005

A federal shield law would set national and consistent standards for a privilege that currently exists under statute, constitutional or common law in 49 states and the District of Columbia, and under the case law in all but two of the federal circuits. The specifics may differ somewhat around the country, but all recognize that the proper functioning of the press in a democratic society — and its essential role in keeping the citizenry informed — depends on the existence of a privilege.

A federal shield law is intended to enable the press to hold government and other institutions accountable for their actions and to establish reasonable and reasonably predictable standards for both shielding and compelling disclosure of sources and information.

Promises of confidentiality, protected by a shield law, allow journalists to obtain and report information from sources who only speak on condition of anonymity — information that might otherwise never be revealed. The accounting fraud at Enron and abuse of Iraqi prisoners at Abu Ghraib are but two recent national stories that required confidential sources.

But confidences in newsgathering are just as important in local coverage. Thanks to the press' receipt of information from confidential sources, most communities in America can point to a significant risk revealed or fraud uncovered, such as stories exposing toxic-waste dumping in local waterways, sexual misconduct at a youth shelter and failing infrastructure of an urban transit system.

Subpoenas to journalists, whether for confidential or non-confidential sources and information, risk:

- reducing reporters to routine, involuntary participants in the judicial and investigatory process;
- allowing government interference with the ability of reporters to do their jobs;
- disrupting press/source relationships; and
- encouraging potential sources simply to refuse to come forward.

A federal shield law is urgently needed that protects confidential sources and adequately balances the public interest in the fair administration of justice against the press' need to remain free of too-easy access to their non-confidential newsgathering and testimony.

## NO
**Bruce Fein**
*Constitutional lawyer, Washington, D.C.*

Written for *CQ Researcher*, March 2005

The law frowns on evidentiary privileges. Thus, confidential communications of even the president of the United States must bow to the needs of criminal justice.

Privilege claims should defeat truth only when absolutely necessary to advance compelling interests. By that yardstick, a federal newsman's privilege statute falls short of the mark. A shield law is superfluous to investigative reporting and the exposure of government abuses.

The Free Flow of Information Act of 2005 is sponsored by Sen. Richard Lugar, R-Ind., joined by cosponsors Sens. Lincoln Chafee, R-R.I., Lindsey Graham, R-S.C., and Christopher Dodd, D-Conn. It is not partisan legislation, but it is wrongheaded.

The bill does not find that a single government scandal or a single media investigation into private misconduct has been derailed or impaired by the absence of a federal privilege law. That omission speaks volumes. For 33 years since the United States Supreme Court spoke in *Branzburg v. Hayes* (1972), newsmen have been vulnerable to compelled testimony or notes in federal criminal or civil proceedings. Despite the inability of reporters to guarantee ironclad anonymity to sources, investigations of Watergate, the Iran-contra affair, Whitewater and other government scandals were thorough and pivoted on anonymous sources and classified information. Indeed, a day seldom passes without a confidential-source news story in the *New York Times*, the *Washington Post* or the *Wall Street Journal*.

The political incentive to leak or to curry favor with the press by passing along "breaking news" ordinarily dwarfs any foolproof guarantee of anonymity. Experience also teaches that the probability of discovering leakers approaches zero. Finally, Department of Justice guidelines permit prosecutors to subpoena the press only as a last, desperate measure.

States are divided over newsmen's privilege laws. Yet no evidence has been assembled indicating that the press in privilege states is more robust or muscular than in non-privilege states.

The Free Flow of Information Act would subvert the mission of a free press to reveal government crimes or malfeasance. Suppose a government official violates the Intelligence Identity Protection Act by leaking to several reporters the name of a covert CIA operative to discredit a government critic. A grand jury subpoenas the reporters to identify the criminal culprit. Under Section 4 of the act, the effort to punish the government crime would be thwarted. It crowns the media with an absolute privilege to refuse disclosure of any anonymous source.

The truth is too important to law enforcement to be left to the press.

Attorney General John Ashcroft directed government agencies in October 2001 to take a more skeptical view of press requests for the release of government records under the Freedom of Information Act. The action reversed a Clinton administration policy that called for releasing government records unless disclosure would be "harmful." The Reporters Committee and other groups complained about the directive.

Peter Osnos, a senior fellow at the Century Foundation, a liberal think tank, says the Bush administration's attempts "to intimidate and punish the media, or at least manipulate and mislead it, represents one of the most concerted assaults on the First Amendment since it was written." [41]

### Civil Matters

A surprising fallout from the investigation into President Clinton's affair with former White House intern Monica Lewinsky has been the increase in plaintiffs in civil cases seeking to compel testimony from journalists — or demanding recompense from media companies. Linda Tripp, Lewinsky's erstwhile friend and confidante, sued the Pentagon, where she had worked, for violating the 1974 Privacy Act, which was meant to prevent disclosure of unauthorized government records. In 2003, the government settled with her for $595,000. Although the

Privacy Act is complicated, it's proven to be a lucrative tool for victims of leaks.

Five news organizations — ABC, the Associated Press, the *Los Angeles Times*, the *New York Times*, and the *Washington Post* — in June 2006 agreed to pay $150,000 each to former government nuclear scientist Wen Ho Lee to settle his privacy lawsuit. The federal government also agreed to pay Lee $895,000 to be used to pay taxes and legal fees. During the 1990s, Lee became the targets of a spying probe and media outlets reported that he was suspected of sharing nuclear secrets with China. Virtually all the charges against Lee were dropped, with the judge who accepted his plea bargain apologizing to him for how his case had been handled. Lee subsequently sued the government for having violated the Privacy Act in leaking information from his personnel files to the media. His lawyers demanded that reporters reveal the identity of government officials who leaked information to them, but the journalists refused.

"The civil cases are maybe the scariest of all," said Dalglish, of the Reporters Committee for Freedom of the Press. "You're talking about daily fines for contempt that last the length of a case, which could be years. That's what's really giving editors and publishers indigestion." [42]

## OUTLOOK

The Plame case exposed Washington journalist at its worst, depicting cozy, gossipy relationships between elite capital journalists and their sources inside the government. The case hurt the cause of journalists in the court of public opinion, showing how reporters were willing to pass along spin and coordinate a message with their sources. Many media critics say that journalists have been too protective of their own rights and privileges, and have not done a good enough job of convincing the public that they are crucial conduits of independent information. "Without leaks, without anonymity for some sources, a free press loses its ability to act as a check and a balance against the power of government," wrote former *Los Angeles Times* Washington bureau chief Jack Nelson. [43]

The real danger from the Plame case, though, is the legal fallout. It was a demonstration, said Jane Kirtley, who teaches law and media ethics at the University of Minnesota, that under sufficient pressure, journalists will testify against their sources. They can't expect protection from contemporary courts. "We're seeing outright contempt for an independent press in a free society," Kirtley said." The fact that courts have no appreciation for this is new, is troubling, and you cannot overestimate the impact it will have over time." [44]

The Supreme Court discounted fears of a chilling effect on potential sources when it refused to recognize a reporter's privilege in the *Branzburg* case in 1972. But journalism groups insist the danger is real. Without protection for confidentiality, "whistleblowers and others would be afraid to come forward to expose wrongdoing and to effect change," Barbara Cochran, president of the Radio-Television News Directors Association, said in a 2005 statement after the federal appeals court issued its decision upholding the contempt citations against Cooper and Miller.

Congress may soon lend journalists significant protection. A media shield bill, which would protect journalists from having to reveal their sources in most cases, except for national security, passed the House, 398-21, in October 2007. That same month, the Senate Judiciary Committee passed its version of the bill. The House bill would allow a judge to order disclosure of sources if it were "essential" to the investigation or prosecution of a leak of classified information. It also sought to define who journalists are, limiting protections to people who "regularly" gather and report news "for a substantial portion of the person's livelihood or for substantial financial gain." "In recent years, the press has been under assault," said House Judiciary Committee Chairman John Conyers Jr., D-Mich. "This measure balances the public's right to know against the legitimate and important interests society has in maintaining its public safety." [45]

Patrick Fitzgerald, the U.S. attorney who served as special counsel in the Plame investigation, argued that the bill would harm law enforcement. President Bush threatened to veto the bill. But the leading contenders for president in 2008 all signaled that they would sign such legislation once they were in office.

"Part of a free press is not merely legal requirements and mandates being handed down by the courts," says Davis, the University of Missouri journalism professor. "You have to have a government that sees the press as an integral part of democratic government, as part and parcel of how we run the system, not just as an extraneous pain."

Still, Washington and Lee's Smolla cautions against overemphasizing journalists' legal problems. For one thing, the Supreme Court and other courts have been "very protective" of free-speech issues generally. "That benefits the press in the same way that it benefits anybody who's engaged in expression," Smolla says. "In terms of the large march of history, there's been a steady and constant increase in judicial recognition of freedom of expression, and the press has benefited generally from that," Smolla continues. "There may be little ticks up and down in any given year or in any given decade, but generally speaking the protection for freedom of the press is robust."

## NOTES

1. David Carr, "Subpoenas and the Press," *New York Times*, Nov. 27, 2006, p. C1.

2. Patrick J. Fitzgerald, "Bill Would Wreak Havoc on a System That Isn't Broken," *The Washington Post*, Oct. 4, 2007, p. A25.

3. Adam Liptak, "After Libby Trial, a New Era for Government and Press," *The New York Times*, March 8, 2007, p. A18.

4. 408 U.S. 665 (1972).

5. Nathan Siegel, "Our History of Media Protection," *The Washington Post*, Oct. 3, 2005, p. A17.

6. David G. Savage, "Ex-Reporter Told to Reveal Sources or Pay Daily Fines," *Los Angeles Times*, March 11, 2008, p. A8.

7. The case is *The Baltimore Sun Company v. Ehrlich*, civ. WDQ-04-3822 (U.S.D.C. Md.), Feb. 14, 2005. Ehrlich's order applied to David Nitkin, the Sun's statehouse bureau chief, and columnist Michael Olesker. For coverage, see Stephen Kiehl, "Sun's Challenge of Ehrlich's Order Is Dismissed by a Federal Judge," *The Baltimore Sun*, Feb. 15, 2005, p. 1A.

8. For background see Kenneth Jost, "Civil Liberties Debates," *CQ Researcher*, Oct. 24, 2003, pp. 893-916.

9. For background see Jost, "Civil Liberties Debates," and David Masci and Patrick Marshall, "Civil Liberties in Wartime," *CQ Researcher*, Dec. 14, 2001, pp. 1017-1040.

10. Quoted in Michiko Kakutani, "After Years of Taking Heat, Spokesman Takes Potshots," *New York Times*, March 1, 2005, p. E5. Bush's quote was in a 2003 interview with Brit Hume of Fox News; Card's remark appeared later in *The New Yorker* magazine.

11. Pam Belluck, "Reporter Who Shielded Source Will Serve Sentence at Home," *Providence Journal*, Dec. 10, 2004, p. A28.

12. Quoted in Mark Patinkin, "Media Don't Fare Well in Unscientific Survey of Taricani Case," *Providence Journal*, Dec. 16, 2004, p. G1.

13. "NewsHour with Jim Lehrer," Public Broadcasting Service, Aug. 11, 2004.

14. See "State Appeal Court Refuses to Quash Prior Restraint," Reporters Committee for Freedom of the Press, March 4, 2005 (www.rcfp.org).

15. The charges against Bryant were dropped on Sept. 1, 2004, after the alleged victim refused to testify.

16. The Colorado Supreme Court decision is *In re: People v. Bryant*, July 19, 2004 (www.courts.state.co .us/supct/supctcaseannctsindex.htm). For coverage, see Steve Lipsher and Felisa Cardona, "Media Drop Bryant Lawsuit," *Denver Post*, Aug. 4, 2004, p. B2.

17. The cases are *Nebraska Press Association v. Stuart*, 427 U.S. 539 (1976); *Cable News Network v. Noriega*, 498 U.S. 976 (1990).

18. For a brief historical overview, see T. Barton Carter, Marc A. Franklin, and Jay B. Wright, *The First Amendment and the Fourth Estate: The Law of Mass Media*, 9th ed., (New York: Foundation Press, 2005), pp. 27-34.

19. Leonard W. Levy, *Emergence of a Free Press* (New York: Oxford University Press, 1985), p. 44.

20. Account drawn from Geoffrey R. Stone, *Perilous Times: Free Speech in Wartime: From the Sedition Act of 1798 to the War on Terrorism* (New York: Norton, 2004), pp. 33-78.

21. *Ibid.*, p. 123.

22. The citations are *Gitlow v. New York*, 268 U.S. 652 (1925); *Near v. Minnesota*, 283 U.S. 697 (1931). For an account of the *Near* case, see Fred W. Friendly, *Minnesota Rag: The Dramatic Story of the Landmark Supreme Court Case That Gave New Meaning to Freedom of the Press* (New York: Random House, 1981).

23. The citation is 376 U.S. 254 (1964). For an account, see Anthony Lewis, *Make No Law: The Sullivan Case and the First Amendment* (New York: Vintage Books, 1991).

24. The cases are *Curtis Publishing Co. v. Butts*, 388 U.S. 130 (1967); and *Gertz v. Robert Welch, Inc.*, 418 U.S. 323 (1974). In *Gertz*, the court held that a private figure must prove some measure of fault in order to recover in a libel suit.

25. The cases are *Cox Broadcasting Corp. v. Cohn*, 420 U.S. 469 (1975); and *The Florida Star v. B.J.F.*, 491 U.S. 524 (1989).

26. The cases are *Richmond Newspapers, Inc. v. Virginia*, 448 U.S. 555 (1980); *Press-Enterprise Co. v. Superior Court* (I), 464 U.S. 501 (1984) (jury selection); *Press-Enterprise Co. v. Superior Court* (II), 478 U.S. 1 (1986).

27. The case is *The New York Times Co. v. United States*, 403 U.S. 713 (1971). For an account, see David Rudenstine, *The Day the Presses Stopped: A History of the Pentagon Papers Case* (Berkeley: University of California Press, 1996).

28. The cases are *Zurcher v. Stanford Daily*, 436 U.S. 547 (1978); *Reporters Committee for Freedom of the Press v. American Telephone & Telegraph Co.*, 593 F.2d 1030 (D.C. Cir. 1978).

29. See Mark Fitzgerald, "Suffering for Silence," *Editor & Publisher*, Aug. 13, 2001, p. 11.

30. Todd Shields, "Feds Stir Double Trouble by Using Subpoena Power," *Editor & Publisher*, Sept. 3, 2001, p. 5.

31. See William Glaberson, "Closed Immigration Hearings Criticized as Prejudicial," *New York Times*, Dec. 7, 2001, p. B7.

32. *Detroit Free Press v. Ashcroft*, 303 F.3d 681 (6th Cir. 2002); *North Jersey Media Group v. Ashcroft*, 308 F.3d 198 (3d Cir. 2002); *Center for National Security Studies v. Department of Justice*, 331 F.3d 918 (D.C. Cir. 2003).

33. Ashcroft's memorandum can be found at www .usdoj.gov/04foia/011012.htm. For coverage, see "Critics Say New Rule Limits Access to Records," *New York Times*, Feb. 27, 2002, p. A18.

34. Quoted in "The Cost of Keeping Mum," *Time*, Feb. 28, 2005, p. 44.

35. Adam Liptak, "A Justice's Scribbles on Journalists' Rights," *New York Times*, Oct. 7, 2007, p. 4:4.

36. Jacob Heilbrunn, "The Source With No Name," *New York Times*, Aug. 19, 2007, p. BR14.

37. Howard Kurtz, "Bloggers Makes Deal, Is Released From Jail," *Washington Post*, April 4, 2007, p. C1.

38. "Go to Jail," *The Economist*, April 14, 2007.

39. Philip Shenon, "Leak Inquiry Said to Focus on Calls With Times," *New York Times*, April 12, 2008, p. A16.

40. Adam Liptak, "U.S. Subpoena is Seen as Bid to Stop Leaks," *New York Times*, Dec. 14, 2006, p. A1.

41. "The Tongue Twisters" *The Economist*, Oct. 13, 2007.

42. Jeffrey Toobin, "Name That Source," *The New Yorker*, Jan. 16, 2007, p. 30.

43. Jack Nelson, "Without Leaks, Truth Dries Up," *Los Angeles Times*, July 21, 2005, p. B11.

44. Adam Liptak, "Courts Grow Increasingly Skeptical of Any Special Protections for the Press," *New York Times*, June 28, 2005, p. A1.

45. Noam M. Levey, "House Extends Law to Protect Reporters," *Los Angeles Times*, Oct. 17, 2007, p. A9.

# BIBLIOGRAPHY

## Books

**Carter, T. Barton, Marc A. Franklin and Jay B. Wright,** *The First Amendment and the Fourth Estate: The Law of Mass Media*, **9th ed., (New York: Foundation Press, 2005).**
The legal textbook comprehensively covers the full range of media law issues, including libel, privacy, access, media concentration and regulation of electronic media. Carter is a professor at Boston University, Franklin a professor emeritus at Stanford University and Wright a professor at Syracuse University's S.I. Newhouse School of Public Communication.

**Levy, Leonard W.,** *Emergence of a Free Press*, **(New York: Oxford University Press, 1985).**
The distinguished constitutional historian, a professor emeritus at Claremont Graduate School, traces the development of freedom of the press in England and America in the seventeenth and eighteenth centuries through the writing of the First Amendment and the debate over the Sedition Act.

**Smolla, Rodney A.,** *Suing the Press: Libel, the Media, and Power,* **(New York: Oxford University Press, 1986).**
A leading First Amendment expert, now dean of the University of Richmond Law School, chronicles the evolution of libel law from *New York Times v. Sullivan* through eight high-profile defamation suits and various proposals for reform. Smolla's *Free Speech in an Open Society* (New York: Knopf, 1992) discusses "news-gathering in the international marketplace."

**Stone, Geoffrey R.,** *Perilous Times: Free Speech in Wartime: From the Sedition Act of 1798 to the War on Terrorism,* **(New York: Norton, 2004).**
The prominent University of Chicago law professor details government policies toward freedom of press and speech from the passage of the Sedition Act in the new nation's first decade through the Civil War, two world wars, the Vietnam War, and the current war on terrorism. Includes detailed notes.

## Articles

**Fernandez, Elizabeth, "Slew of journalists under legal siege for not revealing sources,"** *San Francisco Chronicle*, **Dec. 8, 2004, A6.**
The article gives a good overview of the various confidential-source disputes a week before federal appeals court arguments in the Matthew Cooper-Judith Miller contempt of court case.

**Fitzgerald, Patrick F., "Bill Would Wreak Havoc on a System That Isn't Broken,"** *Washington Post*, **Oct. 4, 2007, A25.**
The special counsel in the Valerie Plame case argues that a federal shield law would define journalists too broadly and hamper law enforcement and national security investigations.

**Garcia, Guillermo X, "The Vanessa Leggett Saga,"** *American Journalism Review*, **March 2002, 20.**
The article explains how an academic-turned-true crime author ended up in jail for a record 168 days for refusing to turn over confidential notes and tapes from her investigation of the high-profile killing of a Houston socialite in 1997.

McCollam, Douglas, "Attack at the Source: Why the Plame Case Is So Scary," *Columbia Journalism Review*, March/April 2005, 29-37.
The article opens with a short retelling of the origins of the *Branzburg* decision and then details the various pending cases on confidential-source disputes, focusing on the investigation of the leak of the identity of CIA operative Valerie Plame.

Natta, Don Van Jr, Adam Liptak and Clifford J. Levy, "The Miller Case: A Notebook, a Cause, a Jail Cell and a Deal," *New York Times*, Oct. 16, 2005, 1.
Reporters for the *New York Times* examine reporter Judith Miller's role in the Valerie Plame investigation and determine that she and the paper badly misplayed their hand.

Penrod, Grant, "A Journalist's Home Is His Prison," *News Media and the Law*, winter 2005.
The author details the contempt of court proceeding and home-confinement sentence against Rhode Island television reporter James Taricani for refusing to disclose the confidential source who leaked a videotape in a high-profile local corruption case.

Savage, David G., "Government, News Media Settle Suit by Wen Ho Lee," *Los Angeles Times*, June 3, 2006, A1.
Five major media organizations and the U.S. government agree to pay a former government scientist $1.65 million for divulging and disseminating information from his private government records.

Smolkin, Rachel, "Under Fire," *American Journalism Review*, February/March 2005.
A spate of recent cases in which reporters have been subpoenaed for their confidential sources and recent court decisions rejecting reporters' privileges to withhold information have implications for press freedom.

Thacker, Sara, "Courts split on whether immigration hearings should be open to the public," *The News Media and the Law*, fall 2002, p. 4.
The cover story in the quarterly magazine published by The Reporters Committee for Freedom of the Press details the two cases challenging the closure of immigration hearings for the hundreds of people detained after September 11, 2001. Another story in the issue covers the ultimately unsuccessful effort to obtain the detainees' names through the Freedom of Information Act. See Rebecca Daugherty, "Appeals court must decide whether detainee identities will be released."

Toobin, Jeffrey, "Name That Source," *The New Yorker*, Jan. 16, 2006, p. 30.
A prominent legal journalist examines why courts have grown less favorable to press protections.

### On the Web

Two advocacy groups in particular provide comprehensive, timely coverage of press-related issues in the courts and elsewhere: The Reporters Committee for Freedom of the Press (www.rcfp.org) and the Student Press Law Center (www.splc.org). Thorough and timely coverage can also be found on Media Law Profs Blog (http://law professors.typepad.com/media_law_prof_blog/); the editor is Christine A. Corcos, associate professor of law, Louisiana State University.

# For More Information

**Media Law Resource Center**, 80 Eighth Ave., Suite 200, New York, NY 10011; (212) 337-2000; www.medialaw.org.

**Radio-Television News Directors Association**, 1600 K St., N.W., Suite 700, Washington, DC 20006-2838; (202) 659-6510; www.rtnda.org.

**The Reporters Committee for Freedom of the Press**, 1101 Wilson Blvd., Suite 1100, Arlington, VA 22209;

(703) 807-2100; www.rcfp.org.

**Society of Professional Journalists**, 3909 N. Meridian St., Indianapolis, IN 46208; (317) 927-8000; www.spj.org.

**Student Press Law Center**, 1101 Wilson Blvd., Suite 1100, Arlington, VA 22209-2275; (703) 807-1904; www.splc.org.

# 5

# Video Games

Sarah Glazer

Detroit Lions running back Kevin Jones goes airborne for extra yardage in the 2007 edition of the popular video game "Madden NFL." Some scholars claim video and computer games help literacy, but others say they don't assist with reading literature or understanding the humanities. Experts also remain divided about whether addiction to games is widespread and whether some games produce violent behavior.

Electronic Arts

From *CQ Researcher*, November 10, 2006.

On a hot summer afternoon, eight teenagers gathered in the darkened basement of the Bronx Central Library to play the top-selling football video game "Madden NFL." The Madden tournament in the Bronx, complete with prizes, is part of a growing effort at libraries across the country to lure a client who rarely darkens the door of a public library — the adolescent boy.

"If it wasn't for the gaming stuff dragging me in that first time, I would have gone maybe once in the past two years," says Ian Melcher, 17, a gamer in Ann Arbor, Mich., who had just checked out two calculus books. "I realized the library was pretty cool and had other things I was interested in."

To persuade skeptical libraries to put video games on the shelf next to books, young librarians who grew up on games are drawing support from a surprising source — academic researchers. They claim that playing video games is practically a requirement of literacy in our digital age.

To many parents and baby boomers, playing video games looks like mindless activity. Yet the knowledge built into "Madden," for example, employs a playbook the size of an encyclopedia. To win, players must have a sophisticated understanding of strategy and make split-second decisions about which play to choose.

"Games stress taking your knowledge and applying it. That's pretty crucial in the modern world," says University of Wisconsin Professor of Reading James Gee, author of the 2003 book *What Video Games Have to Teach Us about Learning and Literacy*.

Indeed, the argument that video and computer games are superior to school in helping children learn is gaining currency in academic circles. Claimed benefits include improved problem-solving,

## Sports and Multiplayer Games Most Popular

The 10 highest-selling video games are either about major-league sports, auto racing or "Star Wars," which largely appeal to boys; most are rated suitable for the entire family. Among computer games, four of the top 10 are "Sims" games, which also appeal to girls, and several are warfare games. Multiplayer games like "World of Warcraft" — which has 6 million players — are heavily female.

| Top 10 Video Games, 2005 | | |
|---|---|---|
| **Rank** | **Title** | **Rating*** |
| 1. | Madden NFL 06 (PlayStation version) | E |
| 2. | Gran Turismo 4 | E |
| 3. | Madden NFL 06 (Xbox version) | E |
| 4. | NCAA Football 06 | E |
| 5. | Star Wars: Battlefront II | T |
| 6. | MVP Baseball 2005 | E |
| 7. | Star Wars Episode III: Sith | T |
| 8. | NBA Live 06 | E |
| 9. | Lego Star Wars | E |
| 10. | Star Wars: Battlefront II | T |

| Top 10 Computer Games, 2005 | | |
|---|---|---|
| **Rank** | **Title** | **Rating*** |
| 1. | World of Warcraft | T |
| 2. | The Sims 2: University Expansion Pack | T |
| 3. | The Sims 2 | T |
| 4. | Guild Wars | T |
| 5. | Roller Coaster Tycoon 3 | E |
| 6. | Battlefield 2 | T |
| 7. | The Sims 2 Nightlife Expansion Pack | T |
| 8. | MS Age of Empires III | T |
| 9. | The Sims Deluxe | T |
| 10. | Call of Duty 2 | T |

\* *T = Teens (suitable for ages 13 and older)*

*E = Everyone (suitable for ages 6 and older)*

*Source:* Entertainment Software Assn., "2006 Sales, Demographic and Usage Data"

create their own literary spin-offs or so-called fanfiction.

"Many video games require players to master skills in demand by today's employers," concluded a report released in October by the Federation of American Scientists, citing complex decision-making and team building. The organization urged the federal government to invest in research and development of educational games for K-12 students and for adult work-force training. [1]

Science writer Steven Johnson, who popularized the pro-game argument in his 2005 book *Everything Bad is Good for You*, argues that when a child enters the world of a computer game, he is "learning the scientific method" as he tries out multiple hypotheses. [2] For instance, today's youngsters don't first sit down and read a rule book, the way baby boomers did. They start pushing buttons to see what happens.

That willingness to learn from failure uniquely prepared members of the dot-com generation, giving them an advantage as entrepreneurs and creative thinkers in the new economy, argue business experts John C. Beck and Mitchell Wade in their 2004 book *Got Game.* "A kid in the classroom has to worry about looking like an idiot. In a game, they're raising their hand all the time, and true learning comes from failing," concurs Dmitri Williams, assistant professor of speech communication at the University of Illinois at Urbana-Champaign. "When you strip away all the explosions, blood, magic coins, princesses and castles, video games are problem-solving tasks — puzzles. There's some irony in the fact that kids are bored at school but rush home to solve these games where they learn math and history."

mastery of scientific investigation and the ability to apply information learned to real-life situations. Some of the more complex games, especially multiplayer games like "World of Warcraft" — played online simultaneously with thousands of players — lead some teens to engage in esoteric, online conversations about strategy and to

As evidence that kids are willing to master language and concepts usually considered over their head, Johnson describes an hour spent teaching his nephew to play the urban planning-style game "SimCity." While Johnson was trying to figure out how to save a dying industrial neighborhood, the 7-year-old piped up, "I think we need to lower industrial tax rates." [3]

"SimCity" creator Will Wright says the youngster probably didn't understand tax rates any more than baby boomers understood mortgages when they played "Monopoly" as kids. But he thinks games teach something else. "The ability to reverse-engineer in your head a model of some arbitrarily complex thing is an incredibly valuable skill that you can apply to almost anything in this world," he says, whether that's doing your taxes, programming a new cell phone or predicting the effect of global warming.

Despite the worries of baby-boomer parents, there's no evidence that video gaming is replacing reading among teens. According to a Kaiser Family Foundation survey, reading for pleasure has remained steady in the past five years even as video-gaming time has risen. [4]

But what about teens who seem to spend most of their leisure time on games? Heavy gamers — more than an hour a day — actually spend more time reading for pleasure (55 minutes daily) than teens who play no video games at all (41 minutes), according to the Kaiser survey. And Kaiser found only 13 percent of adolescents were heavy gamers.

Nevertheless, the persistent anecdotes about teens and adults who skip meals, classes and even work to indulge in hours of video-gaming has led some to worry the games are addictive. Clinics have even sprung up claiming to treat "Internet addiction disorder."

But many psychologists remain skeptical. "There's hardly anyone I would class as a genuine video-game addict," says Professor of Gambling Studies Mark Griffiths of Nottingham Trent University in Nottingham, England. Few players, he says, meet a strict definition of addiction, which includes withdrawal symptoms and a preoccupation so single-minded that every other aspect of life is neglected.

Experts are also divided over whether graphic violence in games like "Grand Theft Auto" has any lasting negative effects on players' behavior, despite a few cases in which a teen's murderous frenzy has been blamed on games by the victim's parents. Recent studies indicate that the younger a player is, the more likely he is to be negatively affected by video violence and the longer lasting the effect. (*See sidebar, p. 104.*)

Concerns about both addiction and violence have led to efforts to curb online role-playing games like "World of Warcraft" and "Lineage II." Last year, the Chinese government imposed penalties on gamers who spend more than three hours playing a game by reducing the

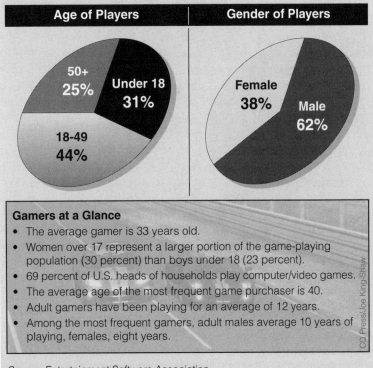

**Most Gamers Are Males**

Sixty-two percent of video-game players are males between 18 and 49, and fully one-quarter are at least 50.

| Age of Players | Gender of Players |
| --- | --- |
| 50+ 25% | Female 38% |
| Under 18 31% | Male 62% |
| 18-49 44% | |

**Gamers at a Glance**
- The average gamer is 33 years old.
- Women over 17 represent a larger portion of the game-playing population (30 percent) than boys under 18 (23 percent).
- 69 percent of U.S. heads of households play computer/video games.
- The average age of the most frequent game purchaser is 40.
- Adult gamers have been playing for an average of 12 years.
- Among the most frequent gamers, adult males average 10 years of playing, females, eight years.

*Source:* Entertainment Software Association

CQ Press/Joe King-Shaw

High-school students in Laramie, Wyo., play "Restaurant Empire," a video game that teaches them about the restaurant industry, in March 2006. Researchers are increasingly urging educators to incorporate games' best learning features into school programs.

AP Photo/Laramie Daily Boomerang/Rob Densmore

abilities of their characters. All the biggest online game operators said they would adopt the new system. The measures were designed to combat addiction in a country where more than 20 million Chinese play games regularly, mainly in net cafes. In one case, a player killed a fellow player who had stolen his virtual sword. (The penalties were later rescinded after widespread protests.)

Aside from worries about addiction and violence, not all scholars are equally enthusiastic about the learning value of video games on the market. In most games, the content is "garbage," according to Harvard Graduate School of Education Professor Christopher Dede, "in the sense that it deals with imaginary situations that are not close to the knowledge and skills people need for the 21st century. To claim that learning magic spells is good preparation for the knowledge-based workplace is just plain silly."

Dede is among those interested in adapting one of the most popular offshoots of gaming — virtual worlds — to educational aims. Player create characters (or avatars) who enter a virtual world. Hundreds of thousands of teenagers now participate in virtual worlds like There.com and Second Life, where they can create a character, buy clothes and real estate and meet other players' avatars. (*See sidebar, p. 109.*)

In "River City," created by Dede's team at Harvard, players try to figure out the cause of a mysterious epidemic in a 19th-century town. Researchers found that middle-schoolers using "River City" improved their biological knowledge and science skills more than peers taught more traditionally. [5]

Another sign of university interest: Colleges now offer courses in "Second Life." Starting this fall, teens entering There.com will be able to take classes in areas like copyright law taught by university professors.

But some advocates worry that all this high-level learning will be limited to middle-class kids, who have access to fancier, faster hardware and to educated parents who can guide their choice of games — creating a new equity gap on top of the existing reading gap between income groups.

While 83 percent of young people ages 8-18 have a video console at home, they may not be using them the same way. [6] A recent study of Philadelphia libraries with computers found that middle-class 12-13-year-olds typically used computers to increase their knowledge, by looking up — for example — Christopher Columbus on the encyclopedia site Encarta. But those from low-income neighborhoods were more likely to play "Magic School Bus," a game for 9-year-olds. [7]

The difference can be traced to the lack of guidance from a parent or other adult, which is as crucial for good games as for good books, says the University of Wisconsin's Gee. "Giving a kid a book [or game] is okay, but with no adult to mentor the child and talk about the material it isn't very helpful," he says.

As video games increasingly become a fact of life in the lives of children and adults, here are some of the questions being debated by parents, academics, the gaming industry and players themselves:

### Does playing video games improve literacy?

For the past year, nearly two-dozen 8-to-13-year-olds from low-income neighborhoods in Madison, Wis., have gathered after school to play the best-selling game

"Civilization," under the watchful eyes of University of Wisconsin researchers. Players rule a society from 4,000 B.C. to the present, building cities, trading, gathering natural resources and waging war. A single game requires about 20 hours to play; achieving high-level mastery requires 100 hours or more.

The children encounter words like "monarchy" and "monotheism" for the first time — but more important, they have to figure out how those and other factors, like natural resources, help a civilization survive or fail, says Kurt Squire, an assistant professor of educational communications and technology, who is directing the study.

"We found when they're expert gamers, they can tell you the differences between civilizations, what technologies they would need, what resources they'd need," he says. To Squire, the game's lifelike simulation is a powerful twist on the progressive-education adage, learning by doing.

Students remember only 10 percent of what they read and 20 percent of what they hear but almost 90 percent if they do the job themselves, even if only as a simulation, according to research cited by the Federation of American Scientists. [8] The University of Wisconsin's Gee even claims that the mind works like a video game in that "effective thinking is more like running a simulation" than forming abstract generalizations. [9]

An academic camp led by Gee argues video games foster a more sophisticated kind of literacy than the simple decoding of words. Video games foster creative thinking — producing "gaming literacies" in the words of Katie Salen, a designer at Parsons The New School for Design in New York City. Gamers not only follow the rules "but push against them, testing the limits of the system in often unique and powerful ways," she says. [10]

Digital literacy also means learning to take information from multiple sources, including Web sites and other players, rather than from one authoritative source like a teacher or textbook.

But Harvard's Dede says that while games may be powerful learning tools, their content leaves much to be desired, and so far no research backs up the claim that games teach kids to think like scientists. To produce

## Gamers Are Not Isolated, Obsessed

Contrary to the stereotype, gamers are not socially isolated people glued to their PlayStations, Xboxes or computers. Players say they spend more than three times as much time each week (23.4 hours) exercising, playing sports, volunteering, attending cultural activities or reading than they spend playing games (6.8 hours).

**Percent of gamers who say they:**

| | |
|---|---|
| Exercise or play sports at least 20 hours a month | 79% |
| Volunteer at least 5.4 hours per month | 45% |
| Regularly read books or daily newspapers | 93% |
| Attend concerts, museums, theater | 62% |
| Play games with others in person at least 1 hr/wk | 51% |
| Play games with others online at least 1 hr/wk | 25% |

*Source:* Peter D. Hart Research Associates, 2004

those results, he argues the engaging qualities of games must be married to scientific content.

Dede developed "River City" to teach basic science skills, such as forming a hypothesis. After 7,000 middle-school students tested the game-like simulation, they improved their scientific-inquiry skills and increased their knowledge of biology at twice the rate of peers using traditional hands-on labs. [11]

But hard data like Dede's is scant, and most studies have been done with only small numbers of children. The Federation of American Scientists, while enthusiastic about games' learning potential, noted that while kids "seem to do better," the research suffers from a lack of concrete measures of learning. [12]

"We don't have anywhere near sufficient evidence about whether playing computer games helps literacy," says Justine Cassell, professor of communication studies and computer science at Northwestern University. On the other hand, she adds, "There's no evidence that computers hurt literacy."

A computer game Cassell has developed for toddlers with a clown-like character can — much like an imaginary friend — help them develop sophisticated language earlier because they must explain what's happening to an absent person. (For example, toddlers get more precise on the phone, saying, "John went to the store" instead of "He went there.") Teens, she says, have a similar experience when blogging because they learn to write like journalists for an unseen audience.

# 'Sims' Inventor Exploring New Frontiers in Creativity

The creator of the most popular PC game of all time is lanky, bespectacled and surprisingly bookish. Will Wright is already famous for creating "The Sims," akin to playing house, which has sold close to 60 million copies. [1] He's also famous for designing one of the most creative games, "SimCity," an urban-planning game so sophisticated it was later used to train city planners.

But the game world is most excited about the new game — "Spore" — that Wright is developing to be released next year by Entertainment Arts. It started out as a game about extraterrestrial life. But in preparation, Wright says, he read 100 books, including many about biology, which led him to a fascination with evolution, the current game's theme.

In "Spore," players create characters who progress from a one-celled organism to an entire race of creatures using principles of evolution. Will your creature be an herbivore or a carnivore? Will you give it two limbs or 5? And will it survive with the claws you've picked out? (If not, go back and pick something different.) Once you've created a creature, you'll move on to creating tribes, communities and planets. Wright estimates it would take 70 years to visit every planet in "Spore."

But the most revolutionary part of "Spore," may be players' ability to access other gamers' creations for their own play. Once players' creations are uploaded onto Spore's server, they can even request their friends' creations.

As a child, Wright was drawn to taking things apart, which got him interested in robots and ultimately computers, he said in an interview at his studio in Emeryville, Calif. Yet Wright, 46, considers himself part of the generation that grew up reading manuals. By contrast, today's kids press buttons in a game to see what happens — a practice he says leads to more creativity. It also gives kids an early experience with testing models in a simulated environment, an important skill as science and other fields increasingly revolve around simulation, he believes.

Wright challenges the basic notion that it's more educational to read a book than to play a game. "You can step back and see that our natural mode of interacting with the world is not to sit back passively, observe it as a movie or book would present it, but to interact with it and actually have effects on the system and study the effects," he says. Play was probably the first educational activity, he suggests, which permitted us to parse out patterns in the world around us.

"I think you can do that to a limited degree with storytelling but not nearly as deeply as with an interactive experience," Wright says. "Yeah, *Harry Potter* is a great universe

The more than 4 million players of "Lineage" compete against one another for castles in a virtual kingdom of wizards, elves and knights. These "castle sieges" engage players in complex arguments online about strategy, according to University of Wisconsin researcher Constance Steinkuehler. [13]

Steinkuehler found players' online posts typically written at a 12th-grade reading level or above and often involve scientific reasoning. "I've watched kids who, in an effort to 'cheat' the game, gather data, build simple mathematical models and argue about those models," which, she adds, educators say "is extremely difficult to get high-schoolers to do."

Parents often despair because their teen is "not sitting on a couch reading a storybook, which is what we think literacy is," says Gee. But "the kids' version of literacy is better for a modern-world understanding of technical language," Gee maintains.

In the best games, players must master a specialized game vocabulary, consulting Web pages for hints on winning that probably use syntax far more complex than their reading in school, Gee argues. "I believe firmly the key to school success is handling technical language," he says.

To see how complex the language can get, Gee suggests looking at a Web site offering hints on playing "Yu-Gi-Oh" (both a video and card game). A typically impenetrable sentence reads, "The effect of 8-Claws Scorpion is a Trigger Effect that is applied if the condition is correct on activation." Seven-year-olds are reading sentences like this, even though its complexity won't be matched in the classroom until middle or high school, Gee says.

But can games produce the kind of literacy we most value? The technical material highlighted by enthusiasts is closer to technical manuals than novels and "more likely to appeal to techies than to dreamers, humanists and conversationalists" and to boys rather than girls, worries Harvard Professor of Cognition and Learning

and all that, but you can't take the stuff you know about *Harry Potter*'s universe and apply it anywhere else."

Players are starting to use his games increasingly for self-expression, not just entertainment, Wright observes, which could help explain their enduring popularity. A feature added to "The Sims" that allows players to write stories in the game and save them on a Web page resulted in several-hundred-thousand short stories, novels and biographical accounts that players "were pouring their heart and soul into," says Wright. Fans "form a very tight community around these games," he observes, as they browse one another's stories, download content and create new elements. A moviemaking feature in "Sims2" led to tens of thousands of movies being created by players.

"Spore" will give players unprecedented room for creation. In "The Sims," players can manipulate the face, but it's still a two-legged creature, Wright points out. "This is designing content in a different way that allows the player to have all the freedom," he says. But when this visitor

Will Wright, creator of "The Sims," loved to take things apart as a child.

played a preview of the game, it was apparent even the most imaginative designers set limits, suggesting that creativity inside a game isn't the same as creativity outside — a major concern of some educators.

First there's the aesthetic style — cute creatures familiar to young watchers of Pixar movies and reminiscent to older viewers of Flintstone dinosaurs. What if one wanted to create something more frightening?

"Within 'Spore' we offer a series of editors that serve as creative toolkits for making everything from creatures and vehicles to plants and buildings," says Executive Producer Lucy Bradshaw. "What these look like is up to the player. So, I might do something cute and cuddly and sort of Teddy Bear-ish, or I might make a really frightening creature with spindly spider legs and an angry-looking beak that looks like it came out of a horror film. It's all about my personal aesthetic. We want Moms to enjoy this just as much as their 15-year-old sons!"

_____
[1] "How to Create a Game About Creating a Universe," *Computer Gaming World*, June 2006, p. 70.

Howard Gardner. Immersing oneself in long novels like *Madame Bovary*, in poetry or in a philosophical text involves a skill many game enthusiasts disparage — linear thinking over many pages. That's "an entirely different mental faculty than is exploited when one surfs the Web from one link to another," Gardner argues.

Moreover, even a good video game can't compete with a great teacher, asserts former teacher Joan Almon, coordinator of the Alliance for Childhood in College Park, Md. "It bothers me that people are using these as the great way of learning. They're a modest alternative to very bad teaching," she says.

In its recent report, however, the Federation of American Scientists urges teachers to change from their "tell and test" method — which encourages passive learning — to incorporating the highly interactive, challenge-reward environment of video games. Game developers have incorporated the best learning features recognized by cognitive science, the report says, including:

- tons of practice;
- continual monitoring and feedback on the player's progress;
- encouragement to seek out information on the game strategy from other gamers, friends and Web sites; and,
- bridging the gap from what's learned to real situations. [14]

Some enthusiasts point out that the Internet is already allowing teenagers to become online creators on a huge scale via blogs, music and mini-films known as *machinima* — often inspired by games. Players have posted several-hundred-thousand stories ranging from 10-page plots to small novels as part of the best-selling computer game of all time, "The Sims," where players create their own family and play virtual house.

Some of that interaction could even raise the level of public discourse. In a study of an international Internet community of 3,000 teens, Northwestern's Cassell found, "the boys came to talk like the girls in a way that would make many of us happy," such as incorporating language that synthesized the ideas of others, and younger teens adopted the language of older teens.

Thanks to the Internet, teens are "no longer just media consumers" but are producing content, which is good for literacy, says Cassell. "We know that media creation — in whatever medium — is good for children's imagination and good for their ability to create a text for someone else."

## Are video games addictive?

Jeffrey Stark, a high-school student from Ontario, Canada, claimed his compulsive playing of the sword-and-sorcery game "EverQuest" ruined his life. He went for a week without bathing or eating a proper meal and stopped going to school for a semester. [15]

Similarly, a 30-year-old registered nurse who plays "EverQuest" with her husband said, "We spend hours — hours! — every single day playing this damn game. My fingers wake me, aching, in the middle of the night. I have headaches from the countless hours I spend staring at the screen. I hate this game, but I can't stop playing. Quitting smoking was never this hard." [16]

About 40 percent of players of multiplayer online games like "EverQuest" say they consider themselves "addicted." [17] Some players call the game "Evercrack." "EverQuest" is an early version of a so-called massively multiplayer online role-playing game (MMORPG), where players create a character who enters a fantasy world and interacts with other players. Online sites like EverQuest Widows, the Yahoo group WOW Widows for spouses of the more than 6 million players of the online "World of Warcraft," and gamewidow.com attest to the despair of gaming spouses and significant others. [18]

In South Korea, the epicenter of online gaming, game addiction reportedly claimed 10 lives in 2005, mainly by cutting off circulation when sitting for hours at the screen. In April, the South Korean government launched a game-addiction hotline, and hundreds of hospitals and private clinics treat the addiction, said to afflict an estimated 2.4 percent of Koreans ages 9-39. [19]

Europe's first clinic for video-game addicts opened in the Netherlands in 2005, and several psychologists treat Internet addicts in the United States. Since starting the Computer Addiction Services program at McLean Hospital — a noted psychiatric facility in Belmont,

Mass. — in 1995, Harvard psychologist Maressa Hecht Orzack has treated many gamers who she said were neglecting their jobs, schoolwork and families. "They have withdrawal symptoms. They can't wait to get back on [the game] again," she said, adding that the games "are made to be addictive." [20]

But some prominent addiction experts say even those who play games excessively rarely meet all the characteristics of addiction — such as developing physical withdrawal symptoms like sweating (true for gambling), needing to play more and more to get the same kick and being preoccupied to the point it is destructive to one's livelihood and family. Even though some psychologists talk about "Internet addiction disorder," the American Psychiatric Association has not recognized it in its official handbook, the *Diagnostic and Statistical Manual of Mental Disorders*.

Psychologist and gambling studies professor Griffiths, at Nottingham Trent University, found in a study that one-in-20 British children reported playing more than 30 hours a week. But Griffiths says very few of those children — or the population generally — meet all of the criteria for addiction. "It's quite clear when a parent rings me and says, 'My little Johnny is addicted,' it's hard to fulfill more than one or two of the criteria," he says. "Their real concern is the vast amount of time they're playing. The real question is: To what extent is it having a negative effect on their life?"

For a 38-year-old man with three children and a good job, playing 14 hours daily will negatively affect his livelihood and family. But for an unemployed 23-year-old with no partner or children, the same amount of time "has nothing but positive effects" if it brings him into a social network and raises self esteem, says Griffiths.

Even if they're not technically addicted, users of multiplayer online role-playing games who play on average 20 hours a week tend to describe their game play as "obligation, tedium and more like a second job than entertainment," according to Stanford University researcher Nick Yee. [21]

For example, if a player wants to engage in pharmaceutical manufacturing, one of many possible career choices in "Star War Galaxies," it takes about three to six weeks of normal game play to acquire the abilities to be competitive. Most such games — which get harder as the player becomes more skilled — use designs based on behavioral conditioning, according to Yee, which conditions players to work harder and faster as they improve, creating a kind of digital treadmill of which players are often unaware. [22]

The work required to advance a character's abilities is so time-consuming that companies like TopGameSeller, based in Shanghai, China, offer services to bring one's character up to a more advanced level. Bringing a character in "World of Warcraft" to a higher level can cost up to $1,488. "We assign two or three expert players to your character to do the leveling," the company promises on its Web site (www.topseller.com), which largely involves "simply killing monsters over and over."

Even Griffiths notes that magazines often rate games on their "addictiveness" as a positive attribute. "It's quite clear that the reward systems in video gaming are similar to gambling," he says. "I don't pick up a video game unless I know I have six hours to burn. If I start now, I'll still be playing at 10 p.m. As soon as you've beaten the high score, you want to beat it again."

Many parents worry that video games are displacing other activities like socializing, creative play and reading. But recent surveys show that teen reading has not declined, even as video-gaming hours have risen. And researchers like Yee find that online gaming takes on a social cast, as players communicate over typed chat.

In any case, game enthusiasts and critics alike say parents must set limits, as with any activity.

### Do video games prepare young people for the future job market?

"You play 'World of Warcraft'? You're hired!" Someday those words may be spoken by employers — if they're not already — two technology experts wrote in *Wired*, praising multiplayer games for teaching important workplace skills. [23]

In "Warcraft," players band together in guilds to share knowledge and manpower in a "quest," such as slaying monsters. To run a large guild, a master must be able to recruit new members, create apprenticeship programs, orchestrate group strategy and settle disputes. One young engineer at Yahoo used to worry about whether he could do his job. "Now I think of it like a quest," he said. "By being willing to improvise, I can usually find the people and resources I need to accomplish the task." [24]

Indeed, becoming a guild master "amounts to a total-immersion course in leadership," argue John Seely Brown, former director of Xerox's Palo Alto Research Center, and Douglas Thomas, an associate professor of communication at the University of Southern California's Annenberg School for Communications. [25]

Business experts Beck and Wade came to similar conclusions after surveying 2,100 young professionals, mainly in business. In their book *Got Game*, they claim those with extensive gaming experience were better team members, put a high value on competence and had more potential to be superior executives. Perhaps most important, they argue, gamers understand that repeated failure is the road to success. They found that 81 percent of those under age 34 had been frequent or moderate gamers. [26]

In their most provocative assertion, Beck and Wade claim the dot-com phenomenon was "structured exactly like a video game" in that it called for entrepreneurial skills and a fearlessness toward failure in a generation that grew up gaming. Among the rules learned from gaming were:

- If you get there first, you win;
- Trial and error is the best and fastest way to learn;
- After failure, hit the reset button; don't shrink away. [27]

As Stanford researcher Yee has discovered, many players view playing multiplayer online games as work. Players in "Star War Galaxies" who pick pharmaceutical manufacturing as a career must decide how to price and brand their products, how much to spend on advertising and whether to start a price war with competitors or form a cartel with them. Once players acquire the skills to be competitive in the market, their business operations require a daily time commitment. [28]

Yet today's schools, obsessed with reading and writing, are preparing children for jobs that soon will be outsourced overseas, claims David Williamson Shaffer, associate professor of learning science at the University of Wisconsin-Madison. "The only good jobs left will be for people who can do innovative and creative work," he writes, arguing that video games that teach professional-level language can accomplish that task better than traditional schooling. [29]

A Federation of American Scientists report recently endorsed that view, urging government, industry and educators to take advantage of video-game features to "help students and workers attain globally competitive skills." [30] It said video games could increase the speed at which expertise is acquired, improve players' ability to apply learning and improve decision-making — all important for the coming "conceptual economy."

Already gamers are running political campaigns, negotiating treaties and building environmentally sensitive communities, the report notes. [31] Ashley Richardson was a middle-schooler when she ran for president of

# CHRONOLOGY

**1950s-1960s** *Pinball becomes popular among young adults. Early video games are included on computers used by computer students.*

**1958** Government physicist William A. Higinbotham invents first computer game — electronic Ping Pong.

**1961** MIT student Steve Russell creates the rocket-ship game "Spacewar!" Loaded into computers used in tech courses, it exposes computer-science students to the first video game.

**1970s** *First commercial video games are marketed to families and young singles in arcades.*

**1972** Magnavox introduces Odyssey, first home video-game console.

**1976** Computer game "Adventure" first allows players to control characters' behavior.

**1977** Atari introduces first video home console with plug-in cartridges.

**1980s** *Video-game popularity spikes with Atari in early 1980s; Atari goes bust and industry collapses; Nintendo revives industry at end of decade.*

**1980** "Pac-Man" is introduced.

**1982** Atari sells almost 8 million units. . . . Surgeon general says games create taste for violence.

**1984** Warner sells Atari as sales wane.

**1985** Popular games "Tetris," "Where in the World is Carmen Sandiego?" and "Super Mario Bros" are introduced.

**1989** Nintendo introduces Game Boy; "SimCity," popular urban-planning computer game, is released.

**1990s** *"First-person shooter" games introduce realistic violence; as sales spike, juvenile violence declines. Multiplayer online games, complex PC games are introduced.*

**1991** "Civilization," a history game that takes hours to play, is introduced.

**1992** "Wolfenstein 3D" is introduced — the first first-person shooter game.

**1993** Introduction of "Doom," with more blood and gore.

**1994** Sony PlayStation is introduced.

**1997** "Grand Theft Auto," a gang-member survival game, is introduced.

**1999** "EverQuest," early online multiplayer game, is introduced.

**2000s** *Concern about excessive game violence and potential for game addiction leads to calls for curbs; number of female gamers rises.*

**2000** "The Sims," a game about relationships popular with girls, is introduced; becomes best-selling computer game of all time.

**2002** Microsoft launches Xbox Live, the first online multiplayer console network. . . . U.S. Army launches "America's Army" to recruit and train soldiers.

**Nov. 9, 2004** "Halo2," sci-fi game, creates biggest-grossing media day in history.

**2004** The parents of British teenager Steven Pakeerah, murdered by a friend in England, blame his killer's obsession with violent games.

**2005** Chinese government penalizes gamers who play for more than three hours. . . . American Psychological Association calls on companies to reduce violence in video games for children and teens. . . . Sen. Hillary Rodham Clinton, D-N.Y., introduces bill to ban rentals, sales of Mature or Adult Only games to minors.

**October, 2006** MacArthur Foundation announces grant of $50 million over five years to research how people learn from video games, other digital media. . . . Federation of American Scientists recommends federal research on educational potential of video games.

Alphaville, the largest city in the popular multiplayer game, "The Sims Online." She debated her opponent on National Public Radio in her campaign to control a government with more than 100 volunteer workers, which made policies affecting thousands of people. [32]

By contrast, students who pass typical school tests often can't apply their knowledge to real-life problems, according to research cited by Shaffer. Students who can write Newton's laws of motion down on a piece of paper still can't use them to answer a simple problem like, "If you flip a coin into the air, how many forces are acting on it at the top of its trajectory?" [33]

Shaffer has designed games that teach middle- and high-school students to think like professionals in solving real-life problems. Students who play urban-planning or science games developed by Shaffer soon develop more sophisticated, professional-level language in those areas, he reports. For example in one game, students help the Chicago Transportation Authority choose what type of seats to put on new buses. "Before playing the game, a player was likely to say, 'I'd choose this seat because it looks comfortable,' " says Shaffer. "Afterwards, the same player says, 'I'd choose this one because you get more seats on the bus, it's less expensive and has a higher safety rating.' These were exactly the criteria the bus company was looking at."

Indeed, simulation games have long proven to be effective in training people for a variety of skills, including performing surgery. More than 6 million people have registered to play "America's Army," a game released by the military in 2002 to teach military skills; 3 million completed the basic combat-training course and 3 million completed the three-lecture medic course. [34] And some soldiers in Iraq say playing video games gave them the skills they needed for real battles. [35]

Simulations might be a powerful technique, but they are not the same as real life, observes Harvard's Gardner. "I am happy to have medical students or airplane pilots in training learn as much as they can from simulations — but I also want them to have some real, high-stakes experience," he says. And these are two areas where simulation makes sense, he notes. "I don't think it makes sense for many professions, ranging from poet to priest."

The biggest success stories involve skills associated with science, technology or engineering. "I want my children — indeed all young people — to learn how to think like a historian, a philosopher, an economist, a literary critic," says Gardner. "I want to stimulate their imagina-tions to create their own worlds, not just that conjured up by the makers of 'World of Warcraft.' "

Some critics worry that the game-playing 20-something generation never gained some of the socialization skills and creativity needed in the workplace. The Alliance for Childhood's Almon doubts that chatting online in a multiplayer game can substitute for face-to-face interaction.

"We've been told by one software company that they have to spend so much time teaching the young 20s how to work with others because they've grown up in isolation," she says. The way children traditionally developed those problem-solving skills was by creating their own play situations with one another, which were "extremely complex, nuanced and filled with social learning, problem-solving and creativity," she says. But children don't do that much independent play anymore, she observes.

Some enthusiasts counter that video games can turn gamers into little scientists who have to figure out the rules on their own. Simulation games like "The Sims" help in mastering sciences that utilize computer-based simulation, including biology and cognitive science, suggests the University of Wisconsin's Gee. [36]

But Harvard's Dede is skeptical. "Do kids learn some things about taking a confusing situation and puzzling about it? Sure. But we wouldn't need schooling if learning was as simple as just putting people into experience and letting them figure it out," he says. "That's just as true for gaming experiences as for real-world experiences." The key is to adapt the methods developed for entertainment to educational games so they can be "a powerful vehicle for education."

# BACKGROUND

## Pinball Precursor

Pinball was the mechanical precursor of video games, say some historians, rousing many of the same fears that video games do today. In the 1930s, New York Mayor Fiorello La Guardia smashed pinball machines with a sledgehammer and banned them — a ban that was only lifted in the 1970s. [37]

In 1958, William A. Higinbotham, a physicist at Brookhaven National Laboratory on Long Island, invented a game of electronic Ping-Pong. Although the game was dismantled the next year — its components were needed for other projects — it was remembered by a

# Do Video Games Make Kids More Violent?

After 14-year-old Stefan Pakeerah was savagely murdered in England by a friend, his parents claimed the murderer had been obsessed by the violent computer game "Manhunt," which awards points for savage killings. Warren Leblanc, 17, who pleaded guilty in 2005 to the murder, had beaten Stefan with a hammer and stabbed him repeatedly after luring him to a local park, the press reported.

Stefan's parents blamed the game and asked retailers to stop selling it. "It's a video instruction on how to murder somebody; it just shows how you kill people and what weapons you use," Patrick Pakeerah said last year, after several major British retailers agreed to stop selling the game. [1]

There is substantial debate among psychologists over whether violent behavior can be blamed on video games, since game players are often exposed to violence from other sources, such as TV or their own lives. Although few long-term studies have been done to see if the effects are long-lasting, many U.S. psychologists are alarmed. Last year, the American Psychological Association adopted a resolution recommending that all violence be reduced in video games marketed to children and youth. The policy decision came after an expert committee reviewed research indicating that exposure to video-game violence increases youths' aggressive thoughts and behavior and angry feelings. [2]

In violent scenes, the committee noted, perpetrators go unpunished 73 percent of the time — teaching children that violence is an effective way to resolve conflict. Some studies also suggest that the active participation peculiar to video games may influence learning more than the kind of passive observation involved in watching TV, the panel pointed out.

"Playing video games involves practice, repetition and being rewarded for numerous acts of violence, which may intensify the learning," said Elizabeth Carll, a New York psychologist who co-chaired the committee. "This may also result in more realistic experiences, which may potentially increase aggressive behavior." [3]

Mark Griffiths, a psychologist at Nottingham Trent University in Nottingham, England, agrees. "I've concluded the younger the person, the more likely there is to be an effect," he says. "If children watch or play video games, right afterwards they will mimic what they see on the screen."

But Griffiths is more skeptical about the lasting effects of video-game violence, especially in older teens and adults. "Video games may have a contributory effect, but overall the evidence is quite slim," he says. "I think there's a predisposition of people who play violent video games to violence anyway. Youthful offenders play more violent video games [than average]. My guess is these people already have problems to start with and seek out that kind of game — not that they become more violent as a result of playing those games."

Another leading researcher at the other end of the spectrum, Iowa State University psychologist Craig Anderson, finds some effects persist in young children. In a recent study of third-, fourth- and fifth-graders, he found that those who played more video games than their peers early in the school year became more verbally and physically aggressive over the course of the year. He describes exposure to violent video games as a "risk factor" — one of many — that could contribute to this behavior. [4]

Seven states limit or ban the sale of violent video games to minors. But most such laws have been overturned after legal

---

future editor of *Creative Computing* magazine, David Ahl, who had seen the game during a high school visit. He dubbed Higinbotham the grandfather of video games. [38]

However, Massachusetts Institute of Technology (MIT) student Steve Russell is generally considered the inventor of video games. In 1961, he created a rocket-ship game called "Spacewar!," which could be played on one of MIT's computers. The manufacturer of the computer, Digital Equipment Corp., began shipping its computers pre-loaded with the game, exposing computer-science students across the country to "Spacewar." [39]

In 1972, Magnavox introduced "Odyssey," the first home video-game console, which Magnavox marketed as a family game. Until the early 1980s manufacturers also marketed arcade games to single adults as having sex appeal.

Slow adoption of video games through the 1970s culminated in the 1977 introduction of Atari — the first video-game console to use plug-in cartridges rather than built-in games. Atari became one of the most successful introductions in history, selling about 3 million consoles a year. Atari was considered wildly popular in the early 1980s until its manufacturer collapsed. [40]

challenges by the game industry, usually as unconstitutional infringements on free speech. None of the laws is currently being implemented, according to the Child-Responsible Media Campaign, which advocates restrictions. [5]

Sen. Hillary Rodham Clinton, D-N.Y., introduced a bill in Congress last year that would make it illegal to rent or sell a video game with Mature or Adult Only ratings to minors. Clinton, who said she was disturbed by the sexually explicit content of "Grand Theft Auto," as well as the violence, cited findings that boys as young as 9 often could buy Mature-rated games. [6] But Clinton's bill also could run into constitutional problems, say even those who advocate restrictions. [7]

"Grand Theft Auto: Vice City," which debuted in 2002, drew criticism for its violence. Players can steal vehicles, engage in drive-by shootings and robberies and buy weapons ranging from submachine guns to hand grenades. Members of gangs also engage in shoot-outs.

Courts have been skeptical of a link between video games and violence. For example, a district court in Michigan blocked implementation of a state ban on sales of violent video games to minors. The decision reflected concern that Anderson's studies had "not provided any evidence that the relationship between violent games and aggressive behavior exists. It could just as easily be said that the interactive element in video games acts as an outlet for minors to vent their violent or aggressive behavior, thereby dimming the chance they would actually perform such acts in reality," the court declared. [8]

Yet game-industry spokesmen also point out that juvenile-crime statistics dropped sharply as the violence in video games crested and have not spiked since. (The breakthrough in realistic video-game violence can be traced to the 1992 release of "Wolfenstein 3 D," the first major "first-person shooter" game, where the player saw the game world through the eyes of the character and enemies fell and bled on the floor.)

"Just as violent video games were pouring into American homes on the crest of the personal-computer wave, juvenile violence began to plummet," according to University of Pennsylvania criminologist Lawrence Sherman. "Juvenile murder charges dropped by about two-thirds from 1993 to the end of the decade and show no signs of going back up. If video games are so deadly, why has their widespread use been followed by reductions in murder?" [9]

[1] BBC News, "Manhunt Game Withdrawn by Stores," Feb. 18, 2005; http://news.bbc.co.uk. See also "Grand Theft Auto Sparks Another Lawsuit," *GameSpot*, retrieved Aug. 18, 2006.

[2] American Psychological Association press release, "APA Calls for Reduction of Violence in Interactive Media Used by Children and Adolescents," Aug. 17, 2005; www.apa.org/releases.

[3] Quoted in *Ibid*.

[4] Douglas A. Gentile and Craig A. Anderson, "Violent Video Games: The Effects on Youth, and Public Policy Implications," in N. Dowd, *et al.*, *Handbook of Children, Culture and Violence* (2006), p. 231 (from page proofs.)

[5] Washington, Illinois, Michigan, California, Minnesota, Oklahoma and Louisiana have passed laws restricting the sale of violent games to minors. See www.medialegislation.org. Also see Gentile and Anderson, *op. cit.*, p. 240. In the past five years, U.S. courts have ruled at least eight times that computer games and video games are protected speech under the First Amendment, according to the Entertainment Software Association; on Oct. 11, 2006, a U.S. district judge in Oklahoma issued a preliminary injunction halting implementation of Oklahoma's law, calling the act's language unconstitutionally vague.

[6] News release, "Sens. Clinton, Lieberman and Bayh Introduce Legislation to Protect Children from Inappropriate Video Games"; http://clinton.senate.gov.

[7] The Child-Responsible Media Campaign; www.medialegislation.org.

[8] Entertainment Software Association, "Essential Facts about Video Games and Court Rulings;" www.theesa.com.

[9] Quoted in John C. Beck and Mitchell Wade, *Got Game* (2004), pp. 53-54.

Nintendo revived the industry in the late 1980s, and since then a wide variety of consoles and games have been introduced, including Sony's PlayStation and Microsoft's Xbox. A variety of other games have been designed for personal computers. As computer animation permitted film-like dramas with original scripts and music, computer games became increasingly sophisticated, bearing little resemblance to the black and white blips of Higinbotham's original game.

The late 1980s were a crucial turning point in the social history of video games, according to Williams, at the University of Illinois. Games began moving from bars, nightclubs and arcades to homes as prices dropped, houses expanded and Americans had more disposable income. Driven by Nintendo's marketing, games became the province of children for the next 10 years. [41]

Video games also ushered in a new generation of young people "comfortable and techno-literate enough to accept personal computers, electronic bulletin boards, desktop publishing, compact disks and the Web," he writes, and pushed the development of microprocessors, broadband networks and display technologies. [42]

Software engineer Tammy Yap designs video games at Midway Home Entertainment in San Diego. Some experts blame girls' lower interest in video games on the scarcity of sympathetic female characters and game designers.

Today half of all Americans 8-18 have a video-game player in their bedrooms. [43] They also have less contact with people they know (within the family) but more contact with unknown people from a variety of backgrounds, particularly with the rise of multiplayer games, Williams points out. That gives a 12-year-old boy access to the knowledge of a 40-year-old lawyer playing the same game (and vice versa) but also rouses fears about whom children are meeting online. [44]

Besides worrying that children might meet potential predators online, adults also were concerned about the violent content of video games. In 1982, Surgeon General C. Everett Koop claimed that video games were hazardous, creating aberrant behavior and increasing a taste for violence. Nearly 25 years later, researchers still have not found definitive proof of long-lasting negative effects from video violence, or of the predicted increase in withdrawal and social isolation, according to Williams. But these worries survive.

Meanwhile, video games long ago became more than child's play. Today, the average age of video gamers is 33, a quarter of gamers are over 50 and only 31 percent are under 18, according to the Entertainment Software Association. [45]

### Equity Gap?

With video-game consoles in 83 percent of the homes of the under-18 crowd, one would expect the benefits of gaming to be pervasive. [46] But surveys suggest that low-income children aren't getting the same access to technology as their middle-class peers — a video-gaming "equity gap" that resembles the so-called digital divide between those with and without Internet access. Although 87 percent of teens use the Internet, those who don't are generally from lower-income households with limited access to high-tech hardware and are disproportionately African-American. [47]

That could mean they lack access to some of the more complex games played on computers and online. Convinced of games' educational potential, Global Kids, a nonprofit that provides education on international issues to urban youth, has obtained a Microsoft grant to teach disadvantaged New York City teens to design and play games.

"Some of these kids don't know how to move a cursor into a Web browser," says Global Kids' Online Leadership Director Barry Joseph. Paradoxically, most attend schools with plenty of computer equipment — courtesy of Clinton-era funding. But many of the students are not connected to the Internet because teachers are often unfamiliar with the technology, Joseph says.

"Middle-class homes have multiple gaming consoles, broadband and adults familiar enough with systems to encourage young people" to play games with learning potential, Joseph says. By contrast, lower-income kids may only have access to a computer at the school library, where daily time is limited to 10 minutes, mandatory filters block the ability to blog and computers have no capacity to store kids' creations, notes MIT's Director of Comparative Media Studies Henry Jenkins.

However, surveys about access may not tell the real story about who's benefiting from technology. "Some folks are using the technology in new ways; others are less digitally savvy and are just playing Gameboy. That may be the real divide in who has positive effects," says Connie Yowell, director of educational grant-making at the MacArthur Foundation, which is helping Global Kids and other groups study how young people are using technology.

### Gender Gap Narrows

Boys between 8 and 18 spend more than twice as much time playing video games as girls, according to a recent Kaiser Family Foundation survey. [48] Some have blamed girls' lower interest on the scarcity of sympathetic female characters and game designers.

"Games were built by boys for boys," Northwestern's Cassell found in 1997 when she co-edited *From Barbie to Mortal Kombat,* a book of scholarly essays on the gender slant of video games. [49]

But Cassell and other experts say the gender gap has been narrowing. Today, women over 18 represent 30 percent of U.S. gamers — a greater proportion than do boys 17 and under (23 percent). [50] "Boys may be playing more traditional video games," Cassell says, "but girls are playing more 'Sims,' " which is akin to playing house.

And virtual worlds are much more popular among females. Females make up the majority of the 400,000 subscribers to There.com, a virtual world where participants can create a character to interact with others, according to Michael K. Wilson, CEO of Makena Technologies, the company behind the site. Socializing and shopping seem to be two major draws for teenage girls, he says.

"It's very clear to us that teens are very interested in shopping. There.com is the holy grail of shopping sites. You can try on a dress [or your avatar can] and ask friends how you look in it," says Wilson. There.com has also experimented with Nike and Levi Strauss & Co. to turn that click on a product into a real-world purchase.

In Second Life, another virtual world, companies like Reebok and Amazon have set up shops to sell real-world versions of their products as well as virtual ones. [51]

Another magnet drawing women has been the rise in so-called casual games — which may take as little as 10 minutes to play, such as Solitaire, mahjong and some short action games. In the past few years, thousands of such games have sprung up on the Internet and game consoles.

The typical casual game players are women in their 40s, one of the fastest-growing sectors of the industry, according to the International Game Developers Association. From almost nothing in 2002, casual games grew to a $600 million business by 2004, and by 2008 industry experts expect to see $2 billion in U.S. sales alone. [52]

Female gamers spend an average of two hours more per week playing video games than a year ago, for an average of 7.4 hours a week, according to the Entertainment Software Association. While male gamers still spent more daily time than females on video games in 2003, the gap had narrowed from 18 minutes to six minutes by 2004. [53]

Males still comprise the majority of those who play online, but the games played most often online — puzzle board and trivia games — are among those most favored by females. [54]

Nevertheless, many young girls don't think they're good at games, Cassell says, because they buy the traditional definition that "real" video games involve action or sports. In the late 1990s, many experts feared the gender gap in game playing would further widen the gender gap in access to technology and science generally. But that may be changing as girls become a major presence in games and virtual worlds that emphasize interaction and creativity over competition.

And some researchers, like Harvard's Dede, find girls are just as interested in a game involving science if it minimizes the things that bore them — like scoring points and violence — and stresses personal interaction instead. For instance, girls trying to discover the cause of a mysterious epidemic in the "River City" simulation game approach the problem differently from boys. "Girls on balance try to establish a relationship with the residents of this virtual town," through the characters they create, and use those relationships to solve the mystery, Dede says.

"Typically, research shows girls aren't interested in science," notes "River City" Project Director Jody Clarke, particularly in middle school, the age the Harvard team is observing. But "we're finding girls are interested in open-ended exploration and engaging with teams, so they're doing science differently," she says. Similarly, multiplayer online games that are drawing female players are designed around open-ended exploration that allows team-like player networks to develop, she says.

"I ask girls whether they're good at computers and they say 'No' even though they are," says Northwestern's Cassell, noting their growing presence in games and blogging. "The traditional definition of a game excludes the kinds of things girls like. It's not true that girls don't like games."

## CURRENT SITUATION

### Big Business

Today, about half of all Americans play computer and video games, according to the Entertainment Software Association (ESA), and Americans spend more money on video games each year than they do going to the movies. [55] Americans also spend more time playing video games than watching rented videos. [56]

In the past 10 years, U.S. video-game sales have almost tripled to $7 billion last year — after peaking at $7.4 billion in 2004 — representing nearly 230 million computer and video games. [57]

# Entering the New Virtual World of Education

Students enrolled in "Law in the Court of Public Opinion" at the Harvard Extension School in fall 2006 log onto their computers every Thursday evening and send animated versions of themselves into a virtual classroom. There, a so-called avatar — another animated persona — representing Law Professor Charlie Ness (looking about 20 years younger) teaches the course in real time, using Ness' real voice. An avatar representing Ness' daughter Rebecca, a computer expert, occasionally flies down from the ceiling to help teach the course.

Harvard is one of several universities that have begun entering game-like virtual worlds to reach a wider audience. The audience is large and growing at a rate of 10-20 percent a month by some estimates. [1]

Ness teaches his course in the virtual world of Second Life, which boasts more than 1 million inhabitants. [2] Participants enter the Second Life fantasy world to meet people and buy and sell virtual real estate, clothes and other goods. (Linden Labs, the company behind Second Life, makes most of its money leasing virtual land to tenants.) In spring 2006, the 20 courses offered in Second Life included "Theatre and Culture," from Case Western Reserve University, and Stanford University's "Critical Studies in New Media."

Second Life's virtual library offers monthly book discussions, talks by authors (as avatars, of course) and a reference service. It was created because of college students' tendency to use online resources instead of brick-and-mortar libraries, according to Lori Bell, director of innovation at the Alliance Library System in East Peoria, Ill., which helped create the virtual library. As for being in virtual worlds, she observes, "The library needs to be there or we're going to start losing people."

So far, 2,000-3,000 people a day visit the library, according to Bell. "We get a lot of people coming because it's a safe place." Elsewhere in Second Life, she notes, "There's a lot of sex, gambling and adult places. The library is somewhere you don't have to buy anything, you don't have people hitting on you, and people are friendly."

Much like the real world, people enter a virtual universe for a variety of reasons, and education is not necessarily at the top of the list. Lauren Gelman, associate director of the Stanford Law School's Center for Internet and Society, says when she first entered the popular virtual world of There.com — with 400,000 subscribers between ages 13 and 26 — "the first thing that happened is I got propositioned." With islands populated by avatars in bikinis, she says, "It's a very Club Med kind of environment."

This fall, Gelman became dean of a virtual university in There.com — the State of Play Academy — which will offer courses by experts in technology-related areas of law such as copyright, patents and trade secrets. [3] Eventually, the academy might even offer a degree-like certificate, Gelman says.

Students who come to these classes are expected to bring a better grasp of technology than the law professor, permitting a two-way transfer of information. "Sometimes I'll be the teacher and sometimes the student," says Gelman, who teaches a course on technology and law at Stanford.

The power of virtual worlds to project situations in 3-D means students can "experience" what they're learning. To train health-care professionals in how to deal with bioterrorism and natural disasters, for example, Idaho State University provides simulations in Second Life of earthquakes and fires, injured victims and how to treat them. [4] Recently, the library invited residents to heckle Tudor King Henry VIII of England and ask his wife Ann Boleyn what it felt like to be beheaded. Two librarians acted out the roles as avatars in full 16th-century dress.

This summer, teens in Second Life participated in a virtual summer camp aimed at building awareness of global issues like sex trafficking, sponsored by Global Kids, a New York-based group that teaches urban youth about leadership and global citizenry. [5] "We take real-world issues and do something about it in a way you could never do in real life," says Barry Joseph, online leadership director at Global Kids. "In Second Life, you can click on someone's 'Save Darfur' green wrist band and get information about what's going on right now in Darfur."

The argument that kids learn better in the video universe has been a major influence on pioneers like Gelman. "If we know there's educational value in that kids think differently when they navigate these worlds, could we put it to better use to teach them substantive stuff while they're sitting in front of 'World of Warcraft' for 10 hours on a Saturday?" asks Gelman. "It could be at the cusp of something completely revolutionary in education — or it might not work."

---

[1] Richard Siklos, "A Virtual World But Real Money," *The New York Times*, Oct. 19, 2006. According to the Second Life Web site, $7.4 million changed hands in September.

[2] http://secondlife.com. Regular users — those who logged on in the last 30 days — totaled 427,838 in mid-October 2006.

[3] http://stateofplayacademy.com/

[4] http://www.isu.edu/irh/IBAPP/second_life.shtml.

[5] www.globalkids.org.

# Do video games significantly enhance literacy?

## YES

**James Paul Gee**
*Tashia Morgridge Professor of Reading,
University of Wisconsin*
*Author,* What Video Games Have to Teach Us
about Learning and Literacy

Written for *CQ Researcher*, November 2006

Popular culture today often involves quite complex language, and that matters because the biggest predictor of children's school success is the size of their early vocabularies and their abilities to deal with complex language.

Consider, for example, a typical description of a "Pokemon" ("pocket monsters" found in video games, cards, books, movies and television shows): "Bulbasaur are a combination of Grass-type and Poison-type Pokémon. Because they are Grass-type Pokémon, Bulbasaur have plant-like characteristics." Or consider this from a Web site for "Yu-Gi-Oh" (another card, game, book, movie phenomenon): "The effect of '8-Claws Scorpion' is a Trigger Effect that is applied if the condition is correct on activation." Lots of low-frequency words here; complex syntax, as well. Children as young as 6 and 7 play "Pokemon" and "Yu-Gi-Oh." To play they have to read — and read complex language.

The biggest barrier to school success is the child's ability to deal with complex "academic" language, the sort of language in textbooks. Such language starts to kick in about fourth grade and ever increases thereafter in school. Children who learn to decode, but can't read to learn in the content areas later on, are victims of the well-known "fourth-grade slump." Worse yet, research shows that even children who can pass tests in the content areas often can't apply their knowledge to real problem-solving.

Without lots of practice, humans are poor at learning from words out of their contexts of application. Good video games put young people in worlds composed of problems to be solved. They almost always give verbal information "just in time" — when players need and can use it — and "on demand," when the player asks for it. They show how language applies to the world it is about.

Research suggests that people really know what words mean only when they can hook them to the sorts of actions, images or dialogues to which they apply. That is why a game manual or strategy guide makes much more sense after someone has played a game for awhile than before. So, too, science textbooks, cut off from the images and actions science is about, are like a technical game manual without any game.

But, a warning: Good video games — good commercial ones like "Civilization 4" and good "serious games" made around academic content — will not work by themselves. Mentors are needed to encourage strategic thinking about the game and the complex language connected to them.

## NO

**Howard Gardner**
*Hobbs Professor of Cognition and Education,
Harvard Graduate School of Education*

Written for *CQ Researcher*, November 2006

It's difficult to argue with many of Gee's points, and the jury is still out on others. Yet I'd point to several biases in the cited examples. I) They are oriented toward competition (despite the fact that some also entail cooperation); 2) The literacy highlighted is that used in technical manuals; 3) These games, and the epistemology underlying them, are more likely to appeal to boys rather than to girls, and to "techies" rather than dreamers, humanists and conversationalists; 4) They foreground simulation, a very powerful technique, but it's not the same as real life.

I am happy to have medical students or future airplane pilots train on simulations — but they also require real, high-stake experience. Patients have feelings; simulacra and robots don't. And note that these are two areas where simulation makes sense. In many other professions, from poets to priests, they don't.

Which leads to the most important point. Literacy is far more than expertise in technical manuals or even in understanding science and technology, important as they are. It entails the capacity to immerse oneself and, ultimately, to love long, imaginative pieces of fiction, such as *Madame Bovary* or *One Hundred Years of Solitude*; poring over difficult philosophical texts and returning time and again to key passages (Kant, Wittgenstein); and spending time and exercising emotional imagination with challenging poets (Gerard Manley Hopkins, Jorie Graham).

Literacy involves linear thinking over many pages — an entirely different mental faculty than is exploited when one surfs the Web from one link to another, often randomly encountered one. I want all young persons to learn how to think like a historian, a philosopher, an economist, a literary critic (four very different "frames of mind"). I want to stimulate their imaginations to create their own worlds, not just that conjured up by the makers of "World of Warcraft."

In sum, the treasures and skills entailed in the video games of today are impressive, but they still represent only a very partial sampling of the kinds of minds that young people have and the kinds that can and should be cultivated. Some can be cultivated in front of a screen. But too much time there is not healthy on any criterion — and any slice of life — no matter how engrossing — is only partial at best. So two cheers for Jim Gee — but two cheers as well for Mark Hopkins * on one end of a log, and an eager questioner and listener on the other.

---

* A 19th-century president of Williams College.

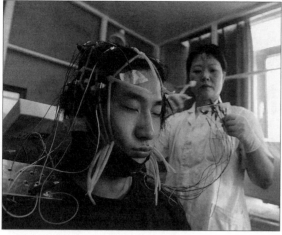

A young man receives an electroencephalogram at a clinic for video-game "addicts" in Beijing in July 2005. Such clinics have opened in several countries, but many psychologists question whether game playing can lead to true addiction.

In fact, the largest-grossing one-day media sale ever occurred on Nov. 9, 2004, when stores sold $125 million worth of "Halo 2" games — the eagerly awaited sequel to the hit Xbox game "Halo", in which individual players defend Earth against alien invaders. [58]

Today, the personal computer is the most popular game machine, contrary to earlier industry predictions that game consoles would dominate. Until recently, Microsoft hadn't marketed games as a core part of its computer. But now it plans to make games easier to install and will emphasize that in its marketing.

Hundreds of millions of people around the world use computers that run the Windows operating system, and about half of them play games, according to Microsoft surveys. The driving force, most analysts say, are subscription-based online multiplayer games played on computers. Games like "World of Warcraft" are expected to take in more than $2 billion worldwide. [59]

Teens have been a big contributor to this growth, with 81 percent of teens — 17 million people — using the Internet to play games online, according to the Pew Internet & American Life Project. That's a 52 percent jump since 2000. [60]

## Social Networking

With 81 percent of all teens playing online video games — up from 66 percent in 2000 — online games have become a widespread form of social networking, according to Amanda Lenhart, senior research specialist at the Pew Internet & American Life Project. [61]

"As with all things on the Internet, it's possible to meet all sorts of people," says Lenhart. "I've heard from a law-enforcement officer about a person who was preyed upon by somebody they met in a game. But the vast majority of people I've talked to have not mentioned any trouble with that sort of thing."

Virtual worlds help teens with two crucial developmental issues — developing an identity and interacting with peers, says Northwestern's Cassell. "That's why they're so popular. They're all about trying on different identities and manifestations," she says.

Although multiplayer games and virtual worlds are clearly places for social networking, they have not become the target of legislation, as have other networking spaces like Myspace.com. [62] Rep. Fred Upton, R-Mich., and others in Congress have proposed restricting children's access to social-networking Web sites. Due to such efforts, as well as entertainment-industry threats to tighten copyright restrictions on kids' variations of games or movies, MIT's Jenkins fears that authorities will "shut down [digital media] before we understand them." [63]

Meanwhile, age, ethnic and social stratifications are breaking down as youngsters play online with older people from cultures around the world. "This is social broadening, which can be scary" to society, says the University of Illinois' Williams. While mixing is positive for diversity, the bonds are different than with a face-to-face friend. "An online friend can console you but can't drive you to the hospital," he points out.

## Libraries Log On

One Friday night each month, nearly 100 Michigan teenagers gather at the Ann Arbor District Library to compete in the Nintendo racing game "Mario Kart." "It's just like story-time, only noisier and smellier," says the library's technology manager, Eli Neiburger.

Libraries increasingly are offering such gaming events, and younger librarians are trying to persuade colleagues that video games are a legitimate part of libraries' mission. A new Young Adult Library Services Association task force is examining whether to recommend video games for teens alongside its annual list of recommended books.

When kids ask, "What can I read?" librarians should give the answer a gaming spin, advises task force member

Beth Gallaway, a trainer/consultant for youth services at the Metrowest Massachusetts Regional Library System in Waltham. "No matter what kind of game kids are playing, they come in genres just like the books we're so familiar with — science fiction, fantasy — and you can pull out these elements from the game," she says.

"There seems to be a lot of interest right now," says Christopher Couzes, director of institutional marketing at Baker and Taylor in Charlotte, N.C., which sells books and other media to libraries. But so far, only about 200 libraries have purchased video games from his firm.

According to the University of Wisconsin's Squire, nearly every student he's met who has played a content-rich game like "Civilization" has checked out a library book on a related topic. But those mind-teaser games are not the games libraries are purchasing. "Libraries want to bring in titles that are popular and that circulate," says Couzes, such as sports games and the popular "Mario Brothers."

## Saying Less?

Although no one knows for sure whether the rising use of video gaming is affecting national literacy and problem-solving abilities, the percentage of U.S. college graduates with proficient English literacy has declined — from 40 percent in 1992 to 31 percent in 2003. [64]

Citing that decline, longtime technology critic Jeremy Rifkin, founder of the Foundation on Economic Trends, blames the increasing use of video games and other electronic media like TV and text messaging. "The human vocabulary is plummeting all over the world, making it more difficult to express ourselves," he says. "It appears that we are all communicating more, but saying less." [65]

However, science writer Johnson observes IQ scores in most developed countries have increased over the past century. He also notes the rate of increase has accelerated in the past 30 years and attributes the rise to the increasing cognitive labor in our mental diet. Compared to the simple children's games of a century ago, today's 10-year-old must master "probing and telescoping through immense virtual worlds," switching from instant-messaging to e-mail and troubleshooting new technologies, Johnson writes. The fact that the U.S. lags behind other countries in educational assessments just shows that students are getting their IQ advantage outside of school, he argues. [66]

A Federation of American Scientists report recently called on the federal government to research the education and work-force-training potential of video games.

The report followed a yearlong evaluation and conference sponsored by the National Science Foundation, which is funding projects to develop educational science games, including multiplayer online games. [67]

While video games could improve learning and motivation, the scientists' report said most commercial games probably will not accomplish those goals, and more educational games should be developed. More research is needed to understand exactly which features of games are important for learning, it said.

High costs and an uncertain market make production of purely educational games too risky for private industry to develop, the federation report said. While some classrooms already use games like "Civilization" for history, "SimCity" for urban planning and "Roller Coaster Tycoon" for physics, schools are unwilling to abandon textbooks and traditional teaching for games whose effectiveness is unknown. The scientists urged educators to develop educational materials around content-rich games like "Civilization" and develop tests to find out what students learn in games.

# OUTLOOK

## Testing the Hypothesis

As video games become more sophisticated and broaden their audience, some cultural observers say it's time to look beyond fears of lurking pedophiles and rotting brains and conduct research to find out what's genuinely good and bad about games.

In October the MacArthur Foundation announced it was committing $50 million to understanding how video games and other digital media affect learning by young people. [68] The foundation is giving grants to game enthusiasts like Wisconsin's Gee and Global Kids' Joseph, as well as to skeptics like Harvard's Gardner.

Unlike school, games are producing "kid-driven learning," says Yowell, noting the foundation will fund innovations based on "what we learn from the kids." MacArthur's hypothesis is that digital media do affect how children learn. "That has huge implications for parents, teachers and policymakers, and we need to understand that," Yowell says.

Edward Castronova, an associate professor of telecommunications at Indiana University, will use his $240,000 grant to build an online game around

Shakespeare's plays, then study how kids' alter-egos dressed in 17th-century costumes learn the bard's words and change their social behavior while living in a very different society. [69]

Some of the enthusiasts' biggest claims will be tested with MacArthur-funded research. Do kids experience failure differently in games? Are they problem-solving differently? What's the effect of giving kids immediate feedback in a game? How do you test what they've learned in a game?

MacArthur grantees will also be asking some of the critics' questions, such as: What's being lost with all the time spent playing? Are players socially isolated? Are they daydreaming less? "We're agnostic," says Yowell.

At least one grant, to Gardner, will examine how kids make ethical decisions about what they share publicly about themselves and their creations. In virtual worlds and multiplayer games, "If I get to pretend to be someone else, what does that mean about how I make ethical decisions?" Yowell asks.

Increasingly, much of our national political debate comes down to disagreements over whether a model is accurate: Will the Earth really suffer from global warming? Did the Iraq war reduce terrorism or stimulate more of it? Since games are all about testing models, they could provide a test-bed for citizenship. Increasingly, they're also about collecting information from many sources — not just rote memorization from a central source.

The big question, enthusiasts say, is whether educators will adapt those techniques to make school as engaging and complex as the best video games. But can games move beyond blood and monsters to become socially positive? Global Kids thinks so and has developed a game about poverty set in Haiti. In a family's struggle to survive, the player has to choose between sending the children to school (and going into debt) or sending them out to work and reaping short-term additional income. [70]

Yet will these kinds of games fly with children who've grown up on the thrills of "Grand Theft Auto"? It's hard to predict, especially as games become ever more realistic and enthralling in this fast-changing industry.

One of the more futuristic visions foresees virtual characters who can respond emotionally to players. "Laura," a computerized exercise trainer developed at MIT, provides empathetic verbal and facial feedback. To technology critic Rifkin, it's hard to know whether to see such attempts as "sadly pathological . . . or whether to be truly frightened." [71]

Ultimately, says MIT's Jenkins, video games are not simply an add-on to mainstream education but a "basic paradigm shift" in how kids learn — one that's here to stay. Parents will have to be actively involved in the digital world to understand it and offer guidance, he says — whether it's questioning the ethics in Second Life or steering kids to the fanfiction sites where they can learn to become better writers.

His advice to parents: Sit down and play a game with your kids. [72]

# NOTES

1. Federation of American Scientists (FAS), "Summit on Educational Games 2006," October 2006; www.fas.org.

2. Steven Johnson, *Everything Bad is Good For You* (2006), p. 45.

3. *Ibid.*, p. 31

4. Kaiser Family Foundation, "Generation M," 2005; www.kff.org. The survey was among children ages 8-18.

5. C. Galas and D.J. Ketelhut, "River City," *Leading with Technology*, 2006, pp. 31-32; http://muve.gse.harvard.edu/rivercityproject/research-publications.htm.

6. Kaiser Family Foundation, *op. cit.*

7. Susan B. Newman and Donna Celano, "The Knowledge Gap," *Reading Research Quarterly*, April/May/June 2006, pp. 176-201; www.reading.org/publications/journals/rrq.

8. FAS, *op. cit.*

9. James Paul Gee, "Reading, Specialist Language Development, and Video Games," unpublished paper, p. 36.

10. MacArthur Open Forum, "Dialogue 2: Gaming Literacies"; http://community.macfound.org.

11. Galas and Ketelhut, *op. cit.*

12. Federation of American Scientists, *op. cit.*, p. 43.

13. Constance A. Steinkuehler, "Massively Multiplayer Online Video Gaming as Participation in A Discourse," *Mind, Culture and Activity*, 2006, 13 (1), pp. 38-52.

14. FAS, *op. cit.*

15. Julia Scheeres, "The Quest to End Game Addiction," *Wired News*, Dec. 5, 2001; www.wired.com.

16. Nick Yee, "The Labor of Fun: How Video Games Blur the Boundaries of Work and Play," *Games and Culture*, January 2006, pp. 68-71. This and other articles/surveys by Yee are at www.nickyee.com/daedalus.

17. www.nickyee.com/daedalus.

18. http://games.groups.yahoo.com/group/WOW_widow/; Scheeres, *op. cit.*

19. Anthony Faiola, "Experts Fear Epidemic of Gaming Addiction," *The Miami Herald*, June 4, 2005, p. A25.

20. Gregory M. Lamb, "Are Multiplayer Games More Compelling, More Addictive?," *The Christian Science Monitor*, Oct. 13, 2005, p. 13.

21. Yee, *op. cit.*, p. 68.

22. *Ibid.*

23. John Seely Brown and Douglas Thomas, "You Play World of Warcraft? You're Hired," *Wired*, April 2006, p. 120.

24. *Ibid.*

25. *Ibid.*

26. John C. Beck and Mitchell Wade, *Got Game* (2004), p. 10.

27. *Ibid.*, p. 42.

28. Yee, *op. cit.*, p. 69.

29. David Williamson Shaffer, *How Computer Games Help Children Learn* (2006).

30. Federation of American Scientists, press release, "Study Recommends Fix to Digital Disconnect in U.S. Education and Workforce Training," Oct. 17, 2006; www.fas.org.

31. Federation of American Scientists, "Summit on Educational Games 2006," *op. cit.*, p. 14.

32. Henry Jenkins, *et al.*, "Confronting the Challenges of Participatory Culture," John D. and Catharine T. MacArthur Foundation, 2006, p. 5; www.digitallearning.macfound.org.

33. *Ibid.*

34. Federation of American Scientists, "Summit on Educational Games 2006," *op. cit.*, p. 12.

35. Jose Antonio Vargas, "Virtual Reality Prepares Soldiers for Real War," *The Washington Post*, Feb. 16, 2006, p. A1.

36. James Gee, *What video games have to teach us about learning and literacy* (2003), p. 48.

37. Chris Suellentrop, "Playing With Our Minds," *Wilson Quarterly*, summer 2006, pp. 14-21.

38. *Ibid.*

39. *Ibid.*

40. Beck and Wade, *op. cit.*, p. 8.

41. Dmitri Williams, in P. Vorderer and J. Bryant, eds., *Playing Computer Games* (2006) in press; https://netfiles.uiuc.edu/dcwill/www/.

42. *Ibid.*, p. 6.

43. Kaiser Family Foundation, press release, "Media Multi-Tasking Changing the Amount and Nature of Young People's Media Use," March 9, 2005.

44. For background see Brian Hansen, "Cyber-Predators," *CQ Researcher*, March 1, 2002, pp. 169-192.

45. Entertainment Software Association; www.theesa.com. See "Facts and Research."

46. Kaiser Family Foundation, "Generation M: Media in the Lives of 8-18 Year Olds: Executive Summary," March 2005; www.kff.org.

47. Pew Internet & American Life Project, "Teens and Technology: Youth are Leading the Transition to a Fully Wired and Mobile Nation," July 27, 2005; www.pewinternet.org. For background see Kathy Koch, "Digital Divide," *CQ Researcher*, Jan. 28, 2000, pp. 41-64.

48. Kaiser Family Foundation, *op. cit.*, March 9, 2005, p. 17. Boys spend an average of 1 hour 12 minutes a day compared to girls' 25 minutes.

49. Justine Cassell and Henry Jenkins, eds., *From Barbie to Mortal Kombat: Gender and Computer Games* (1998).

50. Entertainment Software Association, "Facts and Research"; www.theesa.com.

51. Richard Siklos, "A Virtual World But Real Money," *The New York Times*, Oct. 19, 2006.

52. International Game Developers Association, "2006 Casual Games White Paper"; www.igda.org/casual.

53. *Ibid.*

54. *Ibid.*

55. Suellentop, *op. cit.*, pp. 16-17.

56. Beck and Wade, *op. cit.*, p. 3.

57. The NPD Group, Point-of-Sale Information.

58. Kurt Squire, "From Content to Context," presentation made at Serious Games Summit, Feb. 24, 2004, p. 2.

59. Seth Schiesel, "The PC Embraces Its Gaming Abilities," *The New York Times*, July 18, 2006, Arts Section, pp. 1, 4.

60. Pew Internet & American Life Project, *op. cit.*

61. *Ibid.*

62. For background see Marcia Clemmitt, "Cyber Socializing," *CQ Researcher*, July 28, 2006, pp. 625-648.

63. MacArthur Foundation Webcast of briefing, "Building the Field of Digital Media Learning," Oct. 19, 2006; www.macfound.org.

64. National Center for Education Statistics, "A First Look at the Literacy of America's Adults in the 21st Century," Dec. 15, 2005; http://nces.ed.gov.

65. Jeremy Rifkin, "Virtual Companionship: Our Lonely Existence," *International Herald Tribune*, Oct. 12, 2006, p. 8.

66. Steven Johnson, *Everything Bad is Good for You* (2006), pp. 142-144.

67. Federation of American Scientists, "Summit on Educational Games 2006," *op. cit.*

68. MacArthur Foundation press release, "MacArthur Investing $50 Million in Digital Learning," Oct. 19, 2006; www.macfound.org.

69. Daniel Terdiman, "Shakespeare Coming to a Virtual World," *The New York Times*, Oct. 19, 2006.

70. "Ayiti — the Cost of Life"; thecostoflife.org and www.holymeatballs.org.

71. Rifkin, *op. cit.*

72. MacArthur Foundation Webcast, *op. cit.*

# BIBLIOGRAPHY

## Books

**Beck, John C. and Mitchell Wade, *Got Game: How the Gamer Generation is Reshaping Business Forever*, Harvard Business School Press, 2004.**
Two business experts argue video games provide the kind of leadership, entrepreneurship and team-building skills needed for today's workplace.

**Gee, James Paul, *What Video Games Have to Teach Us About Learning and Literacy*, Palgrave Macmillan, 2003.**
An education professor at the University of Wisconsin-Madison argues that video games provide an intricate learning experience in a modern world where print literacy is not enough.

**Johnson, Steven, *Everything Bad is Good for You*, Riverhead Books, 2006.**
Science writer argues that gamers are learning the scientific method when they try to figure out the "physics" of a game.

**Prensky, Marc, *Don't Bother Me Mom-I'm Learning!* Paragon House, 2006.**
In this enthusiastic book, the founder of an e-learning company urges parents (whom he calls "digital immigrants") to start engaging with digital natives — kids who've grown up with games as a positive learning experience.

## Articles

**Brown, John Seely and Thomas Douglas, "You Play World of Warcraft? You're Hired!" *Wired*, April 2006, p. 120.**
Skills learned in multiplayer games like "World of Warcraft" are training young people for workplace leadership roles.

**Rauch, Jonathan, "Sex, Lies, and Videogames," *The Atlantic Monthly*, November 2006.**
The future of video-game technology includes interactive dramas and Spore, a game coming out next year, that will give players new scope in designing new worlds.

**Rifkin, Jeremy, "Virtual Companionship," *International Herald Tribune*, Oct. 12, 2006, p. 8.**
Technology critic worries that the nation is becoming less literate as video games proliferate, and expresses disgust at futuristic interactive computer characters.

**Shaffer, David Williamson, *et al.*, "Video Games and the Future of Learning," *Phi Delta Kappan*, October 2005, pp. 105-111.**
University of Wisconsin educational researchers argue that video games offer "learning by doing" on a grand scale and that schools need to catch up.

**Siklos, Richard, "A Virtual World But Real Money," *The New York Times*, Oct. 19, 2006.**
The popularity and economies of virtual worlds like Second Life are growing rapidly.

**Suellentrop, Chris, "Playing with Our Minds,"** *Wilson Quarterly,* **summer 2006, pp. 14-21.**
A *New York Times* columnist suggests games do not permit innovation because they force players to play within the system.

**Tompkins, Aimee, "The Psychological Effects of Violent Media on Children," Dec. 14, 2003,** *AllPsych Journal,* **http://allpsych.com.**
So far, research on the effect of violent video games and other media on children only shows evidence of short-term effects.

**Wright, Will, "Dream Machines,"** *Wired,* **April 2006, pp. 111-112.**
The creator of "The Sims," the best-selling PC game of all time, argues that gamers are learning in a "totally new way" and "treat the world as a place for creation." As guest editor, he invited other authors to write about the future and impact of video games for this special issue.

## Reports

**Federation of American Scientists,** *Summit on Educational Games: Harnessing the Power of Video Games for Learning,* **2006; www.fas.org.**
After a yearlong study, the federation recommended that the federal government fund research into the most effective educational features of video games and help develop new educational games.

**Jenkins, Henry,** *et al., Confronting the Challenges of Participatory Culture,* **2006, MacArthur Foundation; www.digitallearning.macfound.org.**
MIT's Jenkins and other technology experts argue that involvement in digital media has given young people new skills and new scope for creativity, and they urge schools to do more to foster "media literacies."

**Kaiser Family Foundation, "Generation M: Media in the Lives of 8-18 Year-olds," 2005; www.kff.org.**
More than 80 percent of adolescents have a video console player at home, and the amount of time spent playing video games has increased in the past five years.

**Pew Internet & American Life Project,** *Teens and Technology,* **July 27, 2005; www.pewinternet.org.**
The vast majority of U.S. teens use the Internet and 81 percent of those play games online.

# For More Information

**Federation of American Scientists**, 1717 K St., N.W., Suite 209, Washington, DC 20036; (202) 546-3300; www.fas.org. Scientists' organization that has called on the federal government to use video games to strengthen education.

**Games, Learning and Society**, University of Wisconsin, Teacher Education Bldg., 225 North Mills St., Madison, WI 53706; (608) 263-4600; http://website.education.wisc.edu/gls/research.htm. Studies the learning potential of video games.

**Global Kids, Inc.**, 561 Broadway, New York, NY 10012; (212) 226-0130; www.globalkids.org. Educates urban youth on international issues and is teaching disadvantaged teens to design and play games.

**Kaiser Family Foundation**, 2400 Sand Hill Rd., Menlo Park, CA 94025; (650) 854-9400; www.kff.org. Conducts surveys on media use by youth and teens.

**MacArthur Foundation**, 140 S. Dearborn St., Chicago, IL 60603; (312) 726-8000; www.macfound.org. Provides grants for research on the learning potential of video games and other digital media.

**www.nickyee.com/daedalus**. The research findings of Stanford researcher Nick Yee, who has surveyed more than 35,000 players of online multiplayer games.

**Pew Internet & American Life Project**, 1615 L St., N.W., Suite 700, Washington, DC 20036; (202) 419-4500; www.pewinternet.org. Surveys youth media use.

# 6

# Media Ownership

David Hatch and Heather Kleba

Protesters in Los Angeles urge the Federal Communications Commission not to ease media-ownership rules. But on June 2, 2003, the FCC voted to allow media corporations to own dramatically more news outlets in any one city. Critics say fewer media conglomerates means fewer choices for consumers. But industry executives say consolidation enables them to stay competitive and provide more selections. The decision was later overturned in an appeals court, and the FCC took up a similar ownership issue in late 2007.

From *CQ Researcher*,
October 10, 2003. (Updated May 23, 2008)

M ajor TV networks pulled out all the stops competing for the first televised interview with Pfc. Jessica Lynch after her dramatic rescue during the Iraq war. Big-name anchors called her on the phone and sent her personalized trinkets, autographed books and photos.

But CBS News offered more than souvenirs. Tapping the synergies of its then parent company, Viacom — whose sprawling media empire at the time included publishing giant Simon & Schuster as well as many cable channels and Paramount Pictures — CBS dangled book deals and music specials before the waifish soldier from West Virginia. [1]

After originally defending its efforts, the network conceded it had overstepped the boundaries of journalistic ethics. Acknowledging the critics who think media companies are too consolidated and powerful, CBS Chairman and CEO Leslie Moonves blamed the aggressive wooing of Lynch on Viacom's sheer size and web of interconnected businesses.

"As these companies become more and more vertically integrated, you know, sometimes you do go over the line," he said. [2] In the end, ABC snared the first TV interview with Lynch, which aired Nov. 11, 2003, with host Diane Sawyer.

Long gone are the days when media companies were one-horse enterprises specializing only in broadcasting or publishing. Today they are multifaceted conglomerates with stakes in everything from television, radio, movies, newspapers and books to the Internet, theme parks, billboards and concert promotion. [3]

Five media powerhouses now control most of America's prime-time TV programming: the Tribune Company; Disney (ABC,

## Inside Big Media

Media conglomerates today own holdings in broadcast, cable, Internet, music, book, video and movie companies. Here is a look at two of the biggest media corporations.*

| News Corp. | CBS Corp. (formerly part of Viacom) |
|---|---|
| **Broadcast Networks** | **Broadcasting** |
| Fox Broadcasting Company<br>35 Fox Television Stations<br>Fox News Channel<br>FX<br>National Geographic Channel<br>Fox Sports Net<br>SPEED<br>DirecTV | 17 CBS television stations |
| **Film** | **Cable** |
| 20th Century Fox<br>Fox Searchlight Pictures<br>Fox Television Studios<br>Blue Sky Studios | The CW (partial ownership)<br>Showtime King World<br>CSTV |
| **Newspapers** | **Radio** |
| New York Post<br>Wall Street Journal<br>5 United Kingdom newspapers<br>20 Australian newspapers<br>5 magazines | Stations located in 40 major metropolitan areas |
| **Publishing Companies** | **Publishing** |
| HarperMorrow Publishers<br>HarperMorrow<br>General Books Group<br>12 Children's Books Groups<br>HarperCollins UK<br>HarperCollins Canada<br>HarperCollins Australia | Simon & Schuster<br>Simon & Schuster Adult Publishing Group<br>Simon & Schuster Children's Publishing<br>Simon & Schuster New Media |
| **Other** | **Other** |
| Los Angeles Kings (NHL, 40% option)<br>Los Angeles Lakers (NBA, 9.8% option)<br>News Interactive<br>Sky Radio Denmark<br>Sky Radio Germany<br>Fox Interactive<br>MySpace.com<br>National Rugby League | CBS Outdoor |

*\* Holdings of other media firms are on the* Columbia Journalism Review's *Web site: www.cjr.org/resources/*

*Source: Columbia Journalism Review,* "Who Owns What," accessed May 7, 2008

ESPN); General Electric (NBC, CNBC, MSNBC); News Corp. (Fox, Fox News) and CBS Corp. [4]

Meanwhile, one company, Clear Channel Communications Inc., dominates radio, owning more than 600 stations — about 350 more than its closest competitor. While Clear Channel owns only half the number of stations it had in 2006 because of its decision to privatize after tiring of low profit margins and catering to Wall Street, it is still a major force in 120 media markets. [5]

Experts note that despite the vast number of media ownership consolidations occurring, there were still 800 local television station owners as of 2007, and no signs of that number dropping off in the near future. [6] However, increasing consolidation could mean that citizens who believe they are consuming different variations of news — for example from Fox News and *The New York Post* — are actually getting the same news, with the same slant, from parent company News Corp. The only difference is the package.

"You're running close to a monopoly or oligopoly situation, there's no question about that," says Michael Copps, a Democratic FCC commissioner and staunch opponent of the 2003 and 2007 moves to loosen media-ownership rules. "It's about the ability of a very small number of companies to control [the content of] our media. To dictate what the entertainment is going to be, to dictate what the civic dialogue is going to be, to dictate that we'll no longer have as much [local news] and diversity as we had before. So it goes to the fundamentals of our democratic life as a country."

While the number of media competitors may be declining, the amount of diversity of content and technologies is not. Today there are six commercial broadcast networks — double the number from a few decades ago — three 24-hour news networks, cable and satellite television, the Internet and a growing number of alternative-media choices, such as low-power FM, satellite radio and Internet "blogs," or Web logs written by everyday citizens. Consumers today have "an overwhelming amount of choice," says NBC lobbyist Bob Okun.

Indeed, the three major networks that dominated prime-time TV for decades have ceded huge chunks of the market to cable and satellite competitors. As of 2005, more than 85 percent of Americans subscribed to cable, satellite and other pay-TV services. [7] "The competition is real from cable," Okun says. "They put on edgier programming."

To fight back, three broadcast TV networks now operate their own studios so they can produce more content themselves, keep tighter control over the creative process and avoid bidding wars over hit shows. Critics say network ownership of studios has forced many independent producers out of business and left those remaining at the mercy of big media. As a result, they say, the broadcast networks are churning out lowbrow, cookie-cutter programming because independent voices have been locked out. Program diversity, creativity and localism — or attention to local needs or tastes — suffer when too few companies control much of what we see, read and hear, the critics say.

But industry executives say consolidation enables them to grow quickly so they can stay competitive. Mergers also create new opportunities for cross-promotion, content repackaging and elimination of redundant offerings, freeing up resources for other areas.

In response to marketplace changes, former Republican Chairman Michael Powell in June 2003 shepherded through the commission a sweeping relaxation of the FCC's media-ownership rules by a narrow 3-2 vote along party lines, with the two Democratic commissioners opposed. In June 2004, Prometheus Radio Project sued the FCC, and won, forcing the FCC to reconfigure those rules and essentially restoring them to their original form. [8]

Among other things, the commission attempted to increase the audience reach of network-owned TV stations, permitting them to reach 45 percent of households, up from 35 percent. It also lifted the ban on a single company owning both a broadcast station and a newspaper in the same market — a combination that previously had only been permitted on a limited basis. In sum, the new rules could allow one company — in a single market — to own three TV stations, one newspaper, eight radio outlets and a cable system. And TV-newspaper mergers would be permissible in about 200 markets, affecting 98 percent of the U.S. population. [9]

The new rules triggered an unexpectedly strong backlash from lawmakers, academics and advocacy groups concerned that media control would fall into too few hands. The rhetoric on both sides was harsh. Critics insisted the new regulations would threaten democracy, while supporters warned that without them, free TV could eventually disappear, as more content migrates to pay TV.

In 2007, the Republican-led FCC voted along party lines, 3 to 2, in favor of reducing ownership restrictions, overturning a 32-year standard in which a single company could not own a newspaper and a radio or television station in the same city. The new rules will drop these restrictions in the 20 largest markets. "The media marketplace has changed considerably since 1975 when the newspaper/broadcast cross ownership was put in place. At that time, cable was a nascent service, satellite television did not exist and there was no Internet," the FCC said in a report accompanying its December decision. [10]

Michael J. Copps, one of two Democrats on the commission, said in response to the overall ruling, "In the final analysis, the real winners today are businesses that are in many cases quite healthy, and the real losers are going to be all of us who depend on the news media to learn what's happening in our communities and to keep an eye on local government. Powerful companies are using political muscle to sneak through rule changes that let them profit at the expense of the public interest." [11]

Immediately after the FCC's decision, lawmakers on Capitol Hill spoke out. A bipartisan group of 25 senators wrote a letter to Chairman Martin, noting that they would seek legislative action to overturn his decision. [12]

Proponents of the FCC's action point out that network broadcasters today are facing more competition than ever before. But critics say the plethora of media choices can be deceptive. A consumer who watches CNN, subscribes to *Time* and *Fortune* and surfs AOL may think he's consulting several independent sources,

# Radio Giant Clear Channel Riles Critics

When a freight train derailed in Minot, N.D, in 2002, releasing toxic fumes into the air, radio station KCJB-AM didn't answer when police phoned to request public alerts.

Critics of media consolidation say no one responded because the station — one of six outlets in Minot owned by Clear Channel Communications — was running on computers after the company consolidated local operations and slashed personnel. [1] But Andrew Levin, senior vice president for government affairs at Clear Channel, says personnel were on hand and blamed Minot police for not knowing how to operate emergency equipment that automatically prompts on-air alerts.

Tiny Minot, it turns out, was the wrong place for Clear Channel to have such problems because North Dakota Democrat Byron Dorgan sits on the powerful Senate panel that oversees the radio industry. The lawmaker wasn't pleased and is now seeking to clamp down on the looser ownership rules passed by the Federal Communications Commission (FCC) on June 2. He often cites the Minot case as a reason why he opposes further deregulation of television, newspapers and other mass media.

To its critics, Clear Channel provides a sobering lesson on the pitfalls of media mergers. Bolstered by the 1996 Telecommunications Act's deregulation of radio, it grew from 40 stations in 1996 to 636 today to become the dominant industry player, with 110 million listeners nationwide and revenue of $3.6 billion annually. [2] It is also one of the nation's largest display-advertising companies, with about 770,000 billboards. [3] Coupled with its nearest competitor, Viacom-owned Infinity Broadcasting, the companies control 42 percent of the U.S. radio market and command 45 percent of the revenue. [4]

Detractors say Clear Channel's homogenized playlists make radio sound the same from coast to coast and that its use of "voice-tracking" — programming local radio stations with deejays and announcers in distant cities — undermines localism. "Only about 9 percent of all our programming is voice-tracked," Levin says, adding that the practice enables small communities to enjoy otherwise unaffordable talent. "We think that folks like it."

Noting that Clear Channel owns less than 12 percent of U.S. radio stations, CEO John Hogan said, "I don't see any way possible to conclude that this is a consolidated industry or that Clear Channel has any real dominance inside that industry." Prior to 1996, he noted, up to 60 percent of radio stations were losing money, and many were in danger of going dark. He said Clear Channel should be heralded as an American success story and that the company helped rejuvenate radio. [5]

Clear Channel says it has increased format diversity in many markets, such as Los Angeles, where it owns stations ranging from nostalgia to Spanish hip-hop. [6] But the watchdog Future of Music Coalition (FMC) found hundreds of redundant radio formats nationwide with songs overlapping up to 76 percent of the time. Some stations altered format names without changing playlists. [7]

"Just because it's a [distinct] format doesn't mean that it's diverse," says FMC Executive Director Jenny Toomey. "The public realizes radio has homogenized since the '96 Act passed."

"Radio consolidation has contributed to a 34 percent decline in the number of owners, a 90 percent rise in the cost of advertising, a rise in indecent broadcasts and the replacement of local news and community programming with voice-tracking and syndicated hollering that ill-serves the public interest," railed Sen. Ernest Hollings, D-S.C., at a January 2003 hearing. [8]

Eric Boehlert, a *Salon* journalist who writes extensively about radio, told National Public Radio, "You can't have a hit without being on Clear Channel stations. You can't have a career without being on Clear Channel stations. So all of a sudden you have a company that is essentially dictating what gets heard on the radio." That was unheard of before the '96 act, he said. [9]

Don Henley, one of several musicians who accuse Clear Channel of heavy-handed, monopolistic practices, told lawmakers this year: "Artists can no longer stand for the exorbitant radio-promotion costs, nor can we tolerate the overt or covert threats posed by companies owning radio stations, venues and [advertising] agencies." [10]

A 2003 report from the watchdog Center for Public Integrity finds that small and medium-sized radio markets have higher levels of radio concentration than large ones. Clear Channel, the report finds, is the main owner in 20 of

but in fact, all are part of media giant *Time* Warner. "You may be hearing many different voices, yes, but they are from the same ventriloquist," said Sen. Byron Dorgan, a North Dakota Democrat. [13]

Because roughly 15 percent of Americans rely on free broadcast TV as their only source of television, a bipartisan coalition of lawmakers is trying to overturn the new FCC regulations, and their decision is expected to pass

the top 25 most-concentrated markets. [11]

Fueling the controversy surrounding the San Antonio, Texas-based company are its close ties to Republicans. CEO Lowry Mays is a friend of President Bush and contributes heavily to GOP causes. Tom Hicks, a Clear Channel board member, purchased the Texas Rangers baseball team from Bush and his associates. The company has made a star of conservative radio host Rush Limbaugh, whose show airs on 180 Clear Channel talk-radio channels. Others are concerned that Clear Channel could unduly influence a combined Hispanic Broadcasting Corp. (HBC) and Univision Communications, which recently won FCC approval to merge. Clear Channel is HBC's largest shareholder. [12]

Meanwhile, Rep. Howard Berman, D-Calif., worries that Clear Channel has "punished" Britney Spears and other artists who bypassed its concert-promotion service by burying radio ads for their concerts and denying airplay to their songs. [13] Competitors allege that Clear Channel secretly purchases radio stations — using front groups and shell companies — and "warehouses" them if there is public opposition to the company's expansion in the hope that regulatory limits will later be lifted. [14]

In September 2003, the watchdog Alliance for Better Campaigns accused Clear Channel and Infinity of limiting the sale of radio ads to candidates in California's gubernatorial recall election. The alliance suggested the companies may be withholding ad space for more lucrative commercial clients. [15]

Clear Channel has strongly denied all of these charges, saying it is the target of criticism because it's the market leader. [16]

The National Association of Broadcasters (NAB) emphasizes there are nearly 4,000 separate owners of 13,000 local radio stations in the U.S. today. "The Hollywood movie studios, the record companies, direct-broadcast satellite, cable systems, newspapers — even the Internet — all have more of their revenue share concentrated among the top 10 owners than does radio," NAB President and CEO Eddie Fritts told lawmakers this year. "Spanish-language formats have increased by over 80 percent in the last decade, and other ethnicities are well represented on the dial." [17]

To some, Clear Channel is a harbinger of television's future. "We're already going that way under the old rules," complains Democratic FCC Commissioner Michael Copps, who already sees signs of the "Clear Channelization" of TV.

"I don't think anybody in the Congress really anticipated the extent of consolidation that has ensued from the 1996 act."

But even Copps sees upsides to concentration, such as the "economies and efficiencies" that have allowed some stations to operate more profitably and avoid going under, depriving listeners of service. [18] Nevertheless, he opposes the FCC's new media-ownership policies.

Clear Channel is now in Washington's crosshairs. Although the FCC loosened ownership rules for newspapers and television stations in June 2003, it limited the number of radio stations that operators can own in certain markets. The FCC wanted to grandfather in existing noncompliant stations, but Sen. John McCain, R-Ariz., offered legislation to force the divestiture of such properties.

---

[1] Marc Fisher, "Sounds Familiar for a Reason," *The Washington Post*, May 18, 2003, p. B1.

[2] Numbers drawn from "The State of the News Media 2008," Center for Excellence in Journalism, March 2008; "Clear Channel Radio Gives Listeners Direct Mobile Access to Favorite Radio Stations," Clear Channel Press Release, May 21, 2007, www.clearchannel.com/Radio/PressRelease.aspx?PressReleaseID=1969; and "The State of the News Media 2007," Center for Excellence in Journalism, 2007.

[3] Eric Boehlert, "Habla usted Clear Channel?" *Salon.com*, April 24, 2003.

[4] See "Radio Deregulation: Has it Served Citizens and Musicians," Future of Music Coalition, www.futureofmusic.org, Nov. 18, 2002, p. 3.

[5] From NPR's "Fresh Air," July 23, 2003.

[6] NPR, *op. cit.*

[7] Future of Music Coalition, *op. cit.*, pp. 42-52.

[8] Hollings, *op. cit.*

[9] NPR, *op. cit.*

[10] From testimony before Senate Commerce Committee hearing on radio consolidation, Jan. 30, 2003.

[11] See "Big Radio Rules in Small Markets: A few behemoths dominate medium-sized cities throughout the U.S," www.openairwaves.org/telecom, released Oct. 1, 2003.

[12] Boehlert, *op. cit.*

[13] See Rep. Howard Berman, D-Calif., letter to U.S. Attorney General John Ashcroft, found at www.house.gov/berman/, Jan. 22, 2002.

[14] Eric Boehlert, "Washington Tunes In," *Salon.com*, March 27, 2002.

[15] See press release, Sept. 3, 2003.

[16] See "Issue Update," www.clearchannel.com, June 2, 2003.

[17] From testimony before Senate Commerce Committee, Jan. 30, 2003.

[18] Copps was speaking at the University of Southern California Media Consolidation Forum in Los Angeles, April 28, 2003, p. 7.

---

both houses of Congress before it faces a presidential veto threat. Meanwhile, the controversy has prompted Congress to re-evaluate whether media deregulation, a trend that has accelerated since Congress enacted the Telecommunications Act of 1996, has met its goal of fostering more competition. [14]

Deregulation advocates say that the Internet will be able to fill the gap left by any news outlets that are forced out, because it is so vast it can hold as much information as Americans will ever need. Critics, however, point out that the most popular Internet news sites are owned by the top media conglomerates.

The 2003 firestorm tainted the image of former Chairman Powell, the son of former Secretary of State Colin L. Powell, and led to his resignation. Martin has not yet succumbed to the backlash that, to this point, has been moderate compared to that of 2003. Lawmakers in both parties are speaking out, but there has been no call for his immediate resignation.

Although cable and satellite television sometimes trigger scrutiny into how much market power they exercise, mergers involving broadcasters are of special concern, because they use the public airwaves and are licensed to serve the "public interest."

Commissioner Copps says public-interest requirements have been relaxed over the years and that license renewals are now largely pro forma. In theory, he says, TV and radio stations are supposed to put the public interest ahead of profit, but in reality, that is not always the case. To deflect congressional pressure, an FCC localism initiative is looking to help broadcasters implement their own localism task forces and will consider license renewal requirements that ensure networks are providing quality local content. [15]

In addition to concerns about content diversity, some critics worry about the ethnic diversity of media owners. According to "Out of the Picture 2007: Minority & Female Ownership in the United States," a recent report put out by media advocacy group Free Press, minorities own only 3.2 percent of the nation's full-power commercial television stations, a decrease of 8.5 percent between 2006 and 2007. Women are being pushed out as well, owning only 80 full-power commercial television stations, or 6 percent. [16]

The report explains that "The pressures of consolidation and concentration brought on by bad policy decisions have crowded out minority owners, who tend to own just a single station and find it difficult to compete with their big-media counterparts fro advertising revenue." Even though the number of television stations has increased about 13 percent since 1998, minority ownership has not increased, and ownership by African Americans has actually decreased 70 percent since 1998. [17]

As Washington politicos debate how the media should be regulated, here are some issues being discussed:

## Is the U.S. media industry too consolidated?

In Tampa, Fla., media consolidation is an everyday reality. Thanks to a waiver of the FCC ban on cross-ownership of local newspapers and TV stations, Media General owns *The Tampa Tribune*, the local NBC affiliate WFLA-TV and TBO.com, a joint-venture Web site produced by the paper and TV station. *

They share a state-of-the-art newsroom, where they sometimes swap story ideas and collaborate on projects. Writers for the paper have appeared on WFLA shows, and some of WFLA's reports make it into the *Tribune*.

Proponents of the Tampa experiment said combining the newsrooms would effectively double the resources available to reporters, producing more in-depth journalism. During an April 2007 forum, former Media General Vice President Dan Bradley told the audience, "Without a doubt, convergence has brought more eyes, ears and feet to the street." He continued, saying that the convergence of the Tampa newsrooms has brought reporting back to the community by allowing reporters to share information and tell local stories in the best way possible. [18] But Robert Haiman, former president emeritus of the Poynter Institute journalism school and former editor of the competing *St. Petersburg Times*, hasn't seen that result. **

"Where are the huge investigative stories that run simultaneously in the newspaper and on the TV station?" he asked. "I'm not seeing incredible feats of journalism," he said. "I see those promotional connections, but I don't see a great leap." [19]

Robert Dardenne, a professor of journalism at the University of South Florida, who also spoke at the April 2007 forum, agrees. "Convergence doesn't enhance strengths, so much as blend them," leading to mediocre stories written by fewer journalists. [20]

But others think Tampa's arrangement benefits the marketplace. "It has given power to both sides," says Barbara Cochran, president of the Radio-Television News Directors Association (RTNDA). The newspaper gets exposure to a broader audience with a younger demographic, and the television station has access to the paper's vast reporting staff, she notes, but "they still make very independent decisions."

---

* The FCC removed the ban in June, but it remains in effect while lawmakers and the courts decide its fate.

** The nonprofit Poynter Institute owns both the St. Petersburg Times and Congressional Quarterly Inc., the former parent company of CQ Press, publisher of *CQ Researcher*.

Does the cross-ownership stifle competition? No, she says, because other voices remain. "You still have competition" in the Tampa television market, she says.

Gauging whether the media is too concentrated boils down to perspective. "Large media companies have become larger, but so has the entire sector," wrote telecom visionary Eli Noam in the *Financial Times*. [21] Industry supporters emphasize that, as of 2007, there are still more than 800 local television station owners, and none of the Big Four networks owns a majority of stations in the local market. Fox (News Corp.) owns 35 local channels, CBS owns 29 and ABC and NBC each own 10. [22]

And while the broadcast networks controlled 90 percent of the audience 25 years ago, today they control less than 50 percent. [23] The networks say the decline is due to the growth of cable, which — because it's a pay service — has fewer content restrictions and thus can offer racier and more violent programming. The major broadcasters insist they're at another disadvantage to cable: It has two revenue streams — advertising and subscriptions — while broadcasters have only advertising.

"You need somehow to create additional forms of revenue," NBC's Okun says, adding that skyrocketing costs for sports, movies, hit TV shows and other marquee programming have forced the networks to consolidate.

But media watchdogs say it's unfair for broadcasters to complain they are losing ground to cable, since broadcasters have migrated most of their channels to cable and satellite for distribution. [24]

Some critics also fear that the news divisions of huge media conglomerates feel pressure to go soft on corporate parents' wrongdoings. "I don't see the problem, frankly. Views are not being suppressed," said Time Warner CEO Ann Moore, noting that *Fortune* has had tough coverage of its parent company. [25]

Public Broadcasting Service (PBS) President and CEO Pat Mitchell complains that companies often justify consolidation by promising that more resources will be available to invest in news and information-gathering, but they rarely deliver. "The American public seems less informed than ever about almost everything," she says.

"That's not diversity of news," responds Marvin Kalb, a senior fellow at Harvard University's Joan Shorenstein Center on the Press, Politics and Public Policy. "That's just multiplicity of news." When TV stations air local newscasts throughout the day they often repeat the same stories, and competing stations usually offer similar coverage, he says.

Real diversity would occur if local stations offered a broader range of stories with more depth, he argues.

In fact, a 2003 study of local TV found that smaller station groups produce better-quality news than network-owned-and-operated stations (O&Os), which have far more resources. [26] In 2005, a similar report found that while news consumption has fallen, 25 percent more people are watching local news over the nightly national news. [27]

Meanwhile, even though there are many more news outlets today, "There's a lot less news being presented to the American people," says Kalb, a former CBS and NBC News reporter.

Nevertheless, the major broadcast networks remain the first place Americans turn for news, especially during times of tragedy, Kalb says. But the networks, assuming the public is getting its hard news from the 24-hour news stations like CNN, are offering less and less hard news. "They feel that you've already got the news elsewhere, so why bother," Kalb says. "But not everybody watches CNN all day. In fact, probably most of us don't watch it at all."

CBS is facing backlash for a similar stance on its nightly news broadcast with new anchor Katie Couric. Critics say that when Couric was brought on, the hard news all but dropped out of the show and was replaced by soft news on celebrities and humanitarians.

MSNBC contributor Michael Ventre wrote in a column that this is the fault of the network more than the anchor. "The people who watch evening news do so because they want the news. . . . They don't care who delivers it, as long as it's somebody they can believe. . . . What it can't be is someone who arrives with much ballyhoo to artificially inject celebrity into a news broadcast." [28]

## Did the FCC loosen its media-ownership rules too much?

It's not often that the National Rifle Association (NRA) and the National Organization for Women (NOW) agree on an issue. But their opposition to the FCC's 2003 decision easing its media-ownership restrictions put them in the same camp. Such diverse alliances spelled trouble for the Republican-led FCC. A broad coalition of regulators, lawmakers and advocacy groups argued that the commission's action threatened consumers, media diversity and democracy.

The commission lifted the cap after heavy lobbying from the Big Four networks, three of which were at — or above — the 35 percent limit due to waivers while the restriction was in limbo.

Former CBS News anchor Walter Cronkite, who lobbied against the 2003 rule changes, warned, "The gathering of more and more outlets under one owner clearly can be an impediment to a free and independent press." [29]

But proponents of the 2003 deregulation were equally ardent: "It has been said that the rules will allow one company to dominate all media in a community," said former GOP Sen. George Allen of Virginia. "It is simply not true. . . . If you look at the availability of information and programming, consumers have an unprecedented abundance of choices." [30]

For the first time in 2003, the FCC permitted triopolies — single ownership of three TV stations in a market — in large metropolitan areas. (It retained its ban on the Big Four broadcast networks merging with each other.) However, this decision was overturned in appeals court, though duopolies remain.

In 2007, the FCC lifted its blanket ban on one company owning both a newspaper and broadcast station in a market in the top 20 markets, so long as there are at least eight other independent news sources and the broadcast station is not in the top four. Before, the combinations were allowed only if they were grandfathered in after being banned in the 1970s or with an FCC waiver to help a struggling outlet.

The 2007 rule change has thus far had the same effect as the 2003 change. Ironically, some of the most outspoken critics have come from Martin's own party. Senator Olympia Snowe (R-ME) joined with Senator Dorgan to introduce the resolution of disapproval that was passed by the Senate on May 15. "We owe it to the American people to restore confidence in the FCC's commitment not only to uphold the public interest but to advance it and strengthen it," Senator Snowe said in a press release after the vote. [31]

On the other side of the political aisle, the comments have been just as negative, In a joint statement, Democratic FCC commissioners Michael Copps and Jonathan Adelstein remarked, "We said the new rules were likely to be about as tough as a bowl of Jell-O. What we didn't realize was that they may turn out to be as tough as a bowl of Jell-O *before* it's put in the fridge." [32]

Senator Byron Dorgan (D-ND), commented late last year on Chairman Martin's decision to go through with the relaxation of ownership rules, indicating that lawmakers in both parties are ready to fight. "There is going

to be a firestorm of protest, and I'm going to be carrying the wood," he said. [33]

Democratic Commissioner Copps complains that the new ownership rules provide no real check on whether the merger is being conducted in the public interest. Before the final FCC vote, he says, commissioners received an e-mail saying that the four factors built into the new ownership standards that would indicate whether a newspaper or broadcast station buy could go through need not be considered in all cases. [34]

Copps says the FCC also failed to consider the impact on minorities, in terms of ownership and employment opportunities and diversity of views. In his statement after the vote, Copps said the FCC commissioners were not even aware of the poor state of minority- and women-owned journalism outlets. In addition, Andrew Jay Schwartzman, President and CEO of the Media Access Project, who appeared before the Senate Subcommittee on Telecommunications, testified that "Nearly half of the TV stations owned by people of color are in the top 20 markets, and not one of them is in the top four of their markets." With the new ownership rules, these stations may be targeted for acquisition. [35]

The FCC is looked into this issue with the help of an advisory committee, and in 2007 adopted rules that will help women and minorities own more broadcast stations by assisting with financing and availability. [36]

"Any further relaxation in the ownership rules is bad for our industry," says Jim Winston, executive director of the National Association of Black-owned Broadcasters, noting, in 2003, a 20 percent decline in minority-owned TV and radio stations since 1996, when the industry was deregulated. Many African-American broadcasters were forced to sell to bigger players that undercut them on ad rates and had more financial leverage. "Minorities have historically had difficulty raising capital," he says.

But NBC's Okun counters that existing media-ownership restrictions undermine diversity more than consolidation does. His network would like to increase the footprint of Telemundo, its Spanish-language broadcast network, but the network is "severely constrained" from doing so under current ownership rules.

### Should Congress reimpose rules limiting television networks' ownership of programming?

Hollywood producer Dick Wolf stood to reap a windfall from NBC — an estimated $1.6 billion over three years

— if the network renewed his series "Law & Order" and its spin-offs, "Special Victims Unit" and "Criminal Intent." But all that changed when NBC announced plans to buy Universal Television, a studio that has a partnership with Wolf.

Observers say that after the sale Universal essentially switched sides in the negotiations and no longer had an incentive to help Wolf get the best deal from NBC. Victoria Riskin, president of the Writers Guild of America, West, said Wolf will still do well. "I'm more worried about what kind of leverage the Dick Wolfs of the future will have," she said. NBC executives insist the merger with Universal created more programming opportunities for Wolf. [37]

For more than two decades, the FCC imposed so-called financial interest and syndication rules — commonly known as fin-syn — on TV broadcasters, curbing their ownership stakes in programming. The rules were intended to protect independent producers and promote program diversity. But as the media universe began to expand, the FCC removed some of its fin-syn rules in 1991 and eliminated them entirely in 1995.

The networks opposed fin-syn for financial reasons. Since they were assuming risk by putting up money on the front-end to help cover production costs, they wanted a slice of the lucrative back-end, or revenue from syndication. "It's the ability to generate content in a cost-effective way," says Okun, explaining why the networks have sought to combine with studios.

Critics blame fin-syn's repeal for ushering in an era of "vertical integration," in which the TV networks increasingly produce shows in-house, and for driving most independent producers out of business. The result, they say, is lowbrow, homogenized content that takes few creative chances. According to Marshall Herskovitz, a television and movie producer, "Today, there are zero independent production companies making scripted television. They were all forced out of business by the networks' insistence — following the FCC's fin-syn ruling — on owning part or all of every program they broadcast." [38]

The networks, however, argue that fin-syn is unnecessary. "There's more production going on today in this country than there ever has been, by a factor of 10 or 20," said NBC Chairman Bob Wright. "American consumers have never had video benefits like they have today." [39]

Testifying before the Senate Commerce Committee in early 2003, Rupert Murdoch, chairman of News Corp., which owns the Fox broadcast network, said, "If anyone comes to us with a show that can get us an audience, we'll be the first to buy." [40]

But Jonathan Rintels, president and executive director of the Center for the Creative Community, an advocacy group for independent producers, says it's time to bring fin-syn back. "The market has completely changed. It's gotten re-concentrated," he says. "Of the 40 new series airing on the four major broadcast networks in the 2002 season, 77.5 percent are owned in whole or part by the same four networks — an increase of over 37 percent in just one year — and up from only 12.5 percent in 1990," the group said in FCC comments. [41]

"The harm to the public is that they don't see the best work that can be put on television," Rintels says.

When veteran producer Norman Lear, for example, developed the now-classic sitcom "All in the Family" for ABC, the network balked at the controversial dialogue — mainly from bigoted paterfamilias "Archie Bunker" — so he took it to CBS, where it became a huge hit. Nowadays, networks lock producers into contracts that bar them from taking their ideas to competitors, Rintels says.

Other groups fighting to restore fin-syn include the Coalition for Program Diversity, whose members include Sony Pictures Television, the Screen Actors Guild, the Directors Guild and Carsey-Werner-Mandabach, a big independent-production company; and the Caucus for Television Producers, Writers & Directors.

In June 2003, the FCC rejected the idea of restoring fin-syn. "In light of dramatic changes in the television market, including the significant increase in the number of channels available to most households today, we find no basis in the record to conclude that government regulation is necessary to promote source diversity," the FCC said. [42]

Some independent producers, tired of waiting for the FCC to reverse its decision, have moved their television shows online. Herskovitz and partner Edward Zwick made an agreement with MySpace last year to offer a program called "quarterlife," which can be viewed exclusively online. [43]

"People are concerned about the gatekeepers," says PBS' Mitchell, who benefited from fin-syn when she worked earlier in her career as an independent producer. "If it's reached a point now where you've got to own the produc-

## CHRONOLOGY

### 1900-1940s *Government limits the influence of radio and television.*

**1901** Italian inventor Guglielmo Marconi sends wireless signals across Atlantic Ocean, paving the way for radio.

**1920** The first radio broadcast debuts at KDKA, in Pittsburgh.

**1927** Philo T. Farnsworth, the inventor of television, demonstrates the technology for the first time. . . . Federal Radio Commission is established.

**1934** Congress passes 1934 Communications Act, setting guidelines for regulating public airwaves.

**1938** Orson Welles' realistic "War of the Worlds" radio broadcast about a Martian invasion creates pandemonium across the country.

**1941** FCC issues National TV Ownership Rule barring companies from owning more than a few TV stations.

**1946** FCC adopts Dual Network Rule, prohibiting companies from owning more than one radio network, later expanded to include TV.

### 1950s-1960s *Television enters its golden age.*

**1950** Cable TV is introduced in rural Pennsylvania and Oregon. . . . FCC institutes the Fairness Doctrine.

**1954** Color TV debuts.

**1969** Public Broadcasting Service is created.

### 1970s *FCC seeks to limit media growth.*

**1970** FCC prohibits companies from owning radio and TV stations in the same market.

**1975** FCC bans cross-ownership of a broadcast and newspaper outlet in the same market.

### 1980s *New networks revolutionize television.*

**1980** Media visionary Ted Turner creates Cable News Network, ushering in an era of 24-hour cable news.

**1985** Australian media mogul Rupert Murdoch launches the Fox network, a feisty upstart to the Big 3.

**1987** FCC eliminates Fairness Doctrine.

### 1990s *Media concentration accelerates after Congress deregulates telecommunications and eases media-ownership rules.*

**1992** Cable Act requires cable systems to carry local broadcasters.

**1995** FCC allows major TV networks to own production studios.

**1996** Disney acquires Capitol Cities/ABC, combining a studio with a TV network. . . . Congress passes landmark Telecommunications Act, loosening broadcast-ownership restrictions and deregulating cable.

### 2000s *Rampant consolidation and FCC action to loosen ownership rules spark national debate.*

**2000** Viacom merges with CBS, continuing the trend of "vertical integration."

**2001** The largest merger in U.S. history joins AOL and Time Warner.

**2002** Comcast and AT&T merge, forming the nation's largest cable company.

**2003** *June 2:* FCC loosens broadcast-ownership restrictions. Three months later, a federal court orders further review. *Sept. 2:* NBC unveils plan to acquire the film, TV and theme-park assets of Vivendi Universal. *Oct. 6:* Federal court in San Francisco rules that cable providers of high-speed Internet access must include competing Internet services on their systems. The FCC vows to appeal.

**2006** Knight Ridder chain of papers sold for $4.5 billion to McClatchy Co. — McClatchy begins selling off Knight Ridder papers. . . . Viacom and CBS split, CBS becomes CBS Corp.

**2007** Real estate magnate Sam Zell purchases the Tribune Company for $8.2 billion. . . . FCC votes to lighten newspaper-broadcast cross-ownership rules. . . . Rupert Murdoch, owner of media giant News Corp., purchases Dow Jones, owner of *The Wall Street Journal*, for $5 billion.

**2008** *March 24:* The Department of Justice approves the merger between Sirius and XM Satellite radio. *April 24:* Senate Commerce Committee votes to support a resolution of disapproval in reaction to the FCC's crow-ownership rule change.

tion as well as the distribution, then what's going to happen to people who are not in that chain? They're going to get left out, and they are getting left out," she says.

"We do need to have some regulatory policy in place," she adds.

## BACKGROUND

### Regulating the Airwaves

The regulatory structure governing America's media industry was born in the early 1900s, when Congress saw a need to restrict the market power of burgeoning broadcasting companies.

The 1927 Federal Radio Act established the Federal Radio Commission, the precursor to the FCC. Seven years later, Congress passed the watershed 1934 Communications Act, creating the FCC as an independent agency and establishing guidelines for regulating the public airwaves — rules that remain the FCC's guiding principles today.

In the early 1940s, the FCC adopted the National TV Ownership Rule, which prevented networks from owning more than a handful of stations, and restricted their ability to buy radio outlets. In 1943, the FCC and the U.S. Supreme Court ordered NBC to divest one of its networks, which later became its competitor, ABC.

In yet another regulatory step, the FCC in 1946 adopted the Dual Network Rule, barring one radio network from owning another. Later amended to include television, it remains largely intact today, though the FCC amended it in the 1990s to let major networks buy smaller ones.

In the late 1940s, cable television emerged to provide TV service in mountainous and rural areas, but it would take three decades to become a serious competitor to broadcast TV. [44]

During a 1961 speech that was to become a harbinger of the regulatory and political battles ahead, FCC Chairman Newton Minnow, a Democrat, described TV as a "vast wasteland." A decade later, the FCC imposed cross-ownership restrictions designed to limit the influence of major media companies. Under the regulations, an individual media company was barred from owning a TV station and radio property in the same market, or a broadcast outlet and newspaper in the same market.

"It was a good rule for 1975," Dick Wiley, the Republican FCC chairman at the time, said recently of the newspaper-broadcast cross-ownership ban. "We were concerned that newspapers would dominate television, which people forget had only really [become popular] 20 years or so earlier. It's almost 30 years later, and many things are different." Wiley's influential Washington law firm represents clients that oppose the ban. [45]

Also in the '70s, with only three commercial networks and PBS available over-the-air, cable television became more competitive. As it grew in popularity, its fare would become more niche-oriented. [46]

### Deregulation Begins

The era of deregulation began in earnest in the 1980s, under the Reagan administration and FCC Chairman Mark Fowler, a Republican who famously likened television to a toaster with pictures — simply another household appliance.

In 1981, the FCC ended its decades-old policy of "ascertainment" for radio stations. The policy required broadcasters to visit community groups and leaders to ascertain what types of programming they wanted and whether broadcasters were serving their needs. The FCC ended ascertainment for TV outlets in 1984. "We determined that it was excessive meddling on our part," says Robert Ratcliffe, deputy chief of the FCC's Media Bureau.

When the idea of requiring ascertainment is broached today with broadcast executives, "Those people jump up and down and say, 'Oh no, that's the heavy hand of regulation coming back. We can't consider something like that,'" Democratic FCC Commissioner Copps says.

In 1985, Fowler oversaw another deregulatory move: The FCC increased from seven to 12 the number of television stations that a single entity was permitted to own. [47]

Fowler also made it his mission to eliminate the Fairness Doctrine. Introduced in 1950, it gave citizens free airtime to reply to criticism leveled against them on TV or radio. [48] Journalists complained that the government should not be dictating editorial content, and the FCC decided that the abundance of media voices made the requirement obsolete. The FCC, which had already concluded that the policy might be unconstitutional, ended it in 1987 after a District of Columbia Circuit Court ruled the agency was no longer required to enforce it. [49]

The prime-time access rule was rescinded along with the Fairness Doctrine. It restricted local TV stations in the top 50 markets to airing only three hours of network programming during prime time, except on Sundays.

# Alternative Media on the Rise

By day, Tony Adragna toils for a Washington-area nonprofit and Will Vehrs works in Virginia's state government. But in their free time they're bloggers, filing constantly updated pontifications on their Web log, an online journal called "Shouting 'Cross the Potomac." In 2004 their blog, at www.quasipundit.blogspot.com, garnered them enough attention to be interviewed on C-SPAN.

"Bloggers are a real window on the world, a really great supplement to reporters who may have trouble . . . getting to . . . a story," Vehrs said, noting that blogs (short for Web logs) provided instant coverage of the Sept. 11, 2001, terrorist attacks and the Aug. 14, 2003, blackout in the Northeast. [1]

Blogs and many other big-media alternatives that have surfaced in recent years don't meet the traditional definitions — or standards — of mainstream news outlets, often providing information that's largely unfiltered by professional editors. But that may be less important to citizens today because the major media — from *The New York Times* to the TV networks — have shown they can still get the facts wrong. [2]

While most blogs feature the writings, rantings and musings of everyday people who simply want to post their thoughts, some bloggers are media stars, such as former *New Republic* Editor Andrew Sullivan, whose "Daily Dish" blog can be found at www.andrewsullivan.com, and Glenn Reynolds, the creator of www.InstaPundit.com. Both sites feature continuously updated commentary on the latest news headlines and, in the case of Reynolds, links to other blogs.

Millions of people now blog, and the number is still growing. Because of its popularity, many are taking a closer look at the economic potential of the medium — i.e., charging for access and running ads.

Seizing on the blog wave, Internet service provider AOL now offers its subscribers blogging at no extra charge. And the Internet search engine Google purchased the company that makes Blogger, a free program to create blogs. [3]

Beyond Web logs, Americans also get their Internet news from sites operated by mainstream news organiza-

tions, such as CNN or *The Washington Post*, Internet-only magazines such as *Slate* and *Salon* and cybergossip Matt Drudge. Breaking e-mail news alerts are now commonplace, and for many Web users, the headlines on RSS feeds or Internet search engines are the first place they get news.

As competition from new and old news media grows, longtime players are becoming more flexible — and in the eyes of some, softening their standards. Consider Baltimore-based Sinclair Broadcasting, which relies on its Central Casting division to provide news and commentary to half of its 58 stations nationwide. From a studio near Baltimore, its news anchors provide newscasts to Pittsburgh, Raleigh, N.C., Flint, Mich., and other cities. Sinclair says Central Casting enables small, limited-resource stations to offer local news, but critics say the arrangement saves money at the expense of local coverage. [4]

Meanwhile, alternative news sites also have emerged. AlterNet.org, created in 1998 to provide its own brand of "investigative journalism," reaches more than 1.7 million readers each month through its Web publications. [5]

So far, however, the Internet is hardly a full-fledged alternative to traditional media. According to Nielsen ratings, the 20 most-popular Internet news sites are dominated by major media conglomerates, such as NBC and Microsoft, which co-own MSNBC.com, and CNN.com, operated by Time Warner. [6]

Apart from news, the Internet also provides alternative, low-cost publishing. Among the newest trends are "online content marketplaces," such as redpaper.com and Lulu.com. The sites provide little editing and let contributors set readership prices as low as pennies a page.

"It's great for grandpa doing his memoirs, and it's great for the family cookbook — people who can't get published anywhere else," said George Farrier, a 73-year old contributor to Lulu.com from Greenfield, Mo. [7] Lulu, which features lengthier writings, including many books, boasts to visitors that it "allows content to flow directly from creator to consumer. That means creators can keep 80 percent of

---

The FCC had hoped the rule would encourage local public-affairs programming in time slots leading into prime time, but instead broadcasters often ran syndicated game shows, sitcom reruns and the like. [50]

As the broadcast industry was being progressively

deregulated, Congress was turning its regulatory sights on the growing cable industry. In 1992, responding to consumer complaints, Congress passed legislation regulating cable rates and imposing other restrictions on cable monopolies. Meanwhile, direct-broadcast satellite

the royalty from each sale, ownership of their work and the rights to sell it anywhere else."

In addition to alternative news and publishing, new technologies also offer alternative entertainment sources. About 250 low-power FM (LPFM) radio stations have cropped up across the country, mostly in small cities and rural areas. Another 600 or 700 of these 100-watt, non-commercial radio stations are expected to be operational soon.

Low-power radio gives a voice to nonprofits, such as religious groups, educational institutions and local governments, similar to the public access provided by local cable channels. Supporters hope LPFM will gain ground now that a recent study finds they would cause very little interference with commercial stations' signals. [8] Full-power radio broadcasters have opposed licensing LPFM stations in major markets because they feared interference, but supporters say the new report should silence those concerns.

Nevertheless, it could take a while for low-power FM to become a popular alternative to commercial radio. "Right now, a minuscule percentage of the public can tune in," says Michael Bracy, co-founder of the Future of Music Coalition, made up of radio and music interests who support LPFM expansion and oppose consolidation by Clear Channel and other big radio players.

Hedging their bets, some mainstream media companies are switching to newer technologies, or at least making investments in them. Clear Channel Communications, the dominant force in broadcast radio, has invested in XM Satellite Radio, the subscription service that more than 170 stations of music and other programming with few commercials and no cackling deejays. As part of the deal, XM carries some Clear Channel stations. [9]

Broadcast television is also evolving, as it slowly switches from analog to digital technology, which provides crisp, high-definition images and allows each broadcaster to offer multiple signals in each market. The transition, which was supposed to be complete by 2006, is expected to take much longer because of slow consumer demand, due in part to pricey digital sets and lack of awareness about digital TV. The FCC has now set a deadline February 17, 2009 for the digital switch to be completed. Squabbles with cable systems over signal carriage, industry bickering over copyright-protection standards and stations' difficulties raising capital to convert equipment have contributed to the delays.

In April 2002, the U.S. General Accounting Office (GAO) said many TV stations would not meet the May 2002 deadline for offering a digital signal. [10] Then in November 2002, the GAO said more federal intervention will be needed for the digital transition to occur. [11]

Meanwhile, some Web-based alternative media have made the jump to more mainstream outlets. Thesmokinggun.com, known for obtaining controversial documents and photos, was born during the dot-com boom of the late 1990s and was later purchased by Court TV. In 2003, it spawned "Smoking Gun TV," on Court TV, as well as a radio program carried by Infinity-owned stations. There was also a twice-monthly column in *People* magazine. [12]

---

[1] See transcript of C-SPAN's "Washington Journal," Aug. 15, 2003.

[2] For background, see Brian Hansen, "Combating Plagiarism," *CQ Researcher*, Sept. 19, 2003, pp. 773-796.

[3] *The Economist*, "Golden Blogs," Aug. 16, 2003.

[4] Jim Rutenberg and Micheline Maynard, "TV News That Looks Local, Even If It's Not," *The New York Times*, p. C1, June 2, 2003, p. C1.

[5] For more information, visit www.alternet.org.

[6] See "Top 20 Internet News Sites," Nielsen Media Research (see www.nielsen-netratings.com for more information), November 2002.

[7] Wailin Wong, "Web Sites Offer Unsung Writers Chance to Sing," *The Wall Street Journal*, Sept. 18, 2003, p. B1.

[8] Mitre Corp., "Experimental Measurements of the Third-Adjacent Channel Impacts of Low-Power FM Stations," released on June 30, 2003; http://hraunfoss.fcc.gov/edocs_public/attachmatch/DA-03-2277A1.doc.

[9] Frank Ahrens, "Why Radio Stinks," *The Washington Post Magazine*, Jan. 19, 2003, p. 24.

[10] "Many Broadcasters Will Not Meet May 2002 Digital Television Deadline," General Accounting Office (02-466), April 2002.

[11] "Additional Federal Efforts Could Help Advance Digital Television Transition," General Accounting Office (03-07), November 2002.

[12] Cesar G. Soriano, "The Smoking Gun Joins High-Caliber Media," *USA Today*, Aug. 18, 2003, p. 3D.

---

(DBS), which made satellite-TV technology more accessible by offering consumers pizza-sized dishes for reception, was introduced in 1994. [51]

In 1995, when the FCC eliminated the fin-syn rules restricting network ownership of programming, it ushered in an era of vertical integration in which the major networks merged with Hollywood studios. Also in the mid-'90s, after months of congressional hearings, debate and intensive lobbying by affected industry parties, Congress passed the sweeping 1996

Telecommunications Act, giving media companies a green light to consolidate and own more radio and TV properties in various markets.

The act also deregulated cable and expanded the audience reach of network-owned stations from 25 percent of U.S. households to 35 percent. In the ensuing years, broadcast TV networks and major cable companies would merge with other huge companies, transforming themselves into vertically integrated media giants controlling both the production and distribution of content.

In yet another loosening of its rules, the FCC in 1999 permitted more duopolies — the single ownership of two TV stations in a market — under certain conditions. Eight independent TV stations had to remain in the market after the combination, and none of the combined stations could be among the top four in the market. Before that, duopolies were permitted on a very limited basis, through waivers intended to aid struggling stations.

In June 2003, the FCC tweaked its duopoly rules again: If eight independent TV stations remain after the combination, a top-four TV station can combine with a non-top-four station in the same market.

Although industry executives insist that duopolies result in better-quality news because of the expanded resources available to the combined stations, critics say that's often not the case. "With the joining together of the two newsrooms, there's not a whole lot of original programming," complained Sylvia Teague, a former news executive and producer with the duopoly involving KCBS-TV and KCAL-TV in Los Angeles. She is now director of a project on broadcast political coverage at the University of Southern California's Annenberg School of Journalism. [52]

In October 2001, the two largest DBS companies — DirecTV and EchoStar — decided to merge, claiming the deal would create a formidable competitor to the cable-TV monopolies. But consumer groups said it would be anticompetitive to create a satellite monopoly. In the end, regulators blocked the deal. Now Murdoch's News Corp. is seeking to buy DirecTV, the nation's largest DBS provider.

Some 88 million Americans subscribe to multichannel video services such as cable and satellite, according to the FCC's 2002 report on video competition. The vast majority — 68.8 million — are cable subscribers. [53]

## Complaints Increase

In recent years, the public has become increasingly dissatisfied with the media, fueled by concerns about everything from too much explicit sex and violence on TV to the botched predictions made by the networks the night of the 2000 presidential election to the recent journalism-fraud scandals at papers such as *The New York Times.* [54]

The public's cynicism was further fueled when big media outlets mostly ignored reporting on the FCC's efforts to relax its media-ownership rules until the agency voted on June 2, 2003. Critics smelled a rat because many media properties lobbied in support of some or all of the new rules and stood to gain financially by their implementation.

"I just have to think there's something we should question about the lack of a national debate, the lack of editorials and really engaged reporting on an issue as important as this until the consumers themselves began to respond," says PBS' Mitchell, whose network was not affected by the FCC decision. The PBS program "Now with Bill Moyers" was among the few news shows that devoted significant coverage to the story.

Further exacerbating suspicions about big media companies, some recent studies suggest that media consolidation has taken a toll on news quality and depth of coverage. A five-year study of local television stations finds that despite the fact that network owned-and-operated stations (O&Os) have far more resources, smaller station groups produce better-quality news — by a "significant" margin. [55]

"Affiliates were more likely to air stories that affected everyone in the community, while O&Os were more likely to air national stories with no local connection — those car chases and exciting footage from far away," the report found.

Meanwhile, television stations have eliminated or dramatically reduced their election coverage. Of the stations that did cover the 2006 midterm elections, most focused only on the "horse race" during the final weeks of the race and ignored the issues being debated. According to a University of Wisconsin study, stories about elections taking place in the Midwest were limited to 76 seconds each, with more than one in 10 of these stories being about campaign ads rather than the campaign issues. [56]

## New Media Landscape

The raging controversy over the FCC's decisions in 2003 and 2007 to relax its media-ownership rules triggered plenty of comparisons between today's media marketplace and TV's so-called golden age a few decades ago.

"Even in small towns, the number of media outlets — including cable, satellite, radio, TV stations and newspapers — has increased more than 250 percent during the past 40 years," wrote former FCC Chairman Powell. [57] But there are fewer media owners. For example, a decade ago there were 12,000 radio stations with 5,100 owners. [58] Today there are more radio stations — 13,000 [59] — but only 3,800 owners. [60]

Two or three decades ago, there were more newspapers in large cities, says Kalb of Harvard's Shorenstein Center. Today there are roughly the same number of newspapers nationwide, but that's because there are more small suburban and small-town newspapers, he says. But today's small-town papers cover mostly local news and are not substitutes for major dailies, Kalb says.

Some industry observers are nostalgic for the days when there were only three major television networks because they feel the news coverage was more in-depth and less sensational. Robert J. Thompson, professor of television and popular culture at Syracuse University, said the comparative lack of choice when only three networks existed paradoxically served the public interest well.

"All three networks would carry presidential debates, State of the Union speeches and the national political conventions," he wrote. [61] Today, coverage of such events on broadcast TV is far more limited.

## CURRENT SITUATION

### TV Industry Split

The FCC's decision to raise the broadcast-ownership cap has cast a spotlight on an embarrassing schism within the television industry that threatens to undermine its lobbying muscle on ownership issues.

In 2003, the networks want the cap upped to 45 percent or removed altogether. But local network affiliates want to preserve the cap at 35 percent, because they worry that if the networks own too many stations, they'll have too much sway over the programs the affiliates air. As the networks grow larger, it's more difficult for local affiliates to resist when the networks want to pre-empt local programming. President George Bush compromised, and signed a law limiting the cap at 39 percent rather than 45 percent, but both caps were overturned in 2004. [62]

"The right to reject or pre-empt network programming must remain at the local level for stations to discharge their duty to reflect what they believe is right for their individual communities," said Jim Goodmon, president and CEO of Capitol Broadcasting Co., which owns five TV stations and radio outlets in the Carolinas. Testifying before a Senate Commerce Committee hearing, Goodmon continued, "Whether it is to reject network programming based on community standards or whether it is to pre-empt national network programming in order to air a Billy Graham special, the Muscular Dystrophy Telethon or local sports, I can't imagine that anyone in this room really wants to take away local control over television programming." [63]

The spat has implications for the National Association of Broadcasters (NAB), the TV industry's fierce lobby, which has been abandoned in recent years by the influential Big Four networks over the ownership issue.

NAB opposed the FCC's 2003 decision to raise the cap and said it supported congressional efforts to roll it back to 35 percent. But NAB did support the FCC's 2007 ownership decision. In a letter to Martin, NAB members wrote, "This order very modestly reformed the complete ban on newspaper/broadcast cross-ownership and made no changes to the television duopoly and local radio-ownership rules. . . . There is no reason for the commission to retreat." [64]

### Reaction to Rules

Angered that the FCC relaxed the ownership rules too much, a growing chorus of lawmakers is aggressively moving to rescind at least key portions of it, including Senators Dorgan, Hillary Clinton (D-NY), Barack Obama (D-IL), John Kerry (D-MA), Olympia Snowe (R-ME) and former Senator Trent Lott (R-MS).

Their major complaint is that, while the FCC did not reverse the entire newspaper-broadcast cross-ownership ban, neither did it take any of the deregulatory steps that many Democrats would have liked to see.

Senator John Dingell (D-MI), chairman of the House Energy and Commerce Committee, was extremely displeased that Chairman Martin went ahead with the FCC vote, giving weight to the comments received from stakeholders. "Despite specific bipartisan and bicameral opposition, the Federal Communications Commission acted arrogantly and brazenly today to weaken the newspaper/broadcast cross-ownership ban. While the Commission did tighten some loopholes in the rule, I am greatly displeased that the Chairman chose to vote on this important issue a mere week after hundreds of pages of comment were submitted on his proposed rule. I question whether the Commission gave adequate, or any, consideration to the public's input. I am also deeply dismayed that the Commission granted dozens of waivers of the new rule without any opportunity for public comment. The Commission has squandered an opportunity to reach agreement on even more meaningful ways to provide concrete benefits to consumers in the form of more minority media ownership and attention to localism. The FCC is a creature of Congress, and these matters will be the subject of rigorous oversight by the Committee on Energy and Commerce." [65]

Martin has fought back, noting after the FCC's vote that "Newspapers in financial difficulty oftentimes have little choice but to scale back local news gathering to cut costs. In 2007 alone, 24 newsroom staff at *The Boston Globe* were fired, including 2 Pulitzer Prize-winning reporters; *The Minneapolis Star Tribune* fired 145 employees, including 50 from their newsroom; 20 were fired by *The Rocky Mountain News*; *The Detroit Free Press* and *The Detroit News* announced cuts totaling 110 employees; and *The San Francisco Chronicle* planned to cut 25 percent of its newsroom staff." He says that the new ownership rules may slow or stop the "erosion in local news coverage by enabling companies to share the high fixed costs of newsgathering across multiple media platforms." [66]

The Senate Commerce Committee voted in late April 2008 to pass a resolution of disapproval in reaction to the rewrite of ownership rules, which would essentially reverse the FCC's decision. While the resolution of disapproval is rarely used, it came up in 2003 when the FCC voted to change the ownership cap. The resolution passed the Senate almost unanimously on May 15, and will now move to the House, where it is expected to be approved. [67] President Bush has already threatened a veto.

When the FCC tried to relax the rules in 2003, the Senate passed just such a resolution of disapproval 55 to 40, but then House Majority Leader Tom DeLay (R-Texas) warned it wouldn't make it past the House — and he was right, though it failed by only a small portion.

## Chairmen Under Fire

The controversy over ownership in 2003 focused on more than just regulation. Former FCC Chairman Powell was under attack from both parties for shepherding the sweeping rule changes through his agency.

Critics said the FCC, which held only one official hearing on media concentration before it voted, rushed to adopt the changes and refused to compromise with Democratic FCC commissioners. [68] Powell countered that the agency issued 12 studies last fall examining the issues.

Critics insist Powell misjudged the guidance of the courts by developing relaxed ownership rules. In fact, a federal appeals court in Washington had struck down the last five media-ownership rules it had reviewed, tossing them back to the agency. Powell said the court told the FCC to get rid of the rules, but critics say the court instructed the agency to justify them, not discard them.

The FCC received at least 2 million e-mails, letters and postcards expressing opposition to the rule changes, though Powell was quick to point out that three-quarters of the messages were sent by NRA members. [69]

Constant rumors in the press that the chairman would resign forced him to repeatedly deny he'd leave the FCC before his term expired.

In the debate over the FCC's 2007 move, Chairman Martin has come under fire for announcing his decision to vote on the measure in a *New York Times* op-ed piece, rather than through traditional means. One day after an interview with the *Times* on the future of the media and deregulation, Martin's op-ed piece explained that newspapers are financially strapped, and unless they are allowed to broadcast via radio or television, they wouldn't be around much longer. So, he said, he wanted to allow "a company that owns a newspaper in one of the largest cities in the country" to "purchase a broadcast TV or radio station in the same market." [70]

Critics also say that Martin is doing exactly what Powell did in 2003. They believe that Martin did not have a sufficient amount of time to look over documents from Congress and other concerned groups in opposition to the rule change before his vote took place, nor did he allow the four other FCC commissioners time to get a full grasp of what his proposal would entail. According to the Media Access Project's Schwartzman, "Between October 22 and November 1 of this year, the FCC has received several thousand pages of highly substantive research which calls into question the studies the FCC released this summer. Between October 1 and October 16, the FCC received hundreds of pages of new filings about the impact of the Commission's ownership rules on minority ownership." He went on to say that a review of all this information would have taken weeks, but Chairman Martin made his decision within days and called for a vote to take place about a month after the final comments were filed. [71]

# Are the major TV networks committed to localism? *

## YES

**Mel Karmazin**
*President and COO, Viacom Inc.*

From testimony before Senate Commerce, Transportation and Science Committee, May 13, 2003

It is utterly unsupportable and unrealistic that broadcasters should be handcuffed in their attempts to compete for consumers at a time when Americans are bombarded with media choices via technologies never dreamed of even a decade ago, much less 60 years ago when some of these rules were first adopted. . . .

Most television stations in this country are held by multi-station groups owned by large corporations headquartered in cities located far from their stations' communities of license. What does it matter that Viacom's main offices are in New York? The corporate group owners are no more "local" in the cities where they own TV stations than is Viacom. Yet, like Viacom and all good broadcasters, group owners work hard to know what viewers want in each market where it has a media outlet. Localism is just good business.

Networks invest billions of dollars in programming, but most of the return on their investment is realized at the station level. Only two of the so-called "Big Four" networks are profitable in any year [compared] to television stations — run by networks and affiliates alike — which operate on margins anywhere from 20 percent to 50 percent.

If networks are precluded from realizing more of the revenue generated by stations, networks' ability to continue their multi-billion-dollar programming investments will diminish, and more and more programming will migrate from broadcasting to cable and satellite TV, where regulation is less onerous. More Americans then will have to pay for what they now get for free.

[The] argument that affiliates provide more local news than do network-owned-and-operated stations is, again, false. In a study commissioned by Viacom, Fox and NBC, Economists Inc. found that the average TV station owned by a network provides more local news per week — 37 percent more — than the average affiliate, a finding consistent with the FCC's own independently conducted study. . . .

Nor is it true that affiliates stand as the bulwark against allegedly inappropriate network programming. . . . Pre-emptions based on content are rare. But in the handful of cases over the past years when an affiliate has determined that a program's subject may be too sensitive for its market — as was the case last week with our Providence affiliate with respect to the "CSI: Miami" episode dealing with fire hazards at nightclubs — we understand and accommodate. Our own stations would do the same thing for their markets' viewers.

## NO

**Tom Daschle, D-S.D.**
*Minority Leader, U.S. Senate*

From a statement on the Senate floor, Sept. 16, 2003

Many argue there are an infinite number of media outlets today, especially given the huge growth in cable channels and Internet addresses.

But the vast majority of Americans get their news and information from television news and/or their local newspaper. None of the cable-news channels has anywhere near the viewership of the broadcast media, and most of the major cable and Internet news outlets are affiliated with the print and broadcast media already controlled in large part by just a handful of companies. Diversity of viewpoints is already in jeopardy, and the new rules would only exacerbate the situation. . . .

If many of those so-called diverse viewpoints are actually controlled by a handful of companies, then one can see that localism, too, is in trouble. The loss of localism in radio is well known, sometimes with dangerous consequences like the famous Minot, N.D., case.

In fact, the lack of localism in radio is so undeniable that even the FCC has agreed to address it in the one aspect of the proposed rules that makes sense.

But localism in television is also at risk — local entertainment choices as well as news. James Goodmon of Capitol Broadcasting in North Carolina explained it well in his testimony before the Commerce Committee.

He owns Fox and CBS stations in Raleigh. Out of respect for his local audience's sensibilities, he has refused to carry either network's "reality TV" shows, including "Temptation Island," "Cupid," "Who Wants to Marry a Millionaire" and "Married by America."

His actions have met with intense resistance from the networks, and he has expressed his grave concern that if the networks' ability to own more and more of the broadcast outlets goes unchecked, local stations and communities won't have any ability to choose their own programming. They will be forced to air the network fare, even when it is offensive to local viewers. . . .

Let me be clear: I don't blame the media companies for advocating for their own interests. They have every right to fight for their interests.

I do blame the chairman of the FCC and the other commissioners who voted for these rules for failing to give the rest of the country the consideration they deserved in this debate.

---

\* Localism refers to serving a community's needs and tastes.

This is not the first time Chairman Martin's FCC has overlooked important information: A pattern came to light in 2006 that it tried to hide two studies about the detrimental impact consolidation can have on local media outlets.

Some are hopeful that Martin won't be around much longer — his term may be up if a Democrat comes into the White House, or if a new Republican president decides to throw him out.

### Cable Debate

While broadcast and newspaper outlets have taken the brunt of the criticism lately, cable is not off the hook. If anything, it could be the next regulatory target, industry observers say. In a recent move, the FCC adopted a rule that bans any cable company from serving more than 30 percent of national pay-TV subscribers. [72] The rule will affect Comcast, which was planning to make a large acquisition. Experts say the cable industry will take the ruling to court, especially after a previous cap was declared unconstitutional by a federal appeals court in 2001.

In November 2007, the two Democratic FCC commissioners and Chairman Martin decided to reduce the rate charged by cable companies to independent programmers to buy time on unused channels. This move was meant to open up more ownership options for minorities and women, as well as promoting competition. The 75 percent cut would mean that cable companies could not charge interested buyers more than 10 cents per month per subscriber. [73] The National Cable & Telecommunications Association argues that cable companies wouldn't make any money or have any incentive to sell the time, and would essentially be giving away their channels, a violation of federal law. It also believes that the move could invite more low-value content. Verizon Communications is suing the FCC over the matter. [74]

According to a 2003 report by the consumer group U.S. PIRG, the top 10 cable operators serve about 85 percent of all cable subscribers and the top three — Comcast, Time Warner and Charter — serve about 56 percent, up 8 percent since 1996. Cable operators also dominate the high-speed Internet-access business, yet the cable industry operates largely unregulated. [75]

In 95 percent of all U.S. households, there is access to only one cable service. [76] In most markets, cable offers little in the way of local news, although regional cable-news channels have sprung up in some large metro areas.

Meanwhile, the average monthly basic-plus-extended cable bill climbed 5.2 percent — from $40.91 to $43.09 — over the 12-month period ending January 1, 2005. During this same period, basic only cable climbed 3.3 percent, from $13.84 to $14.30, and expanded basic climbed 6.2 percent, from $27.07 to $28.74. [77]

Democratic Commissioner Adelstein commented on the FCC's cable price findings, noting, "The price to consumers for cable service increased an average of 5.2 percent this year to bring the 10-year total price increase on cable television rates to a whopping 93 percent. Few other goods and services in America cost nearly twice today what they did in 1995. And as anyone would expect from looking at these ever-rising prices, the cable companies behind them have swelling revenues year in and year out regardless of the overall American economy." [78]

Over the years, allegations have arisen that some cable companies play hardball with programmers and sometimes refuse to carry competing channels. Cox Enterprises, Inc., for example, which has a partial stake in the parent of the Discovery Channel, doesn't carry the rival National Geographic Channel. "We carry more than 200 channels, and we own 10 of them, and we have 55 movie channels and own three," Cablevision spokesman Charles Schueler said. "To suggest that we favor our own programming is absurd." [79]

Robert Sachs, president and CEO of the National Cable and Telecommunications Association, added, "Since 1992, the percentage of program networks in which cable operators have any financial interest has plummeted from 48 percent to less than 21 percent. At the same time, the number of available channels has skyrocketed from 87 to 308. There are more than six times as many non-cable-owned channels as there were a decade ago." [80]

## OUTLOOK

### More Mergers?

There is no question that mergers are on the rise, be they between newspapers or television or radio stations. Even without the FCC's decision to allow some newspaper-broadcast cross-ownership, the recent state of the media has been one of consolidation, buying and selling at many levels. A lot of the "merger mania" has to do with the plummeting value of print news sources now that the Internet is a readily available source of constantly updating news.

In 2003, Merrill media analyst Jessica Reif Cohen wrote, "There may be a bantam wave of media mergers, but surely not the tsunami envisioned." She must not have seen the tidal wave coming. [81]

Within the past few years, quite a few media power companies have been sold, including Knight Ridder, Dow Jones and the Tribune Company. Since 2000, four public newspaper companies have vanished — Dow Jones, Knight Ridder, Tribune and Pulitzer — and two other media corporations are expected to divide up their companies to make them more profitable.

Some owners have had little problem keeping their corporations profitable. Rupert Murdoch's News Corp. seems to be holding off any effects from the slow economy and the evolving newspaper industry. His unsolicited bid to buy Dow Jones, publisher of *The Wall Street Journal*, was a 67 percent increase on the value of Dow Jones' stock, and came on the heels of his purchase of satellite giant DirecTV. [82] While Dow Jones joined Murdoch's already $68-billion empire, he's not completely immune to market forces, recently withdrawing a bid for New York's *Newsday* shortly before the purchase was expected to go through. His spokeswoman hinted that the $580 million price might go higher, which was uneconomical for News Corp. [83]

Real estate baron Sam Zell has so far had a different experience with his purchase of the Tribune Company for $8.2 billion in 2007. He borrowed heavily to finance the purchase and is still in financial trouble. To end his bad luck, Zell has put some pieces of the company on the market, most recognizably the Chicago Cubs baseball organization. [84]

McClatchy seemed to know what was coming when it bought Knight Ridder for $4.5 billion in 2006, and immediately began selling off papers in slow-growth markets, getting rid of 12 in all, including the *San Jose Mercury News*, *Philadelphia Enquirer* and *Akron-Beacon Journal*. [85]

After years of speculation and negotiation, the potential Microsoft-Yahoo merger fell through, after Yahoo rejected Microsoft's bid, and Microsoft said it wouldn't bid over what it thought Yahoo was worth — $33 per share. [86]

Fallout from the FCC's decision, coupled with a court-imposed stay, has created considerable uncertainty and dampened the acquisition fervor. Nevertheless, a few transactions have been announced since the FCC's action, the largest being NBC's acquisition of Vivendi Universal's entertainment assets.

In 2003, the FCC approved the Spanish-television merger between Univision and Hispanic Broadcasting Corp., saying it would not harm diversity of programming for viewers of the networks. But it did require the companies to shed some radio properties to comply with new radio market rules adopted in the summer of 2003. [87]

Meanwhile, FCC Chairman Martin has repeatedly argued that newspapers are in danger of disappearing because of the onslaught of the Internet and around-the-clock news available on cable. In his *New York Times* op-ed, Martin agreed with the paper's publisher that newspapers are in financial trouble. But, according to the Media Access Project's Schwartzman, "newspaper publishing's operating profits are among the highest of any industry." He also goes on to say that Dean Singleton, CEO of MediaNews Group, says the newspaper industry is "not a dying business, it's a changing business." [88]

While Chairman Martin thinks newspapers will lose out to the Internet, Singleton argues that the Internet is beneficial to newspapers in the way they are able to reach more users. A recent study showed that 10 of the nation's top 20 Web sites are maintained by newspapers. [89]

The big worry among Chairman Martin's critics is what will happen to local news if consolidation is allowed to continue at the rate it has. According to FCC data, "89 percent of those surveyed list newspapers or broadcasting as both their first and second important sources of local news." Schwartzman says the increasing consolidation decreases the number of independent voices as well as the number of news sources available. [90]

Ironically, media concentration helped to encourage the strong buying. "The consolidation of sellers and buyers has made it easy to move a market quickly," said Gene DeWitt, president of the Syndicated Network Television Association. [91]

Copps thinks if the consolidation trend continues, the Internet could be a future regulatory battleground. "I'm worried about the openness of the Internet, and companies having control over the gateways to the information there," he says.

## NOTES

1. Jim Rutenberg, "To Interview Former P.O.W., CBS Offers Stardom," *The New York Times*, June 16, 2003, p. A1.

2. Lynn Elber, "CBS May Have Erred in Pursuit of Lynch Interview, Executive Says," Associated Press/TBO.com, July 20, 2003.

3. For background, see Kenneth Jost, "The Future of Television," *CQ Researcher*, Dec. 23, 1994, pp. 1129-1152.

4. Marc Fisher, "Sounds Familiar for a Reason," *The Washington Post*, May 18, 2003, p. B1.

5. The State of the News Media 2008," Center for Excellence in Journalism, March 2008.

6. *Ibid.*

7. Adam Thierer, "Thinking Seriously about Cable & Satellite Censorship: An Informal Analysis of S. 616, The Rockefeller-Hutchison Bill," The Progress & Freedom Foundation, April 2005, www.pff.org/ issues-pubs/ pops/pop12.6cablecensorship.pdf.

8. Media Access Project, *Prometheus v. FCC*, Summary of the Third Circuit Opinion, June 24, 2004, www.mediaaccess.org/prometheus_decision/promet heussummaryfinal062404.pdf.

9. See "Mass Deregulation of Media Threatens to Undermine Democracy," Consumer Federation of America, June 3, 2003.

10. "FCC Adopts Revision to Newspaper/Broadcast Cross-Ownership Rule," FCC Press Release, Dec. 18, 2007, www.fcc.gov/ownership/actions.html.

11. www.nytimes.com/2007/12/18/business/18cnd-fcc .html?_r=1&pagewanted=2&8br&oref=slogin.

12. Ira Teinowitz, "25 Senators Promise to Block Changes to Media Ownership Rules," *TV Week*, Dec. 17, 2007, www.tvweek.com/news/2007/12/25_senators_promise _to_block_c.php.

13. Stephen Labaton, "Senate Debates Repeal of FCC Media Ownership Rules," *The New York Times*, Sept. 12, 2003, p. C3.

14. For background, see David Masci, "The Future of Telecommunications," *CQ Researcher*, April 23, 1999, pp. 329-352.

15. FCC Localism Initiative, www.fcc.gov/localism.

16. "Out of the Picture 2007: Minority & Female TV Station Ownership in the United States," Free Press, October 2007. www.freepress.net/files/otp2007.pdf.

17. "Out of the Picture 2007," *op. cit.*

18. "Big Media: Good, Bad or Both?," Poynter Online, May 1, 2007, www.poynter.org/column.asp?id =101&aid=122318.

19. Paul Farhi, "Mega-Media: Better or More of the Same?" *The Washington Post*, June 3, 2003, p. C1.

20. "Big Media," Poynter Online, *op. cit.*

21. Eli Noam, "The media concentration debate," *Financial Times*, July 31 2003, p. A16.

22. "The State of the News Media 2008," Center for Excellence in Journalism, March 2008.

23. Adam Thierer and Clyde Wayne Crews Jr., "What Media Monopolies?" *The Wall Street Journal*, July 29, 2003, p. B2.

24. See "Free TV Swallowed by Media Giants: The Way It Really Is," Consumer Federation of America, Center for Digital Democracy, Sept. 15, 2003, p. 3.

25. Adam Lashinsky, "Americans Stupid? Media to Blame? Leading thinkers weigh in at Fortune's Brainstorm 2003 conference," *Fortune*, July 31, 2003.

26. See "Does Ownership Matter in Local Television News: A Five-Year Study of Ownership and Quality," Project for Excellence in Journalism, April 29, 2003.

27. "Network vs. Local TV News Consumption," Project for Excellence in Journalism, March 13, 2005, www.journalism.org/node/1381.

28. Michael Ventre, "Lay Off Katie Couric! CBS is to Blame," April 10, 2008, www.msnbc.msn.com/id/ 24054407.

29. Catherine Yang, "FCC's Loner is No Longer So Lonely," *Business Week*, March 24, 2003, p. 78.

30. Labaton, *op. cit.*

31. "Dorgan, Snowe Resolution to Block FCC's Media Ownership Rules Approved by Senate," Senator Snowe press release, May 16, 2008, http:// snowe.senate.gov/public/index.cfm?FuseAction=Press Room.PressReleases&ContentRecord_id=f2a37db0 -802a-23ad-4580-e5ae52448a98.

32. Joint Statement by FCC Commissioners Michael J. Copps and Jonathan S. Adelstein on Release of Media Ownership Order, Feb. 4, 2008.

33. National Journal's CongressDaily, "Dorgan Blasts FCC Plans to Vote on Media Ownership Rules," Oct. 18, 2007.

34. "Dissenting Statement of Commissioner Michael J. Copps," press release, Dec. 18, 2007, www.fcc.gov/ownership/actions.html.

35. "Testimony of Andrew Jay Schwartzman, President and CEO, Media Access Project," Delivered to the Subcommittee on Telecommunications and the Internet, Dec. 5, 2007.

36. FCC Adopts Rules to Promote Diversification of Broadcast Ownership, press release, Dec. 18, 2007.

37. Meg James, "The Vivendi Deal; Creator of 'Law & Order' is Facing Chance of Being Outgunned in Talks," *Los Angeles Times*, Sept. 4, 2003, p. C1.

38. Herskovitz, Marshall, "Are the suits ruining TV?" *The Los Angeles Times*, Nov. 7, 2007.

39. Bill Carter and Jim Rutenberg, "Deregulating the Media: Opponents, Shows' Creators Say Television Will Suffer in New Climate," *The New York Times*, June 3, 2003, p. C1.

40. Bill McConnell, "McCain Weighs in for Fin-Syn," *Broadcasting & Cable*, May 26, 2003, p. 2.

41. See petition for reconsideration filed at FCC by Center for the Creative Community and Association of Independent Video and Filmmakers, available at www.creativecommunity.us, Sept. 4, 2003, pp. 7-8.

42. See "Report and Order," *op. cit.*, p. 15.

43. Michael Cieply, "2 producers head directly to the Internet," *International Herald Tribune*, Sept. 14, 2007.

44. See "Data Gathering Weakness in FCC's Survey of Information on Factors Underlying Cable Rate Changes," General Accounting Office, May 6, 2003, p. 2.

45. Stephen Labaton, "Behind Media Rule and Its End, One Man," *The New York Times*, June 2, 2003, p. C1.

46. For background, see Adriel Bettelheim, "Public Broadcasting," *CQ Researcher*, Oct. 29, 1999, pp. 929-952.

47. See "Media Regulations Timeline" at www.pbs.org/now/politics/mediatimeline.html.

48. *Ibid.*

49. *Ibid.*

50. Robert J. Thompson, "500 Channels, But No Clear Picture of What We Want," *The Washington Post*, May 25, 2003, p. B3.

51. See "Issues in Providing Cable and Satellite Television Services," General Accounting Office, Oct. 2002, p. 1.

52. Greg Braxton, "Rewriting the Rules: Synergies Emerge in TV Duopolies," *Los Angeles Times*, May 30, 2003, p. C1.

53. See FCC "Annual Assessment," *op. cit.*

54. For background, see Brian Hansen, "Combating Plagiarism," *CQ Researcher*, Sept. 19, 2003, pp. 773-796, and Kathy Koch, "Journalism Under Fire," *CQ Researcher*, Dec. 25, 1998, pp. 1121-1144.

55. Project for Excellence in Journalism, *op. cit.*

56. Study: Political ad time trumps election coverage on the tube, Nov. 21, 2006, University of Wisconsin-Madison.

57. Michael K. Powell, "Should Limits on Broadcast Ownership Change?" USA Today.com, Jan. 21, 2003, p. A11.

58. Frank Ahrens, "Why Radio Stinks," *The Washington Post Magazine*, p. 25, Jan. 19, 2003, p. W12.

59. "Broadcast station totals," FCC Audio Division, available at www.fcc.gov, June 30, 2003.

60. Ahrens, *op. cit.*

61. Robert J. Thompson, "500 Channels, But No Clear Picture of What We Want," *The Washington Post*, May 25, 2003, p. B3.

62. John Eggerton, "FCC Officially Raises Station Ownership Cap to 39%," *Broadcasting & Cable*, March 1, 2007, www.broadcastingcable.com/article/CA6420878.html.

63. From testimony before Senate Commerce Committee, May 13, 2003.

64. Erik Sass, "Cross-Ownership Support: NAB Backs FCC Rule Change," Media Post (Free Press), May 8, 2008, www.freepress.net/node/39650.

65. Kaplan, Peter, "FCC Votes to Ease Media Ownership Restrictions," Reuters, December 18, 2007.

66. Statement of Chairman Kevin J. Martin, Dec. 18, 2007, www.fcc.gov/ownership/actions.html.

67. "Dorgan's Resolution to Block FCC's Media Ownership Rules Approved by Senate," Senator Dorgan press release, May 15, 2008, http://dorgan.senate.gov/newsroom/record.cfm?id=297937.

68. Christopher Stern, "Bitter Atmosphere Envelops FCC: Under Chairman Powell, Panel Members Maneuver, Criticize," *The Washington Post*, June 3, 2003, p. E1.

69. Interview on C-SPAN's "Washington Journal," Sept. 3, 2003.

70. Kevin Martin, "The Daily Show," *The New York Times*, Nov. 13, 2007.

71. "Testimony of Andrew Jay Schwartzman, President and CEO, Media Access Project." Delivered to the Subcommittee on Telecommunications and the Internet, Dec. 5, 2007.

72. "FCC Media Ownership Changes," Benton Foundation, last updated Feb. 21, 2008, www.benton .org/node/8499.

73. "New Leased Access Rules Released by FCC," Benton Foundation, Feb. 4, 2008, www.benton.org/ node/8986.

74. "Verizon Appeals FCC's Leased Access Rules," Benton Foundation, April 10, 2008, www.benton .org/node/10435.

75. See "The Failure of Cable Deregulation," at www .uspirg.org, U.S. PIRG, August 2003.

76. "Fighting Media Monopolies 2003," *Consumer Reports*, July 2003, p. 65.

77. See "Report on Cable Industry Prices," FCC-06-179A, Dec. 20, 2006.

78. *Ibid.*

79. David Lieberman, "Media Moguls Have Second Thoughts," *USA Today*, June 2, 2003, p. B1.

80. See Robert Sachs, "Television Ownership" letter to the editor, *The New York Times*, Aug. 1, 2003, p. A20.

81. Sallie Hofmeister and Jube Shiver Jr., "Worry Over FCC Rules Not Shared on Wall Street," *Los Angeles Times*, June 4, 2003, p. C1.

82. Richard Siklos and Andrew Ross Sorkin, "Rupert Murdoch Offers $5 Billion Bid for Dow Jones," *The New York Times*, May 2, 2007.

83. "Murdoch Drops Bid for Newsday," *Time*, May 10, 2008.

84. Richard Pérez-Peña and "Sam Zell: A Tough Guy in a Mean Business," *The New York Times*, April 7, 2008.

85. David Lieberman, "McClatchy to Buy Knight Ridder for $4.5 billion," *USA Today*, March 13, 2006.

86. Michael Liedtke, "Microsoft abandons Yahoo bid, rebuffing higher sale price," Associated Press, May 3, 2008.

87. Press release, Sept. 22, 2003.

88. "Testimony of Andrew Jay Schwartzman, President and CEO, Media Access Project," Delivered to the Subcommittee on Telecommunications and the Internet, Dec. 5, 2007.

89. *Ibid.*

90. *Ibid.*

91. Stuart Elliott, "Trying to sort out the broader trends behind the big surge in spending on TV commercials," *The New York Times*, June 3, 2003, p. C10.

# BIBLIOGRAPHY

### Books

**Chenoweth, Neil, *Rupert Murdoch: The Untold Story of the World's Greatest Media Wizard*, Diane Publishing Company, 2004.**
Chenoweth, an Australian newspaperman, explores Murdoch's access and control around the world.

**Greenwald, Robert and Alexandra Kitty, *Outfoxed: Rupert Murdoch's War on Journalism*, The Disinformation Company, 2003.**
Greenwald and Kitty take an updated look at how consolidating journalism ruins television news. The main focus of the book is placed on the Fox News Channel.

**Klein, Alec, *Stealing Time: Steve Case, Jerry Levin and the Collapse of AOL Time Warner*, Simon & Schuster, 2003.**
Reporter Klein describes how the bursting Internet bubble, conflicting management styles, accounting irregularities and other difficulties devalued the largest merger in American history and forced out top executives.

### Articles

**Fallows, James, "The Age of Murdoch," *The Atlantic*, September 2003.**
Journalist Fallows argues that media baron Rupert Murdoch approaches his media empire as just another business — not one charged with serving the public interest.

Fisher, Marc, "Sounds Familiar for a Reason," *The Washington Post*, May 18, 2003, p. B1.
A Post columnist and the author of an upcoming book on the radio industry takes a critical look at radio giant Clear Channel Communications.

**Kirkpatrick, David D., "Entertainment Industry Faces Problems Mergers Won't Solve," *The New York Times*, Sept. 8, 2003, p. C1.**
Kirkpatrick explores whether NBC's proposed deal with Vivendi Universal signals the end of media mergers.

**Noam, Eli, "The Media Concentration Debate," *Financial Times*, July 31, 2003, p. A11.**
Telecom visionary and Columbia University Professor Eli Noam notes that while media companies are bigger, so is the sector. Local concentration is actually highest among newspapers, not TV stations, and radio-industry growth has slowed in recent years.

**Thierer, Adam, and Clyde Wayne Crews Jr., "What Media Monopolies?" *The Wall Street Journal*, July 29, 2003, p. B2.**
Analysts at the libertarian Cato Institute argue the broadcast networks are far from monopolies because audience share has decreased dramatically, and many non-network station groups own more TV outlets than networks.

**Thompson, Robert J., "500 Channels, But No Clear Picture of What We Want," *The Washington Post*, May 25, 2003, p. B3.**
Consumers have far more media choices today, but the quality of news and the quantity of civic-minded programming often pales compared to decades ago.

### Reports and Studies

**"Big Radio Rules in Small Markets: A few behemoths dominate medium-sized cities throughout the U.S.," Center for Public Integrity, Oct. 1, 2003.**
Radio concentration is highest in small and medium-sized markets, where industry giant Clear Channel is a major player. FCC rules limit companies to owning eight radio outlets per market, but companies sidestep the limit by acquiring stations in adjacent markets that can be heard where they've reached the cap. For a copy, visit www.openairwaves.org/telecom/report.aspx?aid=63.

**"Does Ownership Matter in Local Television News: A Five-Year Study of Ownership and Quality," Project for Excellence in Journalism, April 29, 2003.**
This exhaustive study finds that small-station groups tend to produce better newscasts than large ones, and network affiliates tend to have better news than network-owned stations. Moreover, cross-ownership of a TV station and a newspaper in a market usually results in higher-quality news, but local ownership doesn't guarantee quality. Available at www.journalism.org.

**"Free TV Swallowed by Media Giants: The Way It Really Is," Consumer Federation of America, Consumers Union and Center for Digital Democracy, Sept. 15, 2003.**
Three watchdog groups challenge the argument that free TV is in jeopardy if the FCC's media-ownership rules are not relaxed, pointing out the broadcast networks are strong financially. Available at www.democraticmedia.org.

**Halfon, Jay, and Edmund Mierzwinski, "The Failure of Cable Deregulation," U.S. PIRG, August 2003.**
Cable rates have been rising three times faster than inflation, and even higher. Meanwhile, satellite-TV competition is not resulting in lower rates for cable. For a copy, visit www.uspirg.org.

**"(Media Ownership) Report and Order and Notice of Proposed Rulemaking," Federal Communications Commission, (FCC 03-127), July 2, 2003.**
This 256-page report provides extensive background on the FCC's decision to modify its media-ownership rules. The "Report and Order" can be obtained at www.fcc.gov.

**"Out of the Picture 2007: Minority & Female TV Station Ownership in the United States," Free Press, October 2007. www.freepress.net/files/otp2007.pdf.**

**"Radio Deregulation: Has it Served Citizens and Musicians?" Future of Music Coalition, November 2002.**
The rapid consolidation of the radio industry after deregulation in 1996 is documented in this 147-page report. Available at www.futureofmusic.org.

**"The State of the News Media 2004," Center for Excellence in Journalism, 2004.**
The inaugural look at the state of journalism in America.

**"The State of the News Media 2005," Center for Excellence in Journalism, 2005.**
The center finds that technology is transforming all aspects of journalism — from collection of news to delivery to the preference of consumers in how they like to receive their news.

**"The State of the News Media 2006," Center for Excellence in Journalism, 2006.**
The center takes a look at the ominous situation of journalism, specifically the demise of print media.

**"The State of the News Media 2007," Center for Excellence in Journalism, 2007.**
The center finds that news organizations need to begin thinking about the long-term impacts of the new media environment.

**"The State of the News Media 2008," Center for Excellence in Journalism, March 2008.**
The center finds that the media as a whole is in a more troubled position than it was in 2007.

**"Testimony of Andrew Jay Schwartzman, President and CEO, Media Access Project," Delivered to the Subcommittee on Telecommunications and the Internet, Dec. 5, 2007.**
The text of Andrew Jay Schwartzman's speech before the Senate subcommittee, where he argues that the FCC's coming vote on newspaper/broadcast ownership will be harmful to many sectors of journalism.

# For More Information

**Consumer Federation of America**, 1424 16th St., N.W., Suite 604, Washington, DC 20036; (202) 387-6121; www.consumerfed.org; A vocal advocate of regulating the media; frequently issues reports detailing increased consolidation.

**Consumers Union**, 1666 Connecticut Ave., N.W., Suite 310, Washington, DC 20009-1039; (202) 462-6262; www.consumersunion.org; It has teamed with Consumer Federation to oppose further relaxation of the media-ownership rules.

**Future of Music Coalition**, 1615 L St., N.W., Suite 520, Washington, DC 20036; (202) 429-8855; www.futureofmusic.org; A nonprofit coalition of radio and music interests that opposes radio consolidation and supports fledgling low-power FM.

**National Association of Broadcasters**, 1771 N St., N.W., Washington, DC 20036; (202) 429-5300; www.nab.org; The main trade association representing television and radio broadcasters, though the Big Four TV networks are no longer members.

**National Cable and Telecommunications Association**, 1724 Massachusetts Ave., N.W., Washington, DC 20036; (202) 775-3550; www.ncta.com; The premier trade association for cable TV companies; many also offer high-speed Internet access.

**Radio-Television News Directors Association**, 1600 K St., N.W., Suite 700, Washington, DC 20006-2838; (202) 659-6510; www.rtnda.org; Opposes curbs on press freedoms and promotes journalistic ethics.

7

# Media Bias

Alan Greenblatt and Heather Kleba

I n the 2008 Democratic primary campaign, the media have
made Sen. Barack Obama into an idol and the man to beat.
The treatment of Obama has been so obvious that even his
Democratic opponent, Sen. Hillary Rodham Clinton, has commented on the bias in a recent debate, stating: "Can I just point
out that in the last several debates, I seem to get the first question
all the time? . . . I do find it curious, and if anybody saw 'Saturday
Night Live,' you know, maybe we should ask Barack if he's comfortable and needs another pillow," referring to an SNL sketch in
which the debate moderators appear to be little more than Obama
cheerleaders.

It is hard to determine why the media chose one of the
Democratic candidates over the other-especially because both
Obama and Clinton represent groups that have never before held
the highest office in the nation, making it seem like a win-win either
way. According to Erika Falk in her "Women for President" study,
men receive more coverage than women when they are running in
the same race. But the treatment of Obama harkens back to the
"media darling" effect of his speech in 2004 before the Democratic
National Convention. During a February 28 "Good Morning
America" segment, Sam Donaldson explained it this way: "We're
always looking for that new non-politician. Senator Obama is a
compelling, interesting, charismatic figure. . . . I think there's been
a feeling that the Clintons may have gotten away with a lot of stuff
over a good many years and we're not going to let her get away with
something now if it deserves to be talked about."

Just how biased has the coverage been? According to the Center
for Media and Public Affairs, from December 2007 through

Conservative Fox News commentator Bill O'Reilly,
right, interviews filmmaker Michael Moore during
the Democratic National Convention in July 2004.
Moore's movie "Fahrenheit 9/11" has made him a
leading critic of President Bush. Both liberals and
conservatives are complaining about perceived
bias in news coverage of critical events such as
the war in Iraq.

From *CQ Researcher,*
October 15, 2004. (Updated May 23, 2008)

## Democrats Have Most Faith in the Media

With the sole exception of the Fox News Channel, Republicans believe far less in the credibility of major news organizations than Democrats.

### Partisanship and Credibility

| | Believe all or most of what the news organization says | |
|---|---|---|
| | **Republicans** | **Democrats** |
| **Broadcast and cable outlets:** | | |
| CNN | 26 | 45 |
| CBS News | 15 | 34 |
| NPR | 15 | 33 |
| NewsHour | 12 | 29 |
| 60 Minutes | 25 | 42 |
| ABC News | 17 | 34 |
| MSNBC | 14 | 29 |
| C-SPAN | 22 | 36 |
| NBC News | 16 | 30 |
| Local TV News | 21 | 29 |
| Fox News Channel | 29 | 24 |
| **Print Outlets:** | | |
| The Associated Press | 12 | 29 |
| New York Times | 14 | 31 |
| Time | 15 | 30 |
| Newsweek | 12 | 26 |
| USA Today | 14 | 25 |
| Daily newspaper | 16 | 23 |
| Wall Street Journal | 23 | 29 |

Source: "News Audiences Increasingly Politicized," The Pew Research Center for the People & the Press, June 8, 2004

February 2008, 83 percent of the reports about Senator Obama were positive, while only 53 percent for Senator Clinton were positive. [1]

Of course, nearly every major news network that has displayed a pro-Obama bias, and even those that have not, have come to the same conclusion. The media are not trying to sway voters in one direction or the other; they are simply reporting the news, and right now, the news is that Obama, who last summer looked like he wouldn't make it to the first primary, has won more delegates, more states and more of the popular vote than Senator Clinton.

The Obama situation, though, doesn't look like it's coming to an end any time soon. No matter what problem he has, or what skeleton falls out of his closet, it doesn't seem to dampen the national media's impression. When Obama's former pastor, Jeremiah Wright, surfaced making racially charged comments, the story was reported over and over again, but that never hurt the Obama media image. When Senator Clinton flip-flopped about her current and past support of NAFTA, any excuse she had was quickly overlooked.

Most mainstream journalists are more discreet about their political leanings, but surveys continually show that reporters tend to be more liberal than Americans as a whole, particularly on social issues such as abortion, gun control and gay rights. A 2004 poll by the Pew Research Center for the People & the Press confirmed that there is the perception among conservatives that CBS, NPR, *The New York Times* and other mainstream outlets have a liberal bias. [2]

Journalists insist that they keep their own opinions out of their newspapers or television stories, and that editors monitor their work for fairness.

Moreover, right-leaning bloggers were the first to call into question the authenticity of memos used by CBS News anchor Dan Rather on Sept. 8, 2004, when he reported that Bush had received special treatment during his National Guard career. Within two weeks, Rather had admitted that the documents were fake and that CBS had been gulled by a partisan source. Even though a secretary later confirmed on the air that the allegations in the fake memos were indeed accurate, the damage to CBS' credibility had already been done.

Yet critics on the other side of the political spectrum complain that the mainstream media have become little more than stenographic services for government and corporate power-brokers or — in the case of Fox News — for the Republican Party. Fox and *The Wall Street Journal* have all come under fire for the perceived right-wing slant of their reporters and political commentators. [3]

Many media critics trace the problems to the recent takeover of America's major media outlets by corporate conglomerates and what they see as the press' fear of offending official sources that control access to the White House and other government news. An overdependence on official sources, critics say, was especially evident during coverage of the recent Iraq war. Indeed, in the summer of 2004 after no weapons of mass destruction had been found in Iraq, *The New York Times* and *The Washington Post* questioned the accuracy of their own coverage leading up to the war, and *The New Republic* ran several articles under the cover head-line, "Were We Wrong?" All three publications concluded they had given too much weight to administration claims, and a recent liberal documentary, "Uncovered: The Whole Truth About the Iraq War," implied that the U.S. press did not treat the administration's justification for going to war with enough skepticism. [4]

In the 19th century, American journalists were openly biased, with papers actively promoting the fortunes of one political party over another. In contemporary practice, however, journalists are taught to strive for fairness. But some critics complain that the press lost that appearance of fairness when it adopted a propensity to offer analysis.

"If you don't have any analysis in a story, you haven't done your job," says Martin Johnson, a political scientist at the University of California, Riverside, who has studied the media. "But then you're open to the criticism of injecting bias. We want reporters to be thoughtful and analytical, but at the same time we want them to be objective and not tell us what they really think about things, and those are two entirely contradictory propositions."

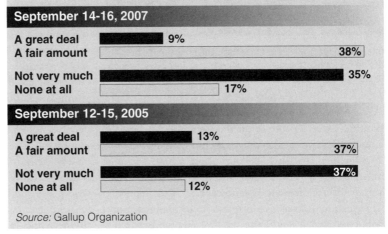

## Confidence in Media Dropped

Americans' confidence in the media dropped 3 percentage points in the past two years, according to a recent Gallup poll. While this number has remained steady over the past couple years, the September 2007 poll concluded that Americans' dissatisfaction with the way the country is headed lends itself to the low levels of confidence in the media.

### Do you have confidence in the media's ability to report news stories accurately and fairly?

**September 14-16, 2007**

| | |
|---|---|
| A great deal | 9% |
| A fair amount | 38% |
| Not very much | 35% |
| None at all | 17% |

**September 12-15, 2005**

| | |
|---|---|
| A great deal | 13% |
| A fair amount | 37% |
| Not very much | 37% |
| None at all | 12% |

*Source:* Gallup Organization

As a result, many Americans today — convinced that news outlets are biased — are seeking out networks and publications that gibe with their own political views. The recent explosion in the availability of multimedia news outlets — with the advent of round-the-clock cable television news and the Internet — enables them to do that easily. Americans who once had to get their news from one or two local newspapers or a 30-minute broadcast by one of three networks can pick their own "politically appropriate" media — from right-leaning talk radio, Internet sites and Fox News to left-leaning independent media sources or newspapers from around the world via the Internet.

And thanks to new technology, news junkies can keep up with the news 24 hours a day, using Blackberries and cell phones or reading headlines on RSS feeds. And Internet users who haven't found a Web blog — as Internet journals are called — that shares their political viewpoint just haven't been looking.

"The old line in broadcasting that there is one message that is going to make sense to everybody is just not the model that we're working under any more," says

Internet bloggers served as credentialed members of the press during the Democratic National Convention in July 2004, helping to change the way news is covered.

Barbie Zelizer, a professor at the Annenberg School of Communications at the University of Pennsylvania.

Some fear that this "Balkanization" of the nation's news media will exacerbate the partisan divide that already afflicts the political landscape. [5] "After Sept. 11, American mainstream culture has become much more politicized than it was before and probably more than it's been in a generation. The media are contributing to that," says Matthew Felling, media director of the Center for Media and Public Affairs.

The splintering of the nation's news media and the profusion of technology have also radically changed the way news is covered, amply demonstrated in the coverage of the 2004 presidential campaign by fully accredited bloggers.

In addition, critics say the political press has expended too much time and energy on charges and counter-charges, rather than investigating the candidates' plans for Medicare, Social Security or national defense. "Bush, Kerry and their operatives drown reporters with an around-the-clock deluge of spin — via e-mail, fax, cell phone and Web blogs — leaving them little time to report and reflect on what is true and what isn't," *The Columbia Journalism Review* complained in 2004. [6]

During the 2004 presidential campaign, some critics said John Kerry had been slow to adapt to the realities of the new media. For instance, in August 2004, he did not immediately respond to commercials by the Swift Boat Veterans for Truth attacking his Vietnam War record. In

a classic example of the modern media "echo chamber" — which can magnify the impact of the smallest news item — the initial ads, despite running in just seven media markets in three states, were heavily covered by the television and cable networks.

Indeed, a Kerry friend said the candidate focused too much on traditional outlets and did not understand the modern media market. "You would think he would have recognized this five years ago," the friend said. [7]

This is not a choice for candidates in the 2008 presidential election, with the proliferation of social networking sites and Web 2.0 tools such as YouTube. If any of the candidates expect to bring in the youth vote-a critically important segment for Democrats-they need to be more accessible and leave an impression that they can communicate through these channels and understand young voters. According to a Pew study, 89 percent of those aged 18 to 39 use a social networking site, and 31 percent of people in this age group get campaign information on these sites. [8]

The Rather affair revealed the new media reality: The traditional media — the three biggest broadcast networks and the large national daily newspapers — no longer control the agenda for the political debate. With the networks ratcheting down their election coverage, outlets that didn't even exist five years ago now dominate the field.

"A big difference is that Democrats continue to try to play within the traditional media, such as the TV networks, *The New York Times*, the *Post* and the major papers," says Elizabeth Wilner, political director for NBC News, "while the Republicans have done a far better job of using alternative news sources and new news sources, such as the Internet and the Fox cable network and talk radio." [9]

"This is potentially a big cultural moment," editorialized *The Wall Street Journal* in September 2004. "For decades, liberal media elites were able to define current debates by all kicking in the same direction, like the Rockettes." [10]

Of course, liberals have long lambasted the editorial page of *The Wall Street Journal*, Fox News and conservative talk radio hosts like Rush Limbaugh as kicking in a distinctly right-wing direction. With so many charges of bias flying in all directions and the growing intensity of media criticism (and self-criticism), many Americans now believe the media simply can't be trusted to tell the truth. The media's credibility also has taken major body blows in recent years after reporters at some of the nation's most venerable news outlets were found to have fabricated news stories. [11]

"The common ground for public understanding and public information may be destroyed in all this," warns Frank Sesno, a communications professor at the George Washington University in Washington, D.C., and former TV broadcaster and CNN executive. "The simple question of 'what happened today?' becomes something we're in danger of arguing over." [12]

"The danger is conveying to people that there's no trustworthy source of news," says the University of California's Johnson. "If that's the message that people ultimately get, that makes it really difficult for them to evaluate the actions of people in government."

As observers consider current changes in the media, here are some of the questions they are asking:

## Bias of the Media

Respondents to the Gallup poll continually believe that the media is too liberal, a trend that can be traced back to the first time this question was asked in 2001. However, over time, the too conservative number has also been growing steadily.

**In general, do you think the media is too liberal, too conservative or about right?**

|                  | Too Liberal | About Right | Too Conservative | Unsure |
|------------------|-------------|-------------|------------------|--------|
| Sept. 14–16, 2007 | 45%         | 35%         | 18%              | 2%     |
| Sept. 7–10, 2006  | 44          | 33          | 19               | 4      |
| Sept. 12–15, 2005 | 46          | 37          | 16               | 1      |
| Sept. 13–15, 2004 | 48          | 33          | 15               | 4      |
| Sept. 2003        | 45          | 39          | 14               | 2      |
| Feb. 2003         | 45          | 36          | 15               | 4      |
| Sept. 2002        | 47          | 37          | 13               | 3      |
| Sept. 2001        | 45          | 40          | 11               | 4      |

*Source:* Gallup Organization

## Is the news audience fracturing along partisan lines?

Patty Cron travels regularly for business and puts up with a lot from hotels, but if there's one thing she can't stand it's a place that offers CNN as the only cable news choice on the room televisions. She prefers Fox News Channel. "When that happens, I check out and switch hotels," she told *The Dallas Morning News.*" [13]

Most people probably wouldn't go to that much effort. But in the increasingly fragmented media world, millions of Americans are seeking a "journalism of affirmation" — news presentations that explain or contextualize events in a way that accords with their political outlook.

"Political polarization is increasingly reflected in the public's news habits," concluded the Pew Research Center for the People & the Press. "In an era of deep-seated political divisions, conservatives and liberals are increasingly choosing sides in their TV news preferences." [14]

A Pew poll of 3,000 adults found that 41 percent of Republicans regularly watched Fox, and 25 percent watched CNN. By contrast, only 20 percent of Democrats watched Fox, while 44 percent watched CNN. In general, Pew found that Republicans were more skeptical about the credibility of major media outlets than Democrats. [15] The public as a whole sees a pro-Democratic bias, according to a 2007 Pew study. While 60 percent of Americans believe there is political bias in the news, 25 percent believe it's a pro-Democratic bias, while only 9 percent see it as a pro-Republican bias. [16]

"The audience is fracturing on partisan lines, and a big contributor to that are 24-hour cable-news networks," says Richard Campbell, director of the journalism program at Miami University in Ohio. Not only do ratings-sensitive cable networks exacerbate partisanship, he says, but they raise the decibel level of the political debate. "If you look at those shows over a long period of time, the goal is conflict, the goal is to create drama by getting people to yell at each other."

When the media, blogs, talk radio and "shouting heads" cable programming accentuate division, it leaves less of a market for straight, seemingly unbiased accounts, such as those appearing on low-key discussion programs like "The NewsHour With Jim Lehrer," "The Charlie Rose Show" and radio's "The Diane Rehm Show."

## Is There an al Qaeda-Iraq Link?

A far higher percentage of people who get their news primarily from Fox than from PBS-NPR incorrectly thought that the U.S. had found clear evidence in Iraq that Saddam Hussein was working closely with the al Qaeda terrorist network.

**Americans Who Thought There Was a Link**
(By percentage of those who depend primarily on each source for news)

| | |
|---|---|
| Fox | 67% |
| CBS | 56 |
| NBC | 49 |
| ABC | 45 |
| Print media | 40 |
| PBS-NPR | 16 |

*Source:* "Misperceptions, the Media and the Iraq War," The PIPA/Knowledge Networks Poll, Oct. 2, 2003

"It's a very lonely business to present the facts, because what sells is opinion-mongering," agrees Felling, at the Center for Media and Public Affairs. He argues that because Americans are so deluged with information, "People are hungry for someone to contextualize the news. They go to opinion-makers because it saves time."

Some media observers see this as a positive development. They believe that all news outlets have their hidden biases and should be upfront about them, like the press in Europe. "For the first time in decades, it's become transparently clear that America has an ideological media, that our TV networks, newspapers, magazines and radio talk shows all represent particular points of view," writes *L.A. Weekly* media columnist John Powers. [17]

Others think the trend is worrisome. If people look for outlets that confirm their preconceived ideas and views and don't trust others, says Charlotte Grimes, who holds Syracuse University's Knight Chair in Political Reporting, it becomes harder for society to reach a general consensus about the meaning of events and the right policy course for responding to them. "When I was growing up, there were far fewer media options, giving Americans a far larger body of shared cultural experience," Powers writes. [18]

While the number of Americans seeking partisan affirmation is growing, it has not reached a critical mass. The majority of the U.S. news audience is not shopping for news outlets with a political bias, say media experts. "The bulk of the population is not necessarily going to be seeking out partisan journalism," says Robert McChesney, a professor of communication at the University of Illinois.

Indeed, a Pew Research Center survey found that 23 percent of Americans prefer news that shares their views while 67 percent prefer news with no point of view. [19] "It's not yet a majority perspective," says Scott Keeter, associate director of the center. "It isn't that a majority of the public really wants to see news with a view, but some do. For some conservatives and Republicans, they may feel they have found that in Fox."

Fox News is now the leading source for news on cable; CNN, for example, gets only a fraction of the Fox News Channel's viewers. But Fox's audience is only a small piece of the broadcast networks' audience share; each network news show gets about three times as many viewers as Fox's top news show.

"At this point, what's called the mainstream news — at the networks and the cable networks aside from Fox — has significant influence about what people think about, if not what they think," McChesney says.

### Does having more news outlets mean the public is better informed?

The function of the news media in a democracy is to produce an informed electorate. Thirty years ago, the electorate had limited choices for news: three newsweeklies, three television networks and the nation's daily newspapers. Today, Americans can choose between a seemingly infinite number of broadcast, cable, newspaper and magazine outlets, both in print and online, domestic and international.

Jack Shafer, a media columnist with the online magazine *Slate*, says the proliferation of news sources makes

Americans better informed. "There is undoubtedly a greater flow of information," he says. "If people have a taste for media and want to spend time with a variety of channels and Web sites, absolutely" they will be better informed than under the "old media" regime.

In addition to having more news outlets, he says, consumers have easier access to everything from raw government data to live coverage of major events, including White House news briefings and daily sessions of Congress. It's not clear, however, how well people are taking advantage of all the information that's available.

"In the same way that you are what you eat, you become what you consume in the news business," says former *Boston Globe* Associate Editor David Nyhan, who worries that shrill sources of information are starving their listeners except for "a cadre of people with an appetite for serious news." He adds: "You can't force people to eat their broccoli."

Tom Rosenstiel, director of the Project for Excellence in Journalism, makes a similar comparison: Even though today more fruits and vegetables and other healthy foods are more readily available year-round, people seem to be eating more junk food than ever.

"There's a similar risk here in our information diet," he says. "Some people are better informed, while some have become expert in the trivial, and some have just engrossed themselves in propaganda. We're faced with a Scandinavian smorgasbord every day, and you don't always eat healthy food at a smorgasbord."

And in addition to finding news that validates their views, the advent of social networking sites like MySpace, Facebook and LinkedIn allows users to find others with whom to discuss that opinion.

Still, cable and the Internet have been a boon to Nyhan's broccoli eaters — those who seek out hard news. Steve Rendall, a senior analyst at Fairness and Accuracy in Reporting (FAIR), a left-leaning media-watchdog group, notes that the British Broadcasting Corporation's (BBC) Web site received a million more hits a day during the run-up to the Iraq war and during the war in Afghanistan.

"They thought the vast majority of the hits were from the United States," he says, adding that Americans were surfing British Web sites because they felt they weren't getting adequate information from the U.S. press.

Critics of the U.S. media complain that it is obsessed with gore and gossip. "If it bleeds, it leads," critics say about local TV news. Similarly, cable networks often dedicate the majority of their 24 hours a day of news to murder trials and celebrity gossip. Seemingly incessant updates about Britney Spears, Lindsay Lohan or the latest reality show sometimes crowd out reporting on the environment, foreign affairs and other serious topics, critics say.

"We have a lot more voices, but I don't know how much journalism we've got going on, at least journalism as it's taught at universities like mine — digging out stories," says the University of Illinois' McChesney. "Most of what they do is regurgitate what someone else has uncovered or what someone in power is talking about."

Felling, at the Center for Media and Public Affairs, agrees. "The paradox of the new media landscape is that there are more outlets and less information." Picking up on the food metaphor, he says, "Print news is the protein of the news diet; all the rest is junk food. The 24-hour news outlets are all sizzle and no steak."

Lee Rainie of the Pew Internet and American Life Project, says the Internet has become a great tool for those who want to know more about serious issues. "It's so much easier now," he says. "The Internet absolutely helps you know more."

But Rainie notes that people can just as easily turn away from general news — accessing information in cyberspace about their church or favorite football team, while their neighbors are turning to Web sites dedicated to knitting or cats. "They're better informed about the things that they care about."

That's not necessarily going to be the great issues of the day. "There are just a lot of people out there who are really inattentive to politics," says the University of California's Johnson. "A lot of people think what's really going on is Spider Man."

Other observers worry that the fracturing of the news audience — combined with media and business changes that are leading to overconcentration on a few big, dramatic stories at the expense of duller government reporting — could cause some real problems for democracy.

Philo Wasburn, a Purdue University political sociologist, told the university's news service that the public's belief in a media bias may affect how many people are involved in politics. "If the public is distrustful, that can lead to disinterest in the media. More importantly, it can also contribute to a lack of political information and discourage participation in the governmental process," he says. [20]

# Documentaries Giving Partisans New Voice

Like many conservatives and critics, Peter Rollins, editor-in-chief of the journal Film & History, takes issue with Michael Moore's portrayal of the Bush administration in his controversial film "Fahrenheit 9/11." Rollins calls Moore "wacky but thrilling" and says he has a "sophomoric, simplistic view."

But unlike other Moore critics, Rollins has no doubts that "Fahrenheit" belongs in the category of documentary film. "They say it's not objective," Rollins says, "but no documentary has ever tried to be objective. Moore's film is very much in the tradition of the persuasive film."

If "Fahrenheit 9/11" has plenty of antecedents, from the late Leni Riefenstal's movies about Nazi Germany to the 1974 anti-Vietnam War documentary "Hearts and Minds," Moore also has plenty of company these days. Every week seems to bring the release of yet another anti-Bush movie, such as "The Oil Factor Behind the War on Terror"; "Hijacking Catastrophe: 9/11, Fear & the Selling of the American Empire" and two recent films by Robert Greenwald that are achieving underground celebrity: "Uncovered: The Whole Truth About the Iraq War," and "Outfoxed: Rupert Murdoch's War on Journalism." Several, including "Bush's Brain," illustrate and elaborate arguments that had already been put forward in books.

"To a certain extent, I believe liberals have found their message vehicle in popular documentaries, just as Republicans did in talk radio," says Matthew Felling, media director at the Washington-based Center for Media and Public Affairs.

Liberals may not hold onto such a monopoly much longer. On Oct. 5, 2004, the day Moore's film was released on DVD, conservative groups released the DVD of "George W. Bush: Faith in the White House," a documentary about Bush's Christian faith — which is being sent to thousands of churches as the conservative response to "Fahrenheit 9/11." Then, conservative Sinclair Broadcasting announced it would broadcast a 90-minute anti-Kerry documentary on its 62 television stations. And two festivals devoted to conservative documentaries have recently been held in Dallas and Los Angeles. "There hasn't been an appetite for it, but I have a feeling that's about to change," says Roger Aronoff, a conservative media critic who has just completed "Confronting Iraq," a documentary about the war.

Liberals and conservatives — and non-political storytellers — are crafting documentaries in unprecedented numbers for two reasons: technology and money. Digital video cameras and editing have made the creation and manipulation of images neater and easier.

There have been numerous instances in recent years of public opinion forcing changes in policy. During the 1980s, Congress repealed major changes in Medicare it had passed the year before after seniors protested. During the 1990s, the lack of public support for a universal health plan proposed by President Bill Clinton led to the death of that proposal — and was a prime contributor to Republicans taking control of Congress in 1995 after years in the minority. Outrage over photographs taken in the Abu Ghraib prison in Iraq and reports of waterboarding prisoners in Guantanamo Bay forced the Bush administration to clarify its anti-torture policies.

For every case in which public opinion was roused, there are hundreds of examples of government decisions that didn't receive press coverage sufficient to awaken constituent ire. There's a cliché in politics —

"sunshine is the best disinfectant" — meaning the more people know about government decisions, the more likely they're going to be made in the public interest. When the press fails to perform its watchdog role, last-minute changes can be made to legislation designed to benefit special interests, or government contracts rewarded to campaign contributors or friends of public officials.

According to a study by the Pew Research Center, since the decline in coverage on the Iraq war, Americans don't have a knowledge of basic facts and figures, such as the approximate number of deaths since the war began. The lack of coverage-down 12 percent between July 2007 and February 2008-reduced the number of those knowledgeable about the number killed in Iraq from 54 percent in August 2007 to only 28 percent early this year.

"It's so quick and inexpensive," says William McDonald, head of the cinematography program at the UCLA School of Theater, Film and Television. "In the past, people might have had an idea for a documentary but wouldn't have known how to pay for it, and production would have been cumbersome. Now you just pick up a camcorder and make a film."

Homemade documentaries are sometimes passed around among partisans on DVD and videotape, similar to the way *samizdat* — underground literature — was circulated in the old Soviet Union. But other, more carefully crafted films are making serious money. Documentary filmmakers used to consider themselves lucky to get a one-time screening at a festival, but now they can set their sights on a long run at the multiplex.

"Supersize Me," which documented the effects of eating a month's worth of meals at McDonald's, spent several weeks among the Top 10 box office leaders in the spring of 2004. "The Fog of War," an Oscar winner about the career of former Defense Secretary Robert S. McNamara, grossed about $10 million. "Fahrenheit 9/11," which made $120 million, shattered Moore's previous record, for 2002's "Bowling for Columbine," as the top-grossing non-Imax documentary of all time.

That kind of financial return will only encourage more people to invest in documentaries, says David Thomson, a film historian in San Francisco. Much of the audience, he suggests, is made up of adults who are tired of the preponderance of Hollywood films targeted at children and teenagers. "There are a lot of people — it's a minority, but still enough to make an audience — who are pretty well sick of the fiction films that are being made in America today," Thomson says.

Rick McKay, director of the recent documentary "Broadway: The Golden Age," agrees. "Feature films these days tend to be for the lowest common denominator, and people are demanding something that makes them think and inspires them," he said in an online chat. "There is a huge void to be filled that documentary filmmakers are filling without the support of a studio. Documentaries are the last vestige of free speech and passion in the film industry that literally one person can make alone."[1]

Thomson says that the documentary tradition in this country, particularly on television, is not as rich as in his native England, but he's not surprised that the medium has become hot in a time of polarization. "Whenever people are politically aroused, and we definitely live in a time when the country is fiercely divided, I think people want to know more about what's going on," he says.

But Thomson warns that, with documentaries, seeing is not necessarily believing. Images can be manipulated and moments captured on film can take on new meanings when put in a different context.

"Documentary is not naturally, inherently factual," Thomson says. "It's very open to trickery of one kind or another."

---

[1] "Film: 'Broadway: The Golden Age,' " Aug. 6, 2004, www.washingtonpost.com/wp-dyn/articles/A43460-2004Aug5.html.

---

"I can't be in Washington or in my statehouse all the time paying attention to politics," says the University of California's Johnson. "I entrust that job to people in the press who can be there, paying attention for me."

But Bruce Bartlett, a senior fellow at the National Center for Policy Analysis, celebrates the proliferation of sources for political information as a vast improvement over the "old paradigm," when information was controlled by a few chosen media outlets.

"Today, cable news, C-SPAN, talk radio and the Internet raise questions and disseminate raw material to millions of people who are no longer bound by the quasi-monopoly of three television networks and one-newspaper towns," Bartlett writes. "They can now get news that otherwise would be suppressed or ignored, check original sources for themselves and draw their own conclusions."[21]

## Has the press been sufficiently skeptical in its coverage of Iraq?

No event in recent years has caused such intense media self-examination as the war in Iraq. And perhaps no other event demonstrates the difficulty the press has in balancing its mandate to report the news — including repeating official statements — while at the same time questioning official sources. Many journalists now wonder whether the media were rigorous enough in challenging Bush administration rationales for war that have proved, in retrospect, mostly wrong.

The conclusions last summer by *The New York Times*, *The Washington Post* and *The New Republic* that they had given too much weight to administration claims may have been unprecedented.

"Before the war, U.S. journalists were far too reliant on sources sympathetic to the administration," wrote Michael

## CHRONOLOGY

**1960s–1970s** *Television comes to dominate the news landscape.*

**1960** KFAX, in San Francisco, is launched as the nation's first 24-hour news radio station but goes out of business after just four months.

**1963** Television surpasses newspapers as the leading source of daily news.

**1969** PBS is created. . . . Moon landing is watched by 94 percent of American households with TV.

**1971** U.S. Supreme Court rules the government cannot prevent *The Washington Post* and *The New York Times* from printing the Pentagon Papers.

**1973** *The Washington Post* wins the Pulitzer Prize for public service for its coverage of the Watergate scandal.

**1980s** *Cable grows exponentially while newspapers continue to decline*

**1980** Ted Turner creates CNN (Cable News Network), ushering in an era of 24-hour news.

**1981** Federal Communications Commission (FCC) determines there are enough radio stations to guarantee sufficient competition and exempts the medium from devoting minimum daily time to news and public affairs programming; the ruling is extended to TV in 1984.

**1982** *USA Today*, a national newspaper with colorful graphics, short stories and less government reporting, is founded and soon widely imitated.

**1988** Cable Communications Act releases cable networks from state and local regulations and many competitive constraints, leading to explosive growth.

**1990s** *Major media companies continue to consolidate, leaving fewer big players.*

**1991** CNN is the only TV news organization with correspondents and a direct satellite hookup in Baghdad during the first Persian Gulf War.

**1992** NBC's "Dateline" rigs explosives under a GM truck to make a fuel tank explosion look more dramatic.

**1995** Former football star O. J. Simpson's trial for murder receives unprecedented coverage from all media.

**1996** Disney acquires Capital Cities-ABC, combining a movie studio with a TV network. . . . Telecommunications Act loosens broadcast ownership restrictions. . . . Fox News Channel founded.

**1997** U.S. Supreme Court finds the Communications Decency Act unconstitutional, extending First Amendment rights to the Internet.

**1998** Plagiarism/fabrication scandals at *The New Republic* and *The Boston Globe* add to journalism's credibility woes.

**2000s** *New players threaten traditional media's audience and credibility.*

**2001** Fox becomes most-watched network in cable news.

**2003** *New York Times* reporter Jayson Blair is fired after fabricating stories.

**2004** FCC recommends a $550,000 fine for CBS stations and calls for tighter decency regulation following a televised glimpse of Janet Jackson's right breast during the Super Bowl. . . . Fox reaps higher ratings during the Republican National Convention than any other network. . . . CBS anchor Dan Rather admits his "60 Minutes" report about President Bush's National Guard service was based on phony documents. . . . FCC proposes record-setting $1.2 million fine against 169 Fox television stations for an April 2003 broadcast of "Married by America" that featured whipped-cream-covered strippers.

**2005** Hurricane Katrina hits the Gulf Coast, leaving over 1,000 dead and millions displaced. Media come under fire for reports of rape and murder in the New Orleans Superdome, where displaced residents were living. However, media are credited with bringing to the administration's attention issues that residents were facing.

**2006** President Bush signs Broadcast Indecency Bill, raising the fines that can be charged to radio and television broadcasters for content deemed indecent by the FCC. . . . Knight Ridder chain of papers sold for $4.5 billion to McClatchy Co.; McClatchy begins selling off Knight Ridder papers.

**2007** Rupert Murdoch, owner of media giant News Corp., purchases *The Wall Street Journal* for $5 billion.

**2008** *Jan. 8:* Presidential primaries begin. *Feb. 12:* Hollywood writers' strike ends after three months.

Massing, a *Columbia Journalism Review* contributing editor. "Despite abundant evidence of the administration's brazen misuse of intelligence in this matter, the press repeatedly let officials get away with it." [22]

But Dana Priest, a national security reporter at the *Post*, says she "never felt any pressure to be on board [with the war], or less skeptical. All these people who criticize the press now — it's not like we had the information that there were no WMD [weapons of mass destruction] and we didn't put it out. We didn't have the information."

In fact, the *Post* and other publications did question the validity of the claim that Iraq had WMD, but the volume and frequency of administration claims — and the front-page treatment they received — tended to drown out the doubt. According to a study by FAIR, the media-watchdog group, 76 percent of the sources in network stories about Iraq during the war were current or former government officials. [23]

"War is far too important to be left to the ex-generals, and that's basically what we were left with," FAIR's Rendall says.

Many reporters point out that part of their job is to report official statements by administration officials and that the skepticism should have started with the opposition party or members of the broader intelligence community. But the Democratic leadership in Congress supported the decision to go to war and, as John Diamond, who covers intelligence issues for *USA Today*, puts it, "Regrettably, there was no country in the world with an intelligence community robust enough to question U.S. and British intelligence."

Diamond says the fact that the Bush administration had ramped up its rhetoric so strongly from earlier Clinton administration claims that Iraq was reconstituting its WMD programs suggested that it must have had some compelling evidence. And when the press demanded proof, the administration's response that America couldn't afford to wait for proof of a smoking gun to emerge in the form of a mushroom cloud was a tacit admission that proof was lacking, he says.

"They were essentially saying we're willing to act without proof," he says. "There was nothing for reporters to hang their hats on other than Iraqi denials, and they had a long history of lying."

Rosenstiel, of the Project for Excellence in Journalism, says covering the run-up to the war in Iraq was different from covering a big domestic story, such as Medicare, which would allow reporters to check for themselves whether the program is working as advertised. Because Iraq was a closed society, it was even different than covering the 1999 war in Kosovo, where reporters could witness for themselves evidence of ethnic cleansing.

"Virtually no one was in Iraq, and if they were, there weren't a lot of people they could ask about WMD," Rosenstiel says. "It's easy to say that they should have known, but the fact is, it may well be that the secretary of State was misled, and he's got a lot more clearance than the national security correspondent of *The Washington Post*."

Reporters and media critics have lamented the fact that major news outlets such as *The New York Times* relied so heavily on self-promoting sources, particularly from Ahmed Chalabi and his defector group, the Iraqi National Congress (INC), while giving little credence to minority voices arguing that there were no WMD. "The INC's agenda was to get us into a war," wrote *New York Daily News* reporter Helen Kennedy. "The really damaging stories all came from those guys, not the CIA." [24]

After the war started, the press focused more on how the war was being fought — highlighting sophisticated new weapons and communications systems, for example — than on why the United States was at war. Once the occupation began to sour, however, press questioning of administration plans and tactics became more aggressive. Indeed, administration officials and some members of Congress have criticized the press for focusing too much on negative stories about Iraq and not highlighting successes there.

Indeed, views of war coverage have become politicized. The press has been criticized from the left for being too slow to break the story of prisoner abuses at the Abu Ghraib prison and from the right for concentrating too much on such stories. Although liberal opponents of the war were chagrined at the U.S. flag emblems regularly displayed as graphics decorating news broadcasts, supporters cheered the literal flag-waving.

Administration defenders note that the belief Saddam Hussein possessed WMD was held not only by the Bush administration but also by foreign leaders. They argued there was an ongoing connection between Hussein and Osama bin Laden's al Qaeda terrorist network for months after the 9/11 Commission report to the contrary. [25]

"I would be willing to bet lunch or dinner at a good restaurant," says Michael Schudson, a professor of media studies at the University of California, San Diego, that the question of whether coverage of the Iraq war and its aftermath has been fair "would break down entirely by party affiliation."

# Is Fox News 'Fair and Balanced'?

As the Republican National Convention was winding down on Sept. 2, 2004, dozens of GOP delegates gathered near the CNN booth and began chanting loudly, "Watch Fox News! Watch Fox News!" [1]

The apparently spontaneous demonstration came just days after protesters of a more liberal persuasion gathered outside Fox's New York headquarters, holding signs that said, "Faux News" and "Shut Up!" (the retort popular Fox commentator Bill O'Reilly sometimes shouts at guests who annoy him).

It may seem surprising that a news outlet could engender such passionate demonstrations from partisans at either end of the ideological spectrum. But, to the extent that the general public concerns itself with questions about media bias, Fox has become the most heated flashpoint — and just a few years after its 1996 founding.

Liberals have decried Fox as the "the most biased name in news," claiming it does little more than spread Republican propaganda. The cable network's owner, Rupert Murdoch, is a media mogul with newspapers, cable and satellite networks and TV stations worldwide, reaching three-quarters of the world's population; he is known for his support of conservative politicians in this country and others. Fox President Roger Ailes was an adviser to Republican presidents from Richard M. Nixon to the first President George Bush.

In fact, some critics charge, Murdoch is using the Fox News Channel (FNC) to import party-affiliated news coverage to the United States. Former Fox producers and reporters claim that they got marching orders each day from management that echoed the Republican Party's line. Rep. Bernie Sanders, I-Vt., contends that Fox pounds away at the GOP's "message of the day," which usually focuses on divisive "wedge" issues like gay rights and abortion instead of issues of concern to the broader population, like the economy, the environment and health care. [2]

Moreover, Sanders and other critics say, Fox reporters and commentators use the same language, word for word, used that day by the GOP on the House or Senate floor and on conservative talk radio, producing an "echo chamber that resonates throughout America."

"I don't think any serious observer at this point does not think Fox leans to the right," says Steve Rendall, senior analyst at Fairness and Accuracy in Reporting (FAIR), a liberal, media-watchdog group.

Jeff Chester, executive director of the Center for Digital Democracy, is blunter: "Fox News is nothing more than a 24/7 political ad for the GOP," he says in the documentary "Outfoxed: Rupert Murdoch's War on Journalism."

Rendall has done studies suggesting that on Fox's flagship news program, "Special Report," Republican guests make up 83 percent of the one-on-one guests vs. 17 percent for Democrats, and that the few Democrats who do appear on the show are centrist or conservative.

"My problem with Fox is not that they are conservative," says Jeff Cohen, a former news contributor to both MSNBC and Fox News. "It's the consumer fraud of them claiming to be 'fair and balanced.' It's nothing of the sort." [3]

But Bill Shine, senior vice president for production at Fox, counters that "fair and balanced" is more than just the network's slogan. He says that Fox goes so far as to take a stopwatch into the studio to ensure that speakers representing different viewpoints get equal time. [4]

Political scientists Tim Groseclose and Jeff Milyo determined in a study that Fox's "Special Report" was more centrist than other sources for news including ABC News' "World News Tonight," *USA Today* and the *Los Angeles Times*. Their study was based on the number of times the outlets quoted various think tanks, comparing these to citations of the same think tanks in speeches by members of Congress. "All of the news outlets, except for Fox News' 'Special Report,' received a score to the left of the average member of Congress," they say. [5]

Groseclose and Milyo, however, acknowledge that their study did not include editorials and commentary. There seems to be little debate that Fox's commentary programs are dominated by conservative voices. Much of the growth of Fox's audience — it has surpassed both CNN and

---

The fact that the debate about Iraq retains its partisan charge has not kept many reporters from wishing they had questioned the Bush administration more critically about its justifications for the war. But, for the most part, they believe they did the best they could, given the unfavorable circumstances.

"It's very difficult in the run-up to a war because a president has access to information that the press does not, but there's probably no more important job for the press than to question the reasons for going to war,"

MSNBC to become the top-rated 24-hour news channel — has come from self-identified conservative viewers. [6]

"There is a group of conservatives dissatisfied by an impression that the mainstream press isn't conservative enough," says Martin Johnson, a political scientist at the University of California, Riverside. "If I'm a conservative and know that Fox is going to present the news from a conservative standpoint, then it makes sense for me to watch it."

Indeed, many viewers applaud Fox's openly patriotic productions, with American flags much in evidence. During the Iraq war, concluded the conservative Media Research Center, "FNC aided viewers by rejecting the standard liberal idea that objective war news requires an indifference to whether America succeeds or fails." [7]

"I have always felt that the major media networks have been liberal in their bias," said Bonnie Dunbar, a delegate to the Republican National Convention from Findlay, Ohio. "Then along comes Fox that presents both sides and gives conservatives their due without putting a negative slant on everything conservatives have to offer." [8]

Even some critics of the news content on Fox acknowledge its skill at transforming television, including the networks' much-imitated moving-graphics style. It presents the news with more emotion than its rivals and understands that conflict makes for good viewing. "Part of Fox News Channel's recipe for success is some of its political agenda, but also its masterful showmanship," says Matthew Felling, director of the Center for Media and Public Affairs. "It presents the news in an entertaining fashion, in a smash-mouth style that's the key to talk radio as well."

Showmanship has its downsides, say Fox critics, who also complain that the network's predominant format of focusing on anchors diminishes news by generating less of it. "Fox is kind of leading the way in cheapening the news in a financial sense," says Robert Greenwald, director of "Outfoxed." "It takes a lot less resources to put two people into a studio screaming at each other than to send reporters all over the world and have them spend months digging."

Regardless of the complaints, Fox News Channel's ratings are a rare area of rapid growth for the beleaguered news industry. The GOP delegates need not have bothered with their catcalling at CNN's convention booth. Fox's ratings for President Bush's acceptance speech that night peaked at more than 7 million viewers — not only higher than any broadcast network but also more than double CNN's 2.7 million viewers. [9]

Seeing the financial success of Fox, other networks are now mimicking its methods, giving more air time to conservative viewpoints, say critics of Fox. "It's called the 'Fox Effect,' " said Cohen, describing how when he was a senior producer for MSNBC's "Phil Donahue Show" he was directed to "out-fox Fox" by putting more conservative guests on the show than liberals. "They mandated that if we had two left-wing guests, we had to have three right-wing guests."

If the "Fox Effect" takes hold of other news outlets, the critics say, objectivity and, eventually, democracy will be the victims.

"Murdoch doesn't believe in objectivity," said David Brock, president and CEO of Media Matters for America. "He has contempt for journalism. He wants all news to be a matter of opinion, because opinion can't be proven false. That's very dangerous, because if people don't have a set of facts they can believe in, it's difficult to reach consensus on public policy." [10]

[1] Alan Murray, "As In Olden Days, U.S. Media Reflect the Partisan Divide," *The Wall Street Journal*, Sept. 14, 2004, p. A4.

[2] Quoted in "Outfoxed: Rupert Murdoch's War on Journalism."

[3] *Ibid.*

[4] See Colleen McCain Nelson, "America's Split Screen: It's Fox News vs. CNN," *The Dallas Morning News*, July 18, 2004, p. 1A.

[5] Tim Groseclose and John Milyo, "A Measure of Media Bias," Stanford University Working Paper, September 2003, p. 2.

[6] "News Audiences Increasingly Politicized," Pew Research Center for the People & the Press, June 8, 2004, p. 1.

[7] Brent Baker and Rich Noyes, "Grading TV's War News," Media Research Center, April 23, 2003, *Executive Summary*, p. 1.

[8] Leon Lazaroff and John Cook, "Fox News scores with GOP, spurs protesters," *Chicago Tribune*, Sept. 3, 2004, p. 14.

[9] Lisa de Morales, "Fox Tops GOP Parley Stats," *The Washington Post*, Sept. 9, 2004, p. C7.

[10] Quoted in "Outfoxed," *op. cit.*

Rosenstiel says. "Throughout American history, if a president misleads the public, or is misled by the intelligence community, the press is not going to catch that. They should, but it's never happened."

Today, news coverage of the Iraq war in the "news hole" has waned from about 15 percent in July 2007 to 3 percent in February 2008, according to the Project for Excellence in Journalism. War news has mainly been usurped by the horse-race coverage of the 2008 primary election. [26]

# BACKGROUND

## Revolutionary Change

At times it seems that the news has not changed at all over the last several hundred years. The type of news once delivered at fairs and markets by balladeers — stories of wars in foreign lands, murder and other crimes — would sound familiar to any contemporary cable viewer.

However, changes in the technology have periodically revolutionized the news business over the course of American history, leading to profound shifts in both the stories being told and the nature of the audience.

During Colonial times, printers, who acted, in effect, as editors and publishers, sometimes allowed governors to approve their copy before going to press. "Printers avoided offending the powerful by keeping divisive issues out of their newspapers, stifling debate rather than promoting it," writes Princeton University sociologist Paul Starr in his book, *The Creation of the Media.* [27]

Such practices changed drastically during the Revolutionary War. The Founding Fathers were great pamphleteers, and newspaper circulation, already higher in America than in England, rose dramatically. Papers took a leading role in disseminating news not only of the conflict but also the texts of essential documents, such as the Declaration of Independence. The central idea of the American Revolution — that ordinary people could govern themselves — made it imperative that information be shared as widely as possible. As Starr notes, democracy gave politicians and parties the incentive to promote a medium that could influence public opinion.

Accordingly, in 1792, the new government — which had created an unusually extensive postal network — set low postal rates for newspapers. By 1832, newspapers accounted for 95 percent of postal weight but contributed only 15 percent of postal revenues. [28] Such postal subsidies helped papers reach a wider area and increase circulation.

When U.S. politics grew more competitive during the 1820s, openly partisan newspapers played a leading role in helping to promote Whigs and other parties.

In the 1830s, the press became more of a popular medium through the rise of "penny papers." Where earlier papers were written mainly for an elite audience and concerned themselves mainly with commercial news, the low, one-cent price of the "penny press" enabled it to reach a broader audience with content focused on political controversies of the day.

But the press' growing reliance on money from advertisers, who didn't want newspapers to offend readers, along with the rise of the telegraph, led to increasing efforts at journalistic objectivity. The Associated Press wire service came to dominate foreign news and contributed a great deal of copy to local newspapers, particularly in the Midwest. Knowing that their client papers held a variety of partisan leanings, AP tried to send out stories that would offend neither advertisers nor readers of any political persuasion.

The falling cost of newsprint, faster presses and improvements in ink and typecasting fostered further growth in the news business. By 1909, about 2,600 daily papers existed in the United States — up from 574 in the 1870s. [29] Editors sought the attention of readers — including new immigrants — with bolder headlines, a greater emphasis on storytelling and occasional crusades and stunts.

Newspaper barons such as Joseph Pulitzer and William Randolph Hearst engaged in circulation wars, running sensational headlines and poaching each other's star reporters.

But newspapers soon faced a major threat from yet another new technology — radio.

## Electronic Media

Americans embraced the radio. Even as the Depression forced many families to drop phone service, the proportion of homes with radios grew from under 25 percent in 1927 to 65 percent in 1934. The Communications Act of 1934 created the Federal Communications Commission (FCC), which regulated radio more tightly than the free-wheeling press.

Anyone could, in theory, print a newspaper, but there was a limited amount of broadcasting spectrum. Much of the radio dial was soon dominated by national networks such as NBC, which tightly controlled affiliated stations and diminished localism by appealing to a broad audience. As with the telegraph, radio helped shape the modern news style, with clear, concise reports. Even then, listeners complained broadcasters were dumbing things down to reach the broadest possible audience.

Technology made political coverage more candidate-centered. With parties unable to influence radio as they had the newspaper business, radio focused more on personalities, especially the incumbent president, which helped President Franklin D. Roosevelt — a natural performer. A study of the 1940 presidential campaign found that the two major parties dominated different media: "In exposure, in congeniality of ideas, in trust and in influence . . . the Republicans inclined in favor of the newspaper and the Democrats in favor of the radio." [30]

During World War II, radio's live broadcasts gave the medium an advantage over newspapers, which were being hurt by a shortage of newsprint. Radio owned the story of Pearl Harbor for about 17 hours, because networks could break into coverage of football games, but no afternoon papers were published on Sundays. By 1943, radio ad revenues surpassed those of newspapers. [31]

As television began to emerge after World War II as the dominant news medium of the second half of the 20th century, broadcasters were subject to regulation aimed at opening the airwaves to all points of view. The so-called "Fairness Doctrine" — formalized by the FCC in 1949 — required radio and television stations to devote a reasonable percentage of time to the coverage of public issues and to provide an opportunity for the presentation of contrasting points of view. The Supreme Court upheld the policy as constitutional in 1969, based largely on the limited number of radio and TV stations. Two decades later, in 1987, the FCC dropped enforcement of the doctrine, citing the growth of broadcast and cable outlets and legal and policy doubts about the rule.

A statutory provision still on the books — Section 315 of the Communications Act — requires any broadcaster that allows a candidate to "use" its facilities to grant "equal opportunities" to all legally qualified candidates for the office. Congress in 1959 amended the "equal time" rule to exempt "bona fide" newscasts and documentaries. But the rule is usually interpreted to apply to entertainment programs so that, for example, the popular NBC comedy show "Saturday Night Live" could not feature one candidate for president without providing equal time to all others. [32]

As early as 1953, about half of U.S. households had a TV. The networks that dominated radio took over television. Radio stations survived through narrowcasting — appealing to limited audiences that advertisers wanted to reach, such as teenagers, African-Americans and farmers, without having to buy ads on the TV networks.

The watershed year for television news may have been 1963, when TV surpassed newspapers as Americans' leading source of daily news. That year, CBS and NBC extended their daily news programs from 15 to 30 minutes. (ABC followed suit four years later.) [33] It was also the year that a stunned nation watched four days of broadcasts surrounding the John F. Kennedy assassination and funeral. A few years later, gruesome war images broadcast into people's homes would help turn public opinion against U.S. involvement in Vietnam.

Relations between the press and the government, strained by Vietnam, worsened with the 1972 Watergate presidential scandal, which led to a more adversarial press culture. *The Washington Post*'s initially lonely pursuit of the story, portrayed as heroic in the 1976 film "All the President's Men," led to a spike in enrollment in college journalism programs, helping to foster the more educated, professional culture of the modern press corps.

## Tabloid Culture

Consistently beaten on breaking stories by the electronic media, newspapers adapted by changing the nature of their content, according to press historian Mitchell Stephens. "[Newspapers] are moving away from pure news reporting toward some hybrid of news, opinion, history and pop sociology," Stephens wrote in 1988. [34] The same changes would later take place in broadcast television, signaling what many see as a decline in the broadcast networks' quality and quantity of news, as well as their commitment to providing news as a public service.

During one 18-month period between 1985 and 1986, non-journalistic corporations purchased each of the three major U.S. broadcast networks. Cost-cutting and staff layoffs in news divisions soon followed.

"When the new generation of owners at ABC, CBS and NBC began to analyze their acquisitions for ways to improve profitability, the news divisions — with their sprawling, highly paid staffs, lavish operating budgets and perishable product and ratings that would prevent ad sales from ever reliably covering costs — presented them with an obvious target," wrote author Susan Bridge, describing a dynamic that was soon dramatized in the satiric 1987 film "Broadcast News." [35]

The networks also cut back dramatically on their foreign coverage, documentaries and investigations and devoted more time to sensationalistic and celebrity news. They devoted extensive coverage in 1986 to the nation's crack epidemic, but when the Drug Enforcement Agency in September released a report calling the attention "excessive," NBC was the only network even to briefly mention it. [36]

The explosive growth of cable television further heightened the single-minded devotion to sensational stories. The Cable Communications Policy Act of 1988 released cable operators from competitive constraints (sought by broadcasters) and from state and local government regulation. Cable penetration of U.S. households leapt from 20 percent in 1980 to 60 percent a decade later. [37]

A wave of mergers, prompted by the 1996 Telecommunications Act, led to further media cost-cutting. Over the next several years, Clear Channel Communications purchased more than 1,200 radio stations, and newspapers declined in both number and circulation. By 1997, only 37 cities had competing dailies (and in 17 of those cities competing papers had joint printing arrangements). [38]

As media consolidation continued, huge fortunes were made, but investment in newsgathering did not keep pace. "The object of these mergers is never to improve the service," said noted journalist and author David Halberstam. "I don't think there's anybody at the head of one of these large corporations that cares very much about journalism." [39]

Cable and satellite technology made possible the proliferation of hundreds of channels, giving birth to tabloid journalism. Faced with 24 hours to fill, all-news channels such as CNN and MSNBC have given wall-to-wall coverage to crime and celebrity stories that cost comparatively little to cover, such as the 1995 murder trial of O. J. Simpson. The line between gossip and reporting became forever blurred, as correspondents rushed to put new information on the air.

"We are a one-story business — there's only room for one big story, because the news managers have decided to cut costs and give less space to difficult, complex and hard-to-understand stories," says former *Boston Globe* Associate Editor Nyhan.

In the late 1990s, the ultimate tabloid story involved President Bill Clinton's affair with White House intern Monica Lewinsky. For the first time, the mainstream press followed up on reports in tabloids like the *National Enquirer*. "We didn't become more like the media — the media became more like us," said *Enquirer* Editor-in-Chief Iain Calder. "I see our DNA in magazines, newspapers and television all over America." [40]

The Lewinsky story took off when *Newsweek* was scooped on its own story through use of the latest technology to alter the news business — the Internet. On Jan. 17, 1998, *Newsweek* editors had decided not to run with the Lewinsky story. Two days later, Matt Drudge posted news of the decision and the content of the story

on his online blog, the Drudge Report. Two days later, *The Washington Post* and ABC News presented their initial stories about the affair, followed by *Newsweek*, which finally posted its story online. [41]

Reflecting the priority now given to such stories, the networks brought home their anchors, who had been in Cuba to cover a papal visit. Over the course of the year, the networks would air on their nightly news programs more than 1,500 stories about the Lewinsky affair. [42]

On March 4, 1999, when ABC broadcast Barbara Walters' interview with Lewinsky, 49 million people tuned in — the largest audience ever for a network news broadcast. [43]

# CURRENT SITUATION

## Merger Mania

On Sept. 8, 2004, CBS anchor Dan Rather reported on "60 Minutes" that CBS had obtained documents showing that President Bush had received favorable treatment during his stint in the Texas Air National Guard. The documents were quickly derided by bloggers and other news organizations as forgeries that could not have been made on the typewriters of the time. After defending its story for nearly two weeks, CBS admitted on Sept. 20 that it had been misled by its source — who turned out to be a former Guardsman who has urged Democrats to wage "war" against Republican "dirty tricks."

The blog chatter that helped sink Rather's account illustrated a curious fact about the modern media: The number of news outlets has grown exponentially, despite the rapid consolidation of media ownership.

Since passage of the 1996 Telecommunications Act, there has been a seemingly unending wave of media mergers, affecting all aspects of the news business. [44] In television, the 10 biggest companies own 30 percent of all stations, reaching 85 percent of U.S. households. The networks make up less than 30 percent of the total business of their new corporate owners. In radio, the top 20 companies control more than a fifth of all stations nationwide. [45] Clear Channel, with its 636 stations, is a presence in 120 of the top 300 markets. [46] Twenty-one companies now control 66 percent of daily newspaper circulation. [47]

More than half the journalists surveyed by the Pew Research Center in spring 2004 thought their profession

# Do mainstream media outlets have a partisan bias?

## YES    Cliff Kincaid
*Editor,* Accuracy in Media Report.

From a Web commentary, June 14, 2004

It's finally starting to dawn on some in the media that diversity should mean something other than hiring minorities and homosexuals. In an article in *The Weekly Standard,* Fred Barnes quoted Tom Rosenstiel of the Project for Excellence in Journalism as saying it's necessary not to think just of diversity that makes newsrooms "look like America," but to create a press corps that "thinks like America."

"In truth," said Barnes, "the effort to hire more minorities and women has had the effect of making the media more liberal. Both these groups tend to have liberal politics, and this is accentuated by the fact that many of the women recruited into journalism are young and single, precisely those with the most liberal views." Rosenstiel says, "By diversifying the profession in one way, they were making it more homogenous in another."

This discussion comes in the wake of a survey by the Pew Research Center and Project on Excellence in Journalism, finding that "news people, especially national journalists, are more liberal, and far less conservative, than the general public." Picking up on the "diversity" problem, Howard Kurtz of *The Washington Post* quoted Rosenstiel as saying that "the growing proportion of self-identified liberals in the national media — and the fact that 'conservatives are not very well represented' — is having an impact." Rosenstiel said, "This is something journalists should worry about."

The survey found a relatively small number of conservatives at national and local news organizations: "Just 7 percent of national news people and 12 percent of local journalists describe themselves as conservatives, compared with a third of all Americans." The liberal bias is most apparent in coverage of social issues. It found, for instance, that "journalists are much more accepting of homosexuality than is the general public."

Thomas Bray of the *Detroit News* suggests that the Pew survey may substantially understate the degree of the bias. Bray suggests that liberal media bias has affected the public's view of Bush and the economy. He notes a Gallup poll of 1,000 Americans showed that 51 percent of Americans say the economy is getting worse, "even as gross domestic product, employment and other indicators continue to forge ahead."

Bray says Bush may be able to overcome this bias, but that he "shouldn't rely too heavily on the notion that voters will be able to sort things out based on what they read, see and hear in the press."

## NO    Charlotte Grimes
*Knight Chair in Political Reporting; S. I. Newhouse School of Public Communications, Syracuse University.*

Written for *CQ Researcher,* October 2004

"Bias" is a four-letter expletive that partisans of all stripes throw at the press. To dispute the accusation is like spitting into a hurricane. The blowback is fierce and ugly. In short, this is an argument that cannot be won. It usually can't even be conducted civilly.

But, to spit into the hurricane: The press does have biases toward conflict and controversy. Reporters and editors are drawn to a verbal brawl like rubberneckers to a highway accident. In our competitive mode, we too often sacrifice accuracy, precision and clarity for speed. In the modern media echo chamber of talk shows, blogs and 24-hour cycle of relentless repetition, the press also plays a part in magnifying and distorting the trivial into the monumental.

Does any or all of that make us partisan? No. So why this widespread — and intensifying — perception of bias?

Partly it's all the above flaws, which partisans and ordinary folks looking for the simplest answers can easily misinterpret as "Aha, bias." Partly it's the bitter fruit of the general decline in public respect for all institutions. Partly it's the age-old "kill the messenger" syndrome. Partly it's the eye of the beholder, with Democrats and Republicans alike making the bias charge ("Why did the press wait so long to publish the Abu Ghraib photographs?" vs. "Why is the press making such a big deal out of the Abu Ghraib photos?") Partly it's the polarization — remember those red and blue states? — of the nation. And partly it's the failures of the press to explain its ethics, professional skills and job — and to make the case that journalists do try to police themselves.

Much is made by partisans, for example, of surveys of journalists showing a majority of respondents have voted for Democrats. Little is said about the independent studies of journalists' work that show, indeed, partisan bias in coverage is generally rare and usually slight. Few, especially among the partisans, notice or credit that often the journalists themselves are those most outraged by the lapses.

Sure, there are some reporters and editors who can't or won't exercise the essential professional skills for impartiality, like asking "What or who's left out?" or "Are any words or phrases loaded?" or "Is this true and accurate?" Those journalists usually end up as columnists or out of the newsroom. True, the press has its sins, weaknesses and flaws. But, if anything, we're bipolar — not partisan.

was being "seriously hurt" by financial pressures brought about by mergers. [48] (Journalists at the Unity conference applauded Kerry vigorously when he stated his opposition to continuing mergers.)

Corporate profits are rising, but newsroom staffs are being cut. More money is being invested in new technologies for disseminating the news than in collecting it. But even as the number of major news companies dwindles, other voices have proliferated. Cable and satellite technology provide hundreds of new channels, offering a much larger choice of programming. And the Internet allows the emergence of new voices in the form of blogs and social networking sites, as well as instant access to newspapers and other sources of information — both reliable and spurious — around the world.

In a decision that displayed both the influence of a single company in the age of media consolidation and the decline of enforcement in equal time and fairness rules, the family-owned Sinclair Broadcasting Corp. in October 2004 ordered the 62 TV stations it owns — many of them in states contested in the 2004 presidential race — to air a documentary highly critical of Kerry. [49] The Kerry campaign called charges made in the documentary about his Vietnam-era activities scurrilous, but it had no recourse for demanding equal time. Equal-time requirements do not apply to news reports, which this documentary is being billed as. Kerry never convinced the FCC that the program didn't constitute news. (Under the equal-time rules, candidates only get to complain if their opponent is being shown and they are not.)

## Blurring the Lines

With the advent of Web blogs, anybody can be a journalist (or consider himself one), as the bloggers who were credentialed at the 2004 party conventions proved. Journalism has become a wide-open market, making it harder for the working press to set itself apart.

Coincidentally, the emergence of bloggers as journalists raises sticky questions about whether journalists can shield their sources. "Do bloggers also have confidentiality of sources?" asks Syracuse University's Grimes, referring to an ongoing investigation into who leaked to reporters the identity of CIA operative Valerie Plame.

"How do we reclaim our distinctive identity in the press," Grimes continues. "People confuse the reporters with the commentators. We've cooperated a lot with that confusion — to our detriment." Grimes, a veteran jour-

nalist, says she became an academic after meeting a woman in a shopping mall who said she loved the news. When Grimes asked what news programs she watched, the woman mentioned Montel Williams and Oprah Winfrey, two talk show hosts.

Talk show programs like that are "virtual journalism," Grimes says, "a combination of innuendo and rumor and factoid, and we're presenting it as the real thing."

Two incidents involving a non-journalist demonstrate just how fuzzy the line between news, gossip and entertainment has become.

James Carville has been a Democratic political consultant for many years. In 2003, he played a fictionalized version of himself as an ongoing character in an HBO series, "K Street," which mixed its narrative with appearances from real Washington insiders. On the show, Carville told former Vermont Gov. Howard Dean, then still a presidential hopeful, a joke about Sen. Trent Lott, R-Miss., that he thought Dean should use in the campaign. Dean went ahead and told the joke at a real-world presidential debate. Carville then watched the actual political debate on a TV monitor in a subsequent "K Street" episode. [50] For many people, it was a demonstration of how the media have helped muddy the distinction between reality and fiction.

More recently, "Saturday Night Live" ran skits regarding the treatment of Obama by the media and more specifically the apparent bias of moderators of a recent CNN debate. An article by the Associated Press says that the "media took a sharper look at Barack Obama the week after" the episode aired. The Project for Excellence in Journalism reports that during the week after the skit, 69 percent of campaign coverage featured Obama, but many of the stories took a hard look at his career in the Senate and previously in the Illinois legislature-insightful coverage that, until this point, had been reserved for Senator Clinton. *The Washington Post, The New York Times* and "Good Morning America" all ran stories regarding whether the media has been treating the two candidates equally. It's hard to say whether the skit had a direct impact on the coverage or whether these stories were already in the works, but there is no question that it had at least a little impact in terms of a wakeup call to major networks as they began to look at Obama in a different light. [51]

Senator Clinton took the SNL story to the campaign trail, adding comments into speeches to urge voters to watch the February 23 episode to see just how biased the media are. Of course, on March 8, the comedy show took a different turn, spoofing Hillary's "3 a.m." ad in which she indirectly criticizes Obama's lack of experience. In the SNL version, "President" Obama calls Clinton to ask her advice at 3 in the morning, noting that he never knew the job of president would be so hard.

Whose corner is SNL in? It's unclear at this point, but the show is definitely having an impact on the campaign. Senator Obama and Senator Clinton have both made guest appearances on the show, hoping to reach out to a younger audience.

Some see today's media environment as topsy-turvy. Major media companies are investing more money in new ways to disseminate information than to gather it. Print reporters appear as commentators on TV and people read their stories as links from other Web sites. It's becoming nearly impossible for the average person to know where they first heard or read a particular story, which makes it more difficult, of course, for them to build up a sense of trust toward a particular outlet. In fact, quality standards now often vary within a single organization, with NBC, for instance, remaining more rigorous than MSNBC.

The diminishing credibility of news institutions, some say, will ultimately prove more damaging than a series of scandals involving individual reporters who plagiarized or fictionalized stories, most notably Jayson Blair of *The New York Times* and Jack Kelley of *USA Today*. [52] Although those were isolated cases, the amount of criticism of the media in general will prove more damaging in the long run, says Felling of the Center for Media and Public Affairs. "Media credibility is spiraling downward because media is eating itself," he says.

Media criticism has become more than a cottage industry. Entire organizations are devoted to critiquing the media. Numerous books such as Bernard Goldberg's *Bias*, Al Franken's *Lies and the Lying Liars Who Tell Them* and Ann Coulter's *Treason and Slander* have been bestsellers. The fact that Goldberg and Coulter impute bias from the left while Franken lampoons pundits on the right hardly matters.

"There are shelves at the bookstore devoted to the idea that the media is horrible because it's liberal," Felling says. "Or because it's conservative. All that tells the average person is that that the media is horrible, period."

"At a time when America's mass media becomes ever more centralized . . . the public's relationship to the media is more decentered than ever before," writes *L.A. Weekly* columnist Powers. "Just as the proliferation of blurbs in movie ads has made all critics appear to be idiots or flacks, so the rabbit like proliferation of news sources — many of them slipshod, understaffed or insanely partisan — has inevitably devalued the authority of any individual source." [53]

## OUTLOOK

### Abandon Objectivity?

Rumors are flying that one of the major broadcast networks may get out of the news business altogether. A recent article by Troy Patterson, *Slate*'s television critic, encourages CBS to get out of the news business, citing that it has television's worst-rated evening and morning newscasts, with a third-rated Sunday news show. [54] Except for the major cable news channels-Fox, CNN and MSNBC-the audience for television news has been in decline and corporate pressures in TV often fall hardest on the labor-intensive newsgathering operations. And with the audience for news fracturing, the only areas of growth lie outside the traditional mainstream media — in Hispanic broadcasting and publications and the Internet.

While it once made sense to aspire to objectivity so as to offend no one, in today's splintered media market it may make more sense to adopt the European model — appealing ardently to partisans of one stripe or another in hopes of securing their allegiance. The popularity of conservative talk radio and Fox News' financial success have prompted other networks — in a trend nicknamed the "Fox Effect" — to change formats and hosts: Both MSNBC and PBS have recently hired more conservative hosts. Meanwhile, in an effort to appeal to liberals, the Air America radio network began broadcasting in 2004. In 2006, however, Air America filed for Chapter 11 bankruptcy after not being profitable in its first two years of operation, mainly because it was blacklisted by prominent advertisers. [55]

In many cases, Americans are changing their news-intake habits to reflect the changing media. As news coverage on local radio stations has shrunk — due to consolidation — National Public Radio has seen its audience more than doubled over the last decade. Niches still exist for serious news, and, even if one of the major networks does shut down its news division, the remaining networks will benefit. The most-viewed Web news pages still belong to well-established media brands.

And in a new trend this election year, both liberals and conservatives who feel the mainstream media is not properly covering the presidential election have turned to books and documentaries for information about their candidates. Bookstore shelves are bulging with titles about both candidates, and the documentary market is flourishing, ranging from Michael Moore's anti-Bush "Fahrenheit 9/11" to "Hillary Uncensored—Banned by the Media," which promises to "expose the truth about her conflicts in the past and her liberal plot for the future." [56]

Meanwhile, the audience for news is shrinking. According to a Pew survey, Americans spend about 66 minutes each day watching, reading or listening to the news — a 10 percent decline since 1994. [57] The future doesn't necessarily look any brighter: Younger Americans are even less likely to pay attention to the news than their elders. During this election cycle, young people are more likely than before to turn for information to entertainment shows such as "The Daily Show" or "The Colbert Report." According to a Pew survey, 39 percent of 18 to 29 year olds learn about the campaign from comedy shows-up from 21 percent in 2004. However, an earlier Pew study indicates that "the regular audiences of the comedy shows were as well informed as the audiences of elite news sources such as the websites of major daily newspapers and "The NewsHour with Jim Lehrer." [58]

All of today's media still rely on mainstream news organizations as primary sources of information, even if they occasionally question the credibility of that information. However, as old-line news organizations invest less and less in newsgathering, and the new media have no budget or inclination to engage in original reporting, the business will diminish, says Rosenstiel, of the Project for Excellence in Journalism.

The new news business likes its information raw, whether it's a Web site linking to documents or TV stations concentrating on events that can be filmed from a helicopter. There is plenty of opinion espoused in the media today, but less analysis that interprets what the staged events of the day really mean. And independent analyses of official statements are increasingly dismissed as partisan.

"As citizens in a democracy, we need access to independent, accurate facts in order to make responsible decisions," says Rendall, the FAIR senior analyst. Rendall says news outlets should own up to their opinions and pursue a more European model in which they announce their biases openly, while presenting solid reporting to back it up.

As "Daily Show" host Jon Stewart commented to ABC newsman Ted Koppel during the 2004 convention, the mainstream press is not doing its job when it merely acts as a referee in partisan debates without providing a "reality check" on the misstatements and exaggerations made by the two parties. [59]

"The major networks and major newspapers are losing ground as agenda-setters and as referees," says Nyhan, the former *Boston Globe* editor. "When the media drop the ball, the politicians go crazy. No one is watching these very complex decisions and mistakes get made."

Jeff Cohen, a television producer and former MSNBC and Fox news contributor, sees a more serious outcome of the media changes. "The media is the nervous system of a democracy," he said. "If it's not functioning well, democracy can't function." [60]

## NOTES

1. Media Boost Obama, Bash "Billary," Center for Media and Public Affairs, Feb. 1, 2008, www.cmpa.com/election%20news%202_1_08.htm.

2. "News Audience Increasingly Politicized," The Pew Research Center for the People & the Press, June 8, 2004, p. 1.

3. David Folkenflik, "More grist for those seeking 'bias' in the news media," *The Baltimore Sun*, Oct. 6, 2004, p. 1E.

4. See "A Pause for Hindsight," *The New York Times*, July 16, 2004, p. 20; Howard Kurtz, "The Post on WMDs: An Inside Story," *The Washington Post*, Aug. 12, 2004, p. A1; and "Were We Wrong?" *The New Republic*, June 28, 2004, p. 8.

5. For background, see Alan Greenblatt, "The Partisan Divide," *CQ Researcher*, April 30, 2004, pp. 373-396.

6. "Summer of Lies," *Columbia Journalism Review*, July/August 2004, p. 3.

7. Jim VandeHei, "Kerry Sharpens Contrast With Bush," *The Washington Post*, Sept. 2, 2004, p. A1.

8. "Social Networking and Online Videos Take Off," The Pew Research Center for the People & the Press, Jan. 11, 2008, http://people-press.org/reports/display.php3?ReportID=384.

9. Elizabeth Wilner, "Outlook: Just Wired Differently," washingtonpost.com, Sept. 21, 2004, www.washington-post.com/wp-dyn/articles/A29834-2004Sep17.html.

10. "A Media Watershed," *The Wall Street Journal*, Sept. 16, 2004, p. A16.

11. For background, see Brian Hansen, "Combating Plagiarism," *CQ Researcher*, Sept. 19, 2003, pp. 773-796.

12. Colleen McCain Nelson, "America's Split Screen: It's Fox News vs. CNN," *The Dallas Morning News*, July 18, 2004, p. 1A.

13. *Ibid.*

14. Pew Research Center, *op. cit.*

15. *Ibid.*, p. 13.

16. "Social Networking and Online Videos Take Off," The Pew Research Center for the People & the Press, Jan. 11, 2008, http://people-press.org/reports/display.php3?ReportID=384.

17. John Powers, *Sore Winners (and the Rest of Us) in George Bush's America* (2004), p. 199.

18. *Ibid.*, p. 247.

19. "Social Networking and Online Videos Take Off," The Pew Research Center for the People & the Press, Jan. 11, 2008, http://people-press.org/reports/display.php3?ReportID=384.

20. Prof: Misconception of media bias causes problems for democracy, Sept. 26, 2007, Purdue University News Service, www.purdue.edu/uns/x/2007b/070926T-WasburnBias.html.

21. Bruce Bartlett, "The Fall of the News Oligopoly," *National Review Online*, Sept. 20, 2004, www.nationalreview.com/nrof.bartlett/bartlett200409200822.asp.

22. Michael Massing, "Now They Tell Us," *The New York Review of Books*, Feb. 26, 2004, p. 43.

23. Steve Rendell and Zara Broughel, "Amplifying Officials, Squelching Debate," *FAIR*, May/June 2003.

24. Quoted in Douglas McCollam, "How Chalabi Played the Press," *Columbia Journalism Review*, July/August 2004, p. 31.

25. Walter Pincus and Dana Millbank, "Al Qaeda-Hussein Link Is Dismissed," *The Washington Post*, June 17, 2004, p. A1.

26. "Political Knowledge Update," The Pew Research Center for the People & the Press, March 12, 2008, http://people-press.org/reports/display.php3?ReportID=401/.

27. Paul Starr, *The Creation of the Media* (2004), p. 61.

28. *Ibid.*, p. 90.

29. Jerry W. Knudson, *In the News* (2000), p. 89.

30. Paul F. Lazarsfeld, Bernard Berelson and Hazel Gaudet, *The People's Choice* (1944), p. 129.

31. Susan Bridge, *Monitoring the News* (1998), p. 7.

32. Harvey Zuckman, *et al.*, *Modern Communications Law* (1999), p. 1234.

33. Edward Bliss Jr., *Now the News: The Story of Broadcast Journalism* (1991), p. 311.

34. Mitchell Stephens, *A History of News* (1988), p. 287.

35. Bridge, *op. cit.*, p. 19.

36. Edwin Diamond, *The Media Show* (1991), p. 100.

37. Bliss, *op. cit.*, p. 435.

38. Knudson, *op. cit.*, p. 89.

39. Quoted in Herbert N. Foerstel, *From Watergate to Monicagate* (2001), p. 19.

40. Quoted in Tom Maurstad, "Enquiring Media: Tabloids Make Vivid Impression on Pop Culture," *The Dallas Morning News*, Aug. 29, 2004, p. 10E.

41. Knudson, *op. cit.*, p. 256.

42. Foerstel, *op. cit.*, p. 122.

43. Leonard Downie Jr. and Robert G. Kaiser, *The News About the News* (2002), p. 28.

44. For background, see David Hatch, "Media Consolidation," *CQ Researcher*, Oct. 10, 2003, pp. 845-868.

45. "The State of the News Media 2004," Project for Excellence in Journalism, March 15, 2004, www.stateofthenewsmedia.org/.

46. "The State of the News Media 2008," Center for Excellence in Journalism, March 2008, www.stateofthenewsmedia.org/2008/chartland.php?id=703&ct=col&dir=&sort=&c1=0&c2=0&c3=0&c4=0&c5=0&c6=0&c7=0&c8=0&c9=0&c10=0&d3=0&dd3=1.

47. "The State of the News Media 2007," Center for Excellence in Journalism, March 12, 2007,

http://stateofthemedia.org/2007/chartland.asp?id=205&ct=pie&dir=&sort=&col5_box=1#.

48. "Bottom-Line Pressures Now Hurting Coverage, Say Journalists," Pew Research Center for the People & the Press, May 23, 2004, p. 1. For background, see Kathy Koch, "Journalism Under Fire," *CQ Researcher*, Dec. 25, 1998, pp. 1121-1144.

49. Howard Kurtz and Frank Ahrens, "Family's TV Clout In Bush's Corner," *The Washington Post*, Oct. 12, 2004, p. 1A.

50. Powers, *op. cit.*, p. 260.

51. "Did SNL Spoof Shift Obama Coverage?" Associated Press, March 4, 2008, www.msnbc.msn.com/id/23472513/.

52. Hansen, *op. cit.*

53. Powers, *op. cit.*, p. 194.

54. Troy Patterson, "Dead Air: Why CBS Should Shutter Its News Division," *Slate*, April 23, 2008, www.slate.com/id/2189815/.

55. "The State of the News Media 2007," Center for Excellence in Journalism, March 12, 2007, www.stateofthenewsmedia.org/2007/narrative_radio_ownership.asp.

56. "Anti-Hillary dirty tricks war hots up," *The Observer*, June 17, 2007, www.guardian.co.uk/world/2007/jun/17/usa.hillaryclinton.

57. Pew Research Center, *op. cit.*

58. "Social Networking and Online Videos Take Off," Pew Research Center for the People & the Press, Jan. 11, 2008, http://people-press.org/reports/display.php3?ReportID=384.

59. "Nightline" ABC News, July 28, 2004.

60. Quoted in "Outfoxed: Rupert Murdoch's War on Journalism."

## BIBLIOGRAPHY

### Books

Alterman, Eric, *What Liberal Media?: The Truth about Bias and the News*, Basic Books, 2003.
*The Nation* columnist argues that accusations of a liberal bias in the mainstream media are not only overstated but miss a tendency toward conservatism.

Boehlert, Eric, *Lapdogs: How the Press Rolled Over for Bush*, Free Press, 2006.
*The Rolling Stone* contributor takes a look at how the national media failed the public while serving the Bush administration.

Bozell III, L. Brent, *Weapons of Mass Distortion: The Coming Meltdown of the Liberal Media*, Crown Forum, 2004.
The president of the Media Research Center offers evidence that major media outlets are liberal and argues that they are going to continue to lose market share as a result.

Downie Jr., Leonard, and Robert G. Kaiser, *The News About the News: American Journalism in Peril*, Knopf, 2002.
Two top *Washington Post* editors worry that good journalism — providing crucial information about government and issues of interest — is too often crowded out by sloppy journalism.

Kuypers, Jim A., *Bush's War: Media Bias and Justifications for War in a Terrorist Age*, Rowman & Littlefield, 2006.
The author discusses the relationship between President Bush and the media in reporting 9/11 and the War on Terror.

Powers, John, *Sore Winners (and the Rest of Us) in George Bush's America*, Doubleday, 2004.
*The L.A. Weekly* editor and columnist explains how Bush's presidency both exemplifies and takes advantage of changes in contemporary media culture.

Starr, Paul, *The Creation of the Media: Political Origins of Modern Communications*, Basic Books, 2004.
A Princeton University sociologist shows how the U.S. government helped make the media vital and competitive through regulatory decisions and investments in technology.

### Articles

Ahrens, Frank, "Murdoch Seizes Wall St. Journal In $5 Billion Coup," *The Washington Post*, Aug. 1, 2007, p. A1.
*The Post* reports the purchase of *The Wall St. Journal* by Rupert Murdoch.

"A Media Watershed," *The Wall Street Journal*, Sept. 16, 2004, p. A16.
An editorial argues that CBS' embarrassment in using fake documents in a report critical of Bush signals the moment when the liberal media lost its power to control the public agenda.

"Anti-Hillary Dirty Tricks War Hots Up," *The Observer*, Sunday June 17, 2007, www.guardian.co .uk/world/2007/jun/17/usa.hillaryclinton.

Kurtz, Howard, "The Post on WMDs: An Inside Story," *The Washington Post*, Aug. 12, 2004, p. A1.
The *Post*'s media critic takes the paper to task for not being sufficiently rigorous of its coverage of the war in Iraq.

Massing, Michael, "Now They Tell Us," *The New York Review of Books*, Feb. 26, 2004, p. 43.
Massing argues that reporters relied too heavily on outside sources arguing the case for war against Iraq and too little on critics.

Menand, Louis, "Nanook and Me," *The New Yorker*, Aug. 9, 2004, p. 90.
Examining "Fahrenheit 9/11" within the documentary tradition, the author concludes that the art of making documentaries tends to be practiced by liberals.

Navarette Jr., Ruben, "Once Journalists Show Their Politics Can They Still Claim Impartiality?" *Chicago Tribune*, Aug. 13, 2004.
The columnist worries that the minority journalists who applauded John Kerry and booed President Bush embarrassed their profession by revealing partisan colors.

Patterson, Troy, "Dead Air: Why CBS Should Shutter Its News Division," *Slate*, April 23, 2008, www.slate.com/id/2189815/.

Samuelson, Robert J., "Picking Sides for the News," *Newsweek*, June 28, 2004, p. 37.
The economics columnist notes that surveys show the public increasingly finds media outlets politically biased.

**Reports and Studies**
Groseclose, Tim and Jeff Milyo, "A Measure of Media Bias," Stanford University Working Paper, September 2003.
Two political scientists devise a way to measure bias in the media.

Kull, Steven, *et al.*, "Misperceptions, the Media and the Iraq War," Program on International Policy Attitudes/Knowledge Networks, Oct. 2, 2003.
Seven polls conducted during 2003 concerning the public's knowledge of the war in Iraq indicate that the audiences for different news outlets have very different grasps of the facts.

Lott Jr., John R. and Kevin A. Hassett, "Is News Coverage of Economic Events Politically Biased?" American Enterprise Institute, Sept. 1, 2004.
The AEI scholars conclude that economic data is about 20 percent more likely to receive positive coverage under Democratic administrations than Republican ones.

"Media Boost Obama, Bash 'Billary,' " Center for Media and Public Affairs, Feb. 1, 2008, www.cmpa .com/election%20news%202_1_08.htm.

"News Audiences Increasingly Politicized," The Pew Research Center for the People & the Press, June 8, 2004.
The group found that political polarization is increasingly reflected in American viewing and reading habits.

"Political Knowledge Update," The Pew Research Center for the People & the Press, March 12, 2008.
The group found that public knowledge of how many Americans have been killed in Iraq has declined considerably.

"Social Networking and Online Videos Take Off," The Pew Research Center for the People & the Press, Jan. 11, 2008.
The group found that the Internet is becoming a staple for all age groups when it comes to news about the 2008 presidential election.

"The State of the News Media 2004," Center for Excellence in Journalism, March 15, 2004.
The center finds the long-term outlook for many traditional news outlets is "problematic."

**"The State of the News Media 2007," Center for Excellence in Journalism, March 12, 2007.**
The center finds that news organizations need to begin thinking about the long-term impacts of the new media environment.

**"The State of the News Media 2008," Center for Excellence in Journalism, March 2008.**
The center finds that the media as a whole is in a more troubled position than it was last year.

# For More Information

**Accuracy in Media**, 4455 Connecticut Ave., N.W., Suite 330, Washington, DC 20008; (202) 364-4401; www.aim.org; A conservative media-watchdog organization.

**Center for Media and Public Affairs**, 2100 L St., N.W., Suite 300, Washington, DC 20037; (202) 223-2942; www.cmpa.com; A nonpartisan research organization.

**Center for Excellence in Journalism**, 1850 K St., N.W., Suite 850, Washington, DC 20006; (202) 293-7394; www.journalism.org. Represents the Committee of Concerned Journalists and the Project for Excellence in Journalism.

**Fairness and Accuracy in Reporting**, 112 W. 27th St. New York, NY 10001; (212) 633-6700; www.fair.org. A progressive national media-watchdog organization.

**Media Research Center**, 325 S. Patrick St., Alexandria, VA 22314; (703) 683-9733; www.mediaresearch.org/welcome.asp. A conservative media-watchdog group.

**Pew Research Center for the People & the Press**, 1150 18th St., N.W., Suite 975, Washington, DC 20036; (202) 293-3126; www.people-press.org; An independent media-research organization funded by the Pew Charitable Trusts.

# 8

# Controlling the Internet

Sarah Glazer

Waving "Orange Revolution" flags, Ukrainians gather in Kiev's Independence Square on Aug. 24, 2005, the 14th anniversary of Ukraine's break from the Soviet Union. During the Orange Revolution, which pressured the government to overturn 2004 election results as fraudulent, community Web sites posted information about where protesters needed assistance.

From *CQ Researcher*, May 12, 2006.

Critics of a proposed, new America Online (AOL) policy discovered in April that AOL apparently was blocking e-mails mentioning DearAOL.com — a Web site set up by 600 organizations opposed to the policy.

"I tried to e-mail my brother-in-law about DearAOL.com, and AOL sent me a response as if he had disappeared," said Wes Boyd, co-founder of MoveOn.org, a liberal political group. "When I sent him an e-mail without the DearAOL.com link, it went right through." [1]

AOL blamed the blockage on a brief technical glitch. "A glitch is a glitch is a glitch," said AOL Communication Director Nicholas Graham. "As many as 65 other domains . . . were impacted," even though they had no connection to DearAOL. [2]

But many DearAOL activists note the timing of the blockage suspiciously coincided with their latest petition drive opposing AOL's plan to allow mass mailers to pay a fee to bypass AOL's spam filters.

Activists fear that under AOL's proposed rule change, messages from "poorer" users — such as nonprofit charities and political groups — would be blocked while commercial ads would sail through. They also worry that major portions of the Internet would be off-limits to citizens of certain countries.

The DearAOL activists note that it's not the first time a big Internet service provider (ISP) has blocked access to content it opposed, nor does the collateral blocking of unaffiliated sites necessarily prove it was an accident, given that last year Telus, a Canadian phone company and ISP, blocked access to a Web site run by its striking employees' union. In the process, access to more than 700 unrelated Web sites was blocked. [3]

## Internet Access Limited by 20 States

Twenty states have laws restricting municipally operated broadband lines and/or laws limiting consumers' right to attach equipment to their Internet lines. Five of the anti-municipal broadband laws were passed in 2005.

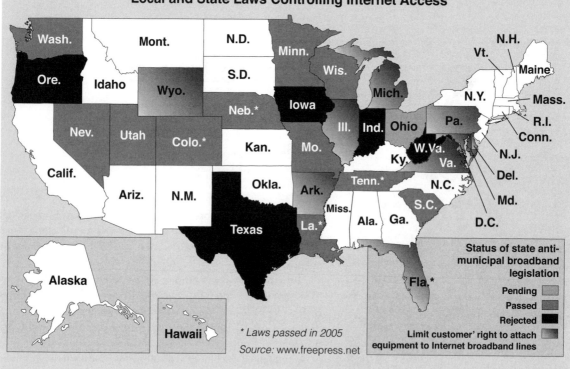

### Local and State Laws Controlling Internet Access

Status of state anti-municipal broadband legislation

- Pending
- Passed
- Rejected
- Limit customer' right to attach equipment to Internet broadband lines

\* Laws passed in 2005

Source: www.freepress.net

In the United States, the battle for Internet control is playing out over revision of the landmark 1996 Telecommunications Act, which deregulated the telecommunications industry to increase competition. [4] Much of the debate centers on so-called Net neutrality — or requiring ISPs to treat all Internet content equally.

Neutrality advocates say the policy has enabled the Internet to foster rapid innovation. With no gatekeeper regulating traffic, tiny start-up companies and college students have created a plethora of innovative products and services — from instant messaging and podcasting to e-Bay, search engines and Amazon.com. "The key to the Net's extraordinary innovation is that it doesn't allow a term like 'allow,' " wrote Lawrence Lessig, a professor of cyberlaw at Stanford University. [5]

But telephone and cable companies, which own the wires over which most Internet traffic travels, want to replace the Net's traditional "open-pipe" structure with a system of priority channels that "sniff" data to determine content and shift some traffic to high-priority lanes. Such a system is needed, the companies say, to ensure higher quality of service for customers downloading bandwidth-gobbling video, for example, and to raise funds to pay for extending fiber-optic cable and other infrastructure to carry today's much faster broadband Internet.

But media advocates say telephone and cable companies mostly want to protect their key businesses — video and voice transmissions — from new competitors offering the same services via broadband.

The big ISPs hope to remake the Internet in the "entertainment model," where big-money players control distribution channels, determining which content makes it onto the movie or television screen, says Jeffrey Chester, executive director of the Center for Digital Democracy. "Phone and cable companies know that if there's an open wire, their business is over," now that broadband connections are fast enough to carry video and voice telephony. "They have to make sure that their own content can receive premium treatment."

Such a model, Chester argues, is dangerous for democracy because the Internet is not just an entertainment medium but also a forum for discussion of public issues. And if some information moves faster, then other information necessarily moves more slowly, he notes. The slower information may never be seen, he adds, which spells death to Web sites where visibility is key. If ISPs can shunt some information to slower lanes while reserving the fast lanes for selected content, what happens to "content necessary for civic participation?" he asks.

David Isenberg, a fellow at Harvard Law School's Berkman Center for the Internet and Society, agrees on the link between Internet freedom and democracy. Freedom of Internet communication is "fundamental to freedom of speech," and "violating it should be anathema to democracy," he says.

Some members of Congress, mostly Democrats, are pushing so-called Net-neutrality legislation that would prohibit ISPs from prioritizing service by content. But after heavy lobbying by the cable and telephone industries, the House Energy and Commerce Committee on April 26 defeated a Net-neutrality amendment while finalizing its version of the telecom law overhaul. Chairman Joe L. Barton, R-Texas, said that while he supports the Federal Communications Commission (FCC) watching for potentially anti-competitive or censorial ISP treatment of Internet content, he doesn't

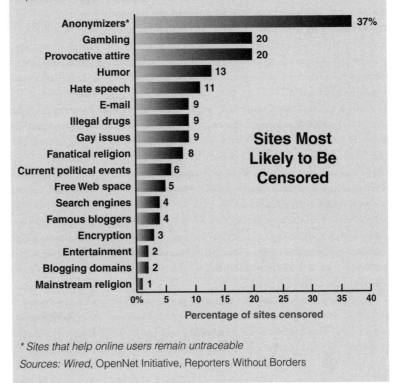

## Off-Limits Web Sites

Sites that help Internet users in non-democratic countries avoid detection and those offering gambling are the most censored — after pornography and political dissent — among nations monitored by the OpenNet Initiative.

**Sites Most Likely to Be Censored**

| Category | Percentage of sites censored |
|---|---|
| Anonymizers* | 37% |
| Gambling | 20 |
| Provocative attire | 20 |
| Humor | 13 |
| Hate speech | 11 |
| E-mail | 9 |
| Illegal drugs | 9 |
| Gay issues | 9 |
| Fanatical religion | 8 |
| Current political events | 6 |
| Free Web space | 5 |
| Search engines | 4 |
| Famous bloggers | 4 |
| Encryption | 3 |
| Entertainment | 2 |
| Blogging domains | 2 |
| Mainstream religion | 1 |

*Sites that help online users remain untraceable*

Sources: *Wired*, OpenNet Initiative, Reporters Without Borders

believe "all the Draconian things" people predict will happen without a Net-neutrality amendment. [6]

A new group — the "Save the Internet" coalition — says it is rapidly gaining individual and institutional supporters. By early May, the group claimed more than a half-million signatures on a petition demanding a Net-neutrality law. Backers range from the liberal MoveOn.org to conservative bloggers like "Instapundit" Glenn Reynolds and "Right Wing News." [7]

"Whenever you see people from the far left and the far right joining together about something that Congress is getting ready to do . . . what Congress is getting ready to do is basically un-American," said Craig Fields, director of Internet operations for Gun Owners of America. [8]

While some worry that powerful corporations want to stifle Internet freedom, others warn that various authoritarian governments in recent years have walled their citizens off from much of the Internet, even as they have promoted broadband use as an economy booster.

Indeed, repressive governments have much to fear from an unfettered Internet. Modern telecommunications played a major role in Ukraine's "Orange Revolution," which "pressured the government to overturn its 2004 election results as fraudulent." [9] Demonstrators used cell phone messaging technology to gather "smart mobs" of protesters, while community Web sites posted information about where protesters needed assistance. [10]

China has promoted Internet use as a tool for economic growth while squelching certain content. With some 111 million Internet users, China is second only to the United States in total users but has strictly limited their access. China blocks Web sites, censors citizens' Web searches and tracks down people who publish critical opinions or information on blogs. The Chinese government — with the acquiescence of Google, Yahoo! and other search engines — not only censors Web sites that question government actions but also those dealing with teen pregnancy, homosexuality, dating, beer and even jokes. [11] (*See sidebar, p. 180.*)

Free-Internet advocates also complain that broadband rollout in the United States has stalled — particularly in rural areas. "This country needs a national goal . . . to have universal, affordable access for broadband technology by the year 2007," said President George W. Bush in March 2004. [12] But critics say that because of phone and cable company foot-dragging and the lack of a national broadband strategy, Bush's goal can't possibly be reached and, in fact, the United States has fallen behind other industrialized countries in access to broadband. (*See graph, p. 178.*)

Installing fiber to carry broadband Internet to rural America is extremely expensive, says David Farber, distinguished career professor of computer science and public policy at Carnegie Mellon University. "I could run fiber to every ranch in Montana, but nobody would pay for it," he says. Nevertheless, private phone and cable companies are trying to block rural governments' efforts to offer residents broadband service on their own if the private market doesn't offer it or the service costs too much.

But low population density is not the obstacle to full broadband penetration so much as the lack of a national strategy to achieve that goal, says the advocacy group Free Press. It notes other low-density countries, such as Iceland and Canada, have more broadband coverage than the United States. [13]

As government, the telecom industry and Internet users debate control of the Net, here are some of the questions being discussed:

## Is the global Internet in danger of being dismantled?

Enthusiasts say the Internet embodies the dream of a global medium allowing people on opposite sides of the planet to communicate as easily as if they were in the same room. Today, however, some say the global Internet is in danger of being fragmented into separate, unconnected networks.

For instance, authoritarian governments are building firewalls to block citizens' access to certain parts of the Net, especially the Web sites of opposition groups. In the past few years, China "has essentially shut its own Internet off from the world Internet," says Jean Camp, associate professor of informatics at Indiana University. "And they're just the first. Other countries could do it," too, increasing the likelihood of Internet fragmentation.

In late February, China set up a master list of new Chinese Internet addresses that will be maintained on Chinese-owned "root servers," according to Michael Geist, chairman of Internet and e-commerce law at the University of Ottawa in Ontario, Canada. [14] Until now, worldwide coordination of Internet addresses has been handled by the U.S.-based Internet Corporation for Assigned Names and Numbers (ICANN). In addition, 13 so-called root-server computers scattered around the globe hold the master list that maps Web site names to the code numbers corresponding to their Internet addresses, or URLs.

China's action "doesn't mark the end of a global, interoperative Internet," but it demonstrates that countries may not always cooperate to keep the global Internet interoperable, said Geist. The global system would "break" if a parallel system duplicated existing addresses and diverted them to different computers, for example, or adopted different technical operating procedures.

The results of such an alternative Internet could be "creepy," says Lauren Weinstein, co-founder of People for Internet Responsibility. Different sites would pop up for the same Web address typed into computers in different countries. International e-mails might not get through, and variable or incompatible standards would stymie those trying to develop new business and communications applications, says Weinstein.

"The Internet . . . exists only if there is agreement about core functionality," he says. "For it to work, there has to be an awful lot of cooperation," and if enough countries become disgruntled with the current system, a split could develop.

But David Gross, coordinator for communications and information policy at the U.S. Department of State, says it's unlikely that a government would risk cutting itself off from the global community by launching an incompatible root system. "I have not heard any government official suggest that there would be benefits . . . in the creation of an independent root system" using existing Internet addresses. Gross said. "Any new network would . . . want to be interoperable with the current system."

Other pressures stem from simple growing pains. Organizations managing Internet technical standards are strained by rapid growth and the competing agendas of Web users and governments. [15]

As Internet users and uses proliferate, issues demanding collaborative solutions also proliferate, but today there is no specific structure to resolve them, says Weinstein. Despite its mind-boggling sophistication, the Internet is, in fact, in its "infancy," he says.

To keep the system interoperable, a new governance structure must develop that is embraced by an unusually diverse group of players, including governments, domestic and international businesses and individual users, says John Mathiason, an adjunct professor for international education and distance learning at Syracuse University. Today the world is just beginning to develop such a system, he says.

Dealing with copyright violations — such as the illegal downloading of music — is only one of many complications that must be worked out, he says. Currently, music copyright laws can be circumvented using servers located in countries that are not party to international copyright treaties, Mathiason says. If the Internet allows circumvention of national boundaries, he says, "You need to work out how conflicting schemes of copyright, commercial transactions and money are going to work."

Such protections don't yet exist, and more unresolved issues keep popping up, Mathiason says. "In a technical sense, the Internet is very robust," he says. "But, from a political point of view, it's very fragile. There is a great motivation by many people to keep it global and open. But when you have a conflict, then the issue is up in the air."

A worker helps install fiber-optic cable onto telephone lines in Louisville, Colo. President George W. Bush has called for "universal, affordable access for broadband technology by the year 2007," but critics say the goal can't be reached because of phone and cable company foot-dragging and the lack of a national broadband strategy.

*Getty Images/Michael Smith*

Today, ICANN is the closest thing to an Internet governing organization, although ostensibly it only manages certain technical parameters — mainly involving Internet addresses — and bases its decisions on input from businesses, governments and users around the world.

"The U.S. has been a very light-handed steward from the beginning," says Susan Crawford, an assistant professor of law at Cardozo Law School in New York City and ICANN board member. "ICANN becomes the issue of contention because the domain name system" — the Internet's system of coordinated address names and their corresponding code numbers — "is one of the very few choke points where you could censor content."

But even ICANN's "light-handed" approach to regulating the Internet has come under fire, in part because, while independent, it operates under the auspices of the U.S. Department of Commerce. For example, last summer, after long deliberation, ICANN announced that it would create a new "dot xxx" Internet domain where pornography Web sites could voluntarily register. The move was controversial worldwide but became more so when, shortly thereafter, ICANN reversed the decision at the behest of the Commerce Department, after heavy lobbying by conservative groups.

Commerce's intervention raised hackles and was seen as "very inappropriate," since it imposed a U.S. policy position on the Internet without consultation, says Crawford. In fact, Commerce's surprise intervention

# A World of Online Communities

Because the Internet developed free of corporate control, it's been a source of innovation, giving rise to new technologies and forums, including some that threaten traditional businesses and values. That's in stark contrast to the "entertainment model" phone and cable companies want to impose on the Internet, which critics say would limit such innovation.

A relative newcomer is **Meetup — www.meetup.com —** which helps people establish interest groups in their local communities. Founded in 2002, it claims 2 million members, including French-, Italian-, Japanese- and Spanish-speakers' groups, stay-at-home-moms' groups and book clubs.

Social-networking sites, where users post profiles and garner "friend" lists, are booming. **MySpace — www.myspace.com** — used by young people and celebrities alike, boasts 50 million members, and **Friendster — www.friendster.com** — 24 million. In South Korea, 15 million people — one-third of the population — belong to CyWorld. [1]

Partisan political networking and blogging sites have flourished over the past few years, but a recent entry, **Essembly — www.essembly.com** — hopes to exploit the social-networking phenomenon on a non-partisan basis. Essembly members post profiles, blog and list friends, as on MySpace, but they also participate in site-wide political dialogue.

Since Hurricane Katrina hit the Gulf Coast in 2005, a volunteer Internet service, the **Katrina People Finder Project — www.katrinalist.net** — has helped people locate missing loved ones. Along with a team of other computer experts, David Geilhufe developed a new computer tool, People Finder Information Formats, to aggregate data from various sources into one searchable, convenient source. [2]

New kinds of people-to-people links — often for the purpose of bypassing banks and other traditional institutions — pop up continually on the Internet. Several new sites feature people-to-people banking. **Kiva — www.kiva.org —** enables individuals in the United States to offer micro-financing help to entrepreneurs in developing countries by partnering with local organizations. Lenders can chip in capital in amounts as small as $25 to help people start bakeries, print shops and hair salons. Kiva reports 100 percent of its loans have been repaid or are being repaid.

**Prosper — www.prosper.com** — links up people who want to borrow money or are willing to lend it, for a return. Would-be borrowers seek cash to attend school, renovate a house, start a business or buy a big present for a 40th anniversary, and Prosper lenders name their own interest rates.

In keeping with the Internet principle that the more people a network links the more value it has, Internet

probably got more people worldwide to come down in favor of the xxx domain than would ever have done so otherwise, says Mathiason.

In another controversial move, ICANN in 2005 at the behest of the U.S. government, transferred ownership of the Internet domain for Kazakhstan — "dot kz" — from a group of Kazakhstan Internet users to an organization owned by the Kazakh government "without requiring consent from the existing owners," said Kieren McCarthy, a British technology writer. It also turned Iraq's domain over to a government-run group. [16]

"Previously, ICANN would take no action . . . unless both sides were in complete agreement," he said. "Now, ICANN had set itself up as the de facto world authority on who should run different parts of the Internet." [17]

Tension between the United States and other governments over non-Internet issues such as the Iraq war are exacerbating disgruntlement with ICANN, say some Internet

scholars. "People just don't have the same good faith now that Washington will stay benevolent and not do anything to abuse its authority," said Lee McKnight, an associate professor of information economics and technology policy at Syracuse University's School of Information Studies. [18]

ICANN — and other organizations being considered to take over Internet management, such as the United Nations — are too likely to become enmeshed with the aims of big business and wealthy governments to make good long-term stewards, say many public-policy analysts. The only way to stave off a fragmented Net lies in civic groups stepping up to develop worldwide consensus on Internet issues, they argue.

"The world is on the path to more globalized governance" though the road is long, says Milton Mueller, a professor of the political economy of communications at Syracuse University and co-founder of ICANN's Noncommercial Users Constituency.

entrepreneurs and activists have long developed applications aimed at bringing more people online, sometimes for free.

For example, **FON software — http://en.fon.com/** — helps Wi-Fi (Wireless Fidelity) users worldwide get access to wireless Internet wherever they go, in return for registering to share their own wireless access with other FON members who pass by.

Internet services to help users get around government censorship also are under continual development by activists around the world.

**Psiphon** — developed by researchers at the University of Toronto — and the **Free Network Project**, or **Freenet**, developed by Scottish network technologist Ian Clarke, use computer networks in non-censoring countries to help people in information-censoring regimes communicate anonymously and freely.

To many Internet enthusiasts, the Net is first and foremost a publishing medium, and as faster broadband connections become the norm, the range of what's published continually expands. At photo-sharing site **Flickr — www.flickr.com** — members file, store and share their photos. And, true to the Internet's community-building tradition, Flickr members engage in plenty of two-way conversation about what they see. For example, in several popular ongoing games, Flickr members snap and post mystery photos in a favorite city, like New York, Chicago or London, and fellow urban-enthusiasts try to guess where the photo was taken.

Among the newest wrinkles are sites where users can upload and share videos. The hot, new video site **YouTube — www.YouTube.com** — started up last year in the garage of two young techies looking to share home videos. Among the current offerings on the site created by Chad Hurley and Steve Chen — a sample guitar lesson posted by a group of music teachers advertising their pay services; a video art installation of a chair that disassembles then reassembles itself to music; performance clips of aspiring comics; and home and travel videos from around the world, from street dancing in Japan to scary driving behavior in India.

And of course, big advertisers also show up on YouTube, counting on the passing traffic — 30 million videos are viewed daily — to drum up interest in everything from new Nike sneakers to upcoming movies like "Superman Returns." [3]

---

[1] Micah L. Sifty, "Essembly.com: Finally, a Friendster for Politics," *Personal Democracy Forum*, March 13, 2006, www.personaldemocracy.com.

[2] Tin Zak, transcript, "Interview with Ethan Zuckerman," *Globeshakers*, Oct. 3, 2005, www.pghaccelerator.org.

[3] "YouTube: Way Beyond Home Videos," *Business Week online*, April 10, 2006, www.businessweek.com.

## Should telephone and cable companies be allowed to control the Internet?

As significantly faster broadband connections become the norm, telephone and cable companies that own the so-called last-mile wires connecting homes and businesses to the Internet say they need more control over how data travels and what kind of data users send in order to improve security, transmission quality and broadband access.

However, Internet-freedom advocates say the Internet only works when it's an "open pipe," with all data treated the same, and when users are free to place whatever software or hardware they want at the "pipe ends" without asking permission — just as electricity customers can plug in either a computer network or a toaster. Without these key qualities, the Internet cannot continue to foster business innovation and the open discussion crucial to democracy, say open-Net advocates.

Cable and telephone companies want permission to alter the open-pipe structure so they can "prioritize" and speed transmission of some data. Allowing companies to speed transmission of some content, such as video, would increase competition by allowing ISPs to specialize, says Chistopher Yoo, a professor of technology and entertainment law at Vanderbilt University Law School.

But others say allowing network owners to slow or speed data will mean that only wealthy individuals and companies would get higher-speed service, leaving poorer, non-commercial users and start-up businesses in slower-moving cyber obscurity. Such a system would also stifle innovation and allow cable and telephone companies to block, slow or charge exorbitant fees to companies like Vonage, which offers Voice Over Internet Protocol (VOIP), or telephone service via the Internet.

"Because the network is neutral, the creators of new Internet content and services need not seek permission

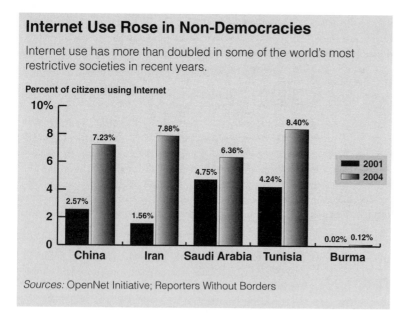

## Internet Use Rose in Non-Democracies

Internet use has more than doubled in some of the world's most restrictive societies in recent years.

Percent of citizens using Internet

Sources: OpenNet Initiative; Reporters Without Borders

use my pipes free, but I ain't going to let them do that. . . . The Internet can't be free in that sense, because we and the cable companies have made an investment and for a Google or Yahoo or Vonage . . . to expect to use these pipes free is nuts!" [21]

But some technology scholars say Whitacre's plan could amount to double-charging. "This is a pretty dumb thing . . . to say," wrote Edward Felten, professor of computer science and public affairs at Princeton University. "If I were an SBC broadband customer, I'd be dying to ask Mr. Whitacre exactly what my monthly payment is buying if it isn't buying access to Google, Yahoo, Vonage and any other $%&^ Internet service I want

. . . or pay special fees to be seen online," said Vinton Cerf, a key Internet software developer and Chief Internet Evangelist for Google. "As a result, we have seen an array of unpredictable new offerings" — from blogging to VOIP — "that might never have evolved had central control of the network been required." [19]

A neutral net is "critical" to America's competitiveness, he adds. "In places like Japan, Korea, Singapore and the United Kingdom, higher bandwidth and neutral broadband platforms are unleashing waves of innovation that threaten to leave the U.S. further and further behind," says Cerf.

In defending their proposal to charge customers more for priority transmission, some phone companies insist that some companies have already asked to be able to pay more for faster service.

"It's probably true that companies are . . . willing to pay for better treatment, but I think they're doing it out of fear," said Jeff Pulver, an Internet analyst. "It's legalized extortion." [20]

As for blocking telephone company competitors like Vonage, Ed Whitacre, CEO of SBC Communications, said he's not worried that his business will be eclipsed by online competitors, because he controls their transmission lines. "How do you think they're going to get to customers?" Whitacre asked. "Through a broadband pipe. Now what [Vonage and other Internet businesses] would like to do is

to use." Many SBC customers sign up for the company's broadband services only to get access to Vonage or Google, so "why should Google pay SBC for this? Why shouldn't SBC pay Google instead?" [22]

Yoo acknowledges that there might be a "limited incentive" for cable Internet providers to discriminate against competing ISPs or for a telephone company to discriminate against VOIP providers. But "since different people want different things from the Internet," he says, encouraging "network diversity" would create a more vibrant marketplace where network providers can "compete on a basis other than price."

Moreover, allowing telecom companies to charge companies extra for priority online treatment would not put innovators at a disadvantage, as many fear, says James Gattuso, a senior fellow at the conservative Heritage Foundation. Instead, start-ups might be first in line to pay for priority transmission, because "if I were starting up a computing application, I would want to be able to say my new service is faster," he says. And start-ups "can get capital to pay for prioritized treatment," Gattuso says. "Money is easier to get than visibility." (See "At Issue," p. 181.)

Verizon's chief technology officer, Mark Wegleitner, says contrary to neutrality-advocates' fears, network owners have a strong incentive to help customers reach as many Web sites as possible. "We think the richest, broadest choice . . . makes for a happier consumer," he said. [23]

But others argue that if companies can "sniff" data packets and speed some information along faster than the rest it will hamper democratic discourse online. Web sites with controversial views might be relegated to the slow lanes, says the Center for Digital Democracy's Chester. And since nonprofits with "dot org" Internet addresses — where much of the civic discourse takes place online — often have little cash, their Internet communications will be shunted to the equivalent of a cyber "dirt road," he says. "This is being framed as a business story, but it's also a battle for the soul of our communications system."

In addition, start-up content providers could be strangled by red tape, he warns. "Today, anyone can open up a Web site and compete" for Internet users' attention. "Tomorrow, you'll have to show up at the office of the phone and cable companies" to get permission to attach your new application to the network, he says.

Advocates of a neutral Internet law say history indicates that phone and cable companies will not respect the Net's open nature on their own. According to Public Knowledge, a nonprofit that advocates for a free and open Internet, ISPs have tried to manipulate how broadband subscribers use the Net and have forbidden subscribers from using their broadband connections to provide content to the public — flying in the face of the Internet's tradition of offering publishing power to ordinary people. [24]

Other broadband contracts forbid home users from logging onto virtual private networks (VPNs), needed by telecommuters to access their workplace networks from home. And, until the FCC intervened last year, Madison River Telephone Co., which serves rural counties in Illinois and several Southern states, blocked subscribers from using Vonage's VOIP service. [25] The wireless company Clearwire, in Kirkland, Wash., blocks broadband services — such as streaming video or VOIP — that use a lot of bandwidth, and broadband providers have successfully lobbied for laws in nine states limiting how broadband consumers can use their own computers. [26]

Content blocking for ideological reasons also has occurred, according to Public Knowledge. Last year the Canadian ISP Telus blocked a Web site set up by a labor union representing Telus employees, who were in a dispute with the company. [27]

## Should local governments be allowed to provide broadband Internet service?

Far fewer Americans have access to affordable broadband than citizens in other developed countries, and too few Americans have a choice of broadband Internet service providers — especially in rural areas. At the end of 2005, only 24 percent of rural households were using high-speed Internet at home, compared to 39 percent of urban and suburban households. [28]

Running TV cables or upgrading phone lines to isolated homes in rural areas costs more and returns less profit than stringing cable or phone lines in high-density urban or suburban areas, so rural areas are usually the last to get new telecom services.

To overcome the problem, many local governments have begun installing or are considering installing their own networks, either on their own or in partnership with private companies. Local groups argue that such government-initiated efforts can spur more competitive broadband markets and widen access. But the cable and phone companies offering Internet services say government-provided broadband services siphon off subscription money that the companies could use to extend their broadband infrastructure.

In Sanborn, Iowa — population 1,300 — "we have lost nearly 50 percent of our subscribers" over the past four years to a municipal broadband service, not because of high prices or poor services but due to unfair competition, said Douglas Boone, CEO of the Premier Communications phone company, told the Senate Commerce Committee on Feb. 14. [29] Private ISPs cannot compete with local governments' broadband offerings, he said, because localities don't pay taxes, which eat up "more than 40 percent of our profits. It is difficult to compete when the local municipality starts . . . with a 40 percent discount." [30]

Furthermore, since most municipal broadband is in rural areas, the projects pose the biggest threat to the smallest ISPs, which generally serve rural areas neglected by the bigger cable and phone companies, according to Brett Glass, owner of a tiny wireless — Lariat.Net — in Laramie, Wyo. Subsidized local broadband networks also crowd out small wireless start-ups, which could mean less competition in the long run because wireless ISPs are potentially the biggest competitive threat to cable and telephone ISPs, he said. [31]

Opponents also argue that locally subsidized broadband is probably an unfair and inefficient use of public

# C H R O N O L O G Y

**1960s–1970s** *Computer researchers develop noncentralized, user-controlled computer networks.*

**1965** MIT researcher Lawrence Roberts creates first long-distance computer network, linking machines in Massachusetts and California.

**1969** University of California at Los Angeles becomes the first node of ARPANET, the Internet's Pentagon-funded precursor.

**1971** Michael Hart starts Project Gutenberg to put copyright-free works online.

**1972** E-mail is invented and dubbed the first Internet "killer app."

**1973** England and Norway become the Net's first international connections.

**1974** AT&T declines invitation to run the Internet.

**1975** First ARPANET mailing lists link people with shared interests.

**1980s–1990s** *Businesses join research institutions online. Internet viruses and spam invented.*

**1982** Sending messages gets easier as a University of Wisconsin server automatically links computer numbers to names, in the prototype of the Domain Name System (DNS).

**1984** Internet-wide DNS introduced. The Net has over 1,000 directly connected computers — called "hosts," or Internet service providers (ISPs).

**1988** Cornell graduate student Robert Morris, son of a network-security expert, sends the first self-replicating virus.

**1989** Internet has over 100,000 hosts.

**1990** "The World" (world.std.com) is the first commercial ISP. The first remotely operable machine — the Internet Toaster — goes online.

**1992** Internet has more than 1 million hosts.

**1993** White House, U.N. go online.

**1994** U.S. immigration lawyers Martha Siegel and Lawrence Cantor send out first spam, advertising their firm.

**1996** Phone companies ask Congress to ban Internet telephones. Congress passes Telecommunications Act but doesn't ban the phones. . . . China requires Net users and ISPs to register with the police. . . . Saudi Arabia confines access to universities and hospitals.

**1998** Private, nonprofit Internet Corporation for Assigned Numbers (ICANN) takes over DNS under a U.S. government contract.

**1999** Somalia gets an ISP; Bangladesh and Palestinian Territories register domains.

**2000s** *Battles over Internet control heat up. Broadband allows voice and video to travel over the Internet. U.S. phone and cable industries consolidate and offer broadband.*

**2000** Yahoo! bans auctions of Nazi memorabilia when it is unable to block French users from the product listings, as ordered by a French court.

**2001** Internet2 — an ultra-fast broadband network for U.S. research institutions — carries a live musical, "The Technophobe and the Madman."

**2002** FCC rules that cable broadband operators don't need to give competing ISPs access to their lines.

**2003** First World Summit on the Information Society discusses global governance and access for developing nations.

**2005** FCC rules phone companies don't need to give competing ISPs free access to broadband connections. India's domain, "dot in," swells from 7,000 sites in 2004 to more than 100,000 in 2005. . . . China jails dissident based on Net writings handed over by Yahoo!

**2006** Google launches controversial Chinese search engine that censors information. . . . Congress considers "Net neutrality" legislation. . . . ICANN contract expires in September, and governments and citizens' groups mull global governance for the Internet.

dollars. "It is unlikely that more than a small number of residents would benefit," wrote Joseph Bast, president of the Chicago-based free-market think tank Heartland Institute, making it hard to "justify the steep cost" that would be borne by all local taxpayers. The cost also can't be justified in the name of overall community improvement, he argued, because "it is fanciful to imagine that municipal broadband is a cost-effective way to promote economic development." [32]

But advocates of municipal broadband point out that many of the projects are not competing against private business. "The overwhelming majority of current projects are the result of a public-private partnership," wrote city officials from four small Texas towns in a Feb. 13 letter to Sen. Kay Bailey Hutchison, R-Texas. They called the claim that the public-sector broadband threatens the private sector "a red herring." [33]

Supporters of municipal broadband also argue that the usual ban against the public sector competing with the private sector does not apply to broadband infrastructure because broadband is a public, not a private, good.

If high-speed Internet services "were a purely private good . . . like, say, golf clubs, I could buy an argument against government provision," said Thomas Rowley, a fellow at the University of Missouri-based Rural Policy Research Institute. But "its benefits go far beyond the individual user to improve an entire community's economy, schools, health care and public safety. As with all these services, if the private sector cannot or will not . . . provide it to all at affordable prices, the public sector must." [34]

# BACKGROUND

## Born in the USA

In the early 1960s, a nuclear clash between the Cold War superpowers, the United States and the Soviet Union, seemed imminent. U.S. researchers wondered: Could they build a communications network that could survive nuclear combat? [35] Their efforts spurred creation of the Internet, whose technological and social ramifications we are only today beginning to understand.

Traditional networks — like the phone system and Post Office — route messages through central switching points and are vulnerable to complete breakdown if vital nodes are knocked out. Paul Baran, an electrical engineer at the RAND Corporation, a think tank focusing on military issues, proposed a network with many nodes, each able to route data on to another network point until the data reached its destination. He also proposed chopping messages into smaller "packets" of digitized information. Each packet is separately addressed and travels on its own to the designated addressee computer.

The network plan — which several other researchers envisioned at the same time — seemed inefficient, but was in truth "extremely rugged," designed with doomsday in mind, explained technology and science fiction writer Bruce Sterling. Each digital packet "would be tossed like a hot potato from node to node to node, more or less in the direction of its destination, until it ended up in the proper place. If big pieces of the network had been blown away, that simply wouldn't matter; the packets would still stay airborne, lateralled wildly across the field by whatever nodes happened to survive." [36]

In 1969, the concept was made operational for the first time, when seven large computers at U.S. research institutions were linked into a non-centralized packet-switching communications network. Funded by the Defense Department's Advanced Research Projects Agency (DARPA), ARPANET allowed researchers to transmit data — and even program each other's computers — via dedicated high-speed lines.

Scientists were enthusiastic about ARPANET, which gave them access to hard-to-come-by user time on remote fast computers. By 1972, the network had 37 nodes. Through the 1970s, other computer networks in the United States and abroad were linked to the so-called ARPANET, and the Internet — the network of networks — was born.

From its earliest days the Internet's radically decentralized structure gave it an unprecedented ability to develop in ways that its inventors never anticipated, a characteristic at the heart of today's battles over the Net.

ARPANET was built to facilitate high-tech computing and government communications. But, to the surprise of many, high-tech users quickly adapted the system to a down-to-earth pursuit — sending mail electronically for free. By 1973 e-mail made up 75 percent of network traffic.

By 1975, users had developed another new application — mailing lists to broadcast individual messages to large numbers of subscribers. These discussion lists gave birth to the first Internet communities — groups around the world connected by networked computers and com-

# Rights Group Names 15 Internet 'Enemies'

Reporters Without Borders, an international organization working to restore the press' right to inform citizens, recently listed the following 15 countries as "enemies of the Internet" because of their restrictive Internet policies:

**Belarus:** President Alexander Lukashenko often blocks access to opposition parties' Web sites, especially at election time. In August 2005, he harassed youths posting satirical cartoons online.

**Burma:** Home Internet connections are prohibited; access to opposition sites is systematically blocked, and Internet café computers record what customers are searching every five minutes for government-spying purposes.

**China:** Censorship technology and spying block all government criticism on the Internet. Intimidation, including the world's largest prison for cyber-dissidents, forces self-censorship by users. Some blogs and discussion groups post real-time news about events in China, but censors remove the postings later. China is exporting its cyber-surveillance expertise to other repressive countries, including Zimbabwe, Cuba and Belarus.

**Cuba:** Citizens may not buy computers or access the Internet without Communist Party authorization. Some Cubans get connected illegally but can only access a highly censored, government-controlled version of the Internet.

**Iran:** Ministry of Information blocks access to hundreds of thousands of Web sites, especially those dealing with sex and providing independent news. Several bloggers were imprisoned recently, including Mojtaba Saminejad, who got a two-year sentence for insulting Ayatollah Ali Khamenei.

**Libya:** There is no independent media, and the government controls the Internet, blocking access to dissident exile sites and targeting cyber-dissidents.

**Maldives:** Several opposition Web sites are filtered by President Maumoon Abdul Gayoom's regime. One of four people arrested in 2002 is still in prison for helping to produce an e-mailed newsletter criticizing government policies.

**Nepal:** King Gyanendra Bir Bikram Shah Dev's regime controls Internet access of citizens. Most online opposition publications, especially those seen as close to Maoist rebels, have been blocked inside the country. Bloggers discussing politics or human rights are under constant pressure from the authorities.

**North Korea:** The government only recently allowed a few thousand privileged citizens access to a highly censored version of the Internet, including about 30 pro-regime sites.

**Saudi Arabia:** The government blocks access to 400,000 sites to protect citizens from content — mainly sex, politics or religion — that violates Islamic principles and social standards.

**Syria:** The government restricts Internet access to a small number of privileged people, filters the Web and closely monitors online activity.

**Tunisia:** President Zine el-Abidine Ben Ali blocks opposition publications and other news sites, discourages e-mail because it is difficult to monitor and jails cyber-dissidents.

**Turkmenistan:** Internet use is essentially prohibited; there are no Internet cafés, and a censored version of the Web is only accessible through certain companies and international organizations.

mon interests. While some lists were work-related, many were not. The most popular of the early unofficial lists was SF-Lovers, a list for discussing science fiction.

As the Internet quietly fostered new ways of communicating, the traditional communications industry remained aloof. Internet users paid for the use of phone lines to transmit their data, but otherwise phone companies paid little attention to the Net. "We were fortunate in that there was absolutely no commercial Internet industry out there," said Robert Kahn, a former DARPA network developer who later founded the nonprofit Corporation for National Research Initiatives to pro-

mote information-infrastructure development. "There were no . . . Internet service providers; there was no commercial anything. So nobody . . . saw the original Internet initiative as a threat to their business." In fact, AT&T made a conscious decision to stay out of computer networking, he pointed out. "They thought they could make more money by selling . . . the underlying circuits." [37]

AT&T — at the time a telephone monopoly — was kept informed of ARPANET's progress but wasn't impressed. AT&T executive Jack Osterman said of one DARPA proposal, "First, it can't possibly work, and if it

**Uzbekistan:** The state security service often asks Internet service providers (ISPs) to temporarily block access to opposition sites. Some Internet cafés warn users will be fined for viewing pornographic or banned political sites.

**Vietnam:** Filters "subversive" Internet content, spies on cyber-café users and jails cyber-dissidents.

## Countries to Watch

**Bahrain:** Has begun to regulate the Internet; requires all online publications, including forums and blogs, to be officially registered.

**Egypt:** Censorship is minor, but the government has taken steps since 2001 to control online material; some criticism of the government is unwelcome.

**European Union (EU):** Holds ISPs responsible for content of Web sites they host, requiring them to block any page considered illegal; EU is studying a proposal to oblige ISPs to retain records of customers' online activity.

**Kazakhstan:** Online publications are under scrutiny because many government scandals have been revealed on Web sites. President Nursultan Nazarbayev's regime blocked two opposition party sites in October 2005.

**Malaysia:** Government intimidation of online journalists and bloggers has increased, notably at the country's only independent Internet daily, whose journalists have been

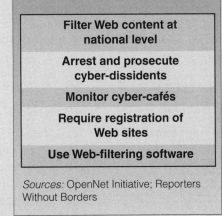

## Controlling Net Traffic

Here are the five most common ways that governments, primarily non-democratic states, control access to the Internet.

> **Filter Web content at national level**
>
> **Arrest and prosecute cyber-dissidents**
>
> **Monitor cyber-cafés**
>
> **Require registration of Web sites**
>
> **Use Web-filtering software**

*Sources:* OpenNet Initiative; Reporters Without Borders

threatened and its premises searched.

**Singapore:** The government intimidates Internet users, bloggers and Web site editors.

**South Korea:** Filters the Internet, blocking pornographic sites and publications that "disturb public order," including pro-North Korea sites; users who go too far in expressing anti-government opinions are punished.

**Thailand:** Filters the Internet to fight pornography, but has extended censorship well beyond this.

**United States:** Laws to prevent intercepting online traffic do not guarantee enough privacy; U.S. Internet firms, including Google, Yahoo!, Cisco Systems and Microsoft, are working with China to censor their material in China.

**Zimbabwe:** The government reportedly is getting Chinese equipment to monitor citizens' Internet usage; state telecom monopoly TelOne asked ISPs in June 2004 to sign contracts allowing it to monitor e-mail traffic and requiring them to block material the government deems illegal.

*Source: Reporters Without Borders, 2005*

did, damned if we are going to allow the creation of a competitor to ourselves." [38]

In 1974, AT&T turned down an offer to run ARPANET. [39]

## Battle of the Band

During the 1980s the decentralized Internet mushroomed from less than 1,000 host computers, mostly in the United States, to millions worldwide, but the telephone and cable companies largely continued to ignore it. The Internet expanded from the research sector to the commercial sector in the mid- to late-'90s and began

spawning e-commerce businesses and new ways to communicate, like the now ubiquitous Web sites. Nervous about potential competition, phone companies asked Congress in the mid-1990s to ban Internet telephony, but legislators refused.

A new world emerged in the late 1990s when broadband technology, using cable and optical fiber to transmit data at high speeds, allowed Internet users to send not just text but video and voice messages. While top speeds get faster all the time, the International Telecommunications Union defines broadband as transmissions of 256 kilobytes per second (Kbps) or faster — for both uploading

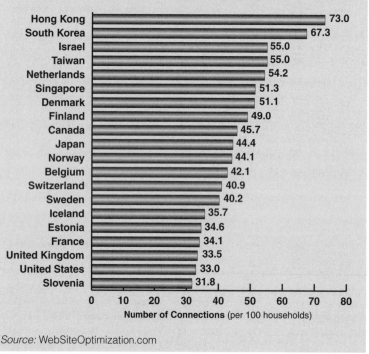

## U.S. Lags in Broadband Penetration

Nearly 75 percent of the households in Hong Kong have broadband Internet connections compared to only one-third in the United States.

**Top 20 Countries With the Most Broadband Penetration**

| Country | Number of Connections (per 100 households) |
|---|---|
| Hong Kong | 73.0 |
| South Korea | 67.3 |
| Israel | 55.0 |
| Taiwan | 55.0 |
| Netherlands | 54.2 |
| Singapore | 51.3 |
| Denmark | 51.1 |
| Finland | 49.0 |
| Canada | 45.7 |
| Japan | 44.4 |
| Norway | 44.1 |
| Belgium | 42.1 |
| Switzerland | 40.9 |
| Sweden | 40.2 |
| Iceland | 35.7 |
| Estonia | 34.6 |
| France | 34.1 |
| United Kingdom | 33.5 |
| United States | 33.0 |
| Slovenia | 31.8 |

*Source:* WebSiteOptimization.com

and downloading — while the U.S. FCC deems broadband as transmissions of 200 Kbps or faster.

As communications digitized and speeded up, the telecommunications landscape changed for its dominant industries — telephone and cable-TV companies.

First, cable operators began offering Internet connections over their lines. Phone companies responded by adding so-called digital subscriber lines (DSL), which are broadband-capable wires with a range of speeds at around 128 Mbps — much slower than cable broadband.

Furthermore, the freewheeling, innovative Internet could now provide the telecommunication industries' two big-money products — video and voice communications.

In 1996, when Congress overhauled federal telecom law for the first time in several years, legislators believed they had created a framework for a competitive telecom marketplace that would last well into the future. [40] However, few foresaw that within a few years Internet companies like Google Video or Vonage would offer video and telephone service that would directly compete with the cable and phone companies — who own the transmission lines over which those competing products would travel.

The 1996 act was "oblivious to the power of the Internet and technology to revolutionize everything," said Michael Powell, who was appointed by President George W. Bush and chaired the FCC from 2001 to 2005. [41]

In the past few years, with Congress not yet willing to wade into telecom law again, the FCC, courts and state legislatures have been left to sort out increasingly bitter battles over broadband.

Phone companies have long been regulated as "common carriers" — open channels required to accept all traffic without discrimination, in return for being free of legal liability for communications they carry. Cable companies were not deemed common carriers; however, prior to 2002, the FCC required them to lease their broadband-Internet lines to competing ISPs on reasonable terms.

But the key principle of the 1996 act — and a guiding principle for the Bush administration — was that the telecom industry would do best if it were freed from government regulation. And, beginning in 2000, cable companies insisted they were unable to expand broadband access because regulation was crippling them. Cable operators' top complaint — the "open access" requirement to lease lines to competing ISPs.

In 2002 the FCC granted their request, saying that when consumers purchase cable-modem service, they are buying only an "information" service, not a traditional two-way communications service like telephone service. The decision exempted cable-modem providers from opening their lines to competing ISPs and from other rules.

Not all FCC commissioners were happy. Commissioner Michael Copps wrote that without open access "the Internet — which grew up on openness — may become the province of dominant carriers, able to limit access . . . to all but their own ISPs," a consequence he called "ironic." [42]

Independent ISPs continued to insist that the Internet is a two-way communications system and fought in court for access to cable lines. But in June 2005, in *National Cable and Telecommunications Association v. Brand X Internet Services*, the Supreme Court sided with cable, overturning a lower court's ruling. [43]

The *Brand X* ruling opened the door for telephone companies to make the same argument — that broadband Internet services carried on phone lines shouldn't be subject to the century-old common-carrier rules. In August 2005, the FCC agreed. Beginning in August 2006, phone companies will no longer have to offer competing ISPs, such as AOL, free access to DSL connections. Phone companies will be able to sell or lease access to their DSL lines for whatever they deem fair value, although they will still be required to offer competitors free access to their slower dial-up connections.

As a result, most non-cable and non-telephone company ISPs "will disappear," says Crawford of Cardozo Law School. "The phone companies will just swallow them up, and there'll be much less choice of Internet providers." Phone and cable companies themselves will begin selling "bundles of services" — such as local and long-distance phone service along with DSL Internet service — that consumers will have no choice but to purchase.

Nevertheless, the FCC's decision will encourage "greater investment in . . . broadband networks," argued James C. Smith, senior vice president of SBC Communications, in defending their decision. [44]

But Internet advocates and some regulators are skeptical. Having one big phone company and one big cable company as the sole broadband providers in an area doesn't foster innovation and low price, says Copps. "I thought the '96 act was pretty clear in saying, 'Let's have competing providers, then deregulate.' But we kind of got it in reverse, deregulating before the competition had materialized."

Indeed, although the '96 law was intended to promote competition, the opposite has happened: The telephone and cable industries have been consolidating ever since — a worrisome fact because the Internet is a key communications channel for democracy, says Copps. In 2005, for example, the FCC approved a merger between SBC Communications and AT&T but bound the com-

A university student in Manila logs onto the new Yahoo! Philippines site. Atypically, more than half the country's Internet users are women. Internet use is growing rapidly in Southeast Asia and the rest of the world, including societies that closely monitor, and censor, citizens' access.

AFP/Getty Images/Romeo Gacad

pany to an enforceable Net-neutrality provision — barring the broadband giant from discriminating among Internet content — for two years. "This allows time for Congress to address the issue and for the American people to become involved," Copps says.

As in many other countries, U.S. phone companies pledged in the 1990s to upgrade infrastructure for high-speed access. In the United States, Congress and the FCC loosened some regulations on the telephone industry, in part because companies argued they would use the extra profits to modernize transmission lines.

Many other governments, such as Japan and South Korea, aggressively monitored infrastructure improvements in their countries to be sure they were made. In many countries, phone companies remained heavily regulated monopolies, which could be compelled to build infrastructure. But the U.S. government relied on what it believed would be market incentives for the private sector to wire the country for broadband, without establishing a clear policy for getting it done or fully debating the economics of doing so.

Meanwhile, in the United States, rural regions, especially, have been fighting back against the big telecom companies' reluctance to extend broadband. With little or no broadband available in some markets or prices too high for lower-income families, local governments have set up their own fiber or wireless "pipes."

# Googling in China Has Its Limits

As governments around the world bring more of their citizens online, they also are censoring information and opinion on the Internet and using networking technology to track down and punish political dissidents, according to Reporters Without Borders, a free-media advocacy group based in France.

Google has drawn press and congressional criticism recently for setting up a Chinese version of its Google.com search engine — Google.cn — which censors search results in line with government information-suppression guidelines. For example, a search for Tiananmen Square on Google.com turns up many images of tanks confronting unarmed demonstrators in 1989. But the same search on Google.cn produces smiling tourists posing for snapshots but few demonstrators.

"In countries such as China, where the mainstream media is subject to censorship, the Internet seemed to be the only way for dissidents to freely express their opinions," Reporters Without Borders Washington representative Lucie Morillon told the House Committee on International Relations on Feb. 15. "But, thanks to some U.S. corporations, Chinese authorities have managed to gradually shut down this 'open window' to the world." [1]

For example, both Google's and Yahoo's China sites have blocked some access to the U.S. government's Voice of America Web site and Radio Free Asia, as well as various other media sites around the world, Morillon said.

Meanwhile, Internet companies take varying approaches to dealing with Chinese-government repression, said Rebecca MacKinnon, a former Beijing bureau chief for CNN and now a fellow at Harvard Law School's Berkman Center for Internet and Society.

The anti-virus capability of Cisco Systems' "router" computers is, in effect, a built-in censorship device, said MacKinnon. By selling routers to China, the company is helping the Chinese government keep its citizens under surveillance and crack down on their political activity, she said, although it's not clear whether Cisco provides Chinese authorities with much training on the machines' capabilities. [2]

Microsoft provides instant messaging and Hotmail e-mail service to China but operates the programs on servers located outside of China to avoid having to hand over data to Chinese authorities. However, Microsoft also runs a Chinese version of its blog site, MSN Spaces, and censors the site according to Chinese requirements. It was widely criticized late last year when it deleted the work of blogger Zhao Jing, not just for Chinese viewers but worldwide. The company has since refined its processes so that global viewers can still read blogs

blocked to Chinese Internet users, according to MacKinnon.

Unlike Microsoft and Google, Yahoo! runs its Chinese-language products on servers inside China and thus must comply with Chinese police requests to hand over information, noted MacKinnon. That compliance has led to the jailing of at least three dissidents, MacKinnon writes. "If I were one of those people or their loved ones, I would never forgive Yahoo!," she said. Recently, Reporters Without Borders reported that Yahoo cooperation also led Chinese officials to a fourth cyber-dissident, Wang Xiaoning, who received a 10-year prison sentence in 2003. [3]

To avoid such dilemmas, Google won't offer some products, such as Gmail or Blogger, on Google.cn "until we're comfortable that we can do so in a manner that respects our users' interest in the privacy of their personal communications," Andrew McLaughlin, Google's senior policy counsel, wrote on the company's blog [4]

"Filtering our search results" on Google.cn in accord with China's censorship requirements "clearly compromises our mission," but "failing to offer Google search at all to a fifth of the world's population . . . does so far more severely," McLaughlin argued.

Google's argument is that Google.cn users actually will get more information if Google itself does the filtering, because Google's filtering tools are more finely developed than the "very broad sweeps" of government censors, says Lauren Weinstein, co-founder of People for Internet Responsibility. While the claim is "not inaccurate technically," Weinstein says, it opens the company up "to a damaging side effect" — charges of hypocrisy. The perception has been created that the company may not be as committed to principles of privacy as it has always claimed, he says.

"And perceptions alone can do a lot of damage," he adds. For example, Google recently fought a U.S. Department of Justice request to turn over millions of search results in the name of protecting users' privacy. But, in the future, skeptics will remember that, in China, "you caved," and they'll ask, in light of that, " 'What happens next time?' " Weinstein says.

---

[1] Testimony before House Committee on International Relations, Feb. 15, 2006, www.rsf.org.

[2] Rebecca MacKinnon, "America's Online Censors," *The Nation*, Feb. 24, 2006.

[3] "Still No Reaction from Yahoo! After Fourth Case of Collaboration With Chinese Police Uncovered," Reporters Without Borders, April 28, 2006, www.rsf.org.

[4] Andrew McLaughlin, "Google in China," Official Google Blog, Jan. 2, 2006, http://googleblog.blogspot.com/2006/01/google-in-china.html.

# Should Congress require Internet service providers to treat all content the same?

## YES
**Rep. Edward J. Markey, D-Mass.**
*Ranking Member, House Subcommittee on Telecommunications and the Internet*

Written for *CQ Researcher*, May 2006

Ever since the Internet was first opened to commercial use in the early 1990s, it has been defined by its open exchange of ideas — an exchange that has fostered tremendous innovation and economic growth.

The Internet's traditional open architecture was protected by rules enforced by the Federal Communications Commission (FCC) that prohibited telecommunications carriers from engaging in discriminatory practices. However, those legal protections, which embodied the notion of "network neutrality," were removed by the FCC in August 2005. The telecommunications legislation now moving through Congress places the very nature of the Internet under attack by failing to provide strong, effective network-neutrality rules.

In essence, network neutrality means that broadband network owners such as AT&T or Verizon cannot discriminate against unaffiliated content providers on the Net but rather have to stay neutral with regard to the content flowing through their networks. Moreover, the phone companies cannot charge access fees to certain companies in exchange for faster content distribution to high-bandwidth customers, or to provide enhanced quality-of-service assurances.

Finally, the principle of network neutrality also protects consumers' freedom to use their choice of gadgets with their broadband connection, from computer modems and VOIP [voice over Internet protocol] phones, to Wi-Fi routers and other whiz-bang gizmos just over the horizon.

Without these protections, the open, free-market nature of the Internet — perhaps the purest example of a level playing field that we have ever seen — would be hijacked by large broadband-network owners and discarded in favor of a tiered superhighway of bandwidth haves and have-nots.

The current debate over network neutrality presents us with a choice: Should we favor the vision for the Internet's future as warped by a small handful of very large companies or should we safeguard the dreams of thousands of inventors, entrepreneurs, small businesses and other independent voices?

Already, we have begun to see the grass roots rise up in opposition to Rep. Joe Barton's telecom bill, with over 250,000 backers of an open and unrestricted Internet signing a petition to Congress. Lawmakers should listen to these voices and ensure that broadband network owners treat all forms of content the same so that we do not lose the open architecture that has allowed the Internet to become such a success.

## NO
**James L. Gattuso**
*Senior Fellow in Regulatory Policy, Heritage Foundation*

Written for *CQ Researcher*, May 2006

Should Internet network owners, such as telephone and cable TV companies, be required to treat all Internet content equally? The idea — known as network neutrality — seems at first glance unobjectionable. What could be wrong with requiring neutrality? A lot, actually.

The key issue is whether network owners should be allowed to offer priority service, for a fee, to content providers who want it. Under a "network-neutral" system, all data is treated the same, with bits being transported to their destinations on a first-come, first-served, basis.

But what if a content provider wants higher-quality service? A firm providing Internet phone calls, for instance, may want to ensure that voice conversations have no delay. Why should it be banned from paying more to the network owner for priority transmission? Such differentiation is hardly a new concept. In the non-Internet world, priority service is offered for everything from package delivery to passenger trains.

Differentiation could also help provide much-needed Internet investment. A content provider, for instance, might contract with a network owner to provide capital for capacity expansion. But the incentive to do so is eliminated if it is required to allocate that new capacity on a first-come, first-served basis.

Regulation proponents argue, nevertheless, that network owners could abuse their power — perhaps blocking specific Web sites to further their own interests. But this is extremely unlikely. No major U.S. network operator has ever blocked a Web site, and if one does, consumers would switch to another operator in a nanosecond.

Rhetoric to the contrary, today's broadband market is a competitive one, with cable and telephone companies fighting each other for customers, and other technologies — such as wireless and satellite — also on offer. Moreover, if a network owner somehow does abuse its power, existing competition law is more than sufficient to address the problem.

Imposing new rules on the Internet would also invite endless litigation. Regulators would be drawn into years-long, lobbyist-driven policy quagmires as to whether this or that action is allowed or banned, and even what prices could be charged. This would be a bonanza for lobbyists and lawyers but would hurt innovation, investment and Internet users.

Proponents of neutrality regulation say the future of the Internet is at stake. They are right. These harmful and unnecessary new rules should be rejected.

## U.S. Lags in Internet Speed

Downloading a typical DVD movie in the United States takes 18 times longer than in Japan.

| Country | Internet Connection | Time |
|---------|--------------------|------|
| Japan | (26Mbit/s) | 20 minutes |
| S. Korea | (20Mbit/s) | 26 minutes |
| Belgium | (3Mbit/s) | 44 minutes |
| Denmark | (2Mbit/s) | 4.5 hours |
| USA | Cable Modem (1.5Mbit/s) | 6 hours |

Note: 1 megabit per second (Mbit/s) = 1 million bits per second

*Source:* International Telecommunication Union, Sept. 26, 2003

The governments often use fiber line already laid by a municipally owned power company or cooperate with private companies. The ISP Earthlink, for instance, is deploying wireless transmitters on light poles in Philadelphia to offer a lower-cost connection, which the city will subsidize for some low-income residents.

But cable and phone companies have been fighting such efforts, lobbying state legislators to stave off what they see as publicly subsidized competition. Fourteen states now have laws restricting localities' ability to offer communications services to residents.

## CURRENT SITUATION

### Fighting for the Net

Congress is overhauling the 1996 telecom law just 10 years after it was enacted. This time, a top priority will be extending the nation's broadband capabilities — barely a blip on the radar screen a decade ago. "Net neutrality" will also be a major new buzzword in the debate.

Over the past year, a growing chorus of advocacy and consumer groups and Internet companies have argued that Congress should require Internet carriers to treat Net content neutrally, rather than shunting chosen data to high-priority — and presumably more expensive — lines. But cable and telephone companies say that preventing them from developing such higher-priced traffic amounts to excessive regulation and that offering priority services is the only way they can afford to roll out broadband to the entire country.

On April 27, the cable and telephone industries won round one of the battle when the House Energy and Commerce Committee approved its telecom bill, after rejecting, 22-34, a Net-neutrality provision sponsored by Rep. Edward J. Markey, D-Mass.

"There is a fundamental choice," said Markey. "It's the choice between the bottleneck designs of a . . . small handful of very large companies and the dreams and innovations of thousands of online companies and innovators." [45]

The final measure, drafted by Texas Republican Barton, instead authorized the FCC to investigate allegations that carriers are treating Internet content unfairly and to fine companies up to $500,000 for blocking or degrading access to Web sites.

The Senate also is expected to debate telecom overhaul legislation this year, although no schedule has been announced. Sen. Ron Wyden, D-Ore., has introduced a bill mandating that ISPs treat all Internet content equally, and Sens. Olympia Snowe, R-Maine, and Byron Dorgan, D-N.D., have drafted a similar bipartisan measure.

Senate Commerce Committee Chairman Ted Stevens, R-Alaska, said he supports neutrality in principle but isn't sure yet what will be in the bill. "We're going to have an enormous number of items that people want to put in," he said. [46]

Not surprisingly in a congressional election year, lobbying has intensified, as have political donations — just as they did in 1996, also an election year.

On April 26, the big computer-chip maker Intel joined a long list of computer and Internet companies — including Microsoft, Google, eBay and Amazon — and advocacy groups from across the political spectrum to push for a neutrality law. The retirees group AARP, the liberal political group MoveOn.org, the American Library Association and the libertarian Gun Owners of America all favor neutrality.

Meanwhile, critics of the telecom industry say phone and cable companies may be paying their way into the hearts of cash-strapped legislators running for re-election. As of March 31, for example, cable giant Comcast was Barton's top 2006 campaign contributor and AT&T was his fourth-biggest donor, according to the political funding Web site OpenSecrets.org. In Barton's 2003-2004 campaign, Comcast was his third-biggest donor and SBC was in second place.

Some Democrats who opposed Markey's Net-neutrality amendment also have financial ties to telecom. Rep. Bobby Rush, D-Ill., cosponsored Barton's telecom bill and is the founder of the Rebirth of Englewood Community Development Corp., a group in his home district that recently received a $1 million grant from the SBC Foundation. [47]

As Congress discusses telecom overhaul, other broadband-related bills are also up for consideration. In the House, Texas GOP Rep. Pete Sessions has introduced legislation to prevent municipalities from setting up broadband networks in localities where private broadband service is available. In the Senate, John McCain, R-Ariz., and Frank R. Lautenberg, D-N.J., are sponsoring a bill to allow local governments to offer broadband service.

However, few expect a comprehensive bill to pass in 2006. The '96 telecom law was several years in the making, and "I don't see why this would be any easier," said Carol Mattey, a former deputy chief of the FCC now with Deloitte & Touche's regulatory consulting practice. [48]

## Whither ICANN?

This year also marks a significant milestone in the quest for global Internet governance. ICANN's current contract with the U.S. government to run the Internet's domain-name addressing system expires in September, and international groups have been discussing a possible new governance structure for several years.

Until the late 1990s, individual U.S. researchers and some small organizations ran the Internet's technical functions on behalf of the U.S. government. That structure was in keeping with the Net's history as a U.S.-developed technology. But as the 21st century neared, the Internet's swelling size and increasing global importance led President Bill Clinton to turn over control of Internet addresses to ICANN, a private, nonprofit group that manages technical aspects of the Net with input from private and public groups worldwide.

The U.S. government's intention, expressed in a

Google CEO Eric Schmidt unveils the firm's Chinese name in Beijing on April 12, 2006. With 111 million Internet users, China is second only to the United States in total number of users. The Chinese government — assisted by Google, Yahoo! and other computer companies — censors Web sites that question government actions or deal with teen pregnancy, homosexuality, dating, beer and even jokes.

series of contracts between ICANN and the Commerce Department, has been to eventually move toward more global control. Last year, however, the Bush administration announced that the international search for an alternate governing body had focused too much on government controls and that the United States would not turn over Net functions to international government bureaucrats — such as the United Nations — who might stifle innovation or be too strongly influenced by repressive governments. [49]

The U.S. government is currently considering all options for the close of the current ICANN contract in September, says a spokesman for the Commerce Department's National Telecommunications and Information Administration, which oversees the agreement. At an international summit in November, participants agreed to create an Internet Governance Forum consisting of government, business and civil-society groups to discuss global Internet governance.

The goal is to create a forum with multiple stakeholders that will meet sometime in mid-2006 in Athens. The group will try to come to global consensus on the top issues involving the Internet, such as spam, cybercrime, the intersection of national law and Internet principles on censorship.

# OUTLOOK

## Wireless Is 'Happening'

If the Internet survives as an open medium, it may be because users — from software engineers to teenagers with pages on MySpace.com — demand security mechanisms that allow innovation while preventing domestic and international threats to Internet freedom, say technology experts.

Today, "the fact that tens of millions of machines in consumer hands are hooked up to networks that can convey reprogramming in a matter of seconds means that those computers stand exposed to near-instantaneous change" by malicious viruses and crippling loads of network-drowning spam, according to Jonathan Zittrain, professor of Internet governance at Oxford University.

The very real threat of Internet meltdown in a world of non-techie users will inevitably lead to a Net "locked down" by governments and ISPs in ways that eliminate user choice and innovation, Zittrain said, unless open-Internet supporters demand or develop improved network security and reliability while retaining users' ability to be creative. [50]

For example, personal computers could be sold with keyboard switches. In "red" mode, a PC would run whatever software it encountered, like PCs today; in "green" mode, it would run only software certified by its ISP. Users would pay more for an Internet connection that allowed them to run "red." [51]

"Corporate mass-market software" that dominates today's Net was developed with little thought to security, says Peter Neumann, principal scientist at the SRI Computer Science Laboratory in Menlo Park, Calif., and co-founder of People for Internet Responsibility. In a universally online world that could lead to a disastrous shutdown of vital Net-based systems, such as power, air-traffic control or electronic voting, he notes.

"The government has typically said the market will solve" security problems, but Microsoft and others "are making scads of money while all but ignoring security," he continues. Meanwhile, the industry has its "head in the sand" and won't change unless "we have enough people who understand the big picture" and take responsibility for it, Neumann says.

For U.S. consumers to make market choices on Internet service, a real market must develop, with three or more competing services available everywhere, not just the phone and cable companies that dominate today,

said former FCC Chairman Powell. "We believe magical things happen at three," he said. [52]

Currently, wireless ISPs remain the best hope, although whether wireless technology is up to the job remains an open question. Some say wireless is poised to emerge strong in urban and rural areas. Nine years ago, "it was a technological curiosity," but today "it's happening," says Steve Stroh, a writer and an analyst for the broadband wireless Internet industry. He cites Trump Tower in Manhattan, which recently installed a wireless network for the entire building, and hundreds of rural wireless ISPs — called WISPs — that increasingly can extend broadband connections over long distances. An operator in eastern Washington state, for example, can reach customers 30-to-40 miles from its transmission point via large antennas, Stroh says.

To flourish, wireless needs access to dedicated bands on the electromagnetic spectrum, says Stroh, which could be a special problem in the United States, where — unlike in some other countries — much prime spectrum is already allocated to users like the Department of Defense. The spectrum issue is on Congress' agenda, with some legislators proposing to dedicate empty spaces in local broadcast TV spectra to wireless ISPs, for example.

The Internet's continued ability to allow unfettered communication and innovation rides on the outcome of all these debates, say longtime Net users like Karl Auerbach, a San-Francisco-based computer-network developer and former ICANN board member.

"These Internet governance debates are the visible aspects of the most significant change in the conception of nation-states, national sovereignty and the relationship of the individual to his/her government since at least the end of the Napoleonic wars," he says.

# NOTES

1. Quoted in "AOL Censors E-Mail Tax Opponents," Electronic Frontier Foundation media release, April 13, 2006.

2. John Byrne, "Update: AOL Says Emails Protesting Its Own Service Blocked By Accident," *The Raw Story* blog, April 14, 2006.

3. Tom Barrett, "To Censor Pro-Union Web Site, Telus Blocked 766 Others," *The Tyee*, Aug. 4, 2005, http://thetyee.ca.

4. For background, see David Masci, "The Future of Telecommunications," *CQ Researcher*, April 23, 1999, pp. 329-352.

5. Lawrence Lessig, "Architecting Innovation," *The Industry Standard*, Sept. 8, 2001.

6. Quoted in Declan McCullagh, "Democrats Lose House Vote on Net Neutrality," ZDNet.com, http://news.zdnet.com.

7. *Save The Internet* blog, www.savetheinternet.com.

8. Quoted in *ibid.*

9. For background, see Kenneth Jost, "Russia and the Former Soviet Republics," *CQ Researcher*, June 17, 2005, pp. 541-564.

10. Daniel Henninger, "Here's One Use of U.S. Power Jacques Can't Stop," *The Wall Street Journal*, Dec. 17, 2004.

11. Declan McCullagh, "No Booze or Jokes for Googlers in China," CnetNews.com, http://news.com, Jan. 27, 2006.

12. "Promoting Innovation and Competitiveness," President Bush's Technology Agenda, March 26, 2004, www.whitehouse.gov.

13. S. Derek Turner, "Why Does the U.S. Lag Behind?" *Free Press*, February 2006.

14. Michael Geist, "The Credible Threat," *Circle ID*, Feb. 28, 2006, www.circleid.com.

15. Quoted in Declan McCullagh, "Internet Showdown in Tunis," CNET News.com, Nov. 11, 2005; http://news.com.com. For background, see Charles S. Clark, "Regulating the Internet," *CQ Researcher*, June 30, 1995, pp. 561-584.

16. Kieren McCarthy, "2005: The Year the U.S. Government Undermined the Internet," *The Register*, Dec. 29, 2005, www.theregister.co.uk.

17. *Ibid.*

18. Amol Sharma, "World Seeks a Wider Web Role," *CQ Weekly*, Nov. 14, 2005, p. 3042.

19. Testimony before Senate Committee on Commerce, Science and Transportation, Feb. 7, 2006.

20. Quoted in Marguerite Reardon, 'Qwest CEO Supports Tiered Internet," ZDNet.com, http://news.zdnet.com.

21. Quoted in "At SBC, All's Well About Scale and Scope," *Business Week Online*, Nov. 7, 2005.

22. Edward Felten, "Net Neutrality and Competition," *Freedom to Tinker* blog, www.freedom-to-tinker.com.

23. Quoted in Marguerite Reardon, "Verizon Says Net Neutrality Overhyped," CNET News.com, March 31, 2006, http://news.com.com.

24. John Windhausen, Jr., "Good Fences Make Bad Broadband," A Public Knowledge White Paper, Public Knowledge, Feb. 6, 2006.

25. *Ibid.*

26. *Ibid.* The nine states are Arkansas, Delaware, Florida, Illinois, Maryland, Michigan, Pennsylvania, Virginia and Wyoming.

27. *Ibid.*

28. John Horrigan, "Rural Broadband Internet Use," Pew Internet and American Life Project, February 2006.

29. Quoted in "Senate Commerce, Science, and Transportation Committee Holds Hearing on Communications Issues," Congressional Transcripts, Feb. 14, 2006, www.cq.com.

30. *Ibid.*

31. Quoted in Dana Blankenhorn, "You Get Muni Broadband by Demanding It," ZDNet blog, April 5, 2006.

32. Joseph L. Bast, "Municipally Owned Broadband Networks: A Critical Evaluation (Revised Edition)," www.heartland.org, October 2004.

33. www.baller.com/pdfs/Texas_2-14-06.pdf.

34. Thomas D. Rowley, "Where No Broadband Has Gone Before," Rural Policy Research Institute, Aug. 19, 2005.

35. For background, see *The Internet's Coming of Age, Committee on the Internet in the Evolving Information Infrastructure* (2001); and Barry M. Leiner, *et al.*, "A Brief History of the Internet," Internet Society, www.isoc.org.

36. Bruce Sterling, "A Short History of the Internet," *The Magazine of Fantasy and Science Fiction*, February 1993.

37. "Putting It All Together With Robert Kahn," *Ubiquity: An ACM IT Magazine and Forum*, www.acm.org.

38. Quoted in Lawrence Lessig, "It's the Architecture, Mr. Chairman," http://cyber.law.harvard.edu/works/lessig/cable/Cable.html.

39. Scott Bradner, "Blocking the Power of the Internet," *Networkworld*, Jan. 6, 2006, www.networkworld.com.

40. For background, see Masci, *op. cit.*; and Kathy Koch, "The Digital Divide," *CQ Researcher*, Jan. 28, 2000, pp. 41-64.

41. Quoted in Elizabeth Wasserman, "The New Telecom Wars: Looking to Update a Landmark Law," *CQ Weekly*, Nov. 14, 2005, p. 3049.

42. Michael Copps, Dissenting Statement, GN. No. 00-185, www.fcc.gov.

43. *National Cable and Telecommunications Association v. Brand X Internet Services*, 543 U.S., 2005.

44. Quoted in "FCC Reclassifies DSL as Data Service," Analyst Views, IT Analyst Information on Demand, Northern Light, Sept. 20, 2005, www.centerformar ketintelligence.com.

45. Quoted in Declan McCullagh, "Republicans Defeat Net Neutrality Proposal," CNet News.com, April 6, 2006, http://news.com.com.

46. Quoted in Declan McCullagh, "Senator: Net Neutrality May Not Happen," ZDNet News, March 22, 2006, http://news.zdnet.com.

47. "Donation Explanation Has Phony Ring," *Chicago Sun-Times*, April 26, 2006.

48. Quoted in Kelly M. Teal, "1996 Telecom Act Turns 10," *New Telephony*, Feb. 8, 2006, www.newtele phony.com.

49. Tim Receveur, "United States Says No UN Body Should Control Internet," *Washington File*, USInfo, U.S. State Department, Oct. 24, 2005, http://usin fostate.gov.

50. Jonathan Zittrain, "The Generative Internet," 2005; www.oiprc.ox.ac.uk/EJWP0306.pdf.

51. *Ibid.*

52. Quoted in "Michael Powell: We Need That Third Pipe," *IP Democracy*, April 3, 2006, www.ipdemoc racy.com.

## BIBLIOGRAPHY

### Books

**Borgman, Christine, *From Gutenberg to the Global Information Infrastructure: Access to Information in the Networked World*, MIT Press, 2003.**
A professor of information studies at the University of California, Los Angeles, describes the technical and policy tradeoffs that libraries, universities, readers and researchers face as they shift from a culture of books to a world of online information.

**Goldsmith, Jack, and Timothy Wu, *Who Controls the Internet? Illusions of a Borderless World*, Oxford University Press, 2006.**
Professors specializing in cyberlaw at Harvard and Columbia, respectively, describe threats the global Internet has posed to national regimes. They argue national government have and are exercising power to control the Internet.

**Thierer, Adam, and Wayne Crews, eds., *Who Rules the Net?: A New Guide to Navigating the Proposed Rules of the Road for Cyberspace*, Cato Institute, 2003.**
Two libertarian analysts assembled essays that discuss the challenges of regulating cyberspace, including how international cyber-disputes should be settled and whether a multinational treaty should govern the Internet.

**Yassini, Rouzbeh, *et al.*, *Planet Broadband*, Cisco Press, 2003.**
An electrical engineer and advocate of cable broadband explains how broadband works and describes how high-speed Internet connections may change how consumers, businesses and researchers use the Net.

### Articles

**Chester, Jeffrey, "The End of the Internet?" *The Nation online*, www.thenation.com, Feb. 1, 2006.**
An advocate of an open-access Internet describes the conflict between traditional Internet values and the economic and policy agendas of the phone and cable industries.

Cukier, Kenneth Neil, "No Joke," *Foreign Affairs*, foreignaffairs.org, Dec. 28, 2005.
A journalist describes U.S. and international views of Internet control and how changes in the way the Internet works are altering those views.

Goldsmith, Jack, and Timothy Wu, "Digital Borders," *Legal Affairs*, January/February 2006, www.legalaffairs.org.
Law professors at Harvard and Columbia, respectively, describe incidents in which national laws collide with traditional Internet principles like freedom of expression.

Hu, Jim, and Marguerite Reardon, "Cities Brace for Broadband War," CNET News.com, May 2, 2005, http:/news.com.com.
Battles are heating up between cities and towns that want to develop government-sponsored broadband networks and regional phone and cable companies that accuse local governments of engaging in unfair competition.

MacKinnon, Rebecca, "America's Online Censors," *The Nation online*, www.thenation.com, Feb. 24, 2006.
A fellow at Harvard Law School's Berkman Center for Internet and Society explores the economics and ethics of U.S. computer companies' cooperation with Chinese-government Internet censorship.

Manjoo, Farhad, "One Cable Company to Rule Them All," *Salon*, Salon.com, March 17, 2004.
A journalist discusses potential threats to Internet access posed by consolidation of media ownership.

Reardon, Margaret, "Broadband for the Masses?" CNET News.com, www.com,com, April 14, 2004.
Jim Baller — a lawyer for local governments — describes court challenges to their attempts to build broadband networks and defends such initiatives.

"Seven Questions: Battling for Control of the Internet," *Foreign Policy*, www.foreignpolicy.com, November 8, 2005.
Stanford University law professor and Internet expert Lawrence Lessig discusses conflicts between the United States and European Union over who should control the granting of Internet domain names.

Zittrain, Jonathan, "Without a Net," *Legal Affairs*, January/ February 2006, www.legalaffairs.org.
An Oxford University professor of Internet governance describes why burgeoning Internet-security threats like computer viruses mean that Internet law and technology require overhaul.

## Studies and Reports

*The Internet's Coming of Age*, Committee on the Internet in the Evolving Information Infrastructure, National Research Council, 2001.
An expert panel recommends policies to accommodate more widespread Internet usage and new technologies.

*Signposts in Cyberspace: The Domain Name System and Internet Navigation, Computer Science and Telecommunications Board*, National Research Council, 2005.
An expert panel explains the Internet's address system and recommends policy to stabilize its future governance.

# For More Information

**Berkman Center for Internet and Society**, Harvard Law School, Baker House, 1587 Massachusetts Ave., Cambridge, MA 02138; (617) 495-7547; http://cyber.law.harvard.edu. A research program investigating legal, technical and social developments in cyberspace, in the United States and worldwide.

**Center for Democracy and Technology**, 1634 I St., N.W., #100, Washington, DC 20006; (202) 637-9800; www.cdt .org. Advocates preservation of constitutional freedoms and democratic values in the developing digital world.

**Center for the Digital Future at the University of Southern California Annenberg School**, 300 South Grand Ave., Suite 3950, Los Angeles, CA 90071; (213) 437-4433; www.digitalcenter.org. A research program investigating the Internet's effects on individuals and societies.

**Electronic Frontier Foundation**, 454 Shotwell St., San Francisco, CA 94110; (415) 436-9333; www.eff.org. A nonprofit organization that advocates for and litigates on technological issues involving privacy, free speech, freedom to innovate and consumer rights.

**Free Press**, 100 Main St., PO Box 28, Northampton, MA 01061; (877) 888-1533; www.freepress.net. A national, nonpartisan organization that promotes public participation in debate on media policy and development of more competitive and public-interest-oriented media.

**ICANN Watch**, www.icannwatch.org. Membership organization of technology experts who study and write about management and policy issues affecting the Internet's domain-name address system.

**Internet Governance Project, School of Information Studies**, Syracuse University, Syracuse, NY 13244; (315) 443-5616; www.internetgovernance.org. An interdisciplinary group of academic researchers analyzing issues of global governance for the Internet.

**National Cable and Telecommunications Association**, 1724 Massachusetts Ave., N.W., Washington, DC 20036; (202) 775-3550; www.ncta.com. Represents the cable industry, the largest single provider of broadband Internet services in the United States.

**Pew Internet and American Life Project**, 1615 L St., N.W., Suite 700, Washington, DC 20036; (202) 419-4500; www.pewinternet.org. Provides data and analysis on Internet usage and its effects on American society.

**Progress and Freedom Foundation**, 1444 I St., N.W., Suite 500, Washington, DC 20005; (202) 289-8928; www.pff.org. A free-market-oriented think tank that studies public policy related to the Internet.

Getty Images/Jamie Squire

FedEx Field, home of the Washington Redskins, is one of dozens of sports stadiums around the country that have sold naming rights to corporate sponsors. Some citizens groups have protested, arguing that putting corporate names on such prominent landmarks is intrusive commercialism.

From *CQ Researcher*,
January 23, 2004. (Updated May 23, 2008)

# 9

# Advertising Overload

Patrick Marshall and Heather Kleba

It's like the Blob that Steve McQueen faced in the 1961 movie of the same name: a formless horror that threatens to engulf us. At least that's how the critics of advertising see things. Advertising and promotions have gotten so out of hand, they say, the glut of ads is threatening our peace of mind, our privacy, and even our health. Consumers today often cannot escape the onslaught of commercialism, as advertisers — competing for attention in an expanding media environment — inundate classrooms, theaters, cyberspace, sports stadiums, police cars, doctors' offices, garbage cans, airports, and even restroom walls. Ads are turning up on parking lot tickets, paper cup insulators, gasoline pump handles, and golf scorecards. "There's an effort to hang an ad in front of our eyes at every waking moment of the day and night," says Gary Ruskin, executive director of Commercial Alert, a nonprofit consumer advocacy group in Portland, Ore. "Americans are sick of it."

And consumers cannot even escape the onslaught in their own homes. TV viewers now see nearly a full hour of commercials during a typical night of primetime broadcasts. In addition, telemarketers invade the dinner hour in millions of homes every night, and spammers daily cram bushels of unsolicited ads into millions of private e-mail boxes. [1] "Advertisements are literally popping up everywhere," says psychologist David Walsh, founder of the National Institute on Media and the Family, in Minneapolis. "It is just overwhelming."

"What advertisers have to come up with each week is the new, new intrusive thing, so we have a steamroller of intrusiveness," said Robert W. McChesney, a professor of communications at the University of Illinois, Urbana-Champaign, and founder of Free

Press, a national media-reform organization. "We're locked in a death-spiral of intrusiveness." [2] Consumers literally can feel like captive audiences of advertisers: Some movie theaters run twenty minutes of ads before showing the movie; airline passengers can find themselves stuck for hours staring at ads plastered across the bottoms of their fold-up trays; and telephone callers must listen to ads repeated over and over while on hold. But the proliferating ads are more than just annoying or unattractive. Many educators and parents are worried about the impact on students of the increasing number of ads in schools. And the literally billions of spam messages and pop-up ads that daily bombard Internet users raise concerns about privacy, cost, and the potential that users will simply be alienated from all ads — even from legitimate retailers.

Seventy percent of e-mail users say spam has made being online unpleasant or annoying, and 80 percent are bothered by what they consider spam's deceptive content, according to the Pew Internet and American Life Project. [3] In a similar 2007 study, Pew found that 37 percent of e-mail users said spam had increased in their personal e-mail accounts, up from 28 percent of e-mail users who said that two years ago. [4]

The amount of spam being sent out, according to the Pew survey, is "mind-boggling." Researchers estimate that nearly 15 billion spam messages are sent out daily. And the costs imposed on the American economy — primarily in lost productivity and in the cost of filtering and deleting spam — have been estimated at from $10 billion to $87 billion per year. [5]

Perhaps fortunately for consumers, however, is that the advertising industry is now in a state of "chaos" according to Greg Smith, chief operating officer of Neo@Ogilvy, a direct-media company. With the onslaught of new technology, which brings hundreds of new ways to deliver ads, advertisers have yet to figure out how best to spend money to maximize results. In fact, as of 2007, only three media categories saw an increase in advertising spending. Magazine advertising was up 4.7 percent, Internet advertising was up 17.2 percent and outdoor advertising increased by 4.4 percent. Television (but not cable) is down overall, with network television advertising down by 3 percent. Radio advertising is down 1.8 percent, and newspapers have seen a decrease in advertising spending of 5.2 percent. [6]

Even though placement decisions are seemingly impossible right now, digital technology does bring advertisers closer to a long sought-after goal — knowing where to place a certain ad to have the greatest impact. Before Internet ads, advertisers couldn't tell whether an increase in revenue came from an ad in the *New York Times* or one placed during a commercial break on *The Office.* Or, as John Wanamaker, a Philadelphia retailer said more than 100 years ago, "Half of the money I spend on advertising is wasted; the trouble is, I don't know which half." Search advertising, such as Google's AdWords, allows advertisers to buy words and then have their ad pop up next to search results when someone using the search engine types in the specific words. For example, if Kraft purchased the word "cheese" from Google, anytime someone searched for that word, the Kraft ad would be listed on the search result screen. With this "click" data, an advertiser can decide how much to spend per ad click, which, in turn, changes the ad's position among other sponsored links. Advertisers also have the benefit of using in-house data or data mining software such as Google Analytics to determine how many clicks a certain ad gets. This makes the digital ad marketplace flexible, allowing companies to test out various ads before settling on one based on the number of people who click on it.

With so much competition for the consumer's attention, advertisers just keep adding more and more ads. "Advertisers are having to work a lot harder to reach their audiences," says James P. Rutherfurd, executive vice president of Veronis Suhler Stevenson, a media research and investment company in New York City. "When you're trying to 'break through the clutter,' you have to do more and more things to get the consumers' attention," David Walsh agrees. "So there is this constant ratcheting up of both the amount and the techniques used to get attention."

Not surprisingly, the ad onslaught has triggered a backlash. In Seattle, moviegoers complained to a theater manager about the interminable advertisements preceding the previews. In 2003, after complaints from the public, San Francisco became the first city to buy back from a corporate sponsor the naming rights of its popular football stadium — tearing down the 3Com Park sign and renaming it Candlestick Park. [7]

While few national-level organizations have yet been formed specifically to fight against the flood of advertising and commercialism, grass-roots groups are springing up, and some national groups are forming to work on specific aspects of the larger issue. The Citizens' Campaign for Commercial-Free Schools, in Washington State, for example, is working toward removing advertising and promotions from schools. And, in Bethesda, Maryland, parents started the Lion and the Lamb Project to crusade against violence in entertainment. [8]

Much of the most recent legislative action has been aimed at telemarketers and e-mail spam. Over the past several years, dozens of states have passed legislation aimed at curbing telemarketers and spammers, including especially tough laws in California and Virginia. In 2003, in fact, Virginia indicted two men under the state's anti-spam law on charges that could result in five years in prison and a $2,500 fine. [9]

In 2002, the public outcry over telephone and e-mail advertising led to major federal action. In 2003 Congress passed legislation authorizing the Federal Trade Commission (FTC) to implement a do-not-call list designed to curb unsolicited calls from telemarketers. Also in 2003, controversial legislation aimed at curbing e-mail spam was enacted. Nonetheless, some activists say not enough is being done to curb the onslaught of advertising and that certain citizens, especially the very young and the elderly, are not adequately equipped to defend themselves. Commercial Alert, a group founded by consumer activist Ralph Nader in 1998 to fight encroaching commercialism, has called for greater restrictions on advertising to children and recently petitioned the FTC and the Federal Communications Commission (FCC) to require pop-up disclosures when product placements are used in TV shows.

Some physicians and public-health experts also are questioning the increasing use of so-called direct-to-consumer (DTC) advertising by pharmaceutical companies to boost drug sales. While advertisers claim such efforts are purely educational, and encourage beneficial conversations between doctors and patients, some experts warn that the advertising may lead to over-prescribing and unnecessary increases in health-care costs. "Drug companies, owing to their clear conflict of interest, are not the ones to educate people about the drugs that they are selling," two former editors of *The New England Journal of Medicine* argue. "DTC ads mainly benefit the bottom line of the drug industry, not the public. They mislead consumers more than they inform them, and they pressure physicians to prescribe new, expensive, and often marginally helpful drugs, although a more conservative option might be better for the patient. That is probably why DTC ads are not permitted in other advanced countries less in the thrall of the pharmaceutical industry." [10]

Others have decried the increasing reliance of government institutions on advertising revenue. Whether it is the Smithsonian Institution soliciting corporate sponsorship for its exhibits or a city government selling advertising space on police cars, "commercial values don't mix with civic values," Nader warns. "The Smithsonian is not a commercial institution. Its job is not to promote General Motors or IBM or whatever company." The former Green Party presidential candidate says that such advertising deals "blur the line" between marketers and government, creating suspicion that government decisions may not be made on merit. "Our country works best when there's a clear distinction, a bright line between civic and commercial values," Nader says.

## Top Ten Advertisers During the First Six Months of 2007
(listed in millions of dollars)

| | |
|---|---|
| Proctor and Gamble | $1,612 |
| AT&T | $1,100 |
| Verizon | $1,041 |
| General Motors | $959 |
| Ford | $865 |
| Time Warner | $793 |
| Johnson & Johnson | $726 |
| Sprint/Nextel | $689 |
| Walt Disney | $664 |
| National Amusements, Inc. | $590 |

*Source:* TNS Media Intelligence

Getty Images/Tina Hager

President Bush signs the "Can Spam Act" in the Oval Office on Dec. 16, 2003, accompanied by Internet executives and congressional sponsors of the measure, which will help consumers, businesses and families combat unsolicited e-mail.

But Adonis Hoffman, senior vice president of the American Association of Advertising Agencies, says advertising is an easy target for consumers and regulators. "When products and services come under scrutiny — whether it is prescription drugs or food products or alcoholic beverages — the most likely and expedient target is to go after the marketing. But when you look at what underlies advertising, in fact, it is simply providing information to consumers so that they can make informed choices on a product or service." Others warn that banning or restricting advertising may run afoul of the First Amendment. "Often, we try to regulate commercial speech because we don't like what the content is," says Marvin Johnson, legislative counsel for the American Civil Liberties Union (ACLU). "That puts us on dangerous territory."

Indeed, says Richard T. Kaplar, vice president of the Media Institute, a nonprofit research foundation, much of the debate over advertising restrictions boils down to the tension between commercial speech and an individual's right to privacy. "We've got two competing values here," Kaplar says. "It's going be the big question in the future."

As Congress and the public debate what to do about the ever-growing presence of advertising in Americans' lives, here are some of the questions being asked:

## Will the new spam-control law work?

Not surprisingly, Congress responded to the public outcry over the deluge of unwanted and often offensive e-mail messages that have clogged cyber mailboxes over the past several years. Stanford University conducted a study in 2004 that found the average Internet user will spend ten business days per year deleting and otherwise dealing with spam. "Industry analysts estimate that the global cost of spam to businesses in 2005, in terms of lost productivity and network maintenance, will be about . . . $17 billion in the United States alone." [11]

Legitimate advertisers and Internet service providers eventually joined consumers in demanding federal anti-spam legislation. They supported federal action partly because they did not want to have to comply with a variety of different state laws and partly because their businesses were being hurt by spammers, most of whom are bent on defrauding the public. "We need federal legislation in part because a patchwork of 50 state laws would be awful," says Jerry Cerasale, senior vice president of the Direct Marketing Association. Moreover, he adds, "Unlike with telephone marketing, with e-mail the fraud element is sadly the core, and legitimate marketers are the fringe." "When you are advertising a legitimate product, the last thing you want is to have your target audience turn off and toss your e-mail out," agrees Hoffman, of the American Association of Advertising Agencies.

By the time Congress took up the issue in earnest, as many as 30 states already had passed anti-spam measures. The toughest is California's, which calls for a $1,000 fine per illegal e-mail. However, the state laws so far have had no noticeable deterrent effect on the flow of spam, partly because enforcing the laws across state borders is virtually impossible, and the added pressure of the federal legislation means that state laws are even less useful.

The cleverly named "Can Spam Act," signed into law by President Bush on December 16, 2003, bans bulk commercial e-mail that falsely identifies senders or uses deceptive subject information. Violators can be fined up to $11,000 per illegal e-mail and sentenced to five years in prison. The law also requires all commercial e-mail to include a valid postal address and to provide recipients an opportunity to opt out of receiving more e-mails.

Some anti-spam advocates wanted the law to require all commercial e-mail to carry a marker that would make it easy to filter out, but the law only requires markers on pornographic e-mails. The law also directs the FTC to study the feasibility of instituting a do-not-spam list comparable to the federal do-not-call list for telemarketers. In 2004, the FTC conducted the study, and concluded, "The Commission therefore strongly believes that implementation of a National Do Not E-mail Registry would not reduce the volume of spam, particularly given currently available technology to authenticate the origin of e-mail messages." Instead of an e-mail registry, the FTC recommended "the widespread adoption of e-mail authentication standards that would help law enforcement and ISPs better identify spammers." [12]

Although major advertisers' organizations supported the Can Spam Act, anti-spam activists and some state officials say it is severely flawed. "The Can Spam Act misses most of the major issues with spam," says Scott Hazen Mueller, chairman of the Coalition Against Unsolicited Commercial E-mail. "There might be one or two prosecutions for show, but we don't anticipate any decreased level of spam. In fact, we anticipate that levels will continue to increase." The act neither creates a do-not-spam registry nor bans unsolicited e-mails, Mueller points out. "The Can Spam Act basically doesn't say that people can't spam," he says. "It actually says that they can spam. We need a stake in the ground that says, 'No, you cannot send unsolicited e-mail advertisements.'"

Critics also complain that the act prohibits individuals from suing spammers, allowing only government agencies to bring actions against senders of e-mails that violate the law. "That pretty much guarantees the law's ineffectiveness," says Jason Catlett, president of Junkbusters, a privacy-advocacy group. The law was "written by online marketers for online marketers. It's going to make for more spam. It's really a tragedy of shortsightedness and corporate lobbying." According to Anne Mitchell, the chief executive of the Institute for Spam and Internet Public Policy, "Most people say it's a miserable failure. But I see it as a lawyer would see it. To think that law enforcement agencies can make spam stop right away is silly. There's no such thing as an instant fix in the law." She also notes that the technology installed on many computers to help stop spam often catches legitimate e-mail. The ever-evolving technology used to keep up, means that spammers are evolving as well. "The more effective the filtering technology . . . the more spam they have to send to get the same dollar rate of return," says Mitchell. [13]

The FTC defends the Can Spam Act, because, as they explain, it is impossible to stop all spammers with any one

Blinking electronic billboards were installed on dozens of subway entrances in New York City after the Metropolitan Transportation Authority sold advertising rights to Clear Channel Communications. After citizens protested the "advertising pollution" in their upper West Side neighborhood, the company replaced the illuminated ad at their subway stop with a non-animated sign.

*Getty Images/Chris Hondros*

piece of legislation, especially since the "methods and motives" have changed, making it hard to keep up with spammers — one example of spammers' methods is their use of botnets, which infiltrate and take over computers, allowing a large volume of spam to be sent from that computer's IP address. Over one million IP addresses "are coordinating spam and virus attacks each day." [14]

Mueller, in fact, believes that concern about the harshness of the California law — which would have allowed individuals to sue spammers — caused advertisers to push for federal legislation. "It was such a strong deterrent that certain parties got a little panicky and pushed Congress to establish new national standards," Mueller says, adding that the impact of the California law would have been felt nationwide, since advertisers wouldn't be able to sort out e-mail to Californians from others. "It would effectively have invoked California standards on the nation," he says.

But the federal law's co-sponsor, Sen. Conrad Burns, R-Mont., says that without preempting state laws, the measure would have been unworkable. "If the rules change once you cross a state line, it would make legislation almost impossible to enforce and essentially

# Do Direct-to-Consumer Drug Ads Raise Health Costs?

When the government relaxed its rules on broadcasting drug commercials in 1997, pharmaceutical companies unleashed a barrage of ads aimed directly at consumers for conditions ranging from arthritis to impotence. In 2007, advertisers spent $5.4 billion on such advertising. [1] The problem with so-called direct-to-consumer (DTC) advertising, critics say, is that it encourages consumers to pressure their doctors to prescribe unnecessary or even inappropriate drugs, inflating healthcare costs and, in some cases, harming patients. "I'm seeing many more people asking for a particular medication based on their own assessments of their conditions," an internist in Haverhill, Mass., said. "They're basically asking me to rubber-stamp their thought processes." [2]

Advertisers disagree. "We believe that prescription-drug advertising has been one of the great success stories in the advertising world, and that it has been providing tremendous benefit to society at large," says Dan Jaffe, executive vice president for governmental affairs at the Association of National Advertisers. "Millions of people have been going to the doctor to discuss health problems they never discussed before after they had seen an ad that raised that issue. We think that's a tremendously valuable benefit."

In fact, some advocates of DTC ads say that such advertising is still being required to say too much by the Food and Drug Administration (FDA). "The FDA should reconsider the notion that all DTC advertisements need to balance information about risks and benefits, writes John E. Calfee, resident scholar at the American Enterprise Institute. "Advertising works best as a dynamic medium, filling the most important relevant holes in consumer awareness and emphasizing different product features as dictated by circumstances. This makes information dissemination more efficient, an essential virtue in information-intensive markets such as pharmaceuticals." [3]

But critics say consumers are not getting enough information in the ads because the FDA now allows TV and radio commercials to advertise drugs' benefits without going into detail about potential side-effects. The advertisements only are required to mention major risks and then provide a Web address and toll-free telephone number for more information. And some researchers contend advertisers are not even adhering to the relaxed requirements. From 1997 when the FDA relaxed its rules for drug ads, allowing them to shorten information on possible side effects, until 2007, $14 billion was spent on cable television and other broadcast drug ads.

Democrats in Congress fought — and lost — last year in an attempt to better regulate television commercials featuring prescription drugs. However, the recent problems that have come to light about prescription drugs such as Vytorin — which didn't let consumers know about research that brought the drug's effectiveness into question; Lipitor — which has come under fire for using Robert Jarvik, inventor of the artificial heart, in its ads, even though he is not licensed to practice medicine; and Procrit — whose manufacturer was warned by the FDA to change its commercial because it was marketing the drug as an anti-fatigue drug, even though it hadn't been approved for that usage — may give the Democrats more fuel to start a new fight.

What is not in dispute, however, is the fact that DTC pharmaceutical ads have paid off big for the pharmaceutical companies. According to the General Accounting Office, "the number of prescriptions dispensed for the most heavily advertised drugs rose 25 percent [from 1999 to 2000], but increased only 4 percent for drugs that were not heavily advertised." [4] There is no question that DTC ads are a billion dollar industry for drug makers and television networks who accept the ads. The problem, according to Bart Stupak (D-MI) is that "Congress needs to decide whether the US should continue to be one of two countries in the world that allow DTC ads, and if we continue to allow such advertising, whether any further limits to DTC ads should be required . . . it appears that we need to enforce significant restrictions on DTC ads." [5]

---

[1] "AMA Calls for Limits on Drug Ads," *Boston Globe*, May 9, 2008.

[2] Phyllis Maquire, "How Direct-to-consumer Advertising is Putting the Squeeze on Physicians," *ACP-ASIM Observer*, American College of Physicians-American Society of Internal Medicine, www.acponline.org/journals/news/mar99/squeeze.htm.

[3] John E. Calfee, "Public Policy Issues in Direct-to-Consumer Advertising of Prescription Drugs," *Journal of Public Policy & Marketing*, vol. 21, no. 2, fall 2002, 174.

[4] "Prescription Drugs: FDA Oversight of Direct-to-Consumer Advertising Has Limitations," General Accounting Office, October 2002, GAO-03-177, 3.

[5] "AMA Calls for Limits on Drug Ads," *Boston Globe*, May 9, 2008.

ineffective," he says. "We needed a federal law to make spam legislation cohesive," says Burns, "which is especially true since e-mail does not stop at a state's border." Moreover, advertising-industry officials say, spammers would pay no attention to a do-not-spam registry, so it wouldn't be effective either. "It would hurt legitimate marketers more than spammers," Hoffman says. Cerasale agrees, adding that a do-not-spam list is administratively much more complicated to do than a do-not-call list because there is no control over e-mail addresses as there is over phone numbers. "It won't work," he says.

Despite critics' doubts, Burns says he expects the act, which went into effect in 2004, to produce real results. "Once someone is caught — and the article hits the front page above the fold — the spammers are going to see there are real consequences for their actions and think twice before they proceed," Burns says. In 2005 Burns said he still thought it was too soon to judge how well the law has worked, but believes the FTC still needs some nudging when it comes to enforcement. "I'll be working to make sure the FTC utilizes the tools now in place to enforce the act and effectively stem the tide of this burden." [15]

But FTC officials say it may take time to track spammers down and prosecute them. [16] Adding to the difficulty: Many illegitimate spammers are located offshore, beyond the reach of the FTC, and the legislation could simply cause more to move overseas. "This is a continuing problem, and one that we have not overlooked," Burns says. "Now that we have passed a law in the United States, it will be important to get other countries on board, and it is clear that many other countries are feeling the same growing pains from the growth of the Internet and the increase in spam. "But legislation is not a silver bullet that will completely rid the world of spam. It is going to take work from industry and strict enforcement to make a dent in the amount of spam out there," Burns says.

The FTC is still fighting an uphill battle. Since the Can Spam act went into effect, spam increased about 20 to 30 percent, making up 80 percent of all e-mail sent. [17] As of November 2007, the FTC has brought over ninety actions against spammers, and the Can Spam Act has brought thirty actions focusing on Can Spam protections like deceptive subject titles and sexually-explicit messages. [18] However, the biggest fine handed out thus far is $900,000.

Federal Trade Commission Chairman Timothy J. Muris, left, and former Federal Communications Commission Chairman Michael K. Powell testify before a Senate committee on the "do-not-call" phone registry created last fall.

## Have existing limits on tobacco advertising worked?

Policymakers considering additional restrictions on advertising for junk food, tobacco or alcohol may be interested in whether earlier restrictions have been effective. In the past, federal and state governments have limited billboard advertising, alcohol commercials and drug ads, but the most restrictive measures have been imposed on cigarette advertising. Limits on tobacco ads have stemmed from a combination of federal mandates and self-regulation. Tobacco companies insist it is company policy not to market their products to children, but critics say the companies often violate those voluntary restrictions.

Then in the early 1970s, in response to new studies about the dangers of smoking, the federal government mandated that cigarette companies print special health warnings on tobacco products and barred tobacco advertising from radio and television. The 1998 Master Settlement Agreement (MSA) between tobacco companies and 46 states prompted cigarette manufacturers to again adopt voluntary restrictions and agree to pay $1.7 billion over 10 years to promote anti-smoking efforts. Specifically, they agreed not to target youth in the advertising, promotion or marketing of tobacco products. [19] Advocates of additional advertising limits often cite falling teen smoking rates between the early 1970s and the early 1990s as proof that restrictions work.

Some tobacco industry officials agree that advertising restrictions may have helped keep teen smoking rates

To try to recoup funding lost in budget cuts, a middle school in Scotts Valley, Calif., allows a financial-services company and other firms to advertise at the school. As advertising expands into virtually every aspect of American life, many educators and parents are worried about the impact on students.

down. "I suspect . . . that [the restrictions] had a positive impact in reducing youth smoking in this country," says Steven Watson, vice president for external affairs at Lorillard Tobacco Co. "Whatever is going on is working, because youth smoking rates are at the lowest level ever recorded. That's good. We remain committed to the effort and have been in complete compliance with the voluntary [and] mandated restrictions now in place."

Clouding the issue is the fact that teen smoking rates climbed between 1992 and 1996 and then started falling again. But no researcher has ever been able to show conclusively that the increase was caused by any particular changes in tobacco advertising, although some suspect it was a factor. At least one group of researchers attributes the rise to a drop in cigarette prices, finding that for every 10 percent drop in price, youth smoking rises nearly 7 percent. [20]

Conversely, some analysts insist that advertising restrictions have no measurable impact on teen smoking. "I don't find that [advertising bans] have been effective at all, which would suggest the primary impact of advertising generally in [the alcohol and tobacco] industries is to alter brand sales or possibly beverage sales and not to influence the total size of the market," Pennsylvania State University economics Professor Jon P. Nelson says. Nelson has also studied tobacco advertising bans in

Europe, which have been in place longer than American restrictions, and he has found no correlation between the bans and smoking rates. "If [advertising bans] really are effective in altering people's behavior as youths, one might expect them to have some longer-run impact, but I don't find evidence of that," Nelson says.

A 2006 study by the *American Journal of Public Health* found that ads that attempt to discourage kids from smoking have, at best, no effect, and ads targeted toward adult smokers actually increase the likelihood that tenth and twelfth graders will smoke. [21] Other researchers find similar results. The Cancer Prevention and Control Program at the University of California, San Diego, found in the early 1990s that "tobacco promotional activities are causally related to the onset of smoking." [22]

Federal researchers found the same results. "Historical analyses show that variations in advertising are associated with concomitant variations in smoking uptake among youths," says a U.S. Department of Health and Human Services report. "A large number of cross-sectional studies have reported associations between exposure to tobacco marketing on the one hand and attitudes toward smoking, susceptibility to smoking, smoking experimentation or regular smoking among youths on the other. These relationships persist even when other factors shown to predict smoking initiation are controlled." [23]

Some analysts say banning tobacco ads has been ineffective because the bans have not been honored. Anti-smoking advocates have charged for years that tobacco companies have continued to target youths in their advertising — in magazines, in-store ads and various other promotions. Indeed, in June 2002, R.J. Reynolds tobacco company was fined $20 million for violating the MSA by running magazine ads aimed at teenagers. [24]

Cheryl Healton, president of the American Legacy Foundation — an anti-smoking organization funded by the agreement — claims tobacco firms recently have begun using product placements to reach youth audiences, a practice activists call "stealth advertising." "No matter how much you restrict advertising, if you cannot address the issue of tobacco product placement in TV and movies, it is almost impossible to counteract that," Healton says. "Right now, every single tobacco company is reporting to the FCC that they do not do that. But it defies logic that there would be so high a prevalence of brands appearing both in TV and in first-run movies, and that those product placements are being provided

AP Photo/Ben Margot

free when virtually no other product placements are ever provided free." Healton suspects "quid pro quo" arrangements, in which a tobacco company, owned by a company that produces other products, might buy a product placement ad — for mints, for instance — on a TV show like *The West Wing* and the quid pro quo would be having President Bartlett smoke. Getting the proof, however, is "impossible without litigation," Healton says.

Lorillard's Watson takes umbrage at Healton's charges. "That's a very serious allegation to make with absolutely no evidence whatsoever," he says. "It's a part of this continuous effort to try to vilify and demonize tobacco companies, rather than deal with the issue of reducing youth smoking. "We do not engage in any type of product placement. Furthermore, as stipulated by the master settlement agreement, when our products are placed in movies and TV programs, producers are in violation of the [MSA and] copyright law if they don't request permission, which we would not give them."

If manufacturers use the money saved on advertising to lower prices, that, too, can lessen the anti-smoking impact of advertising bans. "A ban on advertising tends to force liquor and cigarette competitors to compete on the basis of price, because the sellers find it difficult to project their image without ads," writes Dwight Filley, senior fellow at the Independence Institute, a free-market think tank, in Golden, Colo. "A prohibition of advertising reduces the overall cost of production as their ad budgets plummet." [25]

Moreover, some researchers have found that restricting ads in one medium simply shifts the advertising to other media rather than reducing overall advertising. "If you've got a loose noose, it doesn't do much," says Henry Saffer, an economics professor at Kean University, Union, N.J., and a research associate at the National Bureau of Economic Research. "You have to have fairly draconian restrictions before you get much effect."

### Are tougher limits needed on advertising to children?

Advocacy groups have long called for stricter controls on advertising subtly aimed at children, especially if the products being advertised are illegal for minors to purchase — such as tobacco and alcohol. Now, calls are increasingly being heard for restrictions on targeting children with ads for legal — albeit potentially unhealthy — products, like junk food.

"Is the present system adequately protecting children? No way," says Gary Ruskin of Commercial Alert. "There's an epidemic of marketing-related diseases. Our nation's children are suffering from an epidemic of child obesity. Millions of kids are sick and going to die from the marketing of tobacco. Pathological gambling is a terrible problem." [26]

A March 2007 Kaiser Family study "found that 50 percent of ad time on children's shows is devoted to food. Among the ads aimed at children and teenagers, 72 percent are for candy snacks, sugary cereals or fast food." [27]

Commercial Alert has asked legislators to impose harsher restrictions on advertising to children, including a ban on all TV advertising to children under twelve and revocation of the business-tax deduction for advertising directed at children. But advertisers say advertising is not the culprit, especially for so-called junk foods. "People often blame advertising for people making [bad] choices," says Dan Jaffe, executive vice president for governmental affairs of the Association of National Advertisers. "But many low-salt, low-calorie, low-fat products are languishing on the shelves because the public has not really decided to change its eating behavior. Now people are trying to say, 'Well, then they shouldn't even know about these other foods. We should have the government manipulate the information process.' But that isn't what a free society believes in." Hoffman of the American Association of Advertising Agencies agrees. "The parents are the ultimate decision-makers in the household," Hoffman says. "Kids will be kids, but parents have the responsibility to make sure their kids have a balanced diet, that they're getting foods that have sufficient nutritional content."

The FTC only intervenes if an advertisement is considered misleading or deceptive. An ad hawking junk food to children would not be considered misleading or deceptive by the FTC unless it made claims that it was nutritious, says Mary Engle, associate director for advertising practices at the FTC. "If, in fact, it was not [nutritious] then that could be deceptive and actionable." Still, many advertisers concede that — even if they are within the law in advertising to children — they have a special responsibility to the public. "It does not behoove an advertiser to engage in practices that are going to in any way alienate the consuming public," Hoffman says.

To fend off the blame of childhood obesity, many food manufacturers and fast food chains have worked to

# CHRONOLOGY

**1900s-1960s** *Federal government assembles a regulatory structure to monitor and enforce restrictions on advertising.*

**1906** Food and Drugs Act calls for a federal agency to oversee full labeling of food and drugs, including those containing alcohol, cocaine and heroin.

**1914** Federal Trade Commission is created and charged with ensuring fair competition in business, including regulating advertising, packaging and labeling.

**1934** Federal Communications Commission is created and later monitors and regulates advertising on television and radio.

**1949** Under the power of the so-called Fairness Doctrine, the Federal Communications Commission begins monitoring programming, including advertisements, for balance and fairness.

**1964** A surgeon general's report on the health hazards of smoking prompts the FTC to rule that cigarette advertising is deceptive unless cigarette packages and advertisements bear health warnings.

**1970s-1995** *Supreme Court rules some commercial speech deserves First Amendment protection, launching a steady stream of commercial-speech litigation.*

**1970** Cigarette Smoking Act prohibits cigarette ads on radio and television.

**1975** Supreme Court rules in *Bigelow v. Virginia* that commercial speech has at least partial protection under the First Amendment.

**1980** Supreme Court's *Central Hudson Gas & Electric Corp. v. Public Service Commission* ruling lays out a four-part test — still in use today — for determining whether a federal restriction on commercial speech is permissible under the Constitution.

**1982** After Reese's Pieces are featured in the film "E.T," sales of the candy rise 66 percent, sparking the advertising industry's interest in paid product placements in films and television shows.

**1986** Supreme Court appears to backtrack on protecting commercial speech in *Posada de Puerto Rico Associates v. Tourism Co.*, allowing a Puerto Rican regulation banning advertisements promoting casino gambling — legal in Puerto Rico — to remain in force.

**1989** Channel One educational TV service is launched. In return for loans of television equipment, schools are required to show Channel One programming, including commercials, to students.

**1991** Telephone Consumer Protection Act allows Federal Trade Commission to create the do-not-call phone registry, which is implemented in 2003. The law also prohibits sending unsolicited advertising by fax.

**1995-present** *Supreme Court gradually increases First Amendment protection for commercial speech.*

**1995** In *Rubin v. Coors Brewing Co.* the Supreme Court shows a renewed interest in protecting commercial speech when it agrees with a brewery's challenge to a federal regulation that required disclosure of alcohol content on beer labels and in advertisements. Justice Clarence Thomas's majority opinion says First Amendment prevents restrictions on label content.

**1998** Master Settlement Agreement between tobacco companies and 46 states requires the tobacco companies not to target youth and to spend $1.45 billion to establish an anti-smoking education organization.

**2003** On September 23, a federal judge rules that the FTC is not authorized to implement a do-not-call registry for telemarketers. Congress passes a bill on September 25 authorizing the registry; a U.S. District Court again blocks the registry, after finding its charities exemption violates marketers' free speech. The FTC appeals the ruling on September 26, and the Tenth Circuit Court of Appeals decides to allow the list to go into force pending legal challenges. On September 29 President Bush signs the do-not-call law and signs the "Can Spam" Act on December 16. On December 18 the FCC for the first time cites a company for violating the new do-not-call law. . . . By mid-December more than 54 million telephone numbers have been registered with the FTC.

**2005** Microsoft settles its lawsuit with "Spam King" Scott Richter for $7 million. Richter was also sued by former attorney general Eliot Spitzer in New York for sending e-mails that violated state and federal spam laws.

**2007** Eleven major food manufacturers voluntarily agree to stop advertising foods that do not meet certain nutritional standards during programs aimed at children ages 12 and under.

promote healthier food options and a fitness regimen, including McDonald's new Happy Meal choices including apples and low-fat milk. Fearing the type of scrutiny tobacco companies have faced, regulatory intervention or lawsuits, in 2006 eleven of the biggest food manufacturers agreed to make at least 50 percent of all advertising geared toward children ages twelve and under about healthy food and lifestyles. Companies such as McDonalds, PepsiCo, and Coca-Cola have withdrawn all commercials for the twelve-and-under group that do not meet certain nutritional standards. PepsiCo, for example, will advertise Gatorade, but only in the context of athletic activity-an actual picture of the drink will not be shown-and they will not advertise Pepsi cola. [28] These companies will also open their marketing plans to the Better Business Bureau's Children's Advertising Review Unit. The caveat here for many manufacturers is where they draw the line between children's shows and family shows. Commercials featured during television shows considered "family" programming will still continue to show Pepsi and other sugary foods and drinks that are being voluntarily banned on children's shows.

According to Susan Linn, the co-founder of Campaign for a Commercial-Free Childhood, "This is great public relations for the companies, but it doesn't go nearly far enough . . . It is going to be impossible to monitor if the companies are actually doing what they say." [29]

Some critics say advertisers are increasingly alienating the consuming public to such an extent that the laws eventually will be changed. "I'm not one who wants to lay it all at the feet of the advertisers and the fast-food industry," says Walsh of the National Institute on Media and the Family. "But snack-food companies that advertise effectively are influencing people to consume large quantities of foods that contain trans-fatty acids and high-fructose corn syrup, and that's a health problem."

Other critics complain that advertisers have invaded the schools in many communities through exclusive soft-drink marketing agreements, monopolistic TV programming, use of educational support materials that carry advertising and sponsorship of special activities. "Schools," says Alex Molnar, a professor of education policy at Arizona State University, "have become vectors of marketing." Marketing on school grounds is increasing dramatically, particularly as more school districts face budget crunches, Molnar says. And he warns that there are hidden dangers beyond the mere clutter of brand names. There is

Getty Images/Stephen Chernin

While he was New York Attorney General, Eliot Spitzer sued major spammers for sending unsolicited e-mails to consumers while hiding behind fake identities and forged e-mail addresses. Microsoft General Counsel Brad Smith, at left, supported the action along with other high-tech firms.

an inherent conflict of interest between the role of schools and the role of marketers, he says, and the result goes far beyond children being encouraged to make unhealthy lifestyle choices. "Marketers are special interests," Molnar says. "They're not interested in promoting the welfare of children, which is the charge to schools."

When advertisers sponsor school content through sponsored activities, educational materials or sponsored TV programming, they inevitably control the content of that material, Molnar continues. "School programs get distorted in a variety of ways," he adds. "Either the curriculum content is made incorrect by omission or commission. A corporate point of view is substituted for a kind of objective, disinterested look." Molnar urges state

# Will Advertisers Resort to 'Mind Reading'?

What is scarier than a spammer obtaining your e-mail address? How about advertisers reading your brain waves? While it's a new science, some companies have begun to use neuromarketing to determine how best to advertise their products. During the early years of the new millennium, researchers at some of America's top universities began watching the brain's response to product stimuli placed in front of participants, and even put them in normal shopping scenarios to see how the neurons in the brain respond to certain products and advertisements. Scientists think this breakthrough could be invaluable to big corporations. In 2006, companies spent about $8 billion on market research. [1]

P. Read Montague, a neuroscientist at Baylor College of Medicine in Houston, monitored the brain activity of test subjects as they participated in a blind taste test of Pepsi and Coca-Cola. As in the taste tests performed on TV, Montague found that most subjects preferred Pepsi, and that Pepsi tended to produce a much stronger response in the region of the brain known as the ventral putamen. When Montague ran the test again, but with the subjects knowing the identity of both samples, Coke won the test. Moreover, Montague clearly detected brain activity in the medial prefrontal cortex, the brain's center of higher-level logical thought. While the team has not published any conclusions about the finding, some researchers speculate that the subjects' knowledge they were drinking Coke may have summoned up memories and other logical associations that made it the preferred libation, thus affecting their brain activity. [2]

Similar studies got under way at the Harvard Business School's Mind of the Market Laboratory and the BrightHouse Institute for Thought Sciences at Emory University in Atlanta. BrightHouse, in fact, is testing prospective customers' reactions to an unnamed client's products using a magnetic resonance imaging (MRI) machine. The BrightHouse researchers also detected strong responses in the medial prefrontal cortex when test subjects encountered images of products they liked. Clint Kilts, the scientific director, recently predicted that neuromarketing will soon become a career niche. "You will actually see this being part of the decision-making process, up and down the company," he told the *New York Times*. "You are going to see more large companies that will have neuroscience divisions." [3] Kilts' colleague, Chief Operating Officer Adam Koval, is even more boosterish about the technology. "What it really does," Koval told a reporter, "is give unprecedented insight into the consumer mind. And it will actually result in [advertisers] . . . getting customers to behave the way they want them to behave." [4]

The group's Web site denies any attempts to "read" minds. "We are not capable of, nor do we desire, to 'read' people's private thoughts and feelings or use study infer-

or federal legislators to ban marketing to children in schools. "There is no right to market to children in schools," he says. "Schools are protected spaces."

While conceding there is no "right" to advertise in schools, advertisers say it would be inappropriate to exclude advertising by federal or state legislation. "A top-down approach just isn't realistic," says Clark Rector, senior vice president for government affairs of the American Advertising Federation. "The local officials are more than capable. If they decide they don't want to accept advertising within their local schools, they have that absolute right to do it."

At the same time, Rector points out, "a lot of schools are under increasing financial pressure, and if they think that they can accept advertising on a limited basis and it can help them fund future programs, they ought to be able to do that." School officials say the temptations are great. "Desperate times call for desperate measures," says Bruce Colley, executive director of administrative services for the Bainbridge Island School District in Washington state. "If I'm sitting in a school that doesn't have money available, and some company like Coca-Cola comes up and says they'll put a new scoreboard in there just so long as it says 'Drink Coke,' I can see why people say yes to that." At the same time, he says, "In a perfect world, if education was funded appropriately, this would be a non-issue."

Even some advocacy groups concerned about the impact of ads on children are skittish about implementing government restrictions. "Once we start banning ads from schools, do we then ban them from children's television programming?" Walsh asks. "Do we draw a line at

ences to induce unwilled behavior," says an explanation of the group's research "By watching how different neural circuits light up or go dark during the buying process, the researchers found they could predict whether a person would end up purchasing a product or passing it up. They concluded, after further analysis of the results, that 'the ability of brain activation to predict purchasing would generalize to other purchasing scenarios.' " [5] Some neuroscientists warn, however, that, while this can be seen as a huge benefit for Big Business, it is unlikely that there is any one reason why consumers purchase what they do — it's made up of multiple steps including price, mood, etc. [6]

More recently, an ad agency ran a study involving young whiskey drinkers to decide how to better market Jack Daniels. At Harvard's McLean Hospital, the researches watched the participants' reaction to different whiskey drinking scenarios, and will base some marketing decisions off what they learned. Forbes calls this research a huge milestone and one that will help ad agencies spend money more efficiently, while also helping to influence what people buy. New consulting firms have been springing up, such as NeuroFocus, which specialize in this type of advertising research. The ethical question now, however, is when do these studies cross the line and become consumer manipulation?

While the various studies have yet to undergo scrutiny by the scientific community, they have stirred up some concern among consumer advocacy groups, among them Commercial Alert. In December the group asked Emory President James Wagner to stop the experiments. "Universities exist to free the

mind and enlighten it," wrote Commercial Alert. "They do not exist to find new ways to subjugate the mind and manipulate it for commercial gain. Emory's quest for a 'buy button' in the human skull is an egregious violation of the very reason that a university exists." [7]

After failing to get a response from Emory, Commercial Alert on December 17, 2003, wrote to the federal Office for Human Research Protections, a unit of the Department of Health and Human Services, seeking an investigation of neuromarketing experiments, calling them "unethical because they will likely be used to promote disease and human suffering." [8] Pat El-Hinnawy, public affairs specialist at the Office for Human Research Protections, said January 15, 2004, "We have received their letter and we're looking into it."

---

[1] Alice Park, "Marketing to Your Mind," *Time*, January 19, 2007.

[2] Clive Thompson, "There's a Sucker Born in Every Medial Prefrontal Cortex," *New York Times*, October 26, 2003, section 6, 54.

[3] *Ibid.*

[4] CBC News, www.cbc.ca/consumers/market/files/money/science_shopping.

[5] Nick Carr, "Neuromarketing Could Make Mind Reading the Adman's Ultimate Tool," *The Guardian*, April 3, 2008.

[6] Alice Park, "Marketing to Your Mind," *Time*, January 19, 2007.

[7] www.commercialalert.org/index.php/category_id/1/subcategory_id/82/article_id/205.

[8] www.commercialalert.org/index.php/category_id/1/subcategory_id/82/article_id/211.

fast foods or do we ban all advertising from children's programming?" "I get nervous," he continues. "Some very strong advocacy groups like to keep pushing a line into the next area, and then into the next."

## BACKGROUND

### Protecting the Public

Policymakers and the courts have struggled over the past 100 years to balance the rights of advertisers to market their products against the responsibility of government to protect the public. The first major federal effort to regulate advertising was the 1906 Food and Drugs Act. It required federal regulators to make sure that food and drug labels were not misleading and that eleven dangerous but still legal ingredients — including alcohol, cocaine and heroin — were listed if present. Then in 1914 Congress created the Federal Trade Commission to ensure fair competition. Besides reviewing corporate mergers and preventing unfair business practices, the FTC regulates advertising, packaging and labeling.

The Federal Communications Commission, created in 1934, is charged with protecting the public interest as it regulates broadcast advertisements. In 1949, under what became known as the Fairness Doctrine, the commission began monitoring programming, including advertisements, to ensure that content was balanced and fair. By 1985, the commission reported that the doctrine was not working as intended and that it might actually be chilling free speech. The Reagan administration abolished the doctrine two years later.

## What the Law Says

**Junk mail** — The Federal Trade Commission's (FTC) prohibition againt false or misleading ads is virtually the only regulation affecting the content of mailed advertisements. The volume of ads mailed is restricted only by the willingness of advertisers to pay postal fees.

**Junk fax** — The 1991 Telephone Consumer Protection Act prohibits sending unsolicited faxes. The law has survived multiple challenges in federal courts, largely because faxes, unlike telephone calls, impose a cost on the recipient. The same law prohibits telemarketing to cellular phones.

**Telephone marketing** — The federal government's new do-not-call registry prohibits telemarketers from calling individuals whose phone numbers are listed in the registry. Solicitations from political organizations, charities and telephone surveyors are excempt.

In 1964, the FTC scrutinized cigarette advertising after a U.S. surgeon general's report said smoking was a health hazard. The commission determined that tobacco advertising was deceptive because it failed to inform the consumer of the dangers of smoking and called for warning labels on cigarette packages and advertisements. The next year, Congress passed the Federal Cigarette Labeling and Advertising Act, which required the warning labels. Congress then passed the Cigarette Smoking Act, which prohibited cigarette ads on radio and television beginning in 1971. Although broadcasters challenged the ban, the courts upheld it.

Notably, the unsuccessful challenge was one of only a handful of cases in which the government's ability to restrict or ban commercial speech was questioned. In fact, the Supreme Court did not rule until 1975 that advertisements and other commercial speech were protected by the First Amendment. In *Bigelow v. Virginia*, the court struck down a state law prohibiting ads for abortion-referral services, holding that "the relationship of speech to the marketplace of products or services does not make [commercial advertising] valueless in the marketplace of ideas." [30] At the same time, however, the court made clear that it was not extending protection to all advertisements, but only to speech that contained "material of clear 'public interest.'" [31]

The next year, the Supreme Court extended First Amendment protections for commercial speech a bit further. In *Virginia State Board of Pharmacy v. Virginia Citizens Consumer Council Inc.*, the court held that a state law barring pharmacies from advertising the price of pharmaceuticals was unconstitutional. Significantly, the court noted that "the particular consumer's interest in the free flow of commercial information . . . may be as keen, if not keener by far, than his interest in the day's most urgent political debate." [32] In the same decision, however, the court stressed that commercial speech did not warrant the same level of First Amendment protection as other forms of speech and that states could legitimately regulate advertising in the public interest.

## Commercial Speech

In 1980, the court handed down its most comprehensive and direct ruling aimed at protecting commercial speech. In *Central Hudson Gas & Electric Corp. v. Public Service Commission*, the court considered whether New York state could bar utilities from advertising to promote the use of electricity. [33] While the court still maintained its previous position that commercial speech was entitled to less protection than other speech, it set out a detailed, four-part test government could use to determine whether an advertising restriction was permitted under the Constitution.

The first test is to determine whether the commercial speech in question is non-misleading and concerns a lawful activity. If it does not meet those requirements, the court said, the speech can be silenced. In the second part of the test, the court said the government must demonstrate that restricting the advertisement would serve a substantial public interest, and, thirdly, it must show that the restriction directly advances that public interest. Finally, the government must demonstrate that the restriction is only as extensive as necessary to achieve the specified purpose.

Over the next ten years, the court applied the *Central Hudson* test to a wide variety of cases, with decisions that some analysts have found uneven and potentially confusing. For example, in the 1986 *Posada de Puerto Rico Associates v. Tourism Co.* decision, the court held that the government of Puerto Rico's ban on ads promoting casino gambling — a legal activity in Puerto Rico — was permissible so long as the advertisements were targeted only at residents of Puerto Rico. [34] In several subsequent decisions, the court appeared to favor restrictions. [35] In the mid-1990s, however, the tide turned in favor of protections for commercial speech. In *Rubin v. Coors Brewing Co.*, the court agreed with the Colorado brewery's challenge to a federal regulation that required disclosure of alcohol content on beer labels and in advertisements. [36] Justice Clarence Thomas, who has emerged as a champion of protections for commercial speech, wrote the majority opinion, which said bluntly that label-content restrictions were not permitted under the First Amendment. The *Coors* case "bore the mark of a court bent on ensuring that the *Central Hudson* test be applied with rigor, rather than in a fashion involving unquestioning acceptance of the government's regulatory determinations," an analyst wrote. [37]

Since 1995, the court has shown a decided inclination to strengthen First Amendment protections for commercial speech. "The Supreme Court got away from its sort of muddled thinking and got back on track in confirming the four-part test for commercial speech," says the Media Institute's Kaplar. "I tend to agree with Justice Thomas that the distinction between commercial and non-commercial speech has become sort of artificial, and we should be giving full protection to all kinds of speech — including commercial speech — provided, of course, that it's not false or misleading or unfair or fraudulent."

## Gagging Telemarketers

The one significant setback advertisers have experienced in the courts recently — and perhaps only temporarily — came when the advertising industry was unable to stop implementation of a national do-not-call registry, which allows consumers to block most calls from telemarketers. In 1991, Congress passed the Telephone Consumer Protection Act, which allowed the FTC to create the registry, though it wasn't actually set up to accept consumer telephone numbers until September 2003.

On September 23, 2003 Oklahoma City U.S. District Court Judge Lee R. West ruled in a suit filed by the Direct Marketing Association that the FTC was not authorized to implement the registry. Congress responded two days later with legislation specifically

Telemarketers at Spectrum Marketing Services, in Philadelphia, work their last shift on September 26, 2003. Establishment of the do-not-call phone registry forced the thirty-year-old firm to close.

authorizing the FTC to implement the do-not-call list. The legislation passed the House 412-8 and the Senate 95-0 and was signed by President Bush on September 29, 2003.

But that didn't end the matter. The registry was put on hold yet again by a telemarketing industry lawsuit claiming the registry was an unconstitutional abridgement of marketers' free-speech rights. Judge Edward W. Nottingham of the U.S. District Court in Denver agreed, ruling that exempting charitable organizations from being covered by the registry — as the FTC rule setting up the do-not-call registry permits — would limit what content could be blocked by consumers and would, therefore, violate the free-speech rights of marketers. "Were the do-not-call registry to apply without regard to the content of the speech . . . it might be a different matter," Nottingham wrote in his decision. "For them to fix this, you'd have to apply the do-not-call list to charities," said lawyer Deborah Thoren-Peden, who specializes in privacy issues. "I'm guessing this one is going to be fought out more in the courts." [38] The FTC appealed the ruling to the Tenth Circuit Court of Appeals in Denver and was given the go-ahead to put the registry in force while the issue winds its way through the courts, a matter that may take years. According to the FTC, more than 54 million telephone numbers had been registered by mid-December 2003.

The Qualcomm Stadium scoreboard in San Diego gives a plug to Office Depot and Budweiser beer along with the ball scores. Critics say ads are overrunning American society. Supporters cite their First Amendment rights to commercial free speech.

Between mid-October and mid-December 2003, the FTC had received more than 100,000 complaints about potential violations. And on December 18, the FCC, which shares authority with the FTC for enforcing the registry, cited a company for the first time for violating the new restrictions: CPM Funding Inc., a California-based mortgage company. [39] On November 3, 2003, the FCC followed up quickly by citing AT&T with violations that could result in a fine of $780,000. [40] Under the law, telemarketers can be fined up to $11,000 per violation.

## CURRENT SITUATION

### Protecting Kids?

Apart from what has been happening in the courts, advertisers today operate in a regulatory environment that is generally friendlier to their interests than it has been in decades — a source of frustration for consumer-advocacy groups and regulators alike. "Commercial speech shouldn't be protected under the First Amendment, because corporations aren't people," says Ruskin of Commercial Alert. "Corporations deserve no Bill of Rights protection. The state ought to be able to restrict commercial speech in any way it sees fit."

The FTC is feeling handcuffed, too, Engle says, making it hesitant to take regulatory action in areas such as advertising non-nutritious foods to children. "To regulate, control or prohibit advertising to children we would have to show that the proposed regulation would pass constitutional muster," Engle says. "It's a very high burden on us [since *Central Hudson*]. We can meet the first test, which is to show that there is government interest in preserving children's health. But the next two tests — which are whether the proposed regulation directly advances the government's interest and whether it is narrowly tailored to fit the purpose — would be very hard to meet. You have to show a very strong link between exposure of children to advertising of non-nutritious foods and the health consequences that you're concerned about."

Engle explains that the agency's efforts to regulate advertising to children in the 1970s backfired. "The concern at that time was tooth decay, what with all the sugary foods being advertised," Engle says, pointing out that even twenty-five years ago there was a "groundswell of public concern" about saturating the airways with ads marketing sugar-filled foods to children. The agency proposed banning all advertising to kids under age six, on the theory that advertising to such young children — who lack the cognitive capacity to understand that advertising is trying to sell you something — is unfair. The agency also proposed banning ads for sugary foods directed at children 12 and under, which Congress prohibited the group from issuing. However, some major food companies have taken up the latter proposal voluntarily, after fear of being blamed for childhood obesity.

In the final analysis, Engle says, regulating advertising aimed at children is even more difficult now than in the 1970s. "Since that time, Supreme Court decisions [protecting commercial speech] have only gotten stronger," she says. "It would be much more difficult to construct a rule that wouldn't be overturned."

### New Ad Avenues

Advertisers may face a more welcome reception in the courts, but they nonetheless face serious challenges in reaching overloaded consumers and dealing with rapidly changing technologies. The dual challenges mean advertisers must work ever harder to reach audiences. With the advent of viral video, advertisers are quickly learning that they no longer need to rely on paid advertisements to get products in front of target audiences. In 2007, a Starburst commercial was featured on YouTube and had 10 million views, and not one dollar was put into reaching that audience. [41]

# Should pop-up disclosures be required for product placements in TV shows?

## YES
**Gary Ruskin**
*Executive Director, Commercial Alert*

## NO
**Darryl Nirenberg**
*Counsel, Freedom to Advertise Coalition*

Written for *CQ Researcher*, January 2004

Written for *CQ Researcher*, January 2004

It is a basic principle of law and common morality that advertisers must be honest with viewers. Advertisers can puff and tout and use all the many tricks of their trade. But they must not pretend that their ads are something else.

This principle has been a cornerstone of communications law since the beginning of the broadcast era. Congress first required broadcasters to identify their sponsors in the Radio Act of 1927. The reasoning is obvious: "Listeners are entitled to know by whom they are being persuaded."

Yet current practice in the broadcast industry violates this principle broadly and systematically. Broadcasters not only fail to identify their sponsors; worse, they fail to identify the ads themselves and instead pretend that the ads are merely parts of shows. Such violation has become the new way of doing business.

Put simply, TV networks and stations are shifting advertising from commercial breaks to programming itself. They are inserting branded products directly into programs, in exchange for substantial fees or other consideration. This advertising technique, called "product placement," has become closely integrated into program plots, to the point that the line between programming and "infomercials" has become increasingly blurred. Some commentators see no line at all.

Television networks interweave advertising and programming so routinely that they are, in effect, selling to advertisers a measure of control over aspects of their programming. Some TV programs are so packed with product placements that they approach the appearance of infomercials. The head of a [casino] company that obtained repeated product placements actually called one such program "a great infomercial." Yet these programs typically lack the disclosure required of infomercials to uphold honesty and fair dealing.

Television stations that cram their programs with product placements, yet fail to identify the sponsors in a conspicuous way are brazenly violating the public's right to know who is seeking to persuade them.

This is an affront to basic honesty. We urge the Federal Communications Commission to investigate current TV advertising practices regarding product placement and other embedded ads and to take the steps necessary to restore some honesty and fair dealing to the presentation of these ads by strengthening the sponsorship-identification rules so ads are properly and prominently identified as ads.

The proposal offered by Commercial Alert to require that television programs be continually interrupted with "large" and "conspicuous" pop-ups disclosing placements as they appear represents an unconstitutional infringement on commercial speech rights.

The proposal is impractical, would ruin the entertainment experience for viewers and would be unreasonably burdensome on programmers and advertisers. It ignores the facts that existing Federal Communications Commission regulations adequately address the issue of commercial sponsorship and that the Federal Trade Commission, which examines specific issues regarding product placement disclosure on a case-by-case basis, previously denied a petition similar to Commercial Alert's.

Product placement has occupied a well-accepted place in film and television for decades. In the real world, people eat, drink and wear brand-name products. The visual picture painted for the viewer gains vibrancy when products are portrayed as they are used in everyday life. Such products help tell the story and sometimes become the story.

Longstanding disclosure rules permit a program containing product placement to be broadcast as long as the presence of any product placement is noted. The rules protect the artistic integrity of the program and preserve First Amendment rights while properly informing the public of the presence of this form of commercial speech.

Should Commercial Alert's proposal be adopted, television programming would become virtually impossible to watch as scene after scene would be interrupted by pop-ups flashing the word "advertisement." Its likely result will be to censor or ban this means of commercial speech.

The proposed restriction would run afoul of the Supreme Court's holding that the freedom of speech guaranteed by the First Amendment extends to commercial speech as long as it is not misleading and involves a lawful activity. Advertising may be restricted only if: (1) the government has a substantial interest in restricting it; (2) the restriction materially advances the governmental interest; and (3) the restriction is only as extensive as necessary.

Based on its faulty assumption that Americans are unable to discern fact from fiction, Commercial Alert wants the federal government to abandon precedent, ignore the law and force networks to continually interrupt broadcasts with pop-up disclosures. Fortunately, the Constitution stands in the way.

While advertisers have been exploring new venues for their ads, including schools and the Internet, the advertising arena that has seen the most dramatic growth — mainly deceptive advertising, some critics say — is in product placements in movies and TV programs. Advertisers currently spend about $360 million a year on product placements in films and TV programming, according to the Advertising Research Foundation (ARF). [42] The practice of using product placements grows, ARF says, "as marketers cope with increasing commercial clutter, audience fragmentation, media proliferation and — above all — commercial avoidance" with remotes, DVRs and TiVo devices (though some advertisers have broken into TiVo homes, featuring ads that can only be viewed by those recording and replaying the show — the "slow" button on the TiVo remote must be used to view each frame of the advertisement).

The blockbuster Steven Spielberg movie "E.T." has been credited with starting the boom in paid product placements. When the homesick little alien took a liking to Reese's Pieces, sales of the peanut butter candy jumped 66 percent. That inspired the makers of Huggies diapers to pay filmmakers $100,000 to feature their product in the movie "Baby Boom." Philip Morris reportedly forked over $350,000 to see that James Bond puffed on Lark cigarettes in the movie "License to Kill," [43] and Audi made sure to place their new R8 in the early summer hit "Iron Man." According to the ARF, the No. 1 film in product placement revenues to date is the 2002 James Bond film "Die Another Day." It collected some $160 million by placing 20 products in the feature, including British Airways, Finlandia vodka, Ford, Heineken beer and Sony electronics. [44]

Critics complain that although the filmmaker must disclose that product-placement fees were paid, viewers usually don't notice the announcements, which occur in the quickly scrolling credits at the end of movies and TV programs. Commercial Alert has petitioned the FTC and FCC to require so-called pop-up disclosures when paid product placements occur in TV programs. "To prevent stealth advertising and ensure that viewers are fully aware of the efforts of advertisers to embed ads in programming, the commission should require TV networks and stations to prominently disclose to viewers that their product placements are ads. In addition, product placements should be identified when they occur," Commercial Alert said recently. [45] The group has not sought controls of product placements in films, because

— unlike broadcasts, which use the public airwaves — movies are not regulated by the federal government.

Advertisers are united in opposition to controls on product placements. "Their proposal is unconstitutional," says Jaffe of the Association of National Advertisers, who argues that current disclosure requirements are sufficient. "People will clearly be on notice, and there's no reason to just bombard people with these types of notices." Johnson of the American Civil Liberties Union agrees. "When I see Coca-Cola being prominently featured, I know pretty well that Coca-Cola has probably paid for that," he says. "Is it a function of government to control the speech or is it the function of parents? I'm not sure it's the government's function to be saying you have to say X, Y and Z, particularly when the First Amendment specifically prohibits the government from doing certain things in the area of freedom of speech."

# OUTLOOK

## Schools Targeted

Consumer advocates doubt that either the courts or Congress will protect the public from what they characterize as a flood of advertisements. "Congress is for sale," Commercial Alert's Ruskin says flatly. "Congress is a microcosm of the problem. Congress is basically asleep at the switch." As for the Supreme Court, analysts say it is not likely to reverse course anytime soon and reduce or eliminate First Amendment protections for commercial speech. "If there is any good reason for excluding commercial speech from protection, the Supreme Court hasn't stumbled over it yet," says Roger Marzulla, counsel for Defenders of Property Rights.

Even some consumer groups are leery of regulating commercial speech. "We do not come down on the side of regulation of commercial speech," says psychologist Walsh, of the National Institute on Media and the Family. "The First Amendment is such a fragile thing. Erosion of things like the First Amendment don't happen all at once. They happen an inch at a time." Nevertheless, many consumer groups are beginning to see progress in mobilizing against the onslaught of advertising, especially where it is directed at children. Arizona State University's Molnar says several school districts around the country recently have turned down advertising income after complaints from parents. For example, Molnar notes, districts in Seattle, Rockwell, Texas, and Martin County, Florida, have eliminated their contracts with Channel One, the commercialized in-school television service.

"We found thirty pieces of legislation introduced at either the national or state level that in some way deal with [curbing] school commercialism," Molnar says. "It's a marker of interest. I think we're going to see some kind of legislation shortly, particularly in the area of marketing and nutrition." But ridding schools of advertising may "take a while," he says. In fact, advertisers say local action rather than federal regulation is more appropriate and effective in controlling advertising. "There are currently sufficient guidelines and regulatory mechanisms in place," says Hoffman of the American Association of Advertising Agencies. "I think the industry is searching for solutions now, given the increased attention by consumers, regulators, the media, activist organizations and others. The industry is very, very sensitive to these things."

"We can do a lot; we have done a lot, basically with persuasion, influence and pressure," Walsh agrees. Rather than more government regulations, Walsh argues, more attention to public education, especially where children are concerned, can be effective. "We often look for scapegoats," Walsh says. "Right now, the scapegoat in the obesity epidemic is fast food. Unless we can pry kids away from TV screens [and their sedentary lifestyle], we can keep fast food advertising away from kids from now until the cows come home, but we're not going to affect the obesity problem. All this has to do with education."

Children see advertisements in school on things from book covers to vending machines. To curb part of this problem, in 2004, the Seattle School Board, with help from the Citizens' Campaign for Commercial-Free Schools, approved some of the nation's toughest standards to provide healthy food and beverage options to students during the day, and also got rid of the school district's exclusive contract with Coca-Cola, opting instead to give students local, fresh, unprocessed foods. [46]

## NOTES

1. Steve McClellan, "Ad Clutter Keeps Climbing," *Broadcasting and Cable*, December 22, 2003, 13.

2. Vincent P. Bzdek, "The Ad Subtractors, Making a Difference," *The Washington Post*, July 29, 2003, C9.

3. Deborah Fallows, "Spam: How it is Hurting E-mail and Degrading Life on the Internet," Pew Internet and American Life Project, October 22, 2003, i.

4. Spam 2007, Pew Internet and American Life Project, May 23, 2007.

5. Fallows, "Spam," 7.

6. "The State of the News Media 2008," Center for Excellence in Journalism, March 2008.

7. Vincent P. Bzdek, "The Ad Subtractors, Making a Difference," *Washington Post*, July 29, 2003, C9.

8. *Ibid.*

9. Saul Hansell, "Viginia Indicts Two Under Antispam Law," *New York Times*, December 12, 2003.

10. Arnold S. Relman, and Marcia Angell, "America's Other Drug Problem: How the Drug Industry Distorts Medicine and Politics," *The New Republic*, Dec. 16, 2002, 36. For background, see David Hatch, "Drug Company Ethics," *CQ Researcher*, June 6, 2003, 521-544.

11. Tom Zeller Jr., "Law Barring Junk E-mail Allows a Flood Instead," *New York Times*, February 1, 2005.

12. National Do Not E-mail Registry: A Report to Congress, Federal Trade Commission, June 2004.

13. Zeller, "Law Barring Junk E-mail."

14. Spam Summit: The Next Generation of Threats and Solutions, Federal Trade Commission, November 2007.

15. Zeller "Law Barring Junk E-mail."

16. Saul Hansell, "Spam Keeps Coming, but its Senders are Wary," *New York Times*, January 7, 2004.

17. Zeller "Law Barring Junk E-mail."

18. Spam Summit: The Next Generation of Threats and Solutions, Federal Trade Commission, November 2007.

19. Master Settlement Agreement, 14, www.naag.org/upload/1032468605_cigmsa.pdf. For background, see Kenneth Jost, "Closing in on Tobacco," *CQ Researcher*, Nov. 12, 1999, 977-1000, and "High-Impact Litigation," *CQ Researcher*, Feb. 11, 2000, 89-112.

20. Jonathan Gruber and Jonathan Zinman, "Youth Smoking in the U.S.: Evidence and Implications," National Bureau of Economic Research, *NBER Working Paper No. 7780*, www.nber.org/digest/oct00/w7780.html.

21. New Study Finds Tobacco Industry 'Prevention' Ads Don't Work and Encourage Kids to Smoke; Industry Should Pull Ads and States Should Fund Real Tobacco Prevention, *U.S. Newswire*, October 31, 2006.

22. John P. Pierce, *et al.*, "Tobacco Industry Promotion of Cigarettes and Adolescent Smoking," *Journal of the American Medical Association*, February 18, 1998, vol. 279, no. 7, 511. For background, see Richard L. Worsnop, "Teens and Tobacco," *CQ Researcher*, December 1, 1995, 1065-1088.

23. "Changing Adolescent Smoking Prevalence: Where It Is and Why," U.S. Department of Health and Human Services, November 2001, 2.

24. Alyse R. Lancaster and Kent M. Lancaster, "Teenage Exposure to Cigarette Advertising in Popular Consumer Magazines: Vehicle Versus Message Reach and Frequency," *Journal of Advertising*, September 22, 2003," 70.

25. Dwight Filley, "Forbidden Fruit: When Prohibition Increases the Harm it is Supposed to Reduce," *Independent Review*, December 2, 1999, vol 3, no. 3, 441.

26. For background, see Patrick Marshall, "Gambling in America," *CQ Researcher*, March 7, 2003, 201-224, and Alan Greenblatt, "Obesity Epidemic," *CQ Researcher*, January 31, 2003, 73-104.

27. Elizabeth Olsen, "Study Says Junk Food Still Dominates Youth TV," *New York Times*, March 29, 2007.

28. Brooks Barnes, "Limiting Ads of Junk Food to Children, *New York Times*, July 18, 2007.

29. Ibid.

30. *Bigelow v. Virginia* (421 U.S. 809 [1975]), 826.

31. *Ibid.*, 822.

32. *Virginia State Board of Pharmacy v. Virginia Citizens Consumer Council Inc.* (425 U.S. 748 [1976]), 763.

33. *Central Hudson Gas & Electric Corp. v. Public Service Commission*, 447 U.S. 557 (1980).

34. *Posada de Puerto Rico Associates v. Tourism Co.*, 478 U.S. 328 (1986).

35. Arlen W. Langvardt, "The Incremental Strengthening of First Amendment Protection for Commercial Speech: Lessons from Greater New Orleans Broadcasting," *American Business Law Journal*, June 22, 2000, vol. 37, no 4, 587.

36. *Rubin v. Coors Brewing Co.*, 514 U.S. 476 (1995).

37. Langvardt, "The Incremental Strengthening."

38. Joseph C. Anselmo, "Despite Congress' Best Efforts, Separate Court Rulings Put 'Do Not Call' Registry on Hold," *CQ Weekly*, September 27, 2003, 2358.

39. Griff Witte, "FCC Issues its First 'Do Not Call' Citation," *Washington Post*, December 19, 2003, E3.

40. Matt Richtel, "Telemarketing Fine Proposed for AT&T," *New York Times*, November 4, 2003, C4.

41. "The State of the News Media 2008," Center for Excellence in Journalism, March 2008.

42. Denman Maroney, "Top Topic: Product Placement," Informed, Advertising Research Foundation, vol. 6, no. 4, August 2003.

43. Michael F. Jacobson and Laurie Ann Mazur, *Marketing Madness: A Survival Guide for a Consumer Society* (1995), 67.

44. Maroney, "Top Topic."

45. "Commercial Alert Asks FCC, FTC to Require Disclosure of Product Placement on TV," September 30, 2003, www.commercialalert.org/index.php/category_id/1/subcategory_id/79/article_id/191.

46. "Seattle School Board Approves Comprehensive Suite of Nutrition Policies," Seattle Public Schools News Release, September 3, 2004.

# BIBLIOGRAPHY

### Books

Jacobson, Michael F., and Laurie Ann Mazur, *Marketing Madness: A Survival Guide for a Consumer Society*, Westview Press, 1995.
The president of the Center for Science in the Public Interest offers an entertaining and image-laden history of advertising and U.S. commercial culture.

Kaplar, Richard T., *Advertising Rights: The Neglected Freedom*, The Media Institute, 1991.
The vice president of The Media Institute argues that commercial speech should have the same First Amendment protections as other speech.

Wright, R. George, *Selling Words: Free Speech in a Commercial Culture*, New York University Press, 1997.
A law professor at Samford University in Birmingham, Ala., examines the legal and social issues surrounding First Amendment protections for commercial speech, arguing there is room within the Constitution for greater restrictions.

## Articles

Bosman, Julie, "Do Viewers See Ads? Ratings Coming Soon," *International Herald Tribune*, July 17, 2006.
New Nielsen data will let advertisers know who watches commercials, not just television programs.

Carr, Nick, "Neuromarketing could make mind reading the ad-man's ultimate tool," *The Guardian*, April 3, 2008.
Nick Carr looks at a new up and coming science that marketers could use to better target their audiences.

Hampp, Andrew and Brian Steinberg, "Commercial Ratings? Nets talk TiVo instead; Metric makes debut, but sellers force negotiations back to DVR viewership," *Advertising Age*, June 4, 2007.
Nielsen released its commercial-watching data, but advertisers still don't know who is catching their ads on digital video recorders.

Langvardt, Arlen W., "The Incremental Strengthening of First Amendment Protection for Commercial Speech: Lessons from Greater New Orleans Broadcasting," *American Business Law Journal*, June 22, 2000, 587.
A business law professor at the University of Indiana details the Supreme Court's approach to commercial-speech issues over the past twenty-five years.

McClellan, Steve, "Ad Clutter Keeps Climbing," *Broadcasting and Cable*, Dec. 22, 2003, 13.
A new study of commercial "clutter" on the networks reveals that viewers are now exposed to an average fifty-two minutes of non-program content a night on each of the four major broadcast networks — about seventeen minutes per hour.

Nelson, Jon P., "Cigarette Demand, Structural Change and Advertising Bans: International Evidence, 1970-1995," *Contributions to Economic Analysis & Policy*, vol. 2, issue 1, 2003.
An economist at Pennsylvania State University concludes from international data that advertising bans have no significant impact on cigarette consumption.

Park, Alice, "Marketing to Your Mind," *Time*, January 19, 2007.
Neuromarketing could prove to be a huge benefit to advertisers, but it is an imperfect science.

Pierce, John P., Won S. Choi, Elizabeth A. Gilpin, Arthur J. Farkas and Charles C. Berry, "Tobacco Industry Promotion of Cigarettes and Adolescent Smoking," *Journal of the American Medical Association*, vol. 279, no. 7, February 18, 1998, 511.
An influential study at the Cancer Prevention and Control Program at the University of California, San Diego, found no causal effect between cigarette advertising and youths' decisions to begin smoking.

Story, Louise, "A TV Show's Content Calls the Commercial Plays," *New York Times*, Dec. 21, 2006.
Television advertisers have more leeway in how they target audiences during certain programs.

Story, Louise, "Agencies and Networks Ponder Nielsen Ad Ratings," *New York Times*, June 1, 2007.
Advertisers want more data about TiVo and DVR users to figure out who watches their commercials.

Woellert, Lorraine, "Will the Right to Pester Hold Up?" *Business Week*, November 10, 2003, 73.
A U.S. district judge in Denver ruled that the FTC's do not call registry infringes on corporate First Amendment rights, but many question whether commercial free speech doctrine is too permissive.

## Reports

"Changing Adolescent Smoking Prevalence: Where It Is and Why," U.S. Department of Health and Human Services, November 2001.
This 272-page report contains seventeen articles by top researchers examining such issues as smoking rates among various ethnic groups and the effects of advertising on smoking rates.

**"Cigarette Report for 2001," Federal Trade Commission, 2003.**

The FTC's annual report on cigarette advertising and sales shows that sales decreased by 15.6 billion cigarettes from 2000 to 2001, while advertising and promotional expenditures rose $1.62 billion to $11.22 billion.

**"Exposure to Pro-tobacco Messages among Teens and Young Adults: Results from Three National Surveys," The American Legacy, November 2003.**

The anti-smoking group finds that despite restrictions on advertising tobacco products to minors in 1998, youth "continue to be widely exposed to pro-tobacco messages."

**National Do Not E-mail Registry: A Report to Congress, Federal Trade Commission, June 2004.**

The FTC's study finds that a National Do Not E-mail Registry would not be a deterrent to spammers, mainly due to new technologies that can get around spam blockers.

**"No Student Left Unsold: The Sixth Annual Report on Schoolhouse Commercialism Trends, 2002-2003," Commercialism in Education Research Unit, Arizona State University, October 2003.**

The report finds both an increase in marketing activities and "an increasingly vocal resistance to commercializing activities."

**"Reducing Tobacco Use: A Report of the Surgeon General," U.S. Department of Health and Human Services, 2000.**

This detailed history of efforts to reduce smoking includes a thorough recounting of major court action.

**"Spam: How It Is Hurting E-mail and Degrading Life on the Internet," Pew Internet and American Life Project, Oct. 22, 2003.**

Extensive data "suggest that spam is beginning to undermine the integrity of e-mail and to degrade the online experience."

**Spam Summit: The Next Generation of Threats and Solutions, Federal Trade Commission, November 2007.**

The FTC finds that spamming is still a big problem for legitimate advertisers and the public at large — what they don't know is how to fix the issue.

**"The State of the News Media 2008," Center for Excellence in Journalism, March 2008.**

The center finds that the media as a whole is in a more troubled position than it was last year.

# For More Information

**American Advertising Federation**, 1101 Vermont Ave., N.W., Suite 500, Washington, DC 20005-6306; (202) 898-0089; www.ana.net. The AAF is a trade association that represents 50,000 professionals in the advertising industry. Their Web site contains much information on regulatory actions and legislative activity.

**American Association of Advertising Agencies**, 405 Lexington Ave., 18th Floor, New York, NY 10174-1801; (212) 682-2500; www.aaaa.org. The ad industry's lobbying and research organization provides a good deal of accessible information about issues in advertising on its Web site.

**American Civil Liberties Union**, 125 Broad St., 18th Floor, New York, NY 10004; (212) 549-2666; www.aclu.org. The ACLU aims to "defend and preserve the individual rights and liberties guaranteed to all people in this country by the Constitution and laws of the United States." Its Web site contains information on cases involving commercial-speech issues.

**American Legacy Foundation**, 2030 M St., N.W., Sixth Floor, Washington, DC 20036; (202) 454-5555; www.americanlegacy.org. The educational foundation created by the Master Settlement Agreement between the tobacco companies and the states develops programs about the health effects of tobacco use.

**Center for Science in the Public Interest**, 1875 Connecticut Ave. N.W., Suite 300, Washington, DC 20009; (202) 332-9110; www.cspinet.org. The nonprofit advocacy group tracks a broad variety of issues, including advertising and its impacts on nutrition.

**Children's Advertising Review Unit**, 70 West 36th St., 13th Floor, New York, NY 10018; (866) 334-6272; www.caru.org. CARU was founded in 1974 to promote responsible children's advertising as part of a strategic alliance with major advertising trade associations. The Web site contains "Self-Regulatory Guidelines for Children's Advertising" and relevant laws.

**Commercial Alert**, 4110 S.E. Hawthorne Blvd, #123, Portland, OR 97214-5426; (503) 235.8012; www.commercialalert.org. The nonprofit activist organization was founded by consumer advocate Ralph Nader in 1998 to fight encroaching commercialism.

**Federal Communications Commission**, 445 12th St., S.W., Washington, DC 20554; (888) 225-5322; www.fcc.gov. The FCC is the primary federal agency concerned with regulating TV and radio broadcast industries, including advertising on those media.

**Federal Trade Commission**, 600 Pennsylvania Ave., N.W., Washington, DC 20580; (202) 326-2222; www.ftc.gov. The FTC is the primary federal agency concerned with advertising standards. Its Web site offers a broad variety of historical and current information.

**Junkbusters Corp.**, P.O. Box 7034, Green Brook, NJ 08812; (908) 753-7861; www.junkbusters.com. The for-profit firm offers a wealth of information on how to protect against unwanted advertising.

**The Media Institute**, 1800 N. Kent St., Suite 1130, Arlington, VA 22209; (703) 243-5060; www.mediainstitute.org. The research foundation specializes in communications policy and the First Amendment. The Web site provides links to a variety of other useful sites.

**National Institute on Media and the Family**, 606 24th Ave. South, Suite 606, Minneapolis, MN 55454; (612) 672-5437; www.mediafamily.org. The institute is a national resource for information on the impact of media on children and families. Its useful Web site includes movie reviews for parents.

# 10

# Future of Newspapers

Kenneth Jost

James Hill, an assistant managing editor at the *Detroit Free Press*, reacts to the news on Aug. 3, 2005, that Knight Ridder Inc. was selling the paper to the giant Gannett chain, which publishes 99 daily newspapers. Despite healthy profits, Knight Ridder is under pressure from big institutional investors to put itself on the auction block.

From *CQ Researcher*,
January 20, 2006.

Money manager Bruce Sherman didn't waste words in his Nov. 1, 2005, letter to the board of directors of Knight Ridder Inc. — the country's second-largest newspaper chain.

Sherman reminded the board that his Florida-based investment company, Private Capital Management, holds 19 percent of the company's stock and that he had alerted board members in July to his firm's "concerns" with Knight Ridder's stock performance.

Then Sherman dropped his bombshell: He told the board he wanted Knight Ridder put on the auction block, since it was continuing to have "difficulties . . . in realizing the fair value of the company for its shareholders."

Sherman's demand might have led casual readers of the financial pages to surmise that Knight Ridder was bleeding money and losing customers. In fact, its 32 daily newspapers in such cities as Miami, Philadelphia and San Jose, Calif., had a total circulation of 3.4 million — second only to industry giant Gannett. (*See graph, p. 218.*) And the company's 19.4 percent profit margin — up from 14.4 percent in 1994 — would be considered extraordinary in most industries, where the average profit is only about half that high. [1]

But that's not healthy enough for today's Wall Street. The stock price of Knight Ridder, one of the nation's most respected media organizations, peaked near $80 per share in early 2004 but slumped into the low $50s in 2005. And the institutional investors who hold ever-larger stakes in publicly traded newspaper companies care more about stock prices and shareholder returns than about Pulitzer prizes, foreign news coverage or community service.

"There is pressure from Wall Street," says John Morton, a long-time newspaper-industry analyst in Silver Spring, Md., and colum-

## Number of Newspapers Declined

The number of U.S. daily newspapers declined more than 17 percent in the past 50 years, reflecting the demise of afternoon papers.

### No. of U.S. Daily Newspapers
(includes morning and evening papers)

*Source:* Newspaper Association of America, from *Editor & Publisher* data

nist for *American Journalism Review.* "And Wall Street has become notoriously very short-term oriented."

"There is more pressure on companies to increase profit margins every year, to increase shareholder return every year," says Richard Rodriguez, executive editor of the *Sacramento Bee* and president of the American Society of Newspaper Editors (ASNE). "That, in turn, has placed pressure on newsrooms either to hold down or cut spending. It's a trend that over a period of time is going to cut into the quality of journalism."

The Knight Ridder board is meeting Sherman's demand — as required by corporate law — by agreeing to look at offers from prospective purchasers. So far, according to news reports, possible bidders include McClatchy Newspapers, which publishes the *Bee,* and several consortia of private equity firms. But some analysts are predicting no sale will materialize. And Knight Ridder itself could deflect the shareholder revolt by buying back a chunk of its stock. (*See sidebar, p. 224.*)

Whatever the outcome for Knight Ridder, the story dramatizes the seemingly paradoxical state of the U.S. newspaper industry in the early 21st century. Newspaper companies are bigger than ever, newspapers fatter and their bottom lines written in double-digit black ink. Morton says the average profit margin of publicly traded newspaper companies is 20.5 percent.

Newspapers may be making extraordinary profits, but they are competing with a plethora of new print, online

and broadcast competitors. The competition includes all-news, business-news and sports-news cable networks, several prime-time TV news magazines, thousands of newsletters, weeklies and alternative newspapers and hundreds of online news sources.

And newspapers are losing readers. Circulation has been declining in recent years following decades of sub-par growth, including plummeting readership among young people. Currently, only 52 percent of adults read a newspaper on a typical weekday. Lagging circulation has combined with stagnant advertising growth in the past year to trigger layoffs and cutbacks at some of the company's biggest newspapers, including *The New York Times.*

More ominously, newspapers are under pressure from Internet rivals that offer news, information and even classified advertising for free. To young Internet enthusiasts, print newspapers are relics of an earlier age — uncompetitive in so many ways with online media and bad for trees besides.

Newspaper executives and industry officials insist the pessimistic picture is wrong in some respects and overdrawn in others. They say newspaper companies are strong today and will continue to be strong well into the foreseeable future.

"The industry is in very strong shape financially," says John Sturm, president and chief executive officer of the Newspaper Association of America (NAA), the industry's principal trade association. "Operating margins continue to be very healthy compared to other industry sectors. The industry has good access to capital, there's good internal cash flow and there are substantial investments being made in the online world and other products."

"The general financial picture is quite good," agrees Rodriguez. "That's why it's a little surprising to hear all this talk about the death of the newspaper industry. Right now, there's a bit of piling on."

As for the emergence of online media, industry officials say newspapers have been rushing to develop online editions ever since the mid-1990s. They say newspapers are better situated than Internet rivals like Google, Yahoo and AOL to fully exploit the potential uses of the new technology — and make money while doing it.

"We were among the first to get involved online," says John Kimball, the Newspaper Association's senior vice president and chief marketing officer. "Newspapers are in almost any market the best-known brand and the most visited Web site in that market."

Some experts similarly discount dire warnings for the industry. "Newspapers have been the real news utility for the community," says former *New York Times* reporter Alex Jones, director of the Joan Shorenstein Center for the Press, Politics and Public Policy at Harvard University. "That's never been challenged. Newspapers have a lot more information in them than a one-hour or two-hour TV newscast. If they can parlay that news information on the Web, then they can sustain a business."

Other experts are less sanguine. Philip Meyer, a former reporter and

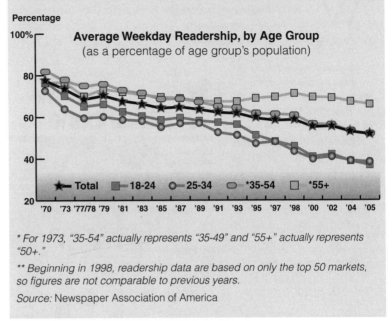

## Readership Declined Among All Age Groups

Newspaper readership in America has been declining among all age groups since 1970. The greatest declines were among readers 18-34. The smallest decline was among readers over 55.

**Average Weekday Readership, by Age Group**
(as a percentage of age group's population)

★ Total   ■ 18-24   ◉ 25-34   ◯ *35-54   ☐ *55+

* For 1973, "35-54" actually represents "35-49" and "55+" actually represents "50+."

** Beginning in 1998, readership data are based on only the top 50 markets, so figures are not comparable to previous years.

Source: Newspaper Association of America

Knight Ridder executive who now holds the Knight professorship in journalism at the University of North Carolina in Chapel Hill, says Wall Street is pushing newspapers too hard for short-term profits while newspaper executives themselves are too timid in meeting the challenges of a new media environment.

"Newspapers had it so good for so long that they developed a risk-averse mentality," Meyer says. "To figure out new ways of delivering the news is going to require some risk-taking."

As the newspaper industry copes with a myriad of editorial and financial challenges, here are some of the questions being debated:

### Is the newspaper industry in financial jeopardy?

Donald Graham, chairman and chief executive officer of the Washington Post Co., was far from upbeat when he reported to investors and analysts in December on the state of the company's flagship newspaper. Circulation at the *Post* was down, advertising revenues were up only modestly, newsprint was more expensive and profits were

diminishing. And just outside the gates, ambitious Web competitors such as Google were creating "clever products . . . designed to make our life harder." [2]

Many of the newspaper executives who spoke at back-to-back media conferences sponsored by financial firms UBS and Credit Suisse First Boston tried to be more positive. In recapping the conferences, however, Goldman Sachs' respected analyst Peter Appert discounted the executives' optimistic predictions on ad revenue and earnings and warned of likely staff cuts in 2006. And to top the week off, Prudential Equity Research Group downgraded its recommendation on New York Times Co. stock to a far-from-enthusiastic "neutral." [3]

The newspaper industry's trade association discounts the gloom-and-doom talk, however — and so do many veteran industry-watchers. "The fundamentals of the business are extremely strong," says Conrad Fink, a professor at the University of Georgia's Grady College of Journalism and Mass Communication in Athens and author of a leading textbook on newspaper management.

# Seeking Ways to Lure Young Readers

When it comes to luring more young readers back to daily newspaper reading, the Readership Institute of Northwestern University in Chicago has good news and bad news.

First, the good news: Newspapers can be reinvented to make them more attractive to people under age 30.

Now, the bad news: It won't be easy.

Institute researchers based their conclusions on six years of investigation into newspaper readers' habits and motivations. In the Front Page Study — completed in May 2005, researchers teamed up with editors and reporters at the *Star Tribune* in Minneapolis to develop two different versions of the front page and an inside page for a typical news day, then tested the reactions of the target audience — self-supporting, childless under-30s with a range of occupations.

The results strongly indicated that the most effective way to reach those readers was through a reader-centered approach to newspaper editing and design, which the Institute calls "editing for experience." The approach begins with "choosing the effects you want to create in your audience, then picking and crafting content to get those results."[1]

Readers liked the lively "Experience" version of the *Star Tribune* front page.

*Courtesy Minneapolis Star Tribune*

Editors were guided by three experiential goals identified by the Readership Institute as feelings, emotions and motivations that cause people to read daily newspapers more: "gives me something to talk about," "looks out for my interests" and "turned on by surprise and humor."

The 140 targeted readers looked at three page versions: the Original Paper that was actually published; the Improved Paper, which included the same stories recrafted to change emphasis, play and approach to enhance the three chosen experiences; and the Experience Paper, in which the three experiences drove both story choice and presentation.

For example, the Experience Paper jettisoned a lead story about a woman who planned to walk every street of Minneapolis as holding little interest for young readers. The replacement, a centerpiece about legalizing Texas Hold 'Em poker, was cast in an engaging pro-con debate format and included information about how to play and where to practice online.

A story about legislation requiring police to collect DNA from any Minnesotan arrested on a felony was reshaped to speak directly to the reader. The original headline, "Broader DNA Collection Law Proposed," became "License, Registration and Saliva please. . . ." The original third-person, institutional account was edited to offer many entry points, to break out useful information in marginalia

As two markers of that strength, Fink notes that newspapers are "almost without exception" the dominant source of news and advertising in their communities and are among the "strongest brand names" in any business. Above all, he emphasizes, newspapers are extremely profitable — with a 20 percent operating margin, almost double the average profits of companies in the benchmark S&P 500.

So why the gloom and doom? Some experts say Wall Street is primarily to blame. "Wall Street wants them to have more," says Morton. "Wall Street is not interested in what you've done in the past. They want to know what you're going to do in the future."[4]

Some experts, however, see more troubling signs for the industry now and in the near future. The economic picture "is changing — obviously," says Tom Rosenstiel,

and boxes and to point readers to a debate in the next day's paper. A new lead, or opening paragraph, addressed readers' interests directly: "If you're ever arrested for a felony in Minnesota, you may soon be asked to open wide and give a sample of saliva along with your fingerprint."

Respondents preferred the Experience Paper over the other two by a ratio of roughly 3-to-1, scoring it much higher on such criteria as: more likely to catch your attention, more visually appealing, more likely to get you to read, more memorable, easier to get information, would cause you to mention when talking with friends, story selection, looks out for your interests and makes the news more interesting.

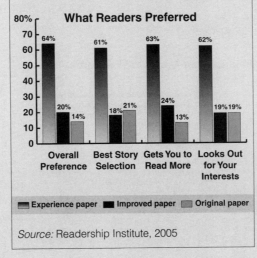

### Emotions Attract Most Readers

Among three versions of a Star Tribune front page, an "experience version" proved the most popular.

**What Readers Preferred**

Legend: Experience paper | Improved paper | Original paper

| | Experience | Improved | Original |
|---|---|---|---|
| Overall Preference | 64% | 20% | 14% |
| Best Story Selection | 61% | 18% | 21% |
| Gets You to Read More | 63% | 24% | 13% |
| Looks Out for Your Interests | 62% | 19% | 19% |

*Source:* Readership Institute, 2005

"What we heard from these young adult Minnesotans is typical of what we hear from young Americans everywhere," the study overview reported. "Newspapers are OK, but they don't compel and engage."

But making them more compelling, while doable, will require altering long-entrenched editorial practices. "Newspapers tend to talk about topics, keeping a distance between themselves, the topic and the reader," noted team leader Nancy Barnes, assistant managing editor at the *Star Tribune*. "In this experiment we actively sought to talk to readers directly, and engage them every step along the way. That makes the newspaper seem more personal. It goes against our natural instinct, however."

"Experiences are a way of converting traditional news judgment from editors' definitions (what's most interesting, what's most important, what you just can't believe happened) to readers' definitions of how they react (what makes readers feel informed, what gives them something to talk about, what tells them the paper is looking out for their interests)," said *Star Tribune* Editor Anders Gyllenhaal.

The young readers' clear preference for the Experience Paper over the Improved Paper supported researchers' contention that reversing the decline in daily newspaper readership will require an editorial revolution within the dailies' hard-news core, not just stylistic changes around the edges.

The overall lesson was "Yes, you can do that," said Mary Nesbitt, managing director of the Readership Institute. But, she continued, "The degree of change you need to make is substantial. It's not just a matter of redesigning the look of the front page. It is that, but it is a lot more than that. You have to consider, given your target audience, how are you defining news in the first place. Where are you going to look for news? What approach or angle do you take with the story? And then how do you present it effectively?"

— *Rachel S. Cox*

[1] "Reinventing the Newspaper for Young Adults," Readership Institute, April 2005, p. 1. Available at www.readership.org/experience/star trib_overview.pdf.

---

a former *Los Angeles Times* reporter who now heads the Project for Excellence in Journalism in Washington. "It's worse in some places than in others."

Rosensteil says the long-term decline in print circulation has accelerated in some places in recent years. "That's really raised questions about whether we're beginning to see the structural shift away from people not reading newspapers in print at all to reading newspa-

pers online or not at all," he says.

In time, shifting to online may be financially advantageous because of the reduced costs of production and distribution, Rosensteil explains — but not yet. "Right now, newspapers can make a lot more from their print editions than from their online editions," he says. "What you can get from the advertiser in an online edition doesn't compare to what you can get for the

## Gannett Is Nation's Largest Newspaper Group

Gannett Co. is the nation's largest newspaper chain in number of daily papers and circulation. Its 99 daily papers include the nation's largest-selling newspaper, *USA Today*, with 2.3 million circulation. Knight Ridder and Tribune Co. trail in second and third places in overall circulation. Knight Ridder is currently looking at offers from prospective purchasers, including the ninth-ranked McClatchy Co., but some experts believe no sale will materialize.

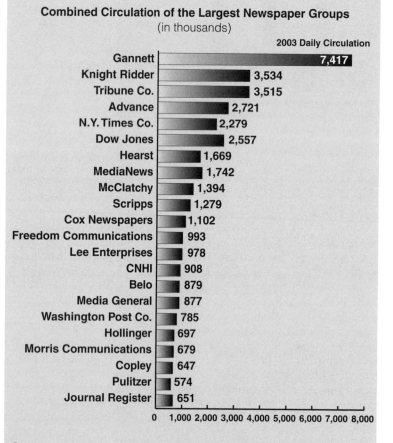

**Combined Circulation of the Largest Newspaper Groups**
(in thousands)

2003 Daily Circulation

| Group | Circulation |
| --- | --- |
| Gannett | 7,417 |
| Knight Ridder | 3,534 |
| Tribune Co. | 3,515 |
| Advance | 2,721 |
| N.Y. Times Co. | 2,279 |
| Dow Jones | 2,557 |
| Hearst | 1,669 |
| MediaNews | 1,742 |
| McClatchy | 1,394 |
| Scripps | 1,279 |
| Cox Newspapers | 1,102 |
| Freedom Communications | 993 |
| Lee Enterprises | 978 |
| CNHI | 908 |
| Belo | 879 |
| Media General | 877 |
| Washington Post Co. | 785 |
| Hollinger | 697 |
| Morris Communications | 679 |
| Copley | 647 |
| Pulitzer | 574 |
| Journal Register | 651 |

0  1,000 2,000 3,000 4,000 5,000 6,000 7,000 8,000

*Sources:* Journalism.org, *Editor and Publisher Yearbook*; *PEJ* Research

deliver content to more people than ever imagined and in a more targeted way than ever before," says Guild President Linda Foley. "It's the fault of these companies in not investing in research and development and not investing in the tools they need."

"For years, they didn't have to worry about that," Foley concludes. "If you were a newspaper, you made money."

Meyer says Wall Street's pressure for exceptionally high earnings clouds the industry's long-term prospects. "Wall Street can't see past its nose," says Meyer. "It is goading companies that don't have some cushion between them and Wall Street into harvesting their assets and running the companies into the ground. It's pushing newspaper companies into sacrificing their long-term interests for short-term gains."

Media-industry consultant Merrill Brown counters that blaming Wall Street is neither justified nor useful. "Public ownership is part of the challenge of management in a difficult media environment," says Brown, a longtime newspaper and magazine journalist before helping found CourtTV and later MSNBC.com. "The public marketplace will reward managements that see the future in clear terms, but the ones that don't will be justifiably punished."

But Jones cautions that both Wall Street and newspaper management may need to lower their expectations for the industry. "With an economic model that is increasingly fragmenting the advertising business and the growth of alternatives in terms of classified-advertising business, newspapers are probably going to have to adjust their expectations as to what is an acceptable level of profit, especially as the transition is made from print to online," he says.

print edition. And right now the online edition is given away."

For its part, the Newspaper Guild-Communications Workers of America — the major union representing the industry — says newspapers' future should be bright, but only if managements invest in the research and planning needed to adapt. "You should be thriving when you can

## Will newspapers succeed online?

As head of the newspaper editors' trade association, *Sacramento Bee* editor Rodriguez naturally worries about the declining circulation of print newspapers. But he worries a bit less about the industry's overall prospects because of what he sees when stopping at a coffee house on a typical Sunday morning.

"Everybody there was looking for information — whether it was the people who were buying the *Bee* or the people reading their computers," Rodriguez says. "There wasn't anyone in that coffeehouse who wasn't looking for information."

A decade after the first surge of online editions, virtually everyone in or around newspapers realizes that computers are a big part of the industry's future — and serving computer users may be key to its long-term survival. But getting to the online *there* from the print *here* is proving to be no easy task.

"They are doing better than the doomsday scenario, but worse than they should be doing," says Pablo Boczkowski, an associate professor at Northwestern University in Evanston, Ill., and author of the recent book *Digitizing the News.* "They are still, to a certain extent, tied to a world that is no longer viable."

"The approach of most newspaper organizations is to put their print product onto the Web," says Mary Nesbitt, managing director of the Readership Institute at Northwestern's Media Management Center. "The platform has changed, the look of it certainly, but it's basically transferring one to the other."

The critique may be generally true, but there were exceptions even in the early days of online newspapers in the late '90s. In his book, Boczkowski notes as one example the "Virtual Voyager" features on HoustonChronicle.com, which used online technologies to take readers along almost in real time on such experiences as a month-long trip on old Route 66. [5]

Today, more and more online newspapers are offering distinctive features that are not — and could not be — published in print editions. Newspaper Web sites commonly combine related editorial or advertising content into extensive packages that would take up way too much space in a print edition.

Newspaper sites also typically include interactive features that allow readers to comment on issues from the serious to the mundane and — unlike letters to the editor — to participate in ongoing dialogues with other readers, and perhaps reporters and editors as well. In early January 2006, for example, visitors to nytimes.com could discuss Israel's pullout from Gaza, the University of Texas' victory in the Rose Bowl, comedian Jon Stewart's selection to host the Oscars or the future of plastic surgery.

Web competitors, however, are busy doing similar things. Google News offers users headlines and news stories from around the world, continuously updated throughout the day (http://news.google.com). Google Groups allows users to create or join a mailing list or discussion forum on topics of individual interest (http://groups.google.com). Users can also track their favorite topics simply by clicking on a star next to the particular subject.

Industry officials insist that newspapers can meet the challenges posed by Internet competitors and note that rivals are in fact pulling much of their content from print sources. "Everybody says the Internet is eating our lunch," says the Newspaper Association's Kimball. "The reality is that newspapers are providing the lunch."

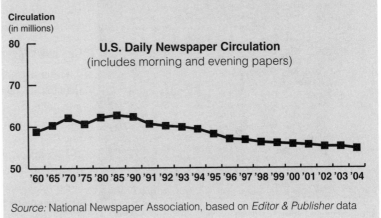

### Newspaper Circulation Declined

The number of papers sold daily in the United States dropped by nearly 10 percent, or more than 5 million papers, from 1960-2004. During the same period, the U.S. population increased 115 million.

**U.S. Daily Newspaper Circulation**
(includes morning and evening papers)

Circulation (in millions)

*Source:* National Newspaper Association, based on *Editor & Publisher* data

Advertising revenue — considered the "bread and butter" of the newspaper business — has been down in recent years, growing less than 3 percent a year compared to about 5 percent historically. Many blame the disappearing ads in newspapers on the emergence of Craigslist.org, a San Francisco-based nonprofit community Web site that offers free, local classified ads on the Internet. Now in many cities, the site was founded by Craig Newmark, left, with CEO Jim Buckmaster.

Kimball and Rodriguez both concede, however, that newspapers have their work cut out for them to make online editions successful. Economically, newspaper companies need to get more revenue from online editions by raising rates and convincing advertisers that the money is well spent. L. Gordon Crovitz, president of Dow Jones' electronic publishing division, alluded to the issue in remarks to the UBS media conference in December. "The challenge for all of us," Crovitz said, "is to do the hard work that's necessary to keep informing advertisers of the value of online advertising." [6]

"We've got a long way to go," Rodriguez says. "We understand as an industry the imperative of getting more technologically savvy. We're still struggling with the structure of how to make that happen."

Industry observers agree on the challenges but offer somewhat different prescriptions. Rosensteil says the future lies online. "In time, you're going to have to let go of that print focus," he says. "To really build a better journalism you have to think of the Internet as the better platform."

But Northwestern's Boczkowski cautions newspapers not to overlook the print product. "The future of newspapers lies in the intersection of print and non-print options," he says. "There is a lot that is wonderful about the print newspaper. It's not that newspaper companies should abandon the print business, but they should reinvent it for our time."

## Can newspapers attract more younger readers?

The demographics of newspaper readership are more than discouraging for the industry. Young people, simply put, are not reading the newspaper as much as their parents or grandparents did — and the numbers keep declining with each new generation. One study found that in 1972 a majority of the people in every age group above the age of 30 read a newspaper every day; three decades later, in 2002, daily newspaper readers were in the majority only among people in their late 50s or older. [7]

"Cohorts of high newspaper readers are being replaced by cohorts who read at lower levels," says Nesbitt of the Readership Institute. "Newspapers still reach a high proportion of the adult population, but it's no longer as entrenched a daily habit as it once was."

Experts offer a variety of explanations for the declining readership. The University of Georgia's Fink suggests that the trend toward waiting to get married is one factor. "Traditionally we waited until they got married, had a household and took on responsibilities, and then they became newspaper readers," and that all once happened at an early age, Fink says. "Now they wait to do all that. And if you haven't read a newspaper by the time you're 30, you're not going to start then."

For his part, David Mindich, a former CNN editor who now chairs the journalism department at St. Michael's College in Colchester, Vt., sees a declining interest among young people in serious news from any media — print, broadcast or online. He blames many institutions besides newspapers. "We no longer use the news in our discussions at the dinner table or in the classrooms as we once did," Mindich says. "We need a total change in our society to change educational expectations, workplace expectations, the expectations of the Federal Communications Commission."

The advent of the Internet further weakens the appeal of the print newspaper. "Our school systems have been training people to get information by computer keyboard and screen," says industry analyst Morton. *Bee* editor Rodriguez says young people especially like the control they can exercise in using online media. "They want it where they want it, when they want it, how they want it," he says. "And they don't want to pay for it."

Newspaper Association officials acknowledge the change in reading habits among young people but point to evidence that young people continue to find newspapers valuable — whether in print or online. "They don't read the newspaper the way their parents or grandparents did," says Kimball. "They don't sit down before or after work and go through the newspaper cover to cover. But if you ask them if they used the newspaper during the course of the day, you get a different picture. Over half of the people ages 12-17 are saying they are using the newspaper on a regular basis."

The Project for Excellence in Journalism's Rosenstiel also believes the declining readership among young people has been somewhat exaggerated and, in any event, says the Internet can help counter the trend. "With the advent of the Internet, there is more reason to believe that young people will be news consumers," he says. "The notion that people under a certain age don't read at all was overstated. They do read, and they now have a medium that they prefer where they can read what they want when they want it."

Other experts, however, fear that over time online newspapers will differ markedly from print editions — and not for the better. Stories online will be shorter, Boczkowski says, because people read them at work or on the run. And online editions will devote less space to substantive news about politics or government and more to entertainment and culture. "There will be far less of the hard news and far more of the soft news — and softer treatment of the hard news," he says.

But Mindich and the Readership Institute's Nesbitt both say newspapers can — and must — find ways to communicate important information to young readers in ways that they will find appealing. "Anecdotally, I've seen that there are many young kids who are following the news closely online," Mindich says. He says editors who substitute soft for hard news are selling young people short.

Nesbitt agrees. She says the key is to present stories in ways that better convey their importance and their interest to readers — both young and old. "Younger adult readers are not stupid," she says. "They react very badly to being talked down to. But they also don't want to be bored to tears by stories that are not well told, stories that are of no interest to them in the first place."

# BACKGROUND

## Growing the Press

Newspapers grew in number, circulation and economic and political importance as the United States itself grew through the 19th and 20th centuries in size, in population and in two other preconditions for a mass medium: industrialization and urbanization. Organizationally, newspapers changed from an "entrepreneurial" model — owned and operated by individuals or families in the community served — to a model of corporate ownership, increasingly in the late 20th century as parts of large newspaper chains. The transformation helped make newspapers a big — and profitable — business, but the effects of corporate ownership on the quality of journalism are sharply debated. [8]

Boston was home of the American Colonies' first newspapers. *Publick Occurrences Both Foreign and Domestick*, a three-page newspaper (with one page deliberately left blank), appeared once in 1690 only to be shut down by authorities; eight years later, the homesick printer returned to London. *The News-Letter* debuted in 1704 and remained as the first continuously published newspaper in the Colonies — one of five in Boston by the time of the Revolutionary War. Most of the early newspapers — more than 2,100 founded between 1690 and 1820 — folded after two years or less, victims of insufficient advertising and unaffordable subscription prices. Still, as historian Frank Luther Mott notes, newspapers played a vital role in spreading news about the war for independence and emerged after the Revolution "with a newly found prestige" that would make them "a power of the first importance." [9]

The number of newspapers increased rapidly in the early years of the Republic — from 37 at the end of the Revolutionary War to 1,258 in 1835 — but most depended on outside financing, for example from political parties. The introduction of the steam-driven press in 1825, along with advances in the manufacture of paper and ink, laid the foundation for mass production. Circulation lagged, however, until the advent of the "penny press," beginning with the *New York Sun* in 1833. *The Sun* and dozens of imitators over the next decade emphasized local crime and court news in newspapers priced to reach a mass audience large enough to attract advertisers. "The penny papers," notes David

# CHRONOLOGY

**1900-1960** *Number of newspapers begins long-term decline; circulation begins to lag behind population growth after end of World War II.*

**1903** Charles L. Knight becomes part owner of *Akron Beacon Journal* in Ohio; buys out partner four years later; brings his sons John S. and James L. into the business as they reach adulthood; leaves paper to them upon his death in 1933.

**1906** Herman Ridder gains complete ownership of German-language daily *Staats Zeitung* in New York; his sons later acquire *Journal of Commerce* (1926) and then begin expanding company with medium-sized papers in Midwest, California, elsewhere.

**1950s** Knight Newspapers has well-regarded daily newspapers in several major cities; Ridder Publications has a dozen dailies in mid-sized cities.

**1960s-1970s** *Major newspaper companies "go public" — raising capital by selling stock on public markets; some create two classes of stock to preserve family control; industry becomes more concentrated.*

**1966** Gannett Co. goes public, with single class of stock.

**1967** New York Times Co. goes public, with control vested in second class of stock held by Ochs-Sulzberger family trust.

**1969** Knight Newspapers and Ridder Publications both go public, each with single class of stock; Knight and Ridder families have sufficient stock holdings for effective control.

**1974** Knight Newspapers and Ridder Publications merge to form country's second-largest newspaper chain.

**1980s** *Newspapers fail with first ventures into electronic products; newsrooms computerized; circulation begins to fall.*

**1980** *Columbus* (Ohio) *Dispatch* debuts "electronic edition" with phone access to contents of *Dispatch* and three other newspapers; folds experiment two years later.

**1982** Gannett launches *USA Today*, national newspaper relying on colorful graphics and ultra-short stories.

**1983** Knight Ridder begins market trial of Viewtron videotext service; folds three years later.

**1987** Nationwide daily newspaper circulation peaks at 62.8 million.

**1990s** *Newspapers aggressively develop online editions as World Wide Web emerges.*

**1993** *New York Times* goes online with "@Times" on AOL; three years later, develops its own site: *New York Times* on the Web.

**1995** P. Anthony "Tony" Ridder advances to chairman and chief executive officer of Knight Ridder; raises company's operating margin over next decade to 19 percent.

**1998** Publicly traded newspaper companies account for nearly half of daily circulation nationwide.

**1999** All but two of 100 biggest newspapers have online editions.

**2000-Present** *Newspapers face increasing competition from online rivals; readership declines, especially among young people.*

**2000** Swedish Metro International launches first youth-oriented commuter tabloid in United States with *Metro Boston*; U.S. companies follow suit: Tribune Co.'s *RedEye* in Chicago (2002), Washington Post Co.'s *Express* (2003).

**2004** Nationwide daily newspaper circulation falls to 54.6 million, 13 percent below 1987 peak.

**2005** Wave of layoffs in industry cuts 2,200 jobs through attrition, buyouts. . . All but two of 20 biggest U.S. newspapers report decline in circulation for period ending Sept. 30. . . . Knight Ridder's biggest institutional investor writes letter on Nov. 1 demanding that board pursue "competitive sale" of company; company mulling bids as of January 2006.

Demers, an associate professor of communications at Washington State University, "were specifically created to make a profit." [10]

More explosive growth followed in the late 19th century: From 1870 to 1900 the number of general-circulation daily newspapers quadrupled from 574 to 2,226, while circulation increased more than fivefold to 15 million. With rapid industrialization and urbanization, manufacturers relied on newspapers to reach buyers, and newspapers reaped the profits. Meanwhile, newspapers' editorial content was also being transformed, first with the birth of "new journalism" in the 1870s — emphasizing better writing, attractive makeup and editorial independence — followed by the mixture of reformism and sensationalism derogatorily labeled "yellow journalism." [11]

Three famous newspaper publishers brought these contrasting approaches to New York City in the 1880s and '90s after buying up struggling papers. Joseph Pulitzer used yellow journalism to turn the *World* into a moneymaker, only to be bested by William Randolph Hearst's yellow journalism at the rival *Journal*. Meanwhile, Adolph Ochs aimed at a higher class of readers at the *Times* with dignified coverage of "All the News That's Fit to Print" — a slogan that still appears every day in the left "ear" of the front page of the paper's print editions.

The newspaper industry continued to mature through the 20th century editorially and financially and — despite some apprehension — continued to prosper even as radio and television emerged as competing news media. Editorially, the 20th century saw the rise of specialized reporters, foreign correspondents and political columnists. Financially, circulation nearly doubled, and advertising revenue more than tripled between 1910 and the last pre-Depression benchmark of 1930. But the number of daily newspapers stood at 2,202 in 1910 and declined slowly and steadily for the rest of the century. [12]

Despite the growth of group ownership, by 1960 only three newspaper chains had achieved national scope: Hearst, Scripps-Howard and Newhouse. More typical of the more than 100 newspaper groups at the time was Gannett, now the nation's largest but then comprising only 16 dailies in medium-sized cities in New York and New Jersey. [13] Among other chains, John S. Knight had expanded beyond his father's *Akron Beacon Journal* to acquire, among others, newspapers in Miami, Detroit, Chicago and Charlotte, N.C. (Knight sold the *Chicago Daily News* in 1956 for a then-record $24 million.)

Meanwhile, Ridder Publications had grown from the family's original property — the New York-based German-language daily *Staats Zeitung* — into a chain with 13 dailies and seven Sundays in such mid-sized cities as St. Paul, Minn.; Wichita, Kan.; and San Jose, Calif. [14]

## Going Public

The consolidation of the newspaper industry proceeded apace in the late 20th century with a continuing decline in the number of dailies and an even sharper decline in the number of independently owned papers. The increasing size of the largest newspaper chains, along with rising fixed costs of newspaper production, drove many of the best-known companies to "go public" — that is, to raise capital by selling stock on publicly traded markets. The increase in public ownership resulted in increased pressure to push profits higher and higher, even at companies still controlled by newspaper-publishing families. [15]

The changes in the industry's economic structure took place against a backdrop of continuing concern about circulation and readership. Circulation had been growing slower than population since the 1960s and began falling in absolute terms for daily papers by the mid-1980s and for Sunday papers by the 1990s, according to industry figures. By 2004, circulation for daily papers had fallen to 54.6 million — 13 percent below the 1987 peak of 62.8 million. Sunday circulation of 57.8 million was 8 percent below the 1993 peak. [16]

Readership figures were even bleaker. The percentage of adults who read a newspaper on an average weekday declined from 78 percent in 1970 to 64 percent in 1989; the figure continued falling through the 1990s and the first years of the 21st century except for a post-9/11 uptick in 2002. By 2005, a bare majority of adults — 51.6 percent — read a newspaper on a typical weekday. The decline was especially sharp among young adults. From 1972 to 1998, the percentage of adults ages 30-39 who read a newspaper on a typical weekday plummeted from 73 percent to 30 percent. [17] (See graph, p. 215.)

Lagging circulation was both cause and effect of the simultaneous decrease in the number of daily newspapers. The number of afternoon papers dropped by nearly half from 1950 to 1998 as people turned to television instead of newspapers for news at the end of the workday. (See graph, p. 214.) On the other hand, the number of morning and Sunday papers both increased — driven largely by the birth of new newspapers in suburbia.

# Knight Ridder's Uncertain Future

Two-and-a-half months after Knight Ridder's biggest investor forced the nation's second-largest newspaper chain to put itself up for sale, its future remains uncertain.

California-based McClatchy Co. and three teams of private equity investors appear to be among the most serious potential bidders. [1] Industry giant Gannett Co. and William Dean Singleton's rapidly growing Denver-based MediaNews Group, may also be interested.

Formal bids for the $4.2 billion company are due after all potential bidders receive financial presentations in January from Knight Ridder (KR). Its board of directors could accept a bid or reject them all and decide not to sell.

In the meantime, KR's news operations, including 32 daily newspapers and a popular Internet news site, continue functioning. But there is speculation that a cost-conscious purchaser might try to cut labor expenses by 5 percent or more. [2]

Florida money manager Bruce Sherman, whose Private Capital Management (PCM) owns 19 percent of KR stock, touched off the corporate turmoil in November 2005, demanding that the KR board "aggressively pursue the competitive sale of the company."

After initial doubt about a sale, speculation is shifting in the direction of an eventual deal. Several other possible scenarios remain, however, including a "buyback" of PCM shares by KR. And any proposed sale might draw opposition from unions or federal antitrust agencies. For example, McClatchy could have problems acquiring KR's *St. Paul Pioneer Press* since it already owns its Twin Cities competitor, the *Star Tribune*.

Depending on the buyer, a sale could extinguish the names of two journalistic families, each with a century of owning newspapers. [3] Charles L. Knight bought the *Akron (Ohio) Beacon Journal* in 1903, guided his sons John S. and James L. into the business, and left it to them upon his death in 1933. With Jack focused on editorial and Jim on business, Knight Newspapers acquired and upgraded papers in bigger cities: the *Miami Herald* (1937), *Detroit News* (1940) and *Chicago Daily News* (1944). The company was profitable, the newspapers respected. *The Herald* picked up

its first Pulitzer in 1950 for a series on organized crime, the *Detroit News* in 1967 for coverage of local race riots.

Herman Ridder, a second-generation German-American, bought the German-language daily *Staats Zeitung* in 1906. His sons kept the paper alive despite anti-German sentiment during World War I, purchased the New York-based *Journal of Commerce* in 1926 and later picked up small- and medium-sized newspapers in monopoly markets. By the mid-1950s, the company had a dozen daily papers, and — in contrast to Knight Newspapers — no overarching philosophy of journalistic excellence.

The merger of the two chains in 1974 stemmed from ordinary corporate considerations. [4] Bernard H. Ridder Jr., president of Ridder Publications, saw no obvious successor among his brothers and cousins. Knight Newspapers, ably guided by Business manager Alvah Chapman, wanted to grow. Chapman called Ridder in March and proposed a merger, and by November it was complete. Headquartered in Miami, the new company had 35 papers with daily circulation of 3.8 million.

Both companies had gone public in 1969, but family members held the biggest blocks: John Knight's two surviving sons held 46 percent of Knight Newspapers; family members owned 50 percent of Ridder Publications. For financial reasons, both companies had gone public with a single class of stock instead of guarding family control with a second, super-voting class of stock. When the companies merged, tax considerations again dictated a single class of stock. The result — unforeseen but foreseeable — was to leave Knight Ridder vulnerable to a shareholder revolt.

At the time of the merger, P. Anthony "Tony" Ridder, one of eight fourth-generation cousins in the business, was business manager of the *San Jose Mercury News*. Two decades later, he had advanced to become KR's chairman and chief executive officer. In the meantime, KR newspapers had earned widespread respect — none more than the *Philadelphia Inquirer*, which collected 17 Pulitzer prizes under an aggressive editor, Eugene Roberts. But in the late 1980s, Ridder had clamped down on Roberts' budget. Frustrated, Roberts unexpectedly resigned in 1990.

Meanwhile, annual newspaper revenue continued to increase by 5 percent or so since the 1960s, even though the industry lost overall advertising revenue with increased competition from radio and television. [18]

The movement toward public ownership began in the 1960s for reasons only partly related to the industry's concerns about circulation and readership. Ben Bagdikian, a former reporter turned industry critic, says tax laws

As head of the company since 1995, Ridder has continued to focus on the company's bottom line — with some success. [5] The company's profit margin has increased to 19.4 percent from 14.4 percent, the stock price from $26 in 1995 to a peak near $80 in May 2004. But the company's price has sagged since then. And three of the papers are pulling down the company's profitability: the *Inquirer*, straining under high labor costs; the *Mercury News*, lagging in advertising revenue because of the dotcom bust; and the competitively pressured *Pioneer Press*. The dip caused concern for Sherman and PCM. Two other big institutional investors are backing Sherman's tactic: Southeastern Asset Management, Inc., and Harris Associates LP. Together, they hold 36 percent of KR stock.

Knight Ridder Chairman P. Anthony "Tony" Ridder.

*Knight Ridder Inc.*

Although the bidding process has been guarded, McClatchy has figured prominently in speculation both because of its recent interest in acquisitions and its positive journalistic reputation. The company began expanding in 1979 beyond its three *Bee* newspapers in California (Sacramento, Modesto, Fresno) to buy papers in Alaska, Washington state, South Carolina and North Carolina. *The Star Tribune* was purchased in 1998.

At first, Gannett was described as uninterested. Then it was reported to have submitted a bid only to withdraw it. A Gannett spokeswoman called that story "ridiculous" but declined to comment further.

Privately owned MediaNews Group, whose more than 40 daily newspapers have a circulation of nearly 2 million, is reportedly planning a bid with two venture capital firms. Since the mid-1980s, Singleton has been buying papers

nationwide and gaining a reputation for journalistic quality.

The other potential bidders identified in published accounts are Blackstone Group LP of New York and Providence Equity Partners, in partnership with the New York buyout firm Kohlberg Kravis Roberts; and Thomas H. Lee Partners LP of Boston in a joint bid with Texas Pacific Group of Dallas and other investment firms. Either of those bids is thought most likely to envision restructuring KR and then selling it — in whole or piece by piece — for a profit.

Despite the inevitable angst among KR employees, industry and labor officials caution against pessimism. "When you look at Knight Ridder, maybe it's not performing as well as it has," says Richard Rodriguez, executive editor of the *Sacramento Bee* and president of the American Society of Newspaper Editors. "But it's still a pretty healthy company."

"You're not going to wind up with those newspapers going out of business," says Linda Foley, president of the Newspaper Guild, a unit of the Communications Workers of America.

---

[1] See Joseph DiStefano, "Potential Buyers of Knight Ridder Still Emerging," *The Philadelphia Inquirer*, Jan. 12, 2006, p. C2; Pete Carey, "Knight Ridder Meets With First Potential Buyer," *San Jose Mercury News*, Jan. 14, 2006, p. 1.

[2] See "Morgan Stanley Pinpoints Knight Ridder's 'Underperforming Papers,' " editorandpublisher.com, Dec. 1, 2005.

[3] See Davis Merritt, *Knightfall: Knight Ridder and How the Erosion of Newspaper Journalism Is Putting Democracy at Risk* (2005), pp. 29-45.

[4] *Ibid.*, pp. 46-59.

[5] Background in part from Joseph Menn, "Moment of Truth for Media Chief," *Los Angeles Times*, Dec. 25, 2005, p. C1; Devin Leonard, "Tony Ridder Just Can't Win," *Fortune*, Dec. 24, 2001, p. 99.

---

encouraged the trend by giving favorable treatment to companies that used retained profits to acquire other companies. [19] But Jones of Harvard's Shorenstein Center says the 19th-century tradition of family-owned newspapers

simply could not be preserved in a 20th-century economy where newspapers were both bigger and more profitable.

"In the 19th century, newspapers went from one family to another," says Jones, who covered the press for the

Newspapers are using more and larger photographs and bolder graphics on their front pages in an effort to hold on to readers, especially younger Americans. Some papers are also distributing free tabloids, such as the Tribune Co.'s *RedEye* in Chicago (bottom, center).

*Times* in the 1980s. "But when newspapers became a way of making money, there came a point where a newspaper could only be acquired by another newspaper because no family could afford it."

The *Times* was, in fact, among the earliest newspaper companies to go public, in 1967. [20] Gannett, still a regional newspaper chain, had gone public a year earlier. Knight and Ridder each went public in 1969 — five years before they merged. Among other major present-day companies, the Washington Post Co. went public in 1971, the Tribune Co. in 1983, McClatchy in 1988 and Scripps-Howard in 1998. By then, the 17 publicly traded newspaper companies owned a total of 313 dailies and 244 Sunday papers, with a combined daily circulation of 24.7 million — or almost 44 percent of total

newspaper circulation (and more than half of the total Sunday circulation).

Many of the companies — including the Times, the Post and McClatchy — structured stock ownership to preserve family control by creating two classes of stock and vesting effective power in stock owned by family members or (in the Times' case) a family-controlled trust. Knight and Ridder, however, both went public in 1969 with a single class of stock. Alvah H. Chapman, a Knight executive who went on to be chairman and CEO of the merged Knight Ridder, later said that the idea of creating two classes of stock was never seriously considered because Jack Knight was expected to hold most of the stock and thus maintain control of the company. When the two companies merged, they again issued only one class of stock. [21]

Simultaneously with the trend toward public ownership, newspapers were moving toward more "soft" news — celebrities, scandals, gossip and human interest stories — and less coverage of government and international news. From 1977 to 1997, the amount of "soft news" in U.S. news media increased to 43 percent from 15 percent, according to a survey by the Project for Excellence in Journalism. [22] Emblematic of the trend was Gannett's nationwide newspaper *USA Today*, founded in 1982, which relied heavily on colorful graphics and ultra-short stories and de-emphasized government reporting.

Jones says going public helped many of the companies, including the Times. "Going public saved the company," he says. "It made it possible for the Times to acquire other companies that allow the business to survive."

But others are more critical. In their study, journalism professors Gilbert Cranberg, Randall Bezanson and John Soloski conclude that investors in publicly traded companies are "concerned with . . . continuously improved profitability" and "indifferent to news or, more disturbingly, its quality." And because publicly traded companies control a large segment of the industry, their practices "are becoming the standards to which all newspapers must subscribe in order to survive." [23]

## Going Online

Newspaper companies began experimenting with non-print technologies in the 1980s, but the ventures were financially unsuccessful. With the advent of the World Wide Web in the 1990s, newspapers intensified their efforts to develop new, non-print products, using several strategies to try to attract readers/users and advertisers. These ventures incurred even bigger losses than the experiments in the '80s. But companies decided to stay with the ventures — viewing the costs as necessary investments for a shift into online distribution essential for the industry's long-term survival. [24]

The various electronic experiments depended first on the computerization of the newsroom: the shift from typewritten copy later set into type by composing room typographers to word-processed copy prepared by newsroom staff on computer screens. By the 1990s, computer terminals were ubiquitous. The technological change reduced labor costs and neutralized composing-room unions; in time, the change also would be seen as giving editorial staff more flexibility and control over the final product.

With content no longer bound to paper, the newspaper industry buzzed with excitement in the 1980s over ways to deliver the news electronically. [25] As Northwestern University's Boczkowski notes, the option that drew the most interest was videotext: transmittal of information stored in a computer database over telephone lines to a dedicated terminal, specially adapted television set or personal computer. The technology — developed by the British Post Office in the 1970s — got its first commercial application in the United States when the *Columbus (Ohio) Dispatch* began publishing an "electronic edition" in 1980 that provided access (at $5 per hour) to the *Dispatch* and three other papers: *The New York Times*, *The Washington Post* and the *Los Angeles Times.* The two-year test was a bust. Boczkowski posits several reasons, including lack of original content and no critical mass of personal computer users. Whatever the reasons, the industry took the failed experiment as proof that electronic delivery posed no threat to established newspapers.

In 1979 Knight Ridder had started its own videotext experiment by creating a separate subsidiary in a joint venture with AT&T. The "Viewtron" service debuted in a field test in 1980, and a market trial began in 1983. By the end of the first year, the service — available through phone lines, not personal computers — had only 2,800 subscribers. Knight Ridder belatedly began offering it to the rapidly growing personal computer market, but not soon enough to salvage the experiment. It folded in 1986 after estimated losses of $50 million.

Other technical alternatives to print newspapers also failed in the 1980s. Teletext transmitted text and rudimentary graphics over television broadcast signals; viewers could then use special decoder equipment to view the content on their TV screens. Several newspapers tried but failed to make it into a profitable business. The *Chicago Sun Times* closed its three-year experiment in 1984 after concluding that cable TV subscribers would not pay extra for the service. Newspapers also experimented with simpler technologies: audiotext, which allowed phone users automated access to newspaper content, and fax delivery of specially customized "papers." But those experiments also proved commercially unsuccessful.

Despite the setbacks, the newspaper industry continued to be interested in electronic delivery and moved quickly to exploit opportunities with the exploding growth of the World Wide Web in the mid-1990s. [26] By

1999 all but two of the 100 largest U.S. dailies had online services. The online papers had their own staffs: 100 people at *The Washington Post*'s Digital Ink as of 1997, 90 at *The Wall Street Journal*'s Interactive Edition and 84 at *USA Today Online*. The online papers also had readers. The editor of *The New York Times* on the Web estimated 250,000 daily visitors to the site as of 1999, compared to the print newspaper's daily circulation of somewhat more than 1 million. One survey indicated that overall the proportion of people who read a newspaper online at least once a week increased from 4 percent in 1995 to 15-26 percent in 1998.

Online papers consisted primarily of "repurposed" content from the print editions — derisively called "shovelware." But newspapers quickly saw that they could do more on the Web than in print — and that they needed to do more to fully exploit the online editions' potential, editorially and financially. One strategy, Northwestern's Boczkowski says, was to "recombine" content — for example, putting together content on a specific subject, sometimes combined with e-mail reminders and updates. Newspaper morgues represented a mother lode of recombinable content, and newspapers quickly recognized that they could sell archived stories once the material was digitized.

A second strategy was (in Boczkowski's phrasing) to "re-create" content — that is, to develop content primarily or exclusively for online sites. He notes as one distinctive example the Web version of the *Philadelphia Inquirer*'s "Blackhawk Down," which expanded the *Inquirer*'s 30-part series on the 1993 battle between U.S. soldiers and Somalian rebels into a 30-part hypermedia package on Phillynews.com.

Despite the bustle and buzz, by the end of the 1990s the online ventures had failed to prove themselves as commercially viable. Several of the biggest newspaper chains reported eight-figure losses at an annual media conference in 1998: $35 million for Tribune Corporation, $23 million for Knight Ridder, $20 million for *Times Mirror* and $10 million to $15 million for the New York Times Co. At the next year's event, Alan Spoon, then president of the Washington Post Co., said the company expected to spend $100 million on online ventures despite previous losses. "This isn't the time for neatness in Internet models," he said. [27]

# CURRENT SITUATION

## Shrinking the Newsroom

The cartoon shows a roaring figure labeled "Accountants" in a King Kong-like pose holding a fistful of money as he appears to topple Chicago's landmark Tribune Tower, corporate headquarters of a newspaper chain now with 11 dailies.

The barbed image by Nick Anderson of Louisville's *Courier-Journal* is one of 100 satirical depictions posted on the Association of American Editorial Cartoonists' Web site in early December 2005 to protest the elimination of staff cartoonist positions at two of the Tribune Co.'s biggest newspapers, the *Los Angeles Times* and *Baltimore Sun*.

The cartoonists' "Black Ink Monday" did nothing to reverse the Tribune Co.'s cost-cutting moves, but the silent protest helped focus attention on two examples of an industrywide wave of cutbacks that eliminated an estimated 2,000 positions at newspapers around the country in 2005. [28]

In the year's biggest cut, the New York Times Co. announced on Sept. 20 that it was reducing its overall work force by 4 percent, or 500 jobs, including 45 positions in the *Times'* newsroom and another 35 editorial jobs at the *Times*-owned *Boston Globe*. On the same day, Knight Ridder's Philadelphia newspapers announced cutbacks that would trim the Inquirer's newsroom by 15 percent — or 75 positions — and the *Daily News*' by nearly 20 percent, or 25 positions.

Two days later, Knight Ridder's *San Jose Mercury News* followed suit with a 15 percent reduction in its newsroom work force from 330 to 280. The *Sun* and the Tribune-owned *Newsday*, the Long Island-based tabloid, had announced job cuts earlier in the year. Tribune Co. had cut some 600 publishing jobs in 2004, most outside the newsrooms. Among others, the *Los Angeles Times*, *Wall Street Journal* and *Washington Post* also had trimmed newsroom staffs in the previous few years.

The job cuts — envisioned coming from buyouts and attrition instead of layoffs — were blamed primarily on lagging advertising revenue. *The Times*, for example, said its ad revenue in August 2005 was 0.8 percent below the figure for August 2004. Analyst Morton says industry-

# Is corporate ownership of newspapers hurting journalism?

## YES

**Robert W. McChesney**
*President, Free Press*
*Co-Author,* Tragedy & Farce: How the
American Media Sell Wars, Spin Elections,
and Destroy Democracy

Written for *CQ Researcher*, January 2006

It is true that from the very beginning of our Republic, the press system has been commercial, in the hands of profit-seeking owners. But the Founders had no illusions that profit-driven journalism would produce the caliber of journalism necessary for the American constitutional experiment to succeed. Behind the leadership of Madison and Jefferson, the government instituted a series of massive public subsidies, in the form of printing contracts and reduced postal rates, to spawn a much more vibrant print culture than would have existed otherwise.

The great strength of private, profit-motivated control over the press has been its structural independence from the government. Its weakness has been a willingness to put commercial gain over public service. The system worked best in competitive markets, when it was relatively easy for people to start a viable, new newspaper if they were dissatisfied with the existing options.

This model collapsed by the end of the 19th century. Newspaper markets increasingly became monopolistic, virtually closing down the option of an individual, even a supremely wealthy individual, of successfully launching a new newspaper in an existing market. U.S. journalism increasingly was awash in profit-obsessed sensationalism and corruption, along with partisan, right-wing politics.

This crisis threatened the legitimacy of the industry and led to the emergence of professional journalism as the solution. Professional journalism has its strengths; it bans explicit corruption and demands factual accuracy while giving journalists some autonomy from the dictates of owners and advertisers. Its main weakness is the uncritical dependence upon "official sources" as the basis of political news.

The strengths of professional journalism have been undermined over the past generation as profit-driven corporate media giants have slashed resources for international, investigative and serious, local journalism. Instead, we have seen more coverage of trivial and salacious stories masquerading as news. Owners have little commercial incentive to challenge the politicians who control the lucrative subsidies and policies upon which they depend.

Regrettably, the Internet will not solve the attack on journalism. It requires more competitive markets with more diverse and local ownership; a commitment to a well-funded and heterogeneous nonprofit and non-commercial media sector; and thoughtful political solutions to the most fundamental of political problems.

## NO

**David Demers**
*Associate professor of communication, Edward R.
Murrow School of Communication, Washington
State University*

Written for *CQ Researcher*, January 2006

Few journalists and scholars would dispute the notion that corporate newspapers wield a great deal of power and, like other bureaucratic institutions, sometimes misuse that power. However, the notion that the transition from the entrepreneurial to the corporate form of organization is destroying good journalism and democratic principles has several major flaws.

To begin with, most of the scholarly research simply fails to support it. Scores of studies have examined the impact of chain ownership or corporate structure on decision-making, editorial content, newsroom behaviors, allocation of resources and organizational values. These studies show that corporate newspapers are more profitable, primarily because they benefit from economies of scale.

But the empirical evidence strongly shows that corporate newspapers place less emphasis on profits as an organizational goal and more on product quality. Chain and corporate newspapers are more vigorous editorially. They produce content that is more critical of traditional or established political and economic power groups and elites.

My own national probability surveys support these findings and also show that editors and reporters at corporate newspapers have more autonomy from owners and supervisors.

So how could the critics be so wrong? They base their arguments on personal experiences or anecdotes, rather than probability surveys, comparative case studies, or historical/longitudinal research. Personal experience can be a valid method for understanding the world. But it can also mislead.

The critical perspective also fails to account for the role newspapers and other news media have played historically as facilitators of change. The critics assume that as a newspaper becomes more "corporatized," the more it promotes the interests of its owners and other corporate and business elites.

All media provide broad-based support for dominant institutions and values, to be sure. But the anti-change position is inconsistent with a large body of historical and empirical research.

During the last century, corporate news media have played a key (if sometimes late) role in promoting the goals of many social movements, including those seeking expansion of rights for women, minorities, the working class, environmentalists, homosexuals and the poor. Such changes certainly have not eliminated discrimination or injustice, but they have altered the power structure and that, in turn, helps explain why our country has a relatively high degree of political stability.

Online newspapers like WashingtonPost.com typically include interactive features that allow readers to participate in ongoing dialogues with other readers, and perhaps reporters and editors as well.

wide advertising revenue has been growing less than 3 percent per year compared to an historic annual growth rate around 5 percent.

The Internet is one big reason for the slump. Some classified advertising is being lost to free online services such as Craigslist.org. Commercial advertisers are also re-evaluating their newspaper ad budgets as consumers do more of their shopping online.

Lagging circulation is also to blame. Among the 20 highest-circulation newspapers in the country, only *The New York Times* and the *Star-Ledger* of Newark, N.J., reported increases in the six months ending Sept. 30 compared to the same period the previous year. The *Inquirer*'s circulation, for example, was down by 3 percent from the previous year, while the *Globe*'s fell 8 percent.

Executives and industry officials generally minimize the importance of the job losses. In an Oct. 14 conference call to investors and analysts, Knight Ridder chairman and CEO Tony Ridder said both Philadelphia papers had been "overstaffed." "We're just bringing them into line," Ridder said. The local newspaper guild president disagreed. "We don't think the staff is too large," said Harry Holcomb, an *Inquirer* business reporter. [29]

"That's a cyclical matter that every industry has gone through in the past," says the NAA's Kimball. "Nobody writes a headline when people add jobs, it's only when they eliminate them."

"It's still in editors' hands what they're going to do," says ASNE President Rodriguez. "Editors don't have their hands tied. They have to make hard decisions and prioritize."

Morton says the cuts reflect Wall Street's emphasis on keeping earnings up, but he is not overly alarmed. "These are not horrible cuts," he said following the *Times*' and Philadelphia announcements. [30] Other industry watchers, however, are more concerned.

"What you've got is a gigantic negative-feedback circle here," says Esther Thorson, a journalism professor at the University of Missouri in Columbia. "You take resources out of the newsroom. As a result, quality goes down, and [then] circulation goes down, and you leave an opportunity for competitors to come into the market, leading to taking more resources out of the newsroom." [31]

## Looking for Readers

Washington, D.C., commuters have a choice of any number of newspapers to read on their morning bus or subway ride. In addition to the long-dominant *Washington Post* and its conservative rival *The Washington Times*, commuters have easy access to the Washington edition of *The New York Times* or *The Wall Street Journal* — all available by home delivery or from newsboxes at most of the busiest bus stops and subway stations.

Nowadays, however, they can also read *Express*, a free tabloid published by the *Post*, edited with a 15-minute commute in mind and aggressively hawked at bus stops and subway stations since its debut in August 2003.

Free papers are one of the newspaper industry's desperate efforts to try to reverse or at least stem the decline in circulation now in its second decade. "It's a way of getting people into the newspaper habit," says Nesbitt of Northwestern's Readership Institute. But a study by a market research firm released in November 2005 raises questions whether giveaway papers are helping established newspapers with their main target: young people between age 18 and 34, most of whom are not daily print newspaper readers.

Free newspapers are not a new idea: many big cities have free, entertainment-oriented weekly newspapers that make their money from movie and music advertising and classifieds. The recently launched commuter and youth papers are different, however, in trying to provide a daily, general-subject-matter alternative to established, paid-circulation newspapers.

A Swedish firm, Metro International, pioneered the quick-read paper for commuters in several European cities before bringing the idea to Boston in January 2000 and Philadelphia a year later. The *Post* is one of several mainstream newspapers that responded by launching free tabloids themselves, both to protect their home turfs and to try to grow their own readership. [32]

*Express* is a tabloid-sized paper, usually around 24 pages, with wire-service copy and some staff-written articles but no stories written by regular *Post* reporters. Publisher Christopher Ma, a Post Co. vice president, said at its launch that *Express* was intended to complement, not compete with, the *Post*. "It's a way for the Post Co. to reach an audience that by virtue of lifestyle and time limitations finds it difficult to read newspapers frequently," Ma said. [33]

Chicago, Cincinnati, Dallas and New York are among the other cities with free tabloids from the same companies that publish paid-circulation dailies. In some cities, there are even rival free papers. In New York, the Tribune Co.'s *amNew York* competes with the Swedish firm's *Metro*. The Tribune's *RedEye* in Chicago prompted the *Sun Times* to launch the *Red Streak*, but it folded in December 2005.

Some newspapers are also giving away classified ads to try to hold readers. The *San Diego Union-Tribune* began in August 2005 to offer free, three-line classified ads for seven days to anyone offering to sell an automobile or merchandise for $5,000 or less. "In this day and age when newspapers are struggling for readership, offering free classifieds can be an enticement to read the paper," says industry analyst Morton. [34]

The Newspaper Association's Sturm says free papers are one of several ways for newspapers to hold and actually grow their audience despite declining circulation. "Readership has been fairly stable," says Sturm. "More people read newspapers than buy one. And newspapers have been adding audience by niche publications, ethnic publications, free publications and, in particular, online with newspaper Web sites."

A study by Scarborough Research, a market research firm, however, may dampen newspaper companies' hopes that the free tabloids are enticing non-readers into the newspaper habit. [35] The study, presented Oct. 26, 2005,

at a symposium in Prague, Czech Republic, dispelled some publishers' concerns that the free tabloids are siphoning readers away from mainstream papers. But it suggested that most of the people reading the giveaway papers are already reading mainstream newspapers. In New York, for example, 78 percent of *amNew York* readers and 71 percent of *Metro* readers said they had also read one or more other newspapers on the previous day.

"Most free daily readers are strong newspapers readers — both free and paid," James Collins, senior vice president of information systems and custom analytics at Scarborough, said in a statement. "Rather than competing with their paid counterparts, free dailies are being used in a complementary fashion by most of their readers."

## OUTLOOK

### Going Private?

If going public is the problem for newspapers, perhaps going private is the solution. That at least is the suggestion of Douglas McCollam, a legal affairs journalist and contributing editor to *Columbia Journalism Review* (*CJR*).

Writing in *CJR*'s January/February 2006 issue, McCollam suggests publicly traded newspaper companies should turn to private investors to avoid the adverse effects that he says result from Wall Street's focus on stock prices and short-term profits. [36] In corporate-finance jargon, a "leveraged buyout" would allow a company to borrow money from private investors in order to buy back all its stock from shareholders, he says.

In comparison to public shareholders, McCollam contends, private equity investors would be less focused on "the quarterly earnings treadmill." And even if some proved to be "every bit as rapacious as the most aggressive fund manager," they would still be better than "the lineup of bloodless managers and mandarins currently squeezing the life out of journalism."

Experienced industry analysts discount the likelihood of any widespread use of the tactic. "The reality of daily newspapers is what it is," says media consultant Brown. "They're not all going to be taken private any time soon." Indeed, McCollam acknowledges that newspaper executives such as New York Times Co. Chairman Arthur O. Sulzberger Jr. and the Washington Post Co.'s Graham say public ownership has benefited their companies.

In their study, professors Cranberg, Bezanson and Soloski proposed a series of corporate and legal reforms to encourage newspaper companies to put more emphasis on journalistic quality than on short-term profit. [37] They would, for example, require that journalistic quality be given a larger role in determining pay incentives for corporate managers and publishers and that it be the only factor in any incentives for editors. They would also require more detailed financial reporting by newspaper companies and reorient government policy to actively foster competition instead of simply protecting existing companies from competition.

Nearly five years after their book's publication, none of their proposals has been widely adopted.

Within the industry, the main question today is not corporate structure or governance but market strategy: how to reposition the print-producing newspaper companies of the 20th century in the increasingly online media environment of the 21st. *Sacramento Bee* Editor Rodriguez believes newspaper companies are up to the challenge.

"Five years from now, you'll see the newspaper industry is very much alive, very strong," he predicts. "You'll see that we've integrated online with print, that we are hiring different kinds of people with multimedia skills and that we're on television more promoting our product as well as doing more direct chats online.

"You'll see a real emphasis on watchdog journalism in which the main emphasis will be newspapers or the newspaper company looking out for readers," he says. "You'll see more participatory events, interactive events with readers, readers' opinions more prominently displaced on Web sites, newspapers acting as a guide to the Web site and more back and forth."

"You'll still see us in a state of confusion about the future of the newspaper industry," Rodriguez concedes in conclusion. "It won't shake out in five years. It's an evolution that will take place over a couple of generations."

No one denies that online is bound to become a more influential medium in the future and that the influence of mainstream newspaper companies is likely to diminish as a result. "They still have a lot going for them," says Northwestern University's Boczkowski. "But their relative importance has decreased dramatically, and I don't think there's any reasonable chance it will go back up in the foreseeable future."

"The big guy is still print. Online is the baby," Boczkowski concludes. "But in 10 to 15 years, it may be the reverse."

Newspaper Guild President Foley echoes management's insistence that newspapers remain the dominant news source, even online. "Where do people go for the news?" she asks rhetorically. "They don't go to Yahoo. They don't go to Google. They go to the newspaper sites."

But Foley also emphasizes that newspapers have to do better at getting revenue from their online products. "They are attracting the eyeballs," she says. "They just need to figure out how to make money out of having those eyeballs."

Former journalists Jones and Meyer are among those who say newspaper companies — and their shareholders — need to adjust their financial expectations downward. "If they can find a way to be satisfied with lower margins, newspapers can survive long enough to make the transition," Meyer says. Nothing in the stock market's recent behavior, however, suggests that investors are following the advice. As newspaper companies' bottom lines have sagged, stock prices have taken a licking.

Still, industry officials and experienced industry-watchers believe newspapers — the print products as well as the companies that produce them — are not about to go extinct. "The newspaper will be one of the instruments you will use to deliver news and information to your readers," says the University of Georgia's Fink. "A lot of Americans will have newsprint ink on their hands for a long time yet — not as many, but a lot."

"I am extremely confident that whatever the content is, it will be coming to the marketplace through the newspapers' brand," says the Newspaper Association's Kimball. "It may be distribution vehicles that we haven't even heard from, but they will be owned by the newspaper."

# NOTES

1. Some background drawn from Joseph Menn, "Moment of Truth for Media Chief," *Los Angeles Times*, Dec. 25, 2005, p. C1; Joseph Menn and James Rainey, "As Knight Ridder Goes, So May News Industry," *Los Angeles Times*, Nov. 8, 2005, p. C1. Sherman's letter was posted on *The Wall Street Journal*'s Web site: www.wsj.com.

2. Graham's prepared remarks to the Credit Suisse First Boston media conference on Dec. 6, 2005, are posted on the Washington Post Co.'s Web site (www.wash

post.com). The quoted remark is from Jay DeFoore, "Print vs. Online Battle at 'Wash Post' with Froomkin in Middle," editorandpublisher.com, Dec. 12, 2005.

3. See Julie Bosman, "Newspapers Offer a Case for Keeping Them Around," *The New York Times*, Dec. 8, 2005, p. C4; Jennifer Saba, "Goldman Sachs Thinks More Job Cuts on the Way," editorandpublisher.com, Dec. 13, 2005; Jennifer Saba, "Prudential Downgrades The New York Times Co.," editorandpublisher.com, Dec. 7, 2005.

4. The Diane Rehm Show, "The Future of Newspapers," WAMU-FM, Jan. 3, 2005.

5. Pablo J. Boczkowski, *Digitizing the News: Innovation in Online Newspapers* (2004), pp. 105-139.

6. Quoted in Bosman, *op. cit.*

7. Data from the study by Wolfram Peiser are cited in David T.Z. Mindich, *Tuned Out: Why Americans Under 40 Don't Follow the News* (2005), p. 28.

8. For a concise history, see David Pearce Demers, *The Menace of the Corporate Newspaper: Fact or Fiction?* (1996), pp. 31-57. See also Michael Emery, Edwin Emery and Nancy L. Roberts, *The Press and America: An Interpretive History of the Mass Media* (9th ed.), 1999; Frank Luther Mott, *American Journalism: A History, 1690-1960* (3d. ed.), 1962.

9. *Ibid.*, p. 108.

10. Demers, *op. cit.*, p. 39.

11. Emery & Emery, *op. cit.*, pp. 162-163 (new journalism), p. 192 (yellow journalism).

12. See Demers, *op. cit.*, p. 47.

13. See Mott, *op. cit.*, pp. 814-817.

14. See Davis Merritt, *Knightfall: Knight Ridder and How the Erosion of Journalism Is Putting Democracy at Risk* (2004), pp. 28-45.

15. Some background drawn from Gilbert Cranberg, Randall Bezanson and John Soloski, *Taking Stock: Journalism and the Publicly Traded Company* (2001). See also Demers, *op. cit.*, pp. 49-53. For additional background, see David Hatch, "Journalism Under Fire," *CQ Researcher*, Oct. 10, 2003, pp. 845-868.

16. "The Source: Newspapers by the Numbers," Newspaper Association of America, 2005, p. 17. Mott notes that circulation did not keep pace with overall population growth in the 1940s and 1950s, but

attributes the lag in part to the high birth rates of the Baby Boom decades. Circulation did slightly exceed the increase in adult population for those two decades, he says. See Mott, *op. cit.*, pp. 804-805.

17. See Patrick G. Marshall, "Hard Times at the Nation's Newspapers," *Editorial Research Reports*, Aug. 24, 1990, p. 481; "The Source," *op. cit.*, p. 7; Merrill Brown, "Abandoning the News," *Carnegie Reporter*, spring 2005.

18. Cranberg, *et al.*, *op. cit.*, pp. 24-25. Cranberg is a professor emeritus, University of Iowa; Bezanson is a professor at the University of Iowa College of Law and Soloski, formerly at the University of Iowa, is now dean of the University of Georgia's Grady College of Journalism and Mass Communication.

19. Cited in Demers, *op. cit.*, p. 50.

20. For details, see Cranberg, *et al.*, *op. cit.*, Appendix A (pp. 155-196).

21. Quoted in Merritt, *op. cit.*, p. 56.

22. Neil Hickey, "Money Lust: How Pressure for Profit is Perverting Journalism," *Columbia Journalism Review*, July/August 1998. For background, see Kathy Koch, "Journalism Under Fire," *CQ Researcher*, Dec. 25, 1998, pp. 1121-1144.

23. Cranberg, *et al.*, *op. cit.*, pp. 8, 10-11.

24. Background drawn largely from Boczkowski, *op. cit.*

25. *Ibid.*, pp. 20-32.

26. *Ibid.*, pp. 51-55.

27. Lucia Moses, "Newspapers, present and future: Good in 1999! Better in 2000?" *Editor & Publisher*, Dec. 11, 1999, p. 30, quoted in Boczkowski, *op. cit.*, p. 67.

28. See Mark Fitzgerald, "The Shrinking Staff," *Editor & Publisher*, Dec. 1, 2005. For other overviews, see Katharine Q. Seelye, "Jobs Are Cut as Ads and Readers Move Online," *The New York Times*, Oct. 10, 2005, p. C1; Frank Ahrens, "N.Y. Times, Philadelphia Papers Plan Job Cuts," *The Washington Post*, Sept. 21, 2005, p. D1.

29. Ridder was quoted in Jennifer Saba, "Philly in Hot Seat on KR Conference Call," editorandpublisher.com, Oct. 14, 2005; Holcomb was quoted in Jennifer Saba, "The Philadelphia Story: 'A Big Disruption,'" *Editor & Publisher*, Dec. 1, 2005.

30. Quoted in Ahrens, *op. cit.*

31. Quoted in Fitzgerald, *op. cit.*

32. Some background drawn from Lucia Moses, "They're Young and Daily Growin,' " *Editor & Publisher*, Nov. 3, 2003, p. 4.

33. Quoted in Frank Ahrens, "Post Co. to Launch Free Tabloid," *The Washington Post*, July 11, 2003, p. E1.

34. Morton's quote, originally given to the Union-Tribune, was repeated in "San Diego Union-Tribune to Offer Free Classifieds," editorandpublisher.com, Aug. 29, 2005.

35. Jennifer Saba, "Study Suggests Free Papers Complement Paid Papers," editorandpublisher.com, Oct. 26, 2005.

36. Douglas McCollam, "A Way Out? How Newspapers Might Escape Wall Street and Redeem Their Future," *Columbia Journalism Review*, January/February 2006, pp. 18-21.

37. Cranberg, *et al.*, *op. cit.*, pp. 141-153.

## BIBLIOGRAPHY

### Books

**Boczkowski, Pablo J.,** *Digitizing the News: Innovation in Online Newspapers*, **The MIT Press, 2004.**
Boczkowski, an associate professor at Northwestern University, recounts the newspaper industry's growing use of online media from the early and largely unsuccessful experiments in the 1980s through the proliferation of newspaper Web sites beginning in the mid-1990s. Includes notes, 27-page bibliography.

**Cranberg, Gilbert, Randall Bezanson, and John Soloski,** *Taking Stock: Journalism and the Publicly Traded Newspaper Company*, **Iowa State University Press, 2001.**
Three well-known professors provide, from a critical perspective, detailed information about ownership, control and "organizational behavior and dynamics" of publicly traded newspaper companies. Cranberg is professor emeritus of journalism, University of Iowa; Bezanson is a professor at the University of Iowa College of Law; and Soloski, formerly at the University of Iowa, is dean of the University of Georgia's Grady College of Journalism and Mass Communication.

**Demers, David Pearce,** *The Menace of the Corporate Newspaper: Fact or Fiction?* **Iowa State University Press, 1996.**
Demers, a professor at Washington State University's School of Communication, argues that the growth of corporate ownership of newspapers has been misunderstood and presents research indicating that corporate ownership has not reduced journalistic professionalism or independence. Includes detailed notes, 22-page bibliography.

**Emery, Michael, Edwin Emery and Nancy L. Roberts,** *The Press and America: An Interpretive History of the Mass Media* **(9th ed.), Allyn and Bacon, 1999.**
The most comprehensive single-volume history of journalism in the United States emphasizes editorial more than financial aspects in recounting the growth and development of newspapers from Colonial times to the present as well as the 20th-century development of radio and television. Includes detailed notes and a 73-page, chapter-by-chapter bibliography. Roberts, a professor of journalism and mass communication at the University of Minnesota, completed the most recent edition following the deaths of Michael Emery and his father Edwin, who were, respectively, professors at California State University, Northridge, and Minnesota.

**Merritt, Davis,** *Knightfall: Knight Ridder and How the Erosion of Newspaper Journalism Is Putting Democracy at Risk*, **Amacom, 2005.**
The longtime Knight Ridder journalist traces the history of the pre-merger Knight and Ridder newspaper chains and critically recounts what he views as an increasing emphasis on corporate profits at the expense of journalistic quality. Merritt had been a reporter or editor with Knight or Knight Ridder for more than 40 years, including 23 years as editor of the *Wichita Eagle*, before he was effectively eased out of that position in the early 1990s. Includes brief chapter notes; Knight Ridder Chief Executive Tony Ridder did not agree to an interview or provide other materials.

**Meyer, Philip,** *The Vanishing Newspaper: Saving Journalism in the Information Age*, **University of Missouri Press, 2004.**
Meyer, a longtime Knight Ridder journalist and now a professor of journalism at the University of North

Carolina-Chapel Hill, describes the book as "an attempt to isolate and describe the factors that made journalism work as a business in the past and that might also make it work with the changing technologies of the present and future." Includes page notes.

**Mindich, David T.Z., *Tuned Out: Why Americans Under 40 Don't Follow the News*, Oxford University Press, 2005.**
Mindich, a former CNN editor and now chair of the journalism department at St. Michael's College, Colchester, Vt., argues that young people have "largely abandoned traditional news" but says they are "ready to interact with the news if [news media] just provide the right conditions for them to do so." Includes notes, nine-page bibliography.

**Mott, Frank Luther, *American Journalism: A History: 1690-1960* (3d ed.), Macmillan, 1962.**
Mott, a longtime professor at the University of Missouri before his death, published the first edition of his comprehensive history of American newspapers in 1940 and updated the work through the 1950s in the last edition. Includes page notes and section-by-section bibliographical notes.

## Article

**Menn, Joseph, "Moment of Truth for Media Chief," *Los Angeles Times*, Dec. 25, 2005, p. C1.**
Menn gives a good overview of the tenure of Knight Ridder chairman and CEO Tony Ridder and the pending demand by the company's biggest institutional investor to put itself up for sale.

## Reports and Studies

**Brown, Merrill, "Abandoning the News," *Carnegie Reporter*, Vol. 3, No. 2 (spring 2005) (www.carnegie .org/reporter).**
The veteran journalist and media-business consultant argues that to survive, news organizations need to work with bloggers and other independent citizens and journalists to develop new products that will be more engaging to readers, particularly young people.

# For More Information

**American Society of Newspaper Editors**, 11690B Sunrise Valley Dr., Reston, VA 20191-1409; (703) 453-1122; www .asne.org. Membership organization for newspaper editors.

**Newspaper Association of America**, 4401 Wilson Blvd., Suite 900, Arlington, VA 22203-1867; (571) 366-1000; www .naa.org. The newspaper industry's principal trade association.

**The Newspaper Guild**, 501 Third St., N.W., 6th Floor, Washington, DC 20001; (202) 434-7177; www.news guild.org. A labor union representing journalists and other media workers.

**Project for Excellence in Journalism**, 1615 L St., N.W., Washington, DC 20036; (202) 419-3650; www.journal ism.org. A Columbia University Graduate School of Journalism initiative aimed at raising journalism standards.

**Readership Institute**, 301 Fisk Hall, Northwestern University, 1845 Sheridan Road, Evanston, IL 60208-2110; (847) 491-9900; www.readership.org. Conducts research for the newspaper industry on readership-building best practices.

# 11

# Future of Television

Alan Greenblatt

Increasing numbers of viewers are watching TV programs via Internet streams and iPod downloads, and millions more are hooked on user-generated videos on sites such as YouTube. Despite all the changes, people are watching more television than ever, including today's most popular show, "American Idol," shown here as host Ryan Seacrest, left, prepares to tap singer Taylor Hicks (right) as the winner of the show's 2006 competition.

From *CQ Researcher,*
February 16, 2007.

Advertisers always pay dearly to run TV commercials during the Super Bowl, and this year was no exception — $2.6 million for a 30-second spot. The commercials themselves are often expensive, over-the top extravaganzas like the famous Michael Jackson ads for Pepsi. But among this year's crop were several that had been shot on cheap digital-video cameras by consumers encouraged by Alka-Seltzer, Chevrolet and Doritos to submit homemade spots.

"These are people who are [accustomed to] personalizing what's important to them, whether it's through their MP3 playlist or their social-site profile," said Doritos spokesman Jared Dougherty. "We wanted to bring that to Doritos, to let them express their love for Doritos in 30 seconds." [1]

In a sense, this was advertising imitating art. Doritos and the other companies were hoping to imitate the sense of free-form buzz that had been generated a few months before by "The Diet Coke & Mentos Experiment," a celebrated Internet film created by a juggler and a lawyer, which showed them sticking mints into plastic bottles of soda and creating fountain effects worthy of the Bellagio in Las Vegas.

Originally distributed on Revver, a video file-sharing Web site, the three-minute film was soon being viewed by millions via such popular video sites as YouTube and MySpace. It also drew enormous "old media" attention and spawned countless imitators. Perhaps most significantly, the ad increased Mentos sales by 15 percent. Partly as a result, the trade publication *Advertising Age* named consumers themselves its "Agency of the Year." [2]

Self-generated video content has become one of the biggest fads of the moment, with hundreds of millions of people around the

**237**

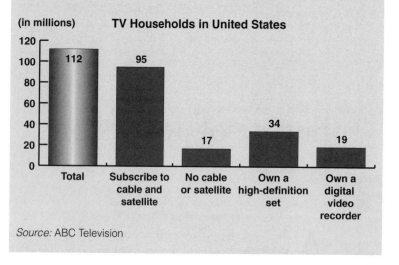

## Most TV Households Have Cable or Satellite

Approximately 85 percent of American households with television are cable or satellite subscribers. Around one-third have high-definition sets, but only one-in-six owns a digital video recorder.

**TV Households in United States**

(in millions)

| | |
|---|---|
| Total | 112 |
| Subscribe to cable and satellite | 95 |
| No cable or satellite | 17 |
| Own a high-definition set | 34 |
| Own a digital video recorder | 19 |

*Source:* ABC Television

"The old idea of a station having to pick up a signal from the network by landline and delivering it to people by antennas on a big hill in your community is about as antiquated as the blacksmith shop," says Robert J. Thompson, founding director of the Center for the Study of Popular Television at Syracuse University.

Clearly, the major networks' near-total hegemony over video distribution is ending. But it's unclear whether they will surrender their dominant position in producing content for most Americans.

The broadcast networks' audience share may be shrinking, and people may be uploading 70,000 videos a day onto YouTube, but even the most popular "viral videos," which spread like a virus — such as the Mentos experiment — are watched by fewer people than a moderately successful network television show. In fact, despite all the new television-viewing devices and platforms, people are watching more traditional TV — game shows, reality TV shows, sitcoms and dramas — than ever before. During the 2005-2006 season, for instance, the average household had the television running for eight hours and 14 minutes a day — up one hour from 1996, according to Nielsen Media Research. [4]

Some industry experts predict that the new platforms — rather than "cannibalizing" traditional TV — will increase its popularity by allowing people to catch up on shows they missed during their regular broadcast time. Television executives' new mantra is that viewers can watch "what they want, when they want it and how they want it."

By failing to embrace such a strategy, the music business squandered a big percentage of its business to illegal file-sharing, says David Poltrack, chief research officer for CBS Corp. [5] "The lesson that the television industry has learned from the music industry is that you can't keep the technology down, so let's use it to make our product ubiquitous," he says. CBS and its competitors are aggressively negotiating with Internet and cell phone companies and anyone else who can keep them a step or two ahead of consumers wanting to watch pop-

world spending hours viewing and sharing short films on the Web. *Time* magazine went so far as to name "You," as in YouTube, its "Person of the Year" — an honor traditionally bestowed on the person who has done the most to shape the news. [3]

Today's proliferation of media platforms is triggering an explosion of user-generated content and challenging the television industry's historic business model. Instead of the age-old concept of "one to many" — in which a network broadcasts a show watched by millions simultaneously — "one" person now can watch a program in "many" different ways, whether downloaded onto a video iPod, clipped into smaller bites for "snacking" on cell phones or YouTube or "streamed" over the Internet on a network's own Web site.* Using digital video recorders (DVRs), such as TiVo, viewers also can decide when to watch a program. Traditional "appointment television" — with viewers settling down at 8 or 9 p.m. to watch a particular program — increasingly appears to be a hopelessly dated concept.

---

* The flow of content across multiple media platforms and the willingness of media audiences to use any platform to enjoy the kind of entertainment they like is known as convergence.

ular shows like "House" or "Lost" on a new platform.

"We are not a television company. We are a sports media company," said John Skipper, ESPN's executive vice president for content. "We're gonna surround consumers with media. We're not gonna let them cut us off and move away from our brand." [6]

Such bold talk has become commonplace, but television types nonetheless remain nervous. After all, there's no reliable way yet to measure how many people have watched an episode of a program recorded by TiVo — or played on an iPod, both of which allow the viewer to easily fast-forward past the commercials. That makes it difficult for advertisers to feel confident that the networks have delivered the promised number of viewers. And that's a serious issue, because advertising is by far the industry's leading source of revenue.

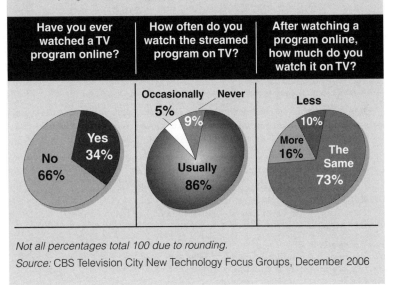

## A Third of Watchers View TV Shows Online

About one-third of regular TV viewers have watched a program on the Web (left), with most viewing a "streaming" program that they regularly watch on TV (middle). Only 10 percent of online viewers watch a program less on TV after viewing it on the Internet (right).

| Have you ever watched a TV program online? | How often do you watch the streamed program on TV? | After watching a program online, how much do you watch it on TV? |
|---|---|---|
| No 66% / Yes 34% | Occasionally 5% / Never 9% / Usually 86% | Less 10% / More 16% / The Same 73% |

*Not all percentages total 100 due to rounding.*

*Source:* CBS Television City New Technology Focus Groups, December 2006

"The marketing community is somewhat dazzled and confused right now," Bob Liodice, president of the Association of National Advertisers, said during a discussion on the future of television in January 2007 in Brooklyn, N.Y. "All the media are shifting, and advertisers are not certain about which ones are working."

TV and ad executives may sound optimistic when they gamely predict that the new platforms will only create additional opportunities for advertisers, but even more neutral observers say predictions about the demise of traditional television will turn out to be misguided.

"We're in a moment in time when media power operates top down from corporate boardrooms and bottom up from teenagers' bedrooms," says Henry Jenkins, director of the comparative media-studies program at the Massachusetts Institute of Technology.

And while there clearly will be no decrease in media — or media choices — in the foreseeable future, the ultimate effect the proliferation of new forms of content and distribution models will have on TV viewing is as yet unknown. "If anyone tells you what the television business is going to look like a decade out," said

Dick Wolf, creator of the "Law & Order" franchise, "they are on drugs." [7]

As television continues to evolve and change, here are some of the questions people in the industry are asking:

### Will the Internet kill television?

No one doubts that technology is rapidly changing the television landscape. But many question whether the new ways to watch video content really threaten traditional television.

"There is so much competition for the time people spend in front of a screen," said Daniel Franklin, executive editor of *The Economist*. "The Internet has behaved like a serial killer. First, the print media suffered, and then the music industry suffered. Perhaps television is next." [8]

Besides making a surfeit of amateur videos universally available, the Internet now provides increased access to professional content. And thanks to its virtually unlimited storage capacity and flexibility, the Web offers better access to certain types of video programming than normal television.

# Home-Grown Videos Open New Frontiers

*Anybody can be a producer — or a journalist*

About a year ago, Will Albino and Brian Giarrocco brought a video camera to Padua Academy, a college-preparatory school for girls in Wilmington, Del. Albino asked students to sign a petition to end women's suffrage, correctly figuring they would mistake the right to vote for "suffering."

They edited the video footage of their prank down to three minutes, posted it on the Internet, and instantly had a hit.

"You hardly need a modicum of talent to create a really entertaining video," says Todd Herman, online video strategist for Microsoft. "That clip in one day sucked 8 million minutes out of people's lives."

Video is becoming about as big a presence on the Web as search engines, turning amateurs into producers, and in some cases, journalists. Last October, Google bought YouTube, the leading video-sharing site, for $1.65 billion. Soon after, *Time* magazine named "You," as in YouTube, its "person of the year." A recent survey found that 38 percent of Americans wanted to create or share content online. [1]

Clearly, the days when Hollywood produced most video entertainment are ending. But what does it mean for everyone in the world to be a potential producer?

A few clips, such as "Evolution of Dance," Justin Laipply's six-minute compression of the last 50 years of steps, have become hugely popular. Laipply's clip has been streamed more than 40 million times. Like most blogs, though, most posted videos get little or no attention. Few people have any real interest in dull footage of cats playing piano. [2]

"The barrier to entry" — the once-formidable cost of shooting and editing footage — "has almost disappeared," says Jeffrey Cole, director of the University of Southern California's Center for the Digital Future. "But what's still in short supply, and always will rise to the top, is good ideas."

Some of those possessed of both camcorders and talent are getting serious offers. Studios and talent agencies are actively scouting and hiring online talent — and sometimes getting turned down. "Hollywood tried to court us," said Kent Nichols, one of the producers of the popular "Ask a Ninja" online series, "and we're like, 'What are you talking about? We already have an established fan base.' " [3]

In addition to serving as a possible farm team for Hollywood, the world of Internet films is opening up production possibilities for professionals. All the TV networks and other content creators are thinking hard about producing shorter films for distribution over Web sites and cell phones.

Merely cutting longer programs or 30-second ads doesn't always work, but the approach pioneered by successful Internet films — great concepts that are instantly understandable — provides a perfect template.

Take sports, for instance. Subscribers to MLB.tv can watch 2,500 baseball games a year and have up to six games showing on their screens at any given time. The site will even send subscribers personalized alerts when pitchers or batters from their Fantasy or Rotisserie league teams are playing in other games not displayed on their screens. *

"People tend to watch on TV," says Michelle Wu, chief executive officer of MediaZone, which offered Internet-based coverage of the Wimbledon tennis tournament last year. But because her service covered more than 300 matches, "People can watch a lot more and at a more convenient time."

The Internet is supplanting traditional TV in numerous other ways as well. For instance, on July 2, 2005, more people worldwide watched the "Live 8" concerts (to fight poverty in Africa) online than via TV. Netflix, the Internet-based DVD-rental company, in January began offering a limited selection of movies and TV shows for direct viewing over the Internet. And the wide availability of video on the Internet in general threatens to end the traditional content monopoly enjoyed by broadcast stations within their particular markets.

For instance, relatively few people sat through the entire Golden Globes telecast this year, writes columnist Andrew Sullivan. "The next day, however, many downloaded clips of the more embarrassing acceptance speeches or the more touching moments. It's more efficient." [9]

---

* Fantasy and Rotisserie leagues involve virtual teams in which players are drafted from multiple teams but their scores depend on real-life statistics.

"It's an opportunity for bigger companies to present material to an audience where the stakes are not so high," says Sue Rynn, vice president for emerging technologies at Turner Broadcasting. "You can migrate successful ideas from some of these niche opportunities into the more traditional space" of broadcast television.

If video entertainment continues to be an area of experiment and uncertainty, it's clear that home-grown video information is having a big impact. Sens. Hillary Rodham Clinton, D-N.Y., and Barack Obama, D-Ill., made their initial presidential campaign announcements on videos they posted on Web sites. They had clearly learned lessons from the paths taken by "viral videos," watching their messages rapidly spread via e-mail as well as replays on traditional media outlets.

In addition, having millions of eyewitnesses capable of capturing what they see on video is changing the nature of news coverage and events. Ordinary people have shot some of the most compelling news footage in recent months, from the famed "Macaca" video of then-Sen. George Allen, R-Va., insulting a dark-skinned volunteer for his opponent's campaign, to the cell phone footage of comedian

Ask A Ninja Question 32 "Ninja Dates"          close

Courtesy AskANinja.com

The producers of the popular Ask a Ninja online series were courted by Hollywood.

Michael Richards slinging racial slurs in a nightclub. The careers of Allen and Richards were brought to a halt in ways that would never have happened before YouTube.

Citizen journalists are now regularly sending footage to Web sites such as Scoopt and NowPublic. From the 2005 London subway bombings to last year's crash of Yankee pitcher Cory Lidle's plane into a Manhattan apartment building, images shot by amateurs dominate news coverage of some events.

"In 1991, when a bystander videotaped the beating of Rodney King in Los Angeles, the incident was almost unbelievable — not the violence but the recording of it," writes media critic James Poniewozik in *Time*. Today, incidents such as the Richards meltdown "are wearing away the distinction between amateur and professional photojournalists." [4]

[1] Bob Garfield, "YouTube vs. Boob Tube," *Wired*, December 2006.

[2] For background, see Kenneth Jost and Melissa J. Hipolit, "Blog Explosion," *CQ Researcher*, June 9, 2006, pp. 505-528.

[3] Matthew Klam, "The Online Auteurs," *The New York Times Magazine*, Nov. 12, 2006, p. 83.

[4] James Poniewozik, "The Beast With a Billion Eyes," *Time*, Dec. 25, 2006-Jan. 1, 2007, p. 63.

What's more, those who depend on the Internet for video are no longer limited to watching on their computers. Apple announced in January that it would soon release a device, called Apple TV, which will wirelessly move video from the Internet onto regular TV sets. Other companies, such as Sony, Microsoft and Sling Media, are working on comparable tools.

"The consumer demand that has currently and historically been served by broadcast television is increasingly being served in other ways by technologies that have more capacity and permit a much more diverse menu of choices," says Bruce M. Owen, a Stanford University economist and author of *The Internet Challenge to Television*. "As a result, the former medium is shrinking."

Those in the television industry are growing more confident about their ability to meet the Internet challenge, because they own the content that people most want to watch, despite the current fad of watching amateur videos on YouTube and other sites. And television presents content in the most watchable format: high definition, which offers a picture quality unequaled on computer screens.

In fact, much of the most popular content on Internet video sites comes from traditional television sources. "So much of YouTube content is still based on repurposing traditional network programming or access to old programming," says Syracuse University's Thompson.

So, rather than television being swallowed by the Internet, things may be going the other way around, says

Most homemade videos posted on the Web get little attention, but "Evolution of Dance," created by 30-year-old Cleveland comedian Judson Laipply, became a global sensation. The hilarious six-minute compression of the last 50 years of dance steps has been streamed on YouTube more than 40 million times.

Chris Pizzurro, vice president of digital and new media advertising sales and marketing for Turner Entertainment. Computers and iPods that play video are becoming, in effect, TV sets. "The TV is actually growing to other devices," he says. "It's because of the programming."

In addition, programming is beginning to migrate from the Web to traditional TV outlets. NBC broadcasts a program based on the popular iVillage site for women, while Warner Brothers just made a deal with Fox to distribute a television version of its even more popular entertainment Web site, TMZ.com.

The networks and production companies are negotiating with YouTube, Yahoo and other Internet companies to show content or at least excerpts of their programs. "Everything is geared toward more individualized consumption," said comedian Jon Stewart, host of

Comedy Central's "The Daily Show." "Getting it off the Internet is no different than getting it off TV." [10] Stewart's program has been among the most-watched shows, in clip form, on the Internet.

But the networks are jealously guarding control of their copyrighted material. On Feb. 2, the media conglomerate Viacom — which owns the MTV and Nickelodeon networks — demanded that YouTube remove 100,000 clips of Viacom content from its site, including "The Daily Show." In addition, Paramount and 20th Century Fox each recently subpoenaed YouTube, forcing the site to disclose the identities of users who had uploaded copyrighted material. Other video-sharing sites have been targets of litigation as well.

Still, given the flow of content between television and computers — and the emergence of devices to expedite that flow — it appears likely that these media will continue to merge, with people watching TV programming via computers and Web sites showing ever more video.

But that doesn't mean TV will disappear. "There will always be a market for consumers who want to watch television in the traditional way, in their living room at a particular time," says Brian Dietz, vice president for communications at the National Cable & Telecommunications Association. "The vast majority of the content that people want is available through the traditional television-viewing service."

## Will television remain a viable medium for advertisers?

Many people in the television industry are wondering whether their longstanding approach — aggregating many viewers to watch a particular show and selling their attention to advertisers — is sustainable.

"That sort of grand bargain — we'll show you the program if you watch the advertising — is breaking down," said *The Economist*'s Franklin.

While television's venerable paradigm may not have broken down completely, it clearly is under pressure due to the changing nature and fragmentation of the audience. Viewers, especially younger ones, are increasingly willing to migrate to new platforms and sources — often allowing the user to bypass commercials — in pursuit of entertainment and information.

New technologies and sources have been chipping away at the broadcast networks' monopoly since the advent of cable. With the explosion of cable channels over the last 30 years, networks today are down to about 42 percent of the viewing audience compared to 80 percent in the 1970s. [11] Today's most popular network shows are lucky to draw half the audience enjoyed by '70s-era TV hits.

During the 1960s, an advertiser could reach 80 percent of adult American women by simply buying a prime-time spot on all three networks; today reaching the same group would require advertising on 100 different channels. [12] The audience is fracturing even more with the advent of new video devices.

"Advertising is suffering because of the sheer amount of it, the lack of innovation within traditional advertising formats and the power that media fragmentation and technology give to consumers to tune out the noise," writes Tom Himpe, author of *Advertising Is Dead: Long Live Advertising.* [13]

For a couple of years now, advertisers have worried that more viewers will use TiVos and other DVRs to skip past their messages. A Ball State University study last year found that viewers do not watch commercials all the way through 59 percent of the time, either because of impatient channel surfing, bathroom breaks or because they have TiVos or other DVRs. [14]

"Only a small percentage of the audience is there during the commercial," says Jeffrey Cole, director of the Center for the Digital Future at the University of Southern California's Annenberg School. "It's not the Internet, it's the bathroom and the remote control."

However, the phenomenon naturally has networks nervous. They also worry about the difficulty of measuring the audience that is watching specific episodes of shows on DVRs, iPods, Internet streams and other new platforms. "It's something everybody in the business is watching, both at the network and affiliate level," says Dennis Wharton, executive vice president for media relations at the National Association of Broadcasters. "We recognize that the model has to evolve."

But he remains optimistic — and with reason. Despite the competition from new media, viewership of traditional television programming continues to rise, and

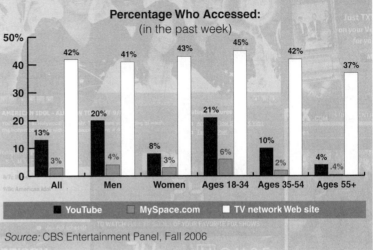

**TV Network Web Sites Outdraw Amateur Sites**

Far more people watched videos on TV network Web sites than on video-sharing sites like YouTube or MySpace, according to a survey conducted by CBS last fall.

**Percentage Who Accessed:**
(in the past week)

| | YouTube | MySpace.com | TV network Web site |
|---|---|---|---|
| All | 13% | 3% | 42% |
| Men | 20% | 4% | 41% |
| Women | 8% | 3% | 43% |
| Ages 18-34 | 21% | 6% | 45% |
| Ages 35-54 | 10% | 2% | 42% |
| Ages 55+ | 4% | 4% | 37% |

*Source:* CBS Entertainment Panel, Fall 2006

with it advertising revenues. Total TV advertising amounted to $47.2 billion during the first nine months of 2006 alone, according to TNS Media Intelligence — an increase of 5.2 percent over the same period the previous year. [15]

Still, networks and advertisers are experimenting with myriad ways to get viewers to think about brands and products. Some, for instance, are turning to product placement — paying to have their products appear as an embedded part of a show. Long common in movies, product placements pop up in many television shows today, often without any subtlety. (*See list, p. 14.*)

Television executives are also trying to "create a good environment for advertising" on new platforms, says Rick Mandler, vice president of digital media advertising at Disney/ABC Media Networks. Several ABC programs are available in their entirety on the company's Web site hours after they have aired on television. They are presented with few commercial interruptions by a single sponsor, but the sponsor's logo appears above the program-viewing window throughout the entire show. Viewers can fast forward through the program itself, but they can't skip past the ads.

The ads run for the traditional 30 seconds but present more information than a traditional commercial.

The TiVo recording device helped revolutionize TV watching by allowing viewers to record their favorite shows and skip over commercials.

Viewers can click on images showing the products being advertised, which will take them to the sponsor's own Web site. These examples illustrate a paradoxical point that Mandler makes. In an age of proliferating video, advertisers need to think of ways of presenting their messages that are not simply 30-second videos.

Ad agencies have said, " 'OK, we'll give you our 30,' " Mandler says. "And we've said, 'We don't want your [traditional] 30.' We want you to create something that leverages the interactivity of the platform."

Interactive advertising, in which viewers navigate their way through a virtual marketplace, has long been talked about but is just now being tried on cable and satellite systems. (It's more common in the United Kingdom and other countries.)

But some television executives believe the real future of TV advertising lies in its past. In the early days of the medium, shows were presented in their entirety — and

sometimes were even produced — by the sponsors. That's why, for instance, comedian Milton Berle's show in the '40s and '50s was not named for him but was called "Texaco Star Theater." Something similar may happen again, with a single sponsor presenting a show, with fewer commercial interruptions, and presenting it not only on network TV but also on every device and Internet platform.

Something like that has already happened with Ford, which has presented two season premieres of "24" without commercial interruption, running two- or three-minute ads at the start and finish of the broadcasts. The carmaker found that consumers had unusually high recall of those ads, despite the fact that they only appeared once. In addition, star Kiefer Sutherland drove a Ford Expedition as part of the show, while other Ford vehicles were woven into the story. "Basically, we own the show," said an advertising executive working with the company. [16]

Sponsors are also heavily integrated into the most popular current TV show, "American Idol," which was pre-sold to sponsors before it won a spot in the Fox network lineup. Contestants appear in little music videos extolling Ford, the judges are never seen without Coke cups nearby, and much viewer voting is done using AT&T's text-messaging service. AT&T Wireless reported that about a third of those voters had never sent a text message before. "Our venture with Fox has done more to educate the public and get people texting than any marketing activity in this country to date," said a company spokesman. [17]

### Are scripted TV shows obsolete?

New media have breathed new life into some network series. Fox began producing fresh episodes of its canceled "Family Guy" cartoon series after it sold well on DVD, and NBC has kept the relatively low-rated comedy "The Office" on the air in large part because it has sold well, at $1.99 an episode, on Apple's iTunes online store.

"I'm not sure that we'd still have the show on the air" without that boost, said Angela Bromstead, president of NBC Universal Television. "When it went on iTunes and really started taking off, that gave us another way to see the true potential other than just Nielsen Media Research." [18]

Typically, though, the shows that perform best in the new platforms are the same ones that are most popular in their regular broadcast time slots. The question facing television executives today is how many stragglers they can afford to keep producing.

With the TV audience continuing to fracture, advertising revenues — even though they are rising — are not keeping up with growing production costs. That leads some in the industry to conclude that the heyday of scripted programming — hour-long dramas and 30-minute situation comedies — may be over.

Scripted shows, after all, are much more expensive to produce than game shows or reality programs. The average scripted drama costs $2.6 million per episode, while the popular "Deal or No Deal" game show, which NBC airs three times a week, only costs about $1 million each, including the prize money. [19]

In October 2006, NBC announced that it would no longer offer scripted shows during the first hour of prime time most nights of the week. Many took it as a sign of things to come. "It's absolutely more bad news for me," TV writer Tim O'Donnell said. "It just eliminates the shelf space available for networks to put on what I pitch." [20]

Although NBC soon backed away from that policy, the network — like its sisters — is producing less scripted programming than a few years ago. The networks have 22 hours of prime time to fill (three hours a night, four on Sunday), and more and more of that time is filled either with game or reality shows or reruns of scripted shows that aired earlier in the week.

Because of dwindling weekend audiences, the networks have essentially ceased offering original programming on Saturday nights and are easing away from broadcasting new material on Fridays as well. "Writers have a lot of reason to be anxious," said Dean Valentine, former head of Disney's television unit. "The world they've been living in no longer exists." [21]

To make matters more uncertain, the contracts covering all the major creative guilds — writing, acting and directing — will expire over the next 18 months. The writers' guild contract expires this summer, and there is a lot of talk in Hollywood that a strike is imminent. Writers and other creative talent — who generally feel they did badly during earlier rounds of negotiation over DVD revenues — now are eyeing a bigger share of the income generated by new media.

A Canadian guild went out on strike in January over similar issues. "We want to be compensated fairly for use of our work on the Internet," the union announced. "We will not have our work put on the Internet for free." [22]

As part of their contingency planning, the networks are developing more reality and game shows. All of the major networks now have multiple prime-time game shows either in production or development. "It's really cheap, and it's a quick way to build an audience," says media consultant Phillip Swann, author of *TV.com*.

But even though the major networks are producing fewer scripted shows, more networks are producing scripted television than ever before. Cable networks such as HBO have stepped up production, as have second-tier broadcast networks such as TNT and The CW (created by CBS and Warner Brothers).

"Yes, CBS and ABC are showing fewer hours a day in scripted entertainment than a decade ago, but there are more networks producing scripted shows today," says MIT's Jenkins. "They're just dispersed across more networks."

What's more, although sitcoms seem to have lost their luster, many hour-long scripted dramas are huge hits. "The success of 'Lost' and 'Desperate Housewives' and 'Heroes' and 'Ugly Betty' suggests there is still an enormous economic value and public interest in scripted programs," Jenkins says.

In fact, many TV people think today's scripted shows are as good or better than ever before. Under challenge from new media, networks have stepped up their game to produce or showcase programs that, in some cases, rival feature films in quality of production and entertainment value.

"Scripted shows to a certain extent are making a comeback," says Wharton, of the National Association of Broadcasters. "Just from the point of view of the craft of television drama, today's shows hold up as well as any shows in the history of television."

Moreover, while reality shows and game shows have proven to be surprisingly durable since their emergence in prime time, even the most popular examples have tended to enjoy fairly limited shelf lives. (A notable exception is the hugely popular "American Idol," averaging about 36 million viewers per episode; the show is in its sixth season.) The limited runs make network executives nervous about abandoning scripted shows, which — when they become hits — can run for years.

Thus, networks realize they must maintain a strong lineup of scripted shows, which have longer half-lives than even the most popular reality shows — whether in syndication, on DVD or across new platforms such as Internet streaming or iTunes downloads.

The shows most often set for automatic, season-long recording on digital video recorders are all scripted programs, including "Law & Order" and "CSI."

# CHRONOLOGY

## 1940s-1960s *Television explodes in popularity.*

**1941** Federal Communications Commission (FCC) authorizes commercial TV operations to start the following year on 10 stations.

**1948** FCC freezes new TV licensing because of flood of applications, effectively preserving oligopoly of NBC, CBS and their affiliates.

**1949** The first cable systems are created in Oregon and Pennsylvania, allowing rural communities too far from broadcast stations to receive programming.

**1952** FCC lifts its licensing freeze, approving plan for 82 new channels (12 on VHF and 70 UHF), opening up the possibility of hundreds of new broadcast stations.

**1965** FCC begins regulating cable TV.

## 1970s-1990s *New competitors challenge broadcast network dominance over home video content.*

**1975** Home Box Office becomes the first cable network to use satellites to send its signal to cable operators, pioneering the concept of a pay-TV channel.

**1984** Congress approves Cable Communications Policy Act, deregulating cable rates and codifying the FCC's ban on telephone companies operating cable systems within their service areas.

**1988** Cable penetration reaches half of U.S. households, with 42.8 million people subscribing to 8,500 cable systems. . . . Congress allows cities to regulate cable systems and home viewers to receive programming via satellite.

**1992** FCC permits local telephone companies to operate video-delivery systems. . . . With cable rates rising sharply, Congress reregulates cable industry — overriding a presidential veto — in order to provide "increased consumer protection."

**1996** For the first time in 62 years, Congress overhauls telecommunications law in effort to increase competition for new broadcasting, cable and other video services. Critics say the new law is a failure.

**1997** DVD players are introduced in the U.S. market.

**1999** TiVo machines (digital video recorders) are released to the public, giving television viewers an easy way to record, store and play back their favorite shows.

## 2000s *The video audience continues to fragment as the Internet opens up new delivery systems and promotes user-generated content.*

**2002** For the first time, cable networks combined draw more viewers than broadcast networks. . . . Major broadcasters lose a record 30 percent of their viewers in the summer.

**2005** More people watch the July 2 "Live 8" charity concerts online than on TV. . . . On Oct. 12 Disney and Apple announce pact to sell TV episodes for downloading and replaying on video iPods. . . . On Nov. 23, the video-swapping Web site BitTorrent agrees to remove links to unlicensed copies of Hollywood films.

**2006** Sen. George Allen, R-Va., is captured on tape on Aug. 11 calling a young man of Indian descent "Macaca"; footage is quickly uploaded onto YouTube and helps to doom Allen's re-election. . . . On Oct. 9, Google buys YouTube for $1.65 billion. . . . NBC Universal announces it will end most scripted programming during the first hour of prime time and cut 700 jobs, applying savings to digital-media investment. It later reconsiders the decision. . . . On Dec. 20, the FCC limits local governments' ability to regulate video services.

**2007** Apple announces on Jan. 9 it will soon release Apple TV, a device to store digital video and transfer it wirelessly from computers to TV sets. . . . On Feb. 2, Viacom demands that YouTube remove more than 100,000 clips of its content from the video-sharing site.

**Feb. 17, 2009** All local TV stations must switch from analog to digital broadcasting, freeing up the analog spectrum for emergency use.

"It's a case of the rich getting richer," says Mark Loughney, vice president of sales and strategy research for ABCTV. "If people are passionate about your programming, they will watch it and find ways of watching it."

## BACKGROUND

### Early TV

The history of television is replete with examples of new devices — color sets, high-definition sets, videotape recorders, flat screens — that burned through years and many iterations before becoming popular. Television itself has been the most important mass medium for so long that it's easy to forget that it, too, was once a newcomer threatening the financial health of older forms of communication.

Television distribution and production were built on the back of radio, with the radio networks — particularly NBC and CBS — seamlessly dominating the newer technology, using many of the same programs and stars. [23]

The concept of sending images over long distances had been discussed for decades prior to the advent of regular television broadcasting. In the 1870s, American inventor Thomas Edison coined the term "telephonescope" to describe the process of converting light and shade into electrical signals that could be transmitted wirelessly. [24] A crude color system was demonstrated as early as 1928. [25]

Television grew rapidly after World War II, which had interrupted its commercial development. In 1946, there were just two TV networks (NBC and CBS) providing 11 hours of programming to a handful of stations that could be watched on one of the 10,000 TV sets then in use. In 1950, four networks (including ABC and DuMont) were sending out 90 hours of weekly programming to about 100 stations serving 10.5 million sets. By the end of the 1950s, 87 percent of U.S. households had a television. [26] National advertisers migrated to the new medium from both radio and from general-interest magazines (*The Saturday Evening Post* and *Collier's* started to fold) and began cutting into the audience for comic books and movies.

Between 1949 until 1952, the FCC protected the oligopoly NBC and CBS had enjoyed in radio by freezing new licenses for broadcasters, essentially making wider competition within the TV industry difficult. The two

networks enjoyed complete dominion over 80 percent of the 60-odd TV markets until 1962, when Congress mandated that all new sets be able to receive both UHF and VHF signals, allowing more competition.

ABC, which had struggled (it had been created in 1943 after a government antitrust suit forced NBC to divest itself of its Blue Network, as ABC was called at the time), came into its own during the 1960s, building an audience through heavy coverage of weekend sports. Fox pursued a similar niche strategy in the 1980s by appealing to viewers ages 18-34 and by broadcasting sports.

For most of their history, however, broadcasters tried to appeal to as wide an audience as possible, pursuing the doctrine of "least objectionable programming" — the belief that out of three choices, viewers will select the one they are least likely to hate. That style of programming fell out of favor by the 1980s, however, when cable began providing viewers with many more options.

### Cable and Video

Cable television had been around, in embryonic form, since the late 1940s. Initially, it evolved as a way to bring television to remote areas that were too far away from the stations to receive broadcast signals. In 1949, E. L. Parson, a radio-station owner in Astoria, Ore., erected an antenna system to receive the signal of a TV station in Seattle, 125 miles away, which he then shared with 25 "subscribing neighbors" via a network of wires. [27] Most early cable systems were similar mom-and-pop operations; by 1957, there were 500 such systems, averaging about 700 subscribers each. [28] A few years later, a San Diego cable operator decided to bring in TV stations from Los Angeles. For the first time, cable service was being offered in cities already served by three or more broadcast stations.

In 1975, Home Box Office (HBO) became the first cable network to use satellites to transmit programs to cable operators, demonstrating the viability of offering a premium channel that subscribers would pay extra to receive. It soon attracted competitors, such as Showtime. Cable revenues grew from $900 million in 1976 to $12.8 billion in 1988 — $3 billion of that from so-called pay-TV channels alone. [29]

Congress had deregulated the cable business in 1984 to offer it protections from certain local government mandates (it would re-regulate the industry in 1992). By 1988, half of U.S. households with television were wired

# Teens' Media Multitasking Raises Questions

*Do they learn? Retain what they learn?*

Several years ago, an ad showed a young man, TV remote control in hand, saying, "You've got 3 seconds. Impress me." [1]

It was meant to underscore the impatience of habitual channel surfers. But what's striking about the ad today is how focused the youth looks. He's only holding a remote control. Where is his iPod, his cell phone and his laptop?

"This is the M Generation," says Ian Rowe, vice president of strategic partnerships and public affairs for MTV Networks. "They want all media all the time."

Cell phones and computers seem to encourage media multitasking, Today's young people watch TV with a computer on their laps and a cell phone by their side, checking their Facebook pages, monitoring eBay auctions, playing fantasy football or video games, sending text messages and phoning their friends. And the young — who grew up using computers from an early age — are more likely than adults to embrace newer media devices and technology.

According to a Kaiser Family Foundation study released in December 2006, anywhere from a quarter to a third of 7th-to-12th-graders say they multitask "most of the time."

A majority of kids multitask some of the time while fewer than 20 percent say they never do. [2]

While today's teens and "tweens" absorb more media than ever and often are interacting with more than one medium at a time, how that affects their attention spans and their ability to learn and retain what they've learned — or whether they will keep up such distractible habits as adults — are all debatable. While multitasking among the young has become a field of serious academic study, most of the basic questions are unanswered.

"One of the great myths is that the 16- or 18-year-old doing six things at once will still be consuming their media that way when they're 30," says Phillip Swann, president of TV Predictions Inc., a consulting firm in North Beach, Md., outside Washington.

"Are we going to reach the point in our culture where people have a hard time listening to a two-and-a-half-minute pop song without channel surfing?" asked New York-based composer R. Luke DuBois. "I see people do that on their iPods all the time. They'll listen to songs only through the first chorus, and then they'll switch to another song." [3]

---

for cable. That year, Congress passed legislation to permit continued transmission of programming to owners of home satellite dishes. [30]

The year 1988 was also a "tipping point" for sales of videocassette recorders (VCRs) — nearly 12 million in the United States alone. Ampex had introduced a videotape machine as early as 1957 and had not been able to keep up with consumer demand — despite a hefty $50,000 price tag. In 1976, Sony introduced its Betamax machines in the United States. Prices had come down a bit — to $1,295 for the machine and $15 for one-hour cassettes. Despite its headstart in the marketplace and superior picture quality, however, Sony lost the "format war" to VHS.

Believing that VCRs would lead to piracy and cut into profits, production companies such as Universal and Disney lobbied Congress and filed lawsuits, claiming their copyrights were being violated.

Eventually, VHS would lose its preeminence to DVD players, which first became available in the U.S. market in 1997. DVD sales and rentals quickly became major sources of profit for television and movie production companies.

## Regulating Competition

By the 1990s, cable systems had attracted a new competitor: the telephone industry, which began clamoring to provide video services to its customers. The FCC had banned telephone companies from owning cable systems in 1970 out of fear that "telcos" would refuse to let a competing cable system use their telephone poles to hang its wires. Congress effectively codified its ban as part of the 1984 cable deregulation act, aiming to prevent discrimination against cable systems and to promote diversity in media ownership.

By the late 1980s, however, Washington policymakers were beginning to advocate allowing telephone compa-

That kind of behavior is bad news for brain development, says Jordan Grafman, chief of the cognitive neuroscience section at the National Institutes of Health. He argues that the inability to focus is a modern version of a primitive response of the brain's frontal lobe to be attracted to novel stimuli.

Some studies suggest multitaskers don't retain as much of what they learn as they would when they are more focused. Divided attention "doesn't allow you to do any deep deliberation," Grafman says. "If you have to invent something, if you have to design something new, if you have to have a different take on an issue, there is no way you are going to be able to do that effectively if you are multitasking."

But research also suggests that young people who have grown up in a media-saturated age "can toggle back and forth between things better than those who are older," says Lee Rainie, director of the Pew Internet & American Life Project. "If you're motivated, you can learn a lot more than you used to, because it's so much easier."

Another school of thought holds that the skills promoted by the convergence of new media — including creativity, peer-to-peer learning and, yes, multitasking — are becoming necessary for success in the modern world. The MacArthur Foundation announced in October 2006 it will devote $50 million over five years to the study of digital media and learning.

Henry Jenkins, a media studies professor at MIT who is working with the foundation, scoffs at those who think multitasking is a bad habit that will be shed with age. "We all live in a world where multitasking is an essential skill," he says. Given the current bombardment of media, "If we can't shift our attention from one piece of information to another, we really will cease to function."

One thing appears to be certain. Despite the way today's young people flock to the latest gadgets and features, including Facebook and MySpace, their primary loyalty is to television. The average young person watches nearly four hours of TV a day — compared to 49 minutes playing video games — and is more likely to give television his or her undivided attention rather than any other media device, according to the Kaiser study. [4]

"Television still completely dominates kids' time with media and is eight times more likely to be a primary activity than a secondary activity," meaning their main focus will be on the TV set rather than on the cell phone or computer, says Ulla G. Foehr, author of the Kaiser study. "So anyone who thinks TV is becoming irrelevant should think again."

---

[1] Henry Jenkins, *Convergence Culture* (2006), p. 64.

[2] Ulla G. Foehr, "Media Multitasking Among American Youth," Kaiser Family Foundation, December 2006, p. 7.

[3] Quoted on "Studio 360," Public Radio International, Jan. 26, 2007.

[4] Foehr, *op. cit.*, p. 8.

---

nies to provide cable services. The FCC permitted phone companies to engage in video programming and recommended that Congress repeal the cross-ownership ban.

Impatient with the lack of action in Congress, Bell Atlantic asked a federal judge to rule that the ban violated the First Amendment. A judge so ruled in 1993, prompting several other telcos to seek legal redress. By late 1994, the legal barriers to competition between telcos and cable had fallen.

In 1996, Congress systematically revamped telecommunications law for the first time in 62 years. The Telecommunications Act of 1996 was intended to open up new delivery systems for both television and telephone to increased competition, lifting most barriers to media ownership. While limiting companies and individuals from owning TV stations that reached more than 35 percent of the national audience, the act abolished many of the cross-market barriers that had prohibited

dominant players from one communications industry, such as telephone, from providing services in other areas, such as cable. [31]

The law's general approach was to replace government regulation with competition as the chief way of assuring that telecommunications services are delivered to customers cheaply and efficiently. It imposed new regulations to help open markets and equalize the burden on competitors, but it also lifted many price controls and other regulations — in some cases before local monopolies are broken. The law eliminated the provision of the 1984 cable act that barred local phone companies from entering the cable-TV market in their service areas, while easing or eliminating the price controls on cable companies.

The law allowed competition, but it did not effectively foster it. Telcos still lag well behind cable companies in providing multichannel video services to consumers.

## TV Advertising Changes With the Times

Changes in television technology — notably the development of devices that allow viewers to bypass commercials — have led some companies to abandon traditional commercials (left) and instead to pay producers to write their products into the show itself (right).

| Top 10 Traditional TV Advertisers (in $ billions spent) | | Top 10 Product Placement Brands (by most appearances) |
|---|---|---|
| 1. Procter & Gamble | $2.9 | 1. Coca-Cola |
| 2. General Motors | 2.0 | 2. Chef Revival Apparel |
| 3. AT&T | 1.4 | 3. Nike Apparel |
| 4. Ford | 1.4 | 4. 24 Hour Fitness |
| 5. DaimlerChrysler | 1.3 | 5. Chicago Bears |
| 6. Time Warner | 1.2 | 6. Cingular Wireless |
| 7. Verizon Communications | 1.1 | 7. Starter |
| 8. Toyota | 1.1 | 8. Dell |
| 9. Altria Group | 1.0 | 9. SLS Electronic Equipment Speakers |
| 10. Walt Disney | 1.0 | 10. Nike Footwear |

*Source:* Nielsen Monitor-Plus, 2006     *Source:* Nielsen Product Placement, 2006

"In truth, the bill promised the worst of both worlds: More concentrated ownership over communications with less possibility for regulation in the public interest," wrote Robert W. McChesney, a University of Illinois communications professor, in his 2004 book *The Problem of the Media.* "Accordingly, both the cable and telecommunication industries have become significantly more concentrated since 1996, and customer complaints about lousy service have hit all-time highs. Cable industry rates for consumers have also shot up, increasing some 50 percent between 1996 and 2003." [32]

## CURRENT SITUATION

### Policy Debates

Regulation typically lags behind technological changes, and that is likely to remain the case for television, since it appears unlikely that the 110th Congress will address the changing landscape of television and telecommunications policy in a comprehensive way.

The House passed a major telecom bill in 2006 that would have made it easier for phone companies to enter the video business, but the Senate never completed its version. [33] Since then the political landscape on Capitol Hill has changed dramatically, with Democrats taking control of both chambers in the 2006 congressional elections. While Congress may take up some narrow issues, "the consensus is that there's won't be a comprehensive bill," says James Brad Ramsay, general counsel for the National Association of Regulatory Utility Commissioners.

Meanwhile, the issues that dominated the telecommunications debate last year have migrated to the Federal Communications Commission (FCC) and the states. For instance, Congress sought to streamline existing rules that require video operators — anyone offering video through cable, broadband or fiber-optic phone lines — to negotiate franchising deals with individual cities and towns. The big phone companies, such as AT&T and Verizon, which are spending billions on new fiber-optic networks to provide broadband video services, say current franchise processes slow the rollout of such services and help preserve a competitive advantage for cable companies.

The FCC on Dec. 20 issued new guidelines that require municipalities to respond to TV franchise requests from phone companies within 90 days. The agency also restricted the limits local governments can place on new video service "build-outs," as well as the franchise fees they can charge. Congress is expected to review the guidelines, which local governments have roundly criticized.

Municipalities say they need discretion to determine which companies would best use public rights of way while digging up roads to install their cables and building their infrastructure, since many vendors are competing for the same valuable space. Many cities also want to require new entrants to guarantee access to low-income or underserved areas.

"We want to be able to negotiate these things, not to have them taken off the table by regulatory framework," says Carolyn Coleman, director of federal relations for the National League of Cities.

Telephone companies have also brought their case to numerous states. Since 2005, nine states have streamlined local franchise rules. The laws vary, but in essence the states have made it easier for the telephone companies to get their franchises and override the protests of local governments.

Not surprisingly, cable companies aren't happy about these new arrangements. "It's not what you think of as a new entrant needing regulatory protection," says Rick Cimerman, vice president for state government affairs at the National Cable & Telecommunications Association. "AT&T alone dwarfs the entire cable industry."

The telephone companies' hope of getting a national franchise bill that would allow them to compete on favorable terms with cable foundered on their own objections — shared by the cable industry — to a provision known as "net neutrality." They even object to the term, saying that it really represents governmental intrusion into the telecommunications business.

Net neutrality bills, which continue to be introduced both in Congress and in a handful of states, would block Internet service providers (ISPs) from charging content providers for priority access. [34] Some companies — including some television companies — want to be able to pay extra to make sure their data can get through quickly and not be slowed by heavy Internet traffic (which can cause video streams to appear jerky). Proponents of the measure say net-neutrality policies would ensure equal access to Internet distribution, preventing a large company from buying up bandwidth and thus blocking or slowing access for competitors or small sites that can't afford to pay for premium treatment.

Another debate likely to rage in Washington this year involves media-ownership rules. In the 1996 Telecommunications Act, Congress barred media companies or individuals from owning television stations serving more than 35 percent of the U.S. population and required the FCC to review media-ownership rules every four years. In 2003, the commission voted to ease the restrictions and allow station owners to reach a combined 45 percent of the national audience. A federal appeals court then struck down the deregulation as "arbitrary and capricious." [35]

As the FCC undertakes its quadrennial review in 2007, broadcasters hope the agency will ease ownership rules. Because the media landscape is shifting so rapidly,

## Most Adults Have Digital TV, Broadband

About two-thirds of U.S. adults have digital televisions and/or high-speed (broadband) Internet connections. Only 35 percent have analog TVs and no broadband or cable connections.

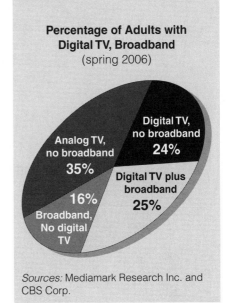

### Percentage of Adults with Digital TV, Broadband
(spring 2006)

Digital TV, no broadband **24%**

Analog TV, no broadband **35%**

Digital TV plus broadband **25%**

Broadband, No digital TV **16%**

*Sources:* Mediamark Research Inc. and CBS Corp.

traditional TV providers cannot be handcuffed if they are to remain competitive, argues Wharton of the National Association of Broadcasters. "We have asked the government to explore some modest changes to some of the rules that would preserve and enhance free, over-the-air broadcasting," he says, "such as rules that bar a newspaper owner from owning stations in the same market, or partnering with another station in same market."

FCC Chairman Kevin J. Martin is sympathetic to calls for deregulation and has said he hopes to revisit the newspaper-broadcast cross-ownership ban. But a strong backlash against the 2003 deregulation has put pressure on Martin and other commissioners to be more sensitive to public opinion. Moreover, Democrats in Congress will be skeptical about attempts to ease media-ownership rules, with House Telecommunications Subcommittee Chairman Edward J. Markey, D-Mass., particularly vocal about the issue.

Apple CEO Steve Jobs introduces the new iPhone at Macworld on Jan. 9, 2007 in San Francisco. The revolutionary device combines a mobile phone and widescreen iPod with touch controls and an Internet communications device with the ability to use e-mail and Web browsing. It starts shipping in the U.S. in June 2007.

"The paradox is that you'll have some people telling you there are fewer and fewer companies owning more and more of the media, so there is really very little access to diversity, yet other people are telling you that we have a world without gatekeepers, that anyone can post anything they want on the Internet," says Jenkins of MIT.

"Both of those statements are true."

## All-You-Can-Eat TV

Outside of the regulatory and policy arena, technology appears to be putting everything about the nature of television up for grabs. A medium that has long been pri-

marily underwritten by advertising is watching its audience crack and break into a million pieces. Viewers accustomed to flipping through channels now are finding that their primary loyalty may be to specific programs, which in turn may be delivered to them through any number of different media. And watching television, which has always been primarily a passive, relaxing activity, is becoming more interactive, with more viewers potentially engaging with content — and trying to find it.

One of the major questions facing the television industry today is whether its traditional means of delivery — networks of affiliated stations — can survive the changes.

"When we see that big box in the living room, we think of channels," says Andrew Kantor, a technology reporter for the *Roanoke Times* and columnist for USAToday.com. "There's no reason for television to be divided by that, other than convention."

It's possible now for viewers to access their favorite shows without giving any thought to what channel it's on. It might help them find a show like "Lost" on the Internet if they know what network presents it, but they certainly need no longer know that it's scheduled to be on their local Channel 5 on Wednesdays at 10 p.m. If they have a TiVo or DVR, they can program it to record "CSI" automatically by series name, not by channel or broadcast time.

"We don't watch Fox, we watch '24,' " says Kantor. "The only reason to have channels today is to help us navigate the content. Who cares if the show is on Fox or CBS or Jimmy's FunStuff channel?"

Some niche networks are considering becoming broadband channels, allowing viewers to watch their programming directly via the Internet without their even having a presence on cable or satellite systems. Companies such as Wal-Mart and Amazon are also lining up to send content directly to viewers. Access will expand even further as new devices become available that can send Internet content to television sets. Apple is expected to release its Apple TV device this month, with major competitors putting out their versions soon. Video game players have already grown accustomed to switching seamlessly from games to live network video feeds on their televisions.

But all the longstanding television services — networks, local affiliates and cable and satellite — have advantages that offer them hope of thriving well into the future, assuming they can adapt to changing circum-

# Should the government preserve limits on media ownership?

## YES  Rep. Edward J. Markey, D-Mass.
*Chairman, House Subcommittee on Telecommunications and the Internet*

From keynote address, National Conference for Media Reform, Jan. 13, 2007

It is often said that our system of democratic self-government relies on an informed citizenry. Informed citizens need to know enough to make decisions in a democracy. And they need to know [not only] raw information but also context as well as the history of issues.

Media ownership is a key tool utilized in this policy context. And that's because diversity of ownership has historically been used as a proxy for diversity of viewpoints and diversity of content. Simply put, therefore, elimination of ownership limits eradicates an important tool we have to help ensure that the public has access to a wide array of viewpoints in local news and information.

In 2003, we were challenged. We were challenged by the drastic and indiscriminate elimination of mass-media ownership rules proposed by the previous Federal Communications Commission [FCC] under its former chairman. In response to pressure from special political and corporate interests, the FCC, on a 3-to-2 vote, rammed through changes to media ownership that would have eviscerated the public-interest principles of diversity and localism.

The FCC's plan did not create more entertainment and information sources for consumers. Nor did it enhance the ability of the broadcasting medium to meet the informational and civic needs of the communities it serves. Instead, it threatened to intensify control of information and opinion in entire cities and regions of the country. The aggregate effect would have encouraged the rapid consolidation of mass-media ownership in this country and the elimination of diverse sources of opinion and expression.

The good news is that the challenge was answered. People took notice, took action and went to court. Congress also responded and enacted some limits, and the court shut down the rest of the sweeping changes and sent the plan back to the FCC. But it was only a temporary reprieve. Today, the FCC is embarked upon another round of analysis and is re-examining whether to change the media-ownership rules.

The communications revolution has the potential to change our society. Unless we continue to revere localism and diversity, we risk encouraging a new round of "communications cannibalism" in mass-media properties on both the national and local levels that would put real progress in bolstering minority ownership of media even further away.

## NO  Bruce M. Owen
*Director, Public Policy Program Stanford University*

Written for *CQ Researcher*, Feb. 15, 2007

Despite the activist hype about "media power," the number of alternatives for viewers is increasing, not decreasing. Economic competition among media for viewers and advertisers is greater now than at any time in history. So is economic competition among the wired and wireless pipelines that carry content to the home.

Competition in the marketplace of ideas, one of the keys to democracy, is more robust than ever, thanks to the ubiquitous Internet. FCC ownership rules, which only apply to the old, regulated media, make it harder for the older media to compete with the new. This will ultimately disadvantage those consumers who still prefer the traditional technologies.

Antitrust laws protect consumers against mergers that reduce competition. The way to tell if competition is threatened is to ask whether consumers will end up with too few choices. Advertisers already have many alternatives to regulated broadcast media, even without considering online advertising. TV viewers use cable or satellite or DSL and online services, each with essentially unlimited channel capacity. These multi-channel media compete among themselves and with newer, wireless high-speed services such as EV-DO and Verizon's BroadbandAccess.

Anyone who thinks media moguls are monolithic gatekeepers standing between freedom of speech and the public should consider how Sen. Hillary Rodham Clinton recently chose to announce her candidacy for the presidency: on her Web site, with an online video. Other candidates did the same. One reason: To bypass any "spin" imparted by traditional media reporting. More generally, as the Federal Election Commission proclaimed last spring: "[T]he Internet's near infinite capacity, diversity and low cost of publication and access has democratized the mass distribution of information, especially in the political context. The result is the most accessible marketplace of ideas in history."

Neither FCC rules nor new laws restricting media ownership make sense. We have perfectly good antitrust laws and enforcers, including the courts, to deal with threats to economic competition in the advertising and video entertainment markets.

Catering to misinformed populist ideas is not a costless indulgence. Traditional media are trying to remain relevant in the new media world. Some consumers would be inconvenienced by their premature demise. This is not the time to increase their costs of operation by maintaining or even increasing regulatory constraints that make them less competitive.

## The Top 10 TV Programs

There's something for almost everyone among the most popular regularly scheduled television shows, from amateur performers to medical and crime dramas to sports and suburban seductresses.

| | |
|---|---|
| 1. | American Idol — Tuesdays (Fox) |
| 2. | American Idol — Wednesdays (Fox) |
| 3. | Dancing with the Stars (ABC) |
| 4. | CSI (CBS) |
| 5. | Dancing with the Stars Results Show (ABC) |
| 6. | NBC Sunday Night Football (NBC) |
| 7. | CSI: Miami (CBS) |
| 8. | Desperate Housewives (ABC) |
| 9. | House (Fox) |
| 10. | Deal or No Deal — Mondays (NBC) |
| 10. | Without a Trace (CBS) |

*Source:* Nielsen Media Research, 2006

stances. For instance, while viewers may soon be able to use the Internet or other means to bypass local affiliate stations, it will take time for traditional viewing habits to change. Local stations are a familiar and easy way to find television shows, and they provide local news, emergency and weather information that Internet providers do not.

As part of a 2005 budget bill, Congress set 2009 as the deadline for broadcasters to switch from analog to digital broadcasting. Lawmakers wanted both to promote digital TV, which provides a crisper picture, and to free up broadcast spectrum for wireless and emergency communications systems.

Although broadcasters opposed the imposition of a specific deadline, they now say it provides them with a competitive advantage. The move to all-digital television broadcasting will enable individual stations to send out multiple signals, essentially providing multiple channels. So, in addition to airing network programs, the station can simultaneously broadcast news, weather and sports coverage produced in-house.

"TV networks have the franchise content people want to watch," says CBS' Poltrack. "The local station is the best way to get it."

That remains true despite the present industry upheaval, Poltrack says, largely because of the advent of

high-definition television, which provides a much clearer picture than standard television. Watching a television show via Internet streaming cannot match the picture quality offered by TV now that most prime time shows are being produced using HDTV technology.

"I can't tell you how many people have told me they'd rather watch grass grow in HD than their favorite show in standard television," says ABC's Mandler.

And networks themselves maintain advantages in the new age, he argues. While content producers may try to sell their products directly to viewers — bypassing the networks and other traditional middlemen — the costs of marketing individual shows can be prohibitive, he points out. While producer-to-consumer programs could become instant word-of-mouth hits just as low-budget videos get e-mailed to millions today, he concedes, they would be exceptional.

Networks also own the rights to decades' worth of old programming. While some people enjoy owning DVDs of their favorite shows, as video-on-demand services become more common more people will prefer to dial up old episodes of "I Love Lucy" or "My Mother the Car" owned by the networks and their partners. Cable services such as Comcast already make hundreds of movies available to subscribers at any time "on demand."

And as the viewing audience continues to fragment, Mandler says, "the folks who can stitch together a national audience and sell it to advertisers are the networks." Even cable and satellite companies — and relatively new broadband services offered by telephone companies — are too fragmented to promise a truly national audience.

Nielsen Media Research, the leading TV audience-measurement company, is working to find new ways to measure the fracturing audience. It will soon offer minute-by-minute ratings that also measure ad and DVR playback viewership, although some in the TV industry are skeptical they can deliver this as quickly as promised. The company is also experimenting with a

400-member video iPod viewership panel and is "moving rapidly" on measuring video viewership on the Web, according to Scott Brown, a Nielsen senior vice president.

"If it's measurable, advertisers will want it," says Jin Kang, an executive producer with NDS, a digital video company. "As long as you can measure viewership, advertisers don't really care how they looked at it."

When industry officials first began to notice the fracturing of the TV audience, the changes in video delivery technology and the growth of user-generated content, "There was a certain amount of panic in the room," concedes Peter Olsen, senior vice president of national ad sales for A&E Television Networks. "Now, there's more enthusiasm. We feel like what we do well — which is produce great content — consumers will continue to enjoy."

## OUTLOOK

### Shifting Landscape

The television industry today feels a bit like the dot-com boom a decade ago. There is endless experimentation, rapid technological change, a host of start-ups and a scramble among established companies to form new partnerships and adapt to a rapidly shifting landscape. There will be plenty of false starts — and big wins, like the sale of YouTube to Google for $1.65 billion last October.

"The changes of the next five years will dwarf the changes of the last 50," said Jeff Zucker, chief executive of NBC Universal's television group, as he announced a restructuring of the company last fall.

But no one really knows what those changes will look like. Viewers may use new devices to access nearly any video content they want, and networks and cable companies may make more and more content available "on demand." Almost everyone agrees that television and the Internet will offer increasingly overlapping experiences.

But all the new technology involves, well, new technology. For now, watching videos through the Internet remains more cumbersome than watching on traditional TV — which also delivers superior picture quality. And millions of people like watching television by simply turning it on and watching.

Some people predict that the big money in future television will be in search engines. "It's great to be given

Shows like ABC's wildly popular "Ugly Betty," starring America Ferrera (right), face new competition for viewers. With higher production costs and a declining viewership, sitcoms and other scripted TV programs are being pushed aside by reality shows such as "American Idol."

the keys to the Library of Congress, but if there's no card catalog, it's not much use," says Todd Herman, a new-media strategist for Microsoft.

For now, despite the advent of consumer-created video and the wide array of choices, most viewers are watching more TV than ever and are using new devices and platforms to keep up with favorite shows by watching at a more convenient time or when "nothing's on."

And networks and advertisers appear increasingly confident that they will be able to measure viewership, and advertisers hope they will be able to more accurately target the right viewers for messages about the appropriate products.

Meanwhile, interactive TV — talked about for years — is just taking root in this country. Interactive TV allows a viewer to make selections to "go" to different places on their set, similar to selecting the movie, special features or language features while watching a DVD. Not too many people are choosing to navigate through an advertiser's showplace on their television set, but enough are starting to do so to make it worthwhile.

But how will the splintering of viewership affect the nation and its culture? "Ultimately, the biggest story of the 21st century will be the fracturing of the 20th-century audience," says Thompson, of the Center for the Study of Popular Television. "We spent the first eight

*Time* selected "You" — as in YouTube — as its 2006 Person of the Year, reflecting the growing popularity of user-generated video content and the increasing participation of everyday citizens in the next Internet generation.

decades of the 20th century putting together the biggest mass audience of all time. You had virtually everybody — old and young, rich and poor — feeding from the same cultural trough at least a few hours a week, if not a few hours a day."

Thompson doesn't think it's a coincidence that the citizenry has become more divided politically at the same time that its main source of popular culture and information has become more splintered. NBC News anchor Brian Williams seems to agree. "It is now possible — even common — to go about your day in America and consume only what you wish to see and hear," he writes. [36]

But others point out that the Internet has also made it easier for people of like-minded interests to find each other and form communities.

And many viewers prefer to make their own entertainment choices, rather than relying on the programming

judgments of network executives. "The common culture of my youth is gone for good . . . splintered beyond repair by the emergence of the Web-based technologies that so maximized and facilitated culture choice as to make the broad-based offerings of the old mass media look bland and unchallenging by comparison," writes critic Terry Teachout. "For all the nostalgia with which I look back on the days of the Top 40, the Book-of-the-Month Club and 'The Ed Sullivan Show,' I prefer to make my own cultural decisions, and I welcome the ease with which the new media permit me to do so." [37]

It's an age of choice, and no one is certain which formats viewers will ultimately favor. But whether people are watching programs on demand, via the Internet or on their local station, it's clear that Americans will continue watching lots of television into the foreseeable future.

"If I had to describe the future of TV in one word," says Mike Bloxham, director of research at Ball State University's Center for Media Design, "it would be 'more.' "

## NOTES

1. Jennifer Mann, "Ads Mimic 'Viral Videos,' " *The Kansas City Star*, Feb. 3, 2007, p. C1.

2. Matthew Creamer, "John Doe Edges Out Jeff Goodby," *Advertising Age*, Jan. 7, 2007, p. S-4.

3. Lev Grossman, "Person of the Year: You," *Time*, Dec. 25, 2006-Jan. 1, 2007, p. 40.

4. Gary Holmes, "Nielsen Media Research Reports Television's Popularity Is Still Growing," Nielsen Media Research, news release, Sept. 21, 2006.

5. For background, see Alan Greenblatt, "Future of the Music Industry," *CQ Researcher*, Nov. 21, 2003, pp. 988-1012.

6. Frank Rose, "ESPN Thinks Outside the Box," *Wired*, September 2005, p. 113.

7. Brian Steinberg, " 'Law & Order' Boss Dick Wolf Ponders Future of TV Ads," *The Wall Street Journal*, Oct. 18, 2006.

8. "Forum With Michael Krasny," KQED, Dec. 16, 2006; available for streaming at www.kqed.org/ep Archive/R612131000.

9. Andrew Sullivan, "Video Power: The Potent New Political Force," *Sunday Times of London*, Feb. 4, 2007, p. 4.

10. Thomas Goetz, "Reinventing Television," *Wired*, September 2005, p. 104.

11. Kevin Downey, "Milestone: Cable Widens Lead in 18-49s," *Medialife Magazine*, April 21, 2006.

12. Henry Jenkins, *Convergence Culture* (2006), p. 66.

13. Quoted in Lewis Lazare, "Changing Face of Ads Examined," *Chicago Sun-Times*, Dec. 4, 2006, p. 63.

14. Marc Ransford, "New Study Has Good and Bad News for Television Advertising Industry," press release, Ball State University, Sept. 26, 2006, www.bsu.edu.

15. Lisa Rockwell, "Web Sparks Advertising Revolution," *Austin American-Statesman*, Dec. 17, 2006, p. H1.

16. Frank Rose, "The Fast-Forward, On-Demand, Network-Smashing Future of Television," *Wired*, October 2003.

17. Jenkins, *op. cit.*, p. 59.

18. Verne Gay, "How iTunes Saved 'The Office,' " *Newsday*, Nov. 1, 2006, p. B21.

19. Gary Levin, "Networks Have Eyes on the Prize," *USA Today*, Dec. 18, 2006, p. 1D.

20. Richard Verrier, "No Time for Making New 'Friends' at NBC," *Los Angeles Times*, Nov. 7, 2006, p. C1.

21. *Ibid.*

22. "Key Issues in ACTRA's Strike," www.actra.ca/actra/control/feature14.

23. For background, see "Radio Development and Monopoly," *Editorial Research Reports*, March 31, 1924; available at *CQ Researcher Plus Archive*, http://library.cqpress.com.

24. Andrew Crisell, *A Study of Modern Television* (2006), p. 17.

25. For in-depth background on the development of television, see "Television," *Editorial Research Reports*, July 12, 1944, available at *CQ Researcher Plus Archive*, http://library.cqpress.com; and Andrew F. Inglis, *Behind the Tube* (1990), p. 237.

26. George Comstock and Erica Scharrar, *Television: What's On, Who's Watching, and What It Means* (1999), p. 6.

27. Inglis, *op. cit.*, p. 360.

28. *Ibid.*, p. 365.

29. *Ibid.*, p. 385.

30. For background, see the following *CQ Researchers*, available at *CQ Researcher Plus Archive*: "Cable Television: The Coming Medium," Sept. 9, 1970, "Television in the Eighties," May 9, 1980; "Cable TV's Future," Sept. 24, 1982; "Cable Television Coming of Age," Dec. 27, 1985; "Broadcasting Deregulation," Dec. 4, 1987; Kenneth Jost, "The Future of Television," Dec. 31, 1994, pp. 1129-1152.

31. For background, see David Masci, "The Future of Telecommunications," *CQ Researcher*, April 23, 1999, pp. 329-352.

32. Robert W. McChesney, *The Problems of the Media* (2004), p. 53.

33. Joelle Tessler, "2006 Legislative Summary: Telecommunications Overhaul," *CQ Weekly*, Dec. 16, 2006, p. 3370.

34. For background, see Marcia Clemmitt, "Controlling the Internet," *CQ Researcher*, May 12, 2006, pp. 409-432.

35. Joelle Tessler, "Diversity Debate Shapes Media Ownership Rules," *CQ Weekly*, Jan. 27, 2007, p. 302.

36. Brian Williams, "Enough About You," *Time*, Dec. 25, 2006-Jan. 1, 2007, p. 78.

37. Terry Teachout, "Culture in the Age of Blogging," *Commentary*, June 2005, www.terryteachout.com/archives20070204.shtml#108419.

# BIBLIOGRAPHY

## Books

**Carter, Bill, *Desperate Networks*, Doubleday, 2006.**
*The New York Times* TV reporter recounts behind-the-scenes stories of how many of today's hottest shows made it on the air (and, in many cases, almost didn't).

**Jenkins, Henry, *Convergence Culture: Where Old and New Media Collide*, NYU Press, 2006.**
The director of MIT's comparative media-studies program looks at how content is flowing across multiple media platforms and how audiences are migrating to watch and interact with it.

**Marc, David, and Robert J. Thompson,** *Television in the Antenna Age: A Concise History*, **Blackwell Publishing, 2005.**
The authors, both affiliated with Syracuse University, summarize both technological evolution and the content presented during TV's first 50 years.

## Articles

**Creamer, Matthew, "John Doe Edges Out Jeff Goodby,"** *Advertising Age*, **Jan. 8, 2007, p. S-4.**
User-generated videos that feature popular consumer products are, in cases such as "The Diet Coke & Mentos Experiment," doing a better job of selling those products than paid advertising, making the consumer the "agency of the year."

**Garfield, Bob, "YouTube vs. Boob Tube,"** *Wired*, **December 2006.**
*Advertising Age*'s editor-at-large argues the fractured media universe means TV will lose its ad-dollar dominance but makes it clear that no one is sure how to make money sponsoring user-generated content.

**Grossman, Lev, "Person of the Year: You,"** *Time*, **Dec. 25, 2006-Jan. 1, 2007.**
The next generation of the Web involves more participation and creativity from users, greater consumer control of video and text content and more news being made and covered by average people.

**Levin, Gary, "Networks Have Eyes on the Prize,"** *USA Today*, **Dec. 18, 2006, p. 1D.**
With scripted-programming costs rising, all the major networks have multiple game shows in production or development.

**McHugh, Josh, "The Super Network,"** *Wired*, **September 2005, p. 107.**
The writer argues that Yahoo! has taken the lead in formulating intuitive ways to help people search through millions of hours of programming in a comprehensible way.

**Rockwell, Lisa, "Web Sparks Advertising Revolution,"** *Austin American-Statesman*, **Dec. 17, 2006, p. H1.**
With so many viewers watching video via the Internet and new devices, advertisers wonder how long a 50-year-old business model built on expensive TV advertising will be sustained.

**Sullivan, Kevin, "Regular Folks, Shooting History,"** *The Washington Post*, **Dec. 18, 2006, p. A1.**
Devices such as cell-phone cameras are making it easier for non-journalists to capture images of the news as it happens, and there is an increasing market for their pictures and videos online and through established news outlets.

**Verrier, Richard, "No Time for Making 'Friends' at NBC,"** *Los Angeles Times*, **Nov. 7, 2006.**
NBC's decision to cut back on scripted programming in prime time is a signal that such programming, which is expensive to produce, is fading fast — particularly sitcoms.

## Reports and Studies

**Berman, Saul J., Niall Duffy and Louisa A. Shipnuck, "The End of Television As We Know It," IBM Institute for Business Value, 2006.**
The generations-old model of a TV audience happily embracing scheduled programming is coming to an end. Over the next several years, programmers, networks and their competitors will have to stay ahead of "gadgeteers," who will lead passive viewers into a more interactive future.

**Foehr, Ulla G., "Media Multitasking Among American Youth: Prevalence, Predictors and Pairings," Kaiser Family Foundation, December 2006.**
More than 80 percent of 7th-to-12th-graders use more than one media device at a time on a regular basis, but their primary loyalty is to television.

**Roberts, Donald F., Ulla G. Foehr and Victoria Rideout, "Generation M: Media in the Lives of 8-18 Year-Olds," Kaiser Family Foundation, March 2005.**
A national survey of children and teens finds that most live in homes with access to multiple media outlets. Since there are only so many hours in a day, kids increase their already heavy "media diets" through multitasking — using a computer or listening to music while watching TV, rather than devoting their attention to one device at a time.

# For More Information

**Association of National Advertisers**, 708 Third Ave., New York, NY 10017; (212) 697-5950; www.ana.net. A trade association for the marketing community that follows industry trends, offers networking and training opportunities and lobbies on behalf of advertisers.

**Center for the Digital Future**, University of Southern California Annenberg School for Communication, 300 S. Grand Ave., Suite 3950, Los Angeles, CA 90071; (213) 437-4433; www.digitalcenter.org. A research and policy institute devoted to the study of mass media and evolving communication technologies.

**Center for the Study of Popular Television**, S. I. Newhouse Communications Center, Syracuse University, 215 University Place, Syracuse, NY 13244; (315) 443-4077; http://newhouse.syr.edu. An academic center that supports research into all aspects of television and popular culture.

**Comparative Media Studies Program**, Building 14N-207, Massachusetts Institute of Technology, 77 Massachusetts Ave., Cambridge, MA 02139; (617) 253-3599; http://cms.mit.edu. Sponsors conferences and encourages students to understand media changes that cut across delivery techniques and national borders.

**Federal Communications Commission**, 445 12th St., S.W., Washington, DC 20554; (888) 225-5322; www.fcc.gov. The federal agency charged with regulating interstate and international communications by radio, television, wire, satellite and cable.

**National Association of Broadcasters**, 1771 N St., N.W., Washington, DC 20036; (202) 429-5300; www.nab.org. A trade association that lobbies Congress, the FCC and the judiciary on behalf of more than 8,300 local radio and television stations and the broadcast networks.

**National Association of Television Program Executives**, 5757 Wilshire Blvd., Penthouse 10, Los Angeles, CA 90036; (310) 453-4440; www.natpe.org. Serves as a clearinghouse for information and convenes meetings for professionals involved in the creation, development and distribution of TV programming.

**National Cable and Telecommunications Association**, 25 Massachusetts Ave., N.W., Suite 100, Washington, DC 20001; (202) 222-2300; www.ncta.com. The principal trade association of the cable television industry, representing 200 cable networks and cable operators who serve more than 90 percent of the nation's cable TV households.

# 12

# Future of the Music Industry

Alan Greenblatt and Karen Foerstel

The rap artist LL Cool J opposes illegal downloading of music from the Internet at a Senate hearing in September. "The majority of artists want to be compensated," he said. To fight piracy, the recording industry has begun filing copyright-infringement suits against consumers and promoting low-cost, legal downloading sites. But many youths say they'll continue illegal downloading because they think CDs are overpriced.

From *CQ Researcher*,
November 21, 2003. (Updated April 25, 2008)

F rustrated with media declarations that they are headed the way of the dinosaurs and are on the brink of extinction, hundreds of independent record stores around the world joined forces on April 19, 2008, to launch the world's first Record Store Day and prove that they are alive and well. In Australia, stores handed out gift bags with music goodies. In Italy, owners kept their shops open late into the night and invited customers to join dance parties. In Washington, D.C., shops offered discounts on merchandise. And in San Francisco, the heavy metal rock group Metallica made their first in-store appearance in nearly a decade.

With digital music downloads, peer-to-peer file-sharing and rampant music piracy, sales of CDs are dropping dramatically and record-store owners are struggling to survive in the new digital age. But the Record Store Day organizers say they're learning to adapt. "We've seen this coming for a long time," says Don Van Cleave, head of the Coalition of Independent Music Stores and one of the organizers of Record Store Day. "The first time we saw a CD burner we said, 'Shit, this ain't good.' " But Van Cleave said independent record stores are diversifying to stay alive, selling everything from T-shirts to piercing accessories to iPods. And their sales of vinyl records are actually on the rise. (*See sidebar, p. 276.*) "We combat the obituaries written for us all the time," Van Cleave says. "We want to be the last cockroaches after the holocaust."

Indeed, the music industry today is facing a digital firestorm that threatens to destroy it, or at the very least change forever how it does business. During the first quarter of 2008, album sales in United States — mainly CDs — dropped 25 percent compared to sales two years ago. [1] While the top ten CDs of 2000 sold a combined 60 million

## Most Downloaders Are Young People

Young consumers are far more likely to use file-sharing software than older consumers. But regardless of age, about half of file sharers say they now buy fewer CDs because they can download songs for free.

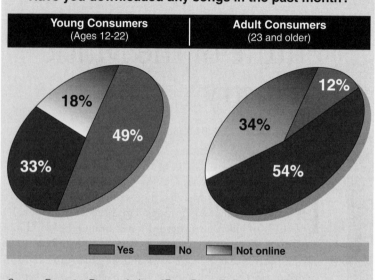

### "Have you downloaded any songs in the past month?"

| Young Consumers (Ages 12-22) | Adult Consumers (23 and older) |
| --- | --- |

Young Consumers: 18%, 49%, 33%

Adult Consumers: 12%, 34%, 54%

Yes    No    Not online

*Source:* Forrester Research, Inc., "From Discs To Downloads," August 2003

more than 1,700 songs on the Web site Kazaa. It was the first time a recording industry lawsuit against an individual for downloading music had gone to trial. "This does send a message, I hope, that downloading and distributing our recordings is not OK," said Richard Gabriel, lead attorney for the music companies involved the suit. [5]

The industry is also targeting college campuses, where they say music piracy is most rampant. Since last year, the Recording Industry Association of America (RIAA) has sent thousands of "pre-litigation" letters to more than 100 universities across the country. The RIAA informs schools it has discovered illegal downloading on their campuses computer networks and requests administrators to identify those responsible. To avoid legal action, the RIAA says those caught downloading could resolve the case for a "discounted rate." [6] Lawyers for universities have said the average settlement between students and the RIAA is about $3,000. [7]

copies, they only sold a combined 25 million in 2006. [2] Most of that decline is blamed directly on the massive amount of music that is being illegally downloaded on the Internet. In 2007 more than one-third — 34 per cent — of Internet users aged fifteen to twenty-four illegally file-shared music. It is estimated that for every track sold, another twenty are illegally downloaded. Some have estimated that 80 percent of all Internet traffic comes from illegal peer-to-peer file-sharing. [3]

Illegal music downloads have cost U.S. record companies $3.7 billion, according to a study by the non-profit think tank Institute for Policy Innovation. The study further found that the piracy of sound recordings has resulted in the loss of 71,060 jobs in the recording industry, retail outlets, and other industries as well as $422 million in lost tax revenue. [4] To fight back, the record industry has filed some 26,000 lawsuits against file-sharers since 2003. In October 2007, six record companies won a $222,000 case against a woman charged with illegally downloading and sharing

Congress is also joining the fight against illegal downloading on campuses. The House of Representatives in March 2008 overwhelmingly passed the College Opportunity and Affordability Act, a bill aimed at making college more affordable to middle- and low-income families. But a two-page section of the 800-page bill mandates that schools develop plans to fight illegal downloading and to use technological deterrents. School officials, however, say the legislation unfairly targets universities and would be extremely costly to implement. They also fear the bill could lead to universities losing federal educational grants if they fail to comply. [8]

While the RIAA is using lawsuits and legislation to fight file-sharing, others in the music industry say adapting — rather than suing — may be the answer to dealing with the new digital age. "There's a set of data that shows that file-sharing is actually good for artists. Not bad for artists. So maybe we shouldn't be stopping it all the time," said Douglas Merrill, the new president of recording label EMI's digital unit. "Obviously, there is piracy that is quite destructive but again I think the data shows that in some cases file-sharing might be okay. What we need to do is understand when is it good, when it is not good. . . . Suing fans doesn't feel like a winning strategy." [9]

Indeed, lawsuits have increased resentment among consumers who see recording labels as greedy corporate monsters who charge too much for CDs. Even some artists have started to push back against recording labels and the cost of music. Trent Reznor, the front man for the rock band Nine Inch Nails last year exhorted fans at a Sydney, Australia, concert to "steal" music to protest high CD prices. [10]

In another sign of the music industry's changing business model, the Grammy-winning British rock group Radiohead in October 2007 avoided going through a record label and released its new album as a digital download that fans could pay as much or as little as they wanted for it. "Almost every core operating principle in the recorded-music business has been shaken or challenged," said Warner Music chairman and chief executive Edgar Bronfman. [11]

In order to compete with illegal downloads, the music industry is being forced to turn to high-tech marketing and distribution tools that were unimaginable just a few years ago. In 2003, music was available in less than ten different formats, mainly CDs and cassettes. But today songs and albums are available in a multitude of formats including video downloads, ringtones, music streams, and downloadable full tracks. Sales of Justin Timberlake's *FutureSex/Love Sounds* album comprised 115 different formats that sold a total of 19 million units, of which only

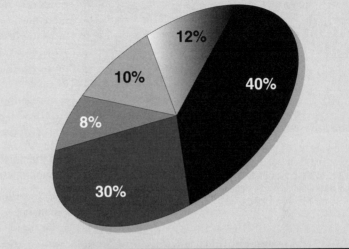

## Where Your Downloading Dollar Goes

Only about 12 cents goes to the artist out of the $1 consumers typically pay to download songs from online services like MusicNet and Pressplay. Most of the money goes to the online site and record company.

**The Site's Cut**
The online music provider gets the biggest share. When sites offer songs for as low as 49 cents, they sacrifice their profit but the label still gets paid.

**The Label's Cut**
A record company receives "performance royalties" that are paid to license an actual recording (not the written music). Some performers run their own labels to keep a larger share of these royalties for themselves.

**The Publisher's Cut**
The music publisher gets a flat fee known as "mechanical royalties," the amount paid to license the written music.

**The Middlemen's Cut**
A small portion is reserved for various intermediaries, such as secondary distributors like Amazon and Sony.

**The Artist's Cut**
The average is 12 percent, but successful bands often get better deals. Many major labels charge artists for "packaging" and promotional copies, leaving them with just 8 percent.

*Source:* Business 2.0

20 per cent were CDs. [12] And every day, new digital technology is allowing consumers greater access to music. In October 2007, Starbucks and Apple announced a partnership that allowed users of the iPhone and iPod Touch to download songs playing in Starbucks shops directly to their portable devices via Wi-Fi. [13]

Falling sales of CDs and the relaunch of the online music site Napster and other legal music downloading sites have forced retailers to slash their prices. The record industry largely blames illegal downloading for $4 billion in lost sales in recent years.

Even the Coalition of Independent Record Store Owners that organized this year's Record Store Day is going digital. Van Cleave says the thirty shops across the country that make up the Coalition's membership are all planning to launch online music stores at the end of this summer. "We're losing some customers to iTunes," says Van Cleave. "Our customers are telling us they want used CDs, new vinyl, and downloads. We can do two of those three. It would be stupid not to do all three and get their money."

While sales of CDs are plummeting, people are listening to more music than ever before — both legally and illegally. Global digital music sales reached $2.9 billion in 2007, a 40 percent increase from 2006 and up from zero just five years ago. The number of legal download sites has grown from less than fifty in 2003 to more than 500 in 2007. More than 6 million tracks are legally licensed for downloads today, compared to just 1 million in 2003. [14]

And the Internet is also allowing performers to bypass historic dependence on industry labels, record stores, and radio stations to reach out to fans. Damian Kulash, lead vocalist for the group OK Go, told the House Judiciary Committee in March 2008 that his Grammy-award winning group would not be where it is today without the Internet. Kulash said that in 2005, before OK Go became internationally well-known, the group produced a low

budget music video that they posted on YouTube.com. Within two days it was viewed one million times and a month later, their album sales jumped 400 percent. To date the video has been viewed on YouTube 30 million times. "Making, distributing, and listening to music is easier now than ever before," Kulash said. "I'd bet that more music is being listened to now than ever before in history. Musical ideas are spreading and combining and growing, even as the rigid structure of the traditional music business is crumbling. All sorts of exciting new things are possible. It's an exhilarating time." [15]

As the music industry tries to evolve with the rapid growth of digital technology, these are some of the questions people are asking:

## Can the music industry recover its profitability through lawsuits?

The Recording Industry Association of America made national news in 2003 when it began suing hundreds of music fans — including a twelve-year-old girl — whom the association alleged had illegally shared a thousand or more songs over the Internet. The press widely publicized the initial 261 lawsuits; a *New Yorker* cover that month showed a child shielding her eyes from the glare of a police spotlight, with CDs and a little teddy bear spilling from her knapsack.

But the bad publicity has not deterred the industry from taking legal action against those who are copying and sharing music without copyright permission. Since it first started taking people to court in 2003, the recording industry has filed 26,000 lawsuits alleging illegal file-sharing. While the vast majority of these cases are settled out of court, the industry won its first case to go to trial in October 2007 against a thirty-year-old Minnesota woman charged with illegally downloading and sharing more than 1,700 songs.

A federal jury ordered that Jammie Thomas, age thirty, pay the six record companies involved in the suit $9,250 for each of the twenty-four songs they focused on in the case — a total of $222,000 in damages. Under copyright law, damages can range from $750 to $30,000 per infringement, or up to $150,000 if the violation is "willful."

Illegal downloads have "become business as usual. Nobody really thinks about it," said Cary Sherman, president of the Recording Industry Association of America, which coordinates lawsuits for recording labels. "This case has put it back in the news. Win or lose, people will understand that we are out there trying to protect our rights." [16] The six recording companies involved in the case were Sony BMG, Arista Records, Interscope Records, UMG Recordings, Capitol Records, and Warner Brothers Records. [17]

The RIAA has also sent thousands of "pre-litigation" letters to universities across the country where they have detected illegal downloading on campus networks. Using software tools, the group can trace illegal file-sharing on campuses, but can generally only identify those responsible by his or her numerical Internet address. The letters sent to schools ask campus officials to track down the students and forward the notifications of copyright infringement onto them. Students can then settle out of court with the RIAA, which provides a Web site where they can pay their "reduced" settlement amount — an average of $3,000 — via a credit card. [18]

Some universities have refused to comply with the RIAA letters, saying it is not their responsibility to serve as the Internet police for the music industry. They also say it is too costly to track down all of the students the RIAA is targeting. In March, after the University of Arizona failed to handover the names of fourteen students accused of copyright infringement, a federal judge granted an RIAA request to subpoena the University for the names. [19] The University of Nebraska last year wrote the RIAA asking to be reimbursed for the cost of tracking down the more than 1,000 students the RIAA was trying to find. The university estimated that each complaint cost about $11 to process. "We're spending taxpayer dollars tracking down the RIAA problems," University of Nebraska spokesperson Walter Weir said. "Are we an agent of the RIAA? Why aren't they paying us for this?" [20]

The RIAA ignored the university's request for reimbursement and said schools do indeed have the responsibility to stop illegal downloads. "It's the university bandwidth that's being abused when students engage in music theft on the campus network," said RIAA spokesperson Jenni Engebretsen. "And it's the university system that is used to offer up content to illegal downloaders around the world. Should that be of concern to taxpayers? Absolutely."

Along with going after individual downloaders, the industry is also taking legal action against the Web sites that allow people to share files among each other.

AFP Photo/Toni Albir

The artist Moby suggests on his Web site that music companies shouldn't treat users of file-sharing services like criminals. "How can a 14-year-old who has an allowance of $5 a week feel bad about downloading music produced by multimillionaire musicians and greedy record companies?" he asked. But he also urged youths to use inexpensive, legal downloading sites.

Four recording labels have filed multi-million dollar lawsuits against two China-based Internet music services. A Chinese court in April agreed to hear the copyright infringement cases against Baidu.com Inc., which is being sued for $9 million, and Sogou, which is being sued for $7.5 million. The companies filing the suits are Sony BMG Music Entertainment Hong Kong Ltd.; Warner Music Hong Kong LTD; Universal Music Ltd.; and Gold Label Internainment Ltd., a Hong Kong company backed by EMI Group PLC. [21]

The case could be precedent-setting, opening up the music sites to future lawsuits running into the billions. The maximum statutory compensation under Chinese law is $71,000 per track. More than 99 percent of all music online in China is not licensed for download, according to the IFPI, which represents the recording industry worldwide, including the RIAA. [22] Critics of the

## CD Sales Continue to Drop

Record companies sold about 140 million fewer compact discs in 2002 than in 2000. The industry blames online sharing of music files, primarily by young people, for most of the 15 percent drop in sales.

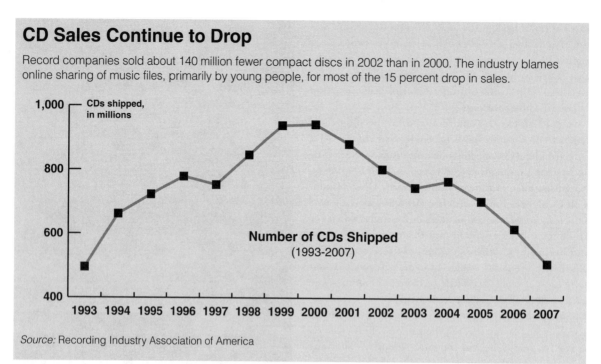

Number of CDs Shipped
(1993-2007)

*Source:* Recording Industry Association of America

RIAA say lawsuits — particularly those against individuals — are one of the most ham-fisted public relations blunders in recent memory. But the RIAA claims the suits are creating just the type of publicity it is seeking. "As much as you tell folks, until you demonstrate a penalty the behavior is not going to change," says RIAA Chairman Mitch Bainwol.

But industry critics argue that the RIAA is trampling on consumers' privacy. "Suing people one at a time is not a business model — it never has been," says Fred von Lohmann, senior staff attorney at the Electronic Frontier Foundation, which advocates free digital expression and defended a file-sharer. "Suing people is unlikely to make people feel warm about spending money on music."

Phil Leigh, founder of the market research firm Inside Digital Media, believes the lawsuits will deter peer-to-peer file-sharing, but doubts they will revive the major music labels. "The end result of this is that you've sued your customers and you've deterred peer-to-peer activity, but you haven't improved sales," Leigh says. "What have you accomplished other than frightening your customers and angering them?"

### Is music overpriced?

With online music sites offering songs for as little as 99 cents per download (legally) and for free (illegally), consumers are increasingly refusing to pay $15 or more for CDs. In February 2008, Apple Inc.'s iTunes vaulted past Wal-Mart to become the country's top music retailer. ITunes has sold more than 4 billion tracks since it launched in 2003. [23] Wal-Mart is now considering a new, lower price structure for CDs in an effort to boost lagging sales. Under the plan, prices for the most popular current albums would drop to $10 and other CDs would go as low as $5. The plan would also require the recording labels to bear a greater share of the cost. "When you look at sales declines with physical product, and you have a category declining like it is, you have to make decisions about what the future looks like," said Wal-Mart divisional merchandise manager for home entertainment Jeff Mass. "If you have a business that is declining and you want to turn it around, it really takes looking at it from all angles." [24]

Negotiations between recording labels and Wal-Mart are still taking place, and while some music executives appear to be scoffing at the proposals, others say they may not have a choice but to go along. "I don't think this is a

Wal-Mart discussion," one top label executive told *Billboard* magazine. "I think this is a future-of-the-business discussion. Right now everyone is paralyzed." [25] Blank discs on sale or after rebates can cost less than a dime apiece. At those prices, and with far more music available on the Internet than in any store, many people complain that prices of new CDs are too high. That's especially true, of course, if the main sources of their music are illegal downloads. Even individuals who feel sheepish about getting their music through illegal means will try to justify their actions by complaining that it's no worse for them to download than for record companies to charge $18 for CDs with only one good song on them.

Stan Liebowitz, a professor of managerial economics at the University of Texas at Dallas who has studied the music industry, calls such arguments "rationalizations" used to make people feel better about violating copyrights laws. He notes that since CD prices dropped in the early 1980s, the average cost of a full-length recording of ten songs has stayed virtually the same, adjusted for inflation. Liebowitz notes that some people think the cost of CDs should have come down even more, given that related products — such as CD players — cost a lot less than they did twenty years ago. Such perceptions are fueled by the fact that blank CDs sell for a fraction of the cost of a prerecorded CD. "There's a misimpression between the fact that a [blank] disk costs $1 and we charge $18, therefore CDs are overpriced," says Amy Weiss, senior vice president of communications for the RIAA. Many other costs are contained within that $18, she notes, including artists' fees, distribution, and retail markup. Even where record companies do make profits, she argues, those go to underwrite other artists whose CDs aren't moving. "It's the one successful artist that pays for the other nine that don't succeed," she says.

But given the slump in today's economy, record storeowners say prices must drop if CDs are going to remain a viable format. "The economy is terrible. When people are having to chose between milk and bread, they're not going to go out and buy four CDs," says Van Cleave of the Coalition of Independent Music Stores. "CDs ought to all be under ten dollars. If all CDs were under ten dollars, we would sell an inordinate amount." He adds: "The industry shot itself in the head with those record clubs from years ago when they were saying CDs were worth one penny. They also shot themselves in the head when they cut out singles. People buy an $18 album for one song they hear on the radio, and the rest of the album is crap."

Other independent storeowners blame both the large record labels for keeping CD prices high and the large retail outlets for driving the little guys out of business. "[Recording labels] have never lowered their wholesale prices on CDs," said Bill Daly, owner of the Crooked Beat record store in Washington, D.C. Independent stores can never sell music as cheaply as the giants like Best Buy or Wal-Mart, who, he says, keep prices low through back-room deals, in which bulk buyers get discounts. And he worries what impact that will have on the music industry. "Best Buy has never broken a new artist," he said. [26]

But others say it is more than high CD prices that are hurting the industry and small record shops. And they question whether efforts by recording labels or big retailers such as Wal-Mart to drop the cost will do anything to increase sales. "I think the consumers that buy CDs these days buy artists that they like, that they want," said Russ Crupnick, vice president and senior industry analyst for the market research firm NPD Group that tracks CD sales. "Price won't get people to buy things they don't want, or don't want in that format." [27]

## Will compact discs become obsolete?

In 2006, the R&B duo Gnarls Barkley made history by becoming the UK's first ever Number-One single to top the chart solely through downloadable sales. The group's song "Crazy" reached the top after the official UK charts company changed its eligibility requirements to include download sales in the tally. [28] "This not only represents a watershed in how the charts are compiled, but shows that legal downloads have come of age," Gennaro Castaldo, spokesman for the music retailer HMV, said at the time. [29]

Last year, the international music association IFPI launched the first-ever a digital-only singles chart, tracking downloads, ringtones, mastertones, full track downloads to mobiles and video mastertones. Avril Lavigne topped the list, selling 7.3 million track downloads of her song "Girlfriend" across the world. [30] CD sales no longer determine the popularity or financial success of musical groups. The explosion of portable digital music devises — from computers to cellphones to iPods — has forever changed the way people listen to music. Nokia sold almost 220 million music-capable mobile phones globally in the first three quarters of 2007. New portable devices are hitting the market each day with Wi-Fi technology that allow music fans to browse the Internet and download music on the go. [31]

CD sales went from a "slow, perhaps manageable but unpleasant decline" in 2006 to "almost a free fall" in 2007, said Crupnick of the NDP Group. "There's no evidence in 2008 that that fall is slowing." His firm estimates that 1 million music fans stopped buying CDs in 2007. [32] "There's a whole generation of people out there who are not learning about that pleasurable shopping experience," of browsing through record stores, says Don Gorder, chairman of the music/business department at the Berklee College of Music in Boston. "What they've learned about music is what they've been able to download off of Kazaa."

Music retailers are feeling the crunch. In 2006, after forty-six years in business, the Tower Records chain went bankrupt and closed its eighty-nine stores in twenty states across the country. [33] Hundreds of independent music stores across the country are shutting their doors. And the ones that are staying open will launch online music stores in the hopes of staying alive. At the end of the summer in 2008 the thirty members of the Coalition of Independent Music Stores plan to offer downloadable sales on their Web sites.

"The CD burner has conditioned people to put music onto their computers and put the tracks in the order that they like," says Phil Leigh, founder of the market research firm Inside Digital Media. "I basically believe that the prepackaged CD is as dead as General Custer." Some analysts predict that retail floor space for CDs will shrink this year by as much as 30 percent. [34] "Like LPs, discs will show up at yard sales," says Josh Bernoff, vice president and principal analyst with the Forrester Research, a technology and market research firm. [35]

But even that pessimistic view still allows for the sales of tens of millions of CDs a year. "In the next couple of years, the vast majority of U.S. consumers — maybe less so in the rest of the world — are still going to be buying their music through CDs," says Mike McGuire of the technology research firm Gartner, Inc. The young may have adapted to downloading, but, for the majority of people, habits die hard, says McGuire, who notes he doesn't use file-sharing software himself. "In terms of the mass of society, we're still looking at physical things, be they CDs or SACDs or DVDs."

In an effort to get consumers to buy physical products rather than just swap tracks, music labels have begun producing DVD-Audio and SACDs, or Super Audio CDs —

which offer higher fidelity reproduction than ordinary CDs. They are also offering "extras," like CDs that come with embedded bonus songs that can be downloaded onto purchasers' computer drives or DVDs of concerts. "The CD is not going away tomorrow, but we know that consumers are demanding other formats and we're giving it to them," says a spokeswoman for the EMI label. "A whole lot of people don't want to throw out their CD collection or their CD players right now, and they're happy with that format." The CD format will not just evaporate, argues Allen Lewites, a manager at Amoeba Music in Berkeley, California "There are just so many players out there — in your house, in your car, your Walkman, and your portable players. There are also home entertainment centers with DVD/CD players," Lewites says. "Plus, it's a good format!" "Will we see the day when there are no more CDs?" asks Gorder. "Yes, I do think that. What I can't say is when that will be. Some will say five years from now, others say fifteen to twenty years."

## BACKGROUND

### Same Old Tune

With sales slipping and piracy on the rise, it is a tumultuous time for the music industry. But every current problem — copyright disputes, fights between record labels and retailers, technological advances creating new competitors and fears that homemade copies of recorded tracks could destroy record companies — has been faced by the industry before. Copyright laws and their enforcement, historically, have tended to lag about fifteen years behind new technological advances, and the industry has typically turned to the courts and Congress for relief before adapting to the new technology.

Before Thomas Edison discovered how to record sound onto a cylinder for playback in 1877, there was no such thing as musical performances without the performer being present. Even after he and other tinkerers improved recorded sound and playback devices over the next few decades, sheet music sales produced more revenue than records.

By the dawn of the twentieth century, however, records were selling well enough to prompt changes in payment schemes. Victor Talking Machine Co. initiated the system of royalty payments to performers: Its 1904 contract with renowned operatic tenor Enrico Caruso paid him $4,000 for his first ten sides and 40 cents per record as they were sold. [36] The Copyright Act of 1909 mandated two-cent royalties for the mechanical reproduction of music through cylinders, recordings and piano paper rolls. It was the first peacetime regulation of the bargaining process between a supplier and a user. [37]

During the 1920s radio's growing popularity represented a major threat to the health of the recording industry, because the superior sound of the live performances that initially dominated broadcasts made older acoustical recordings obsolete. Moreover, the free music pouring into people's homes cut record sales dramatically. Annual record sales dropped from more than 100 million during the late 1920s to just 6 million in the Depression year of 1932. [38]

But, eventually, record companies learned how to use radio as a promotional tool, advertising hit tunes on a scale that the old song pluggers, who gave live demonstrations of songs in piano shops and elsewhere, never could have matched. They marketed the joys of hearing the songs you wanted when you wanted to hear them. Despite years of royalty disputes, radio became the best friend of the record companies.

Warner Music's Stan Cornyn once quipped that if it weren't for radio, record company executives would have to give up the leases on their Mercedes Benzes. A more tangible sign of the recording industry's dependence on radio came with the "payola" scandal of the 1950s, when record companies were caught paying disc jockeys millions of dollars to promote favored songs. Some surveys estimated that disc jockey air-play accounted for 85 percent of all record sales. [39] In response to concerns about payola and threats from record discounters, the major labels in 1951 formed the RIAA.

## Post-war Changes

World War II triggered improvements in recording technology — specifically the discovery of how to record onto plastic tape. A few years later, starting in 1947, music companies began producing records that played at 33 revolutions per minute (rpm) and could play back about twenty minutes of music per side. The previous technology — 78-rpm records — had provided only three minutes per side of playing time. As with many other technological competitions, the so-called speed wars between labels promoting 33-, 45- and 78-rpm records had a lot to do with the various companies trying to sell different playback equipment.

Big stars like Stevie Wonder began demanding the retention of publishing rights to their own songs in the 1970s, finally overcoming the unfair publishing arrangements that had enabled major record companies to take advantage of artists in the '50s.

Getty Images/Kevin Winter

During the postwar boom, record companies diversified their offerings, which until then had typically included adult pop music by singers like Bing Crosby and Frank Sinatra and specialized releases such as country and "race" music, which was what the record labels called records marketed to black audiences. (This term was changed after World War II to rhythm & blues or "R&B.") Companies began marketing directly to children and the older siblings of children. The mid-1950s witnessed the breakthroughs of Elvis Presley and other first-generation performers of rock 'n roll, which would dominate the business for the next four decades.

During the 1950s, companies revised their standard royalty contracts, shifting more expenses onto the artists.

# CHRONOLOGY

**1940s-1950s** *In the period around World War II, recording technology and the music industry become more sophisticated.*

**1947** Long-playing recordings and record players are commercially introduced; "microgroove" 33-rpm records hold three times as many grooves as old 78s and play much more music per side.

**1951** In response to "payola" scandals involving payments to disc jockeys for promoting records and threats from discount retailers, record companies form the Recording Industry Association of America (RIAA).

**1954** Elvis Presley, the most commercially successful rock pioneer, releases his first records; his self-titled debut LP breaks previous sales records held by singer Mario Lanza and bandleader Glenn Miller.

**1960s-1970s** *As rock music becomes the dominant pop music, the record industry concentrates its marketing on youth.*

**1963** Phillips introduces the first commercial cassette recorder in the United States.

**1976** Following a fifteen-year fight, Congress passes the first major overhaul of copyright law since 1909. It raises royalties for songwriters and imposes royalty liability for the first time on new users of copyrighted material, including cable TV.

**1979** Sony introduces the Walkman, a highly portable cassette player, which revolutionizes listening habits and spurs growth in cassette sales.

**1980s-1990s** *New technologies such as cable programming and compact discs fuel continued growth in prerecorded music sales.*

**1981** MTV, a cable channel featuring music videos that help promote new artists, goes on the air.

**1982** Michael Jackson's *Thriller*, the best-selling album of the 20th century, is released.

**1983** Compact discs and players go on sale to the public. Although expensive at first, within four years CDs are selling at the rate of 100 million annually.

**1987** Moving Picture Experts Group develops a standard digital format for storing audio recordings. Called MPEG-3 at first, the name is later shortened to MP3.

**1992** Congress passes the Audio Home Recording Act to combat song piracy through recordings on digital audio-tape machines. The law is soon rendered obsolete by technological developments that move recording onto computers, which the law does not cover.

**1996** Congress passes the Telecommunications Act, leading to massive consolidation of ownership of radio stations.

**1998** Congress passes the Digital Millennium Copyright Act, allowing copyright holders to subpoena the online histories of Internet customers they believe have pirated their products.

**2000s** *Digital technologies pose a serious threat to the music industry as downloading and CD burning become commonplace.*

**2000** The 9th U.S. Circuit Court of Appeals rules in favor of the record industry and against Napster, holding that because Napster maintained a centralized and indexed file-sharing system, the company was liable for copyright infringement.

**2003** *April:* Apple launches its iTunes Music Store, a pay-per-download online site that soon becomes the biggest seller of legally downloaded music. . . . A U.S. District judge in Los Angeles rules that file-sharing companies Grokster and Streamcast do not violate copyright law because they do not have direct control over the files traded on their network. *May:* Kazaa becomes the world's most downloaded software of any kind, with 278 million users. *September:* The Recording Industry Association of America announces lawsuits against 261 individuals for "egregious" copyright violations involving downloading and file-sharing. *October:* Napster reopens for low-fee file-sharing.

**June 2005** In a unanimous decision against the Internet file-sharing service Grokster, the Supreme Court rules that the music industry can file piracy lawsuits against technology companies that encourage customers to steal music and movies over the Internet.

**2007** The music industry wins its first case to go to trial against an individual for illegally downloading songs from the Internet. Six recording labels win a $222,000 judgment against a Minnesota woman charged with downloading songs from the Web site Kazaa. . . . The rock group Radiohead releases its new record as a pay-what-you-wish digital download.

**Feb. 2008** Apple Inc.'s iTunes surpasses Wal-Mart to become the country's top music retailer.

Performers weren't paid until studio time, arrangements, and promotional expenses were recouped. Accounting tricks meant that recording companies could be capricious even when they felt generous. During the early 1960s, for example, Leonard Chess, founder of a Chicago-based blues label, was comparing the royalty statements of jazz pianists Ramsey Lewis and Ahmad Jamal. "He went over Jamal's earnings again," writes his biographer Nadine Cohodas, "and then told the accountant, 'That's too much money for [Lewis] — give some to Jamal.' " [40] Artists, who had long complained that record companies ripped them off, now looked more than ever for concerts and personal appearances to make up the bulk of their incomes.

The new sounds of rock and R&B accompanied even more changes in playback technology. The advent of stereo recording led to the re-recording of the classical music repertoire. The companies fought over both record speeds and tape formats. William Lear, inventor of the car radio, improved tape cartridge recording, doubling playing time and increasing the number of tracks to eight. RCA concentrated on eight-tracks, while Phillips in 1963 released a twin spool cassette system that had the advantage of allowing both playback and recording.

The record companies had consolidated during the 1950s, but the rise of rock and "soul" music led to many new operators. New companies such as Stax, Atlantic, Sun, Chess, and many others discovered important artists ranging from Johnny Cash to Otis Redding before being gobbled up by industry giants. In the 1970s, the big record companies themselves became takeover targets, as major corporations like Transamerica and General Electric entered the field. Meanwhile, artists were becoming more than just cogs in the machine, with big stars like Stevie Wonder able to demand the retention of publishing rights to their own songs.

Transistor radios and cassette players — especially Sony's Walkman, introduced in 1979 — made music portable. Improvements in cassette sound brought about by Ray Dolby's noise reduction experiments in the 1970s helped make it the dominant music format until compact discs took off during the late 1980s.

In 1980, the investment house of Merrill Lynch concluded that there was nothing that could be done to stop the home taping boom that arose from improved technology and complaints about high record prices. Two years

Napster began enabling music lovers to download songs in 1999, but legal challenges forced its closure. It reopened in October 2003 as a legal, low-fee downloading site. However, many sites that have been used for illegal swapping remain online.

later, RIAA President Stanley Gortikov complained that the industry had sold 475 million albums, while 455 million albums were taped at home. "So for every album we sold, one was taped. . . . In our henhouse, the poachers now almost outnumber the chickens," he complained. [41]

## The Digital Age

But studies indicated that home taping did not hurt sales, since people were making copies of records they owned for convenience of playback in their portable devices and cars. In any event, home taping became less of a concern after the introduction of the compact disc in 1983. CD sales skyrocketed from 800,000 units in 1983 to more than 200 million by the decade's end, putting vinyl recordings out to pasture. Rather than relying on lower-quality cassette sound, consumers rushed to buy copies of old favorites cleaned up and released on CDs — notably, the 1987 reissue of the complete recordings of the Beatles. [42]

The record companies continued to worry about new forms of home taping, though, insisting that Congress impose a tax on digital audiotapes and recording equipment to make up for projected lost revenue. They got their wish in 1992, but it didn't matter. The Audio Home Recording Act exempted many forms of recording, including that done on computers, which turned out to be where the real action would occur.

# Colleges Crack Down on File Swapping

When Mike Negra opened his first music and movie rental shop in State College, Pennsylvania, some twenty years ago, he thought he'd hit the mother lode. By 1999, he owned five stores in Pennsylvania and in another college town in Virginia, and his music sales topped $3 million.

"We were experiencing rapid growth, due in large part to the market we were serving — college students," Negra recalls. "Their appetite for entertainment was healthy and recession-proof."

Unfortunately for Negra and the music industry at large, college students also quickly became leading users of Kazaa, Morpheus, and other peer-to-peer (P2P) file-sharing programs that allow them to trade music for free over the Internet. With more time than money, college students can spend hours searching for downloadable versions of favorite songs — thanks to the high-speed Internet access provided by their schools.

Over the years, Negra's sales of CDs and other recordings dropped more than 70 percent. In 2006 the last of his stores stopped selling music and transitioned solely to movie rentals. He blames illegal downloading for the slippage.

According to a survey in 2006 by the research firm Student Monitor, more than half of the country's college students download music and movies illegally. Another study by the market research firm NPD found that college students alone accounted for more than 1.3 billion illegal music downloads in 2006. [1]

In response to declining sales, the music and movie industries have teamed up with major universities to combat illegal downloads on campus. Their Joint Committee of the Higher Education and Entertainment Communities plans to recommend various ways to teach students about the ethical and legal problems associated with downloading — and boot abusers from their computer networks.

"Higher education has a deep and abiding interest in preserving its own bandwidth, which is being occluded by massive amounts of downloading of CDs and motion pictures," says Sheldon Steinbach, a lawyer with the national law firm of Dow Lohnes PLLC, who previously served as general counsel of the American Council on Education.

"Most universities think they should not get in the role of enforcement or policing for the entertainment industry," says John Vaughn, executive vice president of the Association of American Universities. But because piracy is causing computer slowdowns and server overloads on university networks, "there is plenty of need for enforcement and education for their own needs and on their own property," he says.

In addition, Steinbach says, "In terms of our ethical obligations as institutions, if we don't teach young men and women about responsibilities under the copyright law, who will?"

Indeed, universities are often publishers themselves and are considered "marketplaces of ideas" — ideas contained in books, audio presentations and other formats that are usually subject to copyright. A major revenue source for research universities in recent years has been accumulating their own patents on scientific discoveries.

Colleges, as Internet service providers, have been slapped with dozens of music-industry subpoenas demanding information on students believed to be heavily trafficking in illegal downloads. The industry's first lawsuits against individual pirates were filed in 2003 against four college students in Michigan, New Jersey, and New York, each of whom settled for between $12,000 and $17,000. The Recording Industry Association of America now regularly sends out thousands of "pre-litigation" letters to universities

Desktop CD recorders, better known as burners, were available by the early 1990s but their cost was prohibitive until the end of the decade. In 1999, freshman Shawn Fanning dropped out of Northeastern University to found Napster and work on his file-sharing software, which would allow millions of people to easily share audio files over the Internet. The RIAA would soon win injunctions in court that led to Napster shutting down in 2001. The once-controversial site was reborn in October 2003 for legal, fee-service downloading.

## RIAA in Court

Although the RIAA convinced the courts that Napster had violated its member labels' copyrights, it was initially less successful fighting the file-sharing software that followed in Napster's wake, notably Kazaa. The difference: Napster's filing and index systems were centralized, whereas Kazaa, Grokster, Morpheus and other sites simply connected the users of computers they do not own. A federal court ruled in 2003 that because Grokster and the other companies do not have control over the files

across the country, alerting administrators that they have discovered illegal downloading on campus networks. The schools are asked to identify the students, who are then told they can either settle out of court — usually for about a $3,000 fine which is payable by credit card via a Web site created by the RIAA — or face legal action. [2]

For their part, universities have begun cracking down on heavy file-sharing traffic over their systems. At the University of Florida springing 2003, during an average twenty-four-hour period, 3,500 of the 7,500 students living on campus would be using peer-to-peer services such as Kazaa. After the university installed a new system that automatically detects use of file-sharing services, however, traffic on such sites dropped more than 90 percent. In addition, students registering on the network have to certify they will not share copyrighted material. Servers send e-mails to violators and cut off Internet access. The first offense means thirty minutes off the network, the second draws a five-day suspension and the third leads to an indefinite suspension and other penalties. [3]

Universities all have different networks, which means that no one technical solution will work at all of them. Some schools are using "bandwidth shaping" techniques that slow down the speed at which students can access Internet files if they're thought to be illegally downloading material. At the University of California, Berkeley, students are given a warning if they are sharing more than five gigabytes of data per week and can be kicked off the system automatically under some circumstances. The university has an interest in preserving an open network — it doesn't monitor the content students are using — but the expectation is that if someone is sharing six gigabytes of data, it's likely to be music and not just physics notes. Universities also are holding orientation and discussion sessions on the ethics of file-sharing and are sending e-mails and letters to students and staff warning about copyright infringement.

In recent years, more than 100 colleges and universities have contracted with legal music sites, such as Napster, Rhapsody, and Apple's iTunes Music Store, to provide students with streaming audio and downloads. The schools are often able to receive bulk discount rates for the services, which are usually paid for through room and board fees or private grants. [4]

"The unveiling of very legitimate and legal online services for a very small fee really will give the students most of what they want," said Graham Spanier, president of Pennsylvania State University and co-chair of the joint industry-university committee examining the file-sharing problem.

But some studies have found that students are not using the free sites offered by universities, but are instead still illegally downloading. Why? Some universities tell students they can keep the legally downloaded songs only until they graduate. Others students are frustrated by the fact that digital rights management technology allows them only to play songs for free on their laptops but require payments to load songs onto their digital players. [5]

Negra and some others remain skeptical that students will curb their illegal behavior. Every college student interviewed for this report asked that his or her identity not be revealed, indicating they must be continuing to download illegally. "With the climate we live in, please don't use my real name for your article," pleaded "Lance" of Stanford University.

---

[1] "RIAA Sends," press release, Recording Industry Association of America.

[2] Ross, "Recording Industry Group."

[3] Katie Dean, "Florida Dorms Lock Out P2P Users," *Wired News*, Oct. 3, 2003, www.wired.com/news/digiwood/0,1412,60613,00.html.

[4] Nick Timiraos, "Free, Legal and Ignored," *Wall Street Journal*, July 6, 2006.

[5] *Ibid.*

---

being shared through their systems, they are not contributing directly to copyright violations.

Two years later, however, the Supreme Court ruled that the music industry could file piracy lawsuits against Grokster and other technology companies that are caught encouraging customers to steal music and movies over the Internet. In a unanimous ruling in June 2005, the court said Grokster Ltd. and Streamcast Networks Inc., developers of leading Internet file-sharing software, were open to legal action because they deliberately encouraged customers

to download copyrighted files illegally so they could build a larger audience and sell more advertising. Writing for the court, Justice David H. Souter said the companies' "unlawful objective is unmistakable."

The Court, however, said a technology company couldn't be sued if it merely learns its customers are using its products for illegal purposes. [43] Producers of digital devices and their supporters, however, said the ruling threatened future innovation. "This decision relies on a new theory of copyright liability that measures whether manufacturers created their wares with the 'intent' of inducing consumers to infringe," the Electronic Frontier Foundation said in response to the ruling. "It means that inventors and entrepreneurs will not only bear the costs of bringing new products to market, but also the costs of lawsuits if consumers start using their products for illegal purposes." [44]

The ruling put Grokster out of business. Today, if you go to www.grokster.com, a page appears warning that the Supreme Court ruled it was illegal to use the site, and the IP address of your computer "has been logged." "Don't think you can't get caught," the page warns. "You are not anonymous." Along with its win against Grokster, the RIAA is continuing to pursue legal action against individuals caught illegally downloading copyrighted music, such as the 2007 case brought and won by six recording labels against a women charged with illegally downloading more than 1,700 songs on the Web site Kazaa. It was the first time a recording industry lawsuit against an individual for downloading had gone to trial.

## CURRENT SITUATION

### Policing the Internet

For years, the recording industry — with the support of Congress — has successfully blocked efforts to loosen restrictions under the 1998 Digital Millennium Copyright Act. And in the courts, the industry has had big success against online file-sharing services such as Grokster as well as the individuals who use the services. The industry is now increasing pressure on Internet service providers (ISPs) to take greater responsibility for stopping music piracy.

In November, French president Nicolas Sarkozy called for a "three-strikes-and-you're-out" policy for people who illegally download music on the Internet. Internet users caught three times would be cut off by their ISP. The plan still needs to be approved by the French Parliament, but it is gaining support in the U.K. where the British government is pushing major Internet providers to reach an agreement with the British Phonographic Institute. If a voluntary agreement is not met, lawmakers say they will introduce legislation requiring ISPs to take action.

"There is only one acceptable moment for ISPs to start taking responsibility for protecting content — and that moment is now," said John Kennedy, Chairman and CEO of the international music industry group IFPI. "After years of prevarication in the discussion, the French government's decision to seize the day is deeply refreshing. It shows an urgency of approach that is badly needed in every market where music is today being massively devalued by piracy." [45] According to the IFPI, talks are also taking place in the United States between the music industry and ISPs about establishing a similar system. At least six U.S. service providers have agreed to adopt a warning system, according to an IFPI spokesperson. [46]

Many ISPs, consumer groups and lawmakers, however, oppose such measures saying it would erect dangerous obstacles to obtaining information on the Internet. "It's a breach of our civil liberties," said Christofer Fjellner, a Swedish legislator in the European Parliament who sponsored language opposing the three-strikes policy. "When government limits access to the Internet, it's like limiting freedom of speech. It's like banning people from printing books." [47]

### Legislation Battles

Back in the United States, the recording industry is backing a bill introduced last year by Rep. John Conyers (D-MI), chairman of the House Judiciary Committee, which would establish an anti-piracy enforcer in the White House. The bill, which won unanimous approval in March by a Judiciary subcommittee, would also strengthen civil and criminal laws relating to copyright and trademark infringement.

The unanimous approval came only after a provision was dropped that would have allowed prosecutors to seek a separate criminal count against every alleged infringement, meaning multiple counts could be filed for each song on a pirated CD. The provision had drawn the backing of record labels and the opposition of high-tech industries. While it was dropped, Conyers has said he may continue to pursue it. "Just because we took this provision out doesn't mean it is no longer an issue," Conyers said. [48]

High-tech companies that make MP3 recorders and other digital devices say they will step up their efforts this year to fight the recording industry's long-time influence on Capitol Hill. Along with efforts to block the Conyers bill, high-tech electronics companies are working to strengthen the legal doctrine of "fair use," which permits the reproduction of copyrighted material under certain circumstances including academic research, parodies, or journalistic reviews. The high-tech electronics industry believes the 1998 Digital Millennium Copyright Act effectively wiped out most understandings of fair use in its rush to stop people from circumventing encryption copyright protections — also known as "digital rights management." Under the law, they say, even devices that legally reproduce copyrighted materials could face massive court judgments against them.

"[M]illions of Americans are starting to realize that these laws affect them and are beginning to think that it's time to bring some balance back," said Gary Shapiro, head of the Consumer Electronics Association. He added that current law threatens to stunt innovation in the electronics industry. [49] His group is pushing hard for enactment of a fair-use bill sponsored by Democrat Rick Boucher of Virginia, a member of the House Energy and Commerce Committee who originated the House Internet Caucus in 1996.

The Boucher bill would add fair-use exceptions to the 1998 law to allow copying for personal use or for "criticism, comment, news reporting, scholarship, or research." Boucher argues that the measure is long overdue because the copyright law "literally confers on the creator of content the ability to extinguish all fair-use applications." [50]

As they argue for opposing legislation, both the electronics industry and the recording industry say they are the true advocates of artists' interests. Recording companies say they are working to protect performers who are losing millions of dollars in royalties from pirated music. Shapiro counters that the new devices and software his members create provide an outlet for small and independent performers who don't have the financial backing of big recording labels. [51]

Another legislative battle is brewing this year over "net neutrality" — the idea that content on the Internet should not be restricted by network owners. And the issue is dividing traditional political allies. Rep. Ed Markey, D-Mass, chairman of the House Energy and Commerce Committee's telecommunications and Internet subcommittee, has introduced the Internet Freedom Preservation Act that would codify net neutrality principles into law. The bill is gaining support from other Democrats. But the entertainment industry, which has long stood with Democratic lawmakers, opposes such efforts saying it will restrict efforts by ISPs to block illegal downloading. [52]

During a March hearing by the House Judiciary Committee on net neutrality, Rick Carnes, president of the Songwriters Guild of America (SGA), said illegal downloading has severely hurt revenues for songwriters and has forced music-publishing houses to slash in half the number of songwriters they employ. "If a broadband network operator is considering taking technological steps to stop this occurrence, SGA would say 'more power to you.' And, 'the sooner the better.' And finally, 'how can we help?' " Carnes said.

Supporters of the bill, however, say the if the law does not protect neutrality, ISPs could start censoring the kind of information available to the public.

### Entering the Digital Age

As the recording industry fights music piracy in the courts and on Capitol Hill, it is also desperately searching for new ways to compete with both legal and illegal downloading.

In 2007, after years of championing the need for copyright protections on digital music, three of the world's four biggest recording companies — EMI, Universal and Warner — agreed to license their music for sale online as unprotected MP3 files. The fourth, Sony BMG Music Entertainment, is expected to follow soon. [53] The move is likely to encourage even more people to go digital in their music listening habits because songs have traditionally been tied to specific digital devices — for example, iPod players can only play music bought on iTunes.

Record companies also are licensing music in numerous new formats and with hundreds of new partners. In 2007, Amazon partnered with major and independent recording labels to launch its online music download store. [54] Universal Music and Sony BMG are expected in 2008 to start releasing "ringles," CD singles that include mobile phone ringtones and other digital content. [55] And in April 2008, the social networking site MySpace announced plans with three of the four big music companies to sell music, wallpaper, ringtones, and other paraphernalia on its site. [56] Universal Music recently launched a joint venture with global marketing giant WPP to better exploit the links between music and advertisers. [57]

# Vinyl Makes Comeback

While sales of CDs and other "physical" albums are plummeting in this age of digital downloads, one of the oldest music formats — vinyl — is making an unexpected comeback. "Our vinyl inventory is up one-thousand percent," says Don Van Cleave, president of the Coalition of Independent Music Stores. "It's a digital pushback. People want to have something to touch and feel."

And it's not just used records, or even extended dance tracks spun by DJs. Some of today's most popular artists — including the White Stripes, Gnarls Barkley, Amy Winehouse, and even Justin Timberlake — have all released albums on vinyl. Last year, Paul McCartney produced a vinyl-only album of his live performance at the Amoeba Music record store in Hollywood.

"Sales of vinyl hit rock bottom in the 1990s," says Jay Miller manager of sales and marketing at United Record Pressing in Tennessee, one of a handful of vinyl record manufacturers in the United States. "Today our numbers are up quite a bit, mostly full-length vinyl."

Don MacInnis, owner of the record pressing plant Record Technology in California, said production of vinyl in 2007 was up about 25 percent over the previous year. [1]

Sales of record players are also on the rise, especially those with USB connections that allow music fans to listen to vinyl albums through their computers — and even to record them digitally.

Many audiophiles swear that the sound of vinyl is much "richer and warmer" than that of CDs. Although CDs have a wider range of sounds, manufacturers are often encouraged to compress the audio on CDs to make it as loud as possible.

Since the audio on vinyl can't be compressed to such extremes, records generally offer a more nuanced sound.

But acoustics isn't the only — or even the primary — reason vinyl sales are on the rise. "It's become hip," says Van Cleave. "A college student can show off to their friends that they're listening to vinyl." Miller of United Record Pressing agrees: "Collecting [digital] recordings has become effortless. Anyone can go and mass collect files. There's something cold to it. You tend to forget what's there unless you go through your iPod." Vinyl on the other hand has become a respected hobby that requires research and thought. And, unlike CDs, "there's no better artwork then vinyl" covers, Miller says.

Vinyl may prove to be the lifeline of many small and independent record stores who otherwise have been feeling the economic hit from the drop in CD sales. Even larger retailers are getting into the act. Last October, Amazon launched a vinyl-only section stocked with a wide collection of titles and several models of record players. [2]

And because music fans are increasingly listening to portable digital files away from home and vinyl recordings while they are at home, pressing plants are now packaging vinyl albums with coupons for downloadable versions. "You don't need CDs anymore. You can't get more compact then a [digital] file," Miller says. Through the "polar opposite" of vinyl and digital, he says, "you get the best of both worlds."

---

[1] Eliot Van Buskirk, "Vinyl May Be Final Nail in CDs Coffin," *Wired*, Oct. 29, 2007.

[2] *Ibid.*

---

But as recording labels look for new revenue streams to make up for lost CD sales, tensions are also growing with the artists they represent. Last month, the rock band Smashing Pumpkins sued their record label, Virgin Records, for using their name and music in promotional deals with Pepsi and Amazon without permission. The group claimed its only existing agreement with Virgin Records covered the right to sell digital downloads and not the right to use the band's image in promotional campaigns. [58]

The exploding popularity of online social networking sites such as Facebook and YouTube also has led the music industry to rethink how it works. More than 1.2 million rock acts and 1.7 million R&B acts have posted their music and videos on MySpace alone. [59] "Ten years ago I would hear about a potentially great act and spend all day on the phone to everyone I knew," said Mike Smith, managing director of Columbia Records. "Eventually somebody would have a tape and I'd send a bike across town to get it. I'd listen to it and then try and track down the manager, get on the phone to him and arrange to see the band live. Now, if someone mentions a potentially great act I check them out on YouTube or MySpace. You're immediately listening to their music,

# Should the record industry sue copyright infringers?

## YES

**Mitch Bainwol**
*Chairman and CEO, Recording Industry Association of America*

from testimony before the senate governmental affairs permanent subcommittee on investigations, Sept. 30, 2003

The problems facing the music industry will, as broadband expands, soon be the problems of all copyright holders. The decision to enforce our rights against egregious infringers was taken only after suffering years of mounting harm and trying all other avenues.

The music industry first tried to use an aggressive public-education campaign to discourage the unauthorized distribution of recordings, by explaining that online piracy is not only illegal but robs songwriters and recording artists of their livelihoods, stifles the careers of up-and-coming musicians and threatens the jobs of tens of thousands of less celebrated people in the music industry.

The music industry also pursued lawsuits against the peer-to-peer systems, which are knowingly facilitating the illegal distribution of copyrighted recordings on a massive scale. Most important, the music industry has aggressively licensed legitimate online music services to offer legal alternatives to consumers. Only after these steps did not stem the tidal wave of illegal conduct has RIAA resorted to its current course. . . .

The root cause for a drastic decline in record sales is the astronomical rate of music piracy. Computer users illegally download more than 2.6 billion copyrighted files (mostly recordings) every month. At any given moment, well over 5 million users are online offering well over 1 billion files for copying. And unlike traditional music piracy, piracy through networks is viral: Unless the user takes affirmative steps to prevent it, the user automatically and immediately begins offering the files . . . to millions of other users. Moreover, the overwhelming majority of the distribution that occurs on peer-to-peer networks is unauthorized.

Our heightened enforcement efforts are deliberately occurring now when, as a result of the music industry's extensive educational efforts, the public is more aware than ever before of the illegality and consequences of online piracy and, at the same time, the number of legitimate online music sources is exploding. . . .

It is widely recognized and acknowledged that individuals who engage in such unauthorized distribution — either by making recordings available for others to copy or by making copies of others' files — are committing a clear violation of the copyright laws. The courts have been unanimous on this point.

## NO

**Fred von Lohmann**
*Senior Intellectual Property Attorney, Electronic Frontier Foundation*

Written for *CQ Researcher*, November 2003

Everyone agrees that suing music fans one at a time is not a business model. But with one in every five Americans sharing music on the Internet, the record industry claims it has no choice.

Don't you believe it. Let's start with the obvious truths. First, artists and copyright owners deserve to be fairly compensated. No one disputes that. Second, file-sharing is here to stay. Even if you could sue 60 million Americans into submission, that is not going to revive CD sales. Third, the fans do a better job making music available than the corporations. The Apple iTunes Music Store brags about its inventory of over 300,000 songs. Sounds pretty good, until you realize that music fans have made millions of songs available on Kazaa.

So where do we go from here? How about this: the record industry offers fans the opportunity to "get legit" in exchange for a monthly payment of $5 each. So long as they pay, they are free to keep doing what they are going to do anyway — share the music they love using whatever software they like. The money collected gets divided among copyright owners based on the popularity of their music.

It has been done before. This is essentially how songwriters brought broadcast radio in from the copyright cold. Radio stations step up, pay blanket fees and in return get to play whatever music they like. Today, the performing-rights societies like ASCAP and BMI collect the money and pay out millions annually to their artists. Copyright lawyers call it "voluntary collective licensing." No need for changes to copyright law; no need for government intervention.

Five dollars a month might not seem like much, but multiplied by 60 million file-sharers, it would total over $3 billion annually, a number that dwarfs the current profit margins of the entire record industry combined. And it would be pure profit to the labels. No CDs to ship, no online retailers to cut in on the deal, no percentage to Kazaa or anyone else. Best of all, it is an evergreen revenue stream — the money would keep coming, during good times and bad.

It's time to do something daring. After all, it's no more radical than threatening millions of Americans — customers — with ruinous litigation. What court, legislator or regulator is going to get in the way of a new approach that turns fans back into customers?

seeing what they look like and you have all of their contact details in front of you." [60]

## OUTLOOK

The rise of the Internet and the unstoppable popularity of downloadable music has forced the music industry to rethink every aspect of its business model. Throughout the history of recorded music, music labels have provided the financial support to artists to produce, promote, and sell their albums. But with today's online music and social networking sites, performers and consumers can easily bypass the label middleman.

To survive, the recording industry has turned to lawsuits and legislation to bring music back to the last century. But these tactics appear to be having little impact other than to alienate consumers.

Just as the recording labels resisted cassette tapes, CDs and even MTV in years past, they have fought against online music. Only recently has the industry begun understanding that its best strategy is to join the digital bandwagon. "There's no denying that [Warner Music Group] and the industry as a whole have been struggling for almost a decade now with the challenges and opportunities that the digital space presents," Warner Music chairman and CEO Edgar Bronfman Jr. wrote in a recent memo to employees. "The recent trend of dramatic changes in the recorded music market will continue. . . . And though it's a cliché, it's a cliché because it's true: technology will also provide us with new opportunities." [61]

But some argue it may be too late to wean younger listeners off of illegal — or at least — free music. "The majors could have adjusted and reinvented themselves for the digital era," Peter Rojas, co-founder of the free online-only music label RCRD LBL, wrote on the *New York Times* blog Freakonomics. "Instead, they took too long to start selling music online (and even when they did agree to start selling digital downloads, they screwed it up by insisting on digital rights management)." Rojas said a vacuum was created when the labels failed to quickly offer legal downloadable music that people could purchase easily and conveniently.

"A generation of kids got used to the idea that music was free, and given the infinite amount of freely — if illegally — available music out there, it was hard to argue with the facts on the ground. Music seemed free, so it was free," he said. [62]

Indeed, music may soon all become free, with recording labels relying on other products to make a profit. More and more money is now being generated through the licensing of songs for ringtones and videogames, the sale of wallpaper for mobile phones, and the bundling of downloadable music with concert e-tickets. "The record business is turning into a true music entertainment business," said Thomas Hesse, president of Sony BMG Music Entertainment's Global Digital Business. "We are breaking away from the single product format to a vast range of different and complementary products, all centered around the release of an artist." [63]

Record labels are also beginning to realize that free online music can still generate income through ad revenue. Major labels, in fact, are now partnering with the very online services they have condemned for destroying the music industry. Last year, Warner Music Group dropped a copyright infringement lawsuit against imeem, an advertisement-supported social networking Web site which offers free streaming music and videos. Warner instead agreed to license its music and videos to the site for a share of the ad revenues. In exchange, imeem agreed to use audio filtering software to manage copyright protections. [64] Within months of the Warner deal, imeem signed licensing agreements with the other three major labels, Sony BMG, Universal Music Group and EMI. [65] "It's a good outlet for our content," said Alex Zubillaga, Warner's executive vice president of digital strategy and business development. "As far as we are concerned, they are a legitimate business." [66]

The relationship between artists and record labels will also likely never be the same. Performers can now promote themselves over social networking sites like YouTube, MySpace, and imeem. Independent musicians in particular, who could never secure the backing of major labels, can now make it big on their own using the Internet. Imeem alone has about 25 million users and includes about 115,000 independent artists. Bands can track how many people visit their playlists, videos, and photographs. And they can even identify where in the country — and around the world — are their biggest fan bases.

"We're using the Web to manage ourselves and find our audience," said Ryan Divine of the indie rock band Maldroid, which — after winning a music video contest on YouTube in 2006 — was invited to appear on "Good Morning America" and is now launching its first national tour. "We've built this audience having never toured before, except to put up videos and talk to people on the Internet." [67]

Despite the tumultuous changes happening in the music industry, music is more popular and available in more formats than ever before. New digital technology now allows people to listen to their favorite songs at anytime and anywhere they chose. The opportunities for marketing and packaging music in this digital age are almost endless. Traditional music labels will survive as long as they are willing to adapt and even join forces with the online innovators they are fighting. But the traditional music business model of securing artists and making money from the sale of physical products appears destined to soon disappear forever.

## NOTES

1. Ken Barnes, "Album Sales Decline, But Is the Slump Slowing?" *USA Today*, April 3, 2008, p. 1D.

2. Nick Lewis, "Record Store Day Highlights Retailers' Struggle for Survival," *Calgary Herald*, April 19, 2008.

3. "IFPI Digital Music Report 2008," IFPI, January 2008, pp. 15, 18, p. 3.

4. "The True Cost of Sound Recording Piracy to the U.S. Economy," Stephen E. Siwek, Institute for Policy Innovation, August 2007, p. 7, pp. 11, 13.

5. "Minn. Woman to Pay for Illegal Music Downloads," NPR.org, Oct. 5, 2007.

6. *Ibid.*

7. Timberly Ross, "Recording Industry Group Says Piracy Students are Settling," Associated Press, March 24, 2007.

8. Ben Dubose, "Bill Targets Piracy at Colleges; Schools Say They're in the Cross Hairs Unfairly for Illegal Downloads," *Los Angeles Times*, March 16, 2008, p. A26.

9. Greg Sandoval, "Will Former Google Exec Help Save the Music Industry?" CNETNEWS.com, April 2, 2008.

10. Justin Bachman, "The Big Record Labels' Not-So-Big Future," *Business Week Online*, Oct. 11, 2007.

11. *Ibid.*

12. "IFPI Digital Music Report 2008," p. 6.

13. *Ibid.*, p. 12.

14. *Ibid.*, p. 6.

15. Testimony of Damian Kulash, Hearing on Net Neutrality, House Judiciary Anti-Trust Task Force, March 11, 2008.

16. "Minn. Woman," NPR.org.

17. "Music Industry Wins Illegal Downloading Case," Associated Press, Oct. 5, 2007.

18. "RIAA Sends More Law Pre-Lawsuit Letters to Colleges with New School Year," press release, RIAA, Sept. 20, 2007; Ross, "Recording Industry Group."

19. Eric Swedlund, "Recording Industry Wins Subpoenas for Info on 14 at UA," *Arizona Daily Star*, March 5, 2008.

20. Matthew Hansen, "UNL Proves Safe Haven for Music Pirates," *Omaha World-Herald*, March 16, 2007.

21. Sarah McBride and Loretta Chao, "China Opens Door to Music Piracy Cases," *The Globe and Mail* (Canada), April 7, 2008.

22. "Baidu Faces Potential Multi-billion Dollar Liability for Breaching Music Copyrights," press release, IFPI, April 7, 2008, www.ifpi.org/content/section_news/20080407.html.

23. "Apple Passes Wal-Mart in Music Sales," Associated Press, April 3, 2008.

24. Ed Christman, "Wal-Mart Stirs CD Pricing Pot with Multi-tiered Plan," *Billboard*, March 1, 2008.

25. *Ibid.*

26. Angela Valdez, "Will Indie Record Shops Survive?" *Washington City Paper*, April 9, 2008.

27. Steve Painter, "Wal-Mart Looks to Boost Lagging Compact Disc Sales," *Arkansas Democrat-Gazette*, March 20, 2008.

28. Paul Sexton, "Gnarls Barkley Makes U.K. Chart History," *Billboard.com*, April 3, 2006.

29. "Crazy Song Makes Musical History," BBC, April 2, 2006.

30. "IFPI Digital Music Report 2008," p. 6.

31. *Ibid.*, p. 12.

32. Steve Painter, "Wal-Mart Looks to Boost Lagging Compact Disc Sales," *Arkansas Democrat-Gazette*, March 20, 2008.

33. Karen Matthews, "Music Fans in Mourning as Tower Records spins into Final Weeks of 46-year Run," Associated Press, Oct. 13, 2006.

34. Alex Veiga, "Turbulent Year for Recording Industry Points to More Changes in '08," Associated Press, Jan. 7, 2008.

35. Josh Bernoff, "From Discs to Downloads," Forrester Research, August 2003.

36. Russell Sanjek, *Pennies from Heaven*, updated by David Sanjek (1996), p. ix.

37. *Ibid.*, p. 22.

38. David Ewen, *All the Years of American Popular Music* (1977), p. 283.

39. Sanjek, *Pennies from Heaven* (1996), p. 286.

40. Nadine Cohodas, *Spinning Blues Into Gold* (2000), p. 170.

41. Quoted in Peter Titus, "The Man Can't Scotch Our Taping," in Clinton Heylin, ed., *The Penguin Book of Rock & Roll Writing* (1992), p. 496.

42. Michael Fink, *Inside the Music Industry* (1996), p. 23.

43. Ted Bridis, "Court OKs Music-Downloading Lawsuits against Software Firms," Associated Press, June 27, 2005.

44. "Supreme Court Ruling will Chill Technology Innovation" press release, Electronics Frontier Foundation, June 27, 2005.

45. "IFPI Digital Music Report 2008," p. 3.

46. Doreen Carvajal, "Internet Firms Are Wary of New Role as Cybercop," *International Herald Tribune*, April 14, 2008, p. 1.

47. *Ibid.*

48. Brooks Boliek, "White House IPO Czar Bill Clears First Hurdle," *Hollywood Reporter*, March 7, 2008.

49. Shawn Zeller, "Electronics Makers Learning to Lobby," *CQ Weekly*, Oct. 27, 2007.

50. *Ibid.*

51. *Ibid.*

52. Brooks Boliek, "Neutrality Could Divide Hollywood, Democrats," *The Hollywood Reporter*, March 12, 2008.

53. Alex Veiga, "Turbulent Year."

54. "IFPI Digital Music Report 2008," p. 14.

55. Veiga, "Turbulent Year."

56. Ellen Lee, "Changing Music Scene Boosts Indie Bands," *San Francisco Chronicle*, April 21, 2008, p. D1.

57. Owen Gibson, "Smashing Pumpkins Sue Record Label over Use of Songs in Pepsi Promotional Deals," *The Guardian* (London), March 26, 2008, p. 17.

58. *Ibid.*

59. "IFPI Digital Music Report 2008," p. 13.

60. *Ibid.*

61. Veiga, "Turbulent Year."

62. Stephen J. Dubner, "What's the Future of the Music Industry? A Freakonomics Quorum," Freakonomics/*New York Times*, Sept. 20, 2007.

63. "IFPI Digital Music Report 2008," p. 6.

64. Alex Veiga, "Warner Music Drops Suit, Strikes Licensing deal with Web Site," Associated Press, July 13, 2007.

65. Gordon Masson, "Netco Uploads UMG fare," *Daily Variety*, Dec. 11, 2007.

66. Veiga, "Warner Music."

67. Lee, "Changing Music Scene."

## BIBLIOGRAPHY

### Books

**Hammond, John, and Irving Townsend, *On Record*, Ridge Press, 1977.**
The memoirs of a celebrated talent scout who signed and recorded stars from Count Basie to Bruce Springsteen.

**Kempton, Arthur, *Boogaloo: The Quintessence of American Popular Music*, Pantheon Books, 2003.**
A history of African-American music written as a series of profiles of key figures from gospel to hip hop.

**Krasilovsky, M. William, Sidney Schemel and John M. Gross, *This Business of Music: The Definitive Guide to the Music Industry*, 9th edition, Watson-Guptill, 2003.**
The updated edition of the industry's legal bible covers contracts, royalties, loans and copyright issues.

Kuske, Dave and Gerd Leonhard, *The Future of Music: Manifesto for the Digital Music Revolution*, Berklee Press, 2005.
Published by the Music Research Institute at Berklee College of Music, the book explores how digital technology has forever changed the music industry.

Sanjek, Russell, *Pennies From Heaven: The American Popular Music Business in the Twentieth Century*, Da Capo Press, 1996.
A narrative history of the music business from Thomas Edison to the digital age.

## Articles

Anderman, Joan, "The Music Business: What's Next?" *The Boston Globe*, Feb. 23, 2003, p. N1.
A survey of changes to the music business includes the proliferation of sites for downloading songs for a fee and the possible extinction of retailers.

Goodale, Gloria, " 'Don't Call Me a Pirate. I'm an Online Fan,' " *The Christian Science Monitor*, July 18, 2003, p. 13.
"Whitney," a Los Angeles teenager, downloads music on Kazaa for convenience and to avoid what she sees as exorbitant CD prices.

Grossman, Lev, *et al.*, "It's All Free," *Time*, May 5, 2003, p. 60.
A look at the evolving nature of file-sharing and how the content industries are fighting it.

Healey, Jon, "Some Universities Are Welcoming Napster Back to School," *Los Angeles Times*, Nov. 7, 2003, p. 3:1.
Some students don't like Penn State University's plan to provide them with access to contracted music through Napster as part of their dorm fees.

Kot, Greg, "Twilight for the CD," *Chicago Tribune*, March 30, 2003, p. C1.
The future may hold the death of CD stores and the rise of wireless, pocket-sized MP3 players.

Leeds, Jeff, "Universal Music Was Boxed in on CD Prices by Big Retail Chains," *Los Angeles Times*, Sept. 5, 2003, p. 3:1.
Universal had to drop its retail CD prices because big-box retailers had made deeply discounted music prices an ingrained habit with record buyers.

Seabrook, John, "The Money Note," *The New Yorker*, July 7, 2003, p. 42.
Using the promotion of a new artist and the history of the Warner Music Group as a base, a business reporter discusses the transition pangs record labels are experiencing as the MP3 format begins to supercede CDs.

Timberg, Scott, "Lend Them Your Ear," *Los Angeles Times*, Aug. 25, 2003, p. 5:1.
The decline of physical music stores threatens the existence of an important species of proselytizers for good music: the knowledgeable record clerk.

## Reports and Studies

Bernoff, Josh, *et al.*, *From Discs to Downloads*, Forrester Research, August 2003.
A study of Internet downloading finds that file-sharing has already cost the music industry $700 million and predicts CDs will become passé within five years.

Ham, Shane, and Robert D. Atkinson, *Confronting Digital Piracy: Intellectual Property Protection in the Internet Era*, Progressive Policy Institute, October 2003; www.ppionline.org/documents/Digital_Copyright_1003.pdf.
The report argues Congress should take a lead role in allowing copyright holders to deter piracy.

Holden, Blythe, Mike McGuire, *et al.*, *Copyright and Digital Media in a Post-Napster World*, Gartner G2 and the Berkman Center for Internet & Society, August 2003; http://cyber.law.harvard.edu/home/2003-05.
A report outlines key changes in copyright and digital-rights management laws and the changes in business models and consumer behavior that are resulting from digital distribution of music.

"IFPI Digital Music Report 2008," January 2008, www.ifpi.org/content/library/DNR2008.pdf.
The international music association compiles statistics and case studies to show how the music industry is moving into the digital age.

**Liebowitz, Stan, "Will MP3 Downloads Annihilate the Record Industry?: The Evidence So Far," June 2003; www.utdallas.edu/~liebowit/intprop/records.pdf.** An economist looks at the impact of MP3 downloads on sales within the context of a thirty-year history of record sales, as well as changes in income, prices, sale of blank tapes and other benchmarks.

# For More Information

**American Society of Composers, Authors and Publishers**, One Lincoln Plaza, New York, NY 10023; (212) 621-6000; www.ascap.com. Represents music writers worldwide, licenses music and distributes royalties for public performances.

**Berkman Center for Internet & Society**, 1587 Massachusetts Ave., Cambridge, MA 02138; (617) 495-7547; www.cyber.law.harvard.edu/home. A Harvard Law School program that researches Internet issues, including governance, privacy, intellectual property, antitrust, content control and electronic commerce.

**BMI**, 320 West 57th St., New York, NY 10019; (212) 586-2000; www.bmi.com. A performing arts organization that licenses music, collects fees and distributes royalties to writers, composers and copyright holders.

**Digital Media Association**, 1615 L St., N.W., Suite 1120, Washington, DC 20036; (202) 775.2664; www.digmedia.org. An alliance of companies that perform, promote and market music and video content on the World Wide Web and through other digital networks.

**Electronic Frontier Foundation**, 454 Shotwell St., San Francisco, CA 94110; (415) 436-9333; www.eff.org. An organization that promotes unfettered access to digital information.

**National Association of Broadcasters**, 1771 N St., N.W., Washington, DC 20036; (202) 429-5300; www.nab.org. The trade association that represents radio networks and other broadcasters.

**National Association of Recording Merchandisers**, 9 Eves Dr., Suite 120, Marlton, NJ 08052; (856) 596-2221; www.narm.com. A trade association representing the retailers, wholesalers and distributors of prerecorded music in the United States.

**Pew Internet and American Life Project**, 1100 Connecticut Ave., N.W., Suite 710, Washington, DC 20036; (202) 296-0019; www.pewinternet.org; A foundation-sponsored project that researches the impact of the Internet on American society.

**Recording Industry Association of America**, 1330 Connecticut Ave., N.W., Suite 300, Washington, DC 20036; (202) 775-0901; www.riaa.com. Trade group representing the recording industry.